MULTIDIMENSIONAL SCALING

Concepts and Applications

PAUL E. GREEN
Wharton School, University of Pennsylvania

FRANK J. CARMONE, JR.
Drexel University

SCOTT M. SMITH
Brigham Young University

Allyn and Bacon
Boston   London   Sydney   Toronto

Editorial-production service: Technical Texts, Inc.
Text designer: Sylvia Dovner
Cover administrator: Linda Dickinson
Production administrator: Lorraine Perrotta
Manufacturing buyer: William J. Alberti
Series editor: Henry Reece

Copyright © 1989 by Allyn and Bacon
A Division of Simon & Schuster
160 Gould Street
Needham Heights, Massachusetts 02194

Library of Congress Cataloging-in-Publication Data

Green, Paul E.
    Multidimensional scaling : concepts and applications / Paul E. Green, Frank
  J. Carmone, Jr., Scott M. Smith.
        p. cm.
        Bibliography: p.
        Includes index.
        ISBN 0-205-11657-4
    1. Marketing research—Statistical methods. 2. Multidimensional scaling—
Computer programs. 3. Marketing research—Data processing. I. Carmone, Frank
J. II. Smith, Scott M. III. Title.
HF5415.G658   1989
658.8′3′028—dc19   88-20957
ISBN 0-205-11657-4   CIP

Printed in the United States of America

10 9 8 7 6 5 4 3 2 1   93 92 91 90 89

CONTENTS

PREFACE

The earlier version of this book (P.E. Green and F.J. Carmone, *Multi-dimensional Scaling and Related Techniques in Marketing Analysis,* Allyn and Bacon, 1970) was devoted to examining the applicability of multi-dimensional scaling and related techniques to substantive problems in marketing. Now almost twenty years later we have been joined by Scott Smith to bring these procedures into the age of microcomputers. Although most of the techniques discussed in the original book were developed (beginning in 1962) by researchers in the behavioral and life sciences, marketing research practitioners and academics have found them very useful.

The large number of articles appearing in the last twenty years in the professional marketing journals—such as the *Journal of Marketing Research* and the *Journal of Marketing*—using these techniques, attests to their usefulness. This edition continues to provide an applied approach to the presentation of the theory and is more self contained—that is, a selected suite of computer programs is included and discussed in some depth to enable the reader actually to use versions of the algorithms on a personal computer.

It is appropriate to repeat here a statement made in the original text, "... the experience of working in the rapidly evolving field has been both exciting and frustrating. It has been exciting because it seems to us that multi-dimensional scaling methodology provides a new prospective for approaching some particularly thorny behavioral research problems. It has been frustrating because, as this Preface is being written, we are aware that our statement will soon be obsolete—such is the pace with which technical developments in the field are occurring." Almost twenty years later, these comments remain true except we have learned that some of the earlier techniques have not been rendered completely obsolete by later developments. What seems to be happening is an evolution from the isolated, stand-alone algorithms and their associated computer programs to more highly refined decision support systems in the form of computer programs linked together by a common program structure and philosophy. These decision support systems, such as POSSE (Green, Carroll, Goldberg, 1981) and MDS(X) (University of Edinburgh) represent many man years and thousands of dollars in development and, thus, are not readily available to the majority of the student, researcher, or more casual professional users.

This edition of the text, which includes programs for microcomputers, is an attempt to continue to disseminate information about MDS to an ever-increasing group of students, teachers, and practitioners in marketing. The selection of specific computer programs for inclusion was governed by what is publicly available. Most of the older programs are in the public domain and could be converted for use on microcomputers. These versions were originally distributed (for reproduction costs) by Bell Telephone Laboratories, Marketing Science Institute, Forrest Young, James Lingoes, and others. The newer, more integrated and conceptually enhanced versions of these programs are not as easily available and certainly not priced at reproduction cost.

Throughout the text, the reader will note repeated references to computer methodology. Although the technical level of our presentation is not high, the methodology described owes its existence to the types of computation and complex data handling provided only by computer-based algorithms. The increased availability of microcomputers has made this methodology more accessible and useful.

Because we try to write in a simplistic, nonmathematical and easy to understand manner, more advanced readers will probably want to supplement this text with more theoretical books, such as *The User's Guide to Multidimensional Scaling* by A.P.M. Coxon or *Introduction to Multidimensional Scaling: Theory, Methods and Applications* by Susan S. Schiffman, M. Lance Reynolds, and Forrest W. Young; *Multidimensional Scaling* by Joseph B. Kruskal and Myron Wish; *Three-Way Scaling and Clustering* by Phipps Arabie, J. Douglas Carroll, and Wayne S. DeSarbo; and *Multidimensional Scaling* by Mark L. Davison—all published since our earlier edition of this book. These texts contain more detailed discussions of enhanced multidimensional scaling algorithms and their associated computer programs. Detailed comparisons with the programs discussed in these more recent texts are not made here. It is our feeling that the programs included with this book are sufficiently comprehensive to handle the more common types of data collected by marketing research academics and practitioners.

We close this Preface with a reiteration of two caveats regarding the book's scope. First, we did not intend the book to be a state-of-the-art description of the applied MDS field; exposure to newer developments should come from the current journal literature and the books cited above. Second, we have frequently traded off technical precision in favor of intuitive discussions that are more easily grasped by beginning students whose primary interests are applications oriented.

Acknowledgments: In the earlier version of this text, we mentioned a number of our colleagues, friends, and students who had an influence on our thinking about this topic. Many of these individuals have continued to serve as a source of inspiration and encouragement. When possible we have attempted to incorporate their insights and suggestions in this edition. We especially wish to thank Dr. J. Douglas Carroll, Bell Telephone Laboratories, for his continued creativity and patience with the neophytes and Professor Arun Jain, State University of New York at Buffalo, and Professor Larry Richards, University of Oregon, for their detailed and constructive criticism. Proofreading was ably carried out by Jinho Kim, doctoral student, University of Pennsylvania; Dau-Chao Chang, Khalid Dubas, Margaret Liebman, Mary Shoemaker, and Catharine Tang Wong, all doctoral students, Drexel University; and Erica Carmone. Even with all this help, any errors remaining are attributable to the authors.

PART I

Overview

Introduction and Problem Setting

The purpose of this text is to acquaint or update marketing practitioners, teachers, and students with a continually evolving methodology for analyzing choice behavior: multidimensional scaling and related techniques. While some of these techniques can be broadly classified under the traditional rubric of "attitude or image research," the methods extend well beyond the traditional rating scales, semantic differentials, and other such devices used in the measurement of perception and preference.

For the most part, the techniques were developed in the 1960s. Since that time, a sufficient body of research literature has been generated to suggest their great value in modeling both consumer and industrial marketing choice behavior. In this text, we describe a selected subset of these procedures and their implications for marketing analysis. In addition, since the methodology is probably unfamiliar to many readers, we have included a variety of data sets and a detailed case study of soft-drink positioning. These data are used with the following microcomputer programs, which are also included with the text: CLUSTER, CORRESP, INDSCAL, KYST, MDPREF, PREFMAP, PROFIT. In Appendix A we list other computer programs, how they can be used, and their availability.

While our continued enthusiasm about the potential of these techniques is seldom concealed, it should be made clear that the methodology itself continues to evolve, and though much empirical application has been made, more is required if it is to become a "standard" statistical tool. This text has been prepared to further that aim by providing the following:

- — A discussion of analytic techniques heretofore scattered over a variety of journals and unpublished working papers not normally perused by either the practitioner or academic
- — A set of readings identifying the current state of the art in multidimensional scaling
- — A suite of programs to experiment and learn with in studying this methodology

FORMAT OF THE TEXT The main body of the text consists of three parts plus appendixes. In Part II, Section 1 sets the stage for later discussion by reviewing some of the fundamentals of measurement theory and some historical background on multidimensional scaling. In addition, a description of several potential applications of scaling methods is presented for consideration in subsequent chapters.

Section 2 introduces the more formal characteristics of scaling methodology and provides a classification system, due to Coombs (1964), for the analysis of behavioral data. Section 3 describes the analysis of similarities data, including metric, nonmetric conditional, and nonmetric unconditional data analysis. Section 4 introduces the analysis of preference data, including vector and ideal point models. Unfolding analysis and correspondence analysis are also discussed.

The final section in Part II presents reduced space analysis (principal components analysis) and clustering methods. These methodologies, while not multidimensional scaling, are frequently used in conjunction with MDS procedures in many research projects and are thus included for completeness.

Part III of the text includes some of the current literature that reviews and identifies current research in multidimensional scaling (Section 6), correspondence analysis (Section 7), and cluster analysis (Section 8).

Part IV of the text presents case study material for illustrating selected data collection procedures and the running of computer programs included with the text.

There are three appendices: Appendix A contains a listing of available computer programs; Appendix B contains the questionnaire and data set for the soft drink case study; and Appendix C contains a listing of sample data, data matrices from the sample data, and a sample program command file.

HOW MULTIDIMENSIONAL SCALING IS USED IN MARKETING

Two ideas in marketing—the marketing concept and market segmentation—continue to provide the basis for both marketing practice and research. The marketing concept, as evidenced in product positioning strategies, emphasizes the firm's role in developing a uniqueness in the mind of the consumer. In principle, the firm is attempting to better satisfy the needs and wants of a target market segment. This perspective directs corporate research and development, production, finance, and personnel activities to be customer-oriented. As such, the marketing concept is integrative in nature; all activities of the firm are ultimately connected with the identifying and satisfying of the customer. These efforts take place in a variety of competitive and cooperative environments, are intended to create and retain customers, and are expected to lead to growth and profits for the firm.

Market segmentation is the application of the marketing concept. Buyer perceptions are measured, products are developed, and information systems track each segment's response to the various marketing strategies. As such, segmentation is disaggregative in nature; the firm attempts to shape its marketing strategy so as to appeal to specific segments within the diverse market. In so doing, it is assumed that total profits can be increased. Market research applications are founded largely in the identification of relevant segments and the prediction of consequences stemming from the employment of different strategies for the relevant segments.

Perceptions and Preferences in Market Segmentation

Research The analysis of buyer perceptions and preferences of products and services is integral to product positioning and market segmentation research. The scaling of perceptions and preferences can provide operational measures of how the product or service is perceived and evaluated by the firm's clientele—whether actual or potential. Furthermore, that neither perceptions nor preferences need be homogeneous over buyers can suggest opportunities for segmentation strategy. As we shall show, perceptual and preference measurement can provide an operational procedure for implementing both concepts.

Perception and preference are two fundamental phenomena of all human behavior. As we move through the decision-making hierarchy that extends from problem recognition to repeat purchase behavior (problem recognition–product awareness–information search–evaluation–purchase intention–trial–repeat postpurchase evaluation), we are constantly making perceptual judgments about similarities and differences among the myriad of stimuli with which we are confronted. Is Classic Coke more similar to the new Coke than it is to Pepsi? How does Burger King compare to McDonald's for the single head of household who eats fast food three or more times per week? If I'm a Republican from the Midwest running for president of the United States, and I am in favor of farm support, farm products import tariff, increased military spending, but against deficit spending, increases in federal taxes and federal financing of health services for the elderly, will you vote for me? Our perceptions of various entities are the result of our evaluation processes. Perceptions are a necessary part of our choice behavior.

Preferences are no less ubiquitous. Buyers may perceive products or services similarly while displaying differences in preferences. For example, Diet Coke, Diet Pepsi, and Tab could be perceived similarly by two individuals, yet one could prefer Diet Pepsi and the other could prefer Tab. The fact that consumer product markets are rarely dominated by one brand or supplier is partial evidence of the heterogeneity of buyer preferences.

BASIC CONCEPTS OF MULTIDIMENSIONAL

SCALING Multidimensional scaling and related techniques are concerned primarily with the spatial representation of relationships among behavioral data—in our case, buyer perceptions and preferences. While we shall be presenting a somewhat more formal description of multidimensional scaling methods in succeeding chapters, the basic concepts are presented here at an intuitive and content-oriented level.

Attribute Space   Any product or service can be visualized as composed of both physical (objective) and perceived (subjective) attributes or "dimensions." A firm may conduct extensive laboratory tests on its brand, leading to an objective description that employs chemical or physical terms. Such objective attribute "spaces" identify the various brands as points positioned somewhere in the space, where the dimensions of the objective space are defined by the objective measures. The objective space will not necessarily agree with the buyer's perceived space. The perceived space, in contrast, consists of brand or supplier positions that are related to the dimensions reflecting the buyer's perception of the product or service class—those attributes used in making discrimination judgments among brands or suppliers (Boulding, 1968).

Two characteristics of perceived space, and its relationship to objective space, should be mentioned. First, the dimensions of the perceived space need not agree with those of the objective space. Second, even if they do agree with (some subset of) the set of objective dimensions, the projections of the points on the various dimensions may not agree with their objective counterparts. That is, the two configurations of points may differ even if the dimensions agree.

Thus, a set of more or less common stimuli—such as brands of soft drinks, banking services, electric motors, automobiles—can be described in both objective and perceptual space. The perceptual "maps" of brands or specific suppliers of services may, of course, vary both across individuals and over time and context within the same individual. Moreover, the dimensionality of this space—the "richness" of the typical perceptual map—may vary over stimulus classes.

In some settings, such as industrial product applications, the perceived configuration of brands may agree rather closely with an objectively constructed configuration. Measurements of such characteristics as size, speed, efficiency, and reliability can be made rather straightforwardly. In other instances, such as brands of shampoo, headache remedies, toothpastes, and many other consumer-packaged goods, the perceived dimensions may differ markedly from the physical and chemical characteristics of the products. This disparity, of course, is partly a reflection of such factors as advertising content, supplier reputation, and other "external" influences that contribute to the buyer's overall image of the brand or service.

Nonetheless, from the viewpoint of the consumer, the perceived dimensions are the relevant ones in making a product choice; clearly, brands that are physically and chemically identical may be perceived differently and, conversely, chemically and physically distinct brands may be perceived similarly. This possible disparity between objectively measured and perceived attributes suggests the need to consider not only perceptual dimensions but "objective" dimensions, as well and the techniques by which one set can be related to the other.

Ideal Points   Individuals may be characterized as having an ideal stimulus in a perceptual (subjective) attribute space. If so, what is the interpretation? One rather compelling interpretation is that individuals prefer one particular combination of values on the perceived product or service dimensions to all other combinations that are available in the product–service class. Stimuli, such as brands or service suppliers, that are "closer" to an individual's ideal point will tend to be preferred to those farther away. Moreover, the individual may differentially weight the dimensions in terms of their relative importance in the evaluative context. If such is the case, the distance of specific brands or services from the ideal point is assumed to reflect the differential "stretching" that is applied to the dimensions of interest, often termed the importance of the dimensions, as now considered in evaluative space.

   As the reader will probably gather, the concept of attribute space is central to market segmentation and product position, research and strategy, and the techniques to be described in this book. In a positioning strategy sense, the "nearness" of any two brands or services in this space can be formulated as an operational measure of their competitiveness. Stimuli, or products, can be developed for positioning within an attribute space (either perceptual or objective). This strategy may be interpreted as reflecting segment ideal points—that is, the combination of attribute levels that the market segment buyer would tend to prefer to all other combinations. Finally, buyers can be positioned in an evaluative attribute space as well, with the interpretation usually being construed as their respective ideal points—that is, the combination of attribute levels that for a given buyer would tend to be preferred to all other combinations.

   The analytical power of the multidimensional scaling techniques is derived from the above, rather simple geometric notion of attribute space. As we have noted, however, several types of spaces are relevant:

1. The "objective" attribute space in which brands or services are positioned in terms of hard data, such as physical and chemical composition, price, number of service suppliers, and so forth.
2. The set of subjectively determined perceptual attribute spaces that reflect perceived dimensions of the stimuli (brands or suppliers). These may vary:

   — Over individuals at any point in time
   — Over time for any specific individual
   — Over individuals and time by specific situations; for example, how the product is used

3. The set of subjectively determined evaluative attribute spaces that reflect

a common perceived position of stimuli (brands or suppliers). The saliences and/or ideal point positions of individual subjects are not, however, necessarily the same. That is, there exist similar perceptions and corresponding positioning of the brands, but different preferences. These "evaluative" spaces may vary, again:

— Over individuals at any point in time
— Over time for any specific individual
— Over individuals and time by specific situations

Finally, one requires the linking of selected distances in perceptual (evaluative) attribute space to brand preference. In one type of model formulation, this might be accomplished by a function that relates measures of probability of choice to an MDS-produced measure of distance between the stimulus (brand or service) and a buyer's ideal point in evaluative space.

Consequently, predictions of buyer response to corporate policy variables (changes in product, package, promotion, price, and distribution) would thus proceed through a sequence of steps:

— Objective attribute space
— Perceived attribute space
— Evaluative attribute space of stimuli and ideal points
— Choice response function
— Aggregation over individual types of buyers and specific purchase situations

SUMMARY   In this introductory section we have tried to outline, at an intuitive level, the notion of attribute space and its relevance to the spatial description of stimuli. Our interest from a content standpoint primarily consists of the measurement of perceptions and preferences. In so doing, we must distinguish between objective and perceived attribute spaces. Finally, the concepts of attribute importance and ideal point enter as a means of portraying, geometrically, preferred combinations of "scores" on the evaluative dimensions by which stimuli are compared.

In principle, then, the methodology could be used to predict the effect of stimuli changes (in objective space) on: (a) stimuli (brand) positions in perceived space, (b) ideal point or stimulus positions in evaluative space, and ultimately (c) share of brand choices. The remainder of this book will be largely concerned with the implementation of this predictive model and the analytical procedures that are relevant in this implementation.

PART II

Analytic Techniques

Measurement Theory and Overview of Scaling Applications

This section like the previous section, has been prepared at a somewhat intuitive level. Our purpose is to elaborate on the problem setting discussed in the preceding section. As such, the orientation is primarily descriptive rather than methodological.

Specifically, we first introduce some of the rudiments of measurement theory so as to provide background for later discussion of potential scaling applications. This introduction is followed by a brief description of the evolution of multidimensional scaling methods. Two studies are then discussed at an informal level in order to give the reader some idea of the results of applying the methodology. (We leave to later sections a more technical discussion of how and why the techniques work.)

We then turn to a presentation of capsule descriptions of a variety of applied problems that may be researched by means of multidimensional scaling methodology. Our description of these problems is motivated by the desire to provide a substantive base for application of the formal models to be described in subsequent chapters.

AN OVERVIEW OF MEASUREMENT THEORY In its broadest context measurement consists of the assignment of one set of entities, usually mathematical entities such as numbers, to another set of entities, usually empirical phenomena. In making such assignments, the researcher is assuming that the basic ordinal, interval, or ratio relationships among mathematical entities are descriptive of similar relationships among empirical entities. If the correspondence holds well enough to be useful, the known properties of the mathematical measurement system can serve as a model for describing the empirical system.

It is a common observation that people can order objects or other stimulus concepts (such as brands) according to some criterion. That is, they can say whether stimulus (brand) A has more, the same, or less of property (attribute) X than stimulus (brand) B. Such data are collected in a variety of marketing research studies dealing with attitudes, beliefs, and preferences. Any set of numbers that does not violate the ranking relationship is acceptable. Such data are only ordinal-scaled and will be called "nonmetric" in this text.

A more common measurement is the interval scale. The interval scale assumes that the magnitude of the difference between any two objects on a scale (call it X) meaningfully measures their difference on that property called X. Thus, we would like to be able to define a unit that enables numerical comparisons of the difference between any pair of stimulus objects. Such considerations involve an interval or "metric" scale.

If in addition to the properties of the interval scale we can fix a unique zero or natural origin point, we have a ratio scale. This type of scaling is associated with physical properties like height, weight, and length. The ratio scale is a metric scale, but one that is hard to justify in the measurement of perceptions and evaluations. Because the most common forms of statistical tests assume only interval scaled data, the researcher rarely requires the power of the ratio metric [Green, Tull, and Albaum, 1988].

Permissible Transformations Another way of looking at the differences among ordinal, interval, and ratio scales is in terms of their uniqueness under certain types of transformations. Ordinal scales are unique up to a (strictly) monotonic increasing transformation, as shown in Figure 1–1(a). Any transformation that preserves the rank order (monotonicity) is appropriate—that is, any order preserving transformation of the original scale is just as good a representation of the empirical relationships as any other order preserving transformation. Algebraically,

$$x_2 > x_1 \Rightarrow y_2 > y_1.$$

Permissible transformations of interval scales are constrained to be positive linear. That is,

$$y = a + bx; \quad b > 0$$

Figure 1–1(b) illustrates this type of function. A conventional illustration of interval scaling involves temperature, as measured on the Celsius or Fahrenheit scales. We recall that each represents a linear transformation of the other. The linear functions

$$F = 32 + \frac{9}{5}C \quad \text{and} \quad C = -\frac{160}{9} + \frac{5}{9}F = (F - 32) \times \frac{5}{9}$$

permit Celsius conversions to Fahrenheit and from Fahrenheit to Celsius, respectively.

Note that ratio scales are "unique up to"[1] a positive proportionality

---

[1] "Unique up to" means that the scale properties are maintained under the hierarchy of data transformation up to the specified transform. The more powerful the metric, the more constrained the transformation allowed.

_____ *Figure 1–1* _____

Permissible Transformation by Scale Type

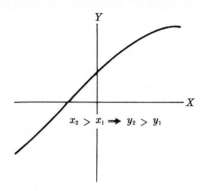

$$x_2 > x_1 \Rightarrow y_2 > y_1$$

(a) Monotonic

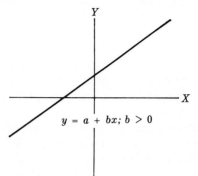

$$y = a + bx; \; b > 0$$

(b) Linear

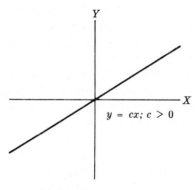

$$y = cx; \; c > 0$$

(c) Proportionality

transformation—that is, we are allowed only to change the unit of measurement:

$$y = cx \qquad c > 0$$

Figure 1–1(c) illustrates this case. Note that the transformation is linear, but the linear function is constrained to pass through the origin. While we would like to be able to measure various classes of psychological and social phenomena on ratio scales, such possibilities are rare. Furthermore, it is often the case that interval scale measurements are sufficiently "strong" for various research purposes and for policy objectives as well.

Ordered Metric Scales   While ordinal, interval, and ratio scales represent the more familiar types, a less common scale of particular significance to certain classes of multidimensional scaling techniques is the ordered metric. An ordered metric scale is one in which all possible intervals between scale positions can be ranked. Suppose we have five stimuli—*A, B, C, D,* and *E*—that are ordered along a continuum. For the $n = 5$ stimuli, ten unique pairs of stimuli exist $[n(n - 1)]/2$. We can order all ten interpoint distances, $AB, AC, \ldots, DE,$ of the five stimuli taken two at a time. The ranking may, for example, be based on perceived similarities between the pairs, with the first pair being most similar and the tenth pair being least similar. The scale is still a ranking or ordinal scale, but the order now applies to all distances separating pairs of points. Moreover, as more and more points are added on the continuum whose end points are *A* and *E,* we will obtain an interval scale (at the limit).

While a single ordering of stimuli on only one attribute provides no basis for developing an interval scale with its stronger representation of the data, it turns out that when we order pairs of points (stimuli), interpoint "distances," may be produced that imply more information about the scale positions of the points than is at first apparent from the original scales. Similarly, several orderings (not all the same) of a set of stimuli by different respondents can (asymptotically) provide metric (interval scaled or stronger) information about both stimuli and subjects by requiring that parameter values of the fitted measurement model be ordinally consistent across the stimuli and subjects of the whole set of data.

The above are both illustrations of what are known as conjoint measurement techniques [Luce and Tukey, 1964]. An outcome or event is conjoint if it represents a combination of two or more elements. Response to pairs of stimuli is conjoint as is also the case of a subject and a stimulus pair of items. If we can establish an ordered relationship for such pairs, we may be able to "upgrade" the data to some stronger form of scale. This is one of the major objectives of nonmetric (or ordinal) multidimensional scaling.

TYPES OF MULTIDIMENSIONAL SCALING
Multidimensional scaling methods generally attempt to represent certain types of data as relations on points in a multidimensional space. The dimensions of the space are assumed to represent attributes or properties along which the stimuli or objects are compared. As we shall see later, the stimuli may be real—for example, brands of toothpaste, corporate names, advertisements—or hypothetical—for example, an "ideal" stimulus [Coombs, 1964] that possesses a particular combination of attribute levels the respondent would prefer to any other combination.

The Development of Nonmetric Scaling
The history of ordinal or nonmetric methods of multidimensional scaling begins with the first conceptual paper and computer program by Roger Shepard (1962). Since that time, however, progress in algorithm development has been rapid. Some appreciation for the versatility of these newer methods might be gained by contrasting them with the more rigid fully metric and fully nonmetric multidimensional scaling approaches.

Fully metric methods, as the name suggests, require that data be in the form of ratio-scaled distances. In practice, however, only interval scale data values are required if a procedure for estimating an "additive constant" is used. These techniques use a factor-analytic approach to find the dimensionality and configuration of points in multidimensional space. More specifically, a data matrix of interpoint distances (normally a square matrix of stimuli × stimuli distances) is used as the starting point to find the appropriate number of dimensions and the configuration of points such that those distances most closely match the original interpoint distances (up to a positive proportionality transformation). Fully metric methods go back to a set of theorems proved by Young and Householder (1938). In general, such methods—since they are based on the linear principal components factor-analysis model—will require a larger number of dimensions in the solution if the relationship between input data and output distances is nonlinear (but still monotonic). Early multidimensional scaling work by Richardson (1938), Klingberg (1941), and Torgerson (1958) used this type of approach and these methods are still in use today.

Fully nonmetric methods do not assume more than a rank order measure of the input "distances." The objective of this class of methods is to find a solution space of minimum dimensionality that maintains the rank order (in the multidimensional case) of each point on each dimension in turn. Fully nonmetric methods do not produce a configuration of point positions that can be mapped—that is, in the defined space. Instead, results consist only of a vector of rank orders representing stimulus projections on each dimension, in turn. These first MDS methods were originally developed by Coombs (1950) and Bennett and Hays (1960). While the techniques require only nonmetric (rank order) input data, they unfortunately also yield only nonmetric output in the multidimensional case.

Nonmetric multidimensional scaling methods (in contrast to *fully* nonmetric methods) are the primary focus of this text and combine the best of each of the previous approaches—ordinal input and metric output. Given only a rank order of "psychological distance" data, the objective of these approaches is to find a configuration whose rank order of (ratio-scaled) distances best reproduces the original input ranks. One tries to do this in the lowest dimensionality that produces a "close enough" ordinal fit.

Sample Applications of Multidimensional Scaling   In order to give the reader some intuitive feel for the results of applying multidimensional scaling techniques, we describe briefly two sample applications of nonmetric methods. At this point we purposely ignore questions of methodology, and focus, instead, on the outcomes of the methodology. In this way the substantive issues are kept uppermost while still enabling us to demonstrate some of the rudiments of the techniques.

In one pilot study, we were interested in how one group of graduate students perceived alternate national brands of soft drinks as being "similar" or "different." Clearly, one could measure various aspects of soft drinks in terms of colaness, dietness, sweetness, fruitiness, aftertaste, and so on. Which of a myriad group of attributes do prospective soft drink consumers actually use in making similarity and difference judgments and what is the outcome of their perceptions?

Approximately sixty graduate business students at two universities were given a questionnaire (Appendix B) in which they were asked to respond to the following kind of question:

Using criteria of your choice, which two of the following soft drinks are most similar? next most similar and so on?

(1) Pepsi	(6) Diet 7-Up
(2) Coke	(7) Dr. Pepper
(3) Coke Classic	(8) Slice
(4) Diet Pepsi	(9) 7-Up
(5) Diet Slice	(10) Tab

The above questions were repeated for all possible pairs of the ten soft drinks. From this simple task, each soft drink pair was evaluated in terms of "subjective" similarity. The resulting average rank order of all possible pairs of soft drinks for all subjects is shown in Table 1–1. These similarities were submitted to the KYST computer algorithm to develop a spatial configuration representing the scaled data.

In subsequent chapters we shall discuss these algorithms more thoroughly. For the moment, however, we show (Figure 1–2) only the two-space configuration derived from the data for a single hypothetical subject.

We note from Figure 1–2 that several soft drinks—Coke, Pepsi, and Coke Classic—are perceived to be very similar—that is, they plot close together.

_____ Table 1–1 _____

Rank Order of Dissimilarities Between Pairs of Soft Drinks

	P	C	CC	DP	DS	D7	DR	S	7	T
Pepsi										
Coke	1									
Coke Classic	3	2								
Diet Pepsi	7	9	8							
Diet Slice	27	28	32	22						
Diet 7-Up	41	42	43	29	13					
Dr. Pepper	18	17	19	20	30	40				
Slice	24	25	26	31	5	16	23			
7-Up	35	36	38	44	15	6	37	14		
Tab	12	11	10	4	33	34	21	39	45	

_____ Figure 1–2 _____

Analysis of Pop Dissimilarities Data

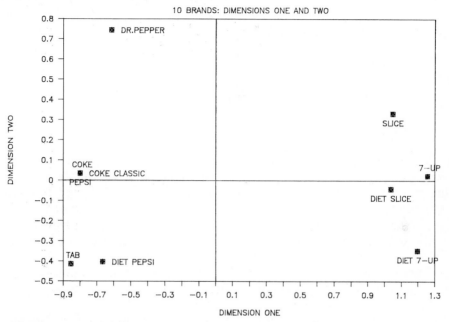

Dimension One = Cola flavor
Dimension Two = Dietness

Additionally, 7-Up and Slice, Diet 7-Up and Diet Slice, and Tab and Diet Pepsi are perceived as similar. The two least similar brands are Dr. Pepper and Diet 7-Up.

From other information obtained from the questionnaire, the horizontal axis can be labeled "Cola Flavor," with Tab being perceived to be the most cola-flavored and 7-Up the least cola flavored. The vertical axis can be labeled as "Dietness," with Tab being perceived to be the most dietetic and Dr. Pepper the most nondietetic. Such "labels," however, are not found by the multidimensional scaling technique; the problem of axis labeling is discussed in subsequent chapters. For purposes of this chapter, the interesting conclusion is that only two attributes were needed to describe the student's perceptions of soft drinks. Moreover, the geometrical distance between each soft drink pair can be viewed as a metric measure of similarity—that is, the notion of brand "image" has been quantified and portrayed geometrically from nonmetric (rank order) input data alone.

Professional Journals Many years ago a sample study was conducted among a small sample of Wharton marketing faculty members and Marketing

Science Institute research personnel [Green and Carmone, 1967*a*]. In this instance the "stimuli" are eight professional journals.

— *Commentary*
— *Harvard Business Review*
— *Journal of Advertising Research*
— *Journal of Business*
— *Journal of Marketing*
— *Journal of Marketing Research*
— *Management Science*
— *Public Opinion Quarterly*

These journals were all familiar to the respondents and, to a greater or lesser extent, still represent sources of professional marketing literature. In this study both similarities and preference data were obtained from each respondent. Thus, in terms of previous discussion, our interest was in developing a similarities–preference space of stimuli and individuals' ideal points with regard to various combinations of journal attributes most preferred by the respondents.

Figure 1–3 shows a two-space map of ideal points and stimuli obtained for a subset of respondents from the analysis of both similarities and preference data. Looking first at the stimuli (professional journals) we note that the *Journal of Advertising Research* and the *Journal of Marketing Research* were perceived to be most alike, while the *Journal of Marketing* and *Management Science* were perceived to be least alike. From other information obtained in the study, one might label the vertical axis "technical level"—*Management Science* being the most technically oriented journal. Similarly, the horizontal axis appears to be "specific–general" with the *Journal of Advertising Research* being the most specific and *Harvard Business Review* being the most general with regard to content material, at least as perceived by this respondent group.

The position of respondent ideal points is also of interest. Respondent 9, for example, most prefers *Management Science* and least prefers the *Journal of Marketing*. Respondent 3, on the other hand, displays a preference for the "general" journals, *Journal of Business* and *Harvard Business Review*. Finally, it is of interest to note that the "average" respondent prefers the technical-specific journals, *Management Science, Journal of Advertising Research,* and *Journal of Marketing Research*.

In later chapters, we shall go into more detail regarding the computer algorithms from which the configuration of Figure 1–3 was prepared. For the present, however, it suffices to say that for this group of respondents, the similarities–preference map yielded fairly straightforward and simple results. Again, we may view distances between stimuli (journals) as (ratio-scaled) measures of their psychological closeness; the smaller the distance between a stimulus and an ideal point, the more it is preferred.

_____ *Figure 1–3* _____

Subjects' Ideal Points and Similarities Configuration of Eight Professional Journals

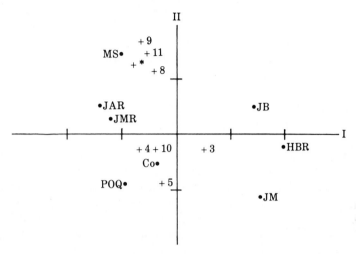

Co   — *Commentary* (Journal of the
            Market Research Society)
HBR — *Harvard Business Review*
JAR — *Journal of Advertising Research*
JB   — *Journal of Business*
JMR — *Journal of Marketing Research*
MS   — *Management Science*
POQ — *Public Opinion Quarterly*
JM   — *Journal of Marketing*

+ * Average Subject's
      Ideal Point
+ Subjects' Ideal Points
• Journals

The foregoing remarks remain at a very general, intuitive level. In subsequent chapters these heuristic notions will be made more precise and operational. At this point, however, it is useful to simply consider some of the problems for which multidimensional scaling may be applicable.

TYPICAL MARKETING PROBLEMS Several perennial marketing problems might be viewed in a new way by using the conceptual framework that underlies the multidimensional scaling methodology. We discuss below a series of illustrative problems in which multidimensional scaling and related methods might be used.

Product Life-Cycle Analysis Traditionally the analysis of product life cycles has used such notions as the "life cycle curve," in which some curve (typically S-shaped) is assumed to represent the behavior of product or brand sales as a function of time. Suppose, alternatively, that we characterize each "brand" as a vector of performance characteristics. In such industrial product classes as electric motors, computers, automobiles, gasoline engines, and so forth, reasonably hard data may exist. (In many consumer products, however, the brand's "scores" on each characteristic may be highly subjective.)

In any event, we might characterize a group of related brands as points in a multidimensional performance shape. Points "near each other" would be presumed to be similar with respect to either objective or subjective characteristics. Indeed, as a first approximation, we might view their perceived closeness or similarity in performance space to be an operational measure of competitiveness or substitutability.

With the above type of representation, one can next conceive of the points shifting over time within the performance space—or, if you will, a series of snapshots of the same performance space. Each snapshot would show the relative positions of competing brands in a specific time period. Finally, one might like to relate movement along various performance axes to some "success" measure like sales or market share. Each of the performance spaces developed at each point in time is derived using multidimensional scaling.

While use of this approach has not appeared in the literature, an earlier analysis of the computer market [Green and Carmone, 1968] has demonstrated its feasibility. We believe that this conceptualization of the product life cycle is particularly useful in the analysis of industrial markets. In our judgment it provides a more meaningful and detailed portrayal of change than that described by empirical representations of product life-cycle curves.

Market Segmentation   A second area of potential application for nonmetric scaling methods is market segmentation. Suppose one could characterize a product class and its buyers as points in a similarities–preference space whose dimensions are perceived product attributes. Each brand could be represented as a stimulus point and each buyer as an ideal point in the same attribute space. Actually, however, market segmentation allows individual buyers to have different perceptual subspaces and, within a given subspace, different ideal point locations. Conceptually, then, each market segment might be viewed as a subspace in which all members of that market segment perceive the stimuli similarly and possess the "same" ideal point position and dimension saliences. One logical next step in the analysis would be to establish the relationship of stimulus and ideal point position to other characteristics of the buyer; for example, the usual socioeconomic, personality, and demographic variables [Green and Morris, 1969].

We could, of course, also have unique spaces for consumers and market segments where the following apply:

1. Individuals exhibit similar perceptions but possess differing dimension saliences and/or ideal point positions.
2. Neither stimulus perception nor ideal point position nor dimension salience is common over individuals.

Partitioning the overall "superspace" of ideal points and stimuli into reasonably homogeneous subspaces and identifying the characteristics of those consumers whose perceptions and preferences characterize those subspaces appears to be in the spirit of market segmentation strategy. Such analyses often show "empty regions" (under-marketed segments) where high concentrations of ideal points exist but no close brands are found. At the very least, the analysis should point out the competitive position of a firm's brand with other brands as viewed perceptually by different market segments.

From the marketer's point of view, the task is to modify the product, package, advertising, and so forth for the purposes of either moving the brand toward some region in the space having a high "concentration" of ideal points and low number of closely related brands, or attempting to move the ideal points themselves toward the brand. We might also conceive of the possibility of reorienting the whole configuration, including its dimensions, as might be the case when a truly "innovative" product enters the market.

Although this approach is somewhat questionable for mature markets, segments may be viewed as spatial representations that may be tracked over time. Thus a perceptions and preferences audit is formed that is both analogous and supplementary to a Nielsen-type audit of physical goods movement.

Allied with the above approach is the potential use of multidimensional scaling in intracorporate research. Are the images of the company's products and services congruent across the advertising department, field sales, product development staff, and the firm's distributors? If so, do these perceptions agree with those of the ultimate buyer? If inconsistency exists, multiple marketing strategies may be modified to increase the effectiveness of pricing, advertising, product, and distribution tactics.

In one such study for a major drug company, the conclusion was that the company sales force had a very different perception of the products, company, and the competition than did the doctors to whom they were selling. Multidimensional scaling was used to document perceptions of the sales force and those of the doctors, and to develop a sales force training program directed at changing physician attitudes.

Vendor Evaluations　　Another intriguing area for potential application is found in the empirical estimation of the importance weights used in multiattribute decision models. (Importance weights are used by people to derive simple brand preference orders from partially ordered alternatives).[2] As an example, consider the industrial purchasing agent who must select a primary vendor. Vendor *A* may be low in price, fair on maintaining delivery promises, poor in technical service, and low in technical innovation. Vendor *B* might be high in price but excellent on delivery promises, and so on. Each vendor might be

---

[2] Partially ordered alternatives refers to the practice of rank ordering alternatives, in turn, by each attribute in a set of attributes. If five alternatives are to be ranked on three attributes, three separate sets of "partially ordered alternatives" would result.

characterized by a summary vector containing the overall rating scores on each attribute dimension. Within the context of the multidimensional scaling problem, only the individual attribute components can be ordered across alternatives.

Clearly, purchasing agents (like other decision makers) implicitly summarize their set of all vendor rating evaluations (called partially ordered alternatives) into an overall rank ordering so as to make a choice. What we would like to determine are the implicit weights that make up the multiattribute decision model. Are some characteristics suppressed entirely, are strong interactions evident—in short, what is the relative importance of each characteristic and how do these weights differ from individual to individual, and over time? Such knowledge would be undoubtedly useful in the design of vendor sales strategies. To date, considerable marketing research has been devoted to the multiattribute decision problem; these approaches have, however, used self-explicated importance measures rather than demand functions from the scaling algorithms.

Advertising Evaluations   The perennial problem of ad pretesting is profitably explored by the use of multidimensional scaling methods. Several basic questions come to mind:

1. Are "good" ads more similar to each other than "good" ads are to "bad" ads?
2. Do predictive experts (advertising personnel) exhibit interperson reliability in making similarity judgments (American Newspaper Publishers Association, 1969)?
3. What are the dimensions along which ads are judged?
4. What are the respective saliences of dimensions in contributing to overall similarity or overall preference?

Related to the above comments is the question of media selection strategy. In one early application, Green and Carmone (1967*b*) were concerned with developing and matching medical journal and physician readership profiles. Nonmetric scaling was used to develop a journal configuration in which medical journals "near" each other in the space tended to "go together" in terms of physician readership. Conversely, a physician profile was also developed in terms of journal readership. In addition, physician readership profiles were related to their prescribing activity in an attempt to determine correspondence between these two classes of behavior.

Studies such as the above could be extended to the problem of matching advertisements with the media vehicle. For example, what advertisements seem to "go with" what magazines? One could investigate this problem through content analysis or through experiments in which the consumer is asked to match specific advertisements with specific magazines. The incidence of such matchings could be taken as a measure of the commonality of specific types of advertisements and specific types of media vehicles. This approach might be useful in getting some quantitative feel for the "vehicle effect" in media selection strategy.

Test Marketing   Another problem area of significance to corporate strategy is product test marketing. Multidimensional scaling methods may be employed both as guides to researching and developing new products and to predicting market share for new entrants. In the first case, similarities and preference mapping may be used to characterize the perceived structure of the product class and to identify clusters of ideal points. The position of a firm's current brand in this space would indicate which brands represent nearest competitors. Moreover, ideal point clusters associated with few surrounding products could suggest opportunities for new product development.

Candidate products could then be evaluated on a test basis by having buyers compare them to existing brands in order to see how product changes are actually perceived. The proportion of preferences going to each new brand represents one indicator of its commercial success [Stefflre, 1960]. Moreover, additional information could be ascertained regarding those existing brands (including the firm's current brand) that are most likely to lose market share to the new entrant.

Sales Force and Store Image Research   In many product classes the company sales force is a dominant influence on increasing product sales. Multidimensional scaling techniques would appear to be just as applicable to evaluating customer perception of our corporate sales representatives as they are to evaluating our perception of brands. It would be interesting to find out if the corporate image projected by the salesperson is congruent with the image produced by other corporate marketing efforts. The question of image congruence (or lack thereof) may hold important implications for market planning and the coordination of promotional activities.

Similar relationships apply to image research in the area of distribution channels. What is the dealer's image of the brand and the consumer's image of both the brand and the dealer? Disparities in image as perceived by the principals in the distribution chain may adversely affect ultimate sales and distributor relations. Such incongruity of image could be ascertained via multidimensional scaling methods.

Brand Switching Research   Considerable interest in the phenomenon of brand loyalty has been generated over the past several years. The availability of large-scale panel data has provided for the identification of brand switching patterns.

Of particular interest is the internalization of brand switching research and the analysis of perceptual similarities and consumer preference. Do brand switchers perceive products differently than brand loyal consumers? What are the preference structures of both brand switchers and brand loyal consumers? Similar questions may be related to identifying "opinion leaders" and other indirect influencers of the brand choice decision.

Attitude Scale Construction   Attitude scaling dominates marketing research. In spite of the importance of attitude research, scales are often developed on an ad hoc basis. A large number of statements are gathered and then subjectively grouped into ordered categories that purport to measure the intensity of each statement along an assumed underlying attitude continuum. However precise this "subjective grouping" approach may be, the selected statements may not meet the stated goal of representing intensity levels on a single unidimensional scale. Instead, statements may tap various portions of an attitude space of two or more dimensions. Furthermore, the positioning of items along this unidimensional scale may be irregular, producing an ordinal scale rather than an interval set of scale descriptors.

In such cases, multidimensional scaling techniques could be used to develop the appropriate dimensionality and configuration of the attitude space. For example, one could obtain judgments of the following type: Assume a person agrees strongly with statement *A,* How likely is it that he will also agree strongly with statement *B*? with statement *C*? and so on. From the similarities data developed from statement pairs, a multidimensional configuration of the statements could be constructed and the dimensions of this configuration could be interpreted as the various components of the multidimensional attitude space. If desired, one could then select subsets of statements whose positions in the space could be approximated by a unidimensional scale.

Of course, many of the above areas of application are mentioned only suggestively and speculatively. Much marketing research using similarities and preference mapping has been conducted, yet relatively little reaches the pages of journal publications. It is primarily in the spirit of application and dissemination that the above topics have been suggested.

SUMMARY   In this chapter, we have tried to portray some of the central notions of measurement theory, attribute space, and similarities–preference mapping in an intuitive manner, emphasizing such applied problem areas as market segmentation, product life-cycle analysis, and test marketing. We leave to later chapters a more formal discussion of the methodology itself. This chapter has been primarily motivational in intent but, it is hoped, suggestive of the breadth of possible applications of multidimensional scaling procedures to the study of consumer and industrial markets.

A Classification of Data
and Scaling Techniques

This section begins the more formal discussion of multidimensional scaling techniques, which is continued in subsequent chapters. As suggested earlier, behavioral data will be viewed as relations on points in some type of geometric space. Stimuli (for example, brands) are typically represented as points in the space, and relationships between stimuli are represented as distances in the space. Historically, the geometric "space" involved only one-dimensional scales, but have since been extended to handle higher dimensional spaces.

In the first part of this section, we discuss multidimensional scaling fundamentals in terms of dominance (similarity or preference) and consonance (equality) relations on subsets of stimuli drawn from the same or different sets. Our portraying of these relations geometrically leads to a discussion of distance functions, including, but not restricted to, Euclidean distances.

We then turn to a discussion of classes of data, as formulated elegantly and succinctly by Coombs. Each of Coombs' four major classes of data are described in turn and illustrated with examples drawn from the behavioral field. We conclude with a discussion of the major types of data matrices and the classes of data implied by these matrices.

With the preceding framework in mind, we then review, in somewhat more detail than in the previous chapter, the various types of multi-dimensional scaling approaches—fully metric, fully nonmetric, and non-metric. We show conceptually how nonmetric scaling can "convert" ordinally scaled dissimilarities rankings into metrically scaled distances. The section concludes with a somewhat more technical discussion of the KYST algorithm that has been developed to execute this task.

MULTIDIMENSIONAL SCALING
FUNDAMENTALS
All of the scaling techniques that we shall be discussing in this section deal with relations on elements or pairs of elements. The term *elements* refers to stimuli, subjects, or both. As described by Coombs (1964), the two basic relations that characterize psychological data are dominance and consonance.

Dominance and Consonance Relationships

Dominance In this case, we create a strict rank order of a set of elements with respect to some property (attribute) level, as would be the case where we are asked to rank a set of fruit drinks in terms of their tartness. For each pair of elements *A* and *B* (for example, orange juice and grape juice), we are asked to say which of the following is true:

A (orange juice) is "higher" than B (grape juice) with respect to property X (cost).

B (grape juice) is "higher" than A (orange juice) with respect to property X (cost).

Consonance In this case we attempt to see if two elements match with respect to some property level, as would be the case, for example, where we are asked to say whether two fruit drinks are alike (or different) in terms of tartness. For each pair of elements *A* and *B,* we are asked to indicate which of the following is true:

A (orange juice) equals B (grape juice) with respect to property X (tartness).

A (orange juice) is not equal to B (grape juice) with respect to property X (tartness).

It is perhaps surprising that virtually all scaling studies involve one or the other of the above tasks. For example, the collection of preference data (if no ties are allowed) is an instance of employing the dominance relation. Consider also the scaling of aptitude scores in which an arithmetic problem is "passed" by a subject if and only if the subject possesses more of the aptitude than the level being tapped by the problem. Data obtained from consonance relationships are no less prevalent. Rating a product as falling into the category of "superior quality" can imply that the perceived attribute level of the product and the evaluation label of "superior quality" represent the best match of the alternative response categories available to the subject.[1] Finally, if one permits ties in the preference ordering, one obtains both dominance and consonance relations on the same data set.

The concept of dominance or ordering implies a common unidimensional continuum for any pair of elements so that the terms "less than" or "greater than" have meaning. The notion of consonance or "equality" can be construed

---

[1] Of course, one could say that the agreement between product and label is greater than that of the same product and any other label in the set; under this interpretation, a dominance relation is appropriate. Thus, an element of possible ambiguity exists in the use of the terms "dominance" and "consonance."

as an interval along a continuum within which the subject assumes that all points are indistinguishable.

So far it would seem that dominance and consonance relationships produce unidimensional rather than multidimensional scales. However, as we shall soon see, we may find it useful to characterize stimuli or subjects in several dimensions in a geometric space. The ordering (or matching) of distances between pairs of points provides the appropriate unidimensional continuum (namely, distance) that leads to the construction of multi-dimensional configurations.

An Example of Dominance and Consonance Relationships Assume that an individual is asked to make certain preference judgments about various automobile models. Figure 2–1 shows a "picture" of the response. Assume that this subject perceives that only two characteristics of cars—their degree of luxuriousness and their degree of sportiness—are important in making evaluative judgments. The ideal point, a concept first proposed by Coombs, is assumed to be located at point I, in the upper right quadrant of the perceptual map. "Ideal point" refers to a hypothetical car model possessing just that preferred combination of luxuriousness and sportiness represented by the amounts measured on each dimension of the chart.

_____ *Figure 2–1* _____

Similarities–Preference Space

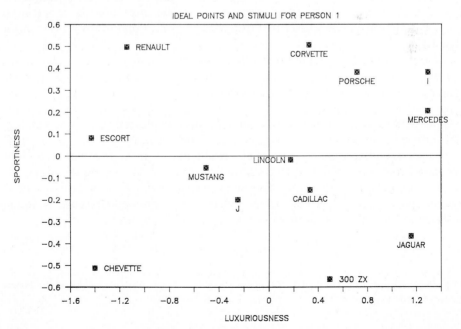

Let us imagine measuring the distance between each car model and the person's ideal point in this two-dimensional space. We would first construct a series of lines of varying lengths connecting each point to the ideal point. Next, we project these eleven distances onto a unidimensional distance scale that ranges from, say, 0 to 3. In doing so, we can compare the length of each line with every other and, ultimately, rank their lengths. Note that in this instance the line connecting the ideal point I to the Chevrolet Chevette would be the longest.

By using interpoint distances as our unidimensional scale, we focus on the difference between the pairs of points—that is, pairs of pairs of points—and we can identify either dominance, if the pairs are of unequal length, or consonance, if the pairs are of equal length. For example, we may say that an individual prefers Jaguar XJ6 to Cadillac Seville if the distance from point I to Jaguar XJ6 is less than that from point I to the Cadillac Seville. We could postulate that individuals will prefer actual automobiles whose combination of attribute levels is closest to their ideal point.

Similarly, we can compare the relative similarities of pairs of real cars in terms of their interpoint distances. For example, Corvette and Nissan 300 ZX could be said to be more similar to each other than, say, Renault Alliance and Porsche 944 if the distance connecting the former pair is less than that connecting the latter.

Notice, further, that a consonance relation is also inherent in this illustration. Assume that some small difference in distances i, P, J exists, representing the (absolute) difference in distances between ideal point I and *P*orsche 944, and ideal point I and *J*aguar XJ6. If this difference in distances is less than some absolute quantity $\epsilon(i)$, then the individual is not able to state a preference. The (absolute) quantity $\epsilon(i)$ is individual i's perceptual threshold.

Many assumptions have been introduced in our discussion of the above example. It seems appropriate now to discuss the nature of some of these assumptions from a more formal point of view.

The Properties of Distance Functions

Earlier we elected to view psychological data as dominance or consonance relations on pairs or pairs of pairs of points in a metric space. The points could all be from the same set—for example, real car models—or from different sets—for example, ideal car models versus real car models. But what do we mean by a metric space? A metric space is one in which there exists a well-defined distance function possessing the following properties for any points x, y, and z.

(1)
$$d(x, x) = 0 \quad \text{and} \quad d(x, y) > 0$$

The distance between a point and itself is zero, whereas the distance between distinct points is positive.

(2)
$$d(x, y) = d(y, x)$$

The distance must be symmetric.

(3) $$d(x, y) \le d(x, z) + d(z, y)$$

The distance from point x to point y must be less than or equal to the distance from x to y indirectly through point z. This property is known as the *triangle inequality* [Figure 2–2(b)].

Euclidean Distances   In order to examine the additional properties of an important subclass of metrics (namely, vector forms) let us introduce an elementary formula for finding the distance between two points in the Euclidean plane. We recall from elementary geometry that the Euclidean distance between two points i and j in the plane is given by

$$d_{ij} = [(x_{i1} - x_{j1})^2 + (x_{i2} - x_{j2})^2]^{1/2}$$

That is, first we compute the difference of each pair of points on each dimension, in turn, and square the differences. We then add these two squared differences together and finally take the square root of the result. Figure 2–2(a) illustrates this procedure in terms of the Pythagorean theorem.[2] This set of operations leads to two additional properties shared by all distance functions (Euclidean or otherwise), which are special cases of the Minkowski metrics.

1. The distance between two points depends only on the (absolute) differences $|x_{i1} - x_{j1}|$ and $|x_{i2} - x_{j2}|$ in their coordinates, dimension by dimension. The distance between two points is not altered when both points are shifted by the same amount in the same direction (since this constant would drop out when differences are taken). This property is known as translation invariance—that is, an interval scale is appropriate for describing the scales (axes), as shown in Figure 2–2(c).
2. If we next imagine two points lying on a vector going through the origin 0 [see Figure 2–2(d)] where point i has coordinates x_{i1} and x_{i2} and point j has coordinates ax_{i1} and ax_{i2} (where $a > 0$), then the distance of point j from the origin 0 is

$$d(0, j) = a[d(0, i)]$$

This characteristic is known as the homogeneity property.

Although our examples have concentrated on two dimensions, we should point out that the Euclidean distance between a pair of points generalizes

---

[2] Recall that the Pythagorean theorem states that the square of the hypotenuse of a right triangle is equal to the sum of the squares of the sides.

Figure 2–2

Illustration of Selected Properties of (Euclidean) Distance Function

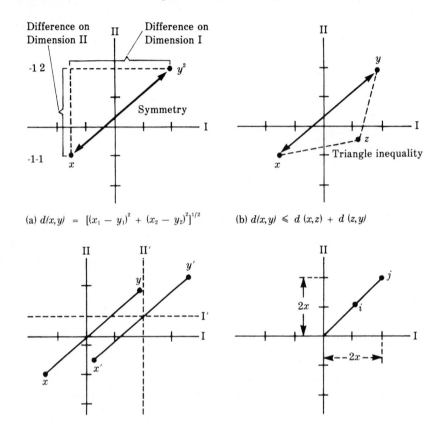

(a) $d(x,y) = [(x_1 - y_1)^2 + (x_2 - y_2)^2]^{1/2}$ (b) $d(x,y) \leqslant d(x,z) + d(z,y)$

(c) Translation Invariance   (d) Homogeneity

easily to more than two dimensions by the formula

$$d_{ij} = \left[\sum_{k=1}^{r} (x_{ik} - x_{jk})^2 \right]^{1/2}$$

where we square each difference in coordinates on dimension $k (k = 1, 2, \ldots , r)$, sum the quantities, and finally take the square root of the total.

Other Distance Functions   While we are most familiar with the Euclidean distance function, it turns out that other distance functions may obey the five properties described above. For example, if in Figure 2–2(a) we could move from point x to point y by only following the dotted line that moves parallel to the axis of movement, we are using a distance called *city block metric*. Like a city block, we must move north, south, east, or west, but cannot cut through "the block" by moving at any other angle. The distance between two points under this metric is merely the sum of the absolute difference of their projections on each separate dimension or $|(x_1 - y_1)| + |(x_2 - y_2)|$. This function and the Euclidean distance function are special cases of a still more general function, the Minkowski p-metric [Shepard, 1966], which possesses the five properties enumerated earlier. (The Euclidean distance, however, is the only one that satisfies the property of rotational invariance.)

The Minkowski p-metric can be written as

$$d_{ij}(p) = \left[\sum_{k=1}^{r} |x_{ik} - x_{jk}|^p \right]^{1/p} \qquad p \geq 1$$

We require $p \geq 1$ to satisfy the triangle inequality. When $p = 1$, we have the city block metric; when $p = 2$, we have the familiar Euclidean metric. While most applications have involved the Euclidean metric, it is appropriate to point out that many nonmetric multidimensional scaling programs provide the flexibility to fit any type of Minkowski p-metric to the data.

Isosimilarity Contours   It is of interest to examine the type of isosimilarity contours implied by various special cases of the Minkowski p-metric. Isosimilarity refers to points equal in distance (and, therefore, similarity) to a given reference point. Figure 2–3 shows graphically the kind of notion we have in mind. For example, suppose we were working with the Euclidean metric curve that results when $p = 2$. Note that all points on the curve are one unit of measure from the center (or origin of the coordinate map.) All points lie on the circumference of a circle with a radius of 1.0. In contrast, the city block metric is identified by a p-metric (where $p = 1$), and results in a diamond-shaped isosimilarity contour. In this case, the city block distance from the origin to any point on the diamond is equal. Finally, if we let p

_____ *Figure 2–3* _____

Isosimilarity Contours for Selected Minkowski p-metrics

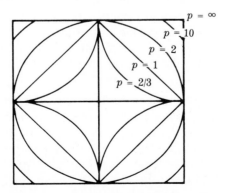

approach infinity, the isosimilarity contour approaches the perimeter square. In this case the largest difference, dimension by dimension, would receive all the weight in the computation of interpoint distance.

At the other extreme, if the concave pattern (for $p = 2/3$) of Figure 2–3 were operative, we would be dealing with the case where the metric is raised to a fractional root. In this case, $p < 1$ and the triangle inequality is violated; hence, we do not have a metric space.

The implied weights given to the various differences on each dimension are also of interest. Only the city block metric gives equal weight to each dimensional difference. The more familiar Euclidean metric actually weights the differences on each dimension by the differences themselves. That is, large differences will receive greater weight than small differences in contributing to the overall distance between two points. In general, the p-th power of distance $d_{ij}(p)$ in a Minkowski p-metric may be viewed as a weighted sum, where each component difference $(x_{ik} - x_{jk})$, is weighted by its own size, raised to the $p - 1$ power [Coombs, 1964]. As p approaches infinity, only the largest difference on any dimension contributes to the interpoint distance d_{ij} ($p = \infty$). The square, shown in Figure 2–3, illustrates this case.

We can also see, in the case of two dimensions, why only Euclidean interpoint distance is invariant under rotation. As can be noted from Figure 2–3, a rotation of 45 degrees would change the city block metric ($p = 1$) into the "supremum" metric ($p = \infty$) if the scalar multiplier 2 were used; that is, the metric would no longer be unique [Coombs, 1964]. (We shall return to a discussion of the rotational "freedom" provided by the Euclidean metric in subsequent sections.)

COOMBSIAN DATA CLASSIFICATION

Now that we have commented on some of the representational aspects of data as relations on points in a metric space, our attention turns to the classes of psychological data that can be represented. We have already used in our previous discussion three descriptors by which data can be organized:

1. Whether the relation is one of dominance or consonance
2. Whether the points are from one set (for example, stimuli) or from two different sets; for example, people's ideal points and stimuli
3. Whether the relation is on a pair of points or on a pair of pairs of points; for example, an order relation on psychological "distances"

Coombs (1964) uses the latter two descriptors to develop an elegant and parsimonious data classification system. Descriptor 1 is used to distinguish various types of data *within* each of the four cells, whereas descriptors 2 and 3 are used to classify the various types of scaling techniques as either a unidimensional or a multidimensional type. Figure 2–4 shows Coombs' fourfold classification scheme. In illustrating the four quadrants, we will

_____ Figure 2–4 _____

Four Main Quadrants of the Coombsian Classification System

	Pairs of Points	Pairs of Pairs
Points from Two Different Sets	Quadrant II Single stimulus	Quadrant I Preferential choice
Points from Same Set	Quadrant III Stimulus comparison	Quadrant IV Similarities

Source: Adapted from C. H. Coombs, *A Theory of Data* (New York: John Wiley & Sons, 1964), p. 21 and p. 28.

focus on dominance relations, but the reader should bear in mind that consonance relations could be established as well on each of the four data classes.

Quadrant I: *Preferential Choice Data*   Data in this quadrant are characterized as involving relations on pairs of pairs of points (for example, relations involving "distances") from two different sets. To illustrate, let us return to the automobile example and the spatial representation of points from two different sets: subject i's ideal point and the set of stimuli (automobile models). The ideal point and stimuli are positioned in a common metric space, and the axes are assumed to represent the salient dimensions underlying the subject's evaluative judgments.

If we again assume that subject i's ideal point is positioned at point I in Figure 2–1 and that the subject prefers Jaguar XJ6 over Cadillac Seville if and only if Jaguar XJ6 is nearer the ideal point, then we can say that we are treating preference data as a dominance relationship on pairs of pairs of points drawn from two different sets. The pairs and sets are defined as follows: Set 1 is the ideal point, set two is the stimuli data, pair 1 is (XJ6-Ideal), and pair 2 is (Cadillac Seville-Ideal). Such pairs of pairs of points are interpreted as defining pairs of psychological distances. If this model holds, we would expect to find the preference ordering: Porsche 944, Jaguar XJ6, . . . , Chevrolet Chevette, Ford Escort, in the order of most to least preferred.

Some other individual, however, may prefer a different combination of the two attributes of luxuriousness and sportiness so as to have an ideal nearest to the Mustang SVO (say, at point J in Figure 2–1). If so, Mustang SVO would be most preferred and Mercedes would be among the least preferred, according to the previous argument.

Quadrant I, then, provides a way of characterizing preference data that is capable of handling a diversity of preferences over individuals for the same set of stimuli. Individual differences in preference orders are handled by assuming different ideal point locations for each person. This lack of commonality of preferences is often observed in marketing research (or, for that matter, behavioral science generally) and constitutes the conceptual basis that underlies the development of a joint space of stimuli and ideal points.

Quadrant II: Single Stimulus Data

Quadrant II data are typed by Coombs as relations on pairs of points from two different sets. To illustrate the characteristics of data described by this quadrant, suppose we had a set of attitude statements used to evaluate a single stimulus, Brand *A*. Each statement is presumed to tap a different *degree* of "favorableness" of attitude toward Brand *A*.

In practice, a large number of individuals, each presumably with a different degree of favorableness of attitude, would be asked to participate in the attitude survey. If the universe of content is scalable along a uni-dimensional continuum (as in a Guttman Scale), we would expect any person possessing a higher degree of favorableness of attitude than is being tapped by a given statement to respond favorably to the statement. Those possessing less would be assumed to respond unfavorably.

The objective of single stimulus data, in which the stimuli (for example, attitude statements) are presented singly for the subject's evaluation, is to arrange *both subject points* and *stimuli points* along a single continuum ranging from, say, very unfavorable to very favorable. Such a joint scale of stimuli and subjects may only be ordinal. While representations of Quadrant II data are not constrained solely to unidimensional scales, most of the applications to date—for example, Guttman scalogram analysis [Richards, 1959]—have involved assumptions of unidimensionality.

Quadrant III: Stimulus Comparisons Data

Data in this quadrant are characterized by relations on pairs of points drawn from the same set. An illustration of this class of data is Thurstone's law of comparative judgment [Green, Tull, and Albaum, 1988], which typically leads to a unidimensional (and in this case interval) scale. The scale is developed from response frequencies that indicate which member of a stimulus pair is evaluated to possess more of some property.

There is no need to review here the mechanics of Thurstonian comparative judgment scaling. For purposes of Coombsian data theory we note that a basic assumption of the Thurstonian model is that the individual says "*i* dominates *j*" if and only if the (momentary) magnitude of the person's "discriminal process" associated with stimulus *i* exceeds that associated with stimulus *j*. For example, such differences in magnitude are assumed to be normally distributed, and the individual, on any specific trial, is also assumed to have selected one "difference" from that distribution.

We note, then, that both Quadrant II and Quadrant III data, involving relations on pairs of points, often lead to unidimensional scales. These two classes of data constituted the main focus of early research in scaling techniques, but are less relevant for the objectives of current research efforts and this book than Quadrants I and IV.

Quadrant IV: Similarities Data   Coombs calls Quadrant-IV data "similarities," which is a way of suggesting that this class of data involves the structure of appearance—that is, how people perceive stimuli as being similar or dissimilar. Such data involve relations on pairs of pairs of points from the same set (usually stimuli). Similarities data are the kinds of data that would be collected by asking a subject to indicate which of the following pairs of automobile models is more similar: (Continental and Mercedes) or (Escort and Mustang SVO). The process is repeated, leading to a ranking of all possible pairs.

Notice here that the criteria constituting "overall similarity" are left to the subject. No attempt is made to specify a particular criterion by which the relative similarity of the two pairs is to be judged. This class of data enables the analyst to develop cartesian maps showing the perceived relationships between the stimuli. The axes of each map are assumed to represent the underlying perceptual dimensions along which each stimulus is compared. In some cases only a single attribute will be involved, but in other cases, a multidimensional characterization of the stimuli is appropriate.

The focus of the following chapters will be on Quadrant IV and Quadrant I data, which deal, respectively, with the structure of perceptions of similarities and evaluation of preferences. Moreover, we shall show that Quadrant IV and Quadrant I representations will often be multidimensional rather than unidimensional.

Proximity Matrices   A second way to present the classes of data useful in multidimensional scaling analysis is to describe the various types of data matrices with which we are dealing. Coombs (1964) describes four main types of proximity matrices, where proximity is defined as an empirical measure of closeness or similarity between pairs of points. Proximity has also been referred to as "psychological distance" and refers to both similarities and dissimilarities measures.

The Stimuli by Stimuli Data Matrix   The four major types of proximity matrices are recognizably displayed in Figure 2–5. To start off consider the simplest case where pairs of stimuli are evaluated and ordered. Suppose we ask an individual to rank the $[n(n-1)]/2$ distinct pairs of soft drink stimuli on the basis of the similarity of the pairs. For the ten soft drink brands, $(10 \times 9)/2 = 45$ distinct pairs would be ranked, each receiving a ranking value from 1 to 45. The resulting proximity matrix is of the type represented by submatrix *A* in Figure 2–5. It is called an *intact unconditional proximity matrix*. The matrix is intact in the sense that each cell (excluding the main diagonal) has an entry that indicates the degree of similarity or dissimilarity of one pair of stimuli relative to all other pairs of stimuli. It is unconditional

_____*Figure 2–5*_____

Major Types of Proximity Matrices

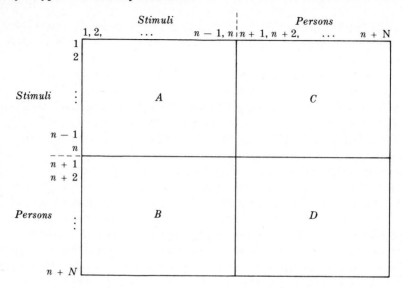

in the sense that each cell value in the symmetric matrix, whether above or below the main diagonal, can be compared to any other. Note that unconditional matrices need not be symmetric.

Now consider an alternate form of the stimuli by stimuli data matrix called the *intact conditional proximity matrix*. This matrix results when, for each row of the matrix, the evaluator ranks the remaining $n-1$ stimuli in terms of decreasing similarity to that row stimulus. In other words, each row displays ranking numbers from 1 to 10, because each row serves in turn as the reference item, and only cell entries within each row of the submatrix A are comparable. Again the points are drawn from the same set and proximities are comparable within but not across rows.

The Person-by-Stimuli Data Matrix   Next, consider submatrix B, where individuals order stimuli. Suppose N individuals rank the n stimuli (say, on the basis of preference or some other "dominance" relation) as indicated in Figure 2–5. In this case, we are dealing with an *off-diagonal conditional proximity matrix* where values are comparable only within each row (each row is the evaluation set for one of the n persons). The pairs of points are drawn from two different sets: the set of persons and the set of stimuli. Finally, if we could collect data of the off-diagonal form, individual i prefers stimulus j more than individual i' prefers stimulus j', we would have the case of an off-diagonal unconditional proximity matrix. In this case, then, we are assuming interpersonal comparisons of utility, a case where such data are often difficult to justify.

Interestingly enough, intact proximity matrices can be related to Quadrants III and IV in the Coombs system (Figure 2–4), while off-diagonal proximity matrices can be related to Quadrants I and II. However, the same set of empirical observations can be analyzed from different viewpoints, as based on the researcher's model of the process assumed to underlie the generation of the observations.

Up to this point we have not discussed submatrices *C* and *D*, where, respectively: (a) stimuli are used as the basis for evaluating and ordering individuals, and (b) pairs of individuals are evaluated and ordered. Empirical situations where stimuli are used to evaluate and order individuals occur, for example, in various types of examination questions or attitude statements. Empirical applications occur where pairs of individuals are ordered, such as in *Q*-type factor analysis and cluster analysis (both *Q*-type factor analysis and cluster analysis group subjects rather than variables).

NONMETRIC MULTIDIMENSIONAL SCALING

Our previous discussions of Coombs' classification system and distance functions have been by way of providing a framework for positioning the various techniques of multidimensional scaling, particularly nonmetric methods. As explained, the term *nonmetric* means that the input data consist only of ordinal relations (usually on pairs of pairs of elements) but the output information is metric—interval scaled or stronger.

From our discussion of distance functions and data matrices, the broad objectives of multidimensional scaling should now be evident. We start out with a set of experimentally obtained proximity measures (similarities, dissimilarities, "psychological distances") that are often of rank order and attempt to represent those empirical data geometrically as points in some type of metric space. We are interested in both the dimensionality of that space and the configuration of points in the space. As will be shown below, the type of algorithm used will depend on what we are willing to assume about the scaling properties of the input data and the type of geometric model "representing" the empirical relations.

The computer algorithms underlying nonmetric scaling date from 1962 with publication of Roger Shepard's innovative paper (1962). Since that time a variety of procedures have been developed for converting nonmetric data into metric output information. In the preceding chapter we discussed briefly the evolution of nonmetric scaling techniques. This earlier discussion is elaborated below.

Fully Metric Methods

As motivation for this discussion, assume that a respondent has been given the task of judging the pairs of car models shown in Figure 2–1 in terms of overall similarity. To be more specific, suppose the respondent is shown a set of 55 cards. On each card appear the names of one pair of the car models: All possible distinct pairs of the 11 items appear only once on the $55 = [11 \times (11-1)]/2$ cards. The subject is first asked to place the cards into two classes, namely, pairs of cars that are more or less similar versus pairs of cars that are more or less different. The criteria on which the choices are made are up to the individual.

After this step, the subject is asked to separate the "similar" pile into two subpiles—highly similar car pairs and somewhat similar car pairs. The subject is then asked to further separate the "different" pile into two piles that identify pairs that are somewhat different and highly different.

The subject is then asked to choose the most highly similar pair within the highly similar subpile, then the next most similar pair, until all cards in the first subpile are ranked. The pairs in subpile two are then ranked, followed by the pairs in subpiles three and four. Before settling on this final ranking, cards may be shifted from subpile to subpile if desired. By means of this stepwise procedure a simple rank order of the 55 car pairs is eventually obtained. One such rank order is shown in Table 2–1.

Now suppose that the 55 rank numbers (1 = most similar; 55 = least similar) are more "strongly" scaled than just ranks—that is, let us assume that the data of Table 2–1 really represent ratio-scaled distances. This crucial assumption is the basis of fully metric methods. Ratio-scaled distances are used as input to find an output configuration (of Euclidean distanced points) whose interpoint distances are proportional to the input.

As shown earlier, it is a simple matter to compute interpoint Euclidean distances between all pairs of points if we know their coordinates—that is, the resulting configuration of points. The converse, however, is not so easy and represents the principal task of fully metric methods: Given a set of interpoint distances, find the dimensionality and configuration of points whose distances most closely match the input values. In our usual appeal for

_____ Table 2–1 _____

Rank Order of Dissimilarities Between Pairs of Car Models

Stimuli	1	2	3	4	5	6	7	8	9	10	11
Mustang SVO	—										
Cadillac Seville	27	—									
Lincoln Continental	26	01	—								
Ford Escort	17	38	39	—							
Corvette	13	28	29	36	—						
Chevrolet Chevette	25	41	42	10	35	—					
Nissan 300 ZX	15	32	30	45	09	48	—				
Renault Alliance	24	40	02	12	43	11	34	—			
Porsche 944	16	33	31	46	08	49	14	44	—		
Jaguar XJ6	37	07	05	50	18	52	19	51	21	—	
Mercedes 500 SEL	47	06	04	53	23	55	22	54	20	03	—

_____ Figure 2–6 _____
Fully Metric Scaling of Automobile Data (based on data in Table 2–1)

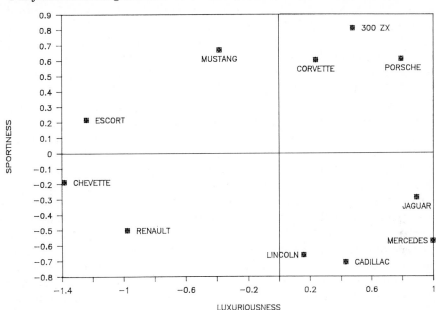

parsimony, we would, of course, like to do this in the smallest number of dimensions.

Computational methods for finding the desired configuration entail the factor analysis of distances. The techniques yield a configuration whose interpoint distances come as close as possible to reproducing (up to a positive proportionality transformation) the numerical values of Table 2–1.

Figure 2–6 shows the configuration resulting from the application of fully metric methods to the Table 2–1 data. Note that it differs from the configuration of Figure 2–1, which, as we shall show, was obtained by a nonmetric procedure from the same input data (but the data were treated only as ranks). The essential point of this discussion is that fully metric methods assume the input data to be ratio-scaled distances. In turn, the analysis yields a metric output configuration of the type illustrated by Figure 2–6. If we were to compute the interpoint distances of all pairs of points in Figure 2–6 and if the configuration were a perfect fit to the data, the resulting numbers would equal those of Table 2–1 up to a positive proportionality transformation.

What happens, however, if we cannot assume that the subject is able to report ratio-scaled distances? Now suppose that the numbers in Table 2–1 merely define a rank order of the 55 pairs (a reasonable assumption given the manner in which data were collected).

Fully Nonmetric Methods The above case is precisely the problem that Coombs attacked. How should data be scaled when one does not assume more than rank order on the input "distances." Coombs (1950) and Bennett and Hays (1960) addressed themselves to solving the nonmetric problem, both unidimensionally and multidimensionally.

Their approaches are known as unfolding methods. Given a matrix of conditional proximities, such as submatrix B in Figure 2–5, the objective of these methods is to find (1) a Euclidean space of minimum dimensionality and (2) the rank order (in the multidimensional case) of each point on each dimension of that Euclidean space (configuration).

But notice here that the output is the rank order of each point on each dimension and is, therefore, nonmetric. By this approach we cannot find a metric configuration, like those shown in Figures 2–1 and 2–6, but only the rank order of the projections of each point on each dimension. We have gained the use of a weaker assumption about the "quality" of the input data, but have given up a metric configuration solution in favor of a set of rank ordered point projections. Moreover, fully nonmetric methods do not appear to lend themselves as readily to precise algorithm development as do either the fully metric procedures or the nonmetric procedures. In a sense, the fully nonmetric methods of Coombs and his colleagues provided a large part of the conceptual groundwork for subsequent, computer-based developments. But from an operational viewpoint, the later developments yield more, producing asymptotically metric output from the same assumption of nonmetric input. Thus, we do not consider fully nonmetric methods beyond this point.

Nonmetric Methods Prior to the publication of Shepard's paper on nonmetric multidimensional scaling, procedures were either fully metric or fully nonmetric. It was Shepard who combined the best of both precursor approaches: rank order input data and metric solutions. Moreover, he provided the first computer algorithm for implementing this objective. (It can truly be said that the development of nonmetric scaling required high-speed computer processing.)

The objective of nonmetric multidimensional scaling can be stated nonrigorously as follows: Given a rank order of proximity data, find a configuration whose rank order of (ratio-scaled) distances, in a specified dimensionality, best reproduces the original rank order of the input data.

As innocuous as this objective may sound, it has spawned a whole progression of research papers and computer programs that are still being expanded to deal with an increasing variety of scaling applications.

The conceptual basis of nonmetric scaling, however, is not difficult to understand. Let us return to the rank order data of Table 2–1. We note that the table is composed of rank numbers, ranging from the most similar pair

(Continental and Cadillac Seville) with rank 1, to the least similar pair (Mercedes Benz 500 SEL and Chevrolet Chevette) with rank 55. As the number of stimuli, n, increases, the number of rank order constraints increases as $[n \times (n-1)]/2$. However, to portray a set of points in an r-dimensional solution we need only $r \times n$ numbers, namely, the coordinate of each point on each dimension.[3]

As the number of pairs of points increases relative to the $r \times n$ numbers needed to specify a configuration, the number of rank order constraints specified between the pairs increases. These constraints are known as inequalities. The rank order constraints, if met in a solution, serve to restrict the movement of the n points so that with "enough" inequalities we obtain, for all practical purposes, a unique configuration. This means that when a large number of relationships are specified by the rank orders, we have little freedom to move one or more points around without violating at least one of the rank order constraints or inequalities. Remember that moving just one point changes its distances with the remaining $n-1$ points.

Shepard demonstrated, via a series of synthetic data analyses, that with as few as 8 points, a 0.99 correlation existed between the interpoint distances of a known two-space configuration and a configuration constructed by his computer program from rank order information alone [Shepard, 1962]. For $n > 15$, the two configurations were virtually indistinguishable.

A word should be said about the meaning of a "unique" configuration in this context. A configuration is unique if the rank order of the interpoint distances is unchanged after undergoing what is known as a similarity transform. In the case of the Euclidean metric, a similarity transform permits:

— Rotation of the configuration about the origin
— Translation of the origin (by adding a constant to each coordinate value)
— Reflection (flipping the configuration across one or more axes of the configuration)
— Uniform stretching (or compression) of the axes

None of these operations will change the rank order of the interpoint distances, and the constraint, under which this class of computer programs operates, is met. Accordingly, multidimensional scaling algorithms try to find a configuration of points, in k dimensions, whose interpoint distances are monotone—that is, they have the same (or possibly the inverse) ranks as the input data.

---

[3] Technically speaking, fewer $(rn - [r(r-1)/2] - 1)$ numbers are needed given the invariance of solution up to a similarity transformation. For example, if $r = 2$, we need only 22 numbers to fix the 11 points. In contrast, we have 55 ranks from the relationships shown in Table 2–1.

In general, as one increases the dimensionality of the space, the chances of finding such a configuration increases. As a matter of fact, any set of rank orders (including ties) on pairs of n points can be satisfied by a configuration in $n - 1$ dimensions [Bennett and Hays, 1960]. The point at issue, however, is to find the lowest dimensionality for which the monotonicity constraint is "closely" met. In application, the researcher may wish to trade off the objective of perfect monotonicity for a solution of lower dimensionality whose distances are almost monotone with the original rank order data.

Currently, a rather wide variety of computer programs exists for performing various types of nonmetric scaling, many of which will be considered in subsequent chapters. We shall primarily emphasize nonmetric methods but shall also discuss fully metric methods where appropriate. The latter set of methods—like fully nonmetric techniques—assumes that the distance function is Euclidean, whereas nonmetric techniques are not so restricted. But in practice, the Euclidean function is most often used, and we shall confine our discussion to that type of metric.

AN ILLUSTRATIVE COMPUTER ALGORITHM Although we shall be

discussing several different nonmetric scaling algorithms in later chapters, it seems useful here to illustrate how a prototypical program works. As will be shown later, most of the programs are quite similar in objective but differ in computational detail. Their theoretical and output correspondences have been pointed out in earlier works, which indicate that the algorithms produce quite similar numerical results when applied to a common set of input data [Gleason, 1967; Green and Wind, 1973; and Green and Rao, 1972]. For illustrative purposes, we describe a general algorithm as representative of these procedures. We follow the Green and Rao (1972) development closely.

For expository purposes assume that we have a set of $[n \times (n - 1)]/2$ ranked pairs of stimuli L_{ij} ($i = 1, 2, \ldots, n - 1; j = 2, 3, \ldots, n$). We can call the L_{ij} the measure of similarity, dissimilarity, or psychological "distances" between the stimuli. Our objective is to find a configuration of points $X = \{x_1, x_2, \ldots, x_n\}$ consisting of n vectors in a space of r dimensions. The r dimensional coordinates of a given stimulus vector x_i can be specified as $x_i = (x_{i1}, x_{i2}, \ldots, x_{ir})$.

For each x_i, x_j in X we can compute a distance d_{ij}. If X is a "good" configuration (in that the ranks of its distances d_{ij} approximately reproduce the input ranks L_{ij}), then that configuration should be "final" or close thereto for representing the L_{ij} in a specified dimensionality.

The appropriate numbers (they may not be distances) that *are* perfectly monotone with the L_{ij} can be denoted as $\hat{d}_{ij}$. The algorithm considers, then, relationships among the three sets:

— L_{ij} = input data ranks
— d_{ij} = computed distances between all pairs of points in the configuration X

— $\hat{d}_{ij}$ = a set of ratio-scaled numbers, chosen to be as close to their respective d_{ij} as possible and subject to being monotone with L_{ij} (that is, $\hat{d}_{ij} < \hat{d}_{kl}$ whenever $L_{ij} < L_{kl}$)

All of these algorithms must then consider two problems:

— The development of an index of fit by which one can tell if the configuration X is an appropriate one for representing the input data, L_{ij}
— A procedure for moving the points x_i, x_j to some "better" configuration if the current index of fit is poor

The algorithm places the j points in an n dimensional space so as to minimize stress. Stress is the measure of badness of fit between the configuration of points whose interpoint distances are monotone with the ranks of the input data. The program finds the minimizing configuration by starting with either a principal components configuration, a random starting configuration, or a user specified configuration. From this starting configuration, points are systematically moved to improve the fit. This procedure is iterated over and over again until the criterion for stopping is reached. Typically, from 10 to 25 iterations may be required.

For the automobile example of Table 2–1, let the data values be entered as a square matrix of size $N = 11$. There will be $n(n - 1) = 110$ entries if no diagonal is included, and for a half matrix $n[(n - 1)/2] = 55$ entries. The distances between pairs of points obtained from an initial (possibly randomly chosen) X matrix of coordinates are first calculated and listed in positions corresponding to those in the data list. Missing data and values in the diagonal entries of the input matrix are set to zero and hence produce corresponding distances of zero.

A least-squares regression of d_{ij} on L_{ij} is next performed. For nonmetric scaling, a monotone ascending regression should be used for dissimilarities data (where rank order increases as distance increases). A monotone descending regression should be performed for similarities data (when a higher rank order number means less distance). For metric scaling, one program (KYST) provides linear or polynomial regression options up to the fourth degree. The regression yields the desired polynomial coefficients.

Index of Fit Most nonmetric scaling algorithms provide an index to fit that represents some variant of Kruskal's stress measure (Kruskal, 1964a).

$$\text{STRESS} = \sqrt{\frac{\sum\limits_{M=1}^{MM} [\text{DIST}(M) - \text{DHAT}(M)]^2}{\sum\limits_{M=1}^{MM} [\text{DIST}(M) - \text{DBAR}]^2}}$$

The numerator of this index consists of DIST(1) to DIST(MM), where MM equals the number of items in the $n \times n$ distance matrix, showing the distances between pairs of points. The DIST values are regressed on the data values: DATA(1) to DATA(MM) to produce the DHAT(1) to DHAT(MM) values of the regression function. The arithmetic average of the DIST values is DBAR. In other words, the numerator contains the sum of squares of the discrepancies between each computed d_{ij} for some configuration X and a set of numbers $\hat{d}_{ij}$ that estimate distances chosen to be as close to their respective d_{ij} as possible, subject to being monotone with the original L_{ij}'s. If the $\hat{d}_{ij}$ equal their d_{ij} counterparts, the numerator of the expression becomes zero and, hence, stress is also zero, indicating a perfect fit.

The denominator of the expression is merely a normalizing value, computed to allow comparisons of the fit measure across different dimensionalities (since, in general, the d_{ij} will increase with increasing dimensionality).

In practice, if the stress of a particular configuration is high—that is, the monotonic fit is poor, the algorithm simply finds a new configuration X whose ranks of interpoint distances are more closely monotone to the original input data ranks L_{ij} than the previously ranked distances.

Earlier versions of the MDS programs offered a slightly different formulation of stress, which is called formula 1 (it is still an option in the KYST program). Stress formula 1 (as opposed to stress formula 2), differs in that the denominator is the sum of the squares of the d_{ij} (that is, DBAR = 0). Both formulas often yield very similar configurations, but in some circumstances (such as the method of unfolding to be explained later) the use of formula 2 is vital.

The interpretation of stress values can be greatly affected by the options used and by various parameters, such as the number of stimuli and number of dimensions.

Improving the Configuration

Assume now that we wish to move the points around to make the ranks of their distances closer to the input data ranks than those found in the previous configuration. In particular, consider a specific point i and its relationship to each of the points j in turn. We would like to move the point i so as to decrease the average discrepancy between the distances d_{ij} and the numbers $\hat{d}_{ij}$, the latter set being monotone with the L_{ij}.

If d_{ij} is larger than $\hat{d}_{ij}$, we could move point i toward point j by an amount proportional to the size of the discrepancy. Conversely, if $\hat{d}_{ij}$ is larger than d_{ij}, then point i is to be moved away from point j by an amount proportional to the discrepancy. Suppose we let α represent the coefficient of proportionality ($0 < \alpha < 1$) or step size. (Often α is set at 0.2).

To find a new coordinate $x'_{ia(j)}$ for point i on axis a, as related to point j, we can use the formula:

$$X'_{ia(j)} = X_{ia(j)} + \alpha\left(1 - \frac{\hat{d}_{ij}}{d_{ij}}\right)(X_{ja} - X_{ia})$$

This formula would move point i in the appropriate direction with respect to point j, but we must consider all $n - 1$ points insofar as their effect on point i is concerned. To do so, we use the expression

$$X'_{ia} = X_{ia} + \frac{\alpha}{n - 1}\sum_{\substack{j=1 \\ j \neq i}}^{n}\left(1 - \frac{\hat{d}_{ij}}{d_{ij}}\right)(X_{ja} - X_{ia})$$

Note that we move point i along axis a in such a way as to take into account the discrepancies involving all other points. This step is, of course, taken for all points in all dimensions.

The procedure can be summarized as involving the following steps:

1. For a given dimensionality, select some initial configuration X_0.
2. Compute d_{ij} between the vectors x_i, x_j of the configuration X_0 and also compute $\hat{d}_{ij}$, chosen to be as close as possible to the original d_{ij} and subject to being monotone with the L_{ij} (input data).
3. Evaluate the fit measure S, the stress of the configuration.
4. If $S > \epsilon$ (ϵ is some small "cutoff" value, say 0.01), find a new configuration X_i whose ranks of the d_{ij} are closer to the L_{ij}.
5. Repeat the process until successive configurations $X_0, X_1, X_2, \ldots, X_p$ converge, such that S is satisfactorily "small"; for example, $S \leq \epsilon$.
6. Repeat the process in the next lower dimensionality, and so on.
7. Choose the lowest dimensionality for which S is satisfactorily "small."

Although specific fit measures and procedures for moving the points differ among the various algorithms, they all seem to be based on the above concepts.

SPECIFIC FEATURES OF THE

KYST PROGRAM KYST can cope with a variety of problems arising in the original data. These include missing data, nonsymmetry, and ties:

1. The program permits solution in any type of Minkowski p-metric, including, of course, the Euclidean and city block metrics as special cases.
2. The program allows various forms of data matrices to be input; for example, full matrix, lower half matrix, upper half matrix, lower corner matrix, upper corner matrix, block diagonal, and so forth.
3. A number of regression options are available, including monotone,

polynomial with and without a constant, and reduced function linear regression.

4. Inherent nonsymmetry of measurement procedures or errors in measurement may cause the d_{ij} and $\hat{d}_{ij}$ to not be equal. In such a situation, the stress function computed over all cells—that is, i, j and j, i—is minimized in the algorithm.

5. There are two ways of treating ties among the data values when performing monotone regression. Consider the fitted regression values corresponding to a group of equal data values. Either no restriction is placed on the size of these fitted values with respect to one another (the "primary" approach), or the fitted values may be required to be equal (the "secondary" approach).

We shall return in subsequent chapters to some of the specific features of the KYST program when we discuss the analysis of similarities and preference data in more detail.

SUMMARY

In this chapter, we constructed a frame of reference that will be useful for more detailed discussion of similarities and preference data, as well as reduced space and cluster analysis—topics to be covered in later sections. We first considered the relations of dominance and consonance as applied to pairs of points or pairs of proximities drawn from the same versus two different sets. This presentation led us into a discussion of distance functions and isosimilarity contours. The Coombsian system of data classification was then described and illustrated by various types of behavioral data. It was then noted that our area of concentration will be on Quadrant I (preference) and Quadrant IV (similarities) data, which lead often, but not necessarily, to multidimensional scales.

We then turned to a comparison of multidimensional scaling approaches, including fully metric, fully nonmetric, and nonmetric techniques. The conceptual rationale of each class was outlined and a prototypical algorithm for performing nonmetric scaling was described in some detail.

Analysis of
Similarities Data

In this section, we describe models for the analysis of similarities data. Our discussion is based on the following progression of topics:

— Conceptual structure and assumptions underlying similarities models
— Computational procedures and the results of analyses of synthetic data
— Empirical problems, including data collection procedures and solution interpretation
— Specific issues, including individual differences models and scenario effects on similarities judgments

We first discuss the general concept of similarity and its relationship to distance models and perception. This discussion leads to a description of various types of similarities matrices and algorithms that have been developed for portraying similarity relations geometrically. The results are then shown using some of the major scaling algorithms in the context of analyzing synthetic data of known characteristics.

The next portion of this section deals with a variety of empirical problems encountered in analyzing similarities data. These include methods of handling various types of data scenarios, including direct judgment data, direct behavioral indexes of similarity, and derived similarity measures. Discussion of data collection alternatives is followed by a description of problems encountered in the interpretation of scaling solutions.

The concluding portion of this section takes up a variety of special issues in similarities analysis, including individual differences models, comparison of alternative scaling solutions by rotation of solutions to congruence, changes in the composition of the stimulus set on configuration stability, and extensions of scaling methods to multiway matrices.

SIMILARITIES RESPONSES AND
DISTANCE MODELS
The major model used in the analysis of similarities data is the distance model, described briefly in the preceding chapter. Certain intuitive niceties link the empirical notion of similarity with the formal notion of distance. For example, it seems reasonable to assume that

an item is more similar to itself than it is to any other item and that the similarity of A to B is the same as the similarity of B to A.

Even more important, it is well to consider the psychological theory that underlies the equating of distance models and similarities (or dissimilarities) judgments. Virtually all distance models considered in mathematical psychology assume that the similarity between two stimuli is some function of their partial similarities on each of several perceptual dimensions. Furthermore, the models assume that partial similarities and dissimilarities do not depend on the actual location of the points but only on their (absolute) similarity or difference, dimension by dimension. While for expository purposes, scaling solutions are called *perceptual maps,* it should be made clear that relatively little research has been done to test the congruence of distance models and psychological models of perception.

When a spatial representation of a set of similarities data is obtained, it is assumed that interpoint distances are ratio scaled and the axes of the configuration are multidimensional interval scaled (with a common unit[1]).

Proximities Matrices as Input to
Similarities Analysis
Two classes of proximity matrices were discussed in Chapter 2, as usually associated with similarities analysis: intact unconditional and intact conditional. Data of the intact-unconditional type assume that all entries in the rows and columns of the (stimuli × stimuli) matrix of the distinct pairs are comparable (recall that each stimulus was ranked relative to all other stimuli in the matrix and would generally receive a number from 1 to $[n(n - 1)]/2$). Data of the intact-conditional type assume that only entries within a given row are comparable (recall that each of n column stimuli are ranked from 1 to n with respect to the row stimulus).

Proximity matrices are constructed by a variety of data collection methods, all of which are said to be *conjoint*[2]—that is, a reference point is identified in the row and all other points are ranked in relation to that reference point (Coombs, 1964). Conjoint data conform to the function $AB < AC$, where the dissimilarity of the pair A and B is less than the dissimilarity of the pair A and C. This, of course, means that B is closer to A than A is to C.

Illustrative forms of proximities matrices are shown in Figure 3–1. Case a, the most common type, assumes that all cell values are comparable and the diagonal is missing (contains zero values). Because data matrix A is

---

[1] As we pointed out in the preceding chapter, the nonmetric model may be transformed at the origin as well as in the choice of a common unit. For the Euclidean metric solution, the axes may be rotated as well, since in this case, interpoint distances do not change with the configuration's orientation in the space.

[2] This is to say that an ordered relation on any pair of pairs always has a common element in each pair. This usage of the term "conjoint" is not to be confused with "conjoint analysis" or the type of data that is required for conjoint analysis.

_____Figure 3–1_____

Alternative Proximities Matrices

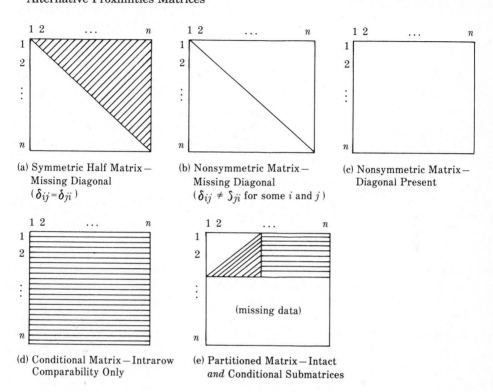

(a) Symmetric Half Matrix —
    Missing Diagonal
    $(\delta_{ij} = \delta_{ji})$

(b) Nonsymmetric Matrix —
    Missing Diagonal
    $(\delta_{ij} \neq \delta_{ji}$ for some i and j)

(c) Nonsymmetric Matrix —
    Diagonal Present

(d) Conditional Matrix — Intrarow
    Comparability Only

(e) Partitioned Matrix — Intact
    and Conditional Submatrices

symmetric, the actual data will often be entered in only the upper half or lower half of the matrix, with the remainder of the matrix left blank. Case b illustrates the situation that may arise in the collection of *confusions* data. (Confusions data indicate the frequency with which object i is matched with object j and is taken to be a behavioral measure of their psychological similarity.) The case b matrix is nonsymmetric with the diagonal missing. The incidence of response to object pair i, j may not be the same as the incidence of response to object pair j, i. Case c, the nonsymmetric matrix with a diagonal, can also arise in the collection of confusions data. Here, however, the incidence of response to the diagonal object pair i, i may be experimentally less than the incidence in which some off-diagonal response is obtained.

Case d represents a common form of original data collection and illustrates the case in which conjoint data are obtained. In case d, $n-1$ stimuli are ranked in terms of decreasing similarity, with each row stimulus serving, in turn, as a reference item. This form of data collection permits intrarow comparability only. Case e typifies a situation where all unconditional proximities are obtained from a subset of the stimuli. This subset is often termed a *core set* and takes the form of a corner matrix. The remaining proximities are obtained on the basis of being conditional on each core stimulus, in turn.

Many other proximity matrix forms are possible, given the possibility of omitting certain stimulus comparisons experimentally. Since most of the scaling algorithms possess "missing data" features, no problem arises so long as the absolute number of data entries is "large" relative to the number of dimensions to be explored. A large number of stimuli is desirable because of the more precise estimation of the subsets associated with the underlying structure of the perceptual space. Evidence indicates that 4 to 6 stimuli per dimension may be adequate. Kruskal and Wish (1978) recommend 9 for 2 dimensions; Spence and Domoney (1974) recommend 6 for 1, 11 for 2, and 17 for 3; Schiffman and coauthors (1981) recommend 6 for 1 and 12 for 3; Davidson (1983) recommends $40 \times$ (number of dimensions)/(number of stimuli − 1). Moreover, the cells that are filled by data values from an experimental design should be chosen to assure connectivity (comparability) over subsets of proximities.

Scaling Algorithms for Proximities Data   A variety of scaling algorithms are used for portraying experimental similarities or dissimilarities as relations on points in geometric space. Those in common use today are identified in Table 3–1. Space limits our discussion of programs not included as software with this text. For a further discussion of other algorithms, see Coxon (1982), Schiffman et al. (1981), and Green and Rao (1972). (Capsule program descriptions appear on diskette and in Part IV of this text.)

_____ *Table 3–1* _____

Alternate Computer Programs Appropriate for Similarities Data

Metric

KYST: Kruskal, Young, and Seery (1973)
INDSCAL: Carroll and Chang (1970); Chang and Carroll (1969)
ALSCAL: Young and Lewyckyj (1979);
             Takane, Young, and de Leeuw (1977)

Factor analysis procedures:
             Green (1978); Harman (1976)

Quasi-nonmetric

KYST: Kruskal, Young, and Seery (1973)
SINDSCAL: Pruzansky (1975)

Monotone

KYST: Kruskal, Young, and Seery (1973)
ALSCAL: Young and Lewyckyj (1979)

Factor Analysis and Simple Scaling Methods As recalled from the preceding section, fully metric methods, using a factor analysis of distances converted to scalar products, are appropriate if the data are considered to be ratio scaled distances to begin. Moreover, if the data are assumed to be only interval scaled, various procedures are available for estimating an additive constant that will convert the input data to distances.

Ordinal Approaches All of the major programs—KYST, MDSCAL, and ALSCAL—can handle the usual symmetric half matrix, as well as cases b and c (Figure 3–1). In the case of nonsymmetric data, a symmetric matrix is constructed by the computer program so that the output of the program—the configuration and its interpoint distances—will obey the metric axioms. Alternatively, if the researchers have obtained a nonsymmetric matrix experimentally, they may wish to assume a symmetric model (coupled with random error) to be most appropriate. If so, this matrix may be made symmetric by summing across the corresponding diagonal entries, $(i,j) + (j, i)$, before scaling the data.

It is often the case that metric methods provide excellent approximations to nonmetric solutions, particularly if the monotonic function can be closely approximated by a linear function. Metric solutions provide additional benefits in that they are not subject to the types of local minima and degeneracy problems sometimes encountered in using ordinal methods.

The KYST program has incorporated a simple scaling feature that enables the researcher to fit a linear function (with or without intercept) as well as prespecified polynomial functions (up to the fourth degree). As such, the KYST program can also be used for metric (as well as nonmetric) analysis.

Exclusive reliance on metric methods may also be questioned since the function linking distance with dissimilarity may be highly nonlinear (but monotonic). Rather than assuming linearity, it is suggested that both metric and nonmetric analyses be run. The menu options for the PC-MDS version of the KYST program permit you to do this quite simply and efficiently.

The conditional proximity matrix [Figure 3–1(d)] is quite common in some data collection methods; for example, the method of n-dimensional rank order. The KYST program can be used to scale such data directly.

The scaling of partitioned matrices [like the one illustrated in Figure 3–1(e)] can arise in cases where core set methods are used. (Core set refers to the set of items that are most important in the study.) For example, if we assume k core items, a subject can be asked to give similarity responses on all $[k(k-1)]/2$ pairs of k items. Assuming n items in total, we obtain similarity responses for the remaining $n - k$ stimuli, by merely rank ordering them relative to each of the k core items, in turn. Other procedures can be used that lead to partitioned matrices in which cell values are comparable only within submatrices. (Actually, the conditional proximity matrix, partitioned by rows, is a special case of this class.) The KYST program, by sublist splitting, permits the scaling of partitioned matrices.

In summary, the KYST and the MDSCAL programs are flexible in their ability to perform both metric and nonmetric analyses as well as being able to scale a variety of special forms of proximity matrices. Other proprietary programs such as ALSCAL also provide these capabilities. Each of the identified programs, of course, handle the most common case [Figure 3–1(a)] of the intact, unconditional half matrix of similarities (dissimilarities) with a missing main diagonal.

SYNTHETIC DATA ANALYSES: RECOVERY

OF THE LETTER R   One useful way to get some intuitive feeling for the behavior of various algorithms in the scaling of similarities data is to examine their application to cases where the characteristics of the input data are known. To illustrate the ability of nonmetric algorithms to recover known configurations, we present in this section the results of a few illustrative analyses.

Input Data   The configuration to be recovered by nonmetric methods is shown in Figure 3–2. It consists of the letter *R* made up of 32 points positioned in two dimensions. The 1,024 interpoint distances from each point to all other points were computed using a PC-based spreadsheet. The pairs of points were then

_____ *Figure 3–2*_____

R Data

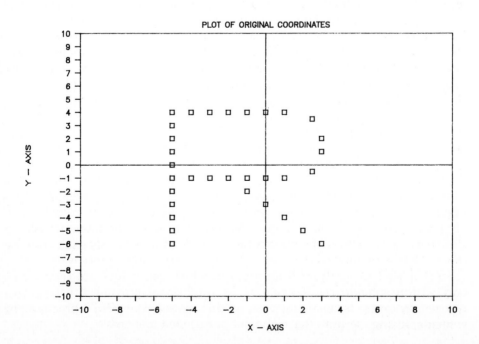

subjected to the simple monotonic transformation

$$y_{ij} = (d_{ij})^2 + 5$$

and submitted independently to full-size versions of the MDSCAL and KYST programs (Figures 3–3A and 3–3B). Solutions were sought in two dimensions and a plot of the monotone function linking dissimilarities with derived interpoint distances was also obtained; see Figures 3–4A and 3–4B.

Scaling Results

We note from Figures 3–4A and 3–4B that each algorithm yields very good recovery of the original configuration, albeit with different orientations.

As might be expected, the fit measures—Kruskal's stress—indicated virtually perfect recovery. The KYST stress value was 0.008, and the MDSCAL stress value was 0.004.

Finally, we note that the monotone transformation function $y_{ij} = (d_{ij})^2 + 5$ is approximated quite accurately as shown by the plots in Figures 3–4A and 3–4B.[3] Moreover, by a transformation made up of a combination of reflection and rotation, each configuration in Figure 3–3 could be oriented to agree with the original orientation of Figure 3–2. While virtually all multidimensional scaling algorithms differ in computational detail, it is evident that they produce quite similar results in the analysis shown here. Schiffman et al. (1981) have observed similar results when comparing POLYCON, KYST, and ALSCAL. Similarity in results is not unexpected given the many commonalities in the algorithms.

Adding Error to the Distances

Earlier work has shown the algorithms to recover known solutions well, not only for known configurations, but also where random error was added to the original data points (Green and Carmone, 1970). Results showed some distortion in the monotone function, but a generally good recovery, even in the presence of moderate amounts of noise.

In order to ascertain the effect of "noise" on configuration recovery, the original 1,024 interpoint distances were next transformed by the function $y_{ij} = (d_{ij})^2 + 5 + e_{ij}$, where e_{ij} represented a uniformly distributed error term with a minimum value of 0 and maximum value of 32.4. The analysis was

---

[3] The Shepard diagrams (Figures 3–4A and 3–4B) are (in general) plots of original data on the Y axis (actual distances in this case) versus two sets of distances (DIST and DHAT) derived by the model. DIST are the distances derived from the configuration before the monotone regression and DHAT are the final distances values from the final monotone regression. The plot points are designated as O if original data values, X if DHAT values, and + if two or more points were plotted on top of each other. Here, however, the observed data have been replaced by the DHAT values so that we have DHAT versus DIST. For a more detailed explanation, see the KYST write-up in Part IV.

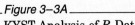

Figure 3–3A

KYST Analysis of R Data

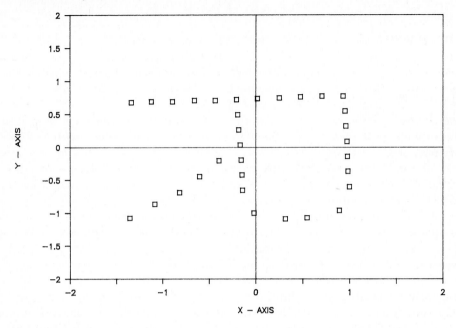

Figure 3–3B

MDSCAL Analysis of R Data

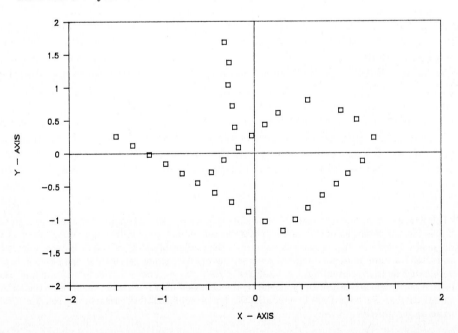

computed using the KYST and MDSCAL programs, and in addition, the INDSCAL program was used to analyze the data with and without the error term. (INDSCAL, INdividual Differences SCALing, is the analysis of data for individual subjects. In this case, error-free data is treated as subject one data and the error data is treated as subject two data.)

Results of Scaling the "Noisy" Data
The results of scaling the noisy data appear in Figures 3–5A, 3–5B, 3–5C, 3–6A, and 3–6B. Again, we note from Figure 3–5 that the orientation of the configurations differs over the three MDS algorithms, but recovery of the original configuration is still quite remarkable. In this case, the KYST stress value was 0.146, the MDSCAL stress value was 0.325, and INDSCAL explained 90.77 percent of variance, all rather "fair" values with regard to goodness of fit. The configuration is recovered with relatively little distortion.

_____ *Figure 3–4A* _____

MDSCAL Analysis of *R* Data with no Error

```
DHAT VERSES DATA FOR    2 DIMENSION(S)
STRESS =     .0035


             .        .1760.    .8212.   1.4664.    2.1116.    2.7569.
                   -.1466       .4986     1.1438    1.7890     2.4343     3.0795
                   *.****.****.****.****.****.****.****.****.****.****.*
       177.20 ..                                                  ..177.20
       170.52 ..                                               X  ..170.52
       163.84 ..                                                  ..163.84
       157.16 ..                                             X    ..157.16
       150.47 ..                                            X     ..150.47
    S  143.79 ..                                          X       ..143.79
    H  137.11 ..                                        X         ..137.11
    E  130.43 ..                                      +X          ..130.43
    P  123.75 ..                                    XX            ..123.75
    A  117.07 ..                                   XX             ..117.07
    R  110.39 ..                                  XX              ..110.39
    D  103.70 ..                                 XX               ..103.70
        97.02 ..                               X                  .. 97.02
        90.34 ..                              X                   .. 90.34
        83.66 ..                            XX                    .. 83.66
        76.98 ..                           XX                     .. 76.98
    D   70.30 ..                          XXX                     .. 70.30
    I   63.61 ..                         XX                       .. 63.61
    A   56.93 ..                       XX                         .. 56.93
    G   50.25 ..                      XXX                         .. 50.25
    R   43.57 ..                     XXX                          .. 43.57
    A   36.89 ..                   X+X                            .. 36.89
    M   30.21 ..                  XXX                             .. 30.21
        23.53 ..               XXX                                .. 23.53
        16.84 ..             XXXX                                 .. 16.84
        10.16 ..          XXXXXXX                                 .. 10.16
         3.48 ..  X  XX                                           ..  3.48
        -3.20 ..                                                  .. -3.20
                   *.****.****.****.****.****.****.****.****.****.****.*
              .        .1760.    .8212.   1.4664.    2.1116.    2.7569.
                   -.1466       .4986     1.1438    1.7890     2.4343     3.0795
```

_____ *Figure 3–4B* _____

KYST Analysis of *R* Data with No Error

```
DHAT VERSES DATA FOR    2 DIMENSION(S)
STRESS =       .0082


                    .     .1765.    .8239.   1.4712.   2.1186.    2.7659.
                  -.1471      .5002     1.1476     1.7949     2.4422      3.0896
                  *.****.****.****.****.****.****.****.****.****.****.*
         177.20 ..                                                    ..177.20
         170.52 ..                                                 X  ..170.52
         163.84 ..                                                    ..163.84
         157.16 ..                                              X     ..157.16
         150.47 ..                                            X       ..150.47
   S     143.79 ..                                         +X         ..143.79
   H     137.11 ..                                        X           ..137.11
   E     130.43 ..                                       X+           ..130.43
   P     123.75 ..                                     +X             ..123.75
   A     117.07 ..                                    XX              ..117.07
   R     110.39 ..                                   +X               ..110.39
   D     103.70 ..                                  +X                ..103.70
          97.02 ..                               XXX                  .. 97.02
          90.34 ..                               X                    .. 90.34
          83.66 ..                             ++X                    .. 83.66
          76.98 ..                            +X                      .. 76.98
   D      70.30 ..                          ++XX                      .. 70.30
   I      63.61 ..                          XX                        .. 63.61
   A      56.93 ..                        ++X                         .. 56.93
   G      50.25 ..                       +XX                          .. 50.25
   R      43.57 ..                     X+X                            .. 43.57
   A      36.89 ..                    X+X+                            .. 36.89
   M      30.21 ..                  XX+                               .. 30.21
          23.53 ..                XX+X                                .. 23.53
          16.84 ..              +XXX                                  .. 16.84
          10.16 ..         XXXXXX+                                    .. 10.16
           3.48 ..   X    X                                           ..  3.48
          -3.20 ..                                                    .. -3.20
                  *.****.****.****.****.****.****.****.****.****.****.*
                    .     .1765.    .8239.   1.4712.   2.1186.    2.7659.
                  -.1471      .5002     1.1476     1.7949     2.4422      3.0896
```

In both cases—error-free and noisy data—all three MDS algorithms performed rather similarly. Since the specific goodness of fit measures differ among the three approaches, one cannot readily use stress to ascertain the relative recovery "power" among the three algorithms. A multiway canonical correlation or factor matching procedure may provide the means to assess the similarity of these recoveries. For the current example, all three approaches yield quite accurate recoveries.

Data Collection Methods   The preceding portions of this section have presented insights into the conceptual and computational aspects of the algorithms. We now discuss a number of empirical problems surrounding their application to the portrayal of similarities data as geometric relations on points in a metric space. One class of such problems concerns the choice of an appropriate data collection method.

Figure 3–5A
MDSCAL Analysis of R Data with Error

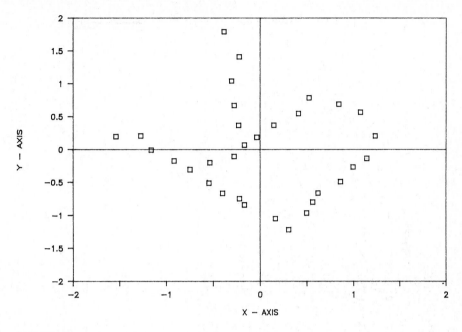

Figure 3–5B
KYST Analysis of R Data with Error

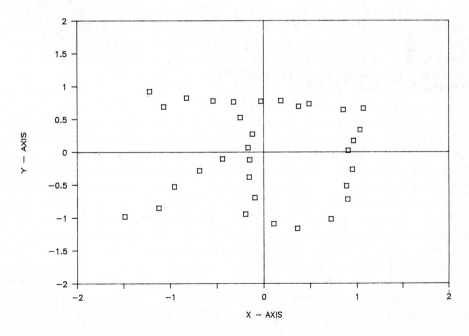

_____ Figure 3–5C _____
INDSCAL Analysis of R Data

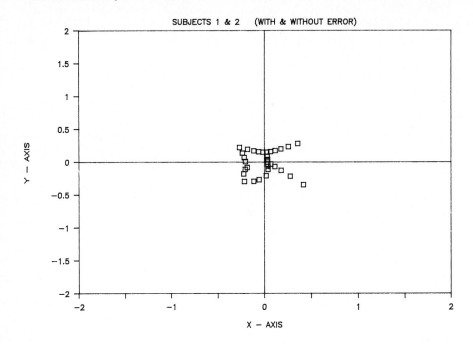

A variety of procedures exist for collecting proximity data, the most common of which entails filling a square symmetric matrix (an $n \times n$ intact conditional matrix where all $[n(n-1)]/2$ stimulus pairs have been evaluated and all cell values are comparable across both rows and columns). This form of data may be derived from measures of similarity, dissimilarity, affinity, substitutability, interaction, correlation, or congruence between the n stimuli [Green and Wind, 1973].

Perhaps the next most common form of the proximity data matrix is the conditional rectangular matrix ($n \times m$ intact conditional, where cell values are often the original data collected by the researcher). This data matrix contains the scores for the proximity relationships between one set of n stimuli (or subjects) and a second set of m stimuli. Each of the n rows of the matrix represents the relationship between one of the n stimuli and each of the m stimuli evaluated. Because the n-th stimulus is common only to the set of row evaluations, comparisons between this row of m similarity measures and the other $n-1$ rows of similarity measures cannot be made.

Given this description of alternate data matrix forms, we shall describe a more detailed set of data categories that result in a complete rank order of all distinct pairs—that is, all pairs in a lower- or upper-half matrix. This scheme for data collection and identification is not exhaustive, but serves to illustrate the large number of data collection procedures that can be employed in gathering similarities data.

Figure 3–7 presents the major descriptors of the classification. This $2 \times 2 \times 2$ cube illustrates the different combinations that can be used to gather data. The first dichotomy, direct versus derived, distinguishes between the pairwise similarity measures that are obtained by making explicit evaluations (such as how similar are these stimulus pairs) and the similarities data that is constructed or "built up" from other rating or evaluations data [such as an $(n \times k)$ matrix of Likert-type scale evaluations collected for n stimuli on each of a set of k attributes].

The second and third dichotomies identify the types of measures that are evaluated—judged similarity measures on the subject's responses that are subjective judgments. In contrast, behavioral measures result from some

_____ *Figure 3–6A* _____

MDSCAL Analysis of *R* Data with Error

```
DIST AND DHAT VERSES DATA FOR   2 DIMENSION(S)
STRESS =     .3245


                   .        .1854.      .8653.   1.5452.    2.2251.    2.9049.
                  -.1545       .5254     1.2052    1.8851     2.5650      3.2449
                  *.****.****.****.****.****.****.****.****.****.****.*
         195.41 ..                                                   ..195.41
         188.07 ..                                              X    ..188.07
         180.73 ..                                           OX  O   ..180.73
         173.39 ..                                          X  X     ..173.39
         166.04 ..                                         OX  O     ..166.04
  S      158.70 ..                                       OX+X  O      ..158.70
  H      151.36 ..                                      000X0         ..151.36
  E      144.02 ..                                   00 X+X  O        ..144.02
  P      136.68 ..                                 0+++X +0           ..136.68
  A      129.34 ..                                000X++0             ..129.34
  R      122.00 ..                                0+X+XO  0           ..122.00
  D      114.65 ..                              ++X0+0                ..114.65
         107.31 ..                          0+++X+ 00                 ..107.31
          99.97 ..                         +++X+++  0                 .. 99.97
          92.63 ..                       0++++XO++  0                 .. 92.63
          85.29 ..                      00+++0X+++                    .. 85.29
  D       77.95 ..                     +0++++X+++                     .. 77.95
  I       70.60 ..                    0+++++X+++  0                   .. 70.60
  A       63.26 ..                   ++++++X++++0                     .. 63.26
  G       55.92 ..                 +++++++X++++   0                   .. 55.92
  R       48.58 ..              0 ++++++X+++++                        .. 48.58
  A       41.24 ..          +0 +++++++++X++++0                        .. 41.24
  M       33.90 ..      + 0++++++++++XX+++++000                       .. 33.90
          26.56 ..      +   0+++++XX+++++00                           .. 26.56
          19.21 ..      +   ++++++X+++++                              .. 19.21
          11.87 ..      + +++X++0 0+                                  .. 11.87
           4.53 ..      +XX+                                          ..  4.53
          -2.81 ..                                                    .. -2.81
                  *.****.****.****.****.****.****.****.****.****.****.*
                   .        .1854.      .8653.   1.5452.    2.2251.    2.9049.
                  -.1545       .5254     1.2052    1.8851     2.5650      3.2449
```

_____ Figure 3–6B _____

KYST Analysis of R Data with Error

```
DIST AND DHAT VERSES DATA FOR    2 DIMENSION(S)
STRESS =     .1463


              .      .1824.     .8512.   1.5200.   2.1887.   2.8575.
              -.1520     .5168    1.1856    1.8543    2.5231    3.1919
             *.****.****.****.****.****.****.****.****.****.****.*
       195.41 ..                                              ..195.41
       188.07 ..                                        X     ..188.07
       180.73 ..                                    0X  0     ..180.73
       173.39 ..                                  0XX         ..173.39
       166.04 ..                                 0 X0         ..166.04
S      158.70 ..                               0X+X  0        ..158.70
H      151.36 ..                              00+X0           ..151.36
E      144.02 ..                            +0XX   0          ..144.02
P      136.68 ..                          0++X +0             ..136.68
A      129.34 ..                          00+X+0             ..129.34
R      122.00 ..                          ++X+X 0            ..122.00
D      114.65 ..                    0 ++X +                  ..114.65
       107.31 ..                    0+++X0 +                 ..107.31
        99.97 ..                 ++++X++00                   .. 99.97
        92.63 ..               0+++X+++ 0                    .. 92.63
        85.29 ..              +0+++X++0+                     .. 85.29
D       77.95 ..               +++++X+++                     .. 77.95
I       70.60 ..             ++++++X++0 0                    .. 70.60
A       63.26 ..            ++++++X+++++                     .. 63.26
G       55.92 ..         00+++++++X++00 0                    .. 55.92
R       48.58 ..          00+++++X+++++                      .. 48.58
A       41.24 ..      0+ 0++++++++++X++++                    .. 41.24
M       33.90 ..   +  ++++0++++X+X++++ +0                     .. 33.90
        26.56 ..   +  0+++++XX+++++00                         .. 26.56
        19.21 ..   +  ++++++X+++ ++                           .. 19.21
        11.87 ..   + +++X++0 000                              .. 11.87
         4.53 ..   +XX+                                       ..  4.53
        -2.81 ..                                              .. -2.81
             *.****.****.****.****.****.****.****.****.****.****.*
              .      .1824.     .8512.   1.5200.   2.1887.   2.8575.
              -.1520     .5168    1.1856    1.8543    2.5231    3.1919
```

behavioral response that is used as an indicant of psychological similarity. The third measurement dichotomy—disjoint versus conjoint comparisons (Coombs, 1964)—refers to whether or not all subjective judgments of objects are made in reference to a specific object. We will now discuss each of the major categories in turn.

Direct Measures of Similarity   By far, the most often used method of obtaining similarities data involves the direct measurement of pairs of stimuli, where respondents evaluate the similarity of stimulus pairs. Several approaches for obtaining direct measures of similarity may be used, namely, direct judged similarities of disjoint pairs of objects, direct judged similarities of conjoint pairs of objects, and direct behavioral methods.

———————— *Figure 3–7*————————————————————————

A Classification of Procedures for Collecting Similarities Data

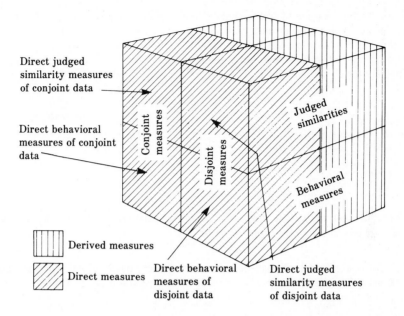

Direct Judged Similarities—Disjoint Pairs   Direct judgments of pairwise similarity is one of the more popular ways of collecting similarities data. A variety of measurement procedures yields disjoint comparisons.

Subjects are often given *all possible pairs* of objects and asked to rank them in terms of decreasing (or increasing) similarity:

Here is a list of 45 pairs of soft drink brands. Please rank them in terms of similarity from most similar to least similar. Assign the number 45 to the pair that is most similar, 44 to the next most similar pair, and so forth, until the value of 1 is assigned to the least similar pair.

Coke—Coke Classic	———
Coke—Diet Pepsi	———
Coke—Diet Slice	———
Coke—Diet 7-Up	———
Coke—Dr. Pepper	———
Coke—Pepsi	———
Coke—Slice	———
Coke—Tab	———
Coke—7-Up	———
Coke Classic—Diet Pepsi	———
⋮	
Tab—7-Up	———

Respondents may also be asked to rate each pair on, say, a 9-point *similarity/dissimilarity* scale:

Listed below are pairs of soft drinks. Please rate each pair on a scale of 1 (not at all similar) to 9 (very similar). Use any value between 1 and 9 to reflect your feelings of the degree of similarity of each pair of beverages. Use criteria of your own choice in making these comparisons, but please try to keep these criteria constant for all comparisons.

Brand Pair	Not at All Similar							Very Similar	
Coke vs. Coke Classic	1	2	3	4	5	6	7	8	9
Coke vs. Diet Pepsi	1	2	3	4	5	6	7	8	9
⋮									
Tab vs. 7-Up	1	2	3	4	5	6	7	8	9

Subjects can be given *pairs of pairs* (2 pairs) as stimuli and asked to indicate which pair is the most similar:

Listed below are sets of pairs of soft drinks. Please evaluate the two pairs and indicate which of the pairs is most similar by circling the number 1 or 2.

Pair 1	Pair 2	Circle 1 or 2
(Coke—Pepsi)	(Pepsi—Coke Classic)	1 2
(Coke—Pepsi)	(Pepsi—Diet Pepsi)	1 2
⋮		
(Slice—Tab)	(7-Up—Tab)	1 2

Alternatively, they may be given three pairs and asked to pick the most and least similar pair, a special case of the rating scale in which response categories are constrained to be dichotomous.

For these techniques, an undifferentiated line scale (a continuous line anchored by bipolar descriptors) is preferred to a scale with verbal descriptors. Difficulties in interpreting a multichotomous verbal scale, or a straight line scale with verbal descriptors, suggests that metric measures are best achieved through a scale having either an undifferentiated straight line, or a marked line scale of equal intervals (Schiffman et al., 1981).

In *subjective clustering methods,* the subject may be asked to sort the stimuli into groups such that those in any given group are thought to be more similar to each other than they are to any stimuli not in the group:

Consider the 10 brands of soft drinks identified below. Please group the brands into three sets, where the brands that are in each set are more similar to each other than they are to any brand in the other two groups. Indicate the group membership of each brand by placing a check in one of the columns.

	Group Assignments		
	1	2	3
Pepsi	___	___	___
Coke	___	___	___
Coke Classic	___	___	___
Diet Pepsi	___	___	___
Diet Slice	___	___	___
Diet 7-Up	___	___	___
Dr. Pepper	___	___	___
Slice	___	___	___
7-Up	___	___	___
Tab	___	___	___

An $n \times n$ "incidence" matrix (where n is the number of brands) could then be constructed in which a number 1 would be inserted if any two stimuli appear in the same group and a 0 otherwise. In this and the immediately preceding procedure, data typically would be aggregated across subjects to overcome the large number of ties, since individual matrices contain only zeros and ones.

All of the preceding methods will yield disjoint data, either for the individual subject or for aggregated groups such as the total sample or sample segments. Since programs can handle missing data, it is also possible for the researcher to eliminate specific comparisons if the number of stimuli is large in order to reduce respondent fatigue. While the problem of which and how many comparisons to forego has not been solved analytically as yet, accepted methodology for experimental design would dictate (a) an equal number of representations of each stimulus and (b) maintenance of "connectivity" among groups of comparisons so that if the stimuli are partitioned into two or more subsets, comparisons can be made across subsets.

Direct Judged Similarities—Conjoint Pairs Many procedures exist for the collection of similarity judgments involving conjoint data. Recall that conjoint data occurs where each pair of pairs has a stimulus in common and the number of pairs of pairs is the number of combinations of the $[n(n-1)]/2$ object pairs. When taken two at a time, the $[n(n-1) \times (n-2) \times (n+1)]/8$ tetrads becomes unwielding with, say, $n > 10$. Conjoint tetrads, each pair of pairs having a stimulus in common, reduces the comparison task markedly to $[n \times (n-1) \times (n-2)]/2$. The trade-off is that disjoint comparisons, where feasible, must be inferred from conjoint comparisons by assuming transitivity. Consider the following conjoint methods:

— Picking k out of $n-1$ items that are most similar to the reference item
— Ordering k out of $n-1$ items in terms of relative similarity to the reference item
— The method of n-dimensional rank order

—The method of anchor point ordering: "Which is more similar to *A*: stimulus *B* or stimulus *C*?"
—The method of triads: "Pick the two stimuli out of the triple that you think are most similar; now pick the two that are least similar."

The pick and order procedures should be mentioned in more detail, as they are frequently used methods of collecting conjoint data. The *anchor point clustering method,* the subject is asked to pick or order those *k* out of *n* − 1 items (where *k* is usually specified by the researcher) that are most similar to the reference or anchor item.

Now consider the brand *Sparkle,* which may not be your current brand. Of the 10 brands below, please choose 5 that, in your opinion, are most similar to *Sparkle.*

Coca Cola	_____	Mountain Dew	_____
Pepsi Cola	_____	Slice	_____
Dr. Pepper	_____	Diet Seven Up	_____
Tab	_____	Diet Slice	_____
Seven Up	_____	Hires Root Beer	_____

Each of the *n* stimuli serves, in turn, as the reference item. The resulting matrix of ones and zeroes (or ranks or average ranks if ordering was asked for) is a conditional proximity matrix and, of course, it need not be symmetric. Moreover, in this approach, responses are usually pooled over subjects in order to mitigate the problem of ties. (A variation of the procedure would entail pooling over subsets of subjects after first partitioning them into subgroups, based on their relative similarity to each other over the whole zero–one response matrix.)

These methods lead to conditional proximity matrices that can be scaled directly (or triangularized, using a program called TRICON (Carmone et al., 1968). In any case, the model being fit obtains interpoint distances for all pairs of points, thus implicitly assuming disjoint as well as conjoint comparisons.

While the above methods are not exhaustive of the many procedures available for collecting direct similarities data, they are representative of the principal ones. Clearly, much more applied research, particularly in the area of interactive computer data collection, is required to ascertain method correspondence over various groups of subjects, stimulus sets, problem setting, and data collection environments.

Direct Behavioral Methods   Direct behavioral methods focus on behavioral tasks that indicate perceived similarity between pairs of objects. This type of data can be collected under a variety of tasks. For example, the subject may be asked to assign individual automobile advertisements (of origin known by the experimenter) to one of several magazines (Green et al., 1968). Or, the subject may be given pairs of samples of unidentified brands of soft drinks and asked to indicate whether each pair is the same or different. An alternate form of this task would be to have the respondent assign each unidentified drink to one of a prespecified set of branded categories. The frequency with which object i is matched with object j is taken to be a behavioral measure of their psychological similarity. Through replication, a confusions or classification matrix can be developed for a single subject, enabling the researcher to obtain the subject's specific similarities configuration. More frequently, however, the data are pooled over subjects and a type of group configuration is obtained. In the latter case, one usually assumes that the respondents are homogeneous with regard to perceptual dimensions and discriminating acuity.

Other behavioral tasks can be developed. For example, slides of two package designs could be flashed momentarily on a screen and the subject asked to indicate whether the members of the pair are the same or different. The mean exposure time required for the subject to discriminate (make some prespecified percentage of correct responses) could be taken as an indicant of each pair's similarity. In still other tasks, the strength (amplitude) of the subject's response (for example, as reported by some physiological response measure such as Galvanic skin response, and so forth could be taken as an indicant of interstimulus response similarity. (It should be noted, that although physiological responses are measurable, cause and effect relationships are difficult to attribute. We may infer the response to be due to similarity, but the response may, in fact, be due to another factor.) It should be noted that one can obtain either unconditional (and symmetric) or conditional proximities, depending on the type of task employed.

DERIVED MEASURES OF SIMILARITY

By derived similarity measures we mean those that are computed for each pair of objects (brands) over the n objects' profile scores. For example, one could construct a series of semantic differentials and have a subject rate a set of stimuli on each of the semantic differential attitude scales. For a given subject, the stimuli-by-attitude scales matrix of attribute ratings can be used to compute interstimulus association measures, such as a simple set of matching coefficients, a correlation matrix, or a matrix of Euclidean distance measures. The derived measures of stimulus pair association could then serve as input to a multidimensional scaling program. A number of problems are encountered with this approach. First, the researcher may not have picked all of the relevant constructs (attribute scales) that people might evoke in making overall similarity responses. Second, there is a question of what weights to assign to each scale in computing overall association measures. Usually, equal weight (of 1.0) is applied to each of the scales for lack of any better procedure. In other instances, however, the interstimulus association measures may be computed on the basis of factor scores obtained from a principal component analysis of an attribute scale × attribute scale correlation matrix of scale pairs across stimuli.

In our own research, we have frequently employed the procedure of evaluating each stimulus on a series of single attribute scales and then having the subject make direct judgments of overall stimulus similarity. This approach not only provides an intermethod comparison, but is useful in interpreting the scaling of the overall similarity measures. Mention should also be made of the possibility of developing a configuration of both objects and scales as obtained by the implied ordering of each object on each scale. Factor analysis is relevant to this objective but involves a point-vector representation.[4]

There are some areas of application where derived measures can be quite useful. For example, if the stimuli can be evaluated on objective rather than subjective properties, association measures can be computed over clusters of stimuli or properties that form performance profiles. This approach is covered in more detail in Section 5.

As a second illustration, the researcher may wish to develop derived measures of intersubject association, as obtained from a subjects-by-similarities matrix. In this case the columns of the matrix would consist of the $[n(n-1)]/2$ pairs of stimuli. This approach can be useful in identifying individual differences in points of view, a topic discussed later in this section.

It is increasingly clear that the variety of procedures available for collecting similarities data may represent a mixed blessing. The choice of which procedure to use depends, as a minimum, on the number of stimuli and the amount of data upgrading that the experimenter is willing to perform. Relatively little research has been conducted on the invariance of proximity measures over alternative data gathering procedures. Such research is surely needed if we are ever to be able to evaluate the suitability of specific techniques for various data gathering objectives.

In addition to field-level comparisons, the study of data collection alternatives can be profitably undertaken by Monte Carlo analysis of synthetic data. This type of study is relatively inexpensive to conduct and should provide results that complement empirical studies dealing with intertechnique comparisons.

SOLUTION INTERPRETATION IN
MULTIDIMENSIONAL SCALING
In Chapter 2 it was indicated that multidimensional scaling solutions involving any type of Minkowski p-metric are invariant even when the axes are subject to translation, reflection, and uniform stretching (or compression). Moreover, in the case of the Euclidean distance measure, the metric most often used in empirical applications, the

---

[4] A point-vector model is based on the projection of stimulus points onto subject vectors (or subject points onto stimulus vectors). This is contrasted to point–point models where distances between points is the relevant criterion.

solution is also invariant when the axes are rotated. Thus, interpretation of the axes, even when uniquely oriented, still presents a problem in all Minkowski p-metrics. In Euclidean space (the metric on which we concentrate here) one needs to both interpret and reorient the configuration.

Some of the scaling programs, such as KYST, conventionally orient the configuration to principal components axes while others orient it to simple structure by means of a Varimax subroutine (Young, 1968). For purposes of this section's discussion, we shall assume that the scaling solution has been rotated to a principal components solution. This orientation might not be the best from the standpoint of axis interpretation, again, because the principal components solution may not produce an exact match with the "true" stimulus axes.

Several methods have been used to assist the researcher in the task of axis identification. They include: (a) research expertise aided by respondents' listings of criteria that they believed they used in making their similarities judgments, (b) property fitting procedures (using the PROFIT program), and (c) experimental design methods. Each approach is discussed in turn.

Researcher Expertise Probably the most common approach to axis interpretation is the use of more or less ad hoc judgments by the researcher. These judgments are formed by examining the configuration itself. Candidate axes may be suggested by having respondents list, at the completion of the similarities task, the main criteria that they believe they used in making their similarity judgments. Sometimes the researcher's judgment may be augmented by enlisting the interpretive aid of the subject after the data have been scaled.

Any of the above procedures entail a large element of subjectivity and perhaps are most appropriately considered as bases for hypothesis formation. Interpretations could be examined in subsequent experiments in which new subjects are asked to give similarities judgments according to these prespecified constructs. The one-dimensional solutions obtained by this means may be tested as possible dimension "labels" by procedures described in the next section.

Property Fitting Procedures If the researcher obtains properties (stimulus ratings based on unidimensional attribute scales) as well as the subject's unstructured judgments of similarities between the constructs, a variety of techniques are possible for axis interpretation. For example, based on prior studies or experimenter judgment, a set of preselected attribute scales can be chosen and the respondent can be asked to rate each stimulus on each attribute according to, say, a 9-point scale. (The constructs themselves might be developed from a preliminary study using Kelly's repertory grid; Kelly (1955).)

In any event, the researcher would have two sets of data for each subject. The first set would consist of the stimulus configuration obtained from scaling the subject's overall similarities data (using KYST or ALSCAL). The second consists of the properties, or respondent's ratings, of each stimulus on each of a prespecified set of attributes. The objective then, would be to "fit" the outside property vectors, which are the unidimensional ratings. Such fitting entails finding, for each property vector separately, a direction (vector) in the stimulus space so that the stimulus projections are, in turn, maximally correlated with each candidate property vector's scale values.

The three procedures widely available for this task are: (a) the max r procedure (Miller et al., 1964); (b) monotone multiple regression (Carroll and Chang, 1967), and (c) Carroll and Chang's PROFIT (Carroll and Chang, 1964). The max r procedure assumes the regression to be linear, while the other two procedures do not require linearity; the third procedure requires "smoothness" (but not necessarily monotonicity). Thus, the procedures make successively weaker assumptions about the form of the psychophysical transform relating the projection sought in the similarities space to the property vector being fitted.

The above approaches fit the property vectors one at a time. In parallel, the researcher may wish to run a canonical correlation between the coordinate values of the stimulus configuration and the whole set of candidate constructs. The canonical weights, so obtained, may then be used to find those linear compounds of the original constructs that are maximally associated with linear compounds of the coordinate values. Successive sets of linear compounds would be uncorrelated with those previously extracted. Examination of construct "loadings" could then suggest candidate labels for describing the new orientation of the transformed coordinates.

An illustration of property fitting by means of the PROFIT procedure is shown in Figure 3–8. In this application, overall similarities judgments were obtained by having subjects rank all possible pairs of 11 brands of automobiles. This was followed by having the same subject rate each of the 11 cars on each of 12 semantic differential scales. Figure 3–8 shows the two-space stimulus configuration obtained from scaling the 11 automobile brands using the average subject's overall similarities data.

We note from Figure 3–8 that the fitting of property vectors provides insight for interpreting the axes. The vertical axis appears to be best labeled "sportiness." The horizontal axis has several property vectors that are almost collinear with it—sophisticated, elegant, strong, complex. Note that many of the scales are not even close to being collinear with either component axis. This suggests that they could be considered as composites of the "basic" dimensions or, alternatively, that an oblique representation of the axes is appropriate for interpretation purposes.

Experimental Design Procedures   In some studies the experimenter may wish to vary the attribute levels of the stimuli themselves; for example, sweetness or degree of carbonation for soft drinks, strength of paper towels, and so on. If the stimuli are designed by the experimenter, a set of objective

_____ *Figure 3–8* _____

Average Subject Configuration and Vectors

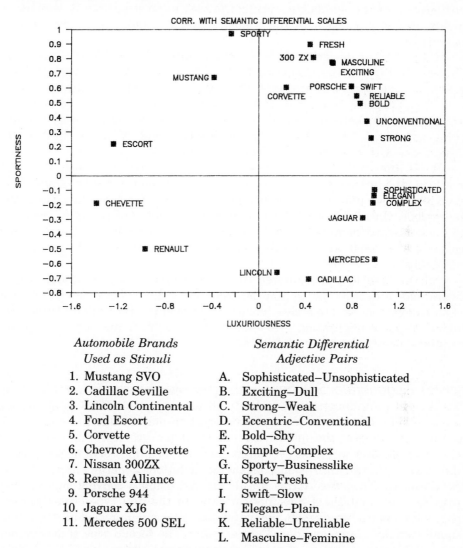

Automobile Brands
Used as Stimuli

1. Mustang SVO
2. Cadillac Seville
3. Lincoln Continental
4. Ford Escort
5. Corvette
6. Chevrolet Chevette
7. Nissan 300ZX
8. Renault Alliance
9. Porsche 944
10. Jaguar XJ6
11. Mercedes 500 SEL

Semantic Differential
Adjective Pairs

A. Sophisticated–Unsophisticated
B. Exciting–Dull
C. Strong–Weak
D. Eccentric–Conventional
E. Bold–Shy
F. Simple–Complex
G. Sporty–Businesslike
H. Stale–Fresh
I. Swift–Slow
J. Elegant–Plain
K. Reliable–Unreliable
L. Masculine–Feminine

property vectors is obtained, against which the perceived stimuli may be measured. Any of the above methods could be used to find appropriate projections in the similarities space, using the objective scales as property vectors. In addition, one could obtain subjective ratings or, possibly, similarities judgments as well, according to the prespecified (objective) constructs.

Green and Carmone, two of the authors of this book, used this type of approach in a pilot study of how Canadian housewives perceived lingerie that varied according to type of fabric, style, color, and price. The objective price vector was found to be poorly correlated with its best-fitting projection in virtually all of the similarities configurations, suggesting that it was not a highly salient dimension in the women's overall similarities judgments of lingerie.

Experimental design procedures might also be used in a sequence of studies, by varying the composition of the stimulus set. For example, if a preliminary experiment suggests that price and style are the two most salient dimensions, additional studies could be run in which the respondents are given stimuli of similar style but varied price or, alternatively, similar price but varied style. The resulting scales could then be checked for congruency with those found in the original study.

While the problem of interpreting scaling solutions is still far from resolved, the property vector fitting and experimental design approaches described above provide a reference point for the subjective expertise of the researcher. Our discussion also underscores the value of running a sequential set of experiments in order to examine the relevance of hypothesized constructs as well as to provide checks on interoccasion or interperson reliability.

Another problem encountered in the interpretation of similarities configurations concerns the appropriateness of a dimensional interpretation itself as opposed, say, to a classlike or categorical interpretation (Torgerson, 1965) of the configuration. We discuss this problem and some proposed solutions at some length in Section 5.

Identifying Degenerate Solutions   As every researcher who has worked in the area of multidimensional scaling will attest, not all MDS solutions are interpretable. Inability to interpret the solution may be due to either a lack of understanding of the underlying judgment process (the stimulus points are arranged in a way that seemingly have no meaning) or a degeneracy in the solution. In two dimensions, degenerate solutions generally appear in one of two forms. These two forms are illustrated using a conventional (rather than folding) analysis of hypothetical data. In the first type of degeneracy, points are arrayed in a circle, indicating that respondents view all stimuli as equally similar to one another (Figure 3–9A). The second type of degeneracy occurs where two clusters of points appear, one at either end of the X axis, and assume a "dumbbell" shape (Figure 3–9B). In the first case, MDS provides little insight into why the points are evaluated as equally similar or dissimilar. In the second case, the data suggest a unidimensional solution and a separate analysis of the clusters of points at each end of the scale. In the separate analysis of each cluster, it is appropriate to look for further multidimensional interpretation. Degenerate solutions most often occur in unfolding analysis when the proper parameters are not selected.

_____ Figure 3–9A _____
Equal Similarity Degenerate Solution (KYST)

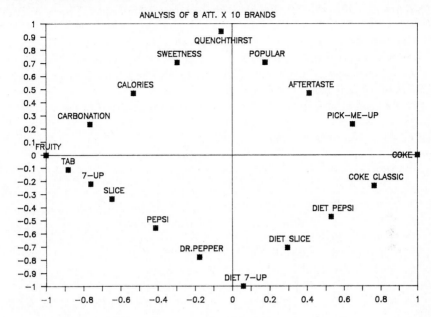

_____ Figure 3–9B _____
"Single" Dimension Degenerate Solution (KYST)

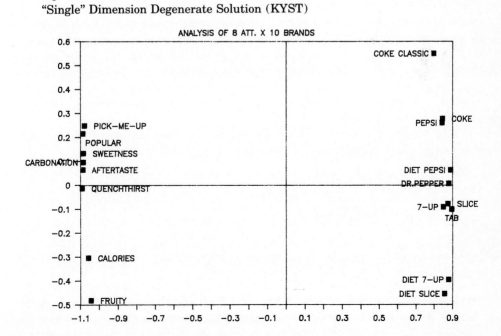

SPECIAL ISSUES IN THE ANALYSIS OF
SIMILARITIES DATA
A number of interesting topics of a rather specialized nature are associated with the analysis of similarities data. These include:

— Methods for dealing with individual differences in similarity judgments and their relationship to market segmentation
— Dependence of similarity judgments on use scenario and changes in the composition of the stimulus set
— Extension of scaling methods to deal with multi-way data matrices

Each of these topics is discussed in turn.

Individual Differences in Similarity Judgments
In a fairly large-size sample, it would be rare indeed if all respondents "perceived" the stimuli in exactly the same way or, on the other hand, used no dimensions in common. In our opinion, it is dangerous to assume homogeneity of similarities judgments across people and then, by simple aggregation, find one configuration that purportedly represents the group. The other extreme would be to develop each individual's configuration separately. Not only is this task unwieldy, but it is predisposed against generalization.

Our own position on the matter is that it is usually best to follow a middle course, namely one of segmentation. We search for the common dimensions or "points of view" in which each point of view may be shared by a number of subjects. Each point of view is, however, presumed to be different from other points of view. If homogeneity across individuals is found by analysis and not just assumed, then aggregation over subjects can be done in a more reasonable manner. Moreover, a second advantage to be gained through the study of individual differences in similarity judgments is the possible identification of market segments. These segments may, in turn, be related to identifiable characteristics (demographic, socioeconomic, psychographic) of the respondents.

Two major approaches (and a hybrid of the two) are available for the systematic study of individual differences in similarities data:

— Q-type factor analytic model [Tucker and Messick, 1963]
— Carroll and Chang's (1969) "INDSCAL" model (for INdividual Differences SCALing).

We discuss each of these briefly and then comment on a dual approach that we have considered. Still other procedures have been proposed by Kruskal and Carmone (1971) and McGee (1968).

Q-Type Factor Analytic Model
This model, applied to similarities data, is simple. It is a metric procedure—although nonmetric analogues can also be used—and it is basically a Q-type principal component analysis of the

(subjects by attribute) similarities matrix. Association measures (cross-products, covariances, correlations) are obtained for each pair of subjects across the whole vector of similarities judgments and the resulting matrix is then factored by principal components. A subject configuration is obtained in component space. This matrix, known as a factor loading matrix, contains subject loadings on the resulting components and is used as the basis for grouping subjects. Various procedures can be employed to choose representative subjects for each component (or "point of view") and separate scalings of each representative subject's data are obtained. An alternate approach might be to conduct an R-type factor analysis and obtain the factor scores matrix, which contains scores of each subject on each of the underlying components. This approach would then be followed by a cluster analysis to produce similar results.

Figure 3–10 shows a hypothetical plot of all subjects and their perceptions of the car brands. The stimulus configuration (for the average subject) has already been shown in Figure 3–8. In this instance, we are interested in whether subjects who are shown a color photograph of each car model, in addition to the brand name, give different similarities responses than those subjects who only receive brand names as stimuli.

Figure 3–10 shows that this is not the case. A two-group discriminant analysis (based on the three-space coordinates for each subject) confirms the

_____ Figure 3–10 _____

Plot of First Two Components—Tucker and Messick Points of View Analysis

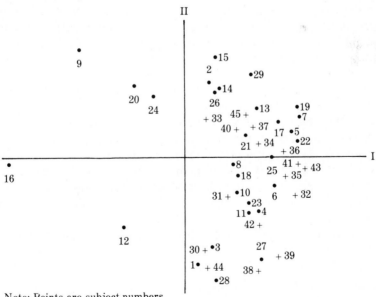

Note: Points are subject numbers.
+ Color photograph
• No photograph

visual evidence. We do note, however, that some subjects (numbers 9, 12, 16, 20, and 24) plot at some distance from the major cluster. As would be expected, their stimulus configurations differ from that obtained from the representative subject closest to the centroid of the major cluster.

After the stimulus configuration associated with each point of view is found, these can be rotated [Cliff, 1966] for maximal congruence with each other in order to get some idea of the degree of correspondence. Moreover, if other characteristics (demographic, socioeconomic) of the subjects are available, one can run canonical correlations between the subject coordinates (from Figure 3–10) and the matrix of subject property vectors. In this way, correlates of points of view may be found that could be useful for market segmentation strategy.

The Carroll and Chang INDSCAL Model   The Carroll and Chang INDSCAL model raises a fundamental issue concerning the factor analysis approach, namely that subsequent scalings of the similarities data associated with each perceptual dimension do not directly show how each dimension is related to the others—that is, the dimensions that subjects (or more often, groups of subjects) may have in common. [See Hauser and Koppelman, 1979, for a discussion of the relative merits of factor analysis and similarity scaling.] Carroll and Chang's approach—also metric but capable of being made quasi-nonmetric—assumes that all subjects share a common, or group, space but that each individual is allowed to weight the dimensions of this space. Moreover, some subjects may assign zero weights to one or more of the axes. Their model develops both the group space and a set of subject weights that represent the different saliences each subject places on each dimension. In this way, an estimate of each subject's stimulus configuration can be obtained by transformation of the group configuration through differential stretching of its axes.

A goodness of fit on each individual stimulus configuration, as estimated by the model, is also obtained. This measure can be used to identify, for separate analyses, those subjects whose similarities data are not well represented by the shared space model.

The problem setting for this example is an evaluation of similarity between musical groups/personalities made by 26 business students (Group *B*) and 26 music students (Group *M*). Figure 3–11 shows a three-space stimulus configuration obtained from the INDSCAL model and Figure 3–12 shows the three two-space projections of the subject weights [Green and Morris, 1969].

Looking first at Figure 3–11, it appears as though appropriate labels for the axes are

> —Axis I, Classical . . . Popular
> —Axis II, Serious . . . Commercial
> —Axis III, Groups . . . Individuals

_____ *Figure 3–11* _____

Three-Dimensional Stimulus Configuration From Carroll–Chang Individual Differences Model

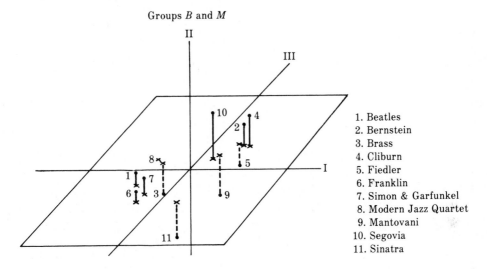

Groups *B* and *M*

1. Beatles
2. Bernstein
3. Brass
4. Cliburn
5. Fiedler
6. Franklin
7. Simon & Garfunkel
8. Modern Jazz Quartet
9. Mantovani
10. Segovia
11. Sinatra

As noted from Figure 3–12, however, individual subject weights differ markedly among subjects. Subject *A,* for example, gives highest weight to axis I, low weight to axis II, and (Figures 3–11, 3–12) moderate weight to axis III. Generally speaking, business students gave more weight to axis I than did music majors. Moreover, greater heterogeneity and higher dimensionality of solution were noted for the music majors.

A Hybrid Approach   A hybrid approach is possible that combines features of both the Factor Analytic and INDSCAL models. A difficulty with the INDSCAL model is the large number of rather unimportant dimensions that might conceivably occur. Scores on these axes would be treated as error variance if not enough subjects were to share the dimensions to make their effect felt in the group stimulus space. In the hybrid approach, the subject by similarities matrix would first be "factored." Subject clusters would then be obtained and subjects assigned to each cluster.

The INDSCAL model would then be applied both within each cluster and across clusters, using data for the representative subjects as the appropriate set of similarities vectors in the latter case. In this way, the fine structure of each cluster would be obtained as well as shared dimensions across clusters for the representative subject of each point of view. So far, our experience with this hybrid approach is too meager for useful evaluation, but its rationale appears to be appropriate for the kinds of empirical problems in which we are interested.

_____ *Figure 3–12* _____
Three-Dimensional Salience Configuration

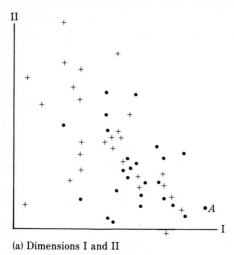

(a) Dimensions I and II

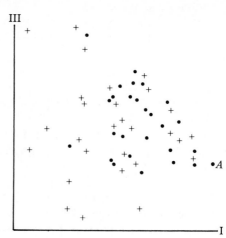

(b) Dimensions I and III

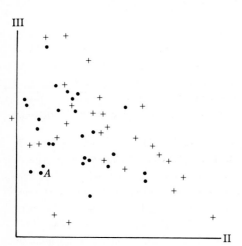

(c) Dimensions II and III

— Group *B*
— Group *M*

Configuration Invariance Over Scenario and
Composition of Stimulus Set
Another special topic of interest to applied
researchers concerns the invariance of stimulus configurations over changes
(a) in scenarios under which the similarities judgments are obtained and (b)
in the composition of the stimulus set. As was discussed in Section 2, in
the Euclidean distance model we mean invariance up to a similarity

transformation—translation, uniform stretching of the axes, reflection, and rotation. None of these transformations will affect the rank order of the derived interpoint distances.

Most similarities judgments are obtained on an unstructured basis where the subject is asked to give responses regarding overall similarity of pairs of stimuli. Indeed, the rationale for this approach is to find out which dimensions are evoked when the subject is not constrained to make comparisons along any preselected set of scales. It seems reasonable to suppose, however, that the evoked dimensions are context bound.

As an example, take the case of brands of soft drinks; if no scenario is specified, it is possible that dimensions like "dietness" or "lightness of taste" may be evoked. However, if the scenario "appropriateness for serving as mixers for alcoholic beverages" is used, other attributes; for example, "degree of carbonation" or "cola versus noncola" might be evoked.

To the authors' knowledge little extensive study of the effect of conditions of product or service use on similarity judgments has been made as yet. From an operational standpoint, it is quite feasible to develop second-order configurations (a "mapping of maps") where the points are scenarios and where scenario similarity is based on the correspondence of stimulus configurations under each scenario.

Such work could lead to a more extensive investigation of consumers' cognitions in which a "basic" configuration—or "superspace"—is related to a set of context-bound subconfigurations. This approach is basic to the development of context-bound artificial intelligence models. The authors have explored this notion in the preference domain (see Section 4), but much more research remains to be done on the question of scenario influence on similarities and preference judgments.

It seems to us that serious study of similarities judgments will have to consider interrelationships among stimulus domains, including those stimulus domains that appear to form nested sets—for example, cola drinks, soft drinks, all beverages. Here one would be interested in the dimensions evoked for within-class discriminations when cola drinks are embedded, say, in the class of all soft drinks.

Multiway Matrices Up to this point our discussion has emphasized the traditional two-way matrix form; for example, stimuli by stimuli or persons by perceptual dimensions (in the case of factor analysis). Many instances arise in the analysis of similarities data where the data entail multiway matrices; for example, persons by concepts by scale ratings or even persons by concepts by scale ratings by occasions.

Two models—both metric—have been proposed for dealing with multiway matrices. Tucker (1964) has advanced a procedure—multimode factor analysis—that is capable of dealing with such multiway matrices. A feature of this procedure is the development of a central or "core" matrix that is operated upon by transformation matrices summarizing data by various components of the multiway matrix.

Carroll and Chang's INDSCAL model is similar in spirit to the Tucker model and can be generalized to quasi-nonmetric form [Arabie, Carroll and De Sarbo, (1987)]. At this writing, neither model has been applied extensively. We speculate, however, that the advent of increased mathematical and computational power will lead to extensions of scaling methods to multiway matrices. This kind of extension appears needed for a more complete understanding of the interconnections among the many facets [Guttman, 1968] by which similarities data can be described.

SUMMARY

Our objective in this section has been to discuss the analysis of similarities data from both a conceptual and empirical point of view. The earlier parts of the section emphasized the assumptions underlying distance models of proximity data, the types of proximity matrices that can be represented by distance models, and the computational features of various algorithms. Some of these algorithms were demonstrated in the analysis of artificial data.

We then turned to empirical matters concerning the analysis of proximities—mainly methods of data collection and procedures for interpreting the scaling solutions. As was described, both of these substantive areas provide extensive opportunities for additional research since little is known about the correspondence of various data collection procedures and alternative methods of configuration interpretation.

The last major topics considered in this section considered a variety of special issues, individual difference models, scenario dependence, and extension of scaling techniques to multiway matrices. These topics reveal both the potential power of scaling methods and, at the same time, the many problems that remain for further study, if the potential of this methodology is to be realized in marketing research.

Analysis of Preference Data

The analysis of preference data is the second major application area for multidimensional scaling methods. The format of this section is similar to that of the preceding section and the following main topics will be discussed:

— Conceptual structure and models for portraying preference judgments
— Computational procedures and results
— Empirical problems, including data collection and solution interpretation
— Special issues, including evaluation function problems and the analysis of preferences for stimulus "bundles"

In the first part of this section, the concept of preference is described and is related to various types of models—the distance model, the vector model, and the compensatory distance model. Included in this introduction is a discussion of preference matrices and the algorithms appropriate for analyzing either preference data alone or a combination of similarities and preference data (covering the same group of stimuli and respondents). We show the behavior of some of these algorithms in the analysis of synthetic data of known characteristics.

Next, this section discusses the major empirical problems associated with the analysis of preferences, including alternative data gathering methods and procedures for the interpretation of joint space configurations.

The concluding portion of this section discusses a variety of special topics in preference analysis, including the relationship of choice probability to ideal point and vector models, the problem of indifference relations, and decision rules used to choose among multiattribute alternatives. Part IV of this text includes the program documentation of the algorithms discussed in this section.

MODELS OF PREFERENCE JUDGMENTS A variety of models have been proposed for the analysis of preference judgments. For our purposes, they are divided into those that may be used only to analyze preference judgments and those that may be used to analyze both similarities data and preference data collected from the same respondents on the same set of stimuli. Each class is discussed in turn.

Models Based on Preference Data Only Historically, psychometricians have focused primarily on models using preference data only. The key objective of these models is to develop a joint space of N subjects and n stimuli that permits the drawing of inferences about the subjects, stimuli, or both. In the case of either metric or nonmetric approaches, nothing further can be done if all subjects give exactly the same preference order to the same set of stimuli. Analysis may be conducted only when disparate scale values or orderings of the same stimuli are observed across subjects.

Basic to all models that analyze preference data alone is the assumption of homogeneity of perception. If this assumption is violated, differences in preference may be confounded with differences in perception. Preference analysis models also assume that the underlying perceptual dimensions constitute the dimensions on which preference is based and that preferences differ across subjects. Given these common assumptions, we may then classify the major models: (a) type of representation—that is, distance models, vector models, or compensatory distance models—and (b) type of algorithm—that is, metric versus nonmetric. Our discussion is organized according to the first descriptor.

Distance Models Distance models have already been encountered in our discussion of similarities data in Section 3. In the context of preference analysis, distance models underlie the conceptual notion of the ideal point [Coombs, 1964]. An ideal point is a hypothetical stimulus (such as a brand, product, or other unit of analysis) possessing a specific combination of "scores" on the underlying (perceptual) dimensions. For the moment we assume that preference is maximum at the ideal point and declines symmetrically along all dimensions as one moves away from the ideal. This conceptualization is pictured in Figure 4–1 for the case of a single subject. The right-hand panel of the figure illustrates the associated isopreference

_____ *Figure 4–1* _____
Illustrative Utility Function and Isopreference Contours

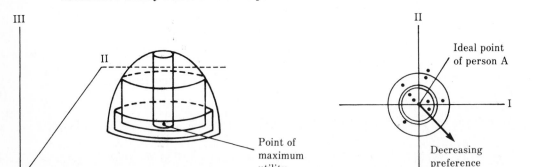

(a) Utility Function of Person A   (b) Isopreference Contours of Person A

curves, in this case a series of concentric circles of increasing radius. All stimulus points on a given isopreference curve are assumed to be equally preferred.

In either the metric or nonmetric case, the assumption is that each of the dimensions of the multidimensional joint space are interval scaled and the interpoint distances between any pair of points, be they ideal to ideal, ideal to stimulus, or stimulus to stimulus, are ratio scaled. Further, the joint space configuration shared by the N subjects and n stimuli is assumed to be unique up to a similarity transform when a Euclidean metric is used (see the discussion of transformations in Section 2).

In short, the structure of the distance model applied to preferences is quite similar to that noted in our discussion of similarities data. The principal distinction is that we deal with a rectangular off-diagonal matrix of input data, consisting of relations on two different sets of points, the first being stimulus points and the second being subject points.

Types of input data may again be conditional or unconditional, as shown in panels (a) and (b) of Figure 4–2. In the case of conditional proximities, we assume that data values are comparable only across columns, and not across rows. In the case of unconditional data, we assume that all cell values in the off-diagonal matrix are comparable, a rather strong assumption. Another way of putting this is to say that the parameters defining the utility function link the subject's preferences to distance and are subject specific in the first case, whereas in the second case all individuals share the same preference function. We do, however, assume in both cases that all individuals share the same monotonic form of the preference utility function.

The selection of a distance model for scaling preference data rests on the distinction of (a) conditional versus unconditional input data and (b) metric versus ordinal assumptions regarding the preference values. In the case of conditional proximities, the KYST, ALSCAL, and MDSCAL programs can be used for ranked data. In addition, KYST and MDSCAL can be used for prespecified preference functions (linear, quadratic, and so forth) and, as such, can perform a metric scaling of the data.

If we allow comparisons across rows [Figure 4–2(b)], a variety of programs, including KYST, ALSCAL, and MDSCAL, can be used in the nonmetric case. Moreover, these same programs can be used for analysis of preference data in which a linear relationship is assumed between preference values and distances from an ideal point.

The objective of using any of these methods is to develop a joint space of $N + n$ points from subject evaluations of only a subset of those points, namely, the $(N \times n)$ off-diagonal input data matrix, conditional or unconditional, as the case may be. We are then using the $(N \times n)$ matrix to estimate the $n \times n$ stimuli matrix and the $N \times N$ subject matrix. If the model holds, all distances are assumed to be comparable, including ideal–ideal and stimulus–stimulus, even though no relations on these pairs of pairs are directly measured.

_____ Figure 4–2 _____

Alternative Forms of Preference Data Matrices

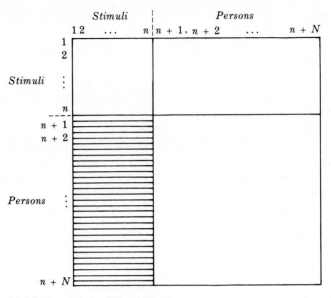

(a) Off-Diagonal, Conditional Matrix

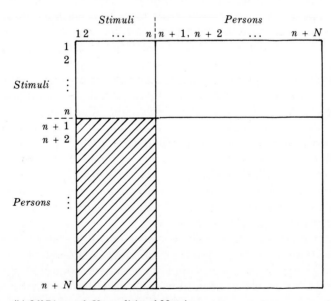

(b) Off-Diagonal, Unconditional Matrix

The principal danger in using nonmetric approaches where so few inequality constraints exist is that the configuration might not be well determined. We later return to demonstrate this point when we use some of the above programs in the context of synthetic data.

Vector Models   The traditional factor analytic model is the metric prototype of this class. The first model of this type for dealing with metrically scaled preferences was proposed by Tucker (1960). This model assumes that all respondents share the same perceptual space. However, within this space each respondent's preferences are assumed to be linearly related to the projections of the *stimulus points* on the individual respondent's uni-dimensional vector. The projections define the points that are interpreted as a set of weights applied to each of the underlying dimensions in the perceptual space. These weights are used in arriving at a unidimensional scale of preference values for the respondent.

In terms of Figure 4–2, we first deal with the *subject × stimuli* submatrix shown in the off-diagonal, conditional proximity matrix of panel (a). We assume that scale comparisons are maintained only within rows. The metric version of the vector model makes the major assumption that preference changes linearly with the saturation of stimulus j on dimension k. As consequences of this assumption, two problems can occur:

1. One can have "mediocre" stimuli that are not preferred by any subject.
2. All "ideal" points lie far outside the range that is achievable for real stimuli (as a matter of fact, the ideal points are infinitely distant in directions defined by the vectors).

Operationally, the vector model assumes that "more is better," a property common to all linear models. Figure 4–3 shows the effect of these assumptions graphically. We note that different preference values are accounted for by different vector directions (the three subject vectors being conventionally scaled to unit length). We see that stimulus C, for example, is neither most nor least preferred by any of the three subjects. Finally, the scale values for each subject are read off by forming a 90-degree projection of each stimulus point on to each vector, in turn.

In this version of the metric vector model, we are free to choose a unit and zero point independently on each coordinate axis of the underlying dimensions. The orthogonal coordinate axes provide independent interval scales along which we can compare stimulus points on a basis of one axis at a time. The projections of stimulus points on each subject's preference vector are defined only up to an interval scale transformation.

On the other hand, if we assume that all preference values are comparable across subjects [Figure 4–2(b)], both the subject weights (projection) on each axis and the stimulus values (projection) on each preference vector are assumed to be interval scaled with fixed zero point.

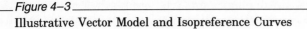

Figure 4–3

Illustrative Vector Model and Isopreference Curves

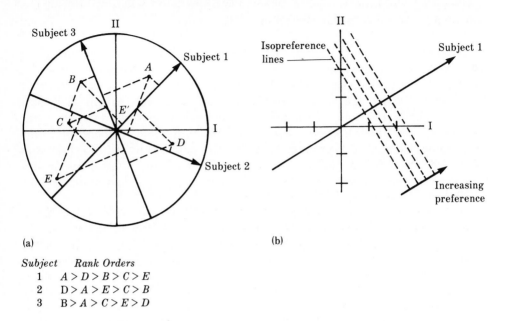

(a)   (b)

Subject	Rank Orders
1	$A > D > B > C > E$
2	$D > A > E > C > B$
3	$B > A > C > E > D$

This is because we assume that all preference scales are comparable across subjects (rows). Even here, however, we can only compare stimulus points on each axis separately, since we are allowed free choice of unit.

Since the development of Tucker's model, others have proposed non-metric versions of the vector model [Shepard and Kruskal, 1964; Roskam, 1968]. The nonmetric formulations first define a space of stimulus points and then find a set of vector directions (in a space of low dimensionality) such that the order of the stimulus point projections on each vector agrees as closely as possible with the orders observed in the off-diagonal, conditional proximity matrix.

The MDPREF model developed by Carroll and Chang [see Chang and Carroll, 1969] uses a vector formulation, but is an internal form of analysis that positions stimulus points and subject vector directions simultaneously in a common space. The notion of an internal approach, such as MDPREF, may be best explained in contrasting MDPREF with an external model, such as PREFMAP. In the internal approach, where only a single data set is analyzed, the stimuli points are interpreted only with respect to the subject vectors lying in principal components space. In the external case, two data sets are required. Stimulus points are interpreted relative to other points defined in the second data set as well as the subject vectors from the first data set.

Both internal and external vector model formulations can be viewed as special cases of the distance model in which the ideal points are found at the "end" of each subject's preference vector, which is assumed to extend to infinity. Under this assumption the rank order of a set of stimulus points from the "ideal" would agree with the rank order of the projections of the stimuli on the subject vector. Analogously, the isopreference "contours" in the two-dimensional case are then represented by a series of parallel lines, each line perpendicular to the subject's vector; this is demonstrated for subject 1 in the panel (a) of Figure 4–3.

MDPREF is designed to handle, metrically, the case of either rank-ordered or paired comparisons data, using the off-diagonal (subject × stimuli) data matrix shown in panel (a) of Figure 4–2. MDPREF uses principal components analysis (Eckart–Young decomposition), and as such, may be used to analyze preference rankings and ratings data. The solution is simultaneous rather than iterative, often producing results that are more stable than other joint space models. In the analysis, the data matrix of size N subjects by n stimuli is decomposed into two smaller matrices, whose matrix product approximates the original data matrix in a least squares sense.

The first of these matrices is an N subject by r dimensions matrix, which contains each of the N subject's score (directional coordinates of the subject vector) in terms of each underlying perceptual dimension. The second matrix is an n stimuli by r dimensions matrix, which contains the coordinates of each stimulus point in the r dimensional perceptual space.

The vector model is most often implemented using data collection procedures that measure subject beliefs. Often referred to as attitude-belief or evaluative-belief models, the models assume that the subject's overall attitude toward a stimulus can be derived by adding up the subject's beliefs about each component or attribute of the stimulus. The ideal point is not explicitly identified, but rather inferred from the stimulus alternatives under consideration. The importance of each of the attributes that sum to overall attitude may or may not be included depending on the complexity of the model desired. Importance is operationalized as a weighted sum of the attributes.

Mathematically, then, this model would appear

$$A_{io} = \sum_{j=1}^{J} a_{ioj} w_{ij}$$

where

A_{io} = attitude of subject i toward stimulus o,

a_{ioj} = evaluation of subject i toward stimulus o with respect to attribute j

w_{ij} = importance of attribute j to subject i

One possible distinction between the vector model (which implicitly assumes an infinitely distant ideal point) and an ideal point model (in which the ideal point is explicitly identified) is the data collection procedures.

Data collection procedures for the vector model often include evaluation measures based on Likert, semantic differential, or continuous rating scales. For example, soft drinks might be evaluated as being low in carbonation–high in carbonation, low in calories–high in calories, very tart–very sweet, or strong aftertaste–no aftertaste.

Compensatory Distance Models   The compensatory distance model is a type of hybrid model, mentioned by Coombs (1964) and formulated for the nonmetric case by Roskam (1968). In the case of preference data, this model assumes that each subject "collapses" the multidimensional evaluation space to a unidimensional preference vector (similar in spirit to the vector model). It is further assumed that an ideal point exists on this vector such that the subject's observed ranking reflects increasing distance of stimulus projections on either side of the ideal point along the compensatory vector; thus, ideal points do not extend to infinity in this case. Figure 4–4 illustrates this type of model.

In the compensatory distance model an independent choice of unit on each coordinate axis is permitted as well as translation of the origin. Also, the unit of each subject's scale is independent but is ratio scaled with an origin located at the ideal point. While coordinates of the stimuli are interval scaled, they are not of common unit; hence, interstimulus comparisons are confined to each dimension separately (unlike the distance model described earlier). If, however, data of the variety noted in Figure 4–2(b) are obtained, one can compare the interpoint distances between pairs of stimulus points.

The compensatory distance model, although intuitively appealing, has received little known use by practitioners. We mention it here only for the

_____ Figure 4–4 _____

Compensatory Distance Model

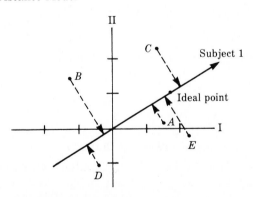

Observed Rank Order:
$E > C > A > B > D$

sake of completeness and refer the reader to a much more extensive account in Roskam (1968).

Models Using Similarities or Similarities-Preference

Data Two approaches are commonly used when representing a joint space of stimuli and ideal points. We may use either similarities or similarities plus preference data. The similarities data approach makes use of the "explicit ideal" concept, whereas the second approach develops a joint space from a combination of similarities and preference data.

Explicit Ideal Point Formulation The notion of an explicit ideal is a simple one and requires no new analytical concepts. Essentially the approach involves including one additional stimulus (total $= n + 1$) that is described as an ideal stimulus (brand, service, company, or other units of analysis). The respondent is asked to imagine what the ideal brand would be like. Operationally, similarities data are collected for all pairs of the $n + 1$ stimuli. When these data are scaled by the usual distance model for describing similarities data, increasing distances from the real stimuli to the hypothetical ideal are assumed to reflect decreasing preference—that is, the greatest preference is found at the ideal and the utility function declines monotonically with distance from the ideal point.

A metric version of the approach using derived measures would consist of having N subjects rate an explicit ideal on the same set of prespecified attributes used to rate the real stimuli. Derived measures of interpoint distance could then be scaled along the lines discussed in Section 3. The stimulus space would consist again of $n + 1$ stimuli plus N subject points with distances from the ideal and would be interpreted as above.

While the use of an explicit ideal is certainly economical in terms of time and effort, some conceptual and empirical problems are associated with this approach. First, it is not clear that respondents can fully conceptualize the notion of an explicit ideal; one may prefer to infer the position of an ideal point from the respondent's simple preference judgments. Second, when subjects shift from a similarities to a preference evaluations context, the (perceptual) axes may be weighted differentially. This effect would not show up clearly if the similarities comparisons involving the explicit ideal are merely mixed in with those involving real stimulus pairs. Finally, some evidence [Neidell, 1968] exists that use of the explicit ideal does not predict (independently obtained) preference orderings, even for the same group of subjects evaluating the same set of real stimuli.

Although we do not want to reject the concept of an explicit ideal, we believe there are more defensible models that exhibit greater flexibility in relating preferences to the geometric representations obtained from similarities data. We comment next on those generalizations of the ideal point concept that have been developed by Carroll and Chang.

Ideal Point Generalization Carroll and Chang [see Chang and Carroll, 1972;

Carroll, 1972; and Carroll and Chang, 1967] have developed the PREFMAP algorithm that incorporates metric and nonmetric models for generalizing the Coombsian concept of ideal point. PREFMAP requires the use of both similarities and preference data for the same group of subjects and stimuli. The metric model assumes that each individual's utility function is linearly related to the weighted squared distance of each of the real stimuli to its ideal. The model is applied in the following way.

1. Similarities data are collected for each of N subjects on n stimuli. This $n \times n$ matrix is first scaled by one of the metric or nonmetric multi-dimensional scaling programs (such as KYST). As a result of scaling the similarities data, a solution, which is known as a configuration, is produced. This similarities configuration identifies the coordinates of the stimulus points. This n stimuli $\times r$ dimensions configuration matrix represents the first set of input to PREFMAP.

2. The second set of input data consists of the preference data for the same stimuli for possibly different scenarios (or use occasions). For example, if five scenarios were used, the preference ranking for each subject on each of the n stimuli would be recorded, in turn, for each of the five scenarios. The preference ranking for each stimulus would be averaged over the N subjects for each scenario.

   As an alternative form of analysis, market segments could be used in place of scenarios. In this case, market segments would be identified a priori and the n stimuli would be ranked according to preference by each person. Next we would compute separate average preference rankings using only those subjects who belonged to each market segment.

3. The approach then entails finding ideal point positions (or, in one case, vectors) for each subject, according to each of four models or phases of the PREFMAP program.

   a. What is called phase IV of the PREFMAP model provides the simplest model of the four. It is a vector model (similar to MDPREF) in which a directional vector is calculated for each subject in the common similarities space. The stimulus points, which are given, are plotted and projected onto the subject vector. The projection of stimulus points onto the subject vector are maximally correlated with the individual subject preference data.

   b. Phase III of the PREFMAP model provides a straightforward Coombsian ideal point model that, like all other models, assumes subjects share the same underlying dimensions of perception ("evaluative" space). Although this model assumes that the same dimensions are used for each individual, subjects may differentially weight the dimensions. The inclusion of weights may lead to a solution that is rotated and differentially stretched from the original similarities configuration.

    c. Phase 2, also an ideal point model, subsumes the above and also permits the use of subject-specific weights to stretch the axes when achieving ideal points for each subject. This stretching involves only changing the scale factors from subject to subject. The importances on each dimension are the same for all subjects. This is all done, however, using the phase 3 solution, which defines the evaluative space as that of the average subject.

    d. Phase 1, is a completely individualistic ideal point model and therefore the most general of the models. Phase 1 includes rotation and differential axis stretching for each subject (though within the framework of a common stimulus space).

4. In addition, the PREFMAP model allows for the possibility of positive ideal points, negative (anti-ideal) points, or combinations whose "signs" vary by dimensions.
5. A goodness of fit measure (multiple correlation) is computed for each subject with regard to each model and F-ratios are also printed out. These can be used for running statistical significance tests on the contribution of more complex models in accounting for variance in the preference data.

Each of the above four models have a different interpretation of the distances to the ideal points. In each model, the distances are the same—that is, the stimuli points are fixed and the ideal points are the same in terms of Euclidean distance in the r dimensions. What does change in each of the four models is the isopreference surface. As the isopreference surface changes, preferences of the n stimuli change.

In order to illustrate the above description more fully, several of the features of the PREFMAP model are shown in Figures 4–5 and 4–6. Figure 4–5 shows the shapes and orientation of isopreference contours (illustrated for the positive ideal point case) while Figure 4–6 shows various ideal point classes for the phase 3 model.

Let us examine Figure 4–5 first. Phase 4, the simple vector model, merely assumes that preferences are linearly related to the projections of the stimulus points in the similarities space on the subject's compensatory vector, which is assumed to extend to infinity. The isopreference "contours" are the series of parallel lines perpendicular to the subject's preference vector. The direction cosines between the vector and the underlying dimensions indicate the relative weights given to changes in each dimension.

Phase 3 shows the case where the similarities space has first been differentially stretched (after possible rotation) to best include the weights reflected in the preference data of the average subject. Phase 3 then assumes that all subjects share this evaluative space, though individual differences are permitted in ideal point location. In two dimensions the isopreference contours around the ideal points are circles, after the space has been rotated

_____ *Figure 4-5* _____

Types of Possible Representations in the Carroll–Chang Generalization of the Unfolding Model

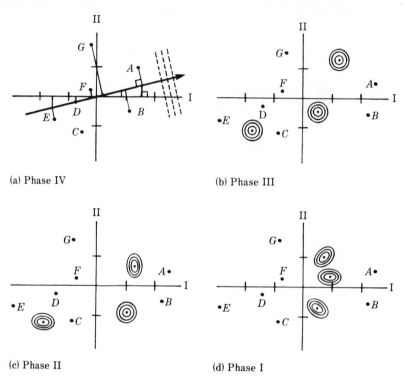

(a) Phase IV

(b) Phase III

(c) Phase II

(d) Phase I

(if necessary) and differentially stretched to reflect the weights of the average subject.

Phase 2 allows individual subject weighting in the space, which is possibly rotated and differentially stretched to reflect the perceptions of average subjects. In this case, the weights are represented (inversely) by the lengths of axes of the isopreference contours (ellipses) that are parallel to the coordinate axes.

Phase 1 shows the completely general case where the individual subjects not only differentially weight the axes of the average subject's configuration (already differentially stretched and rotated), but subjects are allowed their own rotation as well. Thus, the isopreference ellipses need not be parallel to the coordinate axes.

Figure 4–6 shows the variety of ideal points possible with phases 1 through 3, illustrated for the case of two dimensions and phase 3. (The origin has been translated to the ideal point for illustrative purposes.) In the typical

_____ *Figure 4–6* _____

Types of Isopreference Contours, Illustrated in Two Dimensions for Phase III
Model

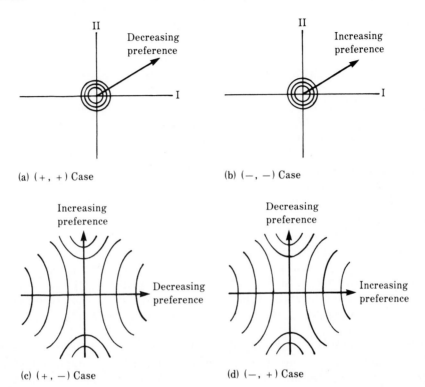

(a) (+, +) Case

(b) (−, −) Case

(c) (+, −) Case

(d) (−, +) Case

Coombsian ideal, or (+, +) case, preference declines with increasing distance
from the ideal along each dimension. In the anti-ideal, or (−, −) case,
preference increases with increasing distance from the anti-ideal. In the
(+, −) or (−, +) cases, the preference function takes the form of a saddle
point with rectangular hyperbolas as isopreference contours.

As can be surmised from the above description, the PREFMAP model is
quite flexible and provides a variety of ways of characterizing preference data
in the (evaluatively transformed) similarities space. In our own research we
have found that the simpler models (phases 3 and 4) are often good
representations of the data. From a psychological standpoint, however, the
possibility of an anti-ideal point is of interest. This formulation allows
respondents to prefer highly dissimilar stimuli, the only constraint being that
dispreferred items must be seen as similar to each other. It is reasonable to
suppose that a number of real world situations could be represented by this
type of model.

The nonmetric option within PREFMAP proceeds along quite similar lines. In this case, however, utility is assumed to be only ordinally related to weighted squared distance from the ideal (in phases 1, 2, and 3). Operationally, the program finds metric solutions for all models and then, by a series of monotone regressions, adjusts the solutions to obey the nonmetric constraints. The model is then parameterized on the basis of the regression weights obtained from the monotone regression.

A Comparison of Models   A number of approaches to the scaling of preferences and/or similarities data have now been presented. As the reader may surmise, the authors display a predilection for the MDPREF and PREFMAP models, both from the standpoint of their ability to avoid problems of local minima and degeneracy (to be discussed in Section 6) and from the viewpoint of their completeness of representation. By completeness we mean, in part, the weights that belong to each of the four PREFMAP models that may be applied to the dimensions of the similarities configuration as one moves from a perceptual (similarity) to an evaluative (preference) frame of reference.

The MDPREF model develops joint-space configurations from preference data alone, making the collecting of similarities judgments unnecessary. The loss of information from not collecting similarity data results in an inability to determine the nature of the transformation associated with moving from a similarities to a preference context, plus the invoking of the strong assumption that all respondents see the stimuli in the same way.

SAMPLE DATA ANALYSES   So the reader can better judge the behavior of various approaches to the analysis of preference data, we again return to an analysis of a sample data set. We employ the Soft Drink data detailed in Appendix B. The first analysis of preference data is conducted using an 8×10 matrix of average preference rankings. The 57 respondents were asked to rank their preference for 10 brands of soft drinks (Coke, Coke Classic, Diet Pepsi, Diet Slice, Diet 7-Up, Dr. Pepper, Pepsi, Slice, Tab, and 7-Up) on each of 8 product attributes (fruitiness, carbonation, calories, sweetness, thirst quenching, popularity with others, aftertaste, and pick-me-up).

This 8×10 matrix of average preference rankings was submitted for MDPREF analysis. Figure 4–7 shows the two-space configuration of stimuli (attributes) and subjects (brands) that explained 90.7 percent of the variance in the preference data. The preference configuration appears to be recovered well.

The attribute vectors have been drawn through the origin and extended through the attribute locations. As has been explained, this is a vector model, where the ideal configuration for this attribute extends infinitely outward to the end of the vector. Each of the brands project onto each attribute vector. In the example, the brands have been projected onto the popularity with others and the calories attribute vectors. The projections are drawn at the 90-degree angle to the vector.

_____ Figure 4–7 _____
MDPREF Analysis of Pop Data

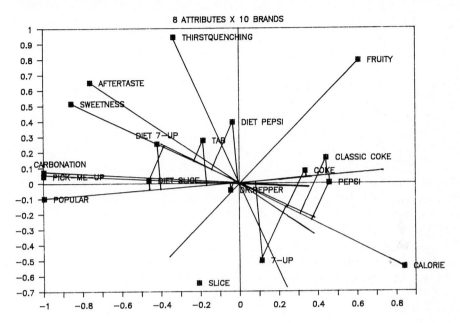

Now, suppose we desire to represent the 10 brands and 8 attributes jointly in a common Euclidean space in such a way that the Euclidean distances between the points reflect the respondent's psychological proximity of the brands to the attributes or their ideals. This type of model is called a point–point model and entails analysis by what is called an unfolding technique. The rectangular matrix described above consisted of 80 data points and is analyzed (Figure 4–8) as a rectangular lower corner matrix by the KYST program. For this specific analysis, a metric algorithm was used, being specified as a second-degree polynomial model.

The joint space analysis with the unfolding model uses only 80 data points and is subject to fewer constraints than would otherwise be employed if the analysis were based on the 153 unique interpoint distances [18(17)/2]. In spite of this reduction in constraints, the brands and attributes are recovered quite well. The underlying assumption of the unfolding model would dictate an accurate recovery of the attributes, but that the 10 brands representing ideal points would be more distorted because they are not as constrained as are the attributes. Inspection of Figure 4–8 somewhat confirms this expectation, showing a minor perturbation of the brand points.

In summary, the MDPREF vector model and the KYST joint-space unfolding models were demonstrated as two approaches to recovery of

_____ Figure 4–8 _____
KYST Unfolding of Pop Preference Data

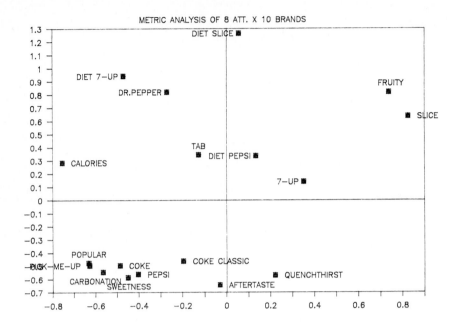

preference evaluations. The differences in the algorithmic approaches (vector versus point–point) was evident in the resulting configurations.

The current example uses metric data (average preference ratings) and produces superior configurations to those for conditional or unconditional rank preference data. While these analysis variations are not shown, test data is easy to construct and results are similar to those observed in Section 3.

DATA COLLECTION METHODS

In Section 3, we discussed at some length the various procedures used in collecting similarities data. In the case of preferences, we are dealing in the Coombsian sense with the problem of creating a rank order of k out of n stimuli. This task may be accomplished using common data collection methods like paired comparisons, triad ordering, and so on, up through a full rank order (where $k = n - 1$).

A second major approach to data collection is to use rating scales in which each stimulus is assigned a numerical value on, say, an 11-point scale. In the nonmetric approaches, we assume that only the ordinal information provided by such data is relevant, whereas in the metric models we assume interval scale properties.

A third principal approach (associated with the notion of an explicit ideal point) involves the rating of both actual stimuli and the subject's explicit ideal on each of a series of attribute scales or constructs prespecified by the researcher. Preferences are then derived by computing some type of distance measure (across attributes) between the explicit ideal and the actual stimuli as positioned in attribute space. We briefly examine, in turn, each of the three approaches.

Ordering Methods   Ordering methods, ranging from paired comparisons to full rank orders are one of the most popular procedures for obtaining preference data. Methods can be distinguished on the basis of the redundancy level the researcher wishes to include in the data collection task (Coombs, 1964). For example, if all $[n(n-1)]/2$ paired comparisons of n stimuli are presented to the subject, checks on the subject's transitivity of preference judgments are provided. In contrast, in the method of simple rank ordering, transitivity must be assumed; the subject is "not allowed" to be intransitive. However, the chances of respondent fatigue and declining motivation are reduced in the case of rank order tasks.

In the past, redundant procedures like paired comparisons or evaluating triplets have been used for data collection. Paired comparison data gives rise to common problems of determining (a) when a subject's responses should be rejected as being "too inconsistent"; and (b) how some "best" complete rank order can be obtained from data that turn out to display some inconsistency. The first problem has been approached by use of Kendall's coefficient of concordance to test the consistency of rank data [Kendall, 1948], while the second problem can be handled in a variety of ways. In our own work, we have favored the use of Slater's i [Slater, 1961] as a procedure for transforming intransitive data into some best complete order.

The problem of respondent fatigue in a highly redundant data collection procedure can be mitigated by the use of various balanced incomplete block designs [Bradley and Terry, 1952]. These designs still permit various consistency checks to be carried out, but reduce considerably the number of independent pairwise comparisons the subject is forced to make.

Rating Methods   Rating procedures of various types permit tied data and interval-scaled information (if the experimenter is willing to assume the latter). A variety of such approaches can be used:

— Two-category assignment; for example, "like" versus "dislike"
— Numerical "thermometer" scales
— Degree of liking (such as Likert, semantic differential, continuous-rating scales) relative to a prespecified standard stimulus
— Hybrid approaches in which, for example, paired comparisons are presented and the subject is asked not only to choose which member of the pair is preferred but also the intensity of preference

Rating scales assume a kind of subjective anchoring on the part of the subject so that the same scale is applied to all stimuli throughout the task. Clearly, it is a prudent procedure to replicate at least a subset of the judgments to provide a check on the stability of the scale. Another problem associated with rating procedures is the tendency for some subjects to use only a small part of the scale. Such response-biasing tendencies may often be handled by standardizing each subject's ratings to, say, zero mean and unit standard deviation.

Rating scales are most appropriately used when a large number of stimuli are involved and ordering methods, including ranking procedures, would place heavy judgmental demands on the subject. Here again, however, a hybrid approach could be used, where stimuli are first assigned to a small set of ordered categories, and then a ranking of stimuli is made within each ordered category.

Rating scales also can be useful in establishing a respondent's neutral or indifference point by the inclusion of such categories as "neither like nor dislike." Here again, this approach can be used in combination with ordering procedures.

Explicit Ideal Ratings   Under this method the actual stimuli and a hypothetical ideal are rated individually on a series of attribute scales; for example, "carbonation," "thirst quenching," and so on. Preferences (or their obverse) are derived by the computation of distance from each real stimulus to the ideal. If the dimensions are all evaluative in the sense of "the more of each attribute, the better," then the method is not particularly revealing since the explicit ideal would always be presumed to score at the top of each attribute scale. In this case, a vector model appears most appropriate.

We have already discussed some of the general limitations of explicit ideal point rating procedures and there is no need to repeat them here. These procedures represent popular data collection techniques in marketing research and, in parallel with some of the procedures already described in this section and in Section 3, may be useful in the interpretation of joint space configurations.

Thurstone's Case V Scaling   A number of other procedures have been used for obtaining value data, including Thurstone case V scaling [Thurstone, 1959], standard gamble methods [Tversky, 1965], indifference mapping, the Churchman–Ackoff value measure [Ackoff, 1962], and the like. Usually these approaches attempt to develop interval or ratio scaled metric data from other data types, such as paired comparisons. The Thurstone case V scaling method is included as part of the PC–MDS computer program.

Thurstone case V scaling provides an algorithm for constructing a unidimensional interval scale using responses from a variety of data types, such as paired comparisons. Thurstone's procedure derives an interval scale from comparative judgment measurement scales, such as "Stimulus 1 is preferable to stimulus 2," or "I am more satisfied with product 1 than product

2." The interval scale values are generated by one individual, whose data represents many repeated judgments on each pair of stimuli. Alternatively, a group of individuals may be used when there are no measurement replications for each subject.

To illustrate the concept, consider a group of subjects who prefer brand 1 to brand 2. In this case, because brand 1 is preferred, the proportion of total comparisons in which brand 1 is preferred is 100 percent. This situation is complicated, however, when brand 2 is compared to brand 3. Suppose a smaller percentage, say 40 percent, prefer brand 2 to brand 3. The differences between preference of brand 1 to 2, and 2 to 3, would lead to the expectation that the differences between scale values for brands 1 and 2 would be greater than for brands 2 and 3. This process might continue for brands 1 through 5. Thurstone's case V scaling provides a means for developing an interval scale from these proportions associated with comparative judgments.

SOLUTION INTERPRETATION IN JOINT
SPACE CONFIGURATIONS
Much of what we have to say on the problem of configuration interpretation has already been said in Section 3 in the context of similarities data. Since the interpretation of joint space configurations of stimuli and ideal points (or vectors) assumes that the perceptual dimensions—possibly transformed in an evaluative context—also underlie the preference judgments, our previous discussion is relevant here as well.

Two problems, however, are relevant to a discussion of the interpretability of joint space configurations. The first problem concerns the interpretation of configurations obtained from preference data alone and, specifically, their correspondence to interstimulus distances obtained from similarities data. The second problem relates to variability of preference across use situations, a topic already discussed in Section 3 in the context of similarities data. Both problems are described from an empirical standpoint and are illustrated with data obtained from past pilot applications of multidimensional scaling.

The Unfolding Problems
As noted in previous sections, unfolding is originally attributed to Coombs (1964). Unfolding applies to procedures used to develop configurations from off-diagonal proximity matrices. In its original formulation, the matrix was of the off-diagonal, conditional variety, the type of data usually obtained when N subjects each rank n stimuli in terms of preference. In the unidimensional case, the subjects and stimuli were assumed to be positioned along a common attribute continuum. Each subject's rank order was assumed to reflect the common scale "folded" at the subject's ideal; the objective of the method was to unfold such data so as to reveal the joint scale of stimuli and subjects. As was noted earlier, the concept was generalized to the multidimensional case by Bennett and Hays (1960). Unfolding is a term that has received dual interpretations as applicable to both intact proximities and off-diagonal proximities matrices.

Nonmetric programs like KYST and ALSCAL represent nonmetric analogues of fully nonmetric methods. As discussed previously, their use in joint space scaling of off-diagonal proximity matrices assumes that all respondents share a common perceptual space, but are allowed idiosyncratic ideal point positions. The empirical question explored here is How does one obtain a derived stimulus configuration from the analysis of preference data alone that agrees with that obtained by the independent scaling of similarities data collected from the same group of respondents?

This question was examined empirically by obtaining both similarities and preference data from each of four respondent groups with regard to seven graduate schools of business [Green and Carmone, 1969]. The stimuli were the graduate business schools of Carnegie-Mellon, Chicago, Columbia, Harvard, MIT, Stanford, and Wharton. The four respondent groups consisted of MIT students, Stanford students, Wharton students, and corporate recruiters.

Figure 4–9 shows, for comparison purposes, each respondent group's

_____ Figure 4–9 _____

Stimulus Configurations from Analysis of Direct Similarities Data by Response Group

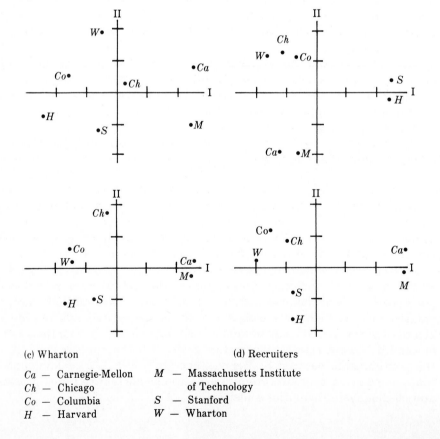

(c) Wharton   (d) Recruiters

Ca — Carnegie-Mellon   M   —   Massachusetts Institute
Ch — Chicago   of Technology
Co — Columbia   S   —   Stanford
H   — Harvard   W   —   Wharton

two-space map as obtained independently from scaling its similarities data. The data in each of the four respondent groups consisted of responses pooled over 15 respondents. Preference data were obtained from each of the four respondent groups and were submitted to the MDSCAL program for the purpose of unfolding the off-diagonal, conditional proximities matrices.

The stimulus interpoint distances derived from the unfolding procedures were then correlated with their counterparts obtained through standard distance calculations, based on direct similarities judgments (Figure 4–9). An almost universally poor recovery of the standard configurations (based on direct similarities data) was observed.

When the same unfolding solutions were canonically correlated (permitting rotation and differential stretching of the perceptual dimensions) with their counterpart coordinate values of Figure 4–9, the results were, with virtually no exceptions, uniformly excellent from a descriptive standpoint—that is, canonical correlations of 0.9 or higher for the first linear compound.

In effect, then, the unfolding solutions were not providing the perceptual configurations (obtained from the similarities data) but rather a configuration that was rotated and differentially stretched so as to reflect the saliences of the perceptual dimensions in the context of preference. This type of transformation is seen graphically in Figure 4–10, which shows an application of the PREFMAP phases III and IV to the combined similarities and preference data.

As will be recalled, PREFMAP permits vectors or ideal point to be positioned in the similarities space by differentially weighting the dimensions so as to best accommodate the preference data. Figure 4–10 shows that the dimensions did indeed receive different saliences as subjects moved from perceived to evaluative spaces.

The above example shows rather forcefully the distinction that can exist between "perceived" and "evaluative" stimulus spaces. This distinction is one of the reasons why we believe the PREFMAP approach provides a more complete and flexible procedure for dealing with preferences, albeit at the expense of requiring the collection of similarities as well as preference data.

Scenario Influence on Preference Judgments

In Section 3, we pointed out a general belief that both similarities and preferences are context bound. In the case of preferences it seems reasonable to suppose that a variety of ideal points could exist, conditional on the use situation or, perhaps, the general problem-solving context confronting the respondent. For example, soft drink preferences could easily be conditional on such scenarios as (a) "when at home watching TV by yourself"; (b) "after exercising"; (c) "appropriateness for entertaining at home," and so on.

If the specific scenario can be described rather precisely, the notion of a single ideal point or vector is more appropriate. However, the experimenter may be interested in the movement of either ideal point or vector in the

_____ Figure 4–10 _____

Joint Space Configurations Obtained from a Combined Analysis of Similarity and
Preference Data (Carroll–Chang Metric Model)

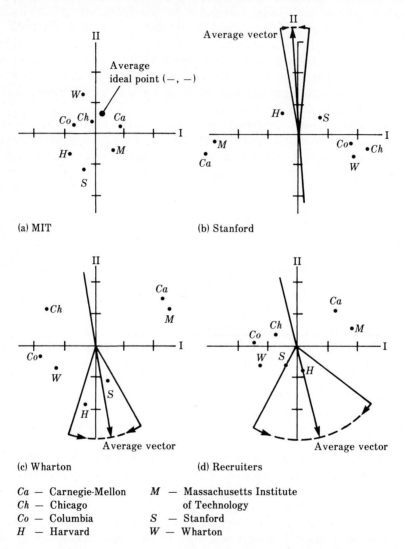

(a) MIT   (b) Stanford

(c) Wharton   (d) Recruiters

Ca	—	Carnegie-Mellon	M	—	Massachusetts Institute
Ch	—	Chicago			of Technology
Co	—	Columbia	S	—	Stanford
H	—	Harvard	W	—	Wharton

evaluative space (or spaces) as the scenario changes. To illustrate this
phenomenon, consider the following hypothetical case study.

The stimuli consist of 10 print advertisements and the respondents are
either professional advertising people (expert group) or graduate students
(control group). Similarities data were collected by asking each respondent to
rank the 10 advertisements according to the relative ability of the ad to draw
coupon responses, given that the magazine is unspecified. Next, the respon-

dent is shown copies of 6 magazines as candidate vehicles for the advertisements: *True, Sports Illustrated, Popular Mechanics, Guy, Women's World,* and *Men Today*. After getting some idea of the general appearance and editorial format of the magazines, the respondent is again asked to rank the same 10 ads with regard to their relative ability to draw coupon responses for each magazine.

The PREFMAP generalization of the unfolding model is to be used for analysis, since similarities data are available for the same subjects. Figure 4–11 shows the effect of vehicle on the joint space configurations of the average subject in each of four subgroups (two clusters of experts and two

_____ *Figure 4–11* _____

Joint Space Configurations of Stimuli and Evaluations—Control Versus Expert Group

C_1, C_2 — Control Group Clusters
E_1, E_2 — Expert Group Clusters

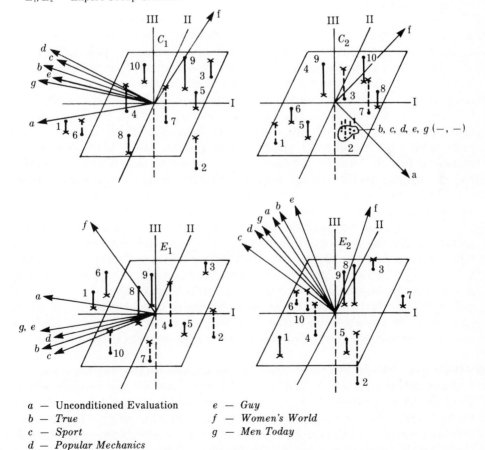

a — Unconditioned Evaluation
b — *True*
c — *Sport*
d — *Popular Mechanics*
e — *Guy*
f — *Women's World*
g — *Men Today*

clusters of students), first partitioned into clusters on the basis of homogeneity of similarities data. We note from the chart that in most cases a vector model is adequate for representing the preference data.

In this example, with the exception of *Women's World,* the preference judgments do not appear to be highly sensitive to vehicle. To these subjects, a "good ad" appears to be a "good ad" independent of vehicle insofar as the five male-audience magazines are concerned. In other stimulus classes, however, it is quite possible that preferences might be highly conditioned on scenario. If so, the PREFMAP approach appears to provide a useful way to portray such ideal point, or vector, "movements" as scenarios are altered.

SPECIAL ISSUES IN PREFERENCE ANALYSIS A number of special topics arise in the analysis of preferences that have involved little substantive research to date. We comment on some of them briefly, more from the standpoint of posing them as areas for future investigation rather than reporting past research results.

Segmentation Based on Joint Space Configurations In Section 3, we discussed the possibility of relating individual differences in perceptual point of view to other respondent characteristics (socioeconomic, demographic, and so forth). The same approach could be used in the case of joint space configurations of subjects' ideal point locations in evaluative space. Thus, in line with our discussion in the Introduction and Problem Setting, subjects could first be partitioned into reasonably homogeneous groups based on commonality of similarities data. These groups could then be further partitioned on the basis of commonality of transforms that lead to evaluative spaces (using the PREFMAP models). Finally, subjects could be further partitioned on the basis of commonality of ideal point position or vector direction, as the case may be.

Various clustering methods (Section 5) could be used to assist in the partitioning task. One might then attempt to describe clusters in terms of other subject characteristics. Since the clusters would be formed on the basis of independent criteria (perceptions and preferences), multiple discriminant analysis might be employed in order to see which components of a vector of external characteristics contribute most highly to cluster discrimination. If such predictor variables are found, knowledge of them, in principle, could be useful in the formation of policy based on market segmentation objectives.

Probability of Choice Models As also discussed in the Introduction and Problem Setting, research needs to be carried out on the relationship of purchase choice probability to distance from ideal point (or in the case of a vector model, relative magnitude of projections on the vector). It is reasonable to assume, in the typical positive ideal point case, that probability of choice would decrease as the distance increased from the ideal point.

One way to estimate the parameter values of the probability function would be to obtain brand switching data from members of a consumer panel, in addition to their similarities and preference data. Empirical fitting procedures could be used to estimate the probability choice function if stability can be assumed over the data collection period.

Another type of modeling approach would be to assume that the stimulus closest to the ideal is always chosen and that observed differences in choice are dependent on the frequency with which various product use scenarios appear. This approach would require a rather extensive collection of preference data that is conditional on various use situations and, of course, that would assume a stable use-generating "mechanism."

Stimulus Bundles   Another topic of substantive interest concerns the prediction of preference for stimulus "bundles"—season tickets, investment portfolios, cereal combination packs, fringe benefit packages, and so forth—from the values of their components. Related to this question is the utility for "variety" and the question of "second choice" preferences, given that the respondent can obtain the first choice [Coombs, 1964].

Again it seems reasonable to suppose that preferences for items are conditional on the assortment already owned by the potential buyer. Little is known, however, concerning the decision procedures used in evaluating bundles as some function of the value of their components. The problem is quite a difficult one, and one that has been examined in part in the current conjoint analysis research literature [Green and Srinivasan, 1978].

Evaluation Functions   Closely allied to the bundles problem are ones concerning the procedures that people use to evaluate multiattribute items such as vendors, houses, schools, and automobiles. As already discussed in this chapter, most stimuli are perceived as multiattribute items where one brand can be better than another on one attribute characteristic and worse on some other attribute characteristic.

The study of people's evaluation functions as processes used to collapse partially ordered alternatives into a complete order is fascinating in its own right. The breadth of application is considerable, ranging all the way from governmental and corporate decision making to decisions made at the household level.

Aside from a few pilot level studies, research in this area is just beginning. We expect, however, that it will assume increasing importance in future research activity, not only by marketing researchers but by operations research analysts, political scientists, and economists as well.

CORRESPONDENCE ANALYSIS   Another relatively new metric technique for exploratory data analysis is correspondence analysis [Carroll, Green, and Schaffer, 1986; Hoffman and Franke, 1986; Lebart, Morineau, and Warwick, 1984; Benzecri, 1969; de Leeuw, 1973].

In correspondence analysis, special representations of the data are formed from the analysis of frequency data that is often in the form of two-way (or higher-way) contingency tables. While the application of correspondence analysis is not limited to preference measures, it is discussed in this chapter as a means of analyzing preference data and for completeness sake. Correspondence analysis is designed for use in developing spatial representations of frequency data, whether preference or nonpreference in application.

The objective of (two-way) correspondence analysis is to show how variables are related and not just that they are not independent in a contingency table analysis sense. Specifically,

— What are the similarities and differences within the rows with respect to a given column category?
— What are the similarities and differences within the column categories with respect to a given row category?
— What is the relationship among the rows and columns?
— Can these relationships be represented graphically in a joint space of low dimensionality?

Correspondence analysis appears, and is interpreted in similar fashion to, principal components analysis, and rightly so, due to the similarity of the algorithms. Output and interpretation of results involves the examination of the eigenvalues associated with each of the principal axes. Coordinates and contributions of the principal axes for the row and column points are produced, as are the relative frequencies and distances (chi-square distances) between the points and the origin of the axes shown.

Just as principal components analysis results in the grouping of independent variables, correspondence analysis involves the grouping of the categories found within the contingency table. The interpretation of the results focuses on proximities among the rows and columns of the contingency table. Correspondence analysis generates the proximities among categories (such as activities, objects, brands, or other stimuli). Those categories having the greatest proximity are those most similar in terms of the underlying structure.

Thus, the row and column variables are portrayed in geometric space as a set of row and column points. These points in derived geometric space are positioned so that the squared chi-square distances between points are transforms of the original tabular entries.

Although correspondence analysis is applicable to most categorical data problems, several common-sense caveats assure the applicability [Lebart, Morineau, and Warwick, 1984].

1. Is the data matrix large enough that visual inspection or simple statistical analysis cannot reveal the underlying structure?

2. Are the variables homogeneous, so that it makes sense to calculate a statistical distance between rows and columns, and so that distances can be interpreted meaningfully?
3. Is the data matrix of unknown structure or poorly understood?

The primary benefit of correspondence analysis not provided by most other multidimensional scaling techniques is the relaxed assumption that allows for binary or categorical input data. Correspondence analysis opens multidimensional scaling methodology to a variety of survey research and data collection techniques that have not previously been subject to advanced levels of analysis. Nominal and ordinal measures that might be used in correspondence analysis include binary (attribute present or absent), pick any that apply, pick k out of n, frequency of rank order, and paired comparisons data.

As examples of correspondence analysis, we refer to two sample problems.

Problem 1:
Preference Groups and
Attribute Matching

Carroll, Green, and Schaffer (1986) report the results of a study of 252 customers of overnight delivery services. Customers were classified into one of ten categories according to their favorite shipper (Alpha, Beta, Gamma, and Delta) and according to the size of their business:

— Alpha, very small (SSA)
— Alpha, small (SA)
— Alpha, large (LA)
— Alpha, very large (LLA)
— Gamma, very small (SSG)
— Gamma, small (SG)
— Gamma, large (LG)
— Gamma, very large (LLG)
— Beta (BTA)
— Delta (DLT)

Respondents were asked to pick any of 15 service attributes describing their favorite shipper:

1. Almost always delivers the package by the promised time
2. Packages almost always delivered in good condition
3. Almost never late in pickup of packages to be shipped
4. Little paperwork required in preparing packages for shipment
5. Will make special trips to pick up packages if needed
6. Easy to calculate the shipping costs
7. Easy to trace a package that has gone astray

8. Sensitive to customer needs in settling claims
9. Capable of shipping packages almost everywhere I want
10. Friendly and congenial employees
11. Extremely efficient in all their business dealings
12. Less expensive than most
13. Responsible and dependable in customer relations
14. Uses the most advanced technology
15. Really interested in the smaller customer

The data input matrix, shown in Table 4–1, identifies the number of times each attribute was associated with each shipper/buyer size category.

The resulting two-dimensional correspondence analysis plot appears in Figure 4–12. Because all interpoint distances are comparable, we observe that Gamma and Delta are most closely associated with (1) Easy to trace a package that has gone astray, (2) Almost always delivers the package by the promised time, (3) Sensitive to customer needs in settling claims, and (4) Friendly and congenial employees. Beta is perceived as inexpensive. Very small customers of Alpha perceive its attributes to be (1) Capable of shipping packages almost everywhere I want, (2) Easy to calculate the shipping costs, and (3) Little paperwork required in preparing packages for shipment.

It is further apparent that four groups of suppliers are present. Delta and Gamma are relatively similar. Somewhat less similar are small, large, and very large users of Alpha. Very small users of Alpha and Beta users appear to be distinct from all other groups.

_____ Table 4–1 _____

Cross Tabulation of Favorite Supplier/Size Category, by Service Attribute

Respondent Category	Service Attribute														
	1	2	3	4	5	6	7	8	9	10	11	12	13	14	15
SSA	4	5	5	20	1	21	2	1	22	8	3	13	1	4	9
SA	2	5	7	13	1	16	4	2	16	10	6	10	7	6	5
LA	9	9	8	12	2	17	5	3	16	11	6	13	10	7	11
LLA	5	11	10	20	1	15	3	2	25	10	6	14	10	6	8
SSG	25	25	19	19	20	11	11	8	19	19	13	2	15	15	10
SG	25	25	21	20	19	14	12	10	18	20	15	3	15	18	14
LG	22	23	18	15	20	12	14	8	15	22	19	2	14	16	11
LLG	17	17	18	11	11	10	11	3	10	14	12	1	13	11	12
BTA	7	11	8	4	3	7	3	2	10	7	8	13	6	3	5
DLT	12	13	13	9	11	8	12	9	9	14	10	1	10	11	7

Source: Data from J. D. Carroll, P. E. Green, and C. M. Schaffer, "Interpoint Distance Comparisons in Correspondence Analysis," *Journal of Marketing Research* **23** (August, 1986), 271–280.

_____ *Figure 4–12* _____
Correspondence Analysis

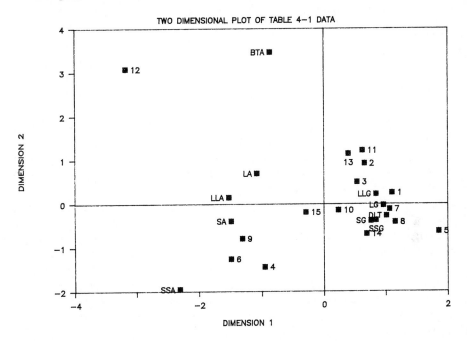

Problem 2:
Purchase Groups and Binary
Purchase Data   Problem 2 employs a different type of measure, but one that is also applicable in preference analysis. Past purchase and consumption of soft drinks were recorded (Table 4–2) as binary variables (purchase = 1 and nonpurchase = 0) for 34 individuals (Hoffman and Frank, 1986). This analysis results in a mapping of respondents and brands rather than brands and attributes (as in the first example).

The resulting two-dimensional (Figure 4–13) plot shows that the axes represent cola–noncola and diet–nondiet selections. In this situation, individual consumers can be identified as purchasers of cola, noncola, diet, nondiet, or other combinations of the categories.

In summary, correspondence analysis does provide perceptual maps of frequency or binary preference measures. It has also been made clear that correspondence analysis is discussed in this section because of the ability to analyze preference data. It is, however, more closely allied with multi-dimensional scaling techniques when evaluated in terms of the research objectives of exploratory data analysis, input data, output configurations, and managerial implications that may be drawn.

_____ Table 4–2 _____

Cross Tabulation of Soft Drink Beverage Purchase and Consumption

Person	Soft Drink*								Person	Soft Drink*							
	1	2	3	4	5	6	7	8		1	2	3	4	5	6	7	8
1	1	0	0	0	1	1	0	1	18	1	1	0	0	1	0	0	0
2	1	0	0	0	1	0	0	0	19	1	0	0	0	0	0	0	1
3	1	0	0	0	1	0	0	0	20	1	1	1	0	1	0	0	0
4	0	1	0	1	0	0	1	0	21	1	0	0	0	1	0	0	0
5	1	0	0	0	1	0	0	0	22	1	0	0	0	1	0	0	0
6	1	0	0	0	1	1	0	0	23	0	1	0	1	0	0	1	0
7	0	1	1	1	0	0	1	0	24	1	1	0	0	1	0	0	0
8	1	1	0	0	1	1	0	1	25	0	1	1	1	0	0	0	0
9	1	1	0	0	0	1	1	1	26	0	1	0	1	0	0	1	0
10	1	0	0	0	1	0	0	1	27	0	1	0	0	0	0	1	0
11	1	0	0	0	1	1	0	0	28	1	0	0	0	0	1	0	1
12	0	1	0	0	0	0	1	0	29	1	0	0	0	0	1	0	0
13	0	0	1	1	0	1	0	1	30	0	1	1	0	0	0	1	0
14	1	0	0	0	0	1	0	0	31	1	0	0	0	1	0	0	1
15	0	1	1	0	0	0	1	0	32	0	1	1	0	0	0	1	0
16	0	0	0	0	1	1	0	0	33	1	0	0	0	1	0	0	1
17	0	1	0	0	0	1	0	0	34	0	1	1	1	0	0	1	0

* 1 = Coke; 2 = Diet Coke; 3 = Diet Pepsi; 4 = Diet 7-Up; 5 = Pepsi; 6 = Sprite; 7 = Tab; 8 = 7-Up.
Source: Data from D. L. Hoffman and G. R. Franke. "Correspondence Analysis: Graphical Representation of Data in Marketing Research," *Journal of Marketing Research* **23** (August, 1986), 23–227.

_____ Figure 4–13 _____

Correspondence Analysis

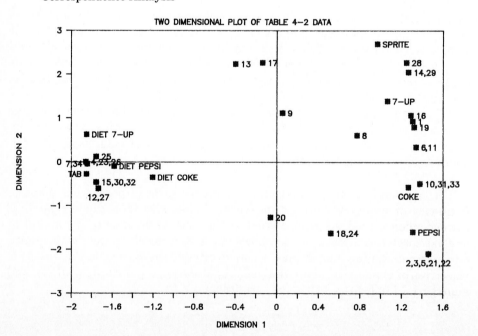

SUMMARY   This section has covered a broad range of topics related to the joint space representation of preference or similarities preference data. We started with a discussion of the conceptual basis and assumption structure underlying the major scaling models—the distance model, the vector model, and the compensatory distance model. This led to a demonstration of the unfolding features of KYST and MDSCAL to generate a joint space in the context of recovering known synthetic data configurations. We then discussed a variety of empirical problems, including various data collection procedures for gathering preference data and some of the limitations associated with attempting to develop joint space representations from preferences alone. The influence of scenario was also described and illustrated by some pilot study results.

Correspondence analysis was discussed as a means of conducting preference analysis where data collection is difficult, resulting in binary or frequency data.

We concluded with brief discussions of special topics and areas for future research. These topics include issues arising in market segmentation, probability of choice models, and decision procedures used in choosing among multiattribute alternatives.

Dimension-Reducing Methods and Cluster Analysis

In preceding sections we have frequently mentioned the phrases objective space and cluster analysis. While our discussion emphasized the use of multidimensional scaling methods in the representation of psychological responses—namely, similarities and preferences—we also indicated from time to time that the methodology can be viewed as a means of data reduction and summarization. In this latter role, our interest is on reducing the subject's evaluation data (evaluations resulting in an attributes × stimuli matrix) into a space of fewer dimensions, with little loss in information.

We can, of course, turn the problem around and consider the dual question of reducing the number of subjects by partitioning them into homogeneous groups, based on their "closeness" to one another in variable space. The first approach may be called reduced space analysis (factor analysis) and the second, cluster analysis.[1] We shall often consider the use of both approaches.

In this section, we first discuss these dual problems of data reduction and clustering in the context of nonpsychological data. After describing some of the basic characteristics of the data matrix, we discuss both metric and nonmetric approaches to reduced space representation. We then turn to the topic of cluster analysis and describe the major characteristics of clustering procedures, including the choice of association coefficient, types of grouping algorithms, cluster description, and problems of statistical inference.

The concluding portion of this section discusses some recent developments in reduced space and cluster analysis, particularly an overlapping clustering technique that appears especially useful in product positioning where products/subjects may belong to several clusters simultaneously.

THE DATA MATRIX   The key concept underlying the use of reduced space and cluster analysis is that in most real-world situations the multiple measure-

---

[1] We note that factor analysis can be used to cluster respondents and cluster analysis can be used to group variables. This is done by transposing the data matrix (i.e., using a variables by subjects data matrix rather than the more common subjects by variables data matrix).

ments collected on a set of subjects are partly redundant—that is, correlated in some way. The dual of this assertion is that some sets of pairs of subjects, when considered across variables, are similar to each other. Geometrically, this could be observed by putting N subjects in $N-1$ dimensional space. We would generally not find all points equidistant from each other, thus indicating that certain sets of points are correlated.

While one can often take advantage of natural association to make predictions—for example, as in regression analysis or discriminant analysis—situations occur in which no variable can be singled out as a dependent or criterion variable. In these situations, we may still wish to summarize the information provided by a whole set of subjects-by-stimuli "scores." We would search for a more parsimonious structure that removes redundancy in the original set of data while preserving most of the information contained in the original data matrix.

In either case, the "raw input" to any such analysis consists of the data matrix. The data matrix is here assumed to be a rectangular matrix of numerical entries whose informational content is to be summarized and portrayed in some way. For example, the computation of the mean and standard deviation of a unidimensional array is often done simply because we are unable to comprehend the meaning of the entire column of values. In so doing, we often (willingly) forego the full information provided by the data in order to understand some of its basic characteristics; for example, central tendency and dispersion. The problem becomes even more complex when we have multiple measurements on a set of objects.

Table 5–1 illustrates a sample data matrix. We note that the array consists of a set of subjects (the N rows) and a set of variables (the n columns). The (i,j) cell entry represents the value of subject i on variable j. The subjects may be people, objects, concepts, or events. The variables are characteristics, properties, attributes, or some other stimuli descriptive or related to the subjects.

Cell values may consist of nominal, ordinal, interval, or ratio-scaled measurements or various combinations of these as we go across columns. The complete (row) vector of values is often called a subject's profile.

In many cases, the investigator is able to partition the data matrix into subsets of columns (or rows) on the basis of prior information. For example, suppose the first column of Table 5–1 is the elapsed time for an automobile to travel from 0 to 100 KPH, and the other columns consist of various automobile performance and physical dimensions for the N automobiles. The researcher may wish to predict quickness or elapsed time from some linear combination of the $n-1$ remaining variables. If so, prior judgment is used to describe how the dependency is to be explained. In this instance, we would probably use a multiple regression of horsepower, torque, weight, and tire size to establish the hypothesized functional relationships.

Quite frequently, however, we may have no reasonable basis for prior partitioning of the data matrix into criterion (dependent) or predictor

_____ *Table 5-1* _____

Illustrative Data and Derived Association Matrices

Observation	X_1	X_{d1}	X_{s1}	X_2	X_{d2}	X_{s2}	X_3	X_{d3}	X_{s3}
1	2	−5.25	−1.92	1	−6.67	−1.85	2	−4.92	−1.29
2	4	−3.25	−1.18	3	−4.67	−1.30	1	−5.92	−1.55
3	6	−1.25	−0.46	7	−0.67	−0.19	5	−1.92	−0.50
4	7	−0.25	−0.09	6	−1.67	−0.46	3	−3.92	−1.02
5	5	−2.25	−0.82	4	−3.67	−1.02	7	0.08	0.02
6	8	0.75	0.27	9	1.33	0.37	6	−0.92	−0.24
7	9	1.75	0.64	8	0.33	0.09	7	0.08	0.02
8	7	−0.25	−0.09	10	2.33	0.65	9	2.08	0.55
9	10	2.75	1.01	11	3.33	0.93	11	4.08	1.07
10	8	0.75	0.27	9	1.33	0.37	8	1.08	0.28
11	12	4.75	1.74	11	3.33	0.93	10	3.08	0.81
12	9	1.75	0.64	13	5.33	1.48	14	7.08	1.85
$\bar{X}_j$	7.25	0	0	7.67	0	0	6.92	0	0
s_j	2.73	2.73	1	3.60	3.60	1	3.83	3.83	1

B: Raw Sums of Squares and Cross Products

	X_1	X_2	X_3
X_1	713	763	688
X_2	763	848	771
X_3	688	771	735

S: Mean-Corrected Sums of Squares and Cross Products

	X_1	X_2	X_3
X_1	82.25	96.00	86.25
X_2	96.00	142.67	134.67
X_3	86.25	134.67	160.92

C: Covariance Matrix

	X_1	X_2	X_3
X_1	7.477	8.727	7.841
X_2	8.727	12.970	12.242
X_3	7.841	12.242	14.629

R: Correlation Matrix

	X_1	X_2	X_3
X_1	1.000	0.886	0.750
X_2	0.886	1.000	0.889
X_3	0.750	0.889	1.000

(independent) variables. The purpose may merely be to group subjects into "similar" subsets (based on their similarity over the whole profile of variables) or to portray the columns of the data matrix in terms of a smaller number of new variables (for example, linear combinations of the original set) that retain most of the information in the original data matrix. These are the cases of concern in this chapter. Both classes of procedures start with the data matrix or some set of measures derived from it.

REDUCED SPACE ANALYSIS   In earlier chapters, we saw how a set of association measures (similarities data, for example) could be "dimensionalized" by multidimensional scaling techniques. We also saw how a set of stimuli in variable space could be converted into a set of "association" measures (e.g., distances) between each stimulus pair. In general, we can go from an association matrix to a dimensional representation and vice versa.

In reduced space analysis we usually, though not necessarily, start off with a data matrix like that conceptualized in Table 5–1. The objective here is to transform this matrix into one having the same number of rows but fewer columns, without serious loss of information.

In finding this reduced space representation, however, we may go through the seemingly roundabout process [Green, 1978]:

— Finding correlation measures
— Rotating the initial configuration of points (objects) to a new orientation of the same dimensionality (this rotated configuration exhibits the characteristic of mutually orthogonal dimensions with sequentially maximal variance—that is, the second dimension displays the next largest variance, subject to being orthogonal to the first, and so on)
— Reducing the dimensionality of this transformed space, usually by discarding those higher dimensions that exhibit the smallest variance of point projections
— Finding still a new orientation of the reduced space that makes the retained dimensions more interpretable from a content point of view
— Interpreting the reoriented dimensions in terms of the variables that show high association with each dimension.

Historically, the methods of factor analysis have been used for a variety of purposes (Rummel, 1970):

— Reducing the dimensionality of a variable space
— Scaling and the spatial representation of perception and preference data
— Untangling complex patterns of intervariable association in multivariate data
— Exploratory research in the identification of latent characteristics for future experimentation
— Developing empirical topologies of variables
— Developing a data-based unidimensional index that maximally separates individuals
— Testing hypothesized relationships between certain variables in specific content areas
— Transforming the matrix of predictor variables prior to applying some other technique like multiple regression or canonical correlation

We shall briefly discuss one type of factoring—principal components analysis—as the major metric technique for reducing the dimensionality of space.

Metric Reduction: *Principal Components Analysis* Factor analysis reduces the dimensionality of a data set to produce a set of underlying dimensions, which are often referred to as components, or factors. Factor analysis then seeks a linear combination of the original variable scores—assumed here to be at least interval scaled—that displays maximum variance if the subject points are projected onto it.

Once this is done, we seek a second linear combination, axis, or underlying dimension that is orthogonal to the first and maximizes residual variance explained. This process continues until all of the variance in the original data is explained. Having done this, we disregard those higher dimensioned linear combinations that account for small amounts of variance.

As we construct the linear combinations, any set of weights, in the linear combination, same or different over each column, plus or minus, might suffice. As a matter of fact, the various types of factoring methods are differentiated in terms of the bases on which the weights defining the factor are selected. Factor scores are obtained by merely finding for each subject the numerical value of the linear combination obtained by substituting original data values in the linear equation of, say, factor one:

$$F_1 = a_1 X_1 + a_2 X_2 + \ldots + a_n X_n$$

where the a_n are the factor weights.

If we then correlate each of these new columns of the (subject × factor) factor score matrix with the original variables, we obtain a set of factor loadings. A factor loading is defined simply as the correlation (across subjects) of an original variable with a factor.

Again, if the method of principal components is used, the weights are chosen in such a way that the successive principal components will account for a maximal portion of total variability in the data, subject to being mutually orthogonal to all previously obtained linear combinations. That is, the first set of weights will lead to a set of component scores that account for maximum variance. Each successive component will account for a decreasing portion of total variance in the original set of data and be orthogonal to all previously existing components.

Some of the geometric aspects of principal components analysis are shown in Figures 5–1 and 5–2. We assume that the original data matrix consists of the measurements of N subjects on three variables. We note from Figure 5–1 that the positions of the actual subject data (from Table 5-1) are portrayed as a somewhat elliptical scatter plot of points. Because variables X_{s1} and X_{s2} are not perfectly correlated, the plot of points forms an ellipse, rather than a straight line. Figure 5-2(a) depicts this more clearly with the principal components being represented by the new set of axes (Z_i) drawn through the major and minor axes of the ellipse.

Z_1, the first principal axis, is the major axis of the ellipse. However, it does not exhaust all of the information in the data, necessitating a second

_____ Figure 5–1 _____

Scatter Plots of Standardized Data of Table 5–1 and the First Principal Component z_1

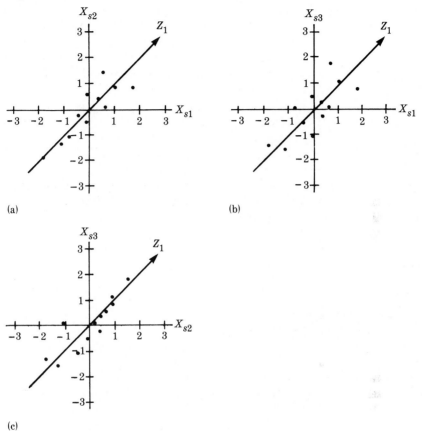

(a)

(b)

(c)

axis, Z_2. Z_2 is the minor axis of the ellipse. We note that most of the information would be preserved if only Z_1 were retained.

Figure 5–2(b) shows the analogous case for three dimensions in which an ellipsoid describes the point scatter. Figure 5-2(b) would appear as a flattened balloon because length (Z_1), width (Z_2), and height (Z_3) have less and less variance (dispersion) to account for.

Figure 5–2(c) reflects the situation where the variables are uncorrelated in three dimensions. The scatterplot appears as a sphere, where each of the dimensions is orthogonal to each other.

Factoring the Association Matrix   In practice, the factors are obtained not by factoring the data matrix itself, but by factoring a set of association measures—cross products, covariances, correlations—that are derived from the data matrix (see Table 5–1).

Figure 5–2
Geometric Aspects of Principal Components Analysis

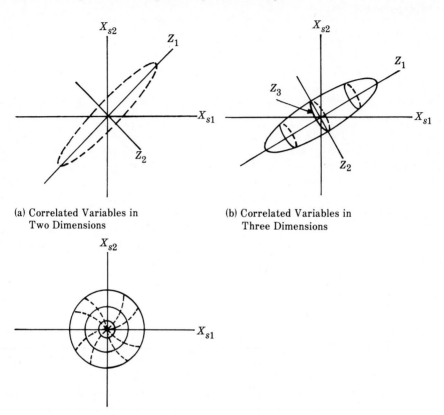

(a) Correlated Variables in
    Two Dimensions

(b) Correlated Variables in
    Three Dimensions

(c) Uncorrelated Variables in
    Three Dimensions

    If as many components are extracted as there are variables, the original association matrix (for example, matrix of correlation coefficients) can be perfectly reproduced by a matrix product of the factor loadings. Of course, in this case no parsimony would be obtained, since one would have as many linear combinations (components) of the variables as there were variables initially.

Metric Approach to Reduced Space Analysis   In terms of our emphasis on reduced space techniques, principal components analysis represents the major metric procedure for reducing the original variable space. In the usual case where a (variable by variable) correlation matrix serves as the starting point for the component analysis (R-type factor analysis), one can compute unit–variance (factor) scores for each object on each component. If weighted squared distances in component space are computed between object pairs, using component eigenvalues as weights, such measures will be proportional to squared interpoint distance in the original variables space if all components are extracted.

Nonmetric Reduced Space Analysis

In general, if the function relating interpoint distance between pairs of points to input data is nonlinear but monotonic, a metric procedure like principal components analysis will lead to a larger number of dimensions in which to portray the point locations in terms of orthogonal axes than would be the case with linear functions. However, if we replace the objective of attempting to reconstruct the actual values of the input matrix with the objective of trying to reproduce only their rank order, we will obtain a space of fewer dimensions. Moreover, it turns out that multidimensional scaling techniques discussed in this book can be used as types of nonmetric factoring procedures. The input data can consist of a symmetric matrix of any type of association measure whose values can be weakly ordered and obey the metric axioms discussed in Chapter 2.

In addition to nonmetric programs that find a dimensional representation of a single set of points (for example, objects) whose ranks of interpoint distances are monotonic with the original input data, other approaches leading to joint spaces can be employed. For example, the vector and unfolding models described in Chapter 4 can be used for the same general objective, depending on the type of representation desired.

CLUSTER ANALYSIS

Cluster analysis, like reduced space analysis, is concerned with data matrices in which the variables have not been partitioned beforehand into criterion versus predictor subsets. In reduced space analysis our interest centered on reducing the variable space to a smaller number of orthogonal dimensions that maintained most of the information—metric or ordinal—contained in the original data matrix. Emphasis was placed on the variables rather than on the subjects (rows) of the data matrix.

In cluster analysis our concern is with the similarity of the subjects, that is, the resemblance of their profiles over the whole set of variables. These variables may be the original set or may consist of a representation of them in reduced space. In either case the objective of cluster analysis is to find similar groups of subjects, where "similarity" between each pair of subjects is usually construed to mean some global measure over the whole set of characteristics, either original variables or derived coordinates, if preceded by a reduced space analysis. In this section we discuss various methods of clustering and the key role that distance functions play as measures of the proximity of pairs of points.

We first discuss the fundamentals of cluster analysis in terms of major questions concerning choice of proximity measure, choice of clustering technique, and descriptive measures by which the resultant clusters can be defined. We show that clustering results can be sensitive to the type of distance function used to summarize proximity between pairs of profiles.

We next discuss the characteristics of various computer programs that have been proposed for grouping profiles—that is, for partitioning the rows (subjects) of the data matrix. This is followed by brief discussions of statistics for defining clusters and the problems associated with statistical inference in this area.

Basic Questions in Cluster Analysis   The most common use of cluster analysis is for classification. That is, subjects are separated into groups such that each subject is more like other subjects in its group than it is to subjects outside the group. Cluster analysis is thus concerned ultimately with classification and represents a set of techniques that are part of the field of numerical taxonomy [Frank and Green, 1968; Punj and Stewart, 1983; Aldenderfer and Blashfield, 1984].

We will initially focus on clustering procedures that result in the assignment of each subject to one and only one class. Subjects within a class are usually assumed to be indistinguishable from one another. Thus, we assume that the underlying structure of the data involves an unordered set of discrete classes. In some cases we may also view these classes as hierarchical in nature, with some classes divided into subclasses.

Clustering procedures can be viewed as "preclassificatory" in the sense that the researcher has not used prior judgment to partition the subjects (rows of the data matrix). However, it is assumed that some of the subjects are heterogeneous; that is, that "clusters" exist. This presupposition of different groups is based on commonalities within the set of independent variables. This assumption is different from that made in the case of discriminant analysis or automatic interaction detection, where the dependent variable is used to formally define groups of objects and the distinction is not made on the basis of profile resemblance in the data matrix itself. Thus, given that no information on group definition is formally evaluated in advance, the major problems of cluster analysis will be discussed as follows.

1. What measure of intersubject similarity is to be used and how is each variable to be "weighted" in the construction of such a summary measure?
2. After intersubject similarities are obtained, how are the classes to be formed?
3. After the classes have been formed, what summary measures of each cluster are appropriate in a descriptive sense—that is, how are the clusters to be defined?
4. Assuming that adequate descriptions of the clusters can be obtained, what inferences can be drawn regarding their statistical significance?

Choice of Proximity Measure   The choice of proximity, similarity, association, or resemblance measure (all four terms will be used synonymously here) is an interesting problem in cluster analysis. The concept of similarity always connotes the question: Similarity with respect to what? Proximity measures are usually viewed in relative terms—two objects are similar, relative to the group, if their profiles across variables are "close" or they share "many" aspects in common, relative to those that other pairs share in common.

Most clustering procedures use pairwise measures of proximity. The choice of which subjects and variables to use in the first place is largely a matter for the researcher's judgment. While these (prior) choices are important ones, they are beyond our scope of coverage. Even assuming that such choices have been made, however, the possible measures of pairwise proximity are many. Generally speaking, these measures fall into two classes: (a) distance-type measures (including correlation coefficients) and (b) matching-type measures. The characteristics of each class are discussed in turn.

Distance-type Measures   A surprisingly large number of proximity measures, including correlation measures, can be viewed as distances in some type of metric space. In Chapter 2, we introduced the notion of Euclidean distance between two points in a space of r dimensions. We recall that the formula was

$$d_{ij} = \left[\sum_{k=1}^{r} (X_{ik} - X_{jk})^2 \right]^{1/2}$$

where x_{ik}, x_{jk} are the projections of points i and j on dimension k; $(k = 1, 2, \ldots, r)$.

Inasmuch as the variables are often measured in different units, the above formula is usually applied after each variable has been standardized to mean zero and unit standard deviation. Our subsequent discussion will assume that this preliminary step has been taken.

The Euclidean distance measure assumes that the space of (standardized) variables is orthogonal—that is, that the variables are uncorrelated. While the Euclidean measure can still be used with correlated variables, it is useful to point out that (implicit) weighting of the components underlying the associated variables occurs with the use of the Euclidean measure.

1. Squared Euclidean distance in the original variable space has the effect of weighting each underlying principal component by that component's eigenvalue.
2. Squared Euclidean distance in the component space (where all components are first standardized to unit variance) has the effect of assigning equal weights to all components.
3. In terms of the geometry of the configuration, in the first case all points are rotated to orthogonal axes with no change in squared interpoint distance. The general effect is to portray the original configuration as a hyperellipsoid with principal components serving as axes of that figure.

Equating all axes to equal length has the effect of transforming the hyperellipsoid into a hypersphere where all axes are of equal length.

The above considerations can be represented in terms of the following squared distance model.

$$d_{ij}^2 = \sum_{k=1}^{r} (y_{ik} - y_{jk})^2$$

where y_{ik}, y_{jk} denote unit variance components of profiles i and j on component axis k ($k = 1, 2, \ldots, r$). If one weights the component scores according to the variances of the components (before standardization) the expression is

$$^*d_{ij}^2 = \sum_{k=1}^{r} \lambda_k (y_{ik} - y_{jk})^2$$

where λ is the kth component variance, or eigenvalue. This expression is equivalent to d_{ij}^2 expressed in original variable space.

The above relationships assume that all principal components are extracted. As described earlier, if such is not the case, squared interpoint distances will be affected by the fact that they are computed in a component space of lower dimensionality than the original variable space.

In summary, both the Euclidean distance measure in original variable space and the Euclidean distance in component space (assuming all components have been extracted) preserve all of the information in the original data matrix. Finally, it should be pointed out that if (in addition to being standardized to mean zero and unit variance) the original variables are uncorrelated, both d_{ij}^2 and $^*d_{ij}^2$ will be equivalent.

Other Euclidean Distance Measures   Two other measures have often been proposed as proximity measures. Both of these measures derive from historical clustering methods that used Q-type factor analysis to cluster subjects. In Q-type factor analysis—as described briefly in our discussion of reduced space analysis—the correlation (or covariance) matrix to be factored consists of intersubject rather than intervariable proximities. In these methods the weights λ_k are left intact.

The effect of Q-type component analysis of either covariance or correlation matrices has been shown by Cronbach and Gleser (1953) to reduce the dimensionality of the space underlying the computation of proximity measures. Both procedures reduce the dimensionality of the original space to one less dimension by equating all profiles to zero mean. As such, profile differences in elevation are removed. In addition, a Q-type analysis applied to the intersubject correlation matrix will remove interprofile variation due to differences in dispersion. The result is a projection of points representing each profile into two fewer dimensions.

Figure 5–3
Effect of Q-Type Component Analysis of Covariance or Correlation Matrix on Profile Means

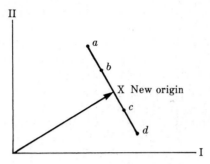

Figures 5–3 and 5–4 show these effects geometrically. In the case of either covariance or correlation matrices the profile mean is subtracted from each vector component which, in the two-component case of Figure 5–3, results in a centroid with a (new) origin located at point X on the figure.

Figure 5–4 shows the effect of removing profile dispersion. If we assume that the profiles were originally positioned in three-space, removal of each profile's mean reduces its dimensionality to two-space. By using a correlation matrix we further reduce dimensionality by projecting all points on to the unit circle, since the standard deviation of a profile can be represented by the

Figure 5–4
Effect of Q-Type Component Analysis of Correlation Matrix on Profile Dispersion

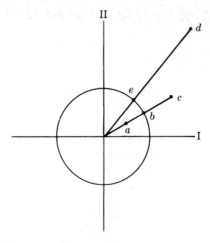

distance of the profile point from the origin (the centroid of the points first having been translated to the origin).

Thus, profiles *a, b,* and *c* would all be identical after the transformation, as would profiles *d* and *e*. The cosine of the angle separating the two vectors represents the *Q*-correlation between them.

Of course, there may be cases where the researcher is not interested in profile differences due to either mean and/or dispersion. If so, a *Q*-type analysis applied to covariance or correlation matrices, as the case may be, is perfectly sensible even though information is (willingly) discarded. In general, however we should expect differences in the derived squared distance measure computed from these procedures—both between themselves and between those computed by the techniques previously discussed.

While the authors have a predilection for the information-preserving measures d_{ij}^2 and $^*d_{ij}^2$, it is well to point out that no universally applicable distance measure exists. The choice of which measure to use depends on which aspect of the data is worth "preserving." A wide variety of distance-type measures is available for cluster analysis. Several of these are compared by Aldenderfer and Blashfield (1984).

Once the researcher has selected a method of measuring pairwise profile similarity, the computational routine for clustering the subjects must be selected. Aldenderfer and Blashfield identify several families of clustering methods, each using a different approach in creating groups: (1) hierarchical agglomerative, (2) hierarchical divisive, (3) factor analytic, and (4) nonhierarchical.

Hierarchical Methods   These procedures are characterized by the construction of an hierarchy or treelike structure. In some methods each point starts out as a unit (single-point) cluster. At the next level the two closest points are placed in a cluster. At the next level a third point either joins the first two or a second two-point cluster is formed, based on various criterion rules for assignment. In application, hierarchical clustering is useful in determining if points are substitutable rather than mutually exclusive.

1. *Single Linkage.*[2] The single linkage or minimum distance rule starts out by finding the two points with the minimum distance. These are placed in the first cluster. At the next stage a third point joins the already-formed cluster of two if the minimum distance to any of the members of the cluster is smaller than the distance between the two closest unclustered points. Otherwise, the two closest unclustered points are placed in a cluster. The process continues until all points end up in one cluster. The distance between two clusters is defined as the shortest distance from a point in the first cluster that is closest to a point in the second.

---

[2]See Jackson (1983) for a step-by-step demonstration of the simple, complete, and average linkage rules.

2. *Complete Linkage.* The complete linkage option starts out in the same way by clustering the two points with the minimum distance. However, the criterion for joining points to clusters or clusters to clusters involves maximum (rather than minimum) distance. That is, a third point joins the already-formed cluster of two if the maximum distance to any of the members of the cluster is smaller than the distance between the two closest unclustered points. In other words, the distance between two clusters is the longest distance from a point in the first cluster to a point in the second cluster.

3. *Average Linkage.* The average linkage option starts out in the same way as the other two. However, in this case the distance between two clusters is the average distance from points in the first cluster to points in the second cluster.

Divisive hierarchical clustering starts out with one (undifferentiated) cluster and proceeds to develop smaller-sized clusters. Agglomerative hierarchical clustering starts out with unit clusters and then builds up to larger-sized clusters.

The Howard–Harris Clustering Method   The Howard–Harris algorithm (1981) is a divisive method that uses the k-means method of assigning cases to the clusters. The k-means method assigns the case to the closest centroid. The approach may take either of the two forms described below.

Approach 1

1. Initially the entire set of observations is considered as one set. The group is split based on the one variable that makes the greatest contribution to within-group sum of squares.

2. Group centroids are recomputed and subject distances to all group centroids are computed. The subject that would best improve the objective function is reassigned. This process is repeated until either a finite number of transfers are performed, no further improvement in within-groups sum of squares is found, or a local optimum is reached.

3. The group with the largest within-groups sum of squares is selected for splitting. Steps 2 and 3 are then repeated until the desired number of clusters are identified.

Approach 2

1. An $m \times m$ covariance matrix is formed and analyzed using principal components analysis. A factor score is computed for each of the n subjects on the first (and most important) dimension or factor.

2. All subjects with factor scores that exceed the mean value of the factor are assigned into a new cluster.

3. After splitting, each observation is reevaluated against all clusters. If the objective function is improved by reassigning a case to another cluster, the case making the greatest improvement is reassigned. Optimization continues until

   a. a finite number of transfers are performed
   b. no further improvement in the objective function is found
   c. a local optimum is reached

4. The next factor is selected as the basis for splitting the next cluster. Steps 2, 3, and 4 are then repeated until the desired number of clusters is identified.

In addition to hierarchical methods, we may identify other clustering methods that dimensionalize the proximity matrix and methods that are nonhierarchical. Dimensionalizing the proximity matrix relies on principal components or factor analysis to find a dimensional representation of the points. Clusters are then identified, based on distances computed in this component space.

Nonhierarchical methods identify clusters directly from the similarity or distance matrices. Nonhierarchical methods do not conform to a strict hierarchical (or nested) tree-like structure, but instead allow points from within clusters to be combined to form a new cluster.

Factor Analytic Methods   These methods analyze an $n \times n$ correlation matrix of similarities between the n cases to find a dimensional representation of the points. Clusters are then developed based on the resulting factor loadings (the correlation between the subject and the underlying dimension).

The use of factor analytic methods for clustering have been criticized because of the use of a linear model that is developed across cases rather than across variables. The linear model tends to moderate the correct identification of anything other than linear additive predictive groups.

Nonhierarchical Methods   These methods have in general been subject to limited use and testing, making their specific operational characteristics difficult to identify. In general, however, these methods start right from a proximity matrix and work in the following fashion (Aldenderfer and Blashfield, 1984).

1. Begin with an initial split of the data into a specified number of clusters.
2. Allocate each data point to the cluster with the nearest centroid.
3. Compute the new centroid of the clusters after all points are assigned to clusters.
4. Iterate steps 2 and 3 until no further changes occur.

Several general types of nonhierarchical clustering designs exist and can be characterized.

1. *Sequential threshold.* In this case, a cluster center is selected and all objects within a prespecified threshold value are grouped. Then a new cluster center is selected and the process is completed. Once points enter a cluster they are removed from further processing.
2. *Parallel threshold.* This method is similar to the one immediately above except that several cluster centers are selected in advance and points within the threshold level are assigned to the nearest center; threshold levels can then be adjusted to admit fewer or more points to clusters.
3. *Parallel partitioning.* This method is similar to the one immediately above except that once several cluster centers are chosen, the whole set of data is partitioned into disjoint sets based on nearest distance to cluster centers being within threshold distance of still other objects.

Matching-type Measures   Quite often the analyst wishing to cluster profiles must contend with data that are only nominal scaled, in whole or in part. While dichotomous data, after suitable transformation, can often be expressed in terms of interpoint distances, the usual approach to nominal-scaled data uses attribute matching coefficients. Intuitively speaking, two profiles are viewed as similar to the extent to which they share common attributes.

As an illustration of this approach, consider the two profiles appearing below.

| | Attribute | | | | | |
	1	2	3	4	5	6
Object 1	1	0	0	1	1	0
Object 2	0	1	0	1	0	1

Each of the above objects is characterized by possession or nonpossession of each of six attributes, where "1" denotes possession and "0" denotes nonpossession. Suppose we count up the total number of matches—either 1, 1 or 0, 0—and divide by the total number of attributes. A simple matching measure could then be stated as

$$S_{12} = M/N = \frac{2}{6} = \frac{1}{3}$$

where M denotes the number of attributes held in common (matching 1's or 0's) and N denotes the total number of attributes. We notice that this measure varies between zero and one.

If weak matches (nonpossession of an attribute) are to be deemphasized, the above measures can be modified to

$$S_{ij} = \frac{\text{No. of attributes that are 1 for both } i \text{ and } j}{\text{No. of attributes that are 1 for either } i \text{ or } j \text{ or both}}$$

In this case, $S_{ij} = \frac{1}{5}$. A variety of such matching-type coefficients is described by Sneath and Sokal (1973) and Everett (1980). Attributes need not be limited to dichotomies, however. In the case of unordered multichotomies, matching coefficients are often developed by means similar to the above by recoding the k-state variables into $k-1$ dummy (zero–one) variables. Naturally such coefficients will be sensitive to variation in the number of states in each multichotomy.

Finally, mention should be made of the case in which the variables consist of mixed scales—nominal, ordinal, and interval. Interval-scaled variables may be handled in terms of similarity coefficients by the simple device of computing the range of the variable R_k and finding

$$S_{ijk}^* = 1 - \frac{|X_{ik} - X_{jk}|}{R_k}$$

This measure has been suggested by Gower (1967) as a device to handle both nominal- and interval-scaled data in a single similarity coefficient.

Mixed scales that include ordinal-scaled variables present greater difficulties. If ordinal and interval scales occur, one can downgrade the interval-scaled data to ordinal scales and use nonmetric procedures. If all three scales—nominal, ordinal, and interval—appear, one is more or less forced to downgrade all data to nominal measures and use matching-type coefficients. An alternative approach would be to compute "distances" for each pair of objects according to each scale type separately, standardize the measures to zero mean and unit standard deviation, and then compute some type of weighted association measure. However, such approaches are quite ad hoc.

While the above classes of clustering algorithms are not exhaustive of the field, most of the currently available routines can be typed as falling into one (or a combination) of the above categories. Criteria for grouping include such measures as average within-cluster distance and threshold cut-off values. The fact remains, however, that even the "optimizing" approaches generally achieve only conditional optima, since an unsettled question in this field is how many clusters to form in the first place.

The recommendation of an algorithm is difficult at best. For classification purposes, clusters should be able to identify distinct separations between different clusters of items. Clusters should also be internally consistent. Because meeting these challenges is often a function of the type of data analyzed, selection of an optimal algorithm is also a function of the characteristics of the data. Overall, the k-means clustering technique appears to perform well [see Punj and Stewart, 1983] when the initial starting configuration is nonrandom. In situations where a random starting configuration is required, the minimum variance type of algorithm often performs well. It is even suggested that clustering might best be approached using a combination of reduced space analysis and clustering techniques, so as to group points in the space obtained from principal components or nonmetric scaling techniques. This approach is particularly beneficial if the number of dimensions is small, allowing the researcher to augment the clustering results with visual inspection of the configuration. If the researcher is more concerned with structure than classification, overlapping clustering ignores the concept of distinct separations between clusters in an attempt to allow products/subjects to belong to more than one cluster.

Describing the Clusters   Once clusters are developed, the researcher still faces the task of describing the clusters. One measure that is used frequently is the centroid; that is, the average value of the objects contained in the cluster on each of the variables making up each object's profile. If the data are interval scaled and clustering is performed in original variable space, this measure appears quite natural as a summary description. If the space consists of principal components' dimensions obtained from nonmetric scaling methods, the axes usually are not capable of being described simply. Often in this case the researcher will want to go back to the original variables and compute average profile measures in these terms.

If matching-type coefficients are used, the cluster may be described by the group's modal profile on each of the attributes; in other cases, arithmetic averages may be computed.

In addition to central tendency, the researcher may compute some measure of the cluster's variability, for example, average interpoint distance of all members of the cluster from their centroid or average interpoint distance between all pairs of points within the cluster.

Statistical Significance   Despite attempts made to construct various tests of statistical significance of clusters, current statistical tests are little more than heuristics offering relatively indefensible procedures. The lack of appropriate tests stems from the difficulty of specifying realistic null hypotheses. First, it is not clear just what the universe of content is. Quite often the researcher arbitrarily selects objects and variables and is often interested in confining attention to only this sample. Second, the researcher is usually assuming that heterogeneity exists in the first place—otherwise, why bother to cluster? Moreover, the clusters are formed from the data and not on the basis of outside criteria. Thus, one would be placed in the uncomfortable statistical position of "testing" the significance between groups formed on the basis of the data itself. Third, the distributions of objects are largely unknown, and it would be dangerous to assume that they conformed to some tractable model like a multivariate normal distribution.

It is indeed likely that different types of clusters may be present simultaneously in the data. It is a major difficulty to specify a priori the type of clustering or homogeneity to be detected.

With these limitations in mind, Arnold (1979) proposed using a statistic originally suggested by Friedman and Rubin (1967). The statistic is given by

$$C = \log \frac{\max |T|}{|W|}$$

where

   $|T|$ is the determinant of the total variance-covariance matrix

   $|W|$ is the determinant of the pooled within-groups covariance matrix.

We continue to believe that, at least in the present state of cluster analysis, the objective of this class of techniques should be to formulate rather than to test categorizations of data. After a classification has been developed and supported by theoretical research and subsequent reformulation of classes, other techniques like discriminant analysis might prove useful in the assignment of new members to groups identified on grounds not solely restricted to the original cluster analysis.

While the above caveats are not to be taken lightly, clustering techniques are useful—in ways comparable to the objectives of factor analysis—as systematic procedures for the orderly preclassification of multivariate data. The results of using these approaches can be helpful and meaningful (after the fact) as will be illustrated next.

AN APPLICATION OF REDUCED SPACE AND CLUSTER ANALYSIS

Thus far, our descriptions of reduced space and clustering methods have largely remained at the conceptual level. In this section, we describe their application to a realistically sized problem—one dealing with the similarities and differences among 90 1987 automobiles, trucks, and utility vehicles whose prices range from $5,000 to $168,000. In this abridged version of the study, we illustrate an application of cluster analysis to 90 vehicles. Figure 5–5 identifies the 90 vehicles for which data was collected on 20 attributes. This 90 vehicle × 20 variable data matrix forms the basis for our analysis directed at grouping the vehicles according to similarity of attributes.

Application of the Howard Harris procedure yielded two different clustering solutions, which, based on the within-group sum of squares for each group, appeared to be worth examining. Figure 5–6 shows the "Scree"-type diagram plotting sum of squares against number of clusters. The curve appears to flatten at 5 clusters and again at 12 clusters.

The 5-cluster solution is shown in Figure 5–7 and the 12-cluster solution is shown in Figure 5–8. As might be surmised, the 5-cluster representation was inferior to the 12-cluster representation.

In Figure 5–6, we note that cluster membership is somewhat more evenly distributed than in Figure 5–8 (12) clusters. The groups are rather homogeneous, though now and again, a vehicle seems to be out of place.

_____ Figure 5–5 _____

Vehicle Performance Characteristics and Listing

VAR	COLUMN	TYPE	EXPLANATION
1	1-3	Real	1987 Model Base Price (In U.S. $)
2-3	4-7	Dummy	Country of Mgf.(1 0 = US;1 1 = Asia;0 1 = Europe)
4	8-9	Real	Number of Doors (2,3,4,5)
5-6	10-13	Dummy	Body Style(0 0=Car;0 1=Truck;1 0=Wagon;1 1=Van)
7	14-15	Real	Number of Passengers (2,3,4,5,6,7,8,9)
8	16-18	Real	Number of Engine Cyl. (4,5,6,8,12)
9-10	19-22	Dummy	Motor Locat.(1 0 = Front;1 1 = Mid-car;0 1 = Rear)
11-12	23-26	Dummy	Drive Location (1 0 = Front;1 1 = 4 WD;0 1 = Rear)
13	27-30	Real	Horse Power Rating
14	31-32	Ord.	Tire Type (1=<175 cm, 2=<200 cm, 3=>200 cm, 4=H/V Rated, 5= Special Racing Tire)
15	33-35	Real	Turning Radius (FT.)
16	36-38	Real	Vehicle Curb Wgt (in 1000 lbs.)
17	39-42	Real	Vehicle Length in inches
18	43-45	Real	Vehicle Width in inches
19	46-48	Real	Vehicle Height in inches
20	49-52	Real	FT./LBS. of Torque

VEHICLES

#	Vehicle	#	Vehicle	#	Vehicle
1	ASTON MARTIN SALOON	31	SHELBY CHARGER GLHS	61	TOYOTA TERCEL
2	FERRARI TESTAROSA	32	TOYOTA CELICA	62	MERCEDES 300E
3	LAMBORGHINI COUNTACH	33	VOLVO 780 COUPE	63	CHEV. G10 SPORTSVAN
4	LOTUS TURBO ESPRIT	34	CHEVROLET CHEVETTE	64	DODGE B250 MAXIVAN
5	PORSCHE 928	35	DODGE COLT	65	FORD E150 CLUB WGN
6	PORSCHE 944	36	FORD ESCORT	66	CHEV ASTRO
7	MAZDA RX7	37	HONDA CIVIC	67	DODGE CARAVAN
8	NISSAN 300ZX	38	HYUNDAI EXCEL	68	FORD AEROSTAR
9	FERRARI 928 GTS	39	ISUZU IMARK	69	NISSAN VAN
10	CORVETTE	40	MAZDA 323	70	TOYOTA VAN LE
11	LINCOLN VII LSC	41	TOYOTA MR2	71	VW VANAGON
12	ROLLS CORNICHE	42	MERKUR XR4TI	72	SUBURBAN R10
13	MERCEDES 560 SEC	43	MITSUBISHI MIRAGE	73	JEEP GRAND WGN
14	CADILLAC SEVILLE	44	NISSAN SENTRA	74	DODGE RAM 50
15	ASTON MARTIN LAGONDA	45	FORD MUSTANG	75	CHEV. S10
16	BMW 730i	46	SUBARU HATCHBACK	76	ISUZU P'UP
17	JAGUAR XJ6	47	TOYOTA COROLLA FWD	77	MAZDA B2000
18	CADILLAC DEVILLE	48	VW GOLF	78	MITSUBISHI
19	BMW 528e	49	YUGO GV	79	NISSAN
20	JAGUAR XJS	50	AUDI 5000	80	TOYOTA
21	MASERATI BITURBO	51	DODGE COLT VISTA	81	DODGE DAKOTA
22	TOYOTA SUPRA	52	TOYOTA CAMRY	82	JEEP COMANCHE
23	MITSUBISHI STARION	53	BUICK SKYHAWK	83	S10 BLAZER
24	ACURA LEGEND	54	CHEV. CELEBRITY	84	BRONCO II
25	AUDI COUPE GT	55	CHRYSLER LEBARON	85	JEEP CHEROKEE
26	CHRYS. LEBARON GTS	56	HONDA CIVIC WAGON	86	JEEP WRANGLER
27	HONDA PRELUDE	57	DODGE ARIES	87	ISUZU TROOPER
28	ISUZU IMPULSE	58	MAZDA 323 WAGON	88	MITSUBIS. MONTERO
29	NISSAN 200 SX	59	NISSAN STANZA	89	TOYOTA LANDCRUISER
30	FIREBIRD TRANS AM	60	SUBARU WAGON	90	SUZUKI SAMURAI

From Figures 5–7 and 5–8 one can get some idea of the current intermanufacturer competition. Market positioning strategies seem to be well developed, with several of the manufacturers having multiple vehicles within the same segments. Product positioning is even more apparent when one recognizes that the vehicles evaluated are distinct models and that minor

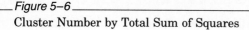

Figure 5–6

Cluster Number by Total Sum of Squares

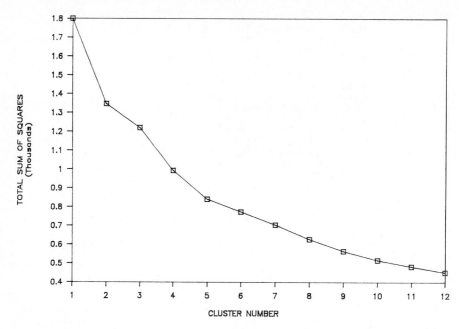

options/product distinctions are present for most vehicles, but are not considered in the data.

Summary of Study   The cluster analysis results constitutes only one of several possible facets in this study. Additional analytical steps may have involved (a) the development of clusters based only on the nominal-scaled data (features), (b) the development of clusters based only on the interval-scaled data, and (c) clustering (involving both features and measured data) on a combined time period basis.

In terms of substantive results, we found that five clusters identified most of the similarities and differences among the vehicle models—VW Vanagon, smaller four-to-five–passenger vehicles and wagons, exotic sports and large-capacity passenger cars and utility vehicles, and popular sports cars and pickups. Of course, the clusters became more detailed as the number of clusters increased. Managerially, the resulting cluster solutions displayed the competitive structure in terms of similarity in the performance profiles of vehicles.

For purposes of this section, suffice it to say that clustering techniques can be used in marketing studies involving large-scale data banks. Moreover, the combination of reduced space (principal components) and cluster analysis can provide a useful dual treatment of the data. The reduced space phase may provide help in summarizing the original variables in terms of a smaller number of dimensions; for example, speed or vehicle size. The

_____ Figure 5–7 _____

Five-Cluster Solution

CLUSTER NUMBER   1   N = 1
   71   VW VANAGON

CLUSTER NUMBER   2   N = 33
   24   ACURA LEGEND
   25   AUDI COUPE GT
   26   CHRYSLER LEBARON GTS
   27   HONDA PRELUDE
   28   ISUZU IMPULSE
   31   SHELBY CHARGER GLH-S
   32   TOYOTA CELICA
   35   DODGE COLT
   36   FORD ESCORT
   37   HONDA CIVIC
   38   HYUNDAI EXCEL
   39   ISUZU IMARK
   40   MAZDA 323
   43   MITSUBISHI MIRAGE
   44   NISSAN SENTRA
   46   SUBARU HATCHBACK
   47   TOYOTA COROLLA FWD
   48   VW GOLF
   49   YUGO GV
   50   AUDI 5000
   51   DODGE COLT VISTA
   52   TOYOTA CAMRY
   53   BUICK SKYHAWK
   54   CHEV. CELEBRITY
   55   CHRYSLER LEBARON
   56   HONDA CIVIC WAGON
   57   DODGE ARIES
   58   MAZDA 323 WAGON
   59   NISSAN STANZA
   60   SUBARU WAGON
   61   TOYOTA TERCEL
   86   JEEP WRANGLER
   90   SUZUKI SAMURAI

CLUSTER NUMBER   3   N = 16
    1   ASTON MARTIN SALOON
    2   FERRARI TESTAROSA
    3   LAMBORGHINI COUNTACH
    4   LOTUS TURBO ESPRIT
    5   PORSCHE 928
    9   FERRARI 928 GTS
   10   CORVETTE
   11   LINCOLN MARK VII LSC
   12   ROLLS ROYCE CORNICHE
   13   MERCEDES 560 SEC
   15   ASTON MARTIN LAGONDA

   16   BMW 730i
   17   JAGUAR XJ6
   20   JAGUAR XJS
   30   FIREBIRD TRANS AM
   62   MERCEDES 300E

CLUSTER NUMBER   4   N = 17
   14   CADILLAC SEVILLE
   18   CADILLAC DEVILLE
   63   CHEV. G10 SPORTSVAN
   64   DODGE B250 MAXIVAN
   65   FORD E150 CLUB WAGON
   66   CHEV ASTRO
   67   DODGE CARAVAN
   68   FORD AEROSTAR
   69   NISSAN VAN
   70   TOYOTA VAN LE
   72   SUBURBAN R10
   73   JEEP GRAND WAGONEER
   83   S10 BLAZER
   84   BRONCO II
   85   JEEP CHEROKEE
   87   ISUZU TROOPER
   89   TOYOTA LANDCRUISER

CLUSTER NUMBER   5   N = 23
    6   PORSCHE 944
    7   MAZDA RX7
    8   NISSAN 300ZX
   19   BMW 528e
   21   MASERATI BITURBO
   22   TOYOTA SUPRA
   23   MITSUBISHI STARION
   29   NISSAN 200 SX
   33   VOLVO 780 COUPE
   34   CHEVROLET CHEVETTE
   41   TOYOTA MR2
   42   MERKUR XR4TI
   45   FORD MUSTANG
   74   DODGE RAM 50
   75   CHEV. S10
   76   ISUZU P'UP
   77   MAZDA B2000
   78   MITSUBISHI
   79   NISSAN
   80   TOYOTA
   81   DODGE DAKOTA
   82   JEEP COMANCHE
   88   MITSUBISHI MONTERO

clustering phase permits one to group vehicles according to their coordinates in this reduced space.

RECENT DEVELOPMENTS IN CLUSTERING
TECHNIQUES Our previous discussion of clustering analysis has tended to emphasize the tandem approach of dimensional and nominal (classlike)

_____ Figure 5–8 _____
Twelve-Cluster Solution

CLUSTER NUMBER   1 N = 1
    71   VW VANAGON
CLUSTER NUMBER   2 N = 8
    14   CADILLAC SEVILLE
    24   ACURA LEGEND
    25   AUDI COUPE GT
    26   CHRYSLER LEBARON GTS
    31   SHELBY CHARGER GLH-S
    50   AUDI 5000
    52   TOYOTA CAMRY
    54   CHEV. CELEBRITY
CLUSTER NUMBER   3 N = 10
     5   PORSCHE 928
    10   CORVETTE
    11   LINCOLN MARK VII LSC
    13   MERCEDES 560 SEC
    16   BMW 730i
    17   JAGUAR XJ6
    18   CADILLAC DEVILLE
    20   JAGUAR XJS
    30   FIREBIRD TRANS AM
    62   MERCEDES 300E
CLUSTER NUMBER   4 N = 8
    68   FORD AEROSTAR
    69   NISSAN VAN
    70   TOYOTA VAN LE
    83   S10 BLAZER
    84   BRONCO II
    85   JEEP CHEROKEE
    87   ISUZU TROOPER
    89   TOYOTA LANDCRUISER
CLUSTER NUMBER   5 N = 12
     6   PORSCHE 944
     7   MAZDA RX7
     8   NISSAN 300ZX
    19   BMW 528e
    21   MASERATI BITURBO
    22   TOYOTA SUPRA
    23   MITSUBISHI STARION
    29   NISSAN 200 SX
    33   VOLVO 780 COUPE
    41   TOYOTA MR2
    42   MERKUR XR4TI
    45   FORD MUSTANG
CLUSTER NUMBER   6 N = 6
    63   CHEV. G10 SPORTSVAN
    64   DODGE B250 MAXIVAN
    65   FORD E150 CLUB WAGON
    66   CHEV ASTRO
    72   SUBURBAN R10
    73   JEEP GRAND WAGONEER

CLUSTER NUMBER   7 N = 3
    86   JEEP WRANGLER
    88   MITSUBISHI MONTERO
    90   SUZUKI SAMURAI
CLUSTER NUMBER   8 N = 4
     2   FERRARI TESTAROSA
     3   LAMBORGHINI COUNTACH 500
     4   LOTUS TURBO ESPRIT
     9   FERRARI 928 GTS
CLUSTER NUMBER   9 N = 9
    74   DODGE RAM 50 PICKUP
    75   CHEV. S10 PICKUP
    76   ISUZU P'UP
    77   MAZDA B2000 PICKUP
    78   MITSUBISHI PICKUP
    79   NISSAN PICKUP
    80   TOYOTA PICKUP
    81   DODGE DAKOTA PICKUP
    82   JEEP COMANCHE PICKUP
CLUSTER NUMBER   10 N = 3
     1   ASTON MARTIN SALOON
    12   ROLLS ROYCE CORNICHE II
    15   ASTON MARTIN LAGONDA
CLUSTER NUMBER   11 N = 18
    27   HONDA PRELUDE
    28   ISUZU IMPULSE
    32   TOYOTA CELICA
    34   CHEVROLET CHEVETTE
    35   DODGE COLT
    36   FORD ESCORT
    37   HONDA CIVIC
    38   HYUNDAI EXCEL
    39   ISUZU IMARK
    40   MAZDA 323
    43   MITSUBISHI MIRAGE
    44   NISSAN SENTRA
    46   SUBARU HATCHBACK
    47   TOYOTA COROLLA FWD
    48   VW GOLF
    49   YUGO GV
    53   BUICK SKYHAWK
    61   TOYOTA TERCEL
CLUSTER NUMBER   12 N = 8
    51   DODGE COLT VISTA
    55   CHRYSLER LEBARON
    56   HONDA CIVIC WAGON
    57   DODGE ARIES
    58   MAZDA 323 WAGON
    59   NISSAN STANZA
    60   SUBARU WAGON
    67   DODGE CARAVAN

representation of data structures. In addition to using multidimensional scaling techniques for reduced space analysis, a number of other nonlinear approaches have been developed, including nonlinear factor analysis [McDonald, 1962], polynomial factor analysis [Carroll, 1969], correspondence analysis [Carroll, Green, and Schaffer, 1986].

Space does not permit anything but brief mention of this interesting work. We do consider in some detail, however, a combination qualitative–quantitative approach to an important problem in reduced space analysis—the interpretation of data structures.

Nominal Versus Dimensional Structures　As mentioned earlier, even a pure class structure—where class membership accounts for all of the information in the data—can be represented spatially. More commonly, however, we consider cluster analysis as a more appropriate technique for characterizing such data. On the other hand, other data structures are inherently dimensional, so that measures of proximity are assumed to vary rather continuously throughout the whole matrix of proximities.

Pure typal and pure dimensional structures represent only two extremes. Since all proximity matrices (that obey certain properties [Gower, 1966]) can be represented spatially, it would seem of interest to consider data structures in terms of the restrictions placed on the points as they are arranged in that space. This motivation underlies many of the most recent developments in cluster analysis.

Torgerson (1965) was one of the first researchers to become interested in the problem of characterizing data as "mixtures" of discrete class and quantitative variables. Several varieties of such structures can be obtained.

1. Data consisting of pure and unordered class structure. Dimensional representation of such data would consist of points at the n vertices of an $n - 1$ dimensional simplex where interpoint distances are all equal. For example, three classes could be represented by an equilateral triangle in two-space, four classes by a regular tetrahedron in three-space, and so on.
2. Data consisting of concentrated masses of points, corresponding to classes, where interclass distances are unequal, thus implying the existence of latent dimensions underlying class descriptions.
3. Data consisting of hierarchical sets of attributes where some classes are nested within other classes; for example, cola and noncola drinks within the diet-drink class.
4. Data consisting of dimensional variables nested within discrete classes; for example, sweet to nonsweet cereals within the class of "processed"-shape (as opposed to "natural"-shape) cereals.
5. Data consisting of mixtures of ideal (mutually exclusive) classes so that one may find; for example, points in the interior of an equilateral triangle whose vertices represent three unordered classes.
6. Data consisting of pure dimensional structure in which, theoretically, all of the space can be filled up by points.

While the above categorizations are neither exclusive nor exhaustive, they are illustrative of the variety of data structures that could be obtained in the analysis of "objective" data or subjective (similarities) data of the sort described in the preceding chapters. From the viewpoint of cluster analysis, some of the above structures could produce elongated, parallel clusters in which average intracluster distance need not be smaller than intercluster distances. Moreover, one could have structures in which the clusters curve or twist around one another along some manifold embedded in a higher dimensional space [Shepard and Carroll, 1966].

Figure 5–9 shows three types of data structures as related to the above categories (Torgerson, 1965). Panel (a) illustrates the case of three un-ordered discrete classes. Panel (b) illustrates the case of discrete class structure where class descriptors are assumed to be orderable. Panel (c) shows the case of three discrete classes and an orthogonal variable that is quantitative. Points occur only along the solid lines of the prism. Figure 5–9(d) illustrates the case where objects are made up of mixtures of discrete classes plus an orthogonal quantitative dimension. In this case, all objects lie on or within the boundaries of the curve prism while "pure" cases would lie at one of the three edges with location dependent on the degree of the quantitative variable that each possesses.

_____ *Figure 5–9* _____

Dimensional Portrayal of Alternative Data Structures

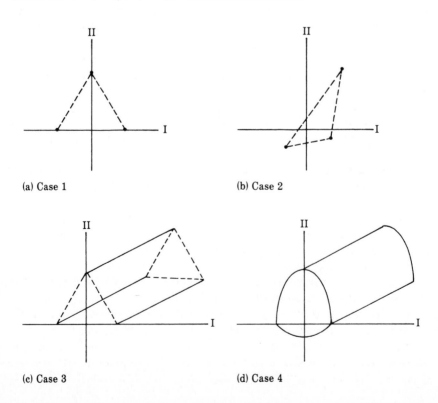

(a) Case 1

(b) Case 2

(c) Case 3

(d) Case 4

Research in cluster analysis and related techniques is proceeding in new directions for dealing with heretofore intractable data structures. The continued development and refinement of interactive display devices should further these efforts by enabling the researcher to visualize various characteristics of the data array as a guide to the selection of appropriate grouping methods.

Overlapping Clustering Techniques   The key element of all clustering techniques discussed so far is the mutually exclusive and exhaustive nature of the clusters developed. While in most cases, managers view segments as mutually exclusive and hierarchical in nature, cases do exist where segments are not mutually exclusive. Indeed, consumers may well fit into several segments. Overlapping clustering is a new clustering model that relaxes the exclusivity constraint of most other hierarchical and nonhierarchical cluster models.

As an example of a cluster analysis of brands of soft drinks, Tab may be perceived as fitting into clusters identifying diet drink, cola, and used by women, whereas Diet Pepsi may fit into only the first two benefit clusters. Brands might compete across product categories. V8 drink competes against other vegetable/fruit drinks, as well as against soft drinks and even as a between-meal snack. A cluster of toothpaste users might show that Aqua-Fresh toothpaste appeals to the fresh breath, decay prevention, and brighteners clusters, while Crest may appeal only to the decay prevention benefit cluster.

Overlapping clustering simply allows for patterns of overlapping to be considered. Arabie (1977), Shepard and Arabie (1979), Arabie and Carroll (1980), Arabie, Carroll, DeSarbo, and Wind (1981) outline methods for overlapping clustering, but point out that limitations do occur in practice. First, it is difficult to develop an algorithm that effectively considers all possible cluster overlap options, especially if the sample size is large. Second, most overlapping clustering algorithms produce too many clusters with excessive overlap. A high degree of overlap results in poor configuration recovery, or in other words, a great mathematical model that is difficult to visualize from the data.

Shepard and Arabie (1979) provide a detailed explanation of their ADCLUS (for ADditive CLUStering) model. The ADCLUS model represents a set of m clusters that may or may not be overlapping. Each cluster is assigned a numerical weight, w_k, where $k = 1, \ldots, m$. The similarity between any pair of points is predicted in the model as the sum of the weights of those clusters that contain the pair. Arabie and Carroll (1980) and Arabie, Carroll, DeSarbo, and Wind (1981) further develop the ability to fit the ADCLUS by presenting the MAPCLUS (for MAthematical Programming CLUStering) algorithm. This implementation appears to meet the needs of clustering items in more than a single cluster. In addition, clusters may be added, deleted, or modified to produce constrained solutions [Carroll and Arabie,

1980], and estimate (in a regression sense) the importance of new sets of clusters in explaining variance in the data.

The importance of overlapping clustering is self-evident, particularly in applications where clusters are not mutually exclusive, but are overlapping. This reality reflects the existence of multiattribute decision rules in decision-making behavior, divergent product application or use scenarios, and even joint decisions made by multiple users within the same household.

SUMMARY   This section has considered a companion objective of the scaling of similarities and preference data—the use of metric and nonmetric approaches in data reduction and taxonomy. We have pointed out that many of the multidimensional scaling programs can serve useful functions as types of nonmetric factoring procedures. Moreover, clustering procedures are often a helpful adjunct in data analysis when one desires to group objects (or variables) according to their relative similarity.

We first discussed metric approaches to reduced space analysis, specifically focusing on principal components. This discussion was followed by brief descriptions of nonmetric analogues to factor analysis, including several of the algorithms originally discussed in the context of similarities and preference data.

We then turned to a description of clustering methods and addressed the topics of association measures, grouping algorithms, cluster descriptions, and statistical inference. This topic led to presentation of some pilot research using cluster analysis in examining the performance structure of the automobile market.

We concluded the section by describing the general problem of portraying data structures that consist of mixtures of categorical and dimensional variables and a discussion of the usefulness of overlapping clustering.

PART III

Literature Review

Multidimensional Scaling Research

INTRODUCTION

A Review of Multidimensional Scaling in Marketing Research

Determining the perceptions of consumers is one of the primary concerns in market research. Multidimensional scaling (along with cluster analysis, factor analysis, multiple discriminant analysis, and conjoint analysis) is an effective way to measure and represent perceptions.

The purpose of the article by Lee G. Cooper is to give an overview of multidimensional scaling in marketing research. The MDS applications covered include product planning, decisions concerning pricing and branding, study of channels of distribution, personal selling, and the effect of advertising in research. The article also includes a discussion of MDS algorithms and product planning models. Each of these areas of discussion is now briefly identified.

Product planning, as a focal point of MDS techniques, concentrates on market structure analysis, the development of product perceptions, and analyzing differences in product perceptions. When applied to new products, MDS may be used to determine relevant product markets, to identify determinant attributes, to create product perceptual spaces, to model individual or market-segment decision making, and to determine the impact of pricing on brand perception.

The selection of trademarks for branding and the effect of these trademarks on consumer perceptions may be evaluated using MDS. Trademarks are visual and semantic images, influencing product perceptions.

Concerning personal selling, two types of MDS studies have been performed. The first deals with the selection criteria that salesmen use in evaluating potential customers, and the second deals with the similarity of salesmen, customers, and noncustomer judgments.

Advertising research is discussed in light of changing brand perceptions and determining the compatibility of attributes and perceptual images.

Multidimensional Scaling

In the second article in this section, J. Douglas Carroll and Phipps Arabie provide a rigorous discussion and review of the current status of multidimensional scaling methodology. The review focuses on the theoretical properties of the data required for MDS analysis, and the properties of specific scaling models. Discussion focuses on specific model types (spatial, nonspatial, and hybrid models), which may have various numbers of sets of points, spaces, and model constraints.

The review article provides a detailed analysis of specific algorithms by model type and specific applications within the social sciences.

A REVIEW OF MULTIDIMENSIONAL SCALING IN MARKETING RESEARCH Lee G. Cooper, *University of California, Los Angeles*

The domain of this review includes the development and application of multi-dimensional scaling (MDS) in product planning; in decisions concerning pricing and branding; in the study of channels of distribution, personal selling, and the effects of advertising; and in research related to the fact finding and analysis mission of marketing research. In research on product planning, specific attention is given to market structure analysis, to the development of a master configuration of product perceptions, to the role of in-dividual differences, to representing con-sumer preferences, to issues in market segmentation, and to the use of asym-metric MDS to study market structure. Regarding fact finding and analysis, this review deals with issues in data collection such as the response rate, time, and accuracy of judgments; the validity, reli-ability, and stability of judgments; and the robustness of data collection techniques and MDS algorithms. A separate section on new-product models deals with the deter-mination of relevant product markets, the identification of determinant attributes, the creation of product perceptual spaces,

and the modeling of individual or market-segment decision making. Three trends are discussed briefly; (1) a trend toward finer grained inspection of individual and group perceptions, (2) a trend toward merging consumer level measurement and market level measurements, and (3) a trend toward the study of the creation of new markets, rather than new products in existing markets.

Understanding the choices people make in the marketplace is the main goal of marketing research. How people perceive the alternatives from which they choose is a fundamental question for this domain. Multidimensional scaling, cluster analysis, factor analysis, multiple discriminant analysis, and conjoint measurement, as methods for representing perceptions, have all received major attention in the marketing research literature.

The professional marketing research community has not lagged behind the academic community. In a survey of American Marketing Association members who were company marketing researchers or suppliers of marketing research to companies, Bateson and Greyser (1982) reported extensive relevant applications of 13 techniques. Almost 70 percent of the company researchers surveyed had used multidimensional scaling (MDS), with two-thirds of these users finding the techniques relevant to their problems. Almost 80 percent had used cluster analysis, 86 percent had used factor analysis, and 56 percent had used conjoint measurement. More than three-quarters of the users of these techniques found them relevant to the problems the researchers confronted. Research suppliers surveyed had slightly higher usage and satisfaction rates.

Such technological diffusion is more likely to occur when there is a symbiosis between the needs of the marketing manager and the curiosity of the marketing researcher. To understand the symbiosis and to help structure a review of the contributions of MDS to marketing research, it is useful to present a classic conceptualization of the role of the marketing manager.

In the late 1940s, a marketing manager was termed a "mixer of ingredients" by Borden (1964), who designed a list of important elements or ingredients that make up a marketing program and a list of forces that bear on the marketing operation of a firm. The marketing mix includes product planning (for example, what product lines are to be offered, what markets to enter, and new product policy), pricing policy, branding, channels of distribution (for example, the paths products take from the manufacturer to the consumer), personal selling, advertising, promotions, packaging, displays, servicing, physical handling, and fact finding and analysis. The market forces that bear on the marketing mix include consumers' buyer behavior (for example, motivation in purchasing, buying habits, and situational influences), the trades' behavior (for example, the structure, practices and attitudes of wholesalers and retailers), competitors' position and behavior (for example, industry structure and direct competition as well as indirect competition), and governmental behavior (for example, the regulatory environment).

On the role of a marketing manager, Borden (1964) stated:

> The skillful marketer is one who is a perceptive and practical psychologist and sociologist, who has keen insight into individual and group behavior, who can foresee changes in behavior that develop in a dynamic world, ... His skill in forecasting response to his marketing moves should well be supplemented by a further skill in devising and using tests and measurements to check consumer or trade response to his program or parts thereof, for no marketer has so much prescience that he can proceed without empirical check [pp. 4–5].

That such a complex and comprehensive mandate for marketing management has fostered the evolution of a specialization in marketing research should come as no surprise. Also contributing to the Zeitgeist were the twin notions that marketing research should not be merely reactive, helping to find a consumer market for the products which spring forth as did Athena, fully grown from the head of Zeus, but rather that marketing research should be proactive in aiding the design of products that better match the needs and desires of consumers.

It was in March of 1964 that Kruskal published his work on nonmetric MDS. By the summer of 1964, data were being collected in six cities to use Kruskal's (1964a, 1964b) algorithm to help design the "perfect cup of coffee" [Brown, Cardozo, Cunningham, Salmon, and Sultan, 1968]. The problem was to array brand-to-brand similarities in a multidimensional space along with the verbal descriptions of product features, then to assess where new products (for example, new blends of coffee) were judged to fall. When the new coffee blend was found that matched the desired feature descriptions in the judgments of consumers, the share of competitive choices for this new coffee, as well as the source of those choices, could be used to help estimate the market potential of a new brand. The linking of brand perceptions with linguistic descriptions was the key contribution of sociologist and linguist Stefflre [Brown et al., 1968; Silk, 1969; Stefflre, 1968]. With a linguistic description to help anchor the perceptions of the new product one could go about trying to design packaging and advertising that conveyed the same or similar image as the new product itself. These are important steps in the design of an entire marketing program to convey a desired image.

Stefflre's similarity judgments came from a simplification of the conditional rank order task. In the conditional rank order task each stimulus serves in turn as the key, and the other stimuli are ranked from the most similar to the key to the least similar to the key. In Stefflre's simplified version each brand served in turn as the key, and the respondents merely checked the other brands in the list that they considered "most similar to" the key. Aggregated over individuals, these data correlated rather well with expensive brand-switching data from consumer purchase panels. Linguistic descriptions (for example, "a very dark rich coffee") were imbedded into the space in a seemingly ad hoc manner, individual differences were aggregated away, no account was taken of the substantive asymmetries of the switching data, and preferences were not formally connected to the spatial representation, but the ideas fit together in a compelling fashion. The work dealt simultaneously with product planning, advertising, and packaging; and with the market forces of the consumer's buyer behavior and the competitors' position and behavior.

The early reviews and overviews [Frank and Green, 1968; Green, 1970; Green and Carmone, 1969; Green, Carmone, and Robinson, 1968; Neidell, 1969] made marketing researchers aware of the broad spectrum of problems to which MDS could be applied. The early books and chapters [Green and Carmone, 1970, 1972, 1973; Green and Greenberg, 1974; Green and Rao, 1972b; Green and Wind, 1973; Greenberg and Green, 1974; Stefflre, 1972] filled in the technical picture, and along with Green (1975a), delineated lingering issues, such as interpretation of MDS configurations, stability and reliability, the relation of perceptual analyses to choices, and issues of individual differences.

This review will deal with the problems and proposed solutions as they developed principally in the journal literature. The marketing mix elements will serve as an organizing theme.

PRODUCT PLANNING

Product planning involves many different stages and problems. In this section the studies have been organized into interrelated subtopics concerning (1) market structure, (2) the evolution of a master configuration for perceptions, (3) individual differences, (4) preferences, (5) market segmentation, and (6) market structure models using asymmetric data. Models for new product planning, and strategic models linking product planning to other elements of the marketing mix, will be reviewed after research on other elements is reported.

Market Structure Analysis

Market structure analysis deals with issues in product planning as well as issues in the understanding of the forces of competition. Two points are illustrated by Klahr's (1970) study of major brands in the cigarette market. Klahr showed that when the dominant distinguishing feature of brands is a binary characteristic (for example, filter tipped versus nonfilter), nonmetric MDS algorithms can produce degenerate results, progressively reducing the within-category distance and increasing the between-category distance until two points in space represent the two categories of brands.

The first point is that marketing researchers received very early warning of this kind of degeneracy. This degeneracy made individual level analysis tenuous, but 5 of the 10 judges in Klahr's study had significant correlations between their preference scales and the distance of each brand from their most preferred brand in the individual spaces. The most preferred brand was used as a surrogate for an ideal brand.

The second point is that it is practically impossible to discuss the structure underlying similarity judgments without dealing with the relations of perceptions to preferences. Klahr's (1969) study of how college admission officers judged applicants served to underscore that not just brands, but the perceived interrelations among many sets of choice alternatives, could be represented with nonmetric MDS. Nonmetric MDS was thus useful in understanding how people make choices.

The Evolution of a Master Configuration for Perceptions

In this subsection is reported a series of studies by Green and his colleagues which have provided leadership in this field and have brought richer meaning to market structure analysis. The Green and Carmone (1968) study of the structure of the computer market over time introduced product life cycle analysis using nonmetric MDS. They compared obverse factor analysis (that is, factor analysis that explores the structure underlying brands rather than the structure underlying descriptive variables) with TORSCA [Young and Torgerson, 1967] and parametric mapping, that is, a nonmetric MDS routine that emphasizes maintaining local monotonicity but relaxes monotonicity for very dissimilar objects [Shepard and Carroll, 1966; Coxon, 1982, pp. 159 ff.]. Rather than just looking at the trends in

aggregate sales over time to reflect where a product was in the cycle of introduction, growth, maturity, and decline, comparisons based on product characteristics in an innovative market, such as computers, could reveal this cyclical structure. Profile distances from 75 normalized characteristics were calculated over the 12 computers, and the 12×12 distance matrix was analyzed by all three methods. Obverse factor analysis and TORSCA found clusters of three generations of computers. Parametric mapping did not. Emphasis was placed on multimethod comparisons when little was known about the match of the functional relations underlying objects to the assumptions implicit in an analysis.

Green and Maheshwari (1969) investigated the perceptions of common stocks as investment vehicles. They used multiple regression to imbed property vectors into the two-dimensional space. The ratings of each object on each property were the dependent measures, and scale values of the objects on each dimension were the independent variables. The multiple regression weights were used as the coordinates of the property vectors. As was also found by Krampf and Williams (1974), the oblique vectors of perceived growth and perceived risk correlated highly with the two dimensions of the configuration. For each of the two groups in this study, preferences were imbedded into the space using Carroll and Chang's (1967) external analysis of preferences. For one group, a vector model indicating the direction of preference gave an adequate representation. For the other group, ideal coordinates were appropriate. On one dimension the closer stocks were to an ideal location, the more preferred they were; whereas on the other dimension the closer stocks were to an anti-ideal location, the less preferred they were.

Green, Maheshwari, and Rao (1969b) used nonmetric MDS to investigate the notion that consumers purchase products that have images similar to their own self-image. By scaling average similarities, imbedding property vectors for interpretation, and using self-image ratings as a surrogate for preference, they found that some consumers do and some do not desire automobiles with images similar to self-images. This equivocal conclusion helped foster an understanding of the need to represent the systematic nature of individual differences in perception and preference.

Again working with automobiles, Green, Maheshwari, and Rao (1969a) collected similarities, preferences, and semantic differential ratings from two groups of respondents. Each group rated 11 cars from a 17-car list, with 5 cars in common across groups. They demonstrated stability for the product spaces derived from the similarity measures compared to the spaces derived from profile distances over 20 semantic sales. The set of 5 cars remained stable over changes in surrounding stimuli. Comparison of TORSCA versus parametric mapping showed at least one stable dimension across the two methods.

Green and Carmone (1971) used a three-way INDSCAL analysis to demonstrate that task-specific ratings tap only a subset of the dimensions in the conceptual space of the individuals. Hustad, Mayer, and Whipple (1975) integrated eight usage occasions and context-specific ideal points into an analysis of market structure. Mauser (1980) scaled political candidates along with campaign themes to discover themes that were highly popular and that appealed to a candidate's current supporters.

Green, Wind, and Jain (1972) demonstrated that heterogeneous collections of stimuli can be meaningfully scaled in a common space. Respondents judged the relevance of common personality traits to "other persons'" choices of automobile brands, occupations, and magazines. For each of five cars a respondent was shown a list of 14 personality traits and asked to rank the traits according to the likelihood

that a person who owned that car would possess that trait. This was repeated for five occupations and then for five magazines. Then each respondent was shown, sequentially, two sets of 25 cards each: All combinations of five magazines and five cars formed the first set and five occupations together with five cars formed the second set. These were sorted into four ordered categories to reflect the probability that a person with a particular occupation would own a particular car or that a person who read a particular magazine would own a particular car.

Even though the data were ranked and ordered categories, all variables were converted to standard scores and the Howard–Harris (1966) clustering routine was used to find four homogeneous groups of individuals. Within each group the original 14 trait rankings were averaged over individuals for the 15 cars, occupations, and magazines. Profile Euclidean distances were computed on these average ranks. Acceptable three-dimensional stresses for the TORSCA-8 solutions were found for each group. The occupation-car and magazine-car ordered category scales were averaged within groups. The complex matrix of associations would have nine sections for the Cartesian product of the set of occupations with the set of magazines and the set of cars. With only the occupation-car and magazine-car sections being of interest, the sublist splitting feature of M-D-SCAL V [Kruskal, 1968] was used so that the nonmetric constraints were maintained only over the two sections. Good fits were again obtained in three dimensions for each group.

The two configurations for each of four homogeneous groups of individuals were used as eight pseudo-subjects of an INDSCAL (Carroll and Chang, 1970) analysis by computing interobject distances in each of the configurations. The three-dimensional INDSCAL solution was comparatively easy to interpret in terms of (1) a prestige dimension, (2) a sportiness-versus-conservatism dimension, and (3) something akin to a masculinity-femininity dimension. The respondents' perceptions of object congruences (occupation-car pairs and magazine-car pairs) "were highly associated with the relative nearness of these objects in an independently obtained (reduced) trait space" (p. 208).

If the Perreault and Young (1980) illustration of ALSOS had been available earlier, the rank-order data would not have forced the methodological choices made here. Averaging rank-order data is not a very desirable methodological alternative. Further, profile distances can produce comparatively low stress solutions while doing a relatively poor job of recovering structure [Drasgow and Jones, 1979]. Despite the information loss inherent in the procedures, it does appear that quite heterogeneous item collections can be meaningfully displayed in a common space.

Green and Rao (1972a) used a similar series of methods to develop a master configuration for 15 bakery items that might be eaten at breakfast. Directly judged similarities for men and women in the respondent pool were averaged separately and scaled in three dimensions using TORSCA. The rating of the bakery items on 7-point bipolar scales was averaged for men and women; Mahalanobis distances were computed over 10 scales and the results also scaled in three dimensions by TORSCA. Finally, preference rankings of the items on each of six different usage occasions were averaged for men and women and parametrically mapped onto a stimulus configuration in three dimensions.

The Euclidean interobject distances from these 16 scaling solutions became the input to an INDSCAL analysis. The resulting dimensions (1) separated the meal type items from the snacks, (2) separated the sweet from the nonsweet items, and (3) separated the cake-like items from the bread-like items. The dimensions were correlated. The pseudo-subject dimensional saliences were easily interpretable and gave a clear representation of how different usage occasions corresponded to different dimensional saliences. It is difficult to assess what impact the averaging of ordinal ranks had on these results. Arabie, Carroll, DeSarbo, and Wind (1981) reanalyzed these data and found five overlapping clusters of pastries, food spread with butter, toasted foods, sweet foods, and relatively simple bread foods.

The last two studies involve the imbedding of features into a product space. Green (1974) collected subjective ratings from respondents regarding (1) the degree of belief that if a particular feature i is present, then feature j would also be present in a typical brand, (2) the degree of belief that a particular brand possesses a particular feature, and (3) the desirability of a particular feature in each of a series of usage occasions. For m features, n brands, and p usage occasions this results in an $(m + n + p) \times m$ data matrix for each respondent. Green based his analysis on the average of the subjects' matrices. The two-dimensional configuration from M-D-SCAL V was interpreted as an approximate radex. The circumplex notion did seem to fit to a certain extent. Associated items frequently showed up as neighbors in an MDS configuration. Neighbors connect to other neighbors, forming something like a circumplex regardless of whether or not a simple interpretation exist for the dimensions. In any case, Green's method of imbedding features into a product space is much less ad hoc than Stefflre's method [Brown et al., 1968, p. 464].

Finally, Green, Wind, and Claycamp (1975) developed a master configuration from the same basic data as described above, but with different analyses. Ross and Cliff's (1964) generalization of the interpoint distance model was used to develop three feature configurations, one from each section of the $(m + n + p)$ data matrix for the average individual. Inter-feature distances in these three configurations became pseudo-individuals in an INDSCAL analysis. A five-dimensional solution resulted, with two common dimensions, (that is, natural-artificial and rich-light), and three solution-specific dimensions. The two common dimensions became the target for fitting brands into the space with PREFMAP (vector model) and then for fitting desirability ratings for features of the favorite brand into the space using the ideal point version of PREFMAP. From this master configuration can be judged the aggregated association of features with brands as well as the features desired in a particular favorite brand. Arabie et al. (1981) suggested that overlapping clustering in this master configuration would be particularly interesting.

Probably the least desired result of an MDS study is a product or brand map that seems uninterpretable. The series of studies just described in this subsection offers ways of enriching the interpretability of a perceptual space by positioning features of products, associated life style items, and preferences into the map alongside the brands.

Individual Differences

Although studies of the systematic differences among individuals appear throughout this review, three studies are reported here to introduce the topic. In the first, Kinnear and Taylor (1973) used a response measure, an ecological concern scale, to segment the sample. In the second, Rao (1972) induced individual differences by an experimental design involving the information each respondent received. In the third study, Ritchie (1974) formed groups of individuals by clustering their dimensional weights from an INDSCAL analysis.

Kinnear and Taylor (1973) studied the effects of ecological concerns on the perceptions of consumers of laundry deter-

gents. At the height of concern about water pollution from phosphates and enzymes in detergent, they sampled 500 members of a consumer panel. A behavioral and attitudinal scale of ecological concern was used to segment the sample into five subgroups expressing increasing ecological concern. Similarities judgments for five phosphate detergents, two nonphosphate products and an explicit rating of an ideal detergent were collected before the attitudinal measures were taken. The three-dimensional INDSCAL solution fit quite well and seemed interpretable in terms of a phosphate dimension and two cleaning power dimensions. The analysis of dimensional weights for the five groups demonstrated that the higher a buyer's ecological concern, the more salient is the ecological dimension in perception and the greater is the perceived similarity of brands that are ecologically nondestructive.

Rao (1972) induced individual differences through experimental manipulation of the amount and kind of explicit information provided as a basis for similarity ranking of 12 cars. The $2 \times 2 \times 2$ design (with two empty cells) varied: brands identified or not, semantic descriptions provided or not, and profile descriptions provided or not. The cell with no brands identified, no semantic description, and no profile description was deleted from the design for obvious reasons; and the condition containing both the semantic descriptions and the profile descriptions was deleted to avoid information overload. The three-dimensional INDSCAL solution was interpreted as (1) luxuriousness, (2) domestic versus foreign manufacture, and (3) size. The absence of brand name de-emphasized salience of the origin of manufacture; whereas without semantic descriptions the luxuriousness was de-emphasized; and without the profile information size was de-emphasized. The nature of the information in each category made these findings quite reasonable. The salience differences were still significant after 10 covariates were introduced to account for (nonexperimental) individual differences among subjects.

Ritchie (1974) studied the nature of individual differences in perception of 12 leisure-time activities. Over three trials he found that there was significantly less variation within individuals in INDSCAL saliences than between individuals. However, when he formed five perceptual groups using Johnson's (1967) hierarchical clustering on dimensional weights, he found that the five groups did not differ between groups in interest or participation in the activities and for the most part did not differ in the 18 Rokeach measures of personal values. The problem here may stem from Ritchie's use of hierarchical clustering on differences in dimensional weights. Two individuals on a vector, just differing in length from the origin, will have the same perceptual configuration. They will differ only in the extent to which the scaling model fits the approximate individual scalar products matrix. So differences in perception are better measured by the angle in radians between the vectors for two individuals.

Preferences

Preference is a key concept for understanding the linkage of perceptions to choices. Four approaches to preference research are considered in this section.

1. The huge marketing literature on conjoint analysis merits its own review and is just briefly mentioned here.
2. The analysis of micropreference structures investigates how individual level utility scales can be developed from preference judgments.
3. Internal analysis of preferences attempts to use the preference judgments alone to develop configurations of brands. Some internal analysis techniques attempt to array directions of increasing preference into the brand

maps (that is, vector preference model); whereas other internal analyses of preference attempt to represent the brand perceptions, along with ideal points for individuals or groups, in a joint space.
4. External analysis of preferences attempts to map preference vectors or ideal points onto predetermined perceptual maps to create joint space representations.

Although the first two approaches are treated in subsections of their own, the last two approaches are considered in three subsections on joint space analysis.

Conjoint Analysis Green and Rao (1971b) introduced the marketing research community to conjoint measurement. They tied the general conjoint analysis model to the specific nonmetric MDS model by multidimensionally scaling law enforcement officers' judgments of the severity of different forms of drug abuse. Green, Wind, and Jain (1972) used MDPREF, Chang and Carroll's (1968) internal analysis of preferences, to represent preference heterogeneity in what was basically a conjoint analysis study of dessert preferences; and Green and Devita (1975) used MDPREF on an interaction preference table to provide a graphical aid for interpreting interaction effects in an extended conjoint analysis model.

Micropreference Structures Bechtel and O'Connor (1979) developed analysis of variance (ANOVA) tests for micropreference structures (Bechtel, 1976). The first test on the graded paired comparison preference ratings (that is, ratings of the strength and direction of preferences) attempts to determine individual level utility scale values for the objects. In an application to soft drink preferences from Cooper (1973), 51 of the 52 respondents had statistically significant utility scales. They were then retained for further tests, which attempted to determine if individual utility scales were mediated by a vector model using perceptual attributes. In this case the perceptual attributes were the first dimension scale values (a cola versus noncola dimension) for the soft drinks from a metric scaling of similarities [Cooper, 1972] and the mean familiarity ratings of the soft drinks. Under the hypothesis of a common perceptual configuration using these two attributes, the ANOVA model rejected the fit of the vector model at the individual level in this example. The preferences seemed too idiosyncratic to be predicted from a common perceptual configuration.

Bechtel and O'Connor (1979) also provided a segment-based analysis of Dutch schoolchildren's national preferences. The preference measures came from the logit of the proportion of children in segment i preferring nation j to nation k. The overall utility scale was statistically significant, as were the segment utility scales for Grades 2 through 6. "Utility scales broaden strikingly with increasing age, indicating better preferential discrimination among older children" (p. 255). There was also a small, but statistically significant, amount of systematic unscalability. (Systematic unscalability was also significant in the aggregate of soft drink preferences.)

Bechtel's (1976) tests allow for very fine grained assessment of the fit of particular multiattribute structures to individual or segment preferences. Bechtel (1981) further developed this logit preference model.

Joint Space Analyses The typical integration of similarities and preferences is illustrated by Green, Carmone, and Fox (1969), who used TORSCA on similarity judgments among 38 television programs and followed with Carroll and Chang's (1967) and Carroll's (1972) external analyses of preferences (PREFMAP). The Doyle and McGee (1973) study of the market structure of convenience foods and Percy's (1975) study of potato side dishes are similar examples.

Best (1976) took a much closer look at joint space modeling as a potential theory of individual choice. Although price considerations did not enter his study, Best did track choices among eight soft drinks over a 12-week period (that is, 2 weeks to adjust to the apparatus and two 5-week consumption periods). At the midpoint of each consumption period, conditional rank order similarity judgments and rank order brand preference were collected. From the first consumption period a readily interpretable three-dimensional INDSCAL solution was selected. PREFMAP was used to imbed ideal points for all 77 individuals.

Inspection of the relation of ideal distances and choice proportions from the first period led to the specification of five different mathematical functions relating distance from the ideal point to product choice. Ten people were represented with a disjunctive model (that is, the brand closest to the ideal point dominated the choices). Forty-five people were represented by a hyperbolic model (that is, choice probability tapered off dramatically with increasing distance from the ideal point). Four people were represented by a conjunctive, relevant set model (that is, all brands within a certain distance from the ideal point had an equal probability of being chosen). Four people were represented by a linear model. A polynomial model was needed to represent 10 people; these people were dieters who had nondiet ideal points for preferences. Brands very near their ideal points had a low probability of being chosen, as did brands that were very far away. The diet brands nearest the nondiet ideals had the greatest probability of being chosen. Finally, four people were represented by a random model.

Thus, 73 of 77 models provided sensible calibration results. Although brand preferences were stable over consumption periods, brand choices were not.

Fifty-seven of the 73 provided significant prediction of future brand choices. The drop-off was partly attributable to six individuals who went off their diets in the second consumption period.

Huber (1975) compared five models for predicting preferences for different levels of tea and sugar in iced tea. All models were developed on 16 experimental compounds in a lattice design (based on the logs of the sugar concentration and tea concentration) and were used to forecast preferences for seven validation examples within the lattice. The three best models were an ideal point model mapped onto the physical space, a naive model that simply averaged preferences for the four nearest neighbors, and an additive part-worth model. Not too far behind in forecasting ability were an ideal point model in a psychological space and an additive model weighted by perceptual scale values. For all but the naive model it was possible to compare metric versions for the forecasts of each model with corresponding nonmetric versions. Although there was considerable congruence between the results within models, the metric version produced consistently superior results.

Marketing researchers have developed alternatives to the multiple regression approach of PREFMAP. Srinivasan and Shocker (1973) developed a linear programming technique for the external analysis of ordinal preference judgments, which they termed LINMAP [see Hopkins, Larreche, and Massy, 1977, for a typical application]. Pekelman and Sen (1974) developed a mathematical programming model that was very similar to LINMAP.

Explicit Versus Implicit Ideal Points in Joint Space Representations Another approach to joint space analysis requests that the respondent explicitly rate an "ideal" product along with the other objects being compared, as was done by Kinnear and Taylor (1973). The ideal point for the respondents is the position of the "ideal" prod-

uct in the perceptual space. Day (1972) compared cognitive consistency theories of attitude structure and multidimensional scaling using this approach. Specifically, he was interested in comparing the representation of preferences obtained from Lehmann's (1971a) ideal distance model (based on specific attribute measurements) with two nonmetric joint space representations: one with an explicit "ideal" product rated along with the other objects and the other representation obtained through external analysis of preferences.

The heuristic comparison between Lehmann's model and the nonmetric MDS approaches favored MDS "because they [MDS approaches] demand less complex and fragmented data from respondents" (p. 284). The explicit versus implicit ideal point comparison revealed a modest displacement between the average explicit and average implicit ideal points. However, the rank orders of the preferences from the two points were almost perfectly correlated. Further, Lehmann obtained considerable variation in preferences depending on the specific usage context (that is, preference judgments were not context-free).

Holbrook and Williams (1978) compared the INDSCAL representation of 12 female singers collected with and without explicit ideal points. Their concern was with the affective halo that sometimes surrounds multiattribute judgments of brands (Fry and Claxton, 1971, went so far as to average scores for only those respondents who did not prefer a brand in order to avoid halo effects in the attribute space they compared to their MDS representation). Holbrook and Williams found that the inclusion of an explicit ideal point did not distort the configuration of the other 12 singers. A clear two-dimensional interpretation (that is, ethnic membership and contemporaneity of style) appeared in both configurations. The 66 intersinger distances correlated around 0.95.

The explicit ideal point approach is quite interesting but does create some problems. It is inappropriate to consider one person's judgments involving explicit ideal points to be comparable to other respondents. Averaging across respondents can distort the position of the explicit ideal point even if the positions of the other products are undisturbed.

Recent Developments in Joint Space Analysis Some of the more recent applications of joint space analyses have come from Moore, Holbrook, and their colleagues. Moore, Pessemier, and Little (1979) applied Schönemann and Wang's (1972) unfolding model in three product classes: cake mixes, household cleaners, and toothpastes. They used Pessemier's dollar metric for graded paired comparison preferences in which respondents estimate a monetary value for the difference in their preference [Pessemier, Burger, Teach, and Tigert, 1971]. After development of the configurations, interpoint distances in the Joint Space were used to estimate purchase probabilities. They noted the tendency of the dollar metric to underpredict preferences for more preferred brands and to overpredict those for less preferred brands. Using a power transformation of the scale values to predict purchase probabilities corrected substantially for the bias. The corresponding predictions were made from the nonmetric unfolding option of KYST. For toothpastes and cake mixes the Schönemann and Wang (1972) model produced statistically superior predictions. For household cleaners KYST was slightly, but not significantly, better.

Holbrook, Moore, and Winer (1982) applied Levine's (1979) procedure for developing joint space solutions from "pick any" data. In marketing research this is like a "relevant" set model in which a consumer picks from a large list or simply recalls all the brands he or she would consider purchasing. In Levine's model a person's ideal point is located at the centroid of all the brands he or she picks, and a brand is located at the centroid of all the people who pick it. Holbrook, Moore, and Winer (1982) applied the model to the representation of radio listenership data, a large stimulus set, which no one person could judge individually. They scaled 1,380 respondents based on 25 radio stations, demonstrating the utility of the method when most other methods are inappropriate or impractical. They also applied the analysis to soft drinks and compared the representation to that obtained using KYST. The results were quite similar when both techniques could be applied. The problems that can be encountered with Levine's (1979) technique stems from (1) individuals who only rate one brand; (2) instability of the much less popular brands (since their positions may be under-determined); and (3) the pulling of the most popular brand to the center of the configuration (for example, Crest was in almost everyone's relevant set and thus positioned at the centroid of the respondents).

Moore (1982) and Moore and Holbrook (1982) studied the predictive power of joint space models using "hold out" brands and hold out concepts. This approach, which was also used in the validation of the Pekelman and Sen (1974) mathematical programming model for attribute weights, tries to validate the predictive ability of a joint space representation by assessing how well preferences or choices for different brands can be forecast once they are placed into existing joint space configurations. Moore and Holbrook found a marked deterioration in predictive power when joint spaces were derived on real objects and used to predict new concepts. They have suggested conjoint analysis as a more sound approach.

Moore (1982) found that perceptual spaces built from discriminant analysis used with external vector models performed better across frequently purchased goods, compact cars, and services. Whereas the conjoint model or multiple discriminant analysis may be superior in these applications, the use of holdout brands is questionable. Without a model for how preferences change over the sets of brands or concepts that form the judgment contexts, one should be wary of holdout brands. Their use basically assumes what is rarely true (that is, that preferences and choices are context-free [Cooper and Nakanishi, 1983]. New-product models, discussed at the end of this review, need to deal specifically with this issue. Even in a new-product context, however, it is most often only one additional choice alternative that the context must absorb, not six breeds of dogs, as in Moore and Holbrook (1982), or an unspecified number of frequently purchased goods, compact cars, and unnamed services, as in Moore (1982).

Market Segmentation

Johnson (1971) said, *"market segmentation analysis refers to examination of the structure of a market as perceived by consumers, preferably using a geometric spatial model, and to forecasting the intensity of demand for a potential product positioned anywhere in the space"* (p. 13). Accordingly, Johnson discussed the uses of MDS and other mapping techniques in a manner very similar to market structure analysis, product positioning analysis, and any of the joint space methods previously discussed.

A more traditional approach to market segmentation has been presented by Wind (1978). He indicated that the classic price discrimination model provides a major theoretical rationale for the segmentation concept. Most simply, the price discrimination model rests on downward sloping demand curves in a plot of price (y) versus quantity (x). Even at a high price, some individuals would demand a product. As price drops, the quantity demanded would increase. With a single fixed price for a product, there is no ability to retrieve the

"consumer surplus" (that is, the area in the plot above the price line but below the demand curve). From this point of view, market segmentation becomes a strategy for differentiating consumers so as to retrieve as much as possible of the consumer surplus. Thus, Wind's discussion of the uses of MDS focused more on the grouping of consumers than the positioning of products. The same physical bundle of benefits may need different packaging, promotion, advertising, pricing, and distribution through different retail outlets to attract different consumer segments. He foresaw great potential for the use of overlapping clustering in this domain.

Young, Ott, and Feigin (1978) differentiated segmentation on generic benefits from product-usage-purpose segmentation and from styling segmentation. The latter case is for products in which "the style, looks, appearance, or image is the overriding criterion of marketing success" (p. 410). It is in this type of segmentation that they deemed multidimensional scaling more appropriate.

Market Structure Models Using Asymmetric Data

Lehmann's (1972) study of market structure using brand switching data demonstrated the different emphasis transition data gave to a nonmetric MDS solution. The emphasis on interbrand substitutability gives results more akin to preference mappings than to similarity scalings [Cooper, 1973]. Lehmann's (1972) analysis, however, actually eliminated the asymmetries by forming a weighted average. MDS analyses that maintained the basic asymmetries of brand-switching data are a very recent development. Harshman, Green, Wind, and Lundy (1982) recently introduced the DEcomposition into DIrectional COMponents (DEDICOM) model to the marketing literature. They reported a reanalysis of part of the free-association data from Green, Wind, and Jain

(1973) and an analysis of car trade-in data from the 1979 model year. Brand-switching data are very important in marketing research, and the DEDICOM model should enjoy wide use. It is, however, quite different from the spatial MDS model that marketing researchers have come to understand in that it requires ratio scale data. Although some discussion of its applicability to interval scale data is presented, marketing researchers would be well advised to apply DEDICOM to the obvious and available frequency-of-purchase data or transition probability data. As a hybrid between MDS and factor analysis, the use of interval scale data calls for "factoring" the double-centered score matrix. The model for the factoring of double-centered score matrices is very complex [Tucker, 1956, 1968]. There should be many applications of DEDICOM in marketing using the data for which it is primarily intended. The analysis of trade-in data for cars is an excellent example of the kind of thinking required to understand asymmetric flows.

New Product Planning

Although the comprehensive new-product models are discussed at the end of this review, there is other research worth noting here. Morgan and Purnell (1969) are often cited for their research on isolating openings for new products in multidimensional space. They actually used factor analysis and cluster analysis to get their product spaces. Lehmann (1974) investigated the usage of TORSCA on linear and polynomial intercorrelations as an alternative to factor analysis in a new product setting. Albers and Brockhoff (1977) structured the new product positioning issue as a mixed integer programming problem [Pekelman and Sen, 1974]. Roberts and Taylor (1975) used multivariate analysis of variance (MANOVA) to show that design effects of new products can be traced by MDS and are open to

statistical confirmation. Silk and Urban (1978) just mentioned the role of MDS in new product development; their illustration of the ASSESSOR model used constant sum scaling of preferences rather than MDS.

PRICING

The two pricing studies reported here rely on the Lancaster model (1966a, 1966b, 1971), Ryans' (1974) description of Lancaster's approach:

> In contrast to the traditional economic theory of consumer demand, which treats the products themselves as the basic unit of analysis, Lancaster's theory is based on viewing products as bundles of product characteristics. Lancaster assumes that these characteristics are objective, measurable attributes of the product [p. 435].

Ryans proceeded by invoking the limited information-processing capacity of consumers. Durable goods have many objective, measurable characteristics, and the consumer will probably rely on only a few "perceived" characteristics. These perceived characteristics were represented with nonmetric MDS in Ryans' study.

Lancaster further assumed that "individuals do not differ in their assessment of the amount of characteristics possessed by a given product" [Ryans, 1974, p. 435]. Ryans dealt with this behaviorally unrealistic assumption by forming clusters that were perceptually homogeneous and by analyzing each cluster separately. Ryans' model assumed that a consumer buying a durable good purchased a brand and the other goods and services that together maximized his/her total satisfaction while meeting his/her budget constraint. Thus, any money conserved is used for utility-generating purposes. The analysis group rated 12 electric blenders. The three validation groups rated 13 blenders, with the last blender presented with three different prices but with the other product characteristics the same. The similarity ratings on which the product space was developed were collected before the price information was introduced. After the introduction of price, rating scale judgments were collected, followed by preference rankings.

The data collection procedure allowed the testing of two assumptions. The first assumption is that the introduction of a dynamically continuous innovation (that is, a new product with a combination of features, that are also present in possibly different amounts in other products in the market) will not affect consumers' perceptions of the characteristics of other products. A good congruence between the 12-product MDS solution and the 13-product solution supported this assumption. The second assumption was that price would not act as a surrogate for quality and thereby affect the perceived amounts of the other characteristics possessed by the new product. That is, the different price tags would not result in different attribute ratings for the same product. Only the attribute scale dealing with high price versus low price varied significantly over validation groups. Ryans (1974) estimated a quadratic utility function [PREFMAP-Model I; Carroll, 1972] on the positions of the brands in a three-dimensional space from M-D-SCAL-5M. The utility function and price were used to predict the rank-order preferences for the new product among the 12 other products. The STRESSes of the solutions for the various clusters seemed somewhat high, and the overall predictions of rankings from the quadratic utility formulation seemed modest. The best prediction, however, occurred in the proportions of first, second, and third rankings, which is the arena of greatest interest.

Hauser and Simmie (1981) postulated a simplified lens model of consumer decision making. Physical features and psychosocial cues lead to perceptions, which in turn lead to preferences. Constraints such as budgets join preferences in

leading to choice, and choice feeds back to perceptions. Expressing the belief that good models exist for the other linkages, Hauser and Simmie concentrated on the mapping of physical features onto perceptions. To generalize the notion of an efficient frontier in perceptual space for the "rational consumer" requires the heroic assumption that an absolute origin can be found for the spatial representation. Thus, in the case of analgesics, gentleness and efficacy dimensions could be transformed into gentleness per dollar and efficacy per dollar. The "per dollar" notion is needed in their analysis to make possible the definition of an efficient frontier for the decisions of a "rational consumer." Since the origin of MDS configurations is arbitrary, MDS does not seem to be a candidate for constructing the perceptual spaces on which the Hauser and Simmie arguments are based. Neither, then, are the spaces derived from factor analysis or multiple discriminant analyses. These are not techniques that yield ratio scaled dimensions.

Although the issue of locating the origin to the perceptual space makes it difficult to understand the applications of rational consumer theory, one of Hauser and Simmie's (1981) theorems deals with consumers, rather than with the convenient fiction of "rational consumers." Their third theorem states:

> If the consumer evaluates products in perceptual space, then any consumer analysis that does not consider the perceptual mapping, F (from physical characteristics to perceptual positions), could identify "consumer optimal" combinations of product which are not efficient ... [p. 41].

This theorem, which they prove by counterexample, has very important implications. Although for the "rational consumer" optimality in the perceptual space implies optimality in the space of physical characteristics, for the real consumer the perceptual analysis holds primacy. Whenever perceptions mediate preferences, the perceptual space is the place in which optimality analysis should occur.

Understanding the impact of pricing on brand perception is problematic within the traditional MDS framework. Price as an attribute of a brand seems much easier to study experimentally by using conjoint measurement designs or by using multiattribute choice models [Cooper and Nakanishi, 1983]. One area seemingly ripe for investigation is how price sensitivity might vary with perceptual position (for example, proximity to an ideal point). Such a study would parallel Clarke's (1978) analysis of advertising effectiveness by perceptual position, discussed below in the section on advertising.

BRANDING

Although selection of a brand name for a new product is one of the tasks Steffire (1968) and others have undertaken within a MDS framework, no studies have been published, to the author's knowledge, which deal solely with other aspects of the problems of branding.

The selection of trademarks is an area in which the relation of visual images and the semantic image they connote could be important. The Young, Ott, and Feigin (1978) study indicating the utility of MDS in segmentation based on style or image seems to highlight some potential uses of MDS in evaluating trademarks. The Green and McMennamin (1973) approach to advertising problems, discussed below in the section on advertising, could also be used for many problems in branding.

The Rao (1972) study, which included a manipulation of whether or not brand information was provided along with semantic descriptions or profile description, indicated some potential uses of MDS in determining the benefits of various branding policies.

CHANNELS OF DISTRIBUTION

Products flow from the manufacturer to the consumer through the channels of distribution. The studies that deal with this topic focus mainly on the relations among different retail outlets. Though market segmentation by types of retail outlets is very clearly within the "price discrimination" approach to segmentation [Wind, 1978], no MDS research was found on this topic.

MacKay and Olshavsky (1975) studied the differences between cognitive maps of retail locations based on MDS of proximity judgments and those based on hand drawings. They found that although hand-drawn maps were more like physical maps than are MDS maps, the MDS maps related more closely to preferences and actual shopping behavior. Olshavsky, MacKay, and Sentell (1975) found that distances from MDS maps correlated better (more negatively) with shopping behavior than did distance from actual maps.

The classic example of a necktie that sells at one price in a department store and at a much higher price in a men's specialty store, indicates some interesting possibilities for MDS research involving channels of distribution. Part of a product or brand image might interact with the images of different retail venues. Research that required judgments on the compatibility of brands with different retail outlets could lead to joint space representations or master configurations that would be useful for marketing decision making.

PERSONAL SELLING

Only two MDS studies related specifically to personal selling. Turner (1971) used nonmetric MDS to infer the number and kinds of criteria that individual salesmen used in evaluating their customers. Such an analysis becomes very similar to Klahr's (1969) study of the evaluation criteria of college admissions officers. Green and McMennamin (1973) took a different approach in one of their examples of market position analysis. A large computer firm hosted a study that first mapped the physical characteristics of the computer and its competition into what they called a "performance space." The similarity judgments on the computer models were collected from salesmen, customers, and noncustomers:

> The sales personnel's perceptions agreed most closely with the objective (performance) positioning of the computer models. However, the firm's customers' perceptions disagreed in significant ways with the sales personnel's perceptions, suggesting that the sales people were not emphasizing certain performance characteristics of the company's line that would enhance customer satisfaction [p. 502].

Interpretation of the separate analyses suggested specific differences in orientation of customers and noncustomers.

ADVERTISING

There are three areas in which MDS has been used as part of advertising research. The first involves how MDS can be used to track the effectiveness of advertisements in repositioning or changing a brand image. The second area deals with the compatibility of attributes or slogans with the perceptual image of a brand and the competitive brands. The third area deals with how advertising effectiveness varies with perceptual position.

In the first area there are two studies: Smith and Lusch (1976) and Perry, Izraeli, and Perry (1976). Smith and Lusch (1976) tried to use nonmetric MDS to assess how advertising can position a brand. Liggett and Myer wanted L&M cigarettes to be considered a "full-flavored" cigarette. They changed the tobacco blend, filter, and

package design, and launched a "massive advertising campaign" (p. 39). The promotion occurred in selected West Coast cities, which enabled Smith and Lusch to study perceptual positions before and after with a control group. Smallest Space Analysis [SSA; Guttman, 1968] on the similarity ratings before the campaign confirmed that L&M was generally not positioned among full-flavored brands. Compared to the "random movements" for the before-and-after measurements of the control group, there was no significant shift in the position of L&M six weeks after the advertising campaign began.

Perry, Izraeli, and Perry (1976) used SSA to track changes in Israeli's perceptions of Canada as a vacation spot before and after the introduction of direct flights to Canada. In this study considerable change in perception was obvious.

The differences between the two studies are instructive. Five months elapsed between measurement occasions in the vacation study. Only six weeks elapsed between measurement occasions in the cigarette study. The increased time alone could produce perceptual changes. The first measurement occurred before the air route was established in the vacation study. Thus, the advertising program for vacationing by air to Canada was much more distinctive than the ads for a reblended cigarette. Only people who indicated that they either had traveled abroad during the last two years or had intended to do so in the subsequent two years were included in the Perry et al. (1976) study. This is a very specific and select audience. (Although only smokers were used in the Smith and Lusch, 1976, study, this was a much less exclusive group.) Finally, no control group was available in the Perry et al. (1976) study. Though the perceptual changes seem large and systematic, Perry et al. did not compare the changes to random movement. The Hanno and Jones (1973) jackknife technique could have been used to test changes against random movements.

In the second area, dealing with the compatibility of brand images and slogans, Green and McMennamin (1973) briefly described three studies in which MDS addressed such advertising problems. The first case dealt with the evaluation of 15 potential new slogans for a soft drink. MDS showed that 11 of the slogans "were perceived as more closely associated with the images of one or more competitive brands than the firm's own brand" (p. 502). In the second case, a cereal marketer found that an advertising campaign emphasizing the good taste and high nutritional value succeeded in positioning their cereal closer to the "good tasting" cereals than any of the other high nutrition cereals. In the third case, five potential advertising copy ideas for an over-the-counter drug were evaluated in an MDS study of physicians, since physicians' recommendations were the source of the early purchases of the drug. The firm's favorite appeal was perceived by the physicians as being more relevant to the leading (competitor's) product. The most popular appeal was thought, before the study, to be too "soft sell." Green and McMennamin (1973) proceeded by providing a detailed illustration of how market position analysis could help develop an advertising strategy for fabric softeners. As indicated earlier, this approach could be useful in problems related to branding.

Finally, one of the most fascinating uses of MDS in marketing was Clarke's (1978) merging of MDS and econometric analysis to expand the scope of competitive advertising models. He conjectured:

> ... it would seem that the advertising of two brands which are considered close substitutes for each other should affect each other's sales more than would the advertising of the third brand which is not viewed by consumers as a near substitute [p. 1687].

He described a situation in which Products A and B are close together in a product space and Product C is relatively far away. A differential cross-elasticity (that is, the advertising expenditures of Product B should have a different impact on sales for Product A than the advertising expenditures of Product C would have on Product A) would be expected. For the case in which an ideal point has been imbedded in the product space, relative distance to the ideal point replaced interproduct distances in Clarke's (1978) analysis. He developed an advertising modification function involving expenditures and either interproduct distance or distance to the ideal point. This is a ratio scale analysis but does not encounter Hauser and Simmie's (1981) problem with arbitrary origins, since Clarke (1978) used ratio distances within the configuration, not scale values for products on the axes. Clarke derived self-elasticities and cross-elasticities for advertising expenditures which do account for perceptual positioning. He also derived an expression for optimal advertising expenditures. His theoretical developments overshadowed his empirical demonstration. The illustration dealt with nine anonymous brands in a 100-brand market. Similarities were collected from students some 10 years after the last data in the econometric stream were gathered. Such an illustration showed only that the estimates could be produced. There is almost no substantive explanation for the fact that particular brands enjoyed differentially effective advertising.

FACT FINDING AND ANALYSIS

Marketing researchers have made many methodological contributions to MDS research. This section reports contributions to understanding response rate, time, and accuracy; validity, reliability, and stability; and robustness of data collection procedures as well as robustness of the scaling algorithms.

Data Collection—Response Rate, Time, and Accuracy

Neidell's (1972) comparison of data collected by triadic combinations, rotating anchors (that is, the conditional rank order task), and semantic differential scales was in much the same style as earlier research on unidimensional methods [Greenberg and Collins, 1966; Kassarjian and Nakanishi, 1967; van de Sandt, 1970]. Neidell (1972) found rotating anchor points were comparable to semantic differential ratings in terms of quality and quantity of responses in mail surveys. Both methods were better than triadic combinations of these criteria.

Henry and Stumpf (1975) and McIntyre and Ryans (1977) added consideration of time and accuracy to their analysis of different data collection techniques for MDS. Henry and Stumpf (1975) varied set size and studied rank ordering, triadic comparison, and anchor point rankings. All were compared in terms of time, and the last two were compared for accuracy in terms of the number of intransitivities. There was no significant difference in accuracy, but the time analysis ranked anchor point methods as fastest, followed by rank ordering and triadic comparisons. McIntyre and Ryans (1977) compared graded paired comparisons to the conditional rank order task used by Henry and Stumpf (1975). Graded paired comparisons turned out to be faster, without significant loss of accuracy. Graded paired comparisons were perceived by respondents to be a less boring and a less difficult task.

Data Collection—Validity, Reliability, and Stability

Summers and MacKay (1976) found only a modest correlation of judgments (rank order similarities) over a 1-month period, only modest congruence in the individual perceptual spaces over this time period, and only modest ability of individuals to select a mapping of their own judgments from an aggregate map. Narayana (1976), on the other hand, found no significant difference in soft drink perceptions over 10 weeks. The major difference between these two studies indicates that if it is desirable to emphasize stability, single analysis should be done (for example, INDSCAL) over occasions, as did Narayana, and changes should be looked for in weights. If it is desirable to emphasize instability, raw judgment vectors should be correlated, as did Summers and MacKay, or individual level perception spaces should be matched.

Moinpour, McCullough, and MacLachlan (1976) showed that if there can be control for structural shifts in frames of reference, INDSCAL analysis of shifts in salience over time can be an effective, conservative method for tracing the impact of persuasive communications. Day, Deutscher, and Ryans (1976) added level of aggregation to their study of reliability. High reliability with relatively poor fits indicated substantial heterogeneity among respondents. Their coefficient of reliability compared the rank order correlation of the original rankings and the later rankings with the rank order correlation of the first ranking and the repeated judgments, assuming their worst possible values. Deutscher (1982) has reviewed these reliability studies in more detail.

Robustness of Data Collection Techniques and MDS Algorithms

Green and Rao (1971a) studied the ability of individual differences models to recover synthetic configurations. The letter R was represented as 15 points in a two-dimensional space. Fifteen subjects were simulated by differentially shrinking or stretching the configuration. Into each configuration eight "property vectors" were imbedded at random angles from the origin, and the eight reflections of those vectors were also imbedded. The "rating" of each point on each vector became one of the 16 elements in each individual's profile. Excellent recovery of the interpoint distances between pairs of profiles could be obtained from the ratings using multiple discriminant analysis, factor analysis of scalar products, INDSCAL analysis, TORSCA on the average distances, and M-D-SCAL IV using the individual differences, nonmetric option. For comparison, the ratings were downgraded to zeros and ones, with mean or higher ratings receiving the one. This was to simulate the effect of Stefflre's [Brown et al., 1968] data collection procedures. For the zero-one data interpoint distance, correlations between final and original configurations ranged from about 0.76 to about -0.02, with factor analysis of scalar products and M-D-SCAL IV showing the worst recovery.

Green (1975b) summarized earlier simulation results on the recovery of structure in structureless data and reported that the simple integer-rank transformations of dissimilarities prior to nonmetric MDS was effective in minimizing the impact of strange transformations of distances. Regarding metric MDS he found that selection of the appropriate additive constant did have a pronounced impact on the recovery of structure. Rao and Katz (1971) simulated large data sets collected by seven different procedures. Although no method recovered structure perfectly, the pick-k-and-order methods produced better recoveries than the subjective grouping methods (for example, sort into k groups). Individual differences models produced poorer recoveries than the group scaling methods, and nonmetric group methods performed better than metric group methods.

Whipple (1976) compared data collection methods and nonmetric MDS algorithms. Four preference rankings and one triadic preference ranking, bipolar ratings, attribute-cued rankings (for example, the objects are ranked on the attribute of product safety), rotating anchor point rankings, and triadic proximity comparisons among seven children's toys formed nine data sets, which were scaled using five nonmetric MDS routines (that is, elastic MDS [EMD; McGee, 1966], M-D-SCAL 5, TORSCA, SSA-I, and KYST). Young and Appelbaum (1968) showed all these routines to be minimized by the same set of scale values even though the objective functions varied for some. A KYST analysis of the 21 interpoint distances from each of the 45 solutions (that is, 9 times 5) showed that there was no algorithmic difference, that all the preference ranking solutions clustered together, and that the bipolar ratings all clustered tightly, as did the attribute-cued rankings and the direct judged proximities.

Green and Maheshwari (1970) simulated conditional rank order data from an underlying configuration and varied the method of analysis (TORSCA versus direct unfolding using M-D-SCAL IV), the extent of ties in the data, and the level of noise. A three-way ANOVA on Fisher's Z from the recovery correlations showed significant interactions between level of ties and level of error; significant interaction between method of analysis and level of error; and significant main effects for analyses, level of ties, and level of error. Jain and Pinson (1976) used MANOVA to investigate the effects of order of presentation, attentional instructions, and degree of commitment. In judging eight U.S. cities, no significant differences were found.

Miscellany

Day and Heeler (1971) compared principal components analysis, hierarchical clustering, and nonmetric MDS as a basis for clustering. The clusters were to be used as a matching device for in-store experiments [Green, Frank and Robinson, 1967a]. Principal components was chosen over nonmetric MDS "because it was more economical and did not appear to distort the data excessively" (p. 346). Hauser and Koppelman (1979) favored factor analysis over discriminant analysis and over similarity scaling for producing perceptual maps. They used predictive validity, interpretability, and ease of use as their criteria. Although some part of their conclusion seems application specific (that is, modeling shopping center images), the controversy regarding the best method for perceptual mapping continues.

Worthy of mention is the early exchange of articles and letters to the editor on distance measures in cluster analysis [Morrison, 1967; Schuchman, 1967] and nonmetric MDS [Green, Frank, and Robinson, 1967b; Green and Rao, 1969]. In response to the very high expectations set by these early discussions of MDS, Green, Frank and Robinson (1967b) ended by noting, "we tried to build a dog house. Already you want to throw a convention in it!" (p. 841).

NEW PRODUCT MODELS

Understanding of the use of MDS in comprehensive new-product models is aided by the delineation of stages given in Shocker and Srinivasan's (1979b) review of product concept generation and evaluation studies. They discussed five stages: (1) determination of the relevant product markets, (2) identification of the determinant attributes, (3) creation of the perceptual product spaces, (4) modeling individual or segment decision making, and (5) evaluation of/search for new product concepts. Since the first four of these directly involve MDS, they will be discussed in turn.

Determination of Relevant Product Markets

The determination of relevant product markets is the stage of defining or articulating the market in which the new product must compete. Srinivasan and Shocker (1973) suggested use of Stefflre's

[Brown et al., 1968] product by usage matrix, which could be multidimensionally scaled to articulate the market. A possibly useful analysis here would be Levine's (1979) analysis of "pick-any" data [Holbrook, Moore, and Winer 1982]. Although the analysis was developed for preference data, its adaption to market definition seems promising. As indicated earlier, respondents would be asked to select all the products they would consider purchasing. Products would be positioned at the center of all the respondents who selected them. Products close together would tend to be those that were the most intersubstitutable.

Srinivasan and Shocker (1973) suggested nonmetric MDS of similarities for market determination. Many illustrations of this type of application have been reviewed earlier, but several methodological problems remain. To allow consumers to generate the market definition should incline researchers to specify an overly large list of potential competitors. At this early stage of development, the focus should be broad. Paired comparisons, conditional rankings, ratings, or other standard data collection techniques would take a great deal of time with long product lists and would lead to a great deal of missing data or ratings of unfamiliar products. The pick-any format of Levine's procedure resolves some of these problems and merits more study.

Identification of the Determinant Attributes

Determinant attributes are traditionally defined as those attributes that distinguish the product alternatives and are probably determinants of brand choice. One should be cautious in emphasizing the need for determinant attributes to distinguish among existing alternatives. If an important attribute does not distinguish among existing alternatives, new alternatives might be positioned so as to be distinct along that attribute.

MDS has obvious uses here. Along with other techniques, MDS was fused for this purpose by Lehmann (1971b), Wind (1973, 1977), Srinivasan and Shocker (1973), Urban (1975), and Hauser and Urban (1977). The advantage of MDS in this context is that it allows the researcher to discover the relevant attributes. The similarities question is probably the most neutral question in the social sciences. It allows the respondent to bring a personal frame of reference to the judgment task, rather than having one imposed by a prescribed list of attributes on which the product alternatives are rated. With this neutrality comes the potential problems of interpretability, the possibility that the results will be a mixture of class and quantitative variation, rather than a strict dimensional representation, and the possibility that dimensions relevant for similarities judgments are not relevant for choice.

The solution of these problems does not come from accepting only a few dimensions in an MDS space. The emphasis of marketing researchers on low-dimensional MDS representations could mean that only the obvious will be discovered. It would be wise to remember the words of Heracleitus of Ephesus, "If you do not expect it, you will not find out the unexpected, as it is hard to be sought out and difficult."

Creation of Perceptual Product Spaces

The creation of perceptual product spaces can be achieved by factor analysis, discriminant analysis, direct measurement of "determinant attributes," or MDS. Wind (1973, 1977), Hustad, Mayer, and Whipple (1975), Urban (1975), and Hauser and Urban (1977) used MDS. All except Urban assumed that different market segments have common perceptual frames of reference. Urban considered clustering individuals on their INDSCAL weights, clustering factor scores, or determining

clusters by obverse factor analysis or by the Tucker and Messick (1963) model. Shocker and Srinivasan (1979b) considered a common framework *obligatory*: "This is because evaluation and/or search for desirable new concepts requires that it be feasible to evaluate a large number of candidates efficiently.... Such tasks are difficult, and would be virtually impossible were it necessary to coordinate multiple customer spaces with a single manufacturer's space" (p. 167).

The emphasis on low dimensionality and the rotational determinacy of techniques such as INDSCAL may not be the allies of the marketing researcher in the creation of perceptual product spaces. What would be beneficial is a representation of individual differences that had some perceptual dimensions common to all and some dimensions that, although relevant to some subsets of individuals, were not relevant to others. Such a representation could create distinct, perceptually homogeneous segments but with a sense of which dimensions were shared over segments and which dimensions were not. Although it might be possible to achieve this representation with a high dimensional INDSCAL solution, it seems that something from the family of individual differences models for MDS [Tucker, 1972; Tucker and Messick, 1963] would be more suited for the task. Evaluation of new concepts in this overall higher dimensional representation might present some problems, but there is no reason to expect them to be insurmountable.

Modeling Individual or Segment Decision Making

Srinivasan and Shocker (1973) imbedded ideal points into the product space with their LINMAP procedure. They modeled the probabilities of all choices as a decreasing function of distance from the ideal point and modeled first choice as the product nearest the ideal point. Hustad et al. (1975) mapped preferences using PREFMAP but did not model choice [Pessemier, 1975; Pessemier and Root, 1973]. Pessemier (1975) mapped his dollar metric preferences into the product space with PREFMAP and implicitly used a Luce (1959) model to represent choice (Pessemier, 1975; Pessemier and Root, 1973). Wind (1973, 1977) imbedded ideal points with PREFMAP and indicated that probability of purchase was not a decreasing function of distance from the ideal point. Urban (1975) also used PREFMAP or LINMAP as a basis for predicting long-run market share. Hauser and Urban (1977) used the same preference mapping but used the multinomial logit model to forecast market share, as did Hauser and Koppelman (1979) and Hauser and Simmie (1981).

The linkages from perceptions of preferences to choice probabilities or market shares are important for marketing research. Forecasts of market-level activity (for example, market share) are best done by procedures that integrate consumer-level measurements (for example, MDS results) with market-level measurements (for example, price, promotional expenditures, availability). This would seem to make the multinomial logit model a robust choice, since information from numerous sources could be combined with MDS results into market forecasts. A very large stumbling block, however, is the independence from irrelevant alternatives (IIA) assumptions that goes along with traditional applications of the multinomial logit model. Particularly in a new product context, it seems more reasonable to model explicitly the effects of changes in the composition of choice sets than to assume, in essence, that there are no effects.

Batsell (1980, 1981) has been working on an MDS approach to the IIA problem. As did Clarke (1978) in his work on differential advertising cross-elasticities, Batsell (1980, 1981) has used interbrand distances as a measure of substitutability

which combines with a measure of utility to predict choice probabilities. Currim (1982) described his own and other recent attacks on the problem of the IIA assumption. Cooper and Nakanishi (1983) have shown how simply standardizing variables in each choice situation overcomes the IIA assumption in logit models or multiplicative competitive interaction (MCI) models.

PROBLEMS AND PROSPECTS

MDS does not answer all the questions which a marketing researcher can pose. Within a less than comprehensive mandate, there seem to be three discernible directions for MDS in marketing research.

The first is toward a finer grained inspection of individual and group perceptions. One of the lingering problems in this direction concerns data omitted through prudence rather than through caprice. If individuals are not familiar enough with some collection of choice alternatives to make judgments about them, it is prudent not to force these judgments. Levine's [1979; Holbrook, Moore, and Winer, 1982] "pick any" MDS model deals well with this issue within its scope of applicability. How relevant set membership is modeled, however, and its impact on spatial representations, requires more general attention. Though Hauser and Koppelman (1979) have cast this as a special problem for MDS, it is no less a problem for factor analysis or discriminant analysis. This is part of a larger problem concerning the representation of individual differences. As marketing researchers move toward basing perceptual spaces on very large samples of consumers, a more richly articulated representation of individual or segment differences will be useful. This will be true for fundamentally symmetric MDS problems as well as fundamentally asymmetric MDS problems.

The second direction deals with merging MDS with other consumer-based measurements (for example, normative beliefs), then, in turn, merging consumer-level measurements with market-level measurements. Although the former data base is primarily cross-sectional (for example, over individuals or segments), the latter is primarily a longitudinal data base. Some of the potential of this merger is communicated by Clarke's (1978) work. In addition to promotions expenditures, there are other market-level influences (for example, price and distribution). A longitudinal analysis of market-level variables might be done to estimate parameters in an MCI model or in a multinominal logit model. These parameters might then be used in a cross-sectional analysis in which parameters for the consumer-level variables are estimated. With market-level choice as the criterion, and the reality of scanner data as a purchase-by-purchase account of market activity, there is much to be explained.

The third direction deals with the representation of change on a broader scale than the introduction of a new product into an existing market. The current new-product models and methods might not have allowed marketing researchers to forecast the video game and home computer revolution. For products that essentially create new markets there needs to be study of the structure and inter-substitutability of product classes or, as in Ritchie (1974), of the relations among alternative uses of leisure time.

In his 1975 review of MDS in marketing, Green (1975a) wondered whether or not MDS had fulfilled its early promise. With eight more years of experience, it seems that it has. The new generation of textbooks on MDS (Coxon, 1982; Davison, 1983; Schiffman, Reynolds, and Young, 1981) promise to prepare the next generation of MDS researchers even better than the pioneers. As long as MDS is not expected to solve all the complex problems of the field, it should continue to be a

powerful and useful methodology in the arsenal of marketing researchers.

REFERENCES

Albers, S., and Brockhoff, B. A procedure for new product positioning in an attribute space. *European Journal of Operational Research,* 1977, *1,* 230–238.

Arabie, P., Carroll, J. D., DeSarbo, W., and Wind, J. Overlapping clustering: A new method for product positioning. *Journal of Marketing Research,* 1981, *23,* 310–317.

Bateson, J., and Greyser, S. *The effectiveness of the knowledge generation and diffusion process in marketing—Some considerations and empirical findings* (Paper No. 82/4). London: The London Business School, July 1982.

Batsell, R. R. *A market share model which simultaneously captures the effects of utility and substitutability* (Working Paper 80-007). Philadelphia: University of Pennsylvania, The Wharton School, 1980.

Batsell, R. R. A multiattribute extension of the Luce model which simultaneously scales utility and substitutability. In J. Huber (Ed.), *The effects of item similarity on choice probability: A collection of working papers from a conference at Quail Roost.* Durham, NC: Duke University, 1981.

Bechtel, G. G. *Multidimensional preference scaling.* The Hague: Mouton, 1976.

Bechtel, G. G. Metric information for group representations. In I. Borg (Ed.), *Multidimensional data representations: When and why.* Ann Arbor MI: Mathesis Press, 1981.

Bechtel, G. G., and O'Connor, P. J. Testing micropreference structures. *Journal of Marketing Research* 1979, *16,* 247–257.

Best, R. J. The predictive aspects of a joint-space theory of stochastic choice. *Journal of Marketing Research,* 1976, *13,* 198–204.

Borden, H. The concept of the marketing mix. *Journal of Advertising Research,* 1964, *4,* 2–7.

Brown, M. P., Cardozo, R. N., Cunningham, S. M., Salmon, W. J., and Sultan, R. G. P. Maxwell House division. In *Problems in marketing.* New York: McGraw-Hill, 1968.

Carroll, J. D. Individual differences and multidimensional scaling. In A. K. Romney, R. N.

Shepard, and S. B. Nerlove (Eds.), *Multidimensional scaling; Theory and applications in the behavioral sciences (Vol. 2). Applications.* New York: Seminar Press, 1972.

Carroll, J. D., and Chang, J. J. Analysis of individual differences in multidimensional scaling via an *N*-way generalization of "Eckart-Young" decomposition. *Psychometrika,* 1970, *35,* 283–320.

Carroll, J. D., and Chang, J. J. *Relating preference data to multidimensional scaling via a generalization of Coombs' unfolding model.* Paper presented at the annual meeting of the Psychometric Society, Madison WI, April 1967.

Clarke, D. G. Strategic advertising planning: Merging multidimensional scaling and econometric analysis. *Management Science,* 1978, *24,* 1687–1699.

Cooper, L. G. A new solution to the additive constant problem in metric multidimensional scaling. *Psychometrika,* 1972, *37,* 311–322.

Cooper, L. G. A multivariate investigation of preferences. *Multivariate Behavioral Research,* 1973, *8,* 253–272.

Cooper, L. G., and Nakanishi, M. Standardizing variables in multiplicative choice models. *Journal of Consumer Research,* 1983, *10,* 96–108.

Coxon, A. P. M. *The user's guide to multidimensional scaling.* Exeter: Heineman, 1982.

Currim, I. Predictive testing of consumer choice models. *Journal of Marketing Research,* 1982, *19,* 208–222.

Davison, M. L. *Multidimensional scaling.* New York: Wiley-Interscience, 1983.

Day, G. Evaluating models of attitude structure. *Journal of Marketing Research,* 1972, *9,* 279–286.

Day, G. S., Deutscher, T., and Ryans, A. B. Data quality, level of aggregation, and nonmetric multidimensional scaling solutions. *Journal of Marketing Research,* 1976, *13,* 92–97.

Day, G. S., and Heeler, R. M. Using cluster analysis to improve marketing experiments. *Journal of Marketing Research,* 1971, *8,* 340–347.

Deutscher, T. Issues in data collection and reliability in marketing multidimensional scaling studies—Implication for large stimulus sets. In R. G. Golledge and J. N. Rayner (Eds.), *Proximity and preference: Problems in the multidimensional analysis of large data sets.* Minneapolis: University of Minnesota Press, 1982.

Doyle, P., and McGee, J. Perceptions of and preferences for alternative convenience foods. *Journal of the Marketing Research Society,* 1973, *15,* 24–34.

Drasgow, F., and Jones, E. Multidimensional scaling of derived dissimilarities. *Multivariate Behavioral Research,* 1979, *14,* 227–244.

Frank, R. E., and Green, P. E. Numerical taxonomy in marketing analysis: A review article. *Journal of Marketing Research,* 1968, *5,* 83–93.

Fry, J. N., and Claxton, J. D. Semantic differential and nonmetric multidimensional scaling descriptions of brand images. *Journal of Marketing Research,* 1971, *8,* 238–240.

Green, P. E. Measurement and data analysis. *Journal of Marketing,* 1970, *34,* 15–17.

Green, P. E., A multidimensional model of product-features association. *Journal of Business Research,* 1974, *2,* 107–118.

Green, P. E. On the robustness of multidimensional scaling techniques. *Journal of Marketing Research,* 1975, *12,* 73–81. (a)

Green, P. E. Marketing application of MDS: Assessment and outlook. *Journal of Marketing,* 1975, *39,* 24–31. (b)

Green, P. E., and Carmone, F. J. The performance structure of the computer market: A multivariate approach. *The Economic and Business Bulletin,* 1968, *21,* 1–11.

Green, P. E., and Carmone, F. J. Multidimensional scaling: An introduction and comparison of nonmetric unfolding techniques. *Journal of Marketing Research,* 1969, *6,* 330–341.

Green, P. E., and Carmone, F. J. *Multidimensional scaling and related techniques in marketing analysis.* Boston: Allyn & Bacon, 1970.

Green, P. E., and Carmone, F. J. The effect of task on intra-individual differences in similarities judgments. *Multivariate Behavioral Research,* 1971, *6,* 433–450.

Green, P. E., and Carmone, F. J. Marketing research applications of nonmetric multidimensional scaling methods. In A. K.

Romney, R. N. Shepard, and S. B. Nerlove (Eds.), *Multidimensional scaling: Theory and applications in the behavioral sciences (Vol. 2). Applications.* New York: Seminar Press, 1972.

Green, P. E., Carmone, F. J., and Fox, L. B. Television program similarities: An application of subjective clustering. *Journal of the Market Research Society,* 1969, *11,* 70–90.

Green, P. E., Carmone, F. J., and Robinson, P. J. Nonmetric scaling methods: An exposition and overview. *Wharton Quarterly,* 1968, 27–40.

Green, P. E., and Devita, M. T. An interaction model of consumer utility. *Journal of Consumer Research,* 1975, *2,* 146–153.

Green, P. E., Frank, R. E., and Robinson, P. J. Cluster analysis in test market selection. *Management Science, Series B,* 1967, *13,* B387–B400. (a)

Green, P. E., Frank, R. E., and Robinson, P. J. Letter to the editor. *Management Science, Series B,* 1967, *13,* B840–B841. (b)

Green, P. E., and Greenberg, M. G. Ordinal methods in multidimensional scaling and data analysis. In R. Ferber (Ed.), *Handbook of marketing research.* New York: McGraw-Hill, 1974.

Green, P. E., and Maheshwari, A. Common stock perception and preference: An application of multidimensional scaling. *Journal of Business,* 1969, *42,* 439–457.

Green, P. E., and Maheshwari, A. A note on the multidimensional scaling of conditional proximity data. *Journal of Marketing Research,* 1970, *7,* 106–110.

Green, P. E., Maheshwari, A., and Rao, V. R. Self-concept and brand preference: An empirical application of multidimensional scaling. *Journal of the Marketing Research Society,* 1969, *11,* 343–360. (a)

Green, P. E., Maheshwari, A., and Rao, V. R. Dimensional interpretation and configuration invariance in multidimensional scaling: An empirical study. *Multivariate Behavioral Research,* 1969, *4,* 159–180. (b)

Green, P. E., and McMennamin, J. L. Market position analysis. In S. H. Britt (Ed.), *The Dartnell marketing managers handbook.* Chicago: The Dartnell Corporation, 1973.

Green, P. E., and Rao, V. R. A note on proximity measures and cluster analysis. *Journal of Marketing Research,* 1969, *6,* 359–364.

Green, P. E., and Rao, V. R. Multidimensional scaling and individual differences. *Journal of Marketing Research,* 1971, *8,* 71–77. (a)

Green, P. E., and Rao, V. R. Conjoint measurement for quantifying judgmental data. *Journal of Marketing Research,* 1971, *8,* 335–363. (b)

Green, P. E., and Rao, V. R. Configuration synthesis in multidimensional scaling. *Journal of Marketing Research,* 1972, *9,* 65–68. (a)

Green, P. E., and Rao, V. R. *Applied multidimensional scaling: A comparison of approaches and algorithms.* New York: Holt, Rinehart, and Winston, 1972. (b)

Green, P. E., and Wind, Y. *Multiattribute decisions in marketing: A measurement approach.* Hinsdale IL: The Dryden Press, 1973.

Green, P. E., Wind, Y., and Claycamp, H. J. Brand features congruence mapping. *Journal of Marketing Research,* 1975, *12,* 306–313.

Green, P. E., Wind. Y., and Jain, A. K. A note on measurement of a social-psychological belief system. *Journal of Marketing Research,* 1972, *9,* 204–208.

Green, P. E., Wind, Y., and Jain, A. K. Analyzing free-response data in marketing research. *Journal of Marketing Research,* 1973, *10,* 45–52.

Greenberg, A., and Collins, S. Paired comparison taste tests: Some food for thought. *Journal of Marketing Research,* 1966, *3,* 76–80.

Greenberg, M. G., and Green, P. E. Multidimensional scaling. In R. Ferber (Ed.) *Handbook of marketing research.* New York: McGraw-Hill, 1974.

Guttman, L. A general nonmetric technique for finding the smallest coordinate space for a configuration of points. *Psychometrika,* 1968, *33,* 469–504.

Hanno, M. S., and Jones, L. E. Effects of a change in reference person on the multidimensional structure and evaluations of trait adjectives. *Journal of Personality and Social Psychology,* 1973, *28,* 368–375.

Harshman, R. A., Green, P. E., Wind, Y., and Lundy, M. E. A model for the analysis of asymmetric data in marketing. *Marketing Science,* 1982, *1,* 205–242.

Hauser, J. R., and Koppelman, F. S. Alternative perceptual mapping techniques: Relative accuracy and usefulness. *Journal of Marketing Research,* 1979, *16,* 495–506.

Hauser, J. R., and Simmie, P. Profit maximizing perceptual positions: An integrated theory for the selection of product features and price. *Management Science,* 1981, *27,* 33–56.

Hauser, J. R., and Urban, G. L. A normative methodology for modeling consumer response to innovation. *Operations Research,* 1977, *25,* 579–619.

Henry, W. A., and Stumpf, R. F. Time and accuracy measures for alternative multidimensional scaling data collection methods. *Journal of Marketing Research,* 1975, *12,* 165–170.

Holbrook, M. B., Moore, W. L., and Winer, R. S. Constructing joint spaces from pick-any data: A new tool for consumer analysis. *Journal of Consumer Research,* 1982, *9,* 99–105.

Holbrook, M. B., and Williams, R. S. A test of the correspondence between perceptual spaces based on pairwise similarity judgments collected with and without the inclusion of explicit ideal objects. *Journal of Applied Psychology,* 1978, *63,* 373–376.

Hopkins, D. S. P., Larreche, J.-C., and Massy, W. F. Constrained optimization of a university administrator's preference function. *Management Science,* 1977, *24,* 365–377.

Howard, N., and Harris, B. *A hierarchical grouping routine, IBM 360/65 FORTRAN program.* Philadelphia PA: University of Pennsylvania Computer Center, 1966.

Huber, J. Predicting preferences on experimental bundles of attributes: A comparison of models. *Journal of Marketing Research,* 1975, *12,* 290–297.

Hustad, T. P., Mayer, C. S., and Whipple, T. W. Consideration of context differences in product evaluation and market segmentation. *Journal of the Academy of Marketing Science,* 1975, *3,* 34–47.

Jain, A. K., and Pinson, C. The effect of order of presentation of similarity judgments on multidimensional scaling results: An empirical examination. *Journal of Marketing Research,* 1976, *13,* 435–439.

Johnson, R. M. Market segmentation: A strategic management tool. *Journal of Marketing Research,* 1971, *8,* 13–18.

Johnson, S. C. Hierarchical clustering schemes. *Psychometrika,* 1967, *32,* 241–254.

Kassarjian, H. H., and Nakanishi, M. A study of selected opinion measurement techniques. *Journal of Marketing Research,* 1967, *4,* 148–153.

Kinnear, T. C., and Taylor, J. R. The effect of ecological concern on brand perceptions. *Journal of Marketing Research,* 1973, *10,* 191–197.

Klahr, D. Decision making in a complex environment: The use of similarity judgments to predict preferences. *Management Science,* 1969, *15,* 595–618.

Klahr, D. A study of consumer's cognitive structure of cigarette brands. *Journal of Business,* 1970, *43,* 190–204.

Krampf, R. F., and Williams, J. D. Multidimensional scaling as a research tool: An explanation and application. *Journal of Business Research,* 1974, *2,* 157–175.

Kruskal, J. B. Multidimensional scaling by optimizing goodness of fit to a nonmetric hypothesis. *Psychometrika,* 1964, *29,* 1–27. (a)

Kruskal, J. B. Nonmetric multidimensional scaling: A numerical method. *Psychometrika,* 1964, *29,* 115–128. (b)

Kruskal, J. B. How to use M-D-SCAL. A program for multidimensional scaling and multidimensional unfolding (Version 4 and 4M of M-D-SCAL, all in FORTRAN IV). Murray Hill NJ: Bell Telephone Laboratories, 1968. (mimeograph)

Lancaster, K. A new approach to consumer theory. *Journal of Political Economy,* 1966, *74,* 132–157. (a)

Lancaster, K. Change and innovation in the technology of consumption. *American Economic Review,* 1966, *56,* 14–23. (b)

Lancaster, L. *Consumer demand: A new approach.* New York: Columbia University Press, 1971.

Lehmann, D. R. Television show preference: Application of a choice model. *Journal of Marketing Research,* 1971, *8,* 47–55.

Lehmann, D. R. Evaluating market strategy in a multiple brand market. *Journal of Business Administration,* 1971, *3,* 15–26. (b)

Lehmann, D. R. Judged similarity and brand-switching data as similarity measures. *Journal of Marketing Research,* 1972, *9,* 331–334.

Lehmann, D. R. Some alternatives to linear factor analysis for variable grouping applied to buyer behavior variables *Jour-*

nal of Marketing Research, 1974, *11*, 206–213.

Levine, J. H. Joint-space analysis of "pick-any" data: Analysis of choices from an unconstrained set of alternatives. *Psychometrika*, 1979, *44*, 85–92.

Luce, R. D. *Individual choice behavior*. New York: Wiley, 1959.

MacKay, D. B., and Olshavsky, R. W. Cognitive maps of retail locations: An investigation of some basic issues. *Journal of Consumer Research*, 1975, *2*, 197–205.

Mauser, G. A. Positioning political candidates—An application of concept evaluation techniques. *Journal of the Marketing Research Society*, 1980, *22*, 181–191.

McGee, V. The multidimensional analysis of "elastic" distance. *The British Journal of Mathematical and Statistical Psychology*, 1966, *19*, 181–196.

McIntyre, S. H., and Ryans, A. B. Time and accuracy measures for alternative multidimensional scaling data collection methods: Some additional results. *Journal of Marketing Research*, 1977, *16*, 607–610.

Moinpour, R. J., McCullough, J. M., and MacLachlan, D. L. Time changes in perception: A longitudinal application of multidimensional scaling. *Journal of Marketing Research*, 1976, *13*, 245–253.

Moore, W. L. Predictive power of joint space models constructed with composition techniques. *Journal of Business Research*, 1982, *10*, 217–236.

Moore, W. L., and Holbrook, M. B. On the predictive validity of joint-space models in consumer evaluations of new concepts. *Journal of Consumer Research*, 1982, *9*, 206–210.

Moore, W. L., Pessemier, E. A., and Little, T. E. Predicting brand purchase behavior: Marketing applications of the Schönemann and Wang unfolding model. *Journal of Marketing Research*, 1979, *16*, 203–210.

Morgan, N., and Purnell, J. Isolating openings for new products in a multi-dimensional space. *Journal of the Marketing Research Society*, 1969, *11*, 245–266.

Morrison, D. G. Measurement problems in cluster analysis. *Management Science, Series B*, 1967, *13*, B775–B780.

Narayana, C. L., The stability of perceptions. *Journal of Advertising Research*, 1976, *16*, 45–49.

Neidell, L. A. The use of nonmetric multidimensional scaling in marketing analysis. *Journal of Marketing*, 1969, *33*, 37–43.

Neidell, L. A. Procedure for obtaining similarities data. *Journal of Marketing Research*, 1972, *9*, 335–337.

Olshavsky, R. W., MacKay, D. B., and Sentell, G. Perceptual maps of supermarket locations. *Journal of Applied Psychology*, 1975, *60*, 80–86.

Pekelman, D., and Sen, S. K. Mathematical programming models for the determination of attribute weights. *Management Science*, 1974, *20*, 1217–1229.

Percy, L. H. Multidimensional unfolding of profile data: A discussion and illustration with attention to badness-of-fit. *Journal of Marketing Research*, 1975, *12*, 93–99.

Perreault, W. D., Jr., and Young, F. W. Alternating least squares optimal scaling: Analysis of nonmetric data in marketing research. *Journal of Marketing Research*, 1980, *17*, 1–13.

Perry, M., Izraeli, D., and Perry, A. Image change as a result of advertising. *Journal of Advertising Research*, 1976, *16*, 45–50.

Pessemier, E. A. Market structure analysis of new product and market opportunities. *Journal of Contemporary Business*. 1975, *4*, 35–67.

Pessemier, E. A., Burger, P., Teach, R., and Tigert. D. Using laboratory brand preference scale to predict consumer brand purchases. *Management Science, Series B*, 1971, *17*, B371–B385.

Pessemier, E. A. and Root, H. P. The dimensions of new product planning. *Journal of Marketing*, 1973, *37*, 10–18.

Rao, V. R. Changes in explicit information and brand perceptions. *Journal of Marketing Research*, 1972, *9*, 209–213.

Rao, V. R., and Katz, R. Alternative multidimensional scaling methods for large stimulus sets. *Journal of Marketing Research*, 1971, *8*, 488–494.

Ritchie, J. R. B. An exploratory analysis of the nature and extent of individual differences in perception. *Journal of Marketing Research*, 1974, *11*, 41–49.

Roberts, M. L. and Taylor, J. R. Analyzing proximity judgments in an experimental design. *Journal of Marketing Research*, 1975, *12*, 68–72.

Ross, J., and Cliff, N. A generalization of the

interpoint distance models. *Psychometrika,* 1964, *29,* 167–176.

Ryans, A. B. Estimating consumer preferences for a new durable brand in an established product class. *Journal of Marketing Research,* 1974, *11,* 434–443.

Schiffman, S. S., Reynolds, M. L., and Young, F. W. *Introduction of multidimensional scaling: Theory, methods, and applications.* New York: Academic Press, 1981.

Schönemann, P., and Wang, M. M. An individual differences model for the multidimensional analysis of preference data. *Psychometrika,* 1972, *37,* 275–309.

Shepard, R. N., and Carroll, J. D. Parametric representation of nonlinear data structures. In P. R. Krishnaiah (Ed.), *International symposium on multivariate analysis, Dayton OH, 1965.* New York: Academic Press, 1966.

Shocker, A. D., and Srinivasan, V. A consumer-based methodology for the identification of new product ideas. *Management Science,* 1979, *20,* 921–937. (a)

Shocker, A. D., and Srinivasan, V. Multiattribute approaches for product concept evaluation and generation: A critical review. *Journal of Marketing Research,* 1979, *16,* 159–180. (b)

Shuchman, A. Letter to the editor. *Management Science, Series B,* 1967, *13,* B688–B691.

Silk, A. J. Preference and perception measures in new product development: An exposition and review. *Industrial Management Review,* 1969, 21–37.

Silk, A. J., and Urban, G. L. Pre-test market evaluation of new packaged goods: A model and measurement methodology. *Journal of Marketing Research,* 1978, *15,* 171–191.

Smith, R. E., and Lusch, R. F. How advertising can position a brand. *Journal of Advertising Research,* 1976, *16,* 37–43.

Srinivasan, V., and Shocker, A. D. Linear programming techniques for multidimensional analysis of preferences. *Psychometrika,* 1973, *38,* 337–367.

Stefflre, V. J. Market structure studies: New products for old markets and new markets (foreign) for old products. In F. Bass and R. Frank (Eds.), *Applications of the sciences in marketing.* New York: John Wiley & Sons, 1968.

Stefflre, V. J. Some applications of multi-dimensional scaling to social science problems. In A. K. Romney, R. N. Shepard, and S. B. Nerlove (Eds.), *Multidimensional scaling: Theory and applications in the behavioral sciences (Vol. 2). Applications.* New York: Seminar Press, 1972.

Summers, J. O., and MacKay D. B. On the validity and reliability of direct similarity judgments. *Journal of Marketing Research,* 1976, *13,* 289–295.

Tucker, L. R. *Factor analysis of double centered score matrices* (ETS RM-56-3). Princeton NJ: Educational Testing Service, 1956.

Tucker, L. R. Comments on "Confounding of sources of variation in factor-analysis techniques." *Psychological Bulletin,* 1968, *70,* 345–354.

Tucker, L. R. Relations between multidimensional scaling and three-mode factor analysis. *Psychometrika,* 1972, *37,* 3–27.

Tucker, L. R., and Messick, S. An individual differences model for multidimensional scaling. *Psychometrika,* 1963, *28,* 333–367.

Turner, R. E. Market measures from salesmen: A multidimensional scaling approach. *Journal of Marketing Research,* 1971, *8,* 165–172.

Urban, G. Perceptor: A model for product positioning. *Management Science,* 1975, *21,* 858–871.

van de Sandt, U. Incomplete paired comparisons using balanced lattice designs. *Journal of Marketing Research,* 1970, *7,* 246–248.

Whipple, T. W. Variation among multidimensional scaling solutions: An examination of the effect of data collection differences. *Journal of Marketing Research,* 1976, *13,* 98–103.

Wind, Y. A new procedure for concept evaluation. *Journal of Marketing,* 1973, *37,* 2–11.

Wind, Y. The perception of a firm's competitive position. In F. M. Nicosia and Y. Wind (Eds.), *Behavioral models for market analysis: Foundations for marketing action.* Hinsdale IL: The Dryden Press, 1977.

Wind, Y. Issues and advances in segmentation research. *Journal of Marketing Research,* 1978, *15,* 317–337.

Young, F. W., and Appelbaum, M. I., Nonmetric multidimensional scaling: The relationship of several methods (Report No. 71). Chapel Hill NC: L. L. Thurstone Psychometric Laboratory, 1968.

Young, F. W., and Torgerson, W. S. TORSCA IV

program for Shepard-Kruskal multidimensional scaling analysis. *Behavioral Science,* 1967, *12,* 498.

Young, S., Ott, L., and Feigin, B. Some practical considerations in market segmentation. *Journal of Marketing Research,* 1978, *15,* 405–412.

MULTIDIMENSIONAL SCALING J. Douglas Carroll, *Bell Laboratories,* and Phipps Arabie, *University of Minnesota and Bell Laboratories*

INTRODUCTION

Perhaps the most salient feature in the progress of multidimensional scaling (MDS) over the past seven years since Cliff's (1973) chapter on Scaling has been the explosive growth in number and variety of models and methods, the proliferation of applications of MDS within many different fields, and a kind of semantic encroachment of the *term* MDS on other domains (for example, factor analysis, test theory, analysis of variance or mathematical models). This semantic expansion of the term, we would argue, is not necessarily undesirable, since "multidimensional scaling," liberally speaking, could be taken to include much that has traditionally been identified with other areas of psychometrics or mathematical psychology. Broadly defined, multidimensional scaling comprises a family of geometric models for multidimensional representation of data and a corresponding set of methods for fitting such models to actual data. A much narrower definition would limit the term to spatial distance models for similarities, dissimilarities or other *proximities data.* The usage we espouse would include nonspatial (for example, discrete geometric models such as tree structures) and nondistance (for example, scalar product or projection) models that apply to nonproximities (for

example, preference or other "dominance") data as well as to proximities.

Because of this methodological and semantic expansion of the field, it seems to us that the major service a reviewer of this literature can do for readers is to attempt to put some order into what may appear as chaos: that is, to impose a taxonomy on the field. This task is our goal. At the outset, we state our disclaimers. Our taxonomy is only one of many possible ways of organizing the field; we view the classification as provisional, relevant to the field as it *now* is and not as it may be some years in the future. In effect, our taxonomy might be regarded as a subjectively derived meta-multidimensional scaling (and/or clustering) of the current state of multidimensional scaling. We hope that the taxonomy will facilitate readers' understanding of the work reviewed herein, as well as of the chapter itself.

A NEW TAXONOMY OF MEASUREMENT DATA AND OF MULTIDIMENSIONAL MEASUREMENT MODELS

The present taxonomy can be viewed as an attempt to update and generalize Coombs' (1964) *A Theory of Data,* although there are many ways in which our tax-

Preparation of this chapter was supported in part by LEAA Grant 78-NI-AX-0142 and NSF Grants SOC 76-24394 and SOC 76-24512.

From J. Douglas Carroll and Phipps Arabie, "Multidimensional Scaling," *Annual Review of Psychology,* M. R. Rosenzweig and L. W. Porter, eds., Vol. 31, 1980. © by Annual Reviews Inc. Reproduced with permission.

onomy departs significantly from Coombs', so that our approach is not, strictly speaking, a generalization. Still, the clearest antecedent is *A Theory of Data,* and Coombs (personal communication) has indicated that except for our use of "data" where he would use "observations," he finds no conflict between his (1964; also see Coombs, 1979) taxonomy and the present one. Our viewpoint has also been influenced by Shepard's (1972b) taxonomy of data and of methods of analysis. Finally, the distinction between "modes" and "ways" is due to Tucker (1972), and the scale types are derived of course from Stevens (1946, 1951).

The main difference between Coombs' and our approach is that we attempt *separate* taxonomies of data and of models, whereas Coombs argued that data cannot be classified independently of the model to which those data are referred, so that the very same data (observations, in Coombs' terms) may fit into different quadrants (or octants) of his schema, depending on which model is assumed. Our attempt to separate the classification of data and of models may be only partially successful, since there is certainly a strong connection between type of data and of model. (There is only a limited class of models suitable for any specific type of data.) We shall nevertheless attempt to maintain the distinction wherever possible.

When one considers the highly important aspect of scale typology, it could be applied exclusively to the data (à la Stevens) or to the model (as suggested by Guttman, 1971), but our view is that the scale typology is decidable separately for the data and for the model. For the former, it seems self-evident that some tasks *ask* the subject to adhere to certain scale types (for example, sorting versus magnitude estimation). However, there can be little doubt that during the years covered by this review, far greater practical emphasis has been placed on incorporating the transformations underlying the scale typology into the model.

The advantages of maintaining the typology for both data and model are apparent from consideration of Shepard's (1972a; Chang and Shepard, 1966) approach that embodied an exponential decay fitting procedure in a metric multidimensional scaling analysis. Unless such a transformation (characteristic of many models of forgetting or confusions) can be accommodated by the scale typology, then it must be claimed that Shepard's analysis produced a new and distinct type of scale. We find it more parsimonious to view the data as ordinal and Shepard's analysis/model as interval with a transformation included. We could explicitly include scale type as a property of such models; however, for the present we are including scale type only as a property of the data. The current version of our new schema is presented below.

I. Properties of Measurement Data: Definitions

A mode is defined as a particular class of entities. Modes will be denoted by capital letters A, B, C,...etc. Entities could be, for example, subjects, stimuli, test items, occasions, experimental conditions, geographical areas, or components of a "multiattribute stimulus." Particular members of the class of entities corresponding to a mode are denoted by subscripts (for example, $A_i, i = 1, \ldots, S$ could denote S subjects).

An N-way array is defined as the cartesian product of a number of modes, some of which may be repeated. For example, an array associated with three-way multidimensional scaling might be of the form $A \times B \times B$, where A denotes subjects, and B stimuli. An element of the array is a particular value of this cartesian product [that is, a combination of particular members of the modes; for example, (A_i, B_j, B_k)]. A *data array* is an assignment of scale values to some or all elements of the array with possible replications.

Having established these definitions,

the taxonomy of data arrays follows straightforwardly, as outlined below:

A. Number of modes

1. One mode
2. Two modes
3. Three or more modes

B. Power of a given mode: A mode's power is the number of times the mode is repeated in the N-way table.

1. Monadic data (for example, single stimulus data, as from an absolute judgment task). Power = 1
2. Dyadic data (for example, proximities data). Power = 2

   a. Symmetric
   b. Nonsymmetric

3. Polyadic data (for example, judgments of homogeneity of sets of three or more stimuli, or similarity of or preference for "portfolios" of a number of items from the same set). Power ≥ 3. (*Note:* In principle each mode could be of power greater than one. In practice only the "stimulus" mode commonly has power greater than one.)

C. Number of ways, defined as total number of factors, whether repeated or not, defining data array; N if table of data is N-way (exclusive of replications, which are not usually thought of as defining a separate mode or way unless there is a structure on the replications and the replications "mode" is explicitly included in the model). (*Note:* The number of ways is clearly redundant with the first two data properties, since it is just the sum over modes of the power of each mode. However, we find it convenient to include this redundant property explicitly in our schema.)

D. Scale type of data (after Stevens, but

with some additions)

1. Nominal
2. Ordinal
3. Interval
4. Ratio (sometimes called "interval with rational origin")
5. Positive ratio
6. Absolute

Note: We have added to Stevens' four scale types what is sometimes called the "interval with rational origin," (which we simply call "ratio") that can be viewed as a ratio scale admitting negative as well as positive values, (and, of course, zero), and the "absolute" scale [for example, Zwislocki, 1978], in which no transformation whatsoever is allowed. At the suggestion of A. Tversky, we are relabeling Stevens' "ratio scale" the "positive ratio scale" (that is, a ratio scale that allows only non-negative values).

E. Conditionality of data

1. Unconditional data
2. Row or column conditional data (Coombs, 1964)
3. Matrix conditional data
4. Other types of conditional data

F. Completeness of data

1. Complete data
2. Incomplete data

G. Number and nature of replications

1. Only one data set comprising the data array
2. Two or more data sets

   a. Same scale type for each replication
   b. Different scale types for different replications

II. Properties of Multidimensional Measurement Models

A. Type of geometric model

1. Spatial

a. Distance models

   i) Euclidean
   ii) Minkowski-p (or l_p) metrics
   iii) Riemannian metrics
   iv) Other non-Euclidean metrics

b. Scalar product (or projection) models

2. Nonspatial (discrete set-theoretic or graph-theoretic models)

a. Nonoverlapping classes (partitions) (for example, standard clustering methods)
b. Overlapping classes (for example, Shepard–Arabie ADCLUS model)
c. Hierarchical tree structure
d. Multiple tree structure

3. Hybrid models (mixtures of continuous and discrete structure)

a. Mixture of (single or multiple) tree structure and spatial structure
b. Mixture of class (overlapping or nonoverlapping) and spatial structure

   i) Dimensions that generalize over all classes
   ii) Some class-specific dimensions
   iii) Both of the above

B. Number of sets of points in space (or other structure)

1. One set
2. Two sets
3. More than two sets

C. Number of spaces or structures (and their interrelations)

1. One space or structure (for example, two-way MDS)
2. Two spaces or structures (for example, stimulus [or other "object"] space and subject [or other "data source"] space in three-way or individual differences MDS)
3. More than two spaces or structures

D. Degree of external constraint on model parameters

1. Purely "internal" solutions in which all model parameters are unconstrained
2. Various kinds of linear, ordinal or other constraints on specific parameters of model
3. "External" models, in which one or more spaces (or other structures), or one or more sets of points in the same structure, is totally fixed

The present survey of multidimensional scaling and related techniques is organized around our taxonomy, but does not conform exactly, owing to space limitations and, of course, uneven progress in various subareas during recent years. We take aspects I-A and I-C ("modes" and "ways" from the properties of data) as the dominant organizing principles. Since we are defining as our goal the imposition of structure on the field as a whole, we shall take somewhat greater liberty than may be usual for *Annual Review* chapters, to cite work that may lie outside the time period we are primarily covering, to cite or refer to unpublished work, or even in some cases work still in progress. We also note that we may underemphasize applications of MDS relative to theoretical and methodological developments. (Some methodological areas are also underemphasized or omitted altogether.) We hope any imbalance that results will be partly corrected by a bibliography now in preparation at Bell Laboratories [also see Bick, Müller, Bauer, and Gieseke, 1977; Nishisato, 1978a].

ONE-MODE TWO-WAY DATA

We began our discussion of MDS data and models with the class of data most frequently encountered: one-mode two-way data, which could otherwise be characterized as two-way dyadic data. These data are typically some form of similarities, dissimilarities, or other proximities data (for example, measures of association between pairs of stimuli or other objects, frequencies of confusions, second order measures of similarity or dissimilarity derived from standard multivariate or other data, etc.). A general overview discussing and interrelating most of the spatial (both distance and scalar product) models and corresponding methods for analysis of such data (as well as two-mode three-way data) is provided by Carroll and Kruskal (1977; see also Carroll and Wish, 1974b). Another type of ostensibly dyadic data are so-called "paired comparisons" data depicting preferences or other forms of dominance relations on members of pairs of stimuli. However, such data are seldom utilized in multidimensional (as opposed to unidimensional) scaling. We do not cover paired comparisons data in this section because we view such data not as dyadic, but as replicated monadic data (having n-2 missing data values within each replication).

Spatial Distance Models (for One-Mode Two-Way Data)

The most widely used MDS procedures are based on spatial *distance models*. These are geometric models in which the similarities, dissimilarities or other proximities data are assumed to relate in a simple and well defined manner to recovered *distances* in an underlying *spatial* representation. If the data are interval scale, the function relating the data to distances would generally be assumed to be inhomogeneously linear; that is, linear with an additive constant as well as a slope coefficient. Data that are interval scale or stronger (ratio, positive ratio, or absolute) are called *metric* data, while the corresponding models and analyses are col-

lectively called *metric* MDS. In the case of ordinal data, the functional relationship is generally assumed to be monotonic—either monotonic nonincreasing (in the case of similarities), or monotonic nondecreasing (for dissimilarities). Ordinal data are often called nonmetric data, and the corresponding MDS models and analyses are also referred to as *nonmetric* MDS. The distinction between metric and nonmetric is based on the presence or absence of metric properties in the data (not in the solution, which almost always has metric properties; Holman (1978) is an exception).

Following Kruskal's (1964b, 1965) innovative work in monotone regression (as the basic engine for fitting most of the ordinal models considered in this review), first devised by Ayer, Brunk, Ewing, Reid, and Silverman (1955), there has been much activity in this area of statistics. In addition to Shepard's (1962a, b) early approach and Guttman's (1968) rank image principle, there have also been alternative and related methods proposed by Barlow, Bartholomew, Bremner, and Brunk (1972), Johnson (1975), Ramsay (1977a), Srinivasan (1975), and de Leeuw (1977b). A provocative comparison between the approaches of Kruskal (1964b) and Guttman (1968) is given by McDonald (1976), and the two methods are subsumed as special cases of Young's (1975b) general formulation. Shepard and Crawford (1975; Shepard, 1974) and Goldstein and Kruskal (1976) have developed techniques for imposing various constraints on ordinal regression functions.

The range of types of data to which MDS analyses are applicable has recently been extended through the use of *nominal* scale techniques of regression (Nishisato, 1971; Hayashi, 1974; Young, de Leeuw, and Takane, 1976; Bouroche, Saporta, and Tenenhaus, 1977; Young and Null, 1978), as found in the ALSCAL program (discussed below) of Takane, Young and de Leeuw (1977).

Unconstrained Symmetric Distance Models (for One-Mode Two-Way Data) Although one of the most intensely developed areas in recent years has been the treatment of nonsymmetric data (discussed in detail below), it is still true that most of the extant data relevant to MDS are symmetric, owing in part to the previous lack of models allowing for nonsymmetric data. Therefore, we first consider recent developments in the scaling of symmetric data (that is, where the proximity of *a* to *b* is assumed identical to that obtained when the stimuli are considered in the reverse order).

Euclidean and Minkowski-p Metric. The most widely assumed metric in MDS work is the Euclidean, in which the distance between two points *i* and *j* is defined as

$$d_{ij} = \left[\sum_{r=1}^{R} (x_{ir} - x_{jr})^2 \right]^{1/2}$$

(where x_{ir} and x_{jr} are the r-th coordinates of points i and j, respectively, in an R-dimensional spatial representation). Virtually all two-way MDS procedures use either the Euclidean metric, or the Minkowski-p (or l_p) metric which defines distances as

$$d_{ij} = \left[\sum_{r=1}^{R} |x_{ir} - x_{jr}|^p \right]^{1/p} \qquad (p \geq 1)$$

and so includes Euclidean distance as a special case in which $p = 2$.

The program KYST (Kruskal, Young, and Seery, 1973, 1977) was christened with an acronym based on the names of Kruskal, Young, Shepard, and Torgerson. KYST is a combination of what were regarded by many as the preferred features of Kruskal's (1964a, b) MDSCAL and Young and Torgerson's (1967) TORSCA, and also includes the new feature of "constrained" or "external" analyses in which a subset of the stimuli are given fixed coordinates by the user while the remaining stimuli are mapped into the constrained configuration.

Other algorithms include the Guttman-Lingoes family of two-way "Smallest Space Analysis" MDS procedures (Lingoes and Roskam's (1975) related series of programs. An informative discussion comparing several of these different algorithmic approaches to MDS is given by Kruskal (1977a; see de Leeuw and Heiser, 1980). Other techniques have also been devised by Young (1972), Johnson (1973) and Hubert and Busk (1976).

Two of the most valuable algorithmic developments in unconstrained two-way (and three-way) MDS within the period covered by this review are the Takane et al. (1977) ALSCAL procedure and Ramsay's (1977b) MULTISCALE. ALSCAL (for Alternating Least squares SCALing) differs from previous two-way MDS algorithms in such ways as (a) its loss function, (b) the numerical technique of alternating least squares (ALS) used earlier by Carroll and Chang (1970) and devised by Wold (1966; also see de Leeuw, 1977a, and de Leeuw and Heiser, 1977), and (c) allowing for nominal scale (or categorical), as well as interval and ordinal data. Both ALSCAL and MULTISCALE are also applicable to two-mode three-way data, and both programs will again be considered under spatial distance models for such data.

MULTISCALE (MULTIdimensional SCAL[E]ing), Ramsay's (1977b; also see Ramsay, 1975) maximum likelihood based procedure, although strictly a metric (or linear) approach, has statistical properties which make it potentially much more powerful as both an exploratory and (particularly) a confirmatory data analytic tool. MULTISCALE, as required by the maximum likelihood approach, makes very explicit assumptions vis à vis distribution of errors, and about the relationship of parameters of this distribution to parameters defining the underlying spatial representation. One such assumption is that the dissimilarity values δ_{ij} are log normally distributed over replications, but other distributional assumptions are also allowed.

The major dividend from Ramsay's (1978) strong assumptions is that the approach enables statistical tests of significance that include, for example, assessment of the correct dimensionality appropriate to the data, via an asymptotically valid chi square test of significance. Another advantage is the resulting confidence regions for gauging the relative precision of stimulus coordinates in the spatial representation. The chief disadvantage is the very strong assumptions that must be made for the asymptotic chi squares and/or confidence regions to be valid. Not least of these is the assumption of ratio scale dissimilarity judgments. In addition there is the assumption of a specific distribution (log normal or normal with specified parameters) and of statistical independence of the dissimilarity judgments.

Applications and Theoretical Investigations of the Euclidean, Minkowski-p, and Other Intradimensionally Subtractive and Interdimensionally Additive Metrics (for One-Mode Two-Way Symmetric Data). While the Euclidean distance formula has certain computational conveniences to recommend it as a statistical model, only within recent years has the formula been viewed as a possible contender for a psychological model. Relevant research has followed along three lines, the earliest of which stems from Beals, Krantz, and Tversky (1968) who provided a set of testable axioms underlying a wide class of distance metrics (including Euclidean and Minkowski-p) as a psychological model. Two of these conditions, intradimensional subtractivity and interdimensional additivity, were extensively violated in the perception of similarity of rectangles in Krantz and Tversky (1975). A very

thorough follow-up by Wiener-Ehrlich (1978) also found an interaction between dimensions for rectangle stimuli. However, for stimuli that were Munsell paper varying along the "separable" dimension of area and brightness, she found that her data did satisfy the relevant axiomatic conditions. Related research has also been reported by Monahan and Lockhead (1977), Schönemann (1977), Zinnes and Wolff (1977), and Chipman and Noma (1978). At present, it seems that no general conclusion can be drawn from this approach to the validity of distance models, but there is certainly no strong support forthcoming.

A major boost for the plausibility of distance models was provided by the elegant work of Rumelhart and Abrahamson (1973), who presented data consistent with a model in which the traditional analogy $a:b::c:x$ implies a parallelogram in a metric space. The study also established that subjects' solutions to certain types of analogical problems were in fact successfully predicted by an independently obtained MDS solution. Other experiments in which the parallelogram rule was verified were designed by Sternberg (1977). Also, a scaling algorithm which takes as input judgments assumed to fit the model (and thus implying linear vector equations à la Rumelhart and Abrahamson) was devised by Carroll and Chang (1972b).

The third stage for questioning the viability of distance models for psychological similarity was set by important papers by Tversky (1977) and Tversky and Gati (1978). While space limitations prohibit an adequate summary or discussion of those papers, the main challenges to distance models were (a) questioning of the minimality ($d_{ii} = 0$) and (b) symmetry ($d_{ij} = d_{ji}$) conditions of the metric axioms, and (c) arguments advocating discrete features as opposed to continuous dimensions as the underlying basis of psychological similarity. Several of these challenges have been eloquently answered by Krumhansl (1978) and will be considered below.

Somewhat oblivious to the validity of the preceding studies, nonmetric (two-way) scaling has continued to grow in popularity, and we are able to mention only a small proportion of the applications in recent years. Scaling has provided representations of structure in memory (Wexler and Romney, 1972; Shepard, 1974; Arabie, Kosslyn, and Nelson, 1975; Holyoak and Walker, 1976). Studies by Shoben (1976, p. 372) and Friendly (1977, p. 206) have demonstrated the utility of the often overlooked option in KYST (Kruskal et al., 1973, 1977) of differentially weighting the stimuli being scaled. The relevance of scaling to memory and other experimental aspects of educational research has been reviewed by Subkoviak (1975).

Many applications of scaling to perceptual phenomena have been covered by Fillenbaum and Rapoport (1971), Carroll and Wish (1974b), Indow (1974), and Gregson (1975). Other scaling studies of visual processes include Heider and Olivier (1972) and Reed (1972). The substantive importance of determining the correct dimensionality of a scaling solution was underscored by the comments of Rodieck (1977) on the investigations of Tansley and Boynton (1976, 1977). Multidimensional scaling has also been found increasingly useful in olfaction (Moskowitz and Gerbers, 1974; Schiffman and Dackis, 1976). In psychoacoustics, two-way scaling has continued to play a prominent role, with examples provided by Shepard (1972a), Wang, Reed, and Bilger (1978), Cermak (1979), and Krumhansl (1979).

Seriation is a term which comes from archaeology and refers to unidimensional representation of a set of objects, where the dimension in question is usually time, so that the result is a chronological ordering of those entities. In several ways, seriation defies our taxonomy, although the original data are typically two-mode two-way, and nonsymmetric. An example in archaeology would be an incidence matrix of artifacts by sites, with the objective of separately ordering (that is, seriating) the objects corresponding to each mode. A corresponding problem in psychology considers a subjects by item response matrix (Hubert, 1974a).

In spite of the description just given of the basic data structure, the actual analysis typically begins with one-mode two-way, symmetric data that are analyzed by KYST (Kruskal et al., 1973, 1977) or some variant of that program. An adequate summary of developments culminating in this practice would greatly exceed the length of this chapter; for an overview, see Hubert (1974b, 1976) or Arabie, Boorman, and Levitt (1978). The central idea of using KYST or related programs to get a Euclidean two-dimensional representation from which the (one-dimensional) seriation is inferred is due to Kendall (1970, 1975; see Shepard, 1974, pp. 385–389 for an example). Refinements in this technique can be found in chapters of Hodson, Kendall, and Tăutu (1971), especially the papers by Kendall (1971a, b) Sibson (1971), and Wilkinson (1971). Important work has also been done by Kupershtokh and Mirkin (1971), Wilkinson (1974), Graham, Galloway, and Scollar (1976), Hubert and Schultz (1976a), Baker and Hubert (1977), and Defays (1978). The applicability of seriation to substantive problems in psychology is cogently illustrated by Coombs and Smith (1973) and Hubert and Baker (1978).

Continuing theoretical interest in non-Euclidean Minkowski-p ($p \neq 2$) metrics is evinced in papers by Fischer and Micko (1972), Carroll and Wish (1974b), Shepard (1974), Arabie et al. (1975), and Lew (1978). While it is not uncommon to find articles oblivious to the difficulties of local minima in non-Euclidean nonmetric scaling, the problems have been documented by various authors and appear not to be limited to specific scaling programs. Arabie and Boorman (1973) reported extensive local minima for non-Euclidean metrics using Kruskal's MDSCAL, and Ramsay (1977, p. 255) found similar difficulties with his MULTISCALE.

Perhaps the first effort explicitly to overcome some of these drawbacks was by Arnold (1971), who obtained Euclidean solutions which were then used as rational initial configurations for Minkowski-p ($p \neq 2$) metrics. The latter solutions served iteratively as initial configurations for p-values increasingly discrepant from 2, in search of the p-value for which stress was least, for a given dimensionality. In unpublished work, some of which is described by Shepard (1974), Arabie replicated Arnold's results, and found that Arnold's approach generally worked well for various data sets, if the declared dimensionality exceeded 2. For reasons still not understood, the Arnold strategy appears not to work well in two-dimensional spaces, where Arabie instead used many different random initial configurations. Also, Shepard (1974) has cautioned that Kruskal's (1964a, b) measure of badness-of-fit, stress, may not be comparable across different Minkowski p-values when the data are heavily tie-bound.

The extent to which Shepard's caveat is applicable to real data is presently unknown. However, it is clear that obtaining a lower stress value for a non-Euclidean metric is a necessary but not sufficient condition for declaring data to be non-Euclidean. Shepard and Arabie (1979, p. 115) presented a city-block solution possessing a least stress value for that particular Minkowski metric as well as a substantive interpretation for the unrotated axes. Another instance of a best-fitting city-block metric was given by Wiener-Ehrlich (1978, p. 405).

Metrics Other Than Euclidean or Minkowski-p. There have been some interesting developments in MDS involving more general metrics. Perhaps the most general of these is Holman's (1978) "completely nonmetric" MDS procedure. This approach can in some ways be viewed as an explicit algorithm to accomplish what Coombs (1964) attempted more heuristically and less algorithmically in his "nonmetric scaling" approach. That is, Holman's approach is nonmetric both vis à vis the data and the solution (the latter in the sense that only the rank order of coordinate values are defined).

Recently considerable interest has focused on another class of metrics—the Riemannian metrics. Motivated largely by Luneburg's (1947, 1950) theory, Indow (1974, 1975, n.d.) has made various attempts to fit Riemannian metrics with constant negative curvature to data relevant to the geometry of visual space (for example, judgments of distances among fixed light sources), but has not developed an MDS algorithm involving a Riemannian metric. The first attempt at Riemannian multidimensional scaling was an approach by Pieszko (1975), who first used "classical" metric MDS [Torgerson, 1958] to fit a configuration, limited to two dimensions, to the data and then obtained a very rough approximation for Riemannian distances defined on that configuration. Lindman and Caelli (1978) have criticized the inappropriateness of Pieszko's global approximation, which is only valid locally. Those authors were the first to produce a genuinely Riemannian (metric) MDS procedure, for Riemannian metrics of constant curvature. In some unpublished work, Caelli, Carroll, and Chang have extended this approach to include Riemannian metrics of positive nonconstant curvature.

More general Riemannian metrics can also be considered, involving geodesic metrics defined in very general nonlinear surfaces (or manifolds) embedded in high-dimensional Euclidean space. An interesting paper by Shepard (1978) describes a number of perceptual (and/or judgmental) phenomena that could be represented in terms of such very general geometric models. Weisberg (1974) provides an urbane discussion of the relevance of a priori structures (and the underlying models) to psychology and related behavioral sciences.

Constrained Symmetric Euclidean Models (for One-Mode Two-Way Data) A number of approaches have emerged quite recently that allow the imposition of various kinds of constraints on two-way MDS (distance model) solutions. To date, all such research has involved the case of symmetric data and has been restricted to the Euclidean metric. More recent approaches include Bentler and Weeks (1978), in which linear constraints (equality of specified pairs of coordinate values or proportionality to given external values) are imposed, Noma and Johnson (1979) in which inequality constraints are imposed on coordinate values (that is, a given dimension in the solution is constrained to be monotonically related to an external variable), and Borg and Lingoes (1979) in which inequality constraints are imposed on certain distances. Recently de Leeuw and Heiser (1979) have discussed a very general class of algorithms for fitting constrained models of many different kinds. Finally, an approach called CANDELINC [Carroll, Green, and Carmone, 1976; Green, Carroll, and Carmone, 1976; Carroll, Pruzansky, and Kruskal, 1979] includes as a special case a version of "classical" metric two-way MDS in which a very general class of linear constraints are imposed. (See discussion under two-mode three-way constrained models.)

Unconstrained Nonsymmetric Euclidean Models (for One-Mode Two-Way Data) A number of approaches exist for analysis of nonsymmetric dyadic data in terms of a Euclidean model. In the analysis of nonsymmetric data, an important general principle is the following: any *nonsymmetric* m-mode n-way data set can be accommodated by a *symmetric* model designed for $(m + 1)$-mode n-way data. The extra mode arises from considering the "rows" and "columns" as corresponding to *distinct* entities, so that each entity will be depicted twice in the representation from the symmetric model. This principle is valid throughout our discussions of nonsymmetric data, and we will therefore not repeat it in subsequent sections.

An alternative, second general principle in the analysis of nonsymmetric proximities data assumes they are row or column conditional (possibly a correct assumption), but employs a model allowing only one set of entities. Thus the model is symmetric, but nonsymmetry is assumed to result from conditionality of the data. Such analyses are possible in MDSCAL-5 and KYST, as well as in a procedure due to Roskam (1975) called MNCPAEX. (See external distance models for two-mode two-way data.) Takane (1979) has produced a nonmetric maximum likelihood approach that allows conditional rank order data. Takane's algorithm is especially interesting because it is simultaneously *parametric* (in the sense that a specific error distribution is assumed) and *nonmetric* (in that the data are strictly ordinal).

Gower (1978) has recently applied unfolding techniques (discussed under spatial distance models for two-mode two-way data) to nonsymmetric dyadic proximities data. In addition, a general approach for decomposing nonsymmetric data matrices has been developed independently by Tobler (1976) and Gower (1977; Constantine and Gower, 1979), while another has been proposed by Holman (1979), in which nonsymmetric proximities are analyzed (via nonmetric models) into symmetric proximities and row and/or column bias parameters.

Young's (1975a) ASYMSCAL (for ASYMmetric multidimensional SCALing) provides another approach for analysis of nonsymmetric data. ASYMSCAL allows differential weights for dimensions for either the row stimuli or for the column stimuli, or both. In this respect ASYMSCAL closely resembles a weighted generalization of the unfolding model that will be discussed in the section on unfolding.

Theoretical Developments for and Applications of Nonsymmetric Analyses (for One-Mode Two-Way Data). Until very recently, asymmetries in a proximities matrix have often been regarded as a nuisance—something to be averaged out or eliminated by various strategies. The recent proliferation of models for asymmetric data has coincided with increased awareness of the psychological importance of asymmetries in proximities data. Tversky (1977) and Tversky and Gati (1978) cite many examples of psychological processes giving rise to nonsymmetric data (see Sjöberg, 1972) and leave the reader with the impression that the psychological universe may indeed be more nonsymmetric than symmetric.

Tversky (1977) and Tversky and Gati (1978) develop the argument still further in advocating the superiority of feature-theoretic models to continuous spatial dimensions for representing structure in data [for example, Gati, 1979]. However, Krumhansl (1978), drawing extensively on findings from unidimensional psychophysics, has developed a highly ingenious "distance-density" model that assumes similarity is a function of both interpoint distance and the spatial density of other stimulus points in the surrounding region of the metric space. Krumhansl finds support in the literature for various predictions made by her model and suggests that spatial distance models may still be more relevant to nonsymmetric data than Tversky (1977; Tversky and Gati, 1978) argued.

While careful consideration of experimental procedures in order to avoid artifactual asymmetries is still warranted

[Janson, 1977], current practice clearly pays much greater attention to (and respect for) asymmetries in data; for example, Cermak and Cornillon (1976), Zinnes and Wolff (1977), Jones, Roberts, and Holman (1978), Krumhansl (1979). Also, a useful inferential test for symmetry in a proximities matrix has been developed by Hubert and Baker (1979).

Scalar Product (Spatial but Non-distance) Models (for One-Mode Two-Way Data). The scalar product between points i and j (b_{ij}) is defined in terms of their coordinates (x_{ir} and x_{jr}, $r = 1, 2, \ldots R$) as

$$b_{ij} = \sum_{r=1}^{R} x_{ir} x_{jr}$$

Scalar product models are sometimes called "projection models" because the scalar products of a set of points with a fixed point are proportional to the projections of those points onto a vector from the origin of the coordinate system to the fixed point.

After the factor analytic model (not considered in this chapter), probably the most widely known scalar product model for symmetric proximities data is Ekman's "content model." Important articles discussing this class of models, whose popularity has declined within the period covered by this review, are Eisler and Roskam (1977) and Sjöberg (1975). The latter argues strongly against the content model, in favor of the more widely accepted class of distance models for proximities data.

Other scalar product symmetric approaches include Guttman and Lingoes' SSA-III [Lingoes, 1972, 1973] and certain options in Young's (1972) POLYCON (for POLYnomial CONjoint analysis). Both programs are nonmetric factor analytic procedures applicable to symmetric data, usually but not necessarily correlations or covariances. Further discussion of these models will be found under unconstrained scalar product models for two-mode two-way data.

In considering scalar product models for nonsymmetric dyadic data, there is Harshman's (1975, 1978) metric procedure DEDICOM (DEcomposition into DIrectional COMponents), which can also handle two-mode three-way data (see below). The "strong" case of the model assumes a common set of dimensions for the rows and columns, so that the model is in that sense symmetric. Asymmetries are accounted for in this model by a set of indices of "directional relationship" which indicate the degree to which each dimension affects each other dimension. One way of viewing the strong DEDICOM model is as a special case of the factor or components analysis model in which factor loadings and factor scores are constrained to be linearly related to each other. (The "weak" model is precisely equivalent to the factor or components analysis model.)

A model involving a geometrically interesting generalization of scalar products (defined only for two or three dimensions, however) has been formulated by Chino (1978) for one-mode two-way nonsymmetric data.

Nonspatial Distance Models (for One-Mode Two-Way Data)

A development that has occurred almost entirely within the period covered by this review is that of non-spatial or discrete models for proximities data. Of course the vast area of clustering has long allowed such representation of proximities, but such solutions have infrequently been viewed as realistic psychological models for proximities data. Moreover, as is true with factor analysis, the clustering literature is much too vast to be covered here, so we refer the reader to Sneath and Sokal (1973), Hubert (1974c), Hartigan (1975), and Blashfield and Allenderfer (1978) for relevant reviews.

Backtracking somewhat, we first consider an approach by Cunningham and Shepard (1974) that is, in fact, neither spatial nor nonspatial. This "non-dimensional" scaling approach transforms the data so as to satisfy the metric condition of the triangle inequality. The method is useful primarily in converting ordinal proximities into ratio scale distance estimates, which could then be used as data for various *metric* analyses, or for determining the form of the function relating proximities to distances.

One nonspatial model that assumes a discrete geometric model is the Shepard and Arabie (1979; Arabie and Shepard, 1973) ADCLUS (for ADditive CLUStering) model. ADCLUS assumes that similarities data can be represented in terms of discrete but possibly overlapping classes or clusters, and that each of these clusters has a non-negative weight (although an additive constant interpretable as the weight for the cluster corresponding to the complete set is not so constrained). The predicted similarity for any pair of stimuli is just the sum of the weights across the clusters containing that pair of stimuli. Formally stated,

$$\hat{s}_{ij} = \sum_{r=1}^{R} w_r p_{ir} p_{jr}$$

where $\hat{s}_{ij}$ is similarity of stimuli (or other objects) i and j, w_r is the weight for the r-th class, R is the number of classes, analogous to the number of dimensions in various spatial models, and p_{ir} is a binary $(0, 1)$ class membership function ($p_{ir} = 1$ *iff* stimulus i is a member of class r, and 0 otherwise). This model is formally equivalent to the factor analytic model (without commonalities) for correlations or covariances, except for the constraint that the p_{ir} be restricted to the discrete values of 0 or 1. In addition, ADCLUS represents a special (symmetric) case of Tversky's (1977) general features model of similarity, and is in fact the only case for which an analytic procedure is currently operational.

Arabie and Carroll (1978) have provided a different algorithm called MAPCLUS (for MAthematical Programming CLUStering) for fitting the ADCLUS model, since the algorithm used in the Shepard-Arabie (1978) algorithm was very expensive computationally and otherwise unwieldy. Moreover, the MAPCLUS approach is easily generalized to fit the three-way model, called INDCLUS (Carroll and Arabie, 1979).

Tree structures comprise another interesting class of discrete geometric models. For a given tree structure there are at least two (and, in some cases, three) types of metrics that can be defined on the stimuli. In this representation, the stimuli are represented as nodes of the tree, either terminal nodes only, or both terminal and nonterminal. One of the two classes of metrics is the *ultrametric* [Hartigan, 1967; Jardine, Jardine, and Sibson, 1967; Johnson, 1967], in which "heights" are associated with nonterminal nodes of the tree, and "distance" between any two nodes is defined as the "height" of the first nonterminal node at which the two are linked.

An interesting relationship between ultrametric and Euclidean metrics (see above) was formally derived by Holman (1972), who showed that a Euclidean representation of "ultrametric data" requires $n - 1$ dimensions, where n is the cardinality of the largest subset of stimuli satisfying the ultrametric inequality. While this demonstration has somewhat limited applicability to data containing error, Holman's (1972) result should help dispel a lingering misconception from the factor analytic tradition, namely that distance-based scaling models are legitimately serviceable as a clustering method: they are not (Kruskal, 1977b).

A second metric, after the ultrametric, has been given a variety of names, and the same is true for the resulting representations. The metric is simply defined as the shortest path in terms of lengths of the

"branches" or "links" connecting adjacent nodes in the tree. For a tree structure there is only one path connecting any pair of nodes, so the shortest path is trivially defined as the length of that unique path. This metric was designated as "path length" and the associated trees as "path length trees" by Carroll and Chang (1973), Carroll (1976), and Carroll and Pruzansky (1975, 1980). Alternative algorithms for fitting the metric, as well as relevant applications are given by Cunningham (1974, 1978) and Sattath and Tversky (1977). Other important references include Buneman (1971, 1974) and Dobson (1974). We note that some of these authors have also given other names to this metric and/or trees on which it is defined.

Carroll and Chang (1973) also allowed a third type of metric, namely a synthesis of ultrametric and path length metric, in which distances were defined as the sum of the path length and a height value associated with the "least common ancestor" node. It can be shown that this "combined" metric can be meaningfully defined only in the case [allowed by Carroll and Chang, 1973] of trees in which the stimuli or other objects are associated with at least some non-terminal as well as terminal nodes.

The approach of Carroll and Pruzansky (1975, 1980; see also Carroll, 1976) utilized mathematical programming techniques, analogous in some ways to those used in the Arabie-Carroll (1978) MAPCLUS approach, to fit either ultrametric or path length trees to proximities data via a least squares criterion. The essential new feature of the Carroll-Pruzansky approach, however, is the generalization to multiple tree structures, for which proximities data are represented by composite distances summed over distances (either ultrametric or path length) from two or more trees. Carroll and Pruzansky applied this approach to a number of data sets, with interpretable results, and conjectured that there may be a relatively well defined sense in which a single tree structure is approximately equivalent to a two-dimensional spatial structure [Sattath and Tversky, 1977].

A constrained nonmetric analysis in terms of (single) path length tree structure models has been described by Roskam (1973), and also allows such options as constraining certain branch lengths to be equal. Constrained analyses are also possible by using appropriate options in most of the procedures designed for unconstrained fitting of the ADCLUS or tree structure models.

Hybrid Distance Models (for One-Mode Two-Way Data)

By hybrid geometric models we denote models that in some way combine continuous spatial structure of the type classically associated with MDS with discrete nonspatial structure such as assumed in ADCLUS, tree structure, other more general graph theoretic structures, or combinations of these. Carroll and Pruzansky (1975) have produced the only approach known to us of "wholistic" fitting of a hybrid model, where both components are simultaneously fitted to the data. This hybrid model combines a tree structure component (either single or multiple) with an R-dimensional spatial component, and uses an alternating least squares procedure for fitting the model. Very good results were obtained in such a hybrid analysis of some kinship data obtained from a sorting task by Rosenberg and Kim (1975). We expect to see other hybrid models formulated and the associated analytic procedures implemented in the future [Carroll, 1975, 1976].

TWO-MODE TWO-WAY DATA

We now consider two-way data in which the two ways correspond to distinct modes (for example, subjects and stimuli). The data array in this case will correspond (in general) to a rectangular matrix which is generally nonsymmetric (even in the case when, by coincidence or design, the matrix is square).

Spatial Distance Models (for Two-Mode Two-Way Data)

The principal distance model for studying individual differences in preference judgments (as a case of two-mode two-way data) is the unfolding model. This approach was originally formulated by Coombs (1950), with a multidimensional generalization provided by Bennett and Hays (1960). The hallmark of this model is that both stimuli and subjects' ideal points are simultaneously mapped into the same spatial configuration. As such, this approach constitutes what we have called an internal (unconstrained) analysis of preference data. The original developments by Coombs (1950) and Bennett and Hays (1960) assumed the data were ordinal and conditional, the latter by subjects for subjects by stimuli preference data. Subsequent proposals and corresponding computer programs have allowed for interval (metric) and/or unconditional data. Also, more recent procedures include external analyses, which are constrained in that the stimulus space is given a priori, while the subjects' ideal points are fitted on the basis of the preference data.

It should be emphasized that the unfolding model is not limited only to subjects by stimuli preference data, but may be applied to any two-mode two-way data matrix for which a distance model is appropriate. Recall, in particular, the first principle given above for representing nonsymmetric data. For a general and more detailed discussion of unfolding models, see Carroll (1972, 1980).

Internal (Unconstrained) Distance Models (for Two-Mode Two-Way Data) Procedures that allow internal unfolding analysis include KYST [Kruskal et al., 1973, 1977] as well as its predecessors MDSCAL-5 and TORSCA-9 (cited above), Guttman and

Lingoes' SSAR-I and SSAR-II procedures [Lingoes, 1972, 1973] and a procedure by Roskam (1971; see also Lingoes and Roskam, 1973). Of these, only KYST and MDSCAL-5 (or 6) use an appropriate loss function and/or allow use of a loss function (stress "formula two") with a variance-like normalization (for conditional analyses) or metric unfolding options (for unconditional analyses). Those two programs thus are the only theoretically valid implementations, since trivial "degenerate" solutions (with a zero value of the loss function) occur when a loss function like stress formula one (having a normalizing factor resembling the sum of squared distances) is used, or when nonmetric conditional analysis is done (irrespective of what loss function is used). The rationale for a loss function like stress formula two can be found in Kruskal and Carroll (1969; see also Carroll, 1980). Programs other than KYST and MDSCAL-5 sometimes yield what appear to be good solutions despite this theoretical problem, but such findings are generally the results of convergence to substantively acceptable local minima, rather than the global minimum corresponding to a degenerate solution. An example of the latter is a configuration in which the entities corresponding to the two modes are each mapped into a single point.

In addition to the metric (internal or external) analyses discussed above, there is a metric unfolding procedure [Schönemann, 1970], that attains an analytic internal solution for a very strong case of the unfolding model. Carroll and Chang's PREFMAP-2 (1971; Chang and Carroll, 1972), which is primarily designed for external analyses (as discussed below; see also Carroll, 1980), also allows an internal solution for a model similar to but slightly more general than Schönemann's (1970). Schönemann and Wang (1972) combine the metric unfolding model with the Bradley-Terry-Luce choice model (Luce, 1959), to produce a stochastic unfolding approach that is applicable to paired comparisons data. The MDPREF model, which can be viewed as a special case of the unfolding model (in which the subjects' ideal points are infinitely distant from the stimulus points [Carroll, 1972, 1980]) will be discussed in the section on scalar product models.

External (Constrained) Distance Models (for Two-Mode Two-Way Data) External analyses in terms of the unfolding model (and some of its generalizations) are provided by the PREFMAP procedure of Carroll and Chang (1967; see also Chang, 1969, and Carroll, 1972, 1980), by KYST [Kruskal et al., 1973, 1977], as well as other programs described below. PREFMAP (and its successor PREFMAP-2, described in Carroll, 1980) is based on a general linear least squares approach, involving quadratic regression procedures, and allows both metric and nonmetric options.

PREFMAP and PREFMAP-2 also allow fitting of two models more inclusive than the standard unfolding model. One of these models, for "weighted unfolding," allows a more general weighted Euclidean metric, with a different pattern of dimension weights as well as different location of ideal points for each subject. A second generalization allows the most general form of Euclidean metric, defined by a different quadratic form for each subject, thus allowing a different rigid (or orthogonal) rotation of the reference frame for individual subjects, followed by differential weighting of the resulting idiosyncratically defined dimensions. An alternative strategy for implementing nonmetric external unfolding analyses is given by the linear programming approach of Srinivasan and Shocker (1973), which also includes non-negativity constraints for the dimension weights. The same constraints are provided in a metric procedure using quadratic programming described by Davison (1976).

During the years covered by this

chapter, substantive applications of both internal and external unfolding include Levine (1972), Coombs, Coombs, and McClelland (1975), Davison (1977), Seligson (1977). Coombs and Avrunin (1977) provided a theoretical derivation of the unfolding model from fundamental psychological principles. There also have been several studies making extensive comparisons (with interesting psychological results) of the structures found when subjects give similarity as well as preference judgments for the same stimulus domain [Cermak and Cornillon, 1976; Nygren and Jones, 1977; Sjöberg, 1977, 1980; also see Carroll, 1972, for an early discussion of this question]. A new methodological approach for combining proximities with preference (and possibly other rating scale) data has been discussed by Ramsay (1979b). The corresponding model lies somewhere between our categories of "internal" and "external" models.

Scalar Product Models (for Two-Mode Two-Way Data)

By far, the dominant class of models for two-mode two-way data are scalar product models, which include factor analysis and principal components analysis. One approach seeks to fit the score matrix, another to fit correlations or covariances; Kruskal (1978) refers to these as the direct and indirect approaches, respectively.

Internal (Unconstrained) Models (for Two-Mode Two-Way Data) The program SSA-III (Lingoes, 1972, 1973) can be viewed as a form of nonmetric factor analysis, differing markedly in rationale from the Kruskal–Shepard (1974) variety of nonmetric factor analysis. SSA-III generally assumes correlations or covariances (but can use other proximities data) and seeks a representation involving vectors such that the scalar products between vectors reproduce the order of the proximities. In contrast, the Kruskal–Shepard approach starts with a general rectangular (two-mode as well as two-way) data matrix, and seeks a representation in terms of two sets of vectors such that the scalar products reproduce (as well as possible) the conditional rank orders (within one of the two modes) of the scores. Thus, Kruskal and Shepard's method uses the direct approach, while Guttman and Lingoes' SSA-III or Young's POLYCON uses the indirect approach. The theoretical rationale of the latter approach is less clear, since, aside from Guttman's simplex structure, it is difficult to envision conditions where correlations or covariances are only defined ordinally.

In passing, we would like to note that when the Kruskal and Shepard (1974) method is applied to two-mode two-way data, it is often expedient to depict the objects of one mode as vectors and the other as points. This representation has various advantages over the more conventional display of both modes as points in a joint space, particularly when the data are conditional with respect to the mode represented by vectors.

A particular type of data to which a factor or component analytic type of model has been very usefully applied comprises a subjects by stimuli matrix of preference (or other dominance) data. In this case the scalar product or projection model has come to be known as the "vector model," because of the very convenient pictorial representation of stimuli as points and subjects as vectors. We view this technique as the "right" way to depict such solutions, since in the case of such data, the matrices are conditional with respect to subjects. Thus, the order of projections of (stimulus) points onto a (subject) vector, but not that of vectors onto a point, is meaningfully defined both in the data and in the geometric representation.

Tucker (1960) and Slater (1960) were the first to propose (independently) somewhat limited versions of such a model for preferences [see also Nishisato, 1978b]. Probably the most widely used method of analysis involving this model is Carroll and Chang's (1964; see also Carroll, 1972, 1980) MDPREF (for MultiDimensional PREFerence analysis), which is actually a special type of factor analysis of either a derived or given preference score matrix. While MDPREF applied to paired comparisons preference data is computationally a metric technique, there is a reasonable index of ordinal agreement with the paired comparisons preference data which is optimized by this procedure [Carroll, 1972].

It is possible, at least in principle, to effect a multidimensional analysis of "classical" paired comparisons data, in which the paired comparisons judgments are aggregated over different subjects or over replications for a single subject. As argued earlier, the result of such preprocessing can be viewed as replicated two-mode two-way data. A multidimensional model for such a matrix, called the "wandering vector" model, is discussed by Carroll (1980). de Leeuw and Heiser (1979) independently proposed a mathematically equivalent model based on Thurstone's Case I model.

External (Constrained) Scalar Product Models (for Two-Mode Two-Way Data) In scalar product external models for two-mode two-way data (as with external unfolding models) one set of points is fixed and the other "mapped in." In the case of conditional data, it is almost always the points corresponding to the conditional mode (the one typically represented as vectors) that are mapped in. One metric means of implementation is multiple linear regression, where the regression coefficients (possibly after some normalization) define the coordinates of the second set of points or vectors. In the case of nonmetric data, some form of what has variously been called nonmetric, ordinal, or monotonic multiple linear regression is necessary. Carroll and Chang's (1971; Chang and Carroll, 1972) PREFMAP and PREFMAP-

2 both provide metric and nonmetric options for such mapping.

One class of models and methods not usually viewed in this way, but which can be characterized as external analysis in terms of a scalar product or vector model (see discussion below, and Carroll, 1980), is the class including approaches variously called conjoint measurement [Luce and Tukey, 1964], functional measurement [Anderson, 1974, 1977], and/or conjoint analysis [Green and Wind, 1973; Green and Srinivasan, 1978]. While all three approaches allow more general models, in the most widely known and used versions of these three closely related approaches, a simple additive model is assumed to relate a (metric or nonmetric) dependent variable to a set of qualitative independent variables that form a (complete or fractional) factorial design. In conjoint measurement, the dependent variable is always assumed to be ordinal, in functional measurement it is assumed metric (usually interval scale), while conjoint analysis includes both metric and nonmetric alternatives.

The additivity analysis central to these three approaches can be viewed as fitting a "main effects only" analysis of variance model to the data either metrically (via classical ANOVA procedures) or nonmetrically. Such additivity analysis can be viewed as an external one in terms of a scalar product model by expressing the main effects ANOVA model in the now widely known form of a multiple linear regression model with appropriately defined (usually binary) "dummy" variables, which play the role of the external dimensions. One widely used procedure for fitting a nonmetric version of this model is Kruskal's (1965; Kruskal and Carmone, 1965) MONANOVA, and other nonmetric procedures for fitting this simple additive model include ADDIT [Roskam and Van Glist, 1967], POLYCON [Young, 1972], CM-I [Lingoes, 1972, 1973], and ADDALS [de Leeuw, Young, and Takane, 1976]. ADDALS also allows more general cases in which, say, the factors of the factorial design are treated as ordinal or interval scale, rather than (necessarily) nominal scale variables, (or mixtures of scale types are allowed for factors) or in which the dependent variable is nominally scaled. Carroll's (1969) categorical conjoint measurement and Nishisato's (1971) optimal scaling approach also provide options for dealing with nominal scale dependent variables.

In recent years there have been increasingly frequent applications of conjoint measurement to data from experimental and other judgmental tasks [for example, Cliff, 1972; Ullrich and Painter, 1974; Falmagne, 1976], as well as relevant theoretical developments (for example, Fishburn, 1975; Falmagne, Iverson, and Marcovici, 1979), which generally fall under the purview of a forthcoming chapter on unidimensional scaling and psychophysics in the *Annual Review*. However, conjoint analysis remains one of the most underemployed techniques for data analysis in psychology. In contrast, the method has enjoyed extensive usage in marketing research, where Green and Wind (1973) provided a practitioner's handbook. Although applications are too numerous to cite at length, the following serve as examples: Johnson (1974), Green and Wind (1975), Green, Carroll, and Carmone (1975), Bouroche (1977), Green (1977), Green and Carmone (1977). Helpful overviews of current developments in the application of conjoint analysis in marketing can be found in Green and Srinivasan (1978) and Wind (1976, 1978a, b).

A general procedure, called ORDMET, that is applicable to nonmetric external analysis in terms of a scalar product model, is described by McClelland and Coombs (1975). Given data sufficiently close to being errorless, ORDMET's linear programming approach can be applied to fitting any external scalar product model, conjoint measurement model, and even

external versions of the unfolding model.

Nonspatial Distance Models (*for Two-Mode Two-Way Data*)

The only nonspatial model proposed to date (outside the clustering literature) that is directly applicable to two-mode two-way data is Tversky and Sattath's (1979) "Preference Trees" model. This model is applicable to a paired comparisons preference matrix aggregated over subjects (or, more appropriately, over replications by a single subject), and so can be viewed (see above) as a two-mode two-way model. The Preference Tree (PRETREE) model follows as a special case of the elimination by aspects (EBA) model [Tversky 1972a, b], and subsumes Luce's (1959, 1977) constant ratio model. Although there is no program for fitting the PRETREE model to data, it has been tested by utilizing trees derived from similarity data or on a priori grounds.

TWO-MODE THREE-WAY DATA

As mentioned under one-mode two-way data, Carroll and Kruskal (1977) have provided a general overview of spatial models and data analytic methods falling under the present heading.

Spatial Distance Models (*for Two-Mode Three-Way Data*)

Unconstrained Symmetric Euclidean Models (for Two-Mode Three-Way Data) The principal type of data falling under this classification is three-way dyadic data, comprising two or more square symmetric proximities matrices for pairs of stimuli, from two or more subjects (or other data sources). The dominant type of model is a distance model (only Euclidean models to date) for stimuli, with a set of individual differences parameters characterizing subjects. The models extend from the "points of view" approach of Tucker and Messick (1963) through various forms of a weighted Euclidean model [Bloxom, 1968; Horan, 1969; Carroll and Chang, 1969, 1970], frequently called the INDSCAL (for INdividual Differences SCALing) model (but called a "subjective metrics" model by Schönemann, 1972).

Yet further generalizations of this model include Tucker's (1972) "three-mode scaling" model, Carroll and Chang's (1972a) IDIOSCAL model, and Harshman's (1972b) PARAFAC2 model. Of these, IDIOSCAL is the most general, as it includes the other two as special cases. IDIOSCAL assumes a different generalized Euclidean metric, which for each subject is defined by a quadratic form described by a symmetric $R \times R$ matrix. Three-mode scaling is essentially a special case of Tucker's (1964) model for three-mode factor analysis, applied to an array of estimated scalar products derived from three-way proximities data. Tucker's approach can be viewed as a special case of the IDIOSCAL model, in which a special structure is imposed on the quadratic form matrices (namely, the individual quadratic forms are linear combinations of a small set of symmetric $R \times R$ matrices). Recent statistical developments in three-mode factor analysis are given by Bentler and Lee (1978, 1979). Harshman's (1972b) PARAFAC2 provides an interesting special case of both IDIOSCAL and three-way scaling. In terms of a geometric interpretation due to Tucker (1972), PARAFAC2 assumes that differential weights are applied to correlated dimensions, but that the correlations are the same for all subjects.

All three of these models have the simple weighted Euclidean model, INDSCAL [Carroll and Chang, 1970] as a special case. INDSCAL has an important property, however, that two of these three more general models (IDIOSCAL and three-mode scaling) do not share, and which has only been conjectured but not

proved for PARAFAC2 [Harshman, 1972b]. The specific feature is "dimensional uniqueness," which means that the dimensions are not invariant under orthogonal (or general linear) transformations, but are uniquely defined (or are "identifiable" in current statistical parlance) except for permutations and reflections. (See Harshman (1972a) and Kruskal (1976, 1977c) for uniqueness proofs. It should be noted that these results have actually been proved for the more general three-way CANDECOMP [for CANonical DECOMPosition] model provided by Carroll and Chang (1970) and independently by Harshman (1970) under the name of PARAFAC [for PARAllel FACtor analysis]). A more extensive discussion of these models can be found in Carroll (1973), Carroll and Wish (1974a, b) and Wish and Carroll (1974).

The principal algorithmic advances in this domain during recent years have entailed the procedure already discussed when considering the ALSCAL method of Takane et al. (1977) and Ramsay's (1977b) maximum likelihood approach in MULTISCALE. Each of these programs has both (one-mode) two-way and (two-mode) three-way capability. In the latter case, both techniques assume the weighted Euclidean, or INDSCAL model. The principal new feature of the ALSCAL treatment of three-way data is that the program provides a nonmetric implementation of the INDSCAL model. Another capability, also not available in other approaches (for example, INDSCAL) to fitting the weighted Euclidean model is the provision for missing or replicated data. In the case of MULTISCALE, which is restricted to the metric case, there are some points to be emphasized vis à vis three-way data. First, the asymptotic chi-square criterion for tests of statistical significance of dimensions is more questionable than in the two-way case. Ramsay (1979a) has devised an adjustment in degrees of freedom to expedite more valid nominal levels of significance. In addition, of course, MULTISCALE in the three-way case allows the definition of confidence regions for subject weights as well as for stimulus points. In research currently underway, Sharon Weinberg is comparing the confidence regions produced by MULTISCALE with those produced by straightforward jackknifing of INDSCAL, a less model-specific procedure employed earlier by Cohen (1974a) and Ebbesen (1977).

A mathematical development that has led to some important new algorithms for the INDSCAL model is Schönemann's (1972) "analytic solution for a class of subjective metrics models." This solution, however, is appropriate only for errorless data that fit the model exactly. More robust modifications have been provided by Carroll and Chang (1972a), Schönemann, Carter, and James (1976), and de Leeuw and Pruzansky (1978). These three modifications all have the advantage that they provide approximate solutions for the weighted Euclidean or INDSCAL model in much less time than for the more standard implementations [Carroll and Chang, 1970; Pruzansky, 1975; Takane et al., 1977; Ramsay, 1977b]. The solutions resulting from the more rapid algorithms often provide useful initial configurations for the standard approaches, which have more well defined and probably more stable numerical properties. Another approach providing an initial configuration for the INDSCAL procedure is implemented in a program called SINDSCAL-LS [Carroll and Pruzansky, 1979], based on a special case of CANDELINC (called LINCINDS) providing a linearly constrained version of INDSCAL. SINDSCAL-LS uses the stimulus space and/or subjects space from three-mode scaling to define the constraint matrices [Cohen, 1974b; MacCallum, 1976].

A final approach to be discussed here is one by Lingoes and Borg (1978), based generally on using "Procrustean" configuration matching techniques, called PINDIS (for Procrustean INdividual Differences Scaling). In addition to providing options for fitting models of the INDSCAL and IDIOSCAL variety, PINDIS introduces a new "vector weighting" or "perspective" model.

Applications of Two-Mode Three-Way Symmetric Euclidean Models Along with the increased capabilities of higher-way models, the user must accept the responsibility for offering convincing interpretations of a larger number of fitted parameters. Accordingly the highly elegant work of Bisanz, LaPorte, Vesonders, and Voss (1978) and LaPorte and Voss (1979) closely related the model parameters of INDSCAL solutions to substantive issues in the study of memory for prose. Other interesting results in the area of memory and cognition can be found in Shoben (1974), Howard and Howard (1977), and Friendly (1977). There have been many three-way analyses of perceptual data, including the studies reviewed in Carroll and Wish (1974a, b) and Wish and Carroll (1974). Other such papers include Carroll and Chang (1974), Walden and Montgomery (1975), Fraser (1976), Chang and Carroll (1978), Soli and Arabie (1979), Arabie and Soli (1980). Researchers in social psychology and sociology have been especially active in applying the weighted Euclidean model [for example, Rosenberg and Kim, 1975; Breiger, Boorman, and Arabie, 1975; Wish, 1975, 1976; Wish, Deutsch, and Kaplan, 1976; Wish and Kaplan, 1977; Coxon and Jones, 1978; Wish, 1979a, b]. The studies by Wish and his colleagues used the INDSCAL model and obtained substantive results supportive of Wish's implicit theory of interpersonal communication.

Constrained Symmetric Euclidean Models (for Two-Mode Three-Way Data) A constrained approach to individual differences MDS that takes as its basic model the Tucker three-mode scaling model has been provided by Bloxom (1978), who imposes various equality constraints, so that parameters are equal to each other or to prespecified values. Bloxom (1978) also includes a constrained version of the INDSCAL model as a special case, since INDSCAL itself corresponds to three-mode scaling with all (off diagonal) dimension correlations constrained to zero.

A different approach to a constrained INDSCAL analysis is provided in a procedure called LINCINDS (for LINearly Constrained INDSCAL) that is a special case of the CANDELINC procedure [Carroll, Pruzansky, and Kruskal, 1979] to be discussed in detail under constrained three-mode three-way scalar product models. In LINCINDS the INDSCAL stimulus coordinates, subject weights, or both can be constrained to be linearly related to a set of exogenous ("outside") variables (measured on the stimuli, subjects, or both). Specifically, the coordinate x_{ir} of the i-th stimulus on the r-th dimension can be constrained to be of the form

$$x_{ir} = \sum_{s=1}^{S} b_{rs} v_{is}$$

where v_{is} is the known value of stimulus i on exogeneous variable s, and b_{rs} is a fitted coefficient (analogous to a regression coefficient in the least squares regression equation predicting dimension r from the S exogenous variables). In practice it has been found inappropriate to use this procedure to constrain the subject weights, however, both from empirical experience and for theoretical reasons related to MacCallum's (1977) criticism of applying linear procedures to INDSCAL weights, although we regard his arguments as overstated [see Carroll, Pruzansky, and Kruskal, 1979].

Nonsymmetric Euclidean Models (for Two-Mode Three-Way Data) DeSarbo (1978) has produced a three-way metric unfolding approach, which can accommodate non-symmetric data according to the first general principle listed above for such data. Also, as noted above in the discussion of Young's (1975a) ASYMSCAL, there is a three-way generalization of that model.

Scalar Product Models (for Two-Mode Three-Way Data)

While not originally formulated as such, both the INDSCAL [Carroll and Chang, 1970] and three-mode scaling [Tucker, 1972] procedures have been applied directly to scalar product data. Both methods ordinarily start out with dissimilarities data and, via preprocessing, transform these data into estimated scalar product matrices, which are then analyzed by a symmetric version of three-way CANDECOMP or of three-mode factor analysis, respectively. Either procedure just as easily fits a model directly for two-mode three-way scalar product data. Moreover, the INDSCAL program [Chang and Carroll, 1969] and its successor SINDSCAL [Pruzansky, 1975] both have options to deal with the scalar product data directly.

A scalar product model explicitly formulated for nonsymmetric two-mode three-way data is a three-way version of Harshman's (1975, 1978) DEDICOM model. This is a generalization of the one-mode two-way DEDICOM model to the two-mode three-way case. A set of dimension weights analogous to those assumed in the INDSCAL-CANDECOMP-PARAFAC models are introduced as parameters describing the second mode (and third way), which may correspond to subjects or other data sources.

Another model for this type of non-symmetric data has been formulated by Carroll and Sen (1976), and was explicitly designed for the case of "cross impact" data, in which each of a number of subjects judges the impact of each of a set of events on each other event. See Carroll (1977) for a description of the model and the corresponding analytic procedure, called impact scaling.

THREE-MODE THREE-WAY DATA

Spatial Distance Models (for Three-Mode Three-Way Data)

As already mentioned in the section on distance models for two-mode three-way nonsymmetric data, DeSarbo (1978) has implemented a three-way metric unfolding procedure, which can be interpreted either as a direct generalization of Schönemann's (1972) two-way metric unfolding model and method, or as a nonsymmetric generalization of INDSCAL. The DeSarbo procedure, like Schönemann's is both metric and unconditional (although a case can be made that DeSarbo's approach is matrix conditional). A typical data array to which this three-way unfolding procedure can be applied is a set of subjects by stimuli matrices of preference scale values, one such matrix for each of a number of situations or experimental conditions.

Scalar Product Models (for Three-Mode Three-Way Data)

The two principal unconstrained models appropriate to this section are the Tucker (1964) three-mode factor analysis model and the general three-way case of CANDECOMP-PARAFAC. While there have been some useful applications of three-mode factor analysis (Wiggins and Blackburn, 1976; Redfield and Stone, 1979; Sjöberg, 1979) there have so far been no convincing applications of the general three-mode three-way case of CANDECOMP-PARAFAC. CANDECOMP has mainly been useful, in fact, (in its two-mode three-way symmetric case) as the analytic underpinnings of the Carroll–Chang INDSCAL procedure, and, more recently, as the first step in DeSarbo's (1978) approach to three-way unfolding.

Turning now to constrained models, we note that the CANDELINC approach, which has been referred to previously (Carroll, Pruzansky, and Kruskal, 1979), is directly applicable to the three- or higher-way CANDECOMP model. In the three-way case, CANDELINC allows linear constraints on all modes, or on just one or two of the three modes. In general these constraints take the form that the parameters for a given mode must be linear combinations of a set of a priori external variables. These external variables are defined via a "design matrix" for each of the linearly constrained modes, with the design matrix containing the evaluated external variables.

HIGHER-WAY DATA

Tucker's three-mode factor analysis could easily be generalized to the higher-way case [see Carroll and Wish 1974a, b], but to our knowledge no actual implementation has been achieved. The N-way CANDECOMP model has been so implemented. While it has not been usefully applied to general N-way multivariate data, one particular useful application has been to a least-squares fitting of the Lazarsfeld latent class model [Carroll, Pruzansky, and Green, 1979].

DATA COLLECTION AND RELATED ISSUES

Although we have emphasized the development of models and their algorithms, there has also been much research in the techniques used before the model is to be fitted, including the perennial problem of comparing two or more proximities matrices. The fact that the straightforward approaches (for example, correlating two matrices) encounter formidable difficulties when inferential tests are sought has often caused investigators to feel that only the scaling output (but not the input matrices) could be compared. The consequent practices have recently become less forgivable owing to results [Hubert and Schultz, 1976b; Hubert, 1978] which generalized earlier work of Mantel (1967) to allow significance tests for the correspondence between two or more [Hubert, 1979] input matrices, as well as related applications.

The extensive variety of models (and their associated types of input data) notwithstanding, situations often arise where the data at hand are not immediately compatible with the intended model. A typical example occurs when a one-mode two-way nonmetric scaling representation is sought for either of the modes of a two-mode two-way data set. Shepard (1972b) has labeled as "indirect similarities" (also sometimes called "profile similarities") the secondary data that ultimately serve as input to the program implementing the model. An example consists of computing the squared Euclidean distances (Carroll, 1968) between all pairs of rows/columns of such a two-mode two-way data set.

One relevant area of research concerns the partitions that result when subjects are asked to sort a set of stimuli into "homogeneous groups." For analyses where differences between subjects' sortings are of interest, a variety of measures of distance between such partitions have been developed [Boorman and Arabie, 1972; Arabie and Boorman, 1973]. For situations in which the stimuli being sorted are of greater interest in the analysis, there is an extensive literature on techniques for going from partitions of the stimuli to one-mode two-way (stimuli by stimuli) data: Carroll (1968), Rosenberg and Jones (1972), Rosenberg and Sedlak (1972), Rosenberg and Kim (1975), Wish (1976), Wish et al. (1976), Wish and Kaplan (1977), Drasgow and Jones (1979). Other papers relevant to indirect similarities data include Sibson (1972), Lund (1974), Batchelder and Narens (1977), Arabie and Soli (1980). Finally, R. A. Harshman (personal communication) has reported favorable results when two-way marginals are

subtracted from three-way data in applications of CANDECOMP-PARAFAC, and Kruskal (1977d) has derived least squares properties supporting this strategy.

A related area of activity in scaling concerns the development of incomplete experimental designs to reduce the effort and expense involved in collecting MDS data. For selectively obtaining data on a subset of the $n(n-1)/2$ pairs of n stimuli, the following may serve as useful references: Spence and Domoney (1974), Green and Bentler (1979), Deutscher (1980), Green (1980), Isaac (1980), Kohler and Rushton (1980), Spence (1980), Young, Sarle, and Hoffman (1980). For conjoint analysis, Green, Carroll, and Carmone (1978) have discussed an approach that spares researchers of the need to execute a full factorial design.

MDS: NEW AREAS OF USAGE

In addition to research activities in the United States, Canada, the United Kingdom, the Netherlands, Israel, and Sweden, various other countries have developed their own traditions of MDS. In Japan, Hayashi, Indow, and others have been especially active (see references throughout this chapter), and Okada and Watanabe have translated into Japanese the two volumes of the 1969 Irvine conference [Shepard, Romney, and Nerlove, 1976; Romney, Shepard, and Nerlove, 1977]. Bouroche and his colleagues in France have been responsible for many developments and applications of scaling techniques [Bertier and Bouroche, 1975; Bouroche and Dussaix, 1975]. In Germany, Feger (1978) and Bick and Müller have formed the core of groups actively developing and using MDS and related methods. In the Soviet Union, there is continuing work by Mirkin and others [Terekhin, 1973, 1974; Kamenskii, 1977].

With respect to disciplines, MDS has maintained a strong base in marketing research. There also appear to be possible applications in econometrics [Maital, 1978], and usage in political science [for example, Weisberg, 1972] and sociology [for example, Boorman and White, 1976; Coxon and Jones, 1977] is also apparent from various references cited earlier. From an advocacy point of view, perhaps the greatest gains in areas related to psychology have come from geography [for example, Tobler and Wineburg, 1971; Olshavsky, MacKay, and Sentell, 1975; Golledge and Spector, 1978; Golledge, Spector, and Rivizzigno, 1980]. We view this substantive interest in MDS from related disciplines as providing a salutary diversity of assumptions upon which new models can be formulated.

AIDS TO USERS: TEXTBOOKS

MDS remains an area characterized by a considerable lag between new methodological developments and routine use by non-specialists (namely, the majority of the consumer community). The fact that the two-volume Irvine conference proceedings [Shepard, Romney, and Nerlove, 1972; Romney, and Nerlove, 1972] were never intended to be a textbook has frustrated many instructors, and so have the ongoing developments subsequent to publication of some of the most useful textbooks [Dawes, 1972; Green and Rao, 1972; Green and Wind, 1973]. Fortunately, a monograph by Kruskal and Wish (1978) has recently appeared, and it is eminently usable as a textbook covering two- and three-way MDS of proximities matrices. This monograph provides helpful guidelines to and examples of usage, and has been enthusiastically received by graduate and advanced undergraduate students in courses we have taught.

PROSPECTS

As we stated in our introduction, our primary goal in this chapter has been to impose a taxonomy on current models and methods, so that their interrelationships as well as various lacunae would be more apparent. While reviewing developments and applications in MDS, we have noted several trends. First, there is increased attention to the substantive appropriateness of these models, in contrast to earlier years when the techniques served primarily as convenient vehicles (and sometimes steam rollers) for data reduction. Second, we find increased realization that no particular model, in general, gives "the true representation." Most analyses choose a model that at best captures part of the structure inherent in the data; the part not fitted often awaits another analysis with a different model and perhaps a complementary interpretation as well. Third, we see a strong trend toward the development of three-way models with applications of three- and higher-way methods becoming almost as numerous as two-way applications. A development not unrelated to the two preceding observations is that we see considerable interest in discrete and hybrid models and predict that their coverage will be more extensive in the next *Annual Review* chapter on MDS.

LITERATURE CITED

Anderson, N. H. Information integration theory: A brief survey. In D. H. Krantz, R. C. Atkinson, R. D. Luce, and P. Suppes (Eds.), *Contemporary developments in mathematical psychology*, Vol. II. San Francisco: Freeman, 1974.

Anderson, N. H. Note on functional measurement and data analysis. *Perception & Psychophysics,* 1977, *21,* 201–215.

Arabie, P., and Boorman, S. A. Multidimensional scaling of measures of distance between partitions. *Journal of Mathematical Psychology,* 1973, *10,* 148–203.

Arabie, P., Boorman, S. A., and Levitt, P. R. Constructing blockmodels: How and why. *Journal of Mathematical Psychology,* 1978, *17,* 21–63.

Arabie, P., and Carroll, J. D. MAPCLUS: A mathematical programming approach to fitting the ADCLUS model. Submitted to *Psychometrika*, 1978.

Arabie, P., Kosslyn, S. M., and Nelson, K. E. A multidimensional scaling study of visual memory in 5-year olds and adults. *Journal of Experimental Child Psychology*, 1975, *19*, 327–345.

Arabie, P., and Shepard, R. N. *Representation of similarities as additive combinations of discrete, overlapping properties*. Paper read at Mathematical Psychology Meetings, *Montreal*, 1973.

Arabie, P., and Soli, S. D. The interface between the type of regression and methods of collecting proximities data. In R. Golledge and J. N. Rayner (Eds.), *Multidimensional analysis of large data sets*. Minneapolis: University of Minnesota Press, 1980.

Arnold, J. B. A multidimensional scaling study of semantic distance. *Journal of Experimental Psychology Monograph*, 1971, *90*, 2, 349–372.

Ayer, M., Brunk, H. D., Ewing, G. M., Reid, W. T., and Silverman, E. An empirical distribution function for sampling with incomplete information. *Annals of Mathematical Statistics*, 1955, *26*, 641–647.

Baker, F. B., and Hubert, L. J. Applications of combinatorial programming to data analysis: Seriation using asymmetric proximity measures. *British Journal of Mathematical and Statistical Psychology*, 1977, *30*, 154–164.

Barlow, R. E., Bartholomew, D. J., Bremner, J. M., and Brunk, H. D. *Statistical inference under order restrictions*. London: Wiley & Sons, 1972.

Batchelder, W. H., and Narens, L. A. A critical examination of the analysis of dichotomous data. *Philosophy of Science*, 1977, *44*, 113–135.

Beals, R., Krantz, D. H., and Tversky, A. Foundations of multidimensional scaling. *Psychological Review*, 1968, *75*, 127–142.

Bennett, J. F., and Hays, W. L. Multidimensional unfolding: Determining the dimensionality of ranked preference data. *Psychometrika*, 1960, *25*, 27–43.

Bentler, P. M., and Lee, S.-Y. Statistical aspects of a three-mode factor analysis model. *Psychometrika*, 1978, *43*, 343–352.

Bentler, P. M., and Lee, S.-Y. A statistical development of three-mode factor analysis.

British Journal of Mathematical and Statistical Psychology, 1979, *32*, 87–104.

Bentler, P. M., and Weeks, D. G. Restricted multidimensional scaling models. *Journal of Mathematical Psychology*, 1978, *17*, 138–151.

Bertier, P., and Bouroche, J. M. *Analyse des données multidimensionnelles*. Paris: Presses Universitaires de France, 1975.

Bick, W., Müller, P. J., Bauer, H., and Gieseke, O. *Multidimensional scaling and clustering techniques (theory and applications in the social sciences)—a bibliography*. Cologne: University of Cologne, 1977.

Bisanz, G. L., LaPorte, R. E., Vesonder, G. T., and Voss, J. F. On the representation of prose: New dimensions. *Journal of Verbal Learning and Verbal Behavior*, 1978, *17*, 337–357.

Blashfield, R. K., and Aldenderfer, M. S. The literature on cluster analysis. *Multivariate Behavioral Research*, 1978, *13*, 271–295.

Bloxom, B. Individual differences in multidimensional scaling. *Research Bulletin 68–45*. Princeton, NJ: Educational Testing Service, 1968.

Bloxom, B. Constrained multidimensional scaling in N spaces. *Psychometrika*, 1978, *43*, 397–408.

Boorman, S. A., and Arabie, P. Structural measures and the method of sorting. In R. N. Shepard, A. K. Romney, and S. B. Nerlove (Eds.), *Multidimensional scaling: Theory and applications in the behavioral sciences*. Vol. 1: *Theory*. New York: Seminar Press, 1972.

Boorman, S. A., and White, H. C. Social structure from multiple networks, II. Role structures. *American Journal of Sociology*, 1976, *81*, 1384–1446.

Borg, I., and Lingoes, J. C. Multidimensional scaling with side constraints on the distances. In J. C. Lingoes, E. E. Roskam, and I. Borg (Eds.), *Geometric representations of relational data*. Second edition. Ann Arbor, Michigan: Mathesis Press, 1979.

Bouroche, J. M. *Analyse des données en marketing*. Paris: Masson, 1977.

Bouroche, J. M., and Dussaix, A. M. Several alternatives for three-way data analysis. *Metra*, 1975, *14*, 299–319.

Bouroche, J. M., Saporta, G., and Tenenhaus, M. Some methods of qualitative data analysis.

In J. R. Barra, F. Brodeau, G. Romier, and B. van Cutsem (Eds.), *Recent developments in statistics*. Amsterdam: North-Holland, 1977.

Breiger, R. L., Boorman, S. A., and Arabie, P. An algorithm for clustering relational data, with applications to social network analysis and comparison with multidimensional scaling. *Journal of Mathematical Psychology*, 1975, *12*, 328–383.

Buneman, P. The recovery of trees from measures of dissimilarity. In F. R. Hodson, D. G. Kendall, and P. Tǎutu (Eds.), *Mathematics in the archaeological and historical sciences*. Edinburgh: Edinburgh University Press, 1971.

Buneman, P. A note on the metric properties of trees. *Journal of Combinatorial Theory*, 1974, *17*, 48–50.

Carroll, J. D. *A justification of D-squared as a second-order proximity measure*. Unpublished manuscript, Bell Telephone Laboratories, Murray Hill, NJ, 1968.

Carroll, J. D. *Categorical conjoint measurement*. Unpublished manuscript, Bell Laboratories, Murray Hill, NJ, 1969.

Carroll, J. D. Individual differences and multidimensional scaling. In R. N. Shepard, A. K. Romney, and S. Nerlove (Eds.), *Multidimensional scaling: Theory and applications in the behavioral sciences. Vol. 1: Theory*. New York: Seminar Press, 1972.

Carroll, J. D. Models and algorithms for multidimensional scaling, conjoint measurement and related techniques. Appendix B of P. E. Green and Y. Wind, *Multiattribute decisions in marketing*. New York: Holt, Rinehart and Winston, 1973.

Carroll, J. D. *Models for individual differences in similarities*. Paper presented at the Eighth Annual Mathematical Psychology Meetings, Purdue University, West Lafayette, Indiana, 1975.

Carroll, J. D. Spatial, non-spatial, and hybrid models for scaling. *Psychometrika*, 1976, *41*, 439–463.

Carroll, J. D. Impact scaling: Theory, mathematical model, and estimation procedures. *Proceedings of the Human Factors Society*, 1977, *21*, 513–517.

Carroll, J. D. Models and methods for multidimensional analysis of preferential choice (or other dominance) data. In E. D. Lanter-

mann and H. Feger (Eds.), *Proceedings of Aachen symposia on decision making and multidimensional scaling*. Berlin: Springer-Verlag, 1980.

Carroll, J. D., and Arabie, P. *INDCLUS: A three-way approach to clustering*. Paper presented at Meeting of Psychometric Society, Monterey, CA, 1979.

Carroll, J. D., and Chang, J. J. *Non-parametric multidimensional analysis of paired-comparisons data*. Paper presented at Joint Meeting of Psychometric and Psychonomic Societies, Niagara Falls, 1964.

Carroll, J. D., and Chang, J. J. *Relating preference data to multidimensional solutions via a generalization of Coombs' unfolding model*. Paper presented at Meeting of Psychometric Society, Madison, WI, 1967.

Carroll, J. D., and Chang, J. J. *A new method for dealing with individual differences in multidimensional scaling*. Unpublished manuscript, Bell Telephone Laboratories, Murray Hill, NJ, 1969.

Carroll, J. D., and Chang, J. J. Analysis of individual differences in multidimensional scaling via an N-way generalization of Eckart–Young decomposition. *Psychometrika*, 1970, *35*, 283–319.

Carroll, J. D., and Chang, J. J. *An alternate solution to the metric unfolding problem*. Paper presented at Meeting of Psychometric Society, St. Louis, MO, 1971.

Carroll, J. D., and Chang, J. J. *IDIOSCAL (Individual DIfferences in Orientation SCALing): A generalization of INDSCAL allowing idiosyncratic reference systems as well as an analytic approximation to INDSCAL*. Paper presented at the Meeting of the Psychometric Society, Princeton, 1972. (a)

Carroll, J. D., and Chang, J. J. SIMULES (SIMUltaneous Linear Equation Scaling): A method of multidimensional scaling based on judgments implying linear vector equations. *Proceedings of the 80th Annual Convention of the American Psychological Association*, 1972, *7*, 111–112. (b)

Carroll, J. D., and Chang, J. J. A method for fitting a class of hierarchical tree structure models to dissimilarities data, and its application to some "body parts" data of Miller's. *Proceedings of the 81st Annual*

Convention of the American Psychological Association, 1973, *8,* 1097–1098.

Carroll, J. D., and Chang, J. J. *Is color space three- or six-dimensional? An INDSCAL analysis of color dissimilarities data with normal and color deficient subjects.* Presented at Meeting of American Psychological Association, New Orleans, 1974.

Carroll, J. D., Green, P. E., and Carmone, F. J. *CANDELINC (CANonical DEcomposition with LINear Constraints): A new method for multidimensional analysis with constrained solutions.* Paper presented at the International Congress of Psychology, Paris, 1976.

Carroll, J. D., and Kruskal, J. B. Multidimensional scaling of two-way and three-way arrays. In W. H. Kruskal and J. M. Tanur (Eds.), *The encyclopedia of statistics.* New York: Free Press, 1977.

Carroll, J. D., and Pruzansky, S. *Fitting of hierarchical tree structure (HTS) models, mixtures of HTS models, and hybrid models, via mathematical programming and alternating least squares.* Paper presented at the U.S.–Japan Seminar on Multidimensional Scaling, University of California at San Diego, La Jolla, California, 1975.

Carroll, J. D., and Pruzansky, S. *Use of LINCINDS as a rational starting configuration for INDSCAL.* Unpublished manuscript, Bell Laboratories, Murray Hill, NJ, 1979.

Carroll, J. D., and Pruzansky, S. Discrete and hybrid scaling models. In E. D. Lantermann and H. Feger (Eds.), *Proceedings of Aachen symposia on decision making and multidimensional scaling.* Berlin: Springer-Verlag, 1980.

Carroll, J. D., Pruzansky, S., and Green, P. E. Estimation of the parameters of Lazarsfeld's latent class model by application of canonical decomposition (CANDECOMP) to multi-way contingency tables. Submitted to *Psychometrika,* 1979.

Carroll, J. D., Pruzansky, S., and Kruskal, J. B. CANDELINC: A general approach to multidimensional analysis with linear constraints on parameters. *Psychometrika,* 1979, *44,* in press.

Carroll, J. D., and Sen, T. K. *Impact scaling.* Paper presented at Meeting of the Society for Multivariate Experimental Psychology, Pennsylvania State University, 1976.

Carroll, J. D., and Wish, M. Models and methods for three-way multidimensional scaling. In D. H. Krantz, R. C. Atkinson, R. D. Luce, and P. Suppes (Eds.), *Contemporary developments in mathematical psychology,* Vol. II. San Francisco: Freeman, 1974. (a)

Carroll, J. D., and Wish, M. Multidimensional perceptual models and measurement methods. In E. C. Carterette and M. P. Friedman (Eds.), *Handbook of perception* (Vol. 2). New York: Academic Press, 1974. (b)

Cermak, G. W. Exploratory laboratory studies of the relative aversiveness of traffic sounds. *Journal of the Acoustical Society of America,* 1979, *65,* 112–123.

Cermak, G. W., and Cornillon, P. C. Multidimensional analyses of judgments about traffic noise. *Journal of the Acoustical Society of America,* 1976, *59,* 1412–1420.

Chang, J. J. *MAPREF—preference mapping program* [name subsequently changed to MDPREF]. Unpublished paper, Bell Laboratories, Murray Hill, NJ, 1969.

Chang, J. J., and Carroll, J. D. *How to use INDSCAL, a computer program for canonical decomposition of N-way tables and individual differences in multidimensional scaling.* Unpublished paper, Bell Laboratories, Murray Hill, NJ, 1969.

Chang, J. J., and Carroll, J. D. *How to use PREFMAP and PREFMAP2—Programs which relate preference data to multidimensional scaling solution.* Unpublished manuscript, Bell Laboratories, Murray Hill, NJ, 1972.

Chang, J. J., and Carroll, J. D. *Three are not enough: An INDSCAL analysis suggesting that color space has seven (±one) dimensions.* Unpublished manuscript, Bell Telephone Laboratories, Murray Hill, NJ, 1978.

Chang, J. J., and Shepard, R. N. *Exponential fitting in the proximity analysis of confusion matrices.* Presented at Meeting of the Eastern Psychological Association, New York, 1966.

Chino, N. A graphical technique for representing the asymmetric relationships between *N* objects. *Behaviormetrika,* 1978, *5,* 23–40.

Chipman, S. F., and Noma, E. *Interacting dimensions in multidimensional psycho-*

physics. Paper presented at the First Joint Meeting of the Psychometric Society and the Society for Mathematical Psychology, Hamilton, Ontario, 1978.

Cliff, N. Consistencies of judgments of adjective combinations. In A. K. Romney, R. N. Shepard, and S. B. Nerlove (Eds.), *Multidimensional scaling: Theory and applications in the behavioral sciences*. Vol. 2: *Applications*. New York: Seminar Press, 1972.

Cliff, N. Scaling. In P. H. Mussen and M. R. Rosenzweig (Eds.), *Annual review of Psychology*. Palo Alto: Annual Reviews, 1973.

Cohen, H. S. *Estimating confidence regions for points in multidimensional scaling solutions*. Unpublished manuscript, Bell Laboratories, Holmdel, NJ, 1974. (a)

Cohen, H. S. Three-mode rotation to approximate INDSCAL structure. Paper presented at Meeting of Psychometric Society, Stanford, CA, 1974. (b)

Constantine, A. G., and Gower, J. C. Graphical representation of asymmetric matrices. *Applied Statistics (Journal of the Royal Statistical Society Series C)*, 1979, in press.

Coombs, C. H. Psychological scaling without a unit of measurement. *Psychological Review*, 1950, *57*, 148–158.

Coombs, C. H. *A theory of data*. New York: Wiley, 1964.

Coombs, C. H. Data and scaling theory. In G. Menges (Ed.), *Handbook of mathematical economic sciences*, Vol. 2. Düsseldorf: West Deutscher Verlag, 1979.

Coombs, C. H., and Avrunin, G. S. Single-peaked functions and the theory of preference. *Psychological Review*, 1977, *84*, 216–230.

Coombs, C. H., Coombs, L. C., and McClelland, G. H. Preference scales for number and sex of children. *Population Studies*, 1975, *29*, 273–298.

Coombs, C. H., and Smith, J. E. K. On the detection of structure and developmental processes. *Psychological Review*, 1973, *80*, 337–351.

Coxon, A. P. M., and Jones, C. L. Multidimensional scaling. In C. A. O'Muircheartaigh and C. Payne (Eds.) *The analysis of survey data*, Vol. 1, *Exploring data structures*. New York: Wiley, 1977.

Coxon, A. P. M., and Jones, C. L. *The images of occupational prestige*. New York: Macmillan, 1978.

Cunningham, J. P. *Finding the optimal tree-realization of a proximity matrix*. Paper presented at the Mathematical Psychology Meetings, Ann Arbor, MI, 1974.

Cunningham, J. P. Free trees and bidirectional trees as representations of psychological distance. *Journal of Mathematical Psychology*, 1978, *17*, 165–188.

Cunningham, J. P., and Shepard, R. N. Monotone mapping of similarities into a general metric space. *Journal of Mathematical Psychology*, 1974, *11*, 335–363.

Davison, M. L. Fitting and testing Carroll's weighted unfolding model for preferences. *Psychometrika*, 1976, *41*, 233–247.

Davison, M. L. On a metric, unidimensional unfolding model for attitudinal and developmental data. *Psychometrika*, 1977, *42*, 523–548.

Dawes, R. M. *Fundamentals of attitude measurement*. New York: Wiley, 1972.

de Leeuw, J. Applications of convex analysis to multidimensional scaling. In J. R. Barra, F. Brodeau, G. Romier, and B. van Cutsem (Eds.), *Recent developments in statistics*. Amsterdam: North-Holland, 1977. (a)

de Leeuw, J. Correctness of Kruskal's algorithms for monotone regression with ties. *Psychometrika*, 1977, *42*, 141–144. (b)

de Leeuw, J., and Heiser, W. Convergence of correction-matrix algorithms for multidimensional scaling. In J. C. Lingoes (Ed.), *Geometric representations of relational data: Readings in multidimensional scaling*. Ann Arbor, MI: Mathesis Press, 1977.

de Leeuw, J., and Heiser, W. Multidimensional scaling with restrictions on the configuration. In P. R. Krishnaiah (Ed.), *Multivariate analysis*, Vol. 5. Amsterdam/New York: North Holland, 1979.

de Leeuw, J., and Heiser, W. Theory of multidimensional scaling. In P. R. Krishnaiah and L. Kanal (Eds.), *Handbook of statistics*. New York: North Holland, 1980.

de Leeuw, J., and Pruzansky, S. A new computational method to fit the weighted Euclidean distance model. *Psychometrika*, 1978, *43*, 479–490.

de Leeuw, J., Young, F. W., and Takane, Y.

Additive structure in qualitative data: An alternating least squares method with optimal scaling features. *Psychometrika*, 1976, *41*, 471–503.

Defays, D. A short note on a method of seriation. *British Journal of Mathematical and Statistical Psychology*, 1978, *31*, 49–53.

DeSarbo, W. *Three-way unfolding and situational dependence in consumer preference analysis*. Doctoral dissertation, University of Pennsylvania, Wharton School, 1978.

Deutscher, T. Issues in data collection and reliability in marketing MDS studies—Implications for large stimulus sets. In R. Golledge and J. N. Rayner (Eds.), *Multidimensional analysis of large data sets*. Minneapolis: University of Minnesota Press, 1980.

Dobson, A. J. Unrooted trees for numerical taxonomy. *Journal of Applied Probability*, 1974, *11*, 32–42.

Drasgow, F., and Jones, L. E. Multidimensional scaling of derived dissimilarities. *Multivariate Behavioral Research*, 1979, *14*, 227–244.

Ebbesen, E. B. *Further evidence concerning Fiske's question: "Can personality constructs ever be empirically validated?"* Unpublished manuscript, Bell Telephone Laboratories, Murray Hill, NJ, 1977.

Eisler, H., and Roskam, E. E. Multidimensional similarity: An experimental and theoretical comparison of vector, distance, and set theoretical models. I, II. *Acta Psychologica*, 1977, *41*, 1–46; 335–363.

Falmagne, J. C. Random conjoint measurement and loudness summation. *Psychological Review*, 1976, *83*, 65–79.

Falmagne, J. C., Iverson, G., and Marcovici, S. Binaural "loudness" summation: Probabilistic theory and data. *Psychological Review*, 1979, *86*, 25–43.

Feger, H. *Multidimensional scaling of attitudes: Intra- and inter-individual variations in preferences and cognitions*. Paper presented at the International Symposium on Social Psychophysics, Mannheim, 1978.

Fillenbaum, S., and Rapoport, A. *Structures in the subjective lexicon: An experimental approach to the study of semantic fields*. New York: Academic Press, 1971.

Fischer, W., and Micko, H. C. More about metrics of subjective spaces and attention

distributions. *Journal of Mathematical Psychology*, 1972, *9*, 36–54.

Fishburn, P. C. Nondecomposable conjoint measurement for bisymmetric structures. *Journal of Mathematical Psychology*, 1975, *12*, 75–89.

Fraser, C. O. Cognitive strategies and multidimensional scaling. *British Journal of Psychology*, 1976, *67*, 399–406.

Friendly, M. L. In search of the M-gram: The structure of organization in free recall. *Cognitive Psychology*, 1977, *9*, 188–249.

Gati, I. A hierarchical model for the structure of vocational interests. *Journal of Vocational Behavior*, 1979, in press.

Goldstein, A. J., and Kruskal, J. B. Least-squares fitting by monotonic functions having integer values. *Journal of the American Statistical Association*, 1976, *71*, 370–373.

Golledge, R. G., and Spector, A. N. Comprehending the urban environment: Theory and practice. *Geographical Analysis*, 1978, *10*, 403–426.

Golledge, R. G., Spector, A. N., and Rivizzigno, V. L. Comparing objective and cognitive representations of environmental cues. In R. Golledge and J. N. Rayner (Eds.), *Multidimensional analysis of large data sets*. Minneapolis: University of Minnesota Press, 1980.

Gower, J. C. The analysis of asymmetry and orthogonality. In J. R. Barra, F. Brodeau, G. Romier, and B. van Cutsem (Eds.), *Recent developments in statistics*. New York/Amsterdam: North Holland, 1977.

Gower, J. C. *Unfolding: Some technical problems and novel uses*. Paper presented at European Meeting on psychometrics and mathematical psychology, Uppsala, 1978.

Graham, I., Galloway, P., and Scollar, I. Model studies in computer seriation. *Journal of Archaeological Science*, 1976, *3*, 1–30.

Green, P. E. A new approach to market segmentation. *Business Horizons*, 1977, *20*, 61–73.

Green, P. E., and Carmone, F. J. Segment congruence analysis: A method for analyzing association among alternative bases for market segmentation. *Journal of Consumer Research*, 1977, *3*, 217–222.

Green, P. E., Carroll, J. D., and Carmone, F. J. *Design considerations in attitude measurement*. Paper presented at the Seventh

Annual Conference on Attitude Research, Hilton Head, SC, 1975.

Green, P. E., Carroll, J. D., and Carmone, F. J. Superordinate factorial designs in the analysis of consumer judgments. *Journal of Business Research,* 1976, *4,* 281–295.

Green, P. E., Carroll, J. D., and Carmone, F. J. Some new types of fractional factorial designs for marketing experiments. In J. N. Sheth (Ed.), *Research in marketing,* Vol. I. Greenwich, CT: JAI Press, 1978.

Green, P. E., and Rao, V. R. *Applied multidimensional scaling: A comparison of approaches and algorithms.* New York: Holt, Rinehart and Winston, 1972.

Green, P. E., and Srinivasan, V. Conjoint analysis in consumer research: Issues and outlook. *Journal of Consumer Research,* 1978, *5,* 103–123.

Green, P. E., and Wind, Y. *Multiattribute decisions in marketing: A measurement approach.* Hinsdale, IL: Dryden, 1973.

Green, P. E., and Wind, Y. New way to measure consumers' judgments. *Harvard Business Review,* 1975, *53,* 107–117.

Green, R. S. A multi-measure assessment of reliability for large sets of data. In R. Golledge and J. N. Rayner (Eds.), *Multidimensional analysis of large data sets.* Minneapolis: University of Minnesota Press, 1980.

Green, R. S., and Bentler, P. M. Improving the efficiency and effectiveness of interactively selected MDS data designs. *Psychometrika,* 1979, *44,* 115–119.

Gregson, R. A. M. *Psychometrics of similarity.* New York: Academic Press, 1975.

Guttman, L. A general nonmetric technique for finding the smallest coordinate space for a configuration of points. *Psychometrika,* 1968, *33,* 465–506.

Guttman, L. Measurement as structural theory. *Psychometrika,* 1971, *36,* 329–347.

Harshman, R. A. *Foundations of the PARAFAC procedure: Models and conditions for an "explanatory" multi-modal factor analysis.* Unpublished manuscript, UCLA, 1970.

Harshman, R. A. Determination and proof of minimum uniqueness conditions for PARAFAC1. UCLA: *Working Papers in Phonetics 22,* 1972. (a)

Harshman, R. A. PARAFAC2: Mathematical and technical notes. UCLA: *Working Papers in Phonetics 22,* 1972. (*b*)

Harshman, R. A. *Models for analysis of asymmetrical relationships among N objects or stimuli.* Paper presented at the U.S.–Japan Seminar on Multidimensional Scaling, University of California at San Diego, La Jolla, California, 1975.

Harshman, R. A. *Models for analysis of asymmetrical relationships among N objects or stimuli.* Paper presented at the First Joint Meeting of the Psychometric Society and the Society for Mathematical Psychology, Hamilton, Ontario, 1978.

Hartigan, J. A. Representation of similarity matrices by trees. *Journal of the American Statistical Association,* 1967, *62,* 1140–1158.

Hartigan, J. A. *Clustering algorithms.* New York: Wiley, 1975.

Hayashi, C. Minimum dimension analysis MDA: One of the methods of multidimensional quantification. *Behaviormetrika,* 1974, *1,* 1–24.

Heider [Rosch], E., and Olivier, D. C. The structure of the color space in naming and memory for two languages. *Cognitive Psychology,* 1972, *3,* 337–354.

Hodson, F. R., Kendall, D. G., and Tăutu, P. (Eds.) *Mathematics in the archaeological and historical sciences.* Edinburgh: Edinburgh University Press, 1971.

Holman, E. W. The relation between hierarchical and Euclidean models for psychological distances. *Psychometrika,* 1972, *37,* 417–423.

Holman, E. W. Completely nonmetric multidimensional scaling. *Journal of Mathematical Psychology,* 1978, *18,* 39–51.

Holman, E. W. Monotonic models for asymmetric proximities. *Journal of Mathematical Psychology,* 1979, in press.

Holyoak, K. J., and Walker, J. H. Subjective magnitude information in semantic orderings. *Journal of Verbal Learning and Verbal Behavior,* 1976, *15,* 287–299.

Horan, C. B. Multidimensional scaling: Combining observations when individuals have different perceptual structures. *Psychometrika,* 1969, *34,* 139–165.

Howard, D. V., and Howard, J. H., Jr. A multidimensional scaling analysis of the development of animal names. *Developmental Psychology*, 1977, *13*, 108–113.

Hubert, L. J. Problems of seriation using a subject by item response matrix. *Psychological Bulletin*, 1974, *81*, 976–983. (a)

Hubert, L. J. Some applications of graph theory and related non-metric techniques to problems of approximate seriation: The case of symmetric proximity measures. *British Journal of Mathematical and Statistical Psychology*, 1974, *27*, 133–153. (b)

Hubert, L. J. Some applications of graph theory to clustering. *Psychometrika*, 1974, *39*, 283–309. (c)

Hubert, L. J. Seriation using asymmetric proximity measures. *British Journal of Mathematical and Statistical Psychology*, 1976, *29*, 32–52.

Hubert, L. J. Generalized proximity function comparisons. *British Journal of Mathematical and Statistical Psychology*, 1978, *31*, 179–192.

Hubert, L. J. Generalized concordance. *Psychometrika*, 1979, *44*, 135–142.

Hubert, L. J., and Baker, F. B. Applications of combinatorial programming to data analysis: The traveling salesman and related problems. *Psychometrika*, 1978, *43*, 81–91.

Hubert, L. J., and Baker, F. B. Evaluating the symmetry of a proximity matrix. *Quality and Quantity*, 1979, *13*, 77–84.

Hubert, L., and Busk, P. Normative location theory: Placement in continuous space. *Journal of Mathematical Psychology*, 1976, *14*, 187–210.

Hubert, L., and Schultz, J. A note on seriation and quadratic assignment. *Classification Society Bulletin*, 1976, *3*, 16–24. (a)

Hubert, L. J., and Schultz, J. Quadratic assignment as a general data analysis strategy. *British Journal of Mathematical and Statistical Psychology*, 1976, *29*, 190–241. (b)

Indow, T. Applications of multidimensional scaling in perception. In E. C. Carterette and M. P. Friedman (Eds.), *Handbook of perception*, Vol. 2. New York: Academic Press, 1974.

Indow, T. *An application of MDS to study of binocular visual space*. Paper presented at the U.S.–Japan Seminar on Multi-dimensional Scaling, University of California at San Diego, La Jolla, California, 1975.

Indow, T. *An Approach to geometry of visual space with no a priori mapping functions: Multidimensional mapping according to Riemannian metrics*. Unpublished manuscript, no date.

Isaac, P. D. Considerations in selection of stimulus pairs for data collection in MDS. In R. Golledge and J. N. Rayner (Eds.), *Multidimensional analysis of large data sets*. Minneapolis: University of Minnesota Press, 1980.

Janson, T. Short communication: Asymmetry in vowel confusion matrices. *Journal of Phonetics*, 1977, *5*, 93–96.

Jardine, C. J., Jardine, N., and Sibson, R. The structure and construction of taxonomic hierarchies. *Mathematical Biosciences*, 1967, *1*, 173–179.

Johnson, R. M. Pairwise nonmetric multidimensional scaling. *Psychometrika*, 1973, *38*, 11–18.

Johnson, R. M. Trade-off analysis of consumer values. *Journal of Marketing Research*, 1974, *11*, 121–127.

Johnson, R. M. A simple method for pairwise monotone regression. *Psychometrika*, 1975, *40*, 163–168.

Johnson, S. C. Hierarchical clustering schemes. *Psychometrika*, 1967, *32*, 241–254.

Jones, F. N., Roberts, K., and Holman, E. W. Similarity judgments and recognition memory for some common spices. *Perception & Psychophysics*, 1978, *24*, 2–6.

Kamenskii, V. S. Methods and models of nonmetric multidimensional scaling (survey). *Automation and Remote Control*, [*Avtomatika i Telemekhanika*, 1977, *38*, 8, 118–156.], 1977, *38*, 1212–1243.

Kendall, D. G. A mathematical approach to seriation. *Philosophical Transactions of the Royal Society of London*, 1970, *269*, 125–135.

Kendall, D. G. Maps from marriages: An application of nonmetric multi-dimensional scaling to parish register data. In F. R. Hodson, D. G. Kendall, and P. Tăutu (Eds.), *Mathematics in the archaeological and historical sciences*. Edinburgh: Edinburgh University Press, 1971. (a)

Kendall, D. G. Seriation from abundance matrices. In F. R. Hodson, D. G. Kendall, and P. Tăutu (Eds.), *Mathematics in the archaeological and historical sciences.* Edinburgh: Edinburgh University Press, 1971. (b)

Kendall, D. G. The recovery of structure from fragmentary information. *Philosophical Transactions of the Royal Society of London A,* 1975, *279,* 547–582.

Kohler, J. A., and Rushton, G. Optimal data designs for computing spatial preference functions. In R. Golledge and J. N. Rayner (Eds.), *Multidimensional analysis of large data sets.* Minneapolis: University of Minnesota Press, 1980.

Krantz, D. H., and Tversky, A. Similarity of rectangles: An analysis of subjective dimensions. *Journal of Mathematical Psychology,* 1975, *12,* 4–34.

Krumhansl, C. L. Concerning the applicability of geometric models to similarity data: The interrelationship between similarity and spatial density. *Psychological Review,* 1978, *85,* 445–463.

Krumhansl, C. L. The psychological representation of musical pitch in a tonal context. *Cognitive Psychology,* 1979, *11,* 346–374.

Kruskal, J. B. Multidimensional scaling by optimizing goodness of fit to a nonmetric hypothesis. *Psychometrika,* 1964, *29,* 1–27. (a)

Kruskal, J. B. Nonmetric multidimensional scaling: A numerical method. *Psychometrika,* 1964, *29,* 115–129. (b)

Kruskal, J. B. Analysis of factorial experiments by estimating monotone transformations of the data. *Journal of the Royal Statistical Society B,* 1965, *27,* 251–263.

Kruskal, J. B. More factors than subjects, tests and treatments: An indeterminacy theorem for canonical decomposition and individual differences scaling. *Psychometrika,* 1976, *41,* 281–293.

Kruskal, J. B. Multidimensional scaling and other methods for discovering structure. In K. Enslein, A. Ralston, and H. S. Wilf (Eds.), *Statistical methods for digital computers,* Vol. 3. New York: Wiley-Interscience, 1977. (a)

Kruskal, J. B. The relationship between multidimensional scaling and clustering. In J. Van Ryzin (Ed.), *Classification and clustering.* New York: Academic Press, 1977. (b)

Kruskal, J. B. Three-way arrays: Rank and uniqueness of trilinear decompositions, with application to arithmetic complexity and statistics. *Linear Algebra and Its Applications,* 1977, *18,* 95–138. (c)

Kruskal, J. B. *Some least-squares theorems for matrices and N-way arrays.* Unpublished manuscript, Bell Telephone Laboratories, Murray Hill, NJ, 1977. (d)

Kruskal, J. B. Factor analysis and principal components: Bilinear methods. In W. H. Kruskal and J. M. Tanur (Eds.), *International encyclopedia of statistics.* New York: Free Press, 1978.

Kruskal, J. B., and Carmone, F. J., Jr. *MONANOVA: A FORTRAN IV program for monotone analysis of variance (non-metric analysis of factorial experiments).* Unpublished manuscript, Bell Telephone Laboratories, Murray Hill, NJ, 1965.

Kruskal, J. B., and Carroll, J. D. Geometrical models and badness-of-fit functions. In P. R. Krishnaiah (Ed.), *Multivariate analysis II.* New York: Academic Press, 1969.

Kruskal, J. B., and Shepard, R. N. A nonmetric variety of linear factor analysis. *Psychometrika,* 1974, *39,* 123–157.

Kruskal, J. B., and Wish, M. *Multidimensional scaling.* Beverly Hills, CA: Sage, 1978.

Kruskal, J. B., Young, F. W., and Seery, J. B. *How to use KYST, a very flexible program to do multidimensional scaling and unfolding.* Murray Hill, NJ: Bell Telephone Laboratories, 1973.

Kruskal, J. B., Young, F. W., and Seery, J. B. *How to use KYST 2: A very flexible program to do multidimensional scaling and unfolding.* Murray Hill, NJ: Bell Telephone Laboratories, 1977.

Kupershtokh, V. L., and Mirkin, B. G. Ordering of interrelated objects I, II. *Automation and Remote Control [Avtomatika i Telemekhanika],* 1971, *32,* 924–929; 1093–1098.

LaPorte, R. E., and Voss, J. F. Prose representation: A multidimensional scaling approach. *Multivariate Behavioral Research,* 1979, *14,* 39–56.

Levine, J. H. The sphere of influence. *American Sociological Review,* 1972, *37,* 14–27.

Lew, J. S. Some counterexamples in multidimensional scaling. *Journal of Mathematical Psychology,* 1978, *17,* 247–254.

Lindman, H., and Caelli, T. Constant curvature Riemannian scaling. *Journal of Mathematical Psychology,* 1978, *17,* 89–109.

Lingoes, J. C. A general survey of the Guttman–Lingoes nonmetric program series. In R. N. Shepard, A. K. Romney, and S. B. Nerlove (Eds.), *Multidimensional scaling: Theory and applications in the behavioral sciences.* Vol. 1: *Theory.* New York: Seminar Press, 1972.

Lingoes, J. C. *The Guttman–Lingoes nonmetric program series.* Ann Arbor, MI: Mathesis Press, 1973.

Lingoes, J. C. (Ed.) *Geometric representations of relational data: Readings in multidimensional scaling.* Ann Arbor, MI: Mathesis Press, 1977.

Lingoes, J. C., and Borg, I. A direct approach to individual differences scaling using increasingly complex transformations. *Psychometrika,* 1978, *43,* 491–519.

Lingoes, J. C., and Roskam, E. E. A mathematical and empirical analysis of two multidimensional scaling algorithms. *Psychometrika,* 1973, *38,* Monograph Supplement No. 19.

Luce, R. D. *Individual choice behavior.* New York: Wiley, 1959.

Luce, R. D. The choice axiom after twenty years. *Journal of Mathematical Psychology,* 1977, *15,* 215–233.

Luce, R. D. and Tukey, J. W. Simultaneous conjoint measurement: A new type of fundamental measurement. *Journal of Mathematical Psychology,* 1964, *1,* 1–27.

Lund, T. Comments on the Stone–Coles multidimensional scaling method. *Multivariate Behavioral Research,* 1974, *9,* 343–346.

Luneburg, R. K. *Mathematical analysis of binocular vision.* Princeton, NJ: Princeton University Press, 1947.

Luneburg, R. K. The metric of binocular visual space. *Journal of the Optical Society of America,* 1950, *40,* 637–642.

MacCallum, R. C. Transformation of a three-mode multidimensional scaling solution to INDSCAL form. *Psychometrika,* 1976, *41,* 385–400.

MacCallum, R. C. Effects of conditionality on INDSCAL and ALSCAL weights. *Psychometrika,* 1977, *42,* 297–305.

Maital, S. Multidimensional scaling: Some econometric applications. *Journal of Econometrics,* 1978, *8,* 33–46.

Mantel, N. The detection of disease clustering and a generalized regression approach. *Cancer Research,* 1967, *27,* 209–220.

McClelland, G. H., and Coombs, C. H. ORDMET: A general algorithm for constructing all numerical solutions to ordered metric structures. *Psychometrika,* 1975, *40,* 269–290.

McDonald, R. P. A note on monotone polygons fitted to bivariate data. *Psychometrika,* 1976, *41,* 543–546.

Monahan, J. S., and Lockhead, G. R. Identification of integral stimuli. *Journal of Experimental Psychology: General,* 1977, *106,* 94–110.

Moskowitz, H. R., and Gerbers, C. L. Dimensional salience of odors. *Annals of the New York Academy of Sciences,* 1974, *237,* 1–16.

Nishisato, S. Analysis of variance through optimal scaling. *Proceedings of the First Canadian Conference on Applied Statistics.* Montreal: Sir George Williams University Press, 1971.

Nishisato, S. *Multidimensional scaling: A historical sketch and bibliography.* Ontario Institute for Studies in Education, Department of Measurement, Evaluation, and Computer Applications, Toronto, Canada, 1978. (a)

Nishisato, S. Optimal scaling of paired comparison and rank order data: An alternative to Guttman's formulation. *Psychometrika,* 1978, *43,* 263–271. (b)

Noma, E., and Johnson, J. *Constrained nonmetric multidimensional scaling.* (Tech. Rep. MMPP 1979–4). Ann Arbor, MI: University of Michigan, Michigan Mathematical Psychology Program, 1979.

Nygren, T. E., and Jones, L. E. Individual differences in perceptions and preferences for political candidates. *Journal of Experimental Social Psychology,* 1977, *13,* 182–197.

Olshavsky, R. W., MacKay, D. B., and Sentell, G. Perceptual maps of supermarket locations. *Journal of Applied Psychology,* 1975, *60,* 80–86.

Pieszko, H. Multidimensional scaling in Riemannian space. *Journal of Mathematical Psychology,* 1975, *12,* 449–477.

Pruzansky, S. *How to use SINDSCAL: A computer program for individual differences in multidimensional scaling.* Murray Hill, NJ: Bell Telephone Laboratories, 1975.

Ramsay, J. O. Solving implicit equations in psychometric data analysis. *Psychometrika,* 1975, *40,* 337–360.

Ramsay, J. O. Monotonic weighted power transformations to additivity. *Psychometrika,* 1977, *42,* 83–109. (a)

Ramsay, J. O. Maximum likelihood estimation in multidimensional scaling. *Psychometrika,* 1977, *42,* 241–266. (b)

Ramsay, J. O. Confidence regions for multidimensional scaling analysis. *Psychometrika,* 1978, *43,* 145–160.

Ramsay, J. O. *Some small sample results for maximum likelihood estimation in multidimensional scaling.* Unpublished manuscript, McGill University, 1979. (a)

Ramsay, J. O. *The joint analysis of direct ratings, pair-wise preferences, and dissimilarities.* Unpublished manuscript, McGill University, 1979. (b)

Redfield, J., and Stone, A. Individual viewpoints of stressful life events. *Journal of Consulting and Clinical Psychology,* 1979, *47,* 147–154.

Reed, S. K. Pattern recognition and categorization. *Cognitive Psychology,* 1972, *3,* 382–407.

Rodieck, R. W. Metric of color borders. *Science,* 1977, *197,* 1195–1196.

Romney, A. K., Shepard, R. N., and Nerlove, S. B. *Multidimensional scaling,* Vol. 2: *Applications.* New York: Seminar Press, 1972.

Romney, A. K., Shepard, R. N., and Nerlove, S. B. *Multidimensional scaling: Theory and applications in the behavioral sciences.* Vol. 2: *Applications.* [A. Okada and K. Watanabe, trans., Japanese]. Tokyo: Kyoritsu Shuppan, 1977.

Rosenberg, S., and Jones, R. A method for investigating and representing a person's implicit theory of personality: Theodore Dreiser's view of people. *Journal of Personality and Social Psychology,* 1972, *22,* 372–386.

Rosenberg, S., and Kim, M. P. The method of sorting as a data-gathering procedure in multivariate research. *Multivariate Behavioral Research,* 1975, *10,* 489–502.

Rosenberg, S., and Sedlak, A. Structural representations of perceived personality trait relationships. In A. K. Romney, R. N. Shepard, and S. B. Nerlove (Eds.), *Multidimensional scaling: Theory and applica-*

tions in the behavioral sciences. Vol. 2: *Applications.* New York: Seminar Press, 1972.

Roskam, E. E. *Unfolding van preferentie—en vergelijkbare keuze-data (een gestandaardiseerde en vereenvoudigde versie van MINI-RSA-EX: zie inputbeschrijring dd. 31-1-70).* Unpublished manuscript, Nijmegen, The Netherlands, 1971.

Roskam, E. E. *Fitting ordinal relational data to a hypothesized structure* (Tech. Rep. 73 MA 06). Nijmegen, The Netherlands: Catholic University, Department of Psychology, 1973.

Roskam, E. E. *A documentation of MINISSA (N).* (Tech. Rep. 75 MA 15). Nijmegen, The Netherlands: Catholic University, Department of Psychology, 1975.

Roskam, E. E. C. I., and Van Glist, W. *"ADDIT" 007/02* (Department of Psychology, Computer Bulletin). Nijmegen, The Netherlands: Catholic University, 1967.

Rumelhart, D. E., and Abrahamson, A. A. A model for analogical reasoning. *Cognitive Psychology,* 1973, *5,* 1–28.

Sattath, S., and Tversky, A. Additive similarity trees. *Psychometrika,* 1977, *42,* 319–345.

Schiffman, S., and Dackis, S. Multidimensional scaling of musks. *Physiology and Behavior,* 1976, *17,* 823–829.

Schönemann, P. H. On metric multidimensional unfolding. *Psychometrika,* 1970, *35,* 349–366.

Schönemann, P. H. An algebraic solution for a class of subjective metrics models. *Psychometrika,* 1972, *37,* 4, 441–451.

Schönemann, P. H. Similarity of rectangles. *Journal of Mathematical Psychology,* 1977, *16,* 161–165.

Schönemann, P. H., Carter, F. S., and James, W. L. *Contributions to subjective metrics scaling. I. COSPA, a fast method for fitting and testing Horan's model, and an empirical comparison with INDSCAL and ALSCAL.* Institute Paper No. 587. Purdue University, Krannert Graduate School, 1976.

Schönemann, P. H., and Wang, M. M. An individual difference model for the multidimensional analysis of preference data. *Psychometrika,* 1972, *37,* 275–309.

Seligson, M. A. Prestige among peasants: A multidimensional analysis of preference data. *American Journal of Sociology,* 1977, *83,* 632–652.

Shepard, R. N. Analysis of proximities: Multidimensional scaling with an unknown distance function. I. *Psychometrika,* 1962, *27,* 125–140. (a)

Shepard, R. N. Analysis of proximities: Multidimensional scaling with an unknown distance function. II. *Psychometrika,* 1962, *27,* 219–246. (b)

Shepard, R. N. Psychological representation of speech sounds. In E. E. David, Jr. and P. B. Deenes (Eds.), *Human communication: A unified view.* New York: McGraw-Hill, 1972. Pp. 67–113. (a)

Shepard, R. N. A taxonomy of some principal types of data and of multidimensional methods for their analysis. In R. N. Shepard, A. K. Romney, and S. B. Nerlove (Eds.), *Multidimensional scaling: Theory and applications in the behavioral sciences,* Vol. 1: *Theory.* New York: Seminar Press, 1972. (b)

Shepard, R. N. Representation of structure in similarity data: Problems and prospects. *Psychometrika,* 1974, *39,* 373–421.

Shepard, R. N. The circumplex and related topological manifolds in the study of perception. In S. Shye (Ed.), *Theory construction and data analysis in the behavioral sciences.* San Francisco: Jossey–Bass, 1978.

Shepard, R. N., and Arabie, P. Additive clustering: Representation of similarities as combinations of discrete overlapping properties. *Psychological Review,* 1979, *86,* 87–123.

Shepard, R. N., and Crawford, G. *Multidimensional scaling based on the fitting of constrained difference functions.* Paper presented at the U.S.–Japan Seminar on Multidimensional Scaling, University of California at San Diego, August 20–24, 1975.

Shepard, R. N., Romney, A. K., and Nerlove, S. B. *Multidimensional scaling: Theory and applications in the behavioral sciences.* Vol. 1: *Theory* [A. Okada and K. Watanabe, trans., Japanese]. Tokyo: Kyoritsu Shuppan, 1976.

Shoben, E. J. *Semantic features in semantic memory.* Doctoral dissertation, Department of Psychology, Stanford University, August 1974.

Shoben, E. J. The verification of semantic relations in a same-different paradigm: An asymmetry in semantic memory. *Journal of*

Verbal Learning and Verbal Behavior, 1976, *15,* 365–379.

Sibson, R. Some thoughts on sequencing methods. In F. R. Hodson, D. G. Kendall, and P. Tăutu (Eds.), *Mathematics in the archaeological and historical sciences.* Edinburgh: Edinburgh University Press, 1971.

Sibson, R. Order invariant methods for data analysis (with discussion). *Journal of the Royal Statistical Society B,* 1972, *34,* 311–349.

Sjöberg, L. A cognitive theory of similarity. *Göteborg Psychological Reports,* 1972, *2,* No. 10.

Sjöberg, L. Models of similarity and intensity. *Psychological Bulletin,* 1975, *82,* 191–206.

Sjöberg, L. Choice frequency and similarity. *Scandinavian Journal of Psychology,* 1977, *18,* 103–115.

Sjöberg, L. Similarity and correlation. In E. D. Lantermann and H. Feger (Eds.), *Proceedings of Aachen symposia on decision making and multidimensional scaling.* Berlin: Springer-Verlag, 1980.

Slater, P. The analysis of personal preferences. *British Journal of Statistical Psychology,* 1960, *13,* 119–135.

Sneath, P. H. A., and Sokal, R. R. *Numerical taxonomy.* San Francisco: W. H. Freeman, 1973.

Soli, S. D., and Arabie, P. Auditory versus phonetic accounts of observed confusions between consonant phonemes. *Journal of the Acoustical Society of America,* 1979, *66,* in press.

Spence, I. Incomplete experimental designs for multidimensional scaling. In R. Golledge and J. N. Rayner (Eds.), *Multidimensional analysis of large data sets.* Minneapolis: University of Minnesota Press, 1980.

Spence, I., and Domoney, D. W. Single subject incomplete designs for nonmetric multidimensional scaling. *Psychometrika,* 1974, *39,* 469–490.

Srinivasan, V. Linear programming computational procedures for ordinal regression. *Journal of the Association for Computing Machinery,* 1975, *23,* 475–487.

Srinivasan, V., and Shocker, A. D. Linear programming techniques for multidimensional analysis of preferences. *Psychometrika,* 1973, *38,* 337–369.

Sternberg, R. J. *Intelligence, information processing, and analogical reasoning: The componential analysis of human abilities.* Hillsdale, NJ: Lawrence Erlbaum Associates, 1977.

Stevens, S. S. On the theory of scales of measurement. *Science,* 1946, *103,* 677–680.

Stevens, S. S. Mathematics, measurement and psychophysics. In S. S. Stevens (Ed.), *Handbook of experimental psychology.* New York: Wiley, 1951.

Subkoviak, M. J. The use of multidimensional scaling in educational research. *Review of Educational Research,* 1975, *45,* 3, 387–423.

Takane, Y. *Maximum likelihood multidimensional scaling from directional rankings of similarities.* Paper presented at the Psychometric Society Meeting, Monterey, CA, 1979.

Takane, Y., Young, F. W., and de Leeuw, J. Nonmetric individual differences multidimensional scaling: An alternating least squares method with optimal scaling features. *Psychometrika,* 1977, *42,* 7–67.

Tansley, B. W., and Boynton, R. M. A line, not a space, represents visual distinctness of borders formed by different colors. *Science,* 1976, *191,* 954–957.

Tansley, B. W., and Boynton, R. M. Letter in reply to R. W. Rodieck. *Science,* 1977, *197,* 1196.

Terekhin, A. Y. Methods of multidimensional data scaling and visualization. (a) Survey. *Automation and Remote Control* [*Avtomatika i Telemekhanika,* 1973, *34,* 7, 80–92], 1973, *34,* 1109–1121.

Terekhin, A. Y. Two problems of individual multidimensional scaling. *Automation and Remote Control* [*Avtomatika i Telemekhanika,* 1974, *35,* 4, 135–142], 1974, *35,* 638–644.

Tobler, W. Spatial interaction patterns. *Journal of Environmental Systems,* 1976, *6,* 271–301.

Tobler, W., and Wineburg, S. A Cappadocian speculation. *Nature,* 1971, *231,* 39–41.

Torgerson, W. S. *Theory and methods of scaling.* New York: Wiley, 1958.

Tucker, L. R. Intra-individual and inter-individual multidimensionality. In H. Gulliksen and S. Messick (Eds.), *Psychological scaling: Theory and applications.* New York: Wiley, 1960.

Tucker, L. The extension of factor analysis to three-dimensional matrices. In N. Frederiksen and H. Gulliksen (Eds.), *Contributions to mathematical psychology.* New York: Holt, Rinehart and Winston, 1964.

Tucker, L. R. Relations between multidimensional scaling and three-mode factor analysis. *Psychometrika,* 1972, *37,* 3–27.

Tucker, L. R., and Messick, S. J. Individual difference model for multidimensional scaling. *Psychometrika,* 1963, *28,* 333–367.

Tversky, A. Choice by elimination. *Journal of Mathematical Psychology,* 1972, *9,* 341–367. (a)

Tversky, A. Elimination by aspects: A theory of choice. *Psychological Review,* 1972, *79,* 281–299. (b)

Tversky, A. Features of similarity. *Psychological Review,* 1977, *84,* 327–352.

Tversky, A., and Gati, I. Studies of similarity. In E. Rosch and B. B. Lloyd (Eds.), *Cognition and categorization.* Hillsdale, NJ: Erlbaum, 1978.

Tversky, A., and Sattath, S. Preference trees. *Psychological Review,* 1979, *86,* in press.

Ullrich, J. R., and Painter, J. R. A conjoint-measurement analysis of human judgment. *Organizational Behavior and Human Performance,* 1974, *12,* 50–61.

Walden, B. E., and Montgomery, A. A. Dimensions of consonant perception in normal and hearing-impaired listeners. *Journal of Speech and Hearing Research,* 1975, *18,* 444–455.

Wang, M. D., Reed, C. M., and Bilger, R. C. A comparison of the effects of filtering and sensorineural hearing loss on patterns of consonant confusions. *Journal of Speech and Hearing Research,* 1978, *21,* 5–36.

Weisberg, H. F. Scaling models for legislative roll-call analysis. *American Political Science Review,* 1972, *66,* 1306–1315.

Weisberg, H. F. Dimensionland: An excursion into spaces. *American Journal of Political Science,* 1974, *18,* 743–776.

Wexler, K. N., and Romney, A. K. Individual variations in cognitive structures. In A. K. Romney, R. N. Shepard, and S. B. Nerlove (Eds.), *Multidimensional scaling: Theory and applications in the behavioral sciences.* Vol. 2: *Applications.* New York: Seminar Press, 1972.

Wiener–Ehrlich, W. K. Dimensional and metric structures in multidimensional stimuli. *Perception & Psychophysics,* 1978, *24,* 399–414.

Wiggins, N. H., and Blackburn, M. C. Implicit theories of personality: An individual differences approach. *Multivariate Behavioral Research,* 1976, *11,* 267–286.

Wilkinson, E. M. Archaeological seriation and the traveling salesman problem. In F. R. Hodson, D. G. Kendall, and P. Tăutu (Eds.), *Mathematics in the archaeological and historical sciences.* Edinburgh: Edinburgh University Press, 1971.

Wilkinson, E. M. Techniques of data analysis-seriation theory. *Archaeo-Physika,* 1974, *5,* 7–142.

Wind, Y. Preference of relevant others and individual choice models. *Journal of Consumer Research,* 1976, *3,* 50–57.

Wind, Y. Introduction to special section on market segmentation research. *Journal of Marketing Research,* 1978, *15,* 315–316. (a)

Wind, Y. Issues and advances in segmentation research. *Journal of Marketing Research,* 1978, *15,* 317–337. (b)

Wish, M. Subjects' expectations about their own interpersonal communication: A multidimensional approach. *Personality and Social Psychology Bulletin,* 1975, *1,* 501–504.

Wish, M. Comparisons among multidimensional structures of interpersonal relations. *Multivariate Behavioral Research,* 1976, *11,* 297–324.

Wish, M. Multidimensional scaling of interpersonal communication. To appear in N. Hirschberg and L. Humphreys (Eds.), *Multivariate applications in the social sciences.* New York: Erlbaum, 1979. (a)

Wish, M. Dimensions of dyadic communication. In S. Weitz (Ed.), *Nonverbal communication* (2nd ed.). New York: Oxford University Press, 1979. (b)

Wish, M., and Carroll, J. D. Applications of "INDSCAL" to studies of human perception and judgment. In E. C. Carterette and M. P. Friedman (Eds.), *Handbook of perception.* Vol. 2. New York: Academic Press, 1974.

Wish, M., Deutsch, M., and Kaplan, S. J. Perceived dimensions of interpersonal relations. *Journal of Personality and Social Psychology,* 1976, *33,* 409–420.

Wish, M., and Kaplan, S. J. Toward an implicit theory of interpersonal communication. *Sociometry,* 1977, *40,* 234–246.

Wold, H. Estimation of principal components and related models by iterative least squares. In P. R. Krishnaiah (Ed.), *Multivariate analysis.* New York: Academic Press, 1966.

Young, F. W. A model for polynomial conjoint analysis algorithms. In R. N. Shepard, A. K. Romney, and S. B. Nerlove (Eds.), *Multidimensional scaling: Theory and applications in the behavioral sciences.* Vol. 1: *Theory.* New York: Seminar Press, 1972.

Young, F. W. *An asymmetric Euclidean model for multiprocess asymmetric data.* Paper presented at the U.S.–Japan Seminar on Multidimensional Scaling, University of California at San Diego, August 20–24, 1975. (a)

Young, F. W. Methods for describing ordinal data with cardinal models. *Journal of Mathematical Psychology,* 1975, *12,* 416–436. (b)

Young, F. W., de Leeuw, J., and Takane, Y. Regression with qualitative and quantitative variables: An alternating least squares method with optimal scaling features. *Psychometrika,* 1976, *41,* 505–529.

Young, F. W., and Null, C. H. Multidimensional scaling of nominal data: The recovery of metric information with ALSCAL. *Psychometrika,* 1978, *43,* 367–379.

Young, F. W., Sarle, W. S., and Hoffman, D. L. Interactively ordering the similarities among a large set of stimuli. In R. Golledge and J. N. Rayner (Eds.), *Multidimensional analysis of large data sets.* Minneapolis: University of Minnesota Press, 1980.

Young, F. W., and Torgerson, W. S. TORSCA, a FORTRAN IV program for Shepard–Kruskal multidimensional scaling analysis. *Behavioral Science,* 1967, *12,* 498.

Zinnes, J. L., and Wolff, R. P. Single and multidimensional same-different judgments. *Journal of Mathematical Psychology,* 1977, *16,* 30–50.

Zwislocki, J. J. Absolute scaling. *Journal of the Acoustical Society of America,* 1978, *63,* (Supplement No. 1), S16.

Cluster Analysis
Research

INTRODUCTION

Cluster Analysis in Marketing Research: Review and Suggestions for Application

Cluster analysis is a statistical method for classification and is an alternative to the other classification techniques such as multidimensional scaling, factor analysis, and discriminant analysis. The article by Girish Punj and David W. Stewart gives a general overview of cluster analysis and its use in marketing. The article discusses the history, algorithms, comparisons, applications, and problems with cluster analysis, and concludes with recommendations that will help yield valid results.

There are many marketing problems in which cluster analysis has had applications. The primary business use has been for market segmentation, where research has focused on identifying groups of entities that share common characteristics. Other cluster applications have included identifying homogeneous groups of buyers, development of potential product opportunities, test market selection, and use as a general data reduction technique. The article cites particular examples in which cluster analysis has been used in each of these areas.

Cluster analysis offers unique statistical problems when analysis and interpretation are considered. Numerous cluster analysis algorithms have been developed, many of which are known by several different names. This multiplicity of approaches poses a problem for the researcher in identifying which technique should be used for a specific application. A second potential problem confronting the user of cluster analysis is cluster identification. Because algorithms differ and because there are no clear guidelines for determining the boundaries of clusters, cluster analysis offers no inherent statistical basis for making statistical inferences.

Each of the major cluster algorithms (along with the various names) is described within the article. The characteristics of data may produce different results under the various algorithms. The selection of the clustering algorithm and solution characteristics is critical to the successful use of cluster analysis. The article contains a comprehensive evaluation of the various clustering techniques, including data transformation issues, solution issues (what algorithm?), validity issues (how to evaluate the solution?), and variable selection issues (what variables will yield a valid decision?).

Overlapping Clustering: A New Method for Product Positioning

The major limitation of traditional cluster analysis algorithms is their preclusion of overlap in cluster membership for individual cluster members. In application, this is to say that cluster members are not allowed to belong to multiple groups. The second article in this section—by Phipps Arabie, J. Douglas Carroll, Wayne DeSarbo, and Jerry Wind—presents a new clustering methodology for overcoming this problem.

CLUSTER ANALYSIS IN MARKETING RESEARCH: REVIEW AND SUGGESTIONS FOR APPLICATION
Girish Punj, *University of Connecticut,* and David W. Stewart, *Vanderbilt University*

Cluster analysis has become a common tool for the marketing researcher. Both the academic researcher and the marketing applications researcher rely on the technique for developing empirical groupings of persons, products, or occasions which may serve as the basis for further analysis. Despite its frequent use, little is known about the characteristics of available clustering methods or how clustering methods should be employed. One indication of this general lack of understanding of clustering methodology is the failure of numerous authors in the marketing literature to specify what clustering method is being used. Another such indicator is the tendency of some authors to differentiate among methods which actually differ only in name.

The use of cluster analysis has frequently been viewed with skepticism.

Green, Frank, and Robinson (1967) and Frank and Green (1968) have discussed problems with determining the appropriate measure of similarity and the appropriate number of clusters. Inglis and Johnson (1970), Morrison (1967), Neidell (1970), and Shuchman (1967) have also expressed concern about the use of cluster analysis. More recently, Wells (1975) has expressed reservations about the use of cluster analysis unless very different, homogeneous groups can be identified. Such skepticism is probably justified in the light of the confusing array of names and methods of cluster analysis confronting the marketing researcher. As this confusion is resolved and as additional information about the performance characteristics of various clustering algorithms becomes available, such skepticism may disappear. Recent work on clustering algorithms

The authors acknowledge the support of the 1981 Dean's Fund of the Owen Graduate School of Management, Vanderbilt University, which facilitated the completion of this article.

From Girish Punj and David W. Stewart, "Cluster Analysis in Marketing Research: Review and Suggestions for Application," *Journal of Marketing Research,* Vol. XX, May 1983. Reprinted with permission of the publisher, American Marketing Association.

affords a basis for establishing some general guidelines for the appropriate use of cluster analysis. It is useful to note that many of the problems associated with cluster analysis also plague multivariate statistics in general: choice of an appropriate metric, selection of variables, cross-validation, and external validation.

Two general sets of issues confront the marketing researcher seeking to use cluster analysis. One set of issues involves theoretical properties of particular algorithms. These issues are considered in the literature on cluster analysis [Anderberg, 1973; Bailey, 1974; Cormack, 1971; Hartigan, 1975], and are not addressed here. The second set of issues is more practical and pertains to the actual use of clustering procedures for data analysis. These issues are the foci of our article, in which we review applications of clustering methodology to marketing problems, provide a systematic treatment of the clustering options open to the marketing researcher, and use both theoretical and empirical findings to suggest which clustering options may be most useful for a particular research problem.

Cluster analysis has most frequently been employed as a classification tool. It has also been used by some researchers as a means of representing the structure of data via the construction of dendrograms [Bertin, 1967; Hartigan, 1967] or overlapping clusters [Arabie et al., 1981; Shepard and Arabie, 1979]. The latter applications are distinct from the use of cluster analysis for classification and represent an alternative to multidimensional scaling and factor analytic approaches to representing similarity data. Whereas classification is concerned with the identification of discrete categories (taxonomies), structural representation is concerned with the development of a faithful representation of relationships. Both uses of cluster analysis are legitimate, but the objectives of these applications are very different. The best clustering algorithm for accomplishing one

of these objectives is not necessarily the best for the other objective. We restrict our treatment of cluster analysis to the more common of the two applications, classification.

Cluster analysis is a statistical method for classification. Unlike other statistical methods for classification, such as discriminant analysis and automatic interaction detection, it makes no prior assumptions about important differences within a population. Cluster analysis is a purely empirical method of classification and as such is primarily an inductive technique [Gerard, 1957]. Though some theorists have not been favorably disposed toward the use of cluster analysis, and criticism of the ad hoc nature of clustering solutions is common, classification is an important and frequently overlooked tool of science. Wolf (1926) has suggested that classification is both the first and last method employed by science. The essence of classification is that certain things are thought of as related in a certain way. Indeed, the final outcome of other methods of study may well be a new classification.

Kemeny (1959) and Kantor (1953), discussing the philosophy of science, point to the fundamental importance of classification. Wold (1926) holds that verification of laws of science may occur only after classification has been completed. Thus, whether the classification exercise is completed explicitly or implicitly, it must occur. Cluster analysis provides one, empirically based, means for explicitly classifying objects. Such a tool is particularly relevant for the emerging discipline of marketing which is still wrestling with the problems of how best to classify consumers, products, media types, and usage occasions.

USES OF CLUSTER ANALYSIS IN MARKETING

The primary use of cluster analysis in marketing has been for market segmentation. Since the appearance of Smith's now-classic article (1956), market segmentation has become an important tool for both academic research and applied marketing. In a review of market segmentation research and methodology, Wind (1978) identifies both the impact of this most fundamental of marketing tools and some rather significant problem areas. Not the least of these problems is the plethora of methods that have been proposed for segmenting markets. This multiplication of techniques has served to confuse many marketers, shift discussions of researchers from more substantive issues to issues of method, and impede the development of meta-research directed at integrating market segmentation research. In concluding his review of the segmentation literature, Wind suggests that one important area of future research should be the "evaluation of the conditions under which various data analytical techniques are most appropriate" (1978, p. 334).

All segmentation research, regardless of the method used, is designed to identify groups of entities (people, markets, organizations) that share certain common characteristics (attitudes, purchase propensities, media habits, and so forth). Stripped of the specific data employed and the details of the purposes of a particular study, segmentation research becomes a grouping task. Wind (1978) notes that researchers tend to select grouping methods largely on the basis of familiarity, availability, and cost rather than on the basis of the methods' characteristics and appropriateness. Wind attributes this practice to the lack of research on similarity measures, grouping (clustering) algorithms, and effects of various data transformations.

A second and equally important use of cluster analysis has been in seeking a better understanding of buyer behaviors by identifying homogeneous groups of buyers. Cluster analysis has been less frequently applied to this type of theory-building

problem, possibly because of theorists' discomfort with a set of procedures which appear ad hoc. Nevertheless, there is clearly a need for better classification of relevant buyer characteristics. Bettman (1979) has called for the development of taxonomies of both consumer choice task and individual difference characteristics. Cluster analysis is one means for developing such taxonomies. Examples of such use may be found in articles by Claxton, Fry, and Portis (1974), Kiel and Layton (1981), and Furse, Punj, and Stewart (1982).

Cluster analysis has been employed in the development of potential new product opportunities. By clustering brands/products, competitive sets within the larger market structure can be determined. Thus, a firm can examine its current offerings vis-à-vis those of its competitors. The firm can determine the extent to which a current or potential product offering is uniquely positioned or is in a competitive set with other products [Srivastava, Leone, and Shocker, 1981; Srivastava, Shocker, and Day, 1978]. Although cluster analysis has not been used frequently in such applications, largely because of the availability of other techniques such as multidimensional scaling, factor analysis, and discriminant analysis, it is not uncommon to find cluster analysis used as an adjunct to these other techniques. Cluster analysis has also been suggested as an alternative to factor analysis and discriminant analysis. In such applications it is important for the analyst to determine whether discrete categories of products are desirable or whether a representation of market structure is desirable. The latter may be more useful in many market structure applications, in which case cluster analysis would not be used as a classification technique and the analyst would face a different set of issues from those addressed here.

Cluster analysis has also been employed by several researchers in the problem of test market selection [Green,

Frank, and Robinson, 1967]. Such applications are concerned with the identification of relatively homogeneous sets of test markets which may become interchangeable in test market studies. The identification of such homogeneous sets of test markets allows generalization of the results obtained in one test market to other test markets in the same cluster, thereby reducing the number of test markets required.

Finally, cluster analysis has been used as a general data reduction technique to develop aggregates of data which are more general and more easily managed than individual observations. For example, limits on the number of observations that can be used in multidimensional scaling programs often necessitate an initial clustering of observations. Homogeneous clusters then become the unit of analysis for the multidimensional scaling procedure. Fisher (1969) discussed the use of cluster analysis for data reduction from the perspective of econometrics and argued that cluster analysis is most appropriate whenever the data are too numerous or too detailed to be manageable. Such data simplification and aggregation are carried out for the convenience of the investigator rather than in the interest of theory building.

Table 7–1 is a brief description of some recent applications of cluster analysis to marketing problems. Although not a complete set of all applications of cluster analysis in marketing, it illustrates several points. First, the array of problems addressed by these studies is striking. Equally striking is the diversity of clustering methods employed. In constructing this table we had difficulty discerning the specific clustering algorithm used by the researchers. Cluster analysis methods were often identified by the name of the program used (for example, BMDP2M, BCTRY, or Howard and Harris) rather than by the specific clustering algorithm used. Only by consulting a particular

program's manual could we identify the method actually employed. For one of the studies cited we could not find any information on the clustering method used.

The lack of specificity about the method of clustering employed in these studies is illustrative of the problems associated with the use of cluster analysis. The lack of detailed reporting suggests either an ignorance of or lack of concern for the important parameters of the clustering method used. Failure to provide specific information about the method also tends to inhibit replication and provides little guidance for other researchers who might seek an appropriate method of cluster analysis. Use of specific program names rather than the more general algorithm name impedes interstudy comparisons.

This situation suggests a need for a sound review of clustering methodology for the marketing researcher. Previous reviews on this subject appeared prior to the publication of much of the research on the performance characteristics of clustering algorithms. Sherman and Sheth (1977) discuss selected similarity measures and clustering algorithms. Though they mention some empirical work on the characteristics of these measures and algorithms, their report is primarily a catalog of techniques and some marketing applications. Relatively little guidance is provided the researcher seeking to discover the characteristics and limitations of various grouping procedures. Indeed, the Sherman and Sheth report may mislead some readers because its categorization of clustering algorithms suggests substantive differences among identical algorithms which differ only in name. Frank and Green (1968) also provide an introduction and review of clustering methodology but make no specific recommendations to guide the user of the methodology. After reviewing the problems and issues facing the user of cluster analytic procedures, we offer clarification of the similarities and differences among various clustering algo-

Table 7-1
Some Recent Applications of Cluster Analysis in Marketing

Application	Purpose of Research	Nature of Data	Clustering Method Used
Anderson, Cox, and Fulcher (1976)	To identify the determinant attributes in bank selection decisions and use them for segmenting commercial bank customers	Determinant attribute scores on several bank selection variables	Iterative partitioning— MIKCA [McRae, 1973]
Bass, Pessemier, and Tigert (1969)	To identify market segments with respect to media exposure	Attribute scores on several media exposure variables	Average linkage cluster analysis [Sneath and Sokal, 1973]
Calantone and Sawyer (1978)	To examine the stability of market segments in the retail banking market	Attribute scores on several bank selection variables	K-means (Howard and Harris, 1966)
Claxton, Fry, and Portis (1974)	To classify furniture and appliance buyers in terms of their information search behavior	Attribute scores on several prepurchase activity measures	Complete linkage cluster analysis [Johnson, 1967; Lance and Williams, 1967a]
Day and Heeler (1971)	To classify stores into similar strata	Factor scores on several store attributes	(1) Complete linkage analysis (2) Iterative partitioning [Rubin, 1965]
Green, Frank, and Robinson (1967)	To identify matched cities for test marketing	Factor scores on several city characteristics	Average linkage cluster analysis [Sneath and Sokal, 1973]

Greeno, Sommers, and Kernan (1973)	To identify market segments with respect of personality variables and implicit behavior patterns	Q sorts on 38 product items	Ward's minimum variance method [Ward, 1963]
Kernan (1968)	To identify groups of people along several personality and decision behavior characteristics	Scores on several personality and decision traits	Ward's minimum variance method [Ward, 1963]
Kernan and Bruce (1972)	To create relatively homogeneous configuration of census traits	Characteristics of census traits	Ward's minimum variance method [Ward, 1963]
Kiel and Layton (1981)	To develop consumer taxonomies of search behavior by Australian new car buyers	Factor scores derived from several search variables	Average linkage cluster analysis [Sneath and Sokal, 1973]
Landon (1974)	To identify groups of people using purchase intention and self-concept variables	Scores on self-image and purchase intention variables	Iterative partitioning [BCTRY; Tryon and Bailey, 1970]
Lessig and Tollefson (1971)	To identify similar groups of consumers along several buyer behavior variables	Scores on several buyer behavior variables	Ward's minimum variance method [Ward, 1963]
Montgomery and Silk (1971)	To identify opinion leadership and consumer interest segments	Scores on several interest and opinion leadership variables	Complete linkage cluster analysis [Johnson, 1967]

(continues)

Table 7–1 (continued)

Application	Purpose of Research	Nature of Data	Clustering Method Used
Moriarty and Venkatesan (1978)	To segment educational institutions in terms of benefits sought when purchasing financial-aid MIS	Importance scores on financial-aid management services	K-means [Howard and Harris, 1966]
Morrison and Sherman (1972)	To determine how various individuals interpret sex appeal in advertising	Ratings of advertisements by respondents	Iterative Partitioning [Friedman and Rubin, 1967]
Myers and Nicosia (1968)	To develop a consumer typology using attribute data	Scores of supermarket image variables	Iterative partitioning [BCTRY; Tryon and Bailey, 1970]
Sethi (1971)	To classify world markets	Macrolevel data on countries	Iterative partitioning [BCTRY; Tryon and Bailey, 1970]
Sexton (1974)	To identify homogeneous groups of families using product and brand usage data	Brand and product usage rate data	Type not specified
Schaninger, Lessig, and Panton (1980)	To identify segments of consumers on the basis of product usage variables	Scores on several product usage variables	K-means [Howard and Harris, 1966]
Green and Carmone (1968)	To identify similar computers (strata in the computer market)	Performance measures for different computer models	K-means [Howard and Harris, 1966]

rithms and some suggestions about their use.

PROBLEMS IN USING CLUSTER ANALYSIS

Unlike other data analytic methods, cluster analysis is a set of methodologies that has developed outside a single dominant discipline. Factor analysis and various scaling methods were developed within the discipline of psychology and one would look to that discipline for guidance in the use of these methods. Regression, though used in a variety of disciplines, has tended to be the special province of econometricians, who have developed a large body of literature on the technique. In contrast, no single discipline has developed and retained clustering methodology. Rather, numerous disciplines (econometrics, psychology, biology, and engineering) have independently approached the clustering problem. Often working in parallel, researchers in these disciplines have arrived at similar solutions but have given them different names. For example, Blashfield (1978) reviewed the literature on hierarchical clustering methods and found as many as seven different names for the same technique. This diversity of names for identical techniques has tended to prevent comparisons of algorithms across disciplines. It has also served to confuse the data analyst by implying a much greater number of available clustering methods than actually exists.

Also confronting the potential user of cluster analysis is the problem of cluster definition. There are currently no clear guidelines for determining the boundaries of clusters or deciding when observations should be included in one cluster or another. Cattell (1978) has suggested that clusters are "fuzzy" constructs. The criterion for admission to a cluster is rather arbitrary. There are no well-established rules for the definition of a cluster. The preferred definition of a cluster seems to vary with the discipline and purpose of the researcher.

Clusters have most frequently been defined by relatively contiguous points in space [Stewart, 1981]. Cormack (1971) suggested that clusters should exhibit two properties, external isolation and internal cohesion. External isolation requires that objects in one cluster be separated from objects in another cluster by fairly empty space. Internal cohesion requires that objects within the same cluster be similar to each other. Everitt (1974) offered a similar concept which he defines as a natural cluster. The requirement of external isolation does not provide for overlapping clusters. Although a few algorithms have been developed for identifying overlapping clusters [Jardine and Sibson, 1971; Peay, 1975; Shepard, 1974], these methods are primarily concerned with the representation of structure rather than classification. Applications of these methods have been few and are not reviewed here.

In the absence of a generally accepted or definitive definition of a cluster, various algorithms have been developed which offer particular operational definitions. Differences among clustering algorithms are frequently related to how the concept of a cluster is operationalized. Thus, to develop a set of recommendations for the application of cluster analysis, we must first develop a recognition of the clustering algorithms available to the marketing researcher and an understanding of the performance of these methods in relation to one another.

CLUSTERING ALGORITHMS

Table 7–2 provides a description of the more common clustering algorithms in use, the various alternative names by which the algorithms are known, and a brief discussion of how clusters are formed by each of these methods. Table 7–2 shows clearly

Table 7-2
Clustering Methods

Primary Name	Alternative Names	Method of Forming Clusters
Hierarchical Methods		
Single linkage cluster analysis	Minimum method [Johnson, 1967]; linkage analysis [McQuitty, 1967]; nearest neighbor cluster analysis (Lance and Williams 1967a); connectiveness method [Johnson, 1967]	An observation is joined to a cluster if it has a certain level of similarity with at least *one of* the members of that cluster. Connections between clusters are based on links between single entities.
Complete linkage cluster analysis	Maximum method [Johnson, 1967]; rank order typal analysis [McQuitty, 1967]; furthest neighbor cluster analysis [Lance and Williams, 1967a] diameter method [Johnson, 1967]	An observation is joined to a cluster if it has a certain level of similarity with *all* current members of the cluster.
Average linkage cluster analysis	Simple average linkage analysis [Sneath and Sokal, 1973]; weighted average method [McQuitty, 1967]; centroid method (Gower, 1967); median method [Lance and Williams, 1967a]	These are actually four similar methods. In all four methods an observation is joined to a cluster if it has a certain average level of similarity with all current members of the clusters. These methods differ in the manner in which the average level of similarity is defined. The weighted average method and median method provide for a priori weighting of the averages based on the number of entities desired in each cluster. The centroid method provides for an initial computation of the centroid of each cluster. Average similarity is based on this centroid. Only the simple average linkage procedure has been widely used.

| Minimum variance cluster analysis | Minimum variance method; Ward's method; error sum of squares method [Ward, 1963]; HGROUP [Veldman, 1967] | The minimum variance method is designed to generate clusters in such a way as to minimize the within-cluster variance. Unlike other hierarchical clustering methods, Ward's method optimizes an objective statistic: it seeks to minimize tr $\mathbf{W}$, where $\mathbf{W}$ is the pooled within-clusters sum of squares and cross-products matrix. Ward's method is somewhat similar to the average method in that variance is a function of deviations from the mean. Some authors have included Ward's method as a special case of the average method (Bailey, 1974). It is an average linkage method because it does not seek to minimize distance between one member of the cluster and the entity, or all members of the cluster and the entity as in single linkage and complete linkage, respectively, but minimizes the average distance within the cluster. |
| *Iterative Partitioning Methods (Nonhierarchical Methods)* | | These methods begin with the partition of observations into a specified number of clusters. This partition may be on a random or nonrandom basis. Observations are then reassigned to clusters until some stopping criterion is reached. Methods differ in the nature of the reassignment and stopping rules.

(continues) |

Table 7–2 (continued)

Primary Name	Alternative Names	Method of Forming Clusters
K-means		Cases are reassigned by moving them to the cluster whose centroid is closest to that case. Reassignment continues until every case is assigned to the cluster with the nearest centroid. Such a procedure implicitly minimizes the variance within each cluster, tr **w**.
Hill-climbing methods		Cases are not reassigned to the cluster with the nearest centroid but are moved from one cluster to another if a particular statistical criterion is obtained. Reassignment continues until optimization occurs. The objective function to be optimized may be selected from one of four options, tr **W**, tr $[(\mathbf{W}^{-1}\mathbf{B}]$, $|\mathbf{W}|$, and the largest eigenvalue of $[(\mathbf{W}^{-1}\mathbf{B}]$, where **W** is the pooled within-cluster covariance matrix and **B** is the between-cluster covariance matrix.
Combined *K*-means and hill-climbing methods		Uses a combination of *K*-means and hill-climbing methods.

that there are relatively few clustering methods from which to choose, far fewer than one might suspect from a reading of the literature on cluster analysis. Four primary hierarchical methods are available, single linkage, complete linkage, average linkage, and Ward's minimum variance method. Although there are several variations of the average linkage method, only one, simple average linkage, is widely used. In addition, two variants of the average method, the centroid and median methods, have very undesirable properties [Aldenderfer, 1977; Sneath and Sokal, 1973] which recommend against their use. The weighted average linkage method has been shown to produce results very similar to those produced by the simple average method [Blashfield, 1977].

There is more variety among the nonhierarchical methods, though all work on similar principles. These iterative partitioning methods begin by dividing observations into some predetermined number of clusters. Observations are then reassigned to clusters until some decision rule terminates the process. These methods may differ with respect to the starting partition, the type of reassignment process, the decision rule used for terminating clustering, and the frequency with which cluster centroids are updated during the reassignment process. The initial partition may be random or based on some prior information or intuition. One method (MIKCA) uses several different random starting partitions to ensure an efficient solution. Two types of reassignment are generally employed, K-means and hill-climbing. These methods are briefly discussed in Table 7–2 as are the termination decision rules used with each method. Cluster centroids may be updated after each membership move or only after a complete pass through the entire data set.

Not included in Table 7–2 are two methods frequently used for cluster analysis: Q-factor analysis and automatic interaction detection (AID) [Morgan and Sonquist, 1963]. Q-factor analysis is not included because Stewart (1981) in the marketing literature and Cattell (1978) in the psychology literature have forcefully argued that factor analysis is inappropriate as a method for identifying clusters. Skinner (1979) discusses some relationships between factor analysis and cluster analysis. AID is not included because it operates on a rather different principle than the clustering procedures. AID requires the prior specification of independent and dependent variables and seeks to identify sets of nominal independent variables which group observations in a manner that minimizes the variance of the dependent variable within each group. Cluster analysis procedures require no such a priori specification of independent and dependent variables.

These clustering algorithms exist in various forms but most have been programmed. Several software programs are currently available for cluster analysis. They differ in their comprehensiveness and ease of use. Table 7–3 briefly describes several of the more common clustering software programs, identifies the types of clustering methods available within each program, and cites the original source of the program. Selecting an appropriate cluster analytic method or software package requires some knowledge of the performance characteristics of the various methods.

EMPIRICAL COMPARISONS OF CLUSTERING METHODS

One method for evaluating clustering methods that has been used with increasing frequency involves comparing the results of different clustering methods applied to the same data sets. If the underlying characteristics of these data sets are known, one can assess the degree to which each clustering method produces results consistent with these known characteristics. For example, if a data set

Table 7–3
Common Clustering Packages/Programs

Name of Package/Program	Where Available/ Authors	Clustering Methods[a]	Comments
ANDERBERG	In the appendices of book entitled *Cluster Analysis for Applications* by M. R. Anderberg (1973).	S, C, A, W, K, H, KH	1. No missing value treatment 2. Only binary data type with octal coding scheme 3. User manual not available
BCTRY	D. Bailey and R. C. Tryon, Tryon-Bailey Associates, Inc., c/o Mr. Peter Lenz, 2222 S. E. Nehalem St., Portland, OR	K	1. No MANOVA statistics are optimized 2. Initial partition has to be user specified 3. Factor analysis of variables may be performed as well
BMDP	W. J. Dixon (ed.), Health Sciences Computing Facility, School of Medicine, UCLA, Los Angeles	S, C, A, K	1. Single and complete linkage available for clustering 2. Binary data not permissible 3. Continuous type similarity measure 4. Method for clustering cases and variables simultaneously is available 5. User cannot supply only similarity matrix for cases
CLUS	H. Friedman and J. Rubin (1967 *JASA* article), IBM SHARE system	K, H	1. Fixed number of clusters 2. Expensive to use

Program	Source	Methods[a]	Comments
CLUSTAN	D. Wishart, Computer Centre, University College of London, 19 Gordon St., London, WC1H OAH, Great Britain	S, C, A, W, K, H	1. High versatility (38 s/dis measures) 2. Initial partition for iterative partitioning methods has to be user specified 3. Binary and continuous data types 4. Binary data in 3 coding schemes 5. Variable transformations not available 6. Permits overlapping clusters
HARTIGAN	In the appendices of book entitled *Clustering Algorithms* by J. J. Hartigan (1975).	S, A, K	1. Fixed number of clusters for iterative partitioning methods 2. No variable transformations available 3. No user manual available
HGROUP	D. J. Veldman (1967), *FORTRAN Programming for the Behavioral Sciences.*	W	1. Part of the University of Texas EDSTAT statistics package
HICLUS	S. C. Johnson (based on 1967 *Psychometrika* article), Bell Telephone Labs, Murray Hill, NJ	SC	1. No user manual available 2. No missing value treatment 3. No standardization of variables 4. No transformation of variables 5. User must supply similarity matrix (hence is versatile in some sense)

[a]S = single linkage; C = complete linkage; A = average linkage; W = Ward's minimum variance method; K = K-means; H = hill climbing; KH = joint K-means, hill climbing.

(continues)

Table 7-3 (continued)

Name of Package/Program	Where Available/ Authors	Clustering Methods[a]	Comments
HOWD (Howard-Harris)	Britton Harris, F. J. Carmone, Jr., University of Pennsylvania, Philadelphia	K	1. No user manual available 2. No MANOVA statistics 3. Number of clusters fixed
ISODATA	Daviel Wolf, SRI, 333 Ravenswood Avenue, Menlo Park, CA	K	1. No user manual available 2. No MANOVA statistics optimized
MIKCA	D. J. McRae, Coordinator, Testing & Computer Applications, Jackson Public Schools, Jackson, MI	K, H, KH	1. No user manual available 2. 4 MANOVA statistics optimized 3. 3 different distance measures
NT-SYS	F. James Rohlf, John Kishapugh, David Kirk, Dept. of Ecology and Evolution, SUNY at Stony Brook	S, C, A	1. Permits overlapping clusters 2. Alphanumeric coding scheme for binary data 3. Moderately versatile
OSIRIS	Institute of Survey Research, University of Michigan, Ann Arbor	C	
SAS	James H. Goodnight, SAS Inst., Inc., P. O. Box 10066, Raleigh, NC	C	1. Continuous similarity measure

[a]S = single linkage; C = complete linkage; A = average linkage; W = Ward's minimum variance method; K = K-means; H = hill climbing; KH = joint K-means, hill climbing.

consists of a known mixture of groups, or subpopulations, the efficacy of a cluster solution can be evaluated by its success in discriminating among these subpopulations. This mixture model approach to the evaluation of clustering algorithms has recently been employed by several researchers. Table 7–4 summarizes the findings of 12 such studies.

The number of clustering algorithms, distance measures, and types of data that might be incorporated in a mixture model study is so large as to preclude any one comprehensive study of the relative efficiency of clustering methods. We can look across the studies in Table 7–4, however, and begin to draw some conclusions about clustering methods. Three procedures seem to warrant special consideration. Ward's minimum variance method, average linkage, and several variants of the iterative partitioning method appear to outperform all other methods. Ward's method appears to outperform the average linkage method except in the presence of outliers. K-means appears to outperform both Ward's method and the average linkage method if a nonrandom starting point is specified. If a random starting point is used K-means may be markedly inferior to other methods, but results on this issue are not consistent. Nevertheless, the K-means procedure appears to be more robust than any of the hierarchical methods with respect to the presence of outliers, error perturbations of the distance measures, and the choice of a distance metric. It appears to be least affected by the presence of irrelevant attributes or dimensions in the data.

One conclusion in several of the studies is that the choice of a similarity/dissimilarity measure, or distance measure, does not appear to be critical. Despite the considerable attention given such measures [Green and Rao, 1969; Morrison, 1967; Sherman and Sheth, 1977], the selection of a similarity measure appears to be less important for determining the outcome of a clustering solution

than the selection of a clustering algorithm. Two cautions should be observed in taking this conclusion at face value, however. First, the number of studies of the relative import of distance measures for determining clustering solutions is small, and many types of data have yet to be examined. There may be types of data for which the selection of a distance measure is critical to the clustering solution. Second, clustering algorithms which are sensitive to the presence of outliers (for example, complete linkage specifically, and more generally all of the hierarchical methods of clustering) seem to produce better solutions when Pearson product moment or intraclass correlation coefficients are used. Such similarity measures tend to reduce the extremity of outliers in relation to Euclidean distance measures. This, in turn, reduces the influence of outliers on the final clustering solution. A similar effect is obtained if data are standardized prior to clustering.

One characteristic of data appears to have a marked decremental effect on the performance of all clustering methods—the presence of one or more spurious attributes or dimensions. A variable that is not related to the final clustering solution (that is, does not differentiate among clusters in some manner) causes a serious deterioration of the performance of all clustering methods, though this problem is least severe with the K-means procedure and is probably less serious for other iterative partitioning methods as well. This finding indicates the need for careful selection of variables for use in clustering and the need to avoid "shotgun" approaches where everything known about the observations is used as the basis for clustering. Clearly one cannot know in advance what variables may differentiate among a set of as yet unidentified clusters. Nevertheless, it is not unreasonable for a researcher to have some rational or theoretical basis for selecting the variables used in a cluster analysis.

A final conclusion can be drawn from

Table 7-4
Empirical Comparisons of the Performance of Clustering Algorithms

Reference	Methods Examined	Data Sets Employed	Coverage[a]	Criteria	Summary of Results
Cunningham and Ogilvie (1972)	Single, complete, average linkage with Euclidean distances and Ward's minimum variance technique	Normal mixtures	Complete	Measures of "stress" to compare input similarity/dissimilarity matrix with similarity relationship among entities portrayed by the clustering method	Average linkage outperformed other methods
Kuiper and Fisher (1975)	Single, complete, average, centroid, median linkage, all using Euclidean distances and Ward's minimum variance technique	Bivariate normal mixtures	Complete	Rand's statistic (Rand 1971)	Ward's technique consistently outperformed other methods
Blashfield (1976)	Single, complete, average linkage, all using Euclidean distance and Ward's minimum variance technique	Multinormal mixtures	Complete	Kappa (Cohen 1960)	Ward's technique demonstrated highest median accuracy

Mojena (1977)	Simple average, weighted average, median, centroid, complete linkage, all using Euclidean distances and Ward's minimum variance technique	Multivariate gamma distribution mixtures	Complete	Rand's statistic	Ward's method outperformed other methods
Blashfield (1977)	Eight iterative partitioning methods: Anderberg and CLUSTAN K-means methods, each with cluster statistics updated after each reassignment and only after a complete pass through the data; CLUS and MIKCA (both hill-climbing algorithms), each with optimization of tr W and W	Multinormal mixtures	Complete	Kappa	For 15 of the 20 data sets examined, a hill-climbing technique which optimized W performed best (that is, MIKCA or CLUS). In two other cases a hill-climbing method which optimized tr W performed best, CLUS.
Milligan and Isaac (1978)	Single, complete average linkage, and Ward's minimum variance technique, all using Euclidean distances	Data sets differing in degree of error perturbation	Complete	Rand's statistic and kappa	Average linkage and Ward's technique superior to single and complete linkage

[a]The percentage of observations included in the cluster solution. With complete coverage, clustering continues until all observations have been assigned to a cluster. Ninety percent coverage could imply that the most extreme 10 percent of the observations were not included in any cluster.

(continues)

Table 7–4 (continued)

Reference	Methods Examined	Data Sets Employed	Coverage[a]	Criteria	Summary of Results
Mezzich (1978)	Single, complete linkage, and *K*-means, each with city-block and Euclidean distances and correlation coefficient, ISO-DATA, Friedman and Rubin method, *Q*-factor analysis, multidimensional scaling with city-block and Euclidean metrics and correlation coefficients, NORMAP/NORMIX, average linkage with correlation coefficients	Psychiatric ratings	Complete	Replicability; agreement with "expert" judges; goodness of fit between raw input dissimilarity matrix and matrix of 0's and 1's indicating entities clustered together	*K*-means procedure with Euclidean distances performed best followed by *K*-means procedure with the city-block metric; average linkage also performed well as did complete linkage with a correlation coefficient and city-block metric and ISO-DATA; the type of metric used (*r*, city-block, or Euclidean distance) had little impact on results.
Edelbrock (1979)	Single, complete, average, and centroid, each with correlation coefficients, Euclidean distances, and Ward's minimum variance technique	Multivariate normal mixtures, standardized and unstandardized	70, 80, 90, 95, 100%	Kappa	Ward's method and simple average were most accurate; performance of all algorithms deteriorated as coverage increased but was less pronounced when the data were standardized or correlation coefficients were used. The latter finding is suggested to result from the decreased extremity of outliers associated with standardization or use of the correlation coefficient.

Edelbrock and McLaughlin (1980)	Single, complete, average, each with correlation coefficients, Euclidean distances, one-way and two-way intraclass correlations, and Ward's minimum variance technique	Multivariate normal mixtures and multivariate gamma mixtures	40, 50, 60, 70, 80, 90, 95, 100%	Kappa and Rand's statistic	Ward's method and the average method using one-way intraclass correlations were most accurate; performance of all algorithms deteriorated as coverage increased.
Blashfield and Morey (1980)	Ward's minimum variance technique, group average linkage, Q-factor analysis, Lorr's nonhierarchical procedure, all using Pearson product moment correlations as the similarity measure	Multivariate normal mixtures	Varying levels	Kappa	Group average method best at higher levels of coverage; at lower levels of coverage Ward's method and group average performed similarly.
Milligan (1980)	Single, complete, group average, weighted average, centroid & median linkage, Ward's minimum variance technique, minimum average sum of squares, minimum total sum of squares, beta-flexible (Lance & Williams 1970a, b), average link in the new cluster, MacQueen's method, Jancey's method, K-means with random	Multivariate normal mixtures, standardized and varying in the number of underlying clusters and the pattern of distribution of points of the clusters. Data sets ranged from error free to two levels of error perturbations of the distance measures, from containing no outliers to two levels of outlier	Complete	Rand's statistic; the point biserial correlation between the raw input dissimilarity matrix and a matrix of 0's and 1's indicating entities clustering together	K-means procedure with a derived point generally performed better than other methods across all conditions 1. Distance measure selection did not appear critical; methods generally robust across distance measures. 2. Presence of random dimensions produced decrements in cluster recovery. 3. Single linkage method strongly affected by

(continues)

Table 7–4 (continued)

Reference	Methods Examined	Data Sets Employed	Coverage[a]	Criteria	Summary of Results
	starting point, K-means with derived starting point, all with Euclidean distances, Cattell's (1949) r_p, and Pearson r	conditions, and from no variables unrelated to the clusters to one or two randomly assigned dimensions unrelated to the underlying clusters.			error-perturbations; other hierarchical methods moderately so; nonhierarchical methods only slightly affected by perturbations. 4. Complete linkage and Ward's method exhibited noticeable decrements in performance in the outlier conditions; single, group average, and centroid methods only slightly affected by presence of outliers; nonhierarchical methods generally unaffected by presence of outliers. 5. Group average method best among hierarchical methods used to derive starting point for K-means procedure. 6. Nonhierarchical methods using random starting points performed poorly across all conditions.

| Bayne, Beauchamp, Begovich, and Kane (1980) | Single, complete, centroid, simple average, weighted average, median linkage and Ward's minimum variance technique, and two new hierarchical methods, the variance and rank score methods; four hierarchical methods: Wolfe's NORMIX, K-means, two variants of the Friedman-Rubin procedure (trace **W** and \|**W**\|). Euclidean distances served as similarity measure. | Six parameterizations of two bivariate normal populations | Complete | Rand's statistic | K-means, trace **W**, and \|**W**\| provided the best recovery of cluster structure. NORMIX performed most poorly. Among hierarchical methods, Ward's technique, complete linkage, variance and rank score methods performed best. Variants of average linkage method also performed well but not as well as other methods. Single linkage performed poorly. |

[a]The percentage of observations included in the cluster solution. With complete coverage, clustering continues until all observations have been assigned to a cluster. Ninety percent coverage could imply that the most extreme 10 percent of the observations were not included in any cluster.

the empirical findings on the performance of clustering algorithms: As a clustering algorithm includes more and more observations, its performance tends to deteriorate, particularly at high levels of coverage, 90 percent and above. This effect is probably the result of outliers beginning to come into the solution. Clustering all observations may not be a good practice. Rather the identification and elimination of outliers or the use of a decision rule to stop clustering short of the inclusion of all observations is probably advantageous. Suggestions for identifying outliers are provided hereafter. The K-means procedure has shown less decrement in performance as coverage increases than have the hierarchical methods.

Though a reasonable amount of evidence suggests that iterative partitioning methods are superior to hierarchical methods, particularly if nonrandom starting points are used, it is not yet clear which of the iterative partitioning methods are superior. K-means procedures and tr **W** and |**W**| hill-climbing procedures all appear to perform well. Some evidence [Blashfield, 1977] suggests that hill-climbing methods which minimize |**W**| have an advantage over other iterative partitioning methods.

RECOMMENDATIONS FOR USING CLUSTER ANALYSIS

It should be clear from the preceding discussion that the research analyst must make several decisions which affect the structure of a cluster solution. These decisions can be grouped in the following broad categories.

1. Date transformation issues

   A. What measure of similarity/ dissimilarity should be used?
   B. Should the data be standardized? How should nonequivalence of metrics among variables be addressed?

   C. How should interdependencies in the data be addressed?

2. Solution issues

   A. How many clusters should be obtained?
   B. What clustering algorithm should be used?
   C. Should all cases be included in a cluster analysis or should some subset be ignored?

3. Validity issues

   A. Is the cluster solution different from what might be expected by chance?
   B. Is the cluster solution reliable or stable across samples?
   C. Are the clusters related to variables other than those used to derive them? Are the clusters useful?

4. Variable selection issues

   A. What is the best set of variables for generating a cluster analytic solution?

Often these decisions are not independent of one another because the choice of a means for addressing one of these issues may constrain the options available for addressing other issues. For example, choosing to use a Pearson product moment correlation coefficient also determines that the data will be standardized because standardization is implicit in the computation of the correlation coefficient. Thus, it is not possible to offer recommendations for the resolution of any one of these issues without an explicit understanding of the interactions among these decisions.

DATA TRANSFORMATION ISSUES

Although issues related to the choice of a similarity/dissimilarity measure have received considerable attention [Green and Rao, 1969; Morrison, 1967] the results of the empirical studies cited above suggest that the choice is not crucial to the final clustering solution. The same appears to be true of the standardization issue. To the extent that a particular measure of similarity or standardization reduces the extremity of outliers, the performance of some algorithms which are sensitive to outliers may be improved. Otherwise the selection of a similarity measure or the standardization of data prior to clustering appears to have minimal effect. We do not suggest that the choice of a similarity measure should be indiscriminant; the measure should be appropriate for the type of data being considered. Rather, the choice of a correlation coefficient, a Euclidean distance, or a city-block metric does not seem to produce much difference in the final outcome, of a clustering exercise involving data for which each of the similarity measures is appropriate.

Some measures of similarity/dissimilarity explicitly correct for interdependencies. Other measures do not consider interdependencies. Interdependencies among variables may exist by design, or, more often, are the unexpected result of the research design. Careful selection of variables may reduce unwanted interdependencies but the problem is likely to remain even in the best of circumstances. Bailey (1974) provides an illustration of the problem, the effect of which is to weight more heavily certain dimensions along which clustering will be carried out. When this is desirable for some theoretical or practical purpose, correcting for interdependencies is inappropriate. When the researcher desires that all dimensions or attributes be given equal weight in the clustering process, it is necessary to correct for interdependencies. This can be achieved by selecting a similarity measure which corrects for interdependencies, Mahalanobis D^2, or partial correlations. Correction may also be achieved by completing a preliminary principal components analysis with orthogonal rotation. Component scores may then be used as input for the computation of a similarity or distance measure. Skinner (1979) gives an example of this latter approach.

SOLUTION ISSUES

The selection of the clustering algorithm and solution characteristics appears to be critical to the successful use of cluster analysis. Empirical studies of the performance of clustering algorithms suggest that one of the iterative partitioning methods is preferable to the hierarchical methods. This holds, however, only when a nonrandom starting point can be specified. In addition, iterative partitioning methods require prior specification of the number of clusters desired. Hierarchical methods require no such specification. Thus, the user is confronted with determining both an initial starting point and the number of clusters in order to use the methods that have demonstrated superior performance. Information for determining starting points in the form of a priori descriptions of expected clusters may be available. In the absence of such information a means for obtaining starting points and an estimate of the number of clusters is required. A two-stage procedure may be employed to cope with this problem.

In the first step one of the hierarchical methods which has demonstrated superior performance, average linkage or Ward's minimum variance method, may be used to obtain a first approximation of a solution. By examining the results of this preliminary analysis, one can determine both a candidate number of clusters and a starting point for the iterative partitioning analysis. In addition, this preliminary analysis can be used for examining the order of clustering of various observations and the distances between individual observations and clusters. This provides an opportunity for the identification of outliers which may be eliminated from further analysis. The remaining cases may then be submitted to an iterative partitioning

_____ Figure 7–1 _____
Two-Stage Clustering

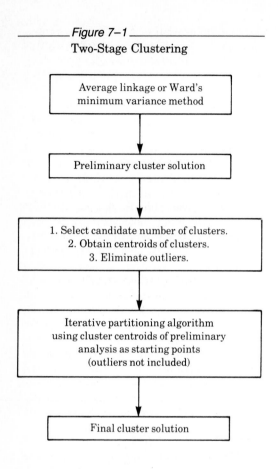

analysis for refinement of the clusters. Similar two-stage clustering approaches have been suggested by Hartigan (1975) and Milligan (1980). Figure 7–1 is a schematic representation of the procedure. Only four cluster analytic software packages provide average linkage or Ward's method and an iterative partitioning algorithm: BMDP, CLUSTAN, and the Anderberg and Hartigan series.

VALIDITY ISSUES

Even after careful analysis of a data set and the determination of a final cluster solution, the researcher has no assurance of having arrived at a meaningful and useful set of clusters. A cluster solution will be reached even when there are no natural groupings in the data. This problem is similar to that encountered with a variety of other procedures ranging from factor analysis to regression analysis. Some test or set of tests must be applied to determine whether the solution differs significantly from a random solution. Milligan and Mahajan (1980) and Milligan (1981) reviewed several such methods for testing the quality of a clustering solution and found them wanting on a number of dimensions. A method suggested by Arnold (1979) appears to overcome the problems of other methods. Arnold (1979) proposed using a statistic first suggested by Friedman and Rubin (1967) as a test of the statistical significance of a cluster solution. The statistic is given by

$$C = \log \frac{\max}{|\mathbf{T}|/|\mathbf{W}|}$$

where $|\mathbf{T}|$ is the determinant of the total variance-covariance matrix and $|\mathbf{W}|$ is the determinant of the pooled within-groups variance-covariance matrix. A number of iterative partitioning methods seek maximization of the ratio of $|\mathbf{T}|$ to $|\mathbf{W}|$: MIKCA, CLUSTAN, and CLUS. For algorithms which do not optimize $|\mathbf{T}|/|\mathbf{W}|$ the test becomes even more conservative. Arnold generated distributions of the C statistic for 2, 4, and 8 group solutions, 10, 20, 50, 100, 200, 500, and 1000 entities, and 5, 10, 20 attributes and indicated values of C which allow rejection of the null hypotheses that the data arise from unimodal or uniform distributions. He presented data to support the use of the statistics and provided formulas for the derivation of other values.

As with other multivariate statistics, one must demonstrate the reliability and the external validity of a cluster solution as well as its statistical significance. Reliability may be established by cross-validation. External validation requires a demonstration that the clusters are useful in some larger sense. Numerous authors have recommended cross-validating cluster solutions [see, for example, Sherman and Sheth, 1977] and several methods of cross-validation have been proposed. One of the more frequently used methods involves dividing the sample in half and carrying out clustering on each half. Descriptive statistics of the two sets of clusters are compared to determine the degree to which similar clusters have been identified. The problem with such an approach is that no objective measure of reliability is obtained.

Several authors have recommended the use of discriminant analysis for cross-validation [Field and Schoenfeldt, 1975; Nerviano and Gross, 1973; Rogers and Linden, 1973]. The approach involves using cluster membership as the group membership variable in a discriminant analysis. After a cluster solution has been developed on one sample, discriminant functions are derived which are applied to a second sample. The degree to which the assignments made with the discriminant functions agree with assignments made by a cluster analysis of the second sample serves as an estimate of the stability of the cluster solution across samples. A coefficient of agreement, such as kappa, may be used to provide an objective measure of such stability. Using discriminant analysis for validating cluster analysis has several drawbacks. Discriminant coefficients may be poor estimates of population values and need to be cross-validated themselves. This procedure is not cost-effective and the sample size available may be insufficient for cross-validating both the cluster analysis and a discriminant analysis.

McIntyre and Blashfield (1980) discussed an alternative approach to cross-validation which is recommended here. The procedure is relatively simple and easy to implement on a computer. Cluster analysis is first carried out on one half of the observations available for analysis. Once a statistically significant clustering solution has been identified, centroids describing the clusters are obtained. Objects in the holdout data set are then assigned to one of the identified clusters on the basis of the smallest Euclidean distance to a cluster centroid vector. The degree of agreement between the nearest-centroid assignments of the holdout sample and the results of a cluster analysis of the holdout sample is an indication of the stability of the solution. A coefficient of agreement, kappa, may be used as an objective measure of stability. If an acceptable level of stability is obtained the data sets may be combined to obtain a final solution.

The demonstration of the statistical significance and stability of a cluster solution is necessary before one can accept and use the classification developed by the methodology. The acceptance of a particular classification system, whether developed through cluster analysis or some other method, requires a further demonstration of utility, however. Classification is only useful if it assists in furthering an understanding of the phenomena of interest. Clusters, or classes, must have demonstrable implications for hypothesis generation, theory building, prediction, or management. The ultimate test of a set of clusters is its usefulness. Thus, the user of cluster analysis should provide a demonstration that clusters are related to variables other than those used to generate the solution. Ideally, only a small number of variables should be required to classify individuals. This classification should then have implications beyond the narrow set of classification variables. The task of classifications is not finished until these broader implications have been demonstrated.

VARIABLE SELECTION ISSUES

The findings of empirical studies of cluster methods suggest that attention to initial variable selection is crucial because even one or two irrelevant variables may distort an otherwise useful cluster solution. The basis for classification must be carefully identified to ensure that extraneous characteristics do not distort an otherwise useful cluster analysis. There should be some rationale for the selection of variables for cluster analysis. That rationale may grow out of an explicit theory or be based on a hypothesis. Clearly more attention needs to be paid to this critical issue. As a science develops, researchers must agree on those dimensions which are most relevant to classification for a particular purpose. Much debate in the science of marketing involves the issue of variable selection. Thus, it is not surprising that a variety of different classification systems has been developed for similar phenomena. Indeed, it is probably unrealistic to expect that a single classification system will emerge in any area of marketing in the foreseeable future. Rather, there are likely to be numerous competing systems. The development of diverse systems is healthy and has been observed in other sciences. Experience with rival systems and a comparison of their usefulness ultimately provide a basis for selection of one system over another. Cluster analysis has much to offer as an aid for developing classification systems. To the extent that classification is both the first and last step in scientific investigation, cluster analysis should have increasing application in marketing.

REFERENCES

Aldenderfer, M. S. (1977), "A Consumer Report on Cluster Analysis Software. 2 Hierarchical Methods," working paper, Department of Anthropology, Pennsylvania State University.

Anderberg, M. R. (1973), *Cluster Analysis for Applications*. New York: Academic Press.

Anderson, W. T. Jr., Cox, E. P. III, and Fulcher, D. G. (1976), "Bank Selection Decisions and Market Segmentation," *Journal of Marketing, 40,* 40–5.

Arabie, P., Carroll, J. D., DeSarbo, W., and Wind, J. (1981), "Overlapping Clustering: A New Method for Product Positioning," *Journal of Marketing Research, 18* (August), 310–7.

Arnold, S. J. (1979), "A Test for Clusters," *Journal of Marketing Research, 16* (November), 545–51.

Bailey, K. D. (1974), "Clusters Analysis," in *Sociological Methodology,* D. Heise, ed. San Francisco: Jossey-Bass.

Ball, G. H. (1970), *Classification Analysis.* Menlo Park, CA: Stanford Research Institute.

Bass, F. M., Pessemier, E. A., and Tigert, D. J. (1969), "A Taxonomy of Magazine Readership Applied to Problems in Marketing Strategy and Media Selection," *Journal of Business, 42,* 337–63.

Bayne, C. K., Beauchamp, J. J., Begovich, C. L., and Kane, V. E. (1980), "Monte Carlo Comparisons of Selected Clustering Procedures," *Pattern Recognition, 12,* 51–62.

Bertin, J. (1967), *Semiology Graphique.* Paris: Gauthier-Villars.

Bettman, J. R. (1979), *An Information Processing Theory of Consumer Choice.* Reading, MA: Addison-Wesley.

Blashfield, R. K. (1976), "Mixture Model Tests of Cluster Analysis: Accuracy of Four Agglomerative Hierarchical Methods," *Psychological Bulletin, 83,* 377–88.

Blashfield, R. K. (1977), "A Consumer Report on Cluster Analysis Software: (3) Iterative Partitioning Methods," working paper, Department of Psychology, Pennsylvania State University.

Blashfield, R. K. (1978), "The Literature on Cluster Analysis," *Multivariate Behavioral Research, 13,* 271–95.

Blashfield, R. K., and Morey, L. C. (1980), "A Comparison of Four Clustering Methods Using MMPI Monte Carlo Data," *Applied Psychology Measurement,* in press.

Calantone, R. J., and Sawyer, A. G. (1978), "Stability of Benefit Segments," *Journal of Marketing Research, 15* (August), 395–404.

Cattell, R. B. (1949), "R_p and Other Coefficients of Pattern Similarity," *Psychometrika, 14,* 279–98.

Cattell, R. B. (1978), *The Scientific Use of Factor Analysis in the Behavioral and Life Sciences.* New York: Plenum Press.

Claxton, J. D., Fry, J. N., and Portis, B. (1974),

"A Taxonomy of Pre-purchase Information Gathering Patterns," *Journal of Consumer Research, 1,* 35–42.

Cohen, J. (1960), "A Coefficient of Agreement for Nominal Scales," *Educational and Psychological Measurement, 20,* 37–46.

Cormack, R. M. (1971), "A Review of Classification," *Journal of the Royal Statistical Society* (Series A), *134,* 321–67.

Cunningham, K. M., and Ogilvie, J. C. (1972), "Evaluation of Hierarchical Grouping Techniques: A Preliminary Study," *Computer Journal, 15,* 209–13.

Day, G. S., and Heeler, R. M. (1971), "Using Cluster Analysis to Improve Marketing Experiments," *Journal of Marketing Research, 8* (August), 340–7.

Dixon, W. J., and Brown, M. B. (1979), *BMDP: Biomedical Computer Programs, P Series, 1979.* Los Angeles: University of California Press.

Edelbrock, C. (1979), "Comparing the Accuracy of Hierarchical Clustering Algorithms: The Problem of Classifying Everybody," *Multivariate Behavioral Research, 14,* 367–84.

Edelbrock, C., and McLaughlin, B. (1980), "Hierarchical Cluster Analysis Using Intraclass Correlations: A Mixture Model Study," *Multivariate Behavioral Research, 15,* 299–318.

Everitt, B. S. (1974), *Cluster Analysis.* London: Halsted Press.

Field, H. S., and Schoenfeldt, L. F. (1975), "Ward and Hook Revisited: A Two-Part Procedure for Overcoming a Deficiency in the Grouping of Two Persons," *Educational and Psychological Measurement, 35,* 171–3.

Fisher, W. D. (1969), *Clustering and Aggregation in Economics.* Baltimore, MD: Johns Hopkins Press.

Frank, R. E., and Green, P. E. (1968), "Numerical Taxonomy in Marketing Analysis: A Review Article," *Journal of Marketing Research, 5* (February), 83–98.

Friedman, H. D., and Rubin, J. (1967), "On Some Invariant Criteria for Grouping Data," *Journal of the American Statistical Association, 62,* 1159–78.

Furse, D. H., Punj, G., and Stewart, D. W. (1982), "Individual Search Strategies in New Automobile Purchase," in *Advances in Consumer Research,* Vol. 9, Andrew Mitchell, ed., 379–84.

Gerard, R. W. (1957), "Units and Concepts of Biology," *Science, 125,* 429–33.

Gower, J. C. (1967), "A Comparison of Some Methods of Cluster Analysis," *Biometrics, 23,* 623–37.

Green, P. E., and Carmone, F. J. (1968), "The Performance Structure of the Computer Market: A Multivariate Approach," *Economic and Business Bulletin, 20,* 1–11.

Green, P. E., Frank, R. E., and Robinson, P. J. (1967), "Cluster Analysis in Test Market Selection," *Management Science, 13,* B-387–400.

Green, P. E., and Rao, V. R. (1969), "A Note on Proximity Measures and Cluster Analysis," *Journal of Marketing Research, 6* (August), 359–64.

Greeno, D. W., Sommers, M. S., and Kernan, J. B. (1973), "Personality and Implicit Behavior Patterns," *Journal of Marketing Research, 10* (February), 63–9.

Hartigan, J. A. (1967), "Representation of Similarity Matrices by Trees," *Journal of the American Statistical Association, 62,* 1140–58.

Hartigan, J. A. (1975), *Clustering Algorithms.* New York: John Wiley & Sons, Inc.

Howard, H., and Harris, B. (1966), "A Hierarchical Grouping Routine, IBM 360/65 FORTRAN IV Program," University of Pennsylvania Computer Center.

Inglis, J., and Johnson, D. (1970), "Some Observations On, and Developments In, the Analysis of Multivariate Survey Data," *Journal of the Market Research Society, 12,* 75–8.

Jardine, H., and Sibson, R. (1971), *Mathematical Taxonomy.* New York: John Wiley & Sons, Inc.

Johnson, S. C. (1967), "Hierarchical Clustering Schemes," *Psychometrika, 32,* 241–54.

Kantor, J. R. (1953), *The Logic of Modern Science.* Bloomington, IN: Principle Press.

Kemeny, J. G. (1959), *A Philospher Looks at Science.* New York: Van Nostrand.

Kernan, J. B. (1968), "Choice Criteria, Decision Behavior, and Personality," *Journal of Marketing Research, 5* (May), 155–69.

Kernan, J. B. and Bruce, G. D. (1972), "The Socioeconomic Structure of an Urban Area," *Journal of Marketing Research, 9* (February), 15–8.

Kiel, G. C., and Layton, R. A. (1981), "Dimensions of Consumer Information Seeking

Behavior," *Journal of Marketing Research, 18* (May), 233–9.

Kuiper, F. K., and Fisher, L. A. (1975), "A Monte Carlo Comparison of Six Clustering Procedures," *Biometrics, 31,* 777–83.

Lance, G. N., and Williams, W. T. (1967a), "A General Theory of Classificatory Sorting Strategies. I. Hierarchical Systems," *The Computer Journal, 9,* 373–80.

Lance, G. N., and Williams, W. T. (1967b), "A General Theory of Classificatory Sorting Strategies. II. Clustering Systems," *The Computer Journal, 10,* 271–7.

Landon, E. L. (1974), "Self Concept, Ideal Self Concept, and Consumer Purchase Intentions," *Journal of Consumer Research, 1,* 44–51.

Lessig, V. P., and Tollefson, J. D. (1971), "Market Segmentation Through Numerical Taxonomy," *Journal of Marketing Research, 8* (November), 480–7.

McIntyre, R. M., and Blashfield, R. K. (1980), "A Nearest-Centroid Technique for Evaluating the Minimum-Variance Clustering Procedure," *Multivariate Behavior Research, 15,* 225–38.

McQuitty, L. L. (1967), "A Mutual Development of Some Typological Theories and Pattern-Analytic Methods," *Educational and Psychological Measurement, 17,* 21–46.

McRae, D. J. (1973), "Clustering Multivariate Observations," unpublished doctoral dissertation, University of North Carolina.

Mezzich, J. E. (1978), "Evaluating Clustering Methods for Psychiatric Diagnosis," *Biological Psychiatry, 13,* 265–81.

Milligan, G. W. (1980), "An Examination of the Effect of Six Types of Error Perturbation on Fifteen Clustering Algorithms," *Psychometrika, 45,* 325–42.

Milligan, G. W. (1981), "A Monte Carlo Study of Thirty Internal Criterion Measures for Cluster Analysis," *Psychometrika, 46,* (2), 187–99.

Milligan, G. W., and Isaac, P. D. (1980), "The Validation of Four Ultrametric Clustering Algorithms," *Pattern Recognition, 12,* 41–50.

Milligan, G. W., and Mahajan, V. (1980), "A Note on Procedures for Testing the Quality of a Clustering of a Set of Objects," *Decision Sciences, 11,* 669–77.

Mojena, R. (1977), "Hierarchical Grouping Methods and Stopping Rules: An Evaluation," *Computer Journal, 20,* 359–63.

Montgomery, D. B., and Silk, A. J. (1971), "Clusters of Consumer Interests and Opinion Leaders' Sphere of Influence," Journal of Marketing Research, *8* (August), 317–21.

Morgan, J. N., and Sonquist, J. A. (1963), "Problems in the Analysis of Survey Data, and a Proposal," *Journal of the American Statistical Association, 58,* 87–93.

Moriarty, M., and Venkatesan, M. (1978), "Concept Evaluation and Market Segmentation," *Journal of Marketing, 42,* 82–6.

Morrison, B. J., and Sherman, R. C. (1972), "Who Responds to Sex in Advertising?" *Journal of Advertising Research, 12,* 15–9.

Morrison, D. G. (1967), "Measurement Problems in Cluster Analysis," *Management Science, 13,* B-775–80.

Myers, J. G., and Nicosia F. M. (1968), "On the Study of Consumer Typologies," *Journal of Marketing Research, 5* (May), 182–3.

Neidell, L. A. (1970), "Procedures and Pitfalls in Cluster Analysis," *Proceedings,* Fall Conference, American Marketing Association, 107.

Nerviano, V. J., and Gross, W. F. (1973), "A Multivariate Delineation of Two Alcoholic Profile Types on the 16PF," *Journal of Clinical Psychology, 29,* 370–4.

Peay, E. R. (1975), "Nonmetric Grouping: Clusters and Cliques," *Psychometrika, 40,* 297–313.

Rand, W. M. (1971), "Objective Criteria for the Evaluation of Clustering Methods," *Journal of the American Statistical Association, 66,* 846–50.

Rogers, G., and J. D. Linden (1973), "Use of Multiple Discriminant Function Analysis in the Evaluation of Three Multivariate Grouping Techniques," *Educational and Psychological Measurement, 33,* 787–802.

Rubin, J. (1965), "Optimal Taxonomy Program (7090-IBM-0026)," IBM Corporation.

Schaninger, C. M., Lessig, V. P., and Panton, D. B. (1980), "The Complementary Use of Multivariate Procedures to Investigate Nonlinear and Interactive Relationships Between Personality and Product Usage," *Journal of Marketing Research, 17* (February), 119–24.

Sethi, S. P. (1971), "Comparative Cluster Analysis for World Markets," *Journal of Marketing Research, 8* (August), 348–54.

Sexton, D. E., Jr. (1974), "A Cluster Analytic Approach to Market Response Functions,"

Journal of Marketing Research, 11 (February), 109–14.

Shepard, R. N. (1974), "Representation of Structure in Similarity Data: Problems and Prospects," *Psychometrika, 39,* 373–421.

Shepard, R. N., and Arabie, P. (1979), "Additive Clustering: Representation of Similarities as Combinations of Discrete Overlapping Properties," *Psychological Review, 86,* 87–123.

Sherman, L., and Sheth, J. N. (1977), "Cluster Analysis and Its Applications in Marketing Research," in *Multivariate Methods for Market and Survey Research,* J. N. Sheth, ed. Chicago: American Marketing Association.

Shuchman, A. (1967), "Letter to the Editor," *Management Science, 13,* B688–96.

Skinner, H. A. (1979), "Dimensions and Clusters: A Hybrid Approach to Classification," *Applied Psychological Measurement, 3,* 327–41.

Smith, W. (1956), "Product Differentiation and Market Segmentation as Alternative Marketing Strategies," *Journal of Marketing, 21,* 3–8.

Sneath, P. H. A. (1957), "The Application of Computer to Taxonomy," *Journal of General Microbiology, 17,* 201–26.

Sneath, P. H. A., and Sokal, R. R. (1973), *Numerical Taxonomy.* San Francisco: W. H. Freeman.

Stewart, D. W. (1981), "The Application and Misapplication of Factor Analysis in Marketing Research," *Journal of Marketing Research, 18* (February), 51–62.

Srivastava, R. K., Leone, R. P., and Shocker, A. D. (1981), "Market Structure Analysis: Hierarchical Clustering of Products Based on Substitution-in-Use," *Journal of Marketing, 45* (Summer), 38–48.

Srivastava, R. K., Shocker, A. D., and Day, G. S. (1978), "An Exploratory Study of Usage-Situational Influences on the Composition of Product-Markets," in *Advances in Consumer Research,* H. K. Hunt, ed. Ann Arbor: Association for Consumer Research, 32–8.

Tyron, R. C., and Bailey, D. E. (1970), *Cluster Analysis.* New York: McGraw-Hill Book Company.

Veldman, D. J. (1967), *FORTRAN Programming for the Behavioral Sciences.* New York: Holt, Rinehart, and Winston.

Ward, J. (1963), "Hierarchical Grouping to Optimize an Objective Function," *Journal of the American Statistical Association, 58,* 236–44.

Wells, W. D. (1975), "Psychographics: A Critical Review," *Journal of Marketing Research, 12* (May), 196–213.

Wind, Y. (1978), "Issues and Advances in Segmentation Research," *Journal of Marketing Research, 15* (August), 317–37.

Wishart, D. (1969), "CLUSTAN IA: A FORTRAN Program for Numerical Classification," Computing Laboratory, St. Andrew's University, Scotland.

Wolf, A. (1926), *Essentials of Scientific Method.* New York: Macmillan Company.

OVERLAPPING CLUSTERING: A NEW METHOD FOR PRODUCT POSITIONING

Phipps Arabie, *University of Illinois at Champagne and Bell Laboratories*; J. Douglas Carroll, *Bell Laboratories*; Wayne DeSarbo, *Bell Laboratories*; and Jerry Wind, *University of Pennsylvania*

Product positioning analysis [Wind, 1977, 1980] of a given brand and its competitors has been based primarily on consumers' evaluations of similarities, perceptions,

Research for this paper was supported in part by LEAA Grant 78-NI-AX-0142 and NSF Grant SOC 76-24512.

From Phipps Arabie, J. Douglas Carroll, Wayne DeSarbo, and Jerry Wind, "Overlapping Clustering: A New Method for Product Positioning," *Journal of Marketing Research,* Vol. XVIII, August 1981. Reprinted by permission of the publishers, American Marketing Association.

and importances of sets of attributes and various usage occasions. Such data traditionally have been analyzed by use of cross-tabulations, profile charts, and multidimensional scaling and/or cluster analysis. More recently, conjoint analysis has been used for assessing both the importance of the attributes and the perceived appropriateness of different brands on various attributes [Green and Srinivasan, 1978]. In addition to these direct approaches for assessing the positioning of a brand, some indirect approaches have been used occasionally: market share data, brand switching matrices, and brand vulnerability analysis [Wind, 1977] which combines purchase patterns with overall attitudes toward the brand to assess the brand's degree of vulnerability and/or opportunities. The indirect approaches focus primarily on the identification of strengths and weaknesses in a brand's positioning, whereas the direct approaches attempt to explain the reasons for these strengths and weaknesses. Common to all these approaches is the identification of a single competitive set and positioning per brand.

Market segmentation analysis typically has included two sets of procedures: one for the identification of segments and one for the determination of the key discriminating characteristics of the various segments. Segment identification methods include simple sorting of respondents on some a priori basis for segmentation (for example, users vs. nonusers) and a variety of clustering procedures for cases in which the segmentation cannot be determined a priori [Wind, 1978]. These clustering procedures have been applied to benefit, need, attitude, and lifestyle segmentation [Frank, Massy, and Wind, 1972]. To assess the key discriminating characteristics of the various segments, a variety of multivariate statistical methods such as multiple discriminant analysis, AID [Morgan and Sonquist, 1963; Sonquist, 1970], multiple regression, and so forth

have been used. Common to all the clustering-based segmentation analyses is the assignment of each consumer to a single segment.

Thus, cluster analysis has been used frequently in product positioning and market segmentation studies. In all these applications, a brand (in positioning studies) or a consumer (in segmentation studies) is identified as a member of one and only one cluster. This classification of brands and consumers into mutually exclusive and collectively exhaustive clusters, although methodologically elegant, is conceptually questionable. Brands can compete against more than one competitive set (that is, have multiple positioning); similarly, consumers can belong to more than one segment. Methodological constraints have precluded consideration of such cases and have restricted conventional positioning/segmentation analysis to the less realistic but technically simpler analysis.

The objective of our article is to describe a new clustering model and algorithm which relaxes the constraint (common to most other clustering algorithms) of clustering objects (brands) or subjects (consumers) into mutually exclusive and exhaustive categories, and which allows for the establishment of *overlapping* clusters. We first discuss the concept of overlapping clusters, then outline a specific overlapping clustering model and algorithm. The method is illustrated in the context of positioning and is compared with more conventional clustering procedures. We conclude with an outline of a possible application to market segmentation and a brief discussion of future applications of overlapping clusters.

THE CONCEPT OF OVERLAPPING CLUSTERS

Hierarchical clustering algorithms are among the most commonly used clustering analyses in marketing research. Users of these approaches, however, tend to discard much of the detail (for example, levels of nesting for specific clusters) found in the dendrogram. The most commonly employed alternative is to obtain a partition of the set of entities being clustered. That is, the objects are segregated into mutually exclusive (and exhaustive) subsets. (As conventionally portrayed, each level or horizontal slice of a dendrogram is also a partition.) For a single partition, there is no nesting of subsets (or clusters—we use the terms interchangeably), so that representation of structure via a partition is necessarily nonhierarchical.

However, in reality, it is typically at least as easy to find examples in which the clusters should *overlap*, without the requirement found in hierarchical clustering that if two distinct clusters overlap, one must be a proper subset of the other. Such a restriction is often unrealistic. A person can belong to more than a single segment. For example, in benefit segmentation studies, a person can desire several different benefits from a particular product. The individual may desire both fresh breath and decay prevention (fluoride) in toothpaste. Similarly, a brand can compete in more than one cluster of products. Dentyne gum may compete with bubble gums as a candy substitute, but also may compete with mouthwash, toothpaste, etc. as a mouth freshener. Such classes (or clusters) of brands will show overlap.

If, rather than using a method of overlapping clustering one seeks to allow all possible patterns of overlap of a set of n entities, there are 2^{n-1} *clusters* to be considered (excluding the null set). As each of these clusters can in turn be present or absent in any given *clustering* solution, there are $2^{2n-1} - 1$ possible clustering solutions when overlap is allowed. To look exhaustively at all possibilities for even moderate n is impossible. What is needed is an heuristic data-oriented approach that selects only those relatively few (potentially overlapping) clusters which contribute to goodness-of-fit and, one hopes, substantive interpretability.

Though methods of overlapping clustering have been available for decades [see reviews by Arabie, 1977; Shepard and Arabie, 1979], these methods [including the B_k method of Jardine and Sibson, 1968, as well as that of Peay, 1974] have been used much less frequently than hierarchical approaches. In addition, the use of these overlapping methods seems to have several drawbacks in practice. First, the methods generally produce too many clusters with too much overlap. In fact, arbitrary constraints often must be used to prevent excessive overlap [Spilerman, 1966]. This problem results in part from the fact that most overlapping clustering methods, like most hierarchical methods, have not used a model or objective function to suggest which clusters are essential to the clustering representation. A second drawback is that if the clusters are too inclusive and/or have too much overlap, embedding them in a spatial solution (via multidimensional scaling techniques) is generally difficult. In such situations, the final result is simply a list of clusters (and, one hopes, their interpretations) without any visualizable graphic representation.

Conceptually, it is desirable to extend the concepts of product positioning and market segmentation to encompass the cases of overlapping clusters. Methodologically, this extension would require a clustering method for representing overlapping structure in data in a parsimonious manner, focusing only on necessary cluster overlaps that can be substantively justified and often spatially presented.

THE METHOD

The ADCLUS Model

Assume n objects to be clustered, with input data of $M = n(n-1)/2$ entries constituting a two-way symmetric (or symmetrized) proximity matrix having no missing entries. Although the raw data may be in the form of either similarities or dissimilarities, we first transform them linearly to be similarities on the interval [0, 1]. (Because the data are assumed to be on an interval scale, this transformation in no way affects the goodness-of-fit, but does allow for the standardization of various parameters in the method described hereafter.) $\mathbf{S} = \|s_{ij}\|$ will refer to these transformed proximities, with which the fitted $\hat{\mathbf{S}}$ matrix is being compared.

The basic equation underlying the ADCLUS (for ADditive CLUStering) model can be written as

$$(1) \qquad \hat{s}_{ij} = \sum_{k=1}^{m} w_k p_{ik} p_{jk}$$

where $\hat{s}_{ij}$ is the theoretically reconstructed similarity between objects i and j, w_k is a non-negative weight representing the salience of the property corresponding to subset k, and

$$P_{ik} = \begin{cases} 1, & \text{if object } i \text{ has property } k \\ 0, & \text{otherwise} \end{cases}$$

Thus, we have a set of m subsets or clusters of the n objects, and these clusters (which are to be "recovered" or fitted by the clustering algorithm) are allowed to overlap, although there is no explicit requirement that they do so. We also associate with each of the m clusters a (typically non-negative numerical) weight, w_k ($k = 1, \ldots, m$). The rationale for the acronym ADCLUS is that the predicted similarity $\hat{s}_{ij}$ of any pair of objects is the sum of the weights of those clusters containing both objects i and j. These weights, which gauge the salience of their respective subsets, are an aspect of the ADCLUS model not found in other approaches to overlapping clustering. Note that the weights and the clusters are both fitted in applying the ADCLUS model.

Moreover, the clustering is of course a discrete representation of the structure in the data, whereas the weights allow for continuous variation in the importance of the clusters. These features of the ADCLUS model, and their intimate relation to the objective function (discussed hereafter), qualify ADCLUS as a model for judgmental tasks in which proximities data are collected.

The MAPCLUS Algorithm

In matrix notation, the ADCLUS model is written

$$(2) \qquad \hat{\mathbf{S}} = \mathbf{PWP}'$$

where $\hat{\mathbf{S}}$ is an $n \times n$ symmetric matrix of reconstructed similarities $\hat{s}_{ij}$ (with ones in the principal diagonal), $\mathbf{W}$ is an $m \times m$ diagonal matrix with the weights w_k ($k = 1, \ldots, m$) in the principal diagonal (and zeroes elsewhere), and $\mathbf{P}$ is the $n \times m$ rectangular matrix of *binary* values p_{ik}. Here, $\mathbf{P}'$ is the $m \times n$ matrix transpose of the matrix $\mathbf{P}$. Note that each column of $\mathbf{P}$ represents one of the m subsets, with the ones of that column defining the constituency of stimuli within the respective subset. Shepard and Arabie (1979) imposed the constraint that the m-th subset (and only that subset) was a column of all ones, whose weight was in effect an additive constant for equation (1), as required for the use of variance accounted for (VAF) as a measure of goodness-of-fit. For our usage, we prefer to express the model as

$$(3) \qquad \hat{\mathbf{S}} = \mathbf{PWP}' + \mathbf{C}$$

where $\mathbf{C}$ is an $n \times n$ matrix having zeroes in the principal diagonal and the (fitted) additive constant c in all the remaining entries. (That constant is simply the weight w_m fitted for the complete subset in equation (2).) Strictly, m in equation 2 and in the Shepard and Arabie (1979) description corresponds to $m - 1$ in equation (3).

However, we believe that this inconsistency is clear enough to allow uniform references hereafter to m as the number of subsets, plus an $(m+1)$st weight as the additive constant.

The Shepard and Arabie (1979) algorithm for fitting the ADCLUS model did not lead to a generally successful algorithm for fitting the model because of computational and numerical difficulties (see pp. 118–19). Subsequently, Arabie and Carroll (1980) devised a different algorithm—MAPCLUS (for MAthematical Programming CLUStering)—for fitting the ADCLUS *model.*

The most obvious difference between the ADCLUS and MAPCLUS programs is that, for the latter, the (fairly small) number of subsets, m, is specified by the user at the beginning of an analysis and does not change throughout the computation. In practice, MAPCLUS has been able to obtain solutions acceptable in terms of both interpretability and goodness-of-fit, using considerably fewer clusters for various data sets than was possible with the ADCLUS program.

Because a detailed description of the MAPCLUS algorithm is given elsewhere [Arabie and Carroll, 1980], we offer the following cursory overview of MAPCLUS. The **P** matrix is *initially* considered to have *continuously* varying p_{ik} in spite of the ultimate binary nature of **P**. The *initial* values of **P** can be taken from any of several sources (detailed hereafter), and **W** is initially all zeroes. We use a gradient approach to minimize a loss function which is the weighted sum of an A- and a B-part. The former is simply a normalized measure of sum of squared error. The more novel B-part consists of a "penalty function" in the form of a polynomial designed to move all pairwise products $p_{ik}p_{jk}$ toward 0 or 1. Thus, the overall algorithm constitutes a "mathematical programming" approach to solving a discrete problem by treating it as a continuous problem with constraints allowing only a particular set of discrete

values of parameters. Another way of describing this specific "penalty function" approach is that we attempt to approach the discrete solution by a sequence of increasingly close continuous approximations.

The subsets and weights are computed as follows. Given whatever estimates we have for the first subset $[p_{(1,1)}, \ldots, p_{(n,1)}]$, univariate regression is used to estimate w_1, and afterward the p_{i1} values are improved iteratively. Then, following an alternating least squares approach, we take residuals and fit them with a second subset, and so on, until the fit of the m-th subset has been iteratively improved and its weight estimated. We also apply multiple linear regression to improve our estimates of all the w_k $(k = 1, \ldots, m)$ weights simultaneously. The whole procedure then is repeated with increases in the weight for the B-part relative to the A-part of the loss function, until asymptotically the $(0, 1)$ constraint holds essentially perfectly. When no further improvement in goodness-of-fit is forthcoming, we apply three additional techniques ("polishing," *de novo* iterations, and combinatorial optimization) to refine the fit still further.

In the present instance, we seek to maximize the variance accounted for, subject to the constraint that **P** is asymptotically binary. Our loss function takes the form

(4) $L_k(\alpha_k, \beta_k, \Delta, \mathbf{P}) = \alpha_k A_k + \beta_k B_k$

Considering first the left side of equation 4, note that the loss function is computed only for subset k. Moreover, we do not sum the penalty function over k. The reason is that we are using an alternating least squares approach [Wold, 1966] which underlies the iterative fitting in turn of each subset $p_{ik}(i = 1, \ldots, n)$ and its associated weight w_k. Wold has shown that for problems posed in a continuous form, the alternating least squares approach (NIPALS) will asymptotically lead to at

least a local optimum (minimum) for the
overall least squares problem for all m
subsets of parameters in a model such as
ours. (If there is only a single optimum this
solution will, under very general conditions, be that global optimum, but this
situation generally will not hold for the
kind of highly nonlinear model we are
fitting.) Because we are only fitting the
k-th subset at any instant, Δ in equation 4
refers to the (centered) residuals computed
for the remaining $m - 1$ subsets and the
reader may wish to associate an implicit
subscript k with Δ. For the present, the
reader is asked only to note this statement
of the procedure, as we believe the
explanation is most easily presented in the
next two subsections which explain in
detail the alternating least squares implementation in MAPCLUS.

In the right side of equation 4, the
term $\alpha_k A_k$ refers to the weight α_k applied to
the normalized sum of squared error, A_k.
Specifically,

$$(5) \qquad A_k = \frac{a_k}{d_k}$$

where

$$(6) \qquad a_k = \sum_{i \ >}^{n} \sum_{j}^{n-1} (\delta_{ij} - w_k P_{ik} P_{jk})^2$$

and

$$(7) \qquad d_k = \frac{4 \sum_{i \ >}^{n} \sum_{j}^{n-1} \delta_{ij}^2}{M}$$

In equation 6, a_k is simply the sum of
squared error, the minimization of which is
equivalent to maximizing VAF. The denominator of A, d_k, is a normalization factor
interpreted as the variance of the residuals, δ_{ij}, computed over the remaining
subsets. The factor of 4 represents the
maximum variance of $\frac{1}{4}$ that could be
obtained from the input data s_{ij} which, as
noted before, are in the range $[0, 1]$.

If our loss function consisted only of

the A term (that is, the B weight $\beta = 0$),
our problem would reduce to performing
principal components analysis, for which
well-known continuous methods are available. However, our model demands that
$p_{ik} = 0$, 1 and the B-part of the loss
function is designed, by successively closer
continuous approximations, to enforce this
discrete constraint. We refer to this as a
"mathematical programming" approach, as
it entails optimizing a nonlinear function
(A_k) with constraints on parameters imposed by use of the "penalty function"
method.

Elaborating on the right side of
equation (4) we have

$$(8) \qquad B_k = \frac{u_k}{v_k}$$

where

$$(9) \qquad u_k = \frac{1}{2} \sum_{i}^{n} \sum_{j}^{n} [(p_{ik} p_{jk} - 1) p_{ik} p_{jk}]^2$$

and

$$(10) \qquad v_k = \sum_{i \ >}^{n} \sum_{j}^{n-1} (p_{ik} p_{jk} - T_k)^2$$

where T_k is simply the mean of the
pairwise products of $p_{ik} p_{jk}$, namely

$$(11) \qquad T_k = \frac{1}{M} \sum_{i \ >}^{n} \sum_{j}^{n-1} p_{ik} p_{jk}$$

The numerator of B, u_k, is designed to
force the pairwise products $p_{ik} p_{jk}$ to be 0, 1.
B is deliberately nonhomogeneous, because
otherwise the p_{ik} could approach *any*
relatively distinct pair of values instead of
only 0, 1. Products of *pairs* of the form
$p_{ik} p_{jk}$ are emphasized to reduce the
likelihood of singleton subsets, that is, all
but one of the p_{ik} ($i = 1, \ldots, n$) being zero.
We deliberately include the diagonal terms
in the numerator of B_k, but exclude them
in the denominator for this reason.

Because MAPCLUS relies on a minimization procedure, we require the gradient of the loss function L_k, ∇L_k, with respect to p_{ik}. It is straightforward that the i-th component of $\nabla L_k (\nabla_i L_k)$ is

$$(12) \quad \nabla_i L_k = \frac{\partial L_k}{\partial p_{ik}} = \frac{\alpha}{d_k} \left[\frac{\partial a_k}{\partial p_{ik}} \right] + \beta \left[\frac{v_k \frac{\partial u_k}{\partial p_{ik}} - u_k \frac{\partial v_k}{\partial p_{ik}}}{v_k^2} \right]$$

where

$$(13) \quad \frac{\partial a_k}{\partial p_{ik}} = -2w_k \sum_{j \neq i} p_{jk} (\delta_{ij} - w_k p_{ik} p_{jk})$$

$$(14)$$

$$\frac{\partial u_k}{\partial p_{ik}} = 2p_{ik} \sum_j \left[(p_{ik} p_{jk} - 1)(p_{jk}^2)(2p_{ik} p_{jk} - 1) \right]$$

and

$$(15) \quad \frac{\partial v_k}{\partial p_{ik}} = 2 \sum_{j \neq i} \left(p_{jk} - \frac{1}{M} \sum_{h \neq i} p_{hk} \right) (p_{ik} p_{jk} - T_k)$$

Finally, returning to the weights α_k and β_k in the loss function of equations (3) and (12), we use the constraint that $\alpha_k + \beta_k = 1$. We typically begin with $\alpha_k = \alpha_0 = 0.50$ and, as computation proceeds, increase the value of β_k relative to α_k (details given hereafter) to ensure that the final values of the $p_{ik} = 0$, 1. This adjustment of α_k and β_k is done according to

$$(16) \quad \alpha_k' = \frac{\alpha_k}{\alpha_k + K_1 \beta_k} \quad \text{and} \quad \beta_k' = \frac{K_1 \beta_k}{\alpha_k + K_1 \beta_k}$$

where K_1 is currently defined as 2.0

We also note that the variance accounted for reported in the following application is given by

$$(17) \quad VAF = 1 - \frac{\sum_{i>j} (s_{ij} - \hat{s}_{ij})^2}{\sum_{i>j} (s_{ij} - \bar{s})^2}$$

and the $\hat{s}_{ij}$ are computed as in equation (1).

AN ILLUSTRATIVE APPLICATION TO PRODUCT POSITIONING

The MAPCLUS algorithm is illustrated on similarity data for 15 breakfast food items studied by Green and Rao (1972). The data constitute row conditional similarity judgments for each of 15 breakfast foods (listed in Table 7–5) given by 21 male Wharton School MBA students and their wives (a total of 42 respondents). The data for each subject were converted to a derived matrix of dissimilarities between all $15(14)/2 = 105$ pairs of the food items. This preprocessing of the data was effected by use of the TRICON computer program [Carmone, Green, and Robinson, 1968] to implement a procedure of Coombs (1964) that searches for the underlying complete pairwise rank order which reconstructs the

_____ Table 7–5 _____

Breakfast Food Items Used by Green and Rao (1972)

Food item	Plotting code used in figures
1. Toast pop-up	TP
2. Buttered toast	BT
3. English muffin and margarine	EMM
4. Jelly donut	JD
5. Cinnamon toast	CT
6. Blueberry muffin and margarine	BMM
7. Hard rolls and butter	HRB
8. Toast and marmalade	TMd
9. Buttered toast and jelly	BTJ
10. Toast and margarine	TMn
11. Cinnamon bun	CB
12. Danish pastry	DP
13. Glazed donut	GD
14. Coffee cake	CC
15. Corn muffin and butter	CMB

preference ordering while minimizing patterns of intransitive preferences. As noted before, the output for TRICON is, for each subject, a triangular halfmatrix of "indirect" dissimilarities (in the form of ranks) for the 105 pairs of stimuli. The ranks were averaged over subjects to produce a two-way (food items by food items, averaged over respondents) matrix, as listed by Green and Rao (1972, p. 26).

MAPCLUS was applied to the data set, and various numbers of clusters ranging from 10 to 4 were specified. In using MAPCLUS, one finds the same tradeoff between interpretability and goodness-of-fit as in models of multidimensional scaling and factor analysis, in contrast to other clustering techniques. In changing from 8 to 5 clusters, trailing off of variance accounted for was slight, but the larger cluster solutions seemed much less interpretable than the 5-cluster solution. Specifically, most of the clusters in the 8-, 7-, and 6-cluster solutions appeared to be much too "large,"—that is, too inclusive. The 4-cluster solution was altogether uninterpretable. The 5-cluster solution, accounting for 84.8 percent of the variance in the input data, was judged the best solution with respect to the tradeoff between the number of clusters and goodness-of-fit. The solution is listed in Table 7–6. The clusters, enclosed by contours, are embedded in a two-dimensional scaling solution (Green and Rao, 1972, p. 31) in Figure 7–2.

Each of the clusters and its interpretation are listed in Table 7.6. The most heavily weighted subset consists of the pastry items. All of the items spread with either butter or margarine are in the second cluster, and all of the toasted items appear in the third cluster. The least sweet items (hard rolls and butter, toast and margarine, and buttered toast) are excluded from the fourth cluster, giving it a "sweet foods" characterization. The subset with the smallest weight consists of the relatively simple bread foods. The additive

_____ Table 7–6 _____

MAPCLUS Representation of the 15 Food Items

Rank by Weight	Weight	Items in Subset	Interpretation
1	0.430	Jelly donut, glazed donut, cinnamon bun, Danish pastry, coffee cake	Pastries
2	0.393	Blueberry muffin and margarine, corn muffin and margarine, English muffin and margarine, hard rolls and butter, toast and margarine, buttered toast	Foods spread with margarine or butter
3	0.313	Toast pop-up, cinnamon toast, toast and marmalade, buttered toast and jelly, buttered toast, toast and margarine	Toasted foods
4	0.264	All but hard rolls and butter, toast and margarine, buttered toast	Sweet foods (compared with those excluded)
5	0.203	English muffin and margarine, hard rolls and butter, toast and margarine, buttered toast, buttered toast and jelly, toast and marmalade	Relatively simple bread foods

Note: Variance accounted for is 84.8 percent, with five subsets and an additive constant of 0.125.

constant (0.125) may be interpreted as the weight for the complete set of stimuli. Alternatively, if that value were added to each of the 105 entries in the input matrix (an allowable transformation, under the assumption of interval-scale data), there would be no need for an additive constant (of zero) for the sixth or complete set of objects.

_____Figure 7–2_____

MAPCLUS Solution for 15 Food Items Listed in Tables 7–5 and 7–6

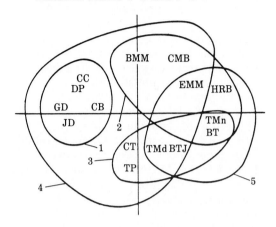

In discussing overlap, we argued for the substantive advantages of being able to portray this real-world aspect of structure in data. Figure 7–3 [Green and Rao, 1972, p. 31] uses the same scaling solution as Figure 7–2 to embed clusters from the complete-link method [see Hartigan, 1975; Hubert, 1974; Johnson, 1967] which is the method of hierarchical clustering most

_____Figure 7–3_____

Complete-Link Hierarchical Clustering Solution for the 15 Food Items

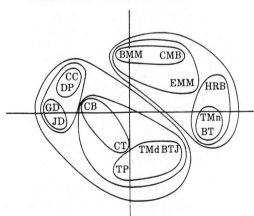

commonly used in marketing research, psychology, and related areas. Although certain levels of embeddedness (see preceding discussion) were discarded by Green and Rao (1972), in their presentation of the complete-link solution, we regard their usage of that method as exemplary. Note, however, the substantive restrictions imposed by the hierarchical constraints. For instance, as soon as buttered toast (BT) is clustered with toast and margarine (TM), there can be no linkage between buttered toast and buttered toast and jelly (BTJ), except at the level of the complete or trivial clustering. In addition, note that although many of the MAPCLUS subsets are also found in the complete-link solution of Figure 7–3, others are not. For instance, the third most heavily weighted cluster, the toasted foods, does not appear at all in the complete-link representation, nor does the fifth MAPCLUS subset.

In addition, without the screening already performed by Green and Rao in removing uninterpretable levels of embedding or nestedness, the difficulties with the complete-link solution compared with Figure 7–2 (MAPCLUS solution) would be all the more apparent. If a cluster at a given level of nestedness in Figure 7–2 is eliminated (that is, the [BMM, CMB] dyad is dropped so that only the [BMM, CMB, EMM] triad appears), there is no objective function against which the resulting change in overall goodness-of-fit can be evaluated. In contrast, for the MAPCLUS solution, the data analyst can add, delete, or modify clusters [to produce a "constrained" solution [see Shepard and Arabie, 1979; Carroll and Arabie, 1980]), and use straightforward multiple linear regression to estimate weights for the new set of clusters and obtain the corresponding variance accounted for.

Finally, the complete-link clustering has no counterpart to the weights for the clusters in the MAPCLUS representation for the Green–Rao (1972) data. That is, the data analyst is given no indication of the relative salience (in the subjects' judgments) of the clusters in the complete-link solution. Although some promising work in this area has been done for hierarchical clustering (Hubert, 1973), there is simply no counterpart in hierarchical clustering, or in other approaches to nonhierarchical clustering, to the weights that are such an integral part of both the ADCLUS model and the interpretation of resulting solutions from the MAPCLUS algorithm.

CONCLUDING REMARKS

The availability of an overlapping clustering model and algorithm [Shepard and Arabie, 1979] makes feasible the clustering of objects (brands) or subjects (customers) in a way that does not require each object or subject to be a member of one and only one cluster, but rather allows for membership in several clusters. This development frees the researcher from the previous methodological limitations of clustering objects or subjects into mutually exclusive and exhaustive categories in spite of the conceptually obvious fact that a person can belong to more than a single segment (that is, multiple role concept) and that a brand can compete in more than one cluster of products. The output of the MAPCLUS overlapping clustering algorithm, compared with the output of the more conventional hierarchical clustering algorithms, clearly illustrates the conceptual advantages of having the flexibility of clustering each brand in more than a single cluster. Similar advantages accrue if segment membership is not limited to a single segment.

Despite the popularity of clustering-based segmentation analysis which focuses on the grouping of respondents into mutually exclusive and exhaustive clusters, in some cases an overlapping segmentation option might be desirable. Overlapping clustering can be applied in market segmentation to cluster individuals

in the same way the procedure has been applied in product positioning to cluster brands (that is, instead of inputting a $k \times k$ matrix of brand similarity one can use any $n \times n$ matrix of subject similarity in the MAPCLUS algorithm). This $n \times n$ subject matrix can be similarity rating or ranking, or importance scores of desired benefits, needs, attitudes, and so forth.

In addition to this straightforward application, which would result in the clustering of individuals but not necessarily with a concomitant interpretable multidimensional space, one can use as input to the MAPCLUS algorithm data which allow the subjects to be clustered in some interpretable space such as brand or product feature space. This procedure can be carried out either in the more conventional manner, with ideal points in a brand space [see, for example, Green and Tull, 1978] or, if more appropriate, with points in a benefit (product feature) space [see, for example, Green, Wind, and Claycamp, 1975]. Once the respondents are located graphically in an appropriate multidimensional space, they can be analyzed with MAPCLUS using the same input (after its adjustment to an $n \times n$ subject matrix), and the resulting configurations can be compared.

In any of these applications of overlapping clustering, one has a problem with the capability of the current version of the MAPCLUS algorithm. Currently, one cannot economically process a matrix larger than 30×30. Although work is underway to develop a more efficient algorithm, one can imagine using in the interim a two-step procedure for clustering of respondents.

1. Clustering of any size sample (100 respondents, for example) by any clustering algorithm, such as hierarchical clustering [Howard and Harris, 1966; Johnson, 1967; or others] and selecting ≤30 pseudosegments. To ensure stable results it might be

desirable to use two clustering algorithms and compare their resulting segments.

2. Take the 30 or so pseudosubjects, develop for them a 30×30 matrix of intersubject similarities (based on their average scores on the variables of interest), and submit the data matrix to the MAPCLUS algorithm.

This procedure is feasible and can result in overlapping segments.

The reported developments in overlapping cluster models and algorithms offer new challenges to marketing researchers.

1. Algorithm developments to overcome the size and cost constraints of MAPCLUS.
2. Model developments to extend the overlapping clustering to three- (or higher) way matrices [Carroll and Arabie, 1979].
3. Reexamination of the segmentation and positioning concepts to assess the implication of an overlapping clustering formulation for marketing strategy considerations. If multiple positioning is desired (that is, positioning a brand against each of the clusters in which the brand competes), how can the strategy be executed in terms of promotion material and distribution?

The concept of overlapping segments is more complex because it can suggest: (1) the selection of several target segments, all of which share some common characteristic, and (2) the selection of a single target segment but the recognition that members of this segment share interest (loyalties?) with other segments as well.

Both interpretations suggest that given the likely presence of overlapping segments (that is, additional evidence of the presence of segment heterogeneity), the selection of a target market segment should not be done in isolation from the positioning decision (whether single or multiple), but rather both should be

undertaken simultaneously. This conclusion is consistent with the recent developments in positioning/segmentation research as seen in the approaches of flexible segmentation (Wind, 1978) and componential segmentation [Green, Wind, and Claycamp, 1978] and its more recent formulation in the context of the POSSE system [Carroll et al., 1980]. Technically, we are urging that because the analyst begins with a two-mode, two-way [see Carroll and Arabie, 1980] data matrix of brands by benefits, it is desirable to seek ADCLUS clusterings of the entities in each mode.

The acceptance of this concept, coupled with the high likelihood of the presence of both overlapping positioning and segments, suggests the need to examine explicitly the relation between the two sets of results. That is, one should select a target segment(s) (with or without overlap) and analyze the overlapping positioning of brands as perceived by members of these segments. Alternatively, one can first select a desirable positioning (with or without overlap) and analyze the various overlapping segments most responsive to the target positioning. Such analyses could better provide insights into the complexity of the marketplace and lead to thoughtful positioning/segmentation decisions. This sequential approach is not as accurate as a decision based on simultaneous analyses of the two decisions (such as the one proposed in the POSSE model). However, to the extent that management is relying on separate positioning and segmentation analysis, making these decisions separately or at best sequentially, it is desirable to consider the fact that a brand is likely to compete in more than a single market against different brands and to attract consumers with diverse benefit preferences. In these cases the methodology we propose is most applicable and could help advance the value of the positioning/ segmentation concepts as guidelines for marketing strategy.

REFERENCES

Arabie, P. (1977), "Clustering Representations of Group Overlap," *Journal of Mathematical Sociology, 5,* 113–28.

Arabie, P., and Carroll, J. D. (1980), "MAPCLUS: A Mathematical Programming Approach to Fitting the ADCLUS Model," *Psychometrika, 45,* 211–35.

Carmone, F. J., Green, P. E., and Robinson, P. J. (1968), "TRICON—an IBM 360/65 FORTRAN IV Program for the Triangularization of Conjoint Data," *Journal of Marketing Research, 5* (May), 219–20.

Carroll, J. D., and Arabie, P. (1979), "INDCLUS: A Three-way Approach to Clustering," paper presented at meeting of Psychometric Society, Monterey, California.

Carroll, J. D., and Arabie, P. (1980), "Multidimensional Scaling," in *Annual Review of Psychology,* M. R. Rosenzweig and L. W. Porter, eds. Palo Alto, California: Annual Reviews.

Carroll, J. D., DeSarbo, W. S., Goldberg, S., and Green, P. E. (1980), "A General Approach to Product Design Optimization via Conjoint Analysis," working paper, Bell Laboratories, Murray Hill, New Jersey.

Coombs, C. H. (1964), *A Theory of Data.* New York: John Wiley & Sons, Inc.

Frank, R., Massy, W., and Wind, Y. (1972), *Market Segmentation.* Englewood Cliffs, New Jersey: Prentice-Hall, Inc.

Green, P. E., and Rao, V. R. (1972), *Applied Multidimensional Scaling: A Comparison of Approaches and Algorithms.* New York: Holt, Rinehart and Winston.

Green, P. E., and Srinivasan, V. (1978), "Conjoint Analysis in Consumer Research: Issues and Outlook," *Journal of Consumer Research, 5,* 103–23.

Green, P. E., and Tull, D. S. (1978), *Research for Marketing Decision,* 4th ed. Englewood Cliffs, New Jersey: Prentice-Hall, Inc.

Green, P. E., Wind, Y., and Claycamp, H. J. (1975), "Brand Features Congruence Mapping," *Journal of Marketing Research, 12* (August), 306–13.

Hartigan, J. A. (1975), *Clustering Algorithms.* New York: John Wiley & Sons, Inc.

Howard, N., and Harris, B. (1966), "A Hierarchical Grouping Routine, IBM 360/65 FORTRAN IV Program." Philadelphia: University of Pennsylvania Computer Center.

Hubert, L. J. (1973), "Monotone Invariant Clustering Procedures," *Psychometrika, 38,* 47–62.

Hubert, L. J. (1974), "Some Applications of Graph Theory to Clustering," *Psychometrika, 39,* 283–309.

Jardine, N., and Sibson, R. (1968), "The Construction of Hierarchic and Non-hierarchic Classifications," *Computer Journal, 11,* 177–84.

Johnson, S. C. (1967), "Hierarchical Clustering Schemes," *Psychometrika, 32,* 241–54.

Morgan, J. N., and Sonquist, J. A. (1963), "Problems in the Analysis of Survey Data and a Proposal," *Journal of the American Statistical Association, 58,* 415–34.

Peay, E. R. (1974), "Hierarchical Clique Structures," *Sociometry, 37,* 54–65.

Shepard, R. N., and Arabie, P. (1979), "Additive Clustering: Representation of Similarities as Combinations of Discrete Overlapping Properties," *Psychological Review, 86,* 87–123.

Sonquist, J. A. (1970), *Multivariate Model Building.* Ann Arbor: Survey Research Center, University of Michigan.

Spilerman, S. (1966), "Structural Analysis and the Generation of Sociograms," *Behavioral Science, 11,* 312–18.

Wind, Y. (1977), "The Perception of the Firm's Competitive Position," in *Behavioral Models of Market Analysis: Foundations for Marketing Action,* F. M. Nicosia and Y. Wind, eds. Hinsdale, Illinois: Dryden Press.

Wind, Y. (1978), "Issues and Advances in Segmentation Research," *Journal of Marketing Research, 15* (August), 317–37.

Wind, Y. (1980), "Going to Market—New Twists for Some Old Tricks," Wharton Magazine (Spring).

Wind, Y. and Robinson, P. J. (1972), "Product Positioning: An Application of Multidimensional Scaling," in *Attitude Research in Transition,* R. I. Haley, ed. Chicago: American Marketing Association.

Wold, H. (1966), "Estimation of Principal Components and Related Models by Iterative Least Squares," in *Multivariate Analysis,* P. R. Krishnaiah, ed. New York: Academic Press.

Correspondence Analysis Research

INTRODUCTION

Correspondence Analysis: Graphical Representation of Categorical Data in Marketing Research

In the article by Donna L. Hoffman and George R. Franke, the correspondence analysis methodology is reviewed, identifying alternative approaches and algorithms. Examples and interpretation are also included. Correspondence analysis is an exploratory data analysis technique for the graphical display of contingency tables and multivariate categorical data. Its history can be traced back at least fifty years under a variety of names, but it has received little attention in the marketing literature. Correspondence analysis scales the rows and columns of a rectangular data matrix in corresponding units so that each can be displayed graphically in the same low-dimensional space. The authors present the theory behind the method, illustrate its use and interpretation with an example representing soft drink consumption, and discuss its relationship to other approaches that jointly represent the rows and columns of a rectangular data matrix. Correspondence analysis is a data analysis technique that permits the geometric mapping of frequency or binary data. Most often correspondence analysis is applied to contingency table data, producing a map identifying the row and column attributes as points in a space of two or more dimensions. Correspondence analysis is analogous to a principal components factor analysis of contingency table data.

Comparing Interpoint Distances in Correspondence Analysis: A Clarification

The research note by J. Douglas Carroll, Paul E. Green, and Catherine M. Schaffer is a clarification of an earlier paper that described a new approach for correspondence analysis. Whereas traditional correspondence analysis models create geometric maps that allow only the comparison of points within rows or within columns of the contingency table, the Carroll, Green, and Schaffer model permits comparisons between the row and column points, given that the user accepts the assumptions underlying the proposal.

In this research note, Carroll, Green, and Schaffer contrast their model with earlier scaling approaches and explain the model using an illustrative example.

CORRESPONDENCE ANALYSIS: GRAPHICAL REPRESENTATION OF CATEGORICAL DATA IN MARKETING RESEARCH   Donna L. Hoffman,

Columbia University, and George R. Franke, *The University of Texas, Austin*

Marketing researchers often need to detect and interpret relationships among the variables in a rectangular data matrix. To facilitate this task, multidimensional scaling and unfolding, discriminant analysis, canonical correlation analysis, factor analysis, and principal components analysis all have been used to represent graphically the rows and/or columns of a data matrix. However, these methods have little applicability to the categorical data that arise in many marketing research applications. The purpose of our article is to direct the attention of the marketing community to correspondence analysis, a multivariate descriptive statistical method that represents graphically the rows and columns of a categorical data matrix in the same low-dimensional space.

In correspondence analysis, numerical scores are assigned to the rows and columns of a data matrix so as to maximize their interrelationship. The scores are in *corresponding* units, allowing all the variables to be plotted in the same space for ease of interpretation. This representation then can be used to reveal the structure and patterns inherent in the data. In this sense, correspondence analysis is in that class of methods known as "exploratory data analysis" [de Leeuw, 1973; Heiser, 1981; Tukey, 1977].

Correspondence analysis has several features that contribute to its usefulness to marketing researchers. Much of its value relates to its multivariate treatment of the data through the simultaneous considera-

tion of multiple categorical variables. The multivariate nature of correspondence analysis can reveal relationships that would not be detected in a series of pairwise comparisons of variables. Correspondence analysis also helps to show how variables are related, not just that a relationship exists. The joint graphical display obtained from a correspondence analysis can help in detecting structural relationships among the variable categories. Finally, correspondence analysis has highly flexible data requirements. The only strict data requirement for a correspondence analysis is a rectangular data matrix with non-negative entries. Thus, the researcher can gather suitable data quickly and easily.

A distinct advantage of correspondence analysis over other methods yielding joint graphical displays is that it produces two dual displays whose row and column geometries have similar interpretations, facilitating analysis and detection of relationships. In other multivariate approaches to graphical data representation, this duality is not present.

Correspondence analysis as a geometric approach to multivariate descriptive data analysis originated in France; Benzécri (1969, 1973a, b) and his colleagues have done much to popularize the technique. The term "correspondence analysis" is a translation of the French "analysis factorielle des correspondances." The technique has received considerable attention in the statistical and psycho-

---

Professor Hoffman gratefully acknowledges support from the Faculty Research Fund of the Graduate School of Business, Columbia University.

From Donna L. Hoffman and George R. Franke, "Correspondence Analysis: Graphical Representation of Categorical Data in Marketing Research," *Journal of Marketing Research,* Vol. XXIII, August 1986. Reprinted by permission of the publisher, American Marketing Association.

metric literature under a variety of names, including dual scaling, method of reciprocal averages, optimal scaling, canonical analysis of contingency tables, categorical discriminant analysis, homogeneity analysis, quantification of qualitative data, and simultaneous linear regression. Complete histories of correspondence analysis are given by de Leeuw (1973), Greenacre (1984), and Nishisato (1980).

Though very few applications of correspondence analysis have been reported in the marketing literature, interest is increasing. Levine's (1979) procedure for the analysis of "pick-any" data, which is related closely to correspondence analysis, has been discussed by Holbrook, Moore, and Winer (1982). Green et al. (1983) use correspondence analysis in a cross-national examination of family purchasing roles. Franke (1983) illustrates the use of "dual scaling" with a reanalysis of data from a study by Belk, Painter, and Semenik (1981) on perceived causes of and preferred solutions to the energy crisis. Franke (1985) also discusses the use of dual scaling in examining measurement-level assumptions and interpreting responses to a measure. Additionally, Benzécri (1973b) describes two marketing-oriented applications of correspondence analysis, one evaluating competing cigarette brands and the other selecting a name for a new brand of cigarettes.

There is virtually no limit to the number of marketing applications for correspondence analysis. In the development of market segments, for example, correspondence analysis could be used to detect relatively homogeneous groupings of individuals. Correspondence analysis also can aid in product positioning studies. For example, suppose interest centers on consumer perceptions of brands as a basis for positioning a particular brand. Correspondence analysis of the categorical brands by attributes matrix gives information on the positioning of each brand vis-à-vis the attributes selected to describe them.

Correspondence analysis has been used to monitor the efficiency of advertising campaigns in France (Marc, 1973). Before the ad campaign, a study is carried out to monitor advertising efficiency. After the campaign, another study is conducted. Together, the results of these studies reveal movement in product positioning attributable to the advertising campaign.

The new method also may prove useful in the design phase of the new-product development process. Suppose a new-product manager gathers (binary) endorsements of consumers on a variety of proposed features of a new offering. Correspondence analysis of this consumers by product features matrix affords guidelines for appropriate segmentation bases and potential marketing mix strategies. The method can be applied also in the concept-testing phase when several concepts are competing for developmental funds. Analysis of the concepts by attributes matrix can indicate those concepts that have the most favorable profiles and, consequently, should be developed further.

In the next two sections we use an artificial example to describe the theory behind the method of correspondence analysis. Appropriate types of data for its use and guidelines for interpretations also are discussed. We then illustrate correspondence analysis with an example that empirically demonstrates practical data considerations and issues of interpretation. The relationship of correspondence analysis to other multivariate methods is examined. In the concluding section we discuss the issues of supplementary variables and outliers, provide some cautions to the researcher, and comment on implementation.

THE METHOD OF CORRESPONDENCE ANALYSIS

An Artificial Example

In marketing research applications, the data collected are categorical, mainly because of the limitations and constraints imposed on the data collection process. For example, a researcher may be interested in the relationship between several brands in a product class and a variety of attributes believed to describe the brands. Frequently the researcher gives consumers a list of brands and asks them to check off the attributes that describe the brands, rather than asking them to rate each brand on a scale. The advantages of this common data collection process are that it is quicker, easier, and less expensive than obtaining rating scale (that is, interval-level) data.

As an example, suppose data were collected from 100 consumers on three brands, and six attributes were hypothesized to describe those brands. For each brand, respondents indicate whether the attribute describes the brand. The data generated from such a procedure might be arrayed as in Table 8–1. We have calculated, by subtraction, the "no" category for each attribute (we explain why subsequently). Twenty-nine percent of the respondents indicated that attribute 1 described brand A, 20 percent said that attribute 2 described brand A, and so on.

These data, originally zeros and ones, have been aggregated over individuals and proportions calculated.

Suppose we are interested in the following questions.

1. What are the similarities and differences among the three brands with respect to the six attributes?
2. What are the similarities and differences among the six attributes with respect to the three brands?
3. What is the relationship among the brands and attributes?
4. Can these relationships be represented graphically in a joint low-dimensional space?

To answer these questions, we present the method of correspondence analysis using as an example the artificial data of Table 8–1. Notation and general data concepts are introduced first. Correspondence analysis involves terminology that may be unfamiliar to marketing researchers. We maintain this terminology in our exposition for consistency with the psychometric and statistical literature. In

____ *Table 8–1* _____

Artificial Data on Three Brands and Six Attributes from 100 Individuals

| | Attribute | | | | | | | | | | | | |
| | 1 | | 2 | | 3 | | 4 | | 5 | | 6 | | |
Brand	Yes	No	Yes	No	Yes	No	Yes	No	Yes	No	Yes	No	Row mass
A	29[a]	71	20	80	18	82	24	76	20	80	13	87	
	(016[b]	039	011	044	010	045	013	042	011	044	007	048)	333
B	26	74	15	85	25	75	30	70	10	90	34	66	
	(014	041	008	047	014	041	016	039	005	050	019	036)	333
C	25	75	26	74	31	69	21	79	15	85	24	76	
	(014	041	014	041	017	038	011	044	008	047	013	042)	333
Column mass	044	122	034	132	042	124	041	125	024	142	040	126	

[a] All entries are proportions. Decimal points are omitted.

[b] Figures in parentheses are rescaled so that their sum equals unity (before rounding).

the following discussion, boldface capital letters represent matrices, boldface lower-case letters represent vectors, and lower-case italic letters represent scalars.

Notation and Data Doubling

Let $\mathbf{X}$ represent the 3×12 brands by attribute categories categorical data matrix displayed in Table 8-1. In general, the matrix is "objects by variable categories." The term "objects" is used to represent the extensive variety of products, commodities, goods, and consumers investigated in marketing research studies. Hence, objects may be brands, individuals, product classes, segments of consumers, and so forth. The term "variables" is used in the broadest sense possible and refers, in general, to characteristics of the objects being studied. These characteristics may be attributes, store locations, marketing mix variables, attitude statements, and so forth.

The general q-variate categorical data matrix $\mathbf{X}$ is $n \times p$, where the q variables (for example, attributes) are represented by sets of columns and categorical measurements of objects (for example, brands) on those variables are represented by rows. Each variable has P_r categories (columns), with $r = 1, \ldots, q$ and $P_1 + \ldots + P_r + \ldots + P_q = p$. The general entry x_{ij} is some categorical measure of the j-th variable category,[1] $j = 1, \ldots, p$, on the i-th object, $i = 1, \ldots, n$.

When the q variables have only two possible responses (for example yes/no, endorse/do not endorse, purchase/do not purchase, and so forth), only two categories are possible for each variable and $P_r = 2$ for all r. In practice, the researcher typically obtains only the positive endorsements and infers the negative by subtraction. In

applications of correspondence analysis to data other than contingency tables the data matrix can be "doubled" to obtain this full set of responses. Doubling creates a symmetry between the two "poles" of each binary variable and renders the correspondence analysis invariant with respect to the direction in which we choose to scale the data (Greenacre, 1984). The artificial example in this and the following section is based on such a doubled data matrix.

Algebraic Considerations in Correspondence Analysis

A variety of approaches lead to the equations of correspondence analysis (Tenenhaus and Young, 1985). As a theoretical basis for developing the logic of correspondence analysis, we use the notion of the singular value decomposition (SVD) of a matrix (Eckart and Young, 1936; Green with Carroll, 1978). This "principal components analysis" approach, due largely to Greenacre (1978, 1984), is useful because it emphasizes the geometric properties of correspondence analysis and illuminates the practical implications of the data analysis. The singular value decomposition embodies the idea of the basic structure of a matrix, consisting of basic values and basic vectors. The eigenstructure (eigenvalues and eigenvectors) of a symmetric matrix is a special case of the SVD.

The philosophy behind correspondence analysis is to obtain a graphical representation of both the rows and columns of the original data matrix in terms of as few dimensions as possible. In correspondence analysis, each row of $\mathbf{X}$ represents a point *profile* in p-dimensional space and each column represents a point profile in n-dimensional space. Attention is directed to the profiles of the frequency distributions rather than their raw occurrence, because the raw frequencies in Table 8–1 do not yield a meaningful interpretation of distances between row points and between column points.

---

[1] Actually, j indexes the l-th category of the r-th variable, $l = 1, \ldots, P_r$, but this level of precision in notation is not required for the exposition we present.

In terms of the n brands, say, in p-dimensional attribute space, it is clear that some brands will "occur" frequently and consequently some attribute categories will be endorsed frequently for those brands. Other brands will have small frequencies of occurrence and hence the attribute categories attributed to them will appear less frequently. The brand profiles are conditional frequencies of attribute category j given brand i. Similarly for the p attributes in n-dimensional brand space, the conditional frequencies of brand i given attribute category j are the quantities of interest.

To perform a correspondence analysis, one rescales the original data matrix $\mathbf{X}$ so that the sum of the elements equals 1.

$$(1) \qquad \mathbf{P} = \mathbf{X}/\mathbf{1}'\mathbf{X}\mathbf{1}, \text{ with } \mathbf{1}'\mathbf{P}\mathbf{1} = 1$$

where $\mathbf{1}' = (1 \ldots 1)'$, either $1 \times n$ or $1 \times p$, depending on the context. $\mathbf{P}$ is the *correspondence matrix* whose elements are the relative frequencies and if $\mathbf{X}$ is a contingency table, $\mathbf{P}$ is the probability density on the cells of $\mathbf{X}$. The row sums of $\mathbf{P}$ are written into $\mathbf{D}_r$, an $n \times n$ diagonal matrix,

$$(2) \qquad \mathbf{D}_r = \text{diag}(\mathbf{r})$$

where $\mathbf{r} = \mathbf{P}\mathbf{1}$, and the column sums of $\mathbf{P}$ are written into $\mathbf{D}_c$, a $p \times p$ diagonal matrix,

$$(3) \qquad \mathbf{D}_c = \text{diag}(\mathbf{c})$$

where $\mathbf{c} = \mathbf{P}'\mathbf{1}$. These row and column sums are referred to as masses in correspondence analysis. The masses enable us to weight each profile point in proportion to its frequency. Again, if we are working with a contingency table, $\mathbf{r}$ and $\mathbf{c}$ are the marginal densities. These densities are only analogies when $\mathbf{X}$ is not a contingency table. The entries of $\mathbf{P}$, with row and column masses $\mathbf{r}$ and $\mathbf{c}$, respectively, are in parentheses in Table 8–1 below the corresponding entries of $\mathbf{X}$.

Note that the brand masses are all equal (0.33) and that each attribute also has equal mass (0.16), though this quantity is distributed differently for each attribute between the yes and no categories, depending on the frequency of responses in each category. In this example, the masses are equal because each row sums to the same constant value and each pair of columns sums to the same constant value, by design. In other situations, such as in contingency tables, the masses will not necessarily be equal.

The row and column profiles of $\mathbf{P}$ are defined as the vectors of row and column elements of $\mathbf{P}$ divided by their respective masses. The n row profiles in p-dimensional space are written in the rows of $\mathbf{R}$ and the p column profiles in n-dimensional space are written in the rows of $\mathbf{C}$.

$$(4) \qquad \mathbf{R} = \mathbf{D}_r^{-1}\mathbf{P}$$

and

$$(5) \qquad \mathbf{C} = \mathbf{D}_c^{-1}\mathbf{P}'$$

Note that a profile (row or column) sums to unity. The correspondence analysis problem is to find a low-rank approximation to the original data matrix that optimally represents both these row and column profiles in k-dimensional subspaces, where k is generally much smaller than either n or p.[2] These two k-dimensional subspaces (one for the row profiles and one for the column profiles) have a geometric correspondence, which we examine hereafter, that enables us to represent both in one joint display.

Because we wish to represent graphically the distances between row (or column) profiles, we orient the configuration of points at the "center of gravity" of

---

[2] Correspondence analysis optimizes several criteria simultaneously. See Tenenhaus and Young (1985) for a detailed discussion.

both sets. The centroid of the set of row points in its space is $\mathbf{c}$, the vector of column masses. This defines the "average" row profile. The centroid of the set of column points in its space is $\mathbf{r}$, the vector of row masses. This is the average column profile. To perform the analysis relative to the center of gravity, $\mathbf{P}$ is centered "symmetrically" by rows and columns, that is, $\mathbf{P} - \mathbf{rc}'$, so that the origin corresponds to the average profile of both sets of points.

The solution to finding a representation of both row and column profiles in a low-dimensional space involves the generalized singular value decomposition (GSVD) and low-rank matrix approximation theory [Seber, 1984]. The GSVD of the symmetrically centered correspondence matrix $\mathbf{P}$ defines the theoretical correspondence analysis problem.

$$(6) \qquad \mathbf{P} - \mathbf{rc}' = \tilde{\mathbf{M}} \mathbf{D}_{\tilde{\mu}} \tilde{\mathbf{N}}'$$

where $\tilde{\mathbf{M}}' \mathbf{D}_r^{-1} \tilde{\mathbf{M}} = \tilde{\mathbf{N}}' \mathbf{D}_c^{-1} \tilde{\mathbf{N}} = \mathbf{I}$, with $\tilde{\mathbf{M}}$ $n \times k$, $\tilde{\mathbf{N}}$ $p \times k$, and $\mathbf{D}_{\tilde{\mu}}$ $k \times k$, and $\tilde{\mu}_1 \geq \ldots \geq \tilde{\mu}_t \geq \ldots \geq \tilde{\mu}_k > 0$.

The columns of $\tilde{\mathbf{M}}$ and $\tilde{\mathbf{N}}$ hold the first k left and right generalized basic vectors of $\mathbf{P} - \mathbf{rc}'$, in the metrics $\mathbf{D}_r^{-1}$ and $\mathbf{D}_c^{-1}$, corresponding to the k largest basic values and define the optimal weighted Euclidean k-dimensional subspaces in terms of weighted sum of squared distances. $\mathbf{D}_{\tilde{\mu}}$ is a diagonal matrix holding the generalized basic values $\tilde{\mu}_1, \ldots, \tilde{\mu}_k$, in descending order, corresponding to the generalized basic vectors. In other words, the principal axes of the attribute category (column) set of points are defined by the columns of $\tilde{\mathbf{M}}$ and the principal axes of the brand (row) set of points are defined by the columns of $\tilde{\mathbf{N}}$. The weighted centers of gravity of each set of points are both at the origin of the principal axes.[3]

The principal coordinates [Gower, 1966] of the brand and attribute category profiles, with respect to their principal axes, are written in the rows of $\mathbf{F}$ and $\mathbf{G}$, respectively.

$$(7) \qquad \mathbf{F} = (\mathbf{D}_r^{-1} \mathbf{P} - \mathbf{1c}') \mathbf{D}_c^{-1} \tilde{\mathbf{N}}$$

and

$$(8) \qquad \mathbf{G} = (\mathbf{D}_c^{-1} \mathbf{P}' - \mathbf{1r}') \mathbf{D}_r^{-1} \tilde{\mathbf{M}}$$

The set of points defined in equation (7) are the n row profiles in weighted Euclidean k-dimensional space, with masses defined by the n elements of $\mathbf{r}$ and principal axis weights defined by the inverses of the elements of $\mathbf{c}$, that is, $\mathbf{D}_c^{-1}$. A similar definition holds for the column set of points defined in equation (8). These are the p column profiles in weighted Euclidean k-dimensional space, with masses defined by the p elements of $\mathbf{c}$ and principal axis weights defined by the inverses of the elements of $\mathbf{r}$, that is, $\mathbf{D}_r^{-1}$. Thus, the principal axes are weighted inversely by the elements of the average profile.

Each set of points can be related to the principal axes of the other set of profile points through rescalings by the basic values.

$$(9) \qquad \mathbf{F} = \mathbf{D}_r^{-1} \tilde{\mathbf{M}} \mathbf{D}_{\tilde{\mu}}$$

and

$$(10) \qquad \mathbf{G} = \mathbf{D}_c^{-1} \tilde{\mathbf{N}} \mathbf{D}_{\tilde{\mu}}$$

In practice, the correspondence analysis problem is restated in an equivalent

---

[3] The centering operation has the effect of removing the *trivial axes* with corresponding basic values of unity. That is, without centering, the first axes (columns) extracted from the left and right generalized basic vectors would correspond to $\mathbf{r}$ and $\mathbf{c}$, respectively, and the first diagonal element of $\mathbf{D}_{\tilde{\mu}}$ would equal 1. In this case, the analysis is performed relative to the origin, rather than from the "center of gravity." Because the GSVD of $\mathbf{P} - \mathbf{rc}'$ is "contained" in the GSVD of $\mathbf{P}$ (Greenacre, 1978, 1984), attention is restricted to $\mathbf{P} - \mathbf{rc}'$.

form in terms of the SVD for computational convenience.

(11) $\mathbf{D}_r^{-1/2}(\mathbf{P} - \mathbf{rc'})\mathbf{D}_c^{-1/2} = \mathbf{M}\mathbf{D}_\mu\mathbf{N'}$

where $\mathbf{M'M} = \mathbf{N'N} = \mathbf{I}$, with $\mathbf{M}$ $n \times k$, $\mathbf{N}$ $p \times k$, $\mathbf{D}_\mu$ $k \times k$, and $\mu_1 \geqslant \ldots \geqslant \mu_t \geqslant \ldots \geqslant \mu_k > 0$. Then,

(12) $\mathbf{F} = \mathbf{D}_r^{-1/2}\mathbf{M}\mathbf{D}_\mu$

where $\mathbf{M} = \mathbf{D}_r^{-1}\tilde{\mathbf{M}}$, and

(13) $\mathbf{G} = \mathbf{D}_c^{-1/2}\mathbf{N}\mathbf{D}_\mu$

where $\mathbf{N} = \mathbf{D}_c^{-1}\tilde{\mathbf{N}}$, and plotting the rows of $\mathbf{F}$ and $\mathbf{G}$ in the same space results in a k-dimensional correspondence analysis.

Correspondence analysis can be considered a dual generalized principal components analysis [Greenacre, 1984]. The columns of $\mathbf{F}$ are the eigenvectors of $\mathbf{RC}$ and the columns of $\mathbf{G}$ are the eigenvectors of $\mathbf{CR}$.

(14) $(\mathbf{D}_r^{-1}\mathbf{P}\mathbf{D}_c^{-1}\mathbf{P'})\mathbf{F} = \mathbf{F}\mathbf{D}_\lambda$

and

(15) $(\mathbf{D}_c^{-1}\mathbf{P'}\mathbf{D}_r^{-1}\mathbf{P})\mathbf{G} = \mathbf{G}\mathbf{D}_\lambda$

The eigenvalues λ_t, are the weighted variances of each principal axis (the weighted sums of squares of the points' coordinates along the t-th principal axis in each set) and are equal to the corresponding squared basic values from the SVD in equation (11).

(16) $\mathbf{F'}\mathbf{D}_r\mathbf{F} = \mathbf{D}_\mu^2 = \mathbf{D}_\lambda$

and

(17) $\mathbf{G'}\mathbf{D}_c\mathbf{G} = \mathbf{D}_\mu^2 = \mathbf{D}_\lambda$

The axes are orthogonal, though the metric is "chi square" and not ordinary Euclidean as in principal components analysis.

The transition formulas relate the brand and attribute category coordinates to each other.

(18) $\mathbf{F} = \mathbf{D}_r^{-1}\mathbf{P}\mathbf{G}\mathbf{D}_\mu^{-1} = \mathbf{R}\mathbf{G}\mathbf{D}_\mu^{-1}$

and

$$\mathbf{G} = \mathbf{D}_c^{-1}\mathbf{P'}\mathbf{F}\mathbf{D}_\mu^{-1} = \mathbf{C}\mathbf{F}\mathbf{D}_\mu^{-1}$$

Hill (1974) considers these the defining formulas for a correspondence analysis.

The transition formulas in equations (18) and (19) are important because they provide the mechanism for obtaining one set of coordinates from the other set. To see the geometric importance of these formulas, consider the i-th row of $\mathbf{F}$, $\mathbf{f}_i'$.

(20) $\mathbf{f}_i' = (\tilde{\mathbf{r}}_i'\mathbf{G})\mathbf{D}_\mu^{-1}$

where $\tilde{\mathbf{r}}_i'$ is the i-th row profile from $\mathbf{R}$ in equation (4). Equation (20) defines a "barycenter," actually a center of mass, of the p column profile points in $\mathbf{G}$, because the sum of the elements of $\tilde{\mathbf{r}}_i$ equals unity. Postmultiplication by $\mathbf{D}_\mu^{-1}$ divides the coordinates of the centroid by the singular values. Geometrically, a particular row profile will be "attracted" to a position in its subspace that corresponds to the column variable categories prominent in that row profile. A corresponding definition and interpretation holds for the rows of $\mathbf{G}$.

Distances (squared) between points in the same set are given by

(21) $$d_{ii'}^2 = \frac{\sum\limits_j 1}{c_j(p_{ij}/r_i - p_{i'j}/r_{i'})^2}$$

for row points i and i' and

(22) $$d_{jj'}^2 = \frac{\sum\limits_i 1}{r_i(p_{ij}/c_j - p_{ij'}/c_{j'})^2}$$

for column points j and j'. These are similar to ordinary Euclidean distances except that each squared term is weighted by the inverse of the relative frequency (mass) corresponding to the term.

These distances, approximated in the k-dimensional subspaces by

$$(23) \qquad d_{ii'}^2 \approx (\mathbf{f}_i - \mathbf{f}_{i'})'(\mathbf{f}_i - \mathbf{f}_{i'})$$

and

$$(24) \qquad d_{jj'}^2 \approx (\mathbf{g}_i - \mathbf{g}_{i'})'(\mathbf{g}_j - \mathbf{g}_{j'})$$

for row and column points, respectively, are defined as chi square distances. This distance measure is chosen because it guarantees invariance according to the property of distributional equivalence.

— If two rows having identical column profiles are aggregated, the distances between columns remain unchanged.
— If two columns having identical row profiles are aggregated, the distances between rows remain unchanged.

Clearly, identical profiles imply equal or proportional raw data.

The Correspondence Analysis Model

The correspondence analysis "model" on $\mathbf{P}$ in k dimensions reveals how an element of $\mathbf{P}$ is approximated in the k-dimensional weighted Euclidean subspace.

$$(25) \qquad \mathbf{P} \approx \mathbf{rc}' + \mathbf{D}_r \mathbf{FD}_\mu^{-1} \mathbf{G}' \mathbf{D}_c$$

From equation (25) it is clear that the model treats rows and columns symmetrically, as nothing changes if we begin with $\mathbf{X}'$ instead of $\mathbf{X}$.

Data Considerations

Because of the inherent symmetry of correspondence analysis, the implied data matrix for analysis is a contingency table. However, the method can be applied to almost any matrix of categorical data, as long as the entries are non-negative. Excellent data classifications for correspondence analysis are given by Benzécri (1973b), Nishisato (1980), and Greenacre (1984).

Many situations in marketing research lead to data at the nominal or ordinal level of measurement [Perreault and Young, 1980]. Such data are often intractable with traditional analytical methods. A common source of this type of data is the evaluation of objects (for example, retail outlets, competing products, individuals) on attributes (for example, product features, attitude statements) with binary judgments rather than 5- or 7-point rating scales. Binary judgments are useful when the researcher has many objects or attributes to measure, when respondent cooperation is difficult to obtain, when it is difficult to make fine distinctions between objects on the attributes, and whenever rating scales are difficult to use.

Another source of data common in marketing research is the open-ended elicitation of attributes, brands, stores, and so on, from respondents—that is, "pick-any" data. With an unconstrained set of alternatives, failure to mention an alternative does not necessarily imply rejection of it. Correspondence analysis is appropriate for such data, whereas standard multi-dimensional scaling methods are not [Holbrook, Moore, and Winer, 1982].

Though correspondence analysis is ideally suited to those research situations in which categorical measurements are the most reasonably obtained, it also can be applied to ordered categories and "discretized" quantitative variables [see Jambu and Lebeaux, 1983], but the original ordering may not be maintained after scaling unless the solution is constrained [Nishisato and Sheu, 1984]. This type of application allows investigation of possible nonlinearities among the categories with respect to the principal axes. It can lead to the discovery of relationships between scale value categories that are obscured if the data are dichotomized, or if methods are used that recognize only the metric properties of the data. Thus, a "loss of information" in ignoring the ordered or interval nature of the data yields a meaningful gain in understanding [Lebart, Morineau, Warwick, 1984].

Correspondence analysis of other forms of data, such as rank-order data, sorting data, paired comparison data, and successive categories data, is discussed by Jambu and Lebeaux (1983), Nishisato (1980), Nishisato and Nishisato (1983), and Nishisato and Sheu (1984). Applications of correspondence analysis are virtually unlimited, but Lebart, Morineau, and Warwick (1984) suggest three conditions that should be satisfied if correspondence analysis is to be most effective.

1. The data matrix must be large enough that visual inspection or simple statistical analysis cannot reveal its structure.
2. The variables must be "homogeneous," so that it makes sense to calculate a statistical distance between rows and columns and so that distances can be interpreted meaningfully.
3. The data matrix must be "amorphous, a priori." In other words, the method is most fruitfully applied to data whose structure is either unknown or only poorly understood.

INTERPRETING A CORRESPONDENCE ANALYSIS

The principal coordinates of the brand and attribute category profile points from the correspondence analysis in two dimensions of the artificial data of Table 8–1 are plotted in Figure 8–1. The plots are merged into one joint display for ease of interpretation.

The overall spatial variation in each set of points can be quantified and assists in interpretation. This variation, the total inertia, is defined as the weighted sum of squared distances from the points to their respective centroids and is equivalent for both sets of points.

$$(26) \quad \text{Inertia (Total)} = \sum_i \sum_j \frac{(p_{ij} - r_i c_j)^2}{r_i c_j}$$

___*Figure 8–1*_____

Two-Dimensional Correspondence Analysis of the Doubled Data Matrix in Table 8–1

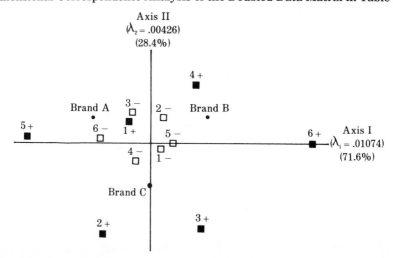

(27)   Inertia (rows) $= \sum_i r_i \left[\dfrac{\sum_j 1}{c_j (p_{ij}/r_i - c_j)^2} \right]$

$= \sum_i r_i (\bar{\mathbf{r}}_i - \mathbf{c})' \mathbf{D}_c^{-1} (\bar{\mathbf{r}}_i - \mathbf{c})$

(28)   Inertia (columns)

$= \sum_j c_j \left[\dfrac{\sum_i 1}{r_i (p_{ij}/c_j - r_i)^2} \right]$

$= \sum_j c_j (\bar{\mathbf{c}}_j - \mathbf{r})' \mathbf{D}_r^{-1} (\bar{\mathbf{c}}_j - \mathbf{r})$

It is because of the geometric correspondence of the two sets of points, in position and inertia, that we can merge the two displays into one joint display. The advantage of this merger is that a concise graphical display representing varied features of the data is obtained in a single picture. The geometric display of each set of points reveals the nature of similarities and variation within the set, and the joint display shows the correspondence between sets. However, distances between points from different sets cannot be interpreted because these distances do not approximate any defined quantity. Distances between points in the same set are equal to the relevant chi square distances in equations (23) and (24), whereas the between-set correspondence is influenced by the barycentric nature of the transition formulas in equations (18) and (19).

The total inertia also can be decomposed along the principal axes. Each eigenvalue, λ_t, indicates the weighted variance (inertia) explained by the t-th principal axis of the display. Summed over all k principal axes, these eigenvalues represent the total inertia of the spatial representation.

The first principal axis in the artificial example accounts for 71.6 percent of the spatial variation in the data ($\lambda_1 = 0.01074$). The second principal axis accounts for the remaining 28.4 percent ($\lambda_2 = 0.00426$). In this artificial example, two dimensions

recover exactly the original data matrix because with three brands there are at most two mutually exclusive dimensions. Real applications involving reduced dimensionalities of larger data matrices will necessarily be approximations.

From Figure 8–1 we see that brands A, B, and C are relatively far from each other in terms of the attributes that describe them. Their relative positions as points in the two-dimensional space indicate the similarities and differences among them with respect to the attributes. The first dimension separates attribute 6+ on the right from attribute 5+ on the left, and also separates brand B on the right from brand A on the left. The second dimension separates attributes 2+ and 3+ on the bottom from attribute 4+ on the top. This dimension, in addition, differentiates brand C on the bottom from brands A and B on the top.

The transition formulas in equations (18) and (19) make clear that, geometrically, a particular brand will tend to a position in its space corresponding to the attribute categories prominent in that brand profile. Similarly, given the display of brand profiles, a particular attribute category will tend along the principal axes in the direction of the brands that are relatively substantial in that category. For example, the attribute category 3+ point is on the negative side of the second principal axis, and brand C, which is relatively high on attribute 3+ (see Table 8-1), is on the negative side of its second principal axis. Points near the center of the display have undifferentiated profile distributions as a consequence of the origin placed at the center of gravity. Notice that we have been careful not to interpret between-set distances.

The interpretation of the correspondence analysis is not yet complete. The two-dimensional display in Figure 8–1 shows the projections of the point profiles onto the plane, but does not indicate which points have had the most impact in

_____Table 8–2_____

Numerical Results of Correspondence Analysis of Table 8–1 Data[a]

Name	Quality	Mass	Inertia[b]	Axis 1			Axis 2		
				Coordinate	Squared correlation	Contri-bution[b]	Coordinate	Squared correlation	Contri-bution[b]
Brand A	1000	333	405	−130	883	500	50	117	167
Brand B	1000	333	405	130	883	500	50	117	167
Brand C	1000	333	190	0	0	0	−90	1000	666
1 + (yes	1000	44	10	−50	519	9	40	481	21
1 − (no)	1000	122	1	20	519	3	−20	481	7
2 +	1000	34	110	−100	206	32	−20	794	307
2 −	1000	132	31	30	206	8	50	794	78
3 +	1000	42	130	120	289	51	−180	711	316
3 −	1000	124	44	−40	289	17	60	711	104
4 +	1000	41	60	100	429	37	110	571	124
4 −	1000	125	20	−30	429	12	−40	571	41
5 +	1000	24	123	−270	1000	172	0	0	0
5 −	1000	142	21	50	1000	30	0	0	0
6 +	1000	40	340	360	999	480	−10	1	1
6 −	1000	126	110	−110	999	149	0	1	1

[a] All values are multiplied by 1000 and decimal points are omitted.

[b] Scaled (before multiplication by 1000) to sum to unity.

determining the orientation of the axes. For a complete and correct interpretation of the graphical display, we must use additional information.

Because the total inertia of each set of points is decomposed along the principal axes and among the points in similar and symmetric fashion, the inertia for each set of points can be decomposed in a manner analogous to the decomposition of variance. These various decompositions are used to assist in the interpretation of the graphical display.

Table 8–2 is the numerical representation of the correspondence analysis depicted in Figure 8–1. Each column represents a particular decomposition of the variation in each set of points and is discussed in turn. The two columns headed "Coordinate" contain the coordinates of the points on the first and second principal axes, respectively. The weights for each point (column headed "Mass") are repeated from Table 8–1 for completeness.

Inertia of the Points

The inertia of the i-th brand point is equal to

$$(29) \qquad r_i \left[\frac{\sum_j 1}{c_j (p_{ij}/r_i - c_j)^2} \right] = r_i \sum_t f_{it}^2$$

Equation (29) represents the contribution of the i-th brand to the total inertia, with r_i the mass of that brand and the quantity in brackets the squared chi squared distance of the brand profile to the center of gravity **c** in the brand space—that is, $\sum_t f_{it}^2$. A similar definition holds for each attribute category point. These contributions, summed over all brands (or attribute categories), equal the total inertia.

The inertias for each point are in the column headed "Inertia" in Table 8–2. Brand A's inertia in the set of brand points is 40.5 percent of the total inertia, as is brand B's. Brand C accounts for 19 percent of the total inertia in this set. Attribute category 6+ has an inertia that is 34 percent of the total inertia in the attribute set of points and accounts for by far the largest proportion.

Absolute Contributions to Inertia

The inertia along the t-th axis, λ_t, consists of the weighted sum of squared distances to the origin of the displayed row (or column) profiles, where the weights are the masses for each row (or column) point. For the brand profiles, this inertia can be expressed as

$$(30) \qquad \lambda_t = \sum_i r_i f_{it}^2$$

A similar definition holds for the attribute category profiles. Thus, each eigenvalue also represents the inertia of the projections of the brand set (or attribute category set) of points on each axis.

If each term in the summation is expressed as a percentage relative to the inertia "explained" by each axis. That is,

$$(31) \qquad r_i f_{it}^2 / \lambda_t$$

the absolute contribution of the i-th brand to the t-th principal axis is obtained. The absolute contributions quantify the importance of each point in determining the direction of the principal axes and serve as guides to interpretation of each axis. They are interpreted as the percentage of (weighted) variance explained by each point in relation to each axis.

It is clear from the decomposition that a point can contribute to a principal axis—that is, make a high contribution to the inertia of that axis—in two ways: when

it has a large mass and/or when it is a large distance from the centroid, even if it has relatively low mass.

Because all the brands have equal mass, it is their distance from the centroid that determines their contributions to the inertia of each axis. The absolute contributions, in the columns headed "Contribution" in Table 8–2, indicate that brands A and B contribute equally and solely to the direction of axis 1 and brand C contributes primarily to axis 2.

Similarly for the attributes, categories 6+, 5+, and 6− define the first principal axis whereas categories 3+, 2+, 4+, and 3− define the second principal axis. Attribute categories 1−, 5−, and to a lesser extent 1+ contribute essentially nothing to the inertia of each axis and consequently are near the origin (note that their profiles are virtually identical to the average column profile **r**).

Relative Contributions to Inertia

After the dimensional interpretation, the next step in a correspondence analysis is to determine the "quality" of the representation of each point in the display. The quantity

$$(32) \qquad \frac{f_{it}^2}{\sum_t f_{it}^2}$$

gives the relative contribution of the t-th principal axis to the inertia of the i-th brand. A similar definition holds for the relative contributions of the attribute categories. These values are independent of the point's mass and indicate how well each point is "fit" by the representation.

A relative contribution is actually a squared correlation, because it is equal to the $\cos^2$ of the angle θ between the point and the t-th principal axis. High values of $\cos^2\theta$ indicate that the axis explains the point's inertia very well; θ is low and the profile point lies in the direction of the axis and correlates highly with it. Summed over all the axes of interest (in this case two), the relative contributions give the quality of the representation. This is just the $\cos^2$ of the angle the point makes with the subspace. Thus, the relative contribution gives that part of the variance of a point explained by an axis, and the quality gives the goodness of fit of each point's representation in the subspace. The sum of the relative contributions over all axes (not just those used for the display) equals unity (as in Table 8–2).

The relative contributions are in the columns headed "Correlation in Table 8–2. The first axis explains 88.3 percent of the inertia of brands A and B and nothing of brand C, whereas the second axis explains 11.7 percent of the inertia of brands A and B and 100 percent of that of brand C. Similarly, the first axis explains 51.9 percent of attribute 1 and the second axis explains the remaining 48.1 percent. The relative contributions are equal for each attribute category pair because the doubling procedure gives each pair of attribute categories equal mass. The qualities of each point in the two-dimensional space (all equal to unity) are in the column headed "Quality."

The various decompositions of the total inertia, in conjunction with the principal coordinate values for the brands and attribute categories, make possible a complete interpretation of the correspondence analysis of the data in Table 8–1. As discussed hereafter, external information can be fit into the display through the transition formulas in equations (18) and (19) and also can be helpful in interpreting correspondence analysis results. Another aid is cluster analysis, which with large data matrices may be useful in detecting homogeneous groups and in presenting results (Jambu and Lebeaux 1983). Whatever aids are used, we emphasize that visual inspection of the graphical display is a key step in interpreting the results.

ILLUSTRATING CORRESPONDENCE ANALYSIS

Empirical Example: Beverage Purchase and Consumption

A group of male and female MBA students from Columbia University were asked to indicate, for a variety of popular soft drinks, the frequency with which they purchased and consumed the soft drinks in a 1-month period. For illustrative purposes, the scale used to collect the information was coded 1 to indicate purchase and consumption at least every other week and 0 to indicate purchase and consumption less than every other week. The data about eight soft drinks from 34 of the students were used for our example. The soft drinks are Coke, Diet Coke, Diet Pepsi, Diet 7-Up, Pepsi, Sprite, Tab, and 7-Up. The 34×8 binary indicator matrix is displayed in Table 8-3.

A correspondence analysis was performed on the 34×16 matrix obtained by doubling Table 8–3 about the columns. The resulting eigenvalues equal their corresponding proportions of inertia because the total inertia equals unity (in this example). The eigenvalues for the first three principal axes are 0.482, 0.151, and 0.099, with cumulative proportions of inertia equaling 0.482, 0.633, and 0.732. Eight dimensions recover perfectly the 34×16 doubled data matrix—that is, $\sum \lambda_t = 1$—hence the other five axes account for the remaining 26.8 percent of the inertia.

In a doubled binary data matrix with q variables, the row sums equal a constant value (8 in this case) and the row masses equal $1/n$. The row profiles define n points in $2q$-dimensional space, but q linear dependencies are present among the columns so the dimensionality of the rows is really equal to q.

Figure 8–2 is the joint display of individuals and soft drinks in the plane

____ Table 8–3 _____

The 34 × 8 Binary Indicator Matrix of
Beverage Purchase and Consumption

Soft drink

Individual	Coke	Diet Coke	Diet Pepsi	Diet 7-Up	Pepsi	Sprite	Tab	7-Up
1	1	0	0	0	1	1	0	1
2	1	0	0	0	1	0	0	0
3	1	0	0	0	1	0	0	0
4	0	1	0	1	0	0	1	0
5	1	0	0	0	1	0	0	0
6	1	0	0	0	1	1	0	0
7	0	1	1	1	0	0	1	0
8	1	1	0	0	1	1	0	1
9	1	1	0	0	0	1	1	1
10	1	0	0	0	1	0	0	1
11	1	0	0	0	1	1	0	0
12	0	1	0	0	0	0	1	0
13	0	0	1	1	0	1	0	1
14	1	0	0	0	0	1	0	0
15	0	1	1	0	0	0	1	0
16	0	0	0	0	1	1	0	0
17	0	1	0	0	0	1	0	0
18	1	1	0	0	1	0	0	0
19	1	0	0	0	0	0	0	1
20	1	1	1	0	1	0	0	0
21	1	0	0	0	1	0	0	0
22	1	0	0	0	1	0	0	0
23	0	1	0	1	0	0	1	0
24	1	1	0	0	1	0	0	0
25	0	1	1	1	0	0	0	0
26	0	1	0	1	0	0	1	0
27	0	1	0	0	0	0	1	0
28	1	0	0	0	0	1	0	1
29	1	0	0	0	0	1	0	0
30	0	1	1	0	0	0	1	0
31	1	0	0	0	1	0	0	1
32	0	1	1	0	0	0	1	0
33	1	0	0	0	1	0	0	1
34	0	1	1	1	0	0	1	0

defined by the first two principal axes. These two axes account for 63.3 percent of the total inertia in the data. We chose two axes for display on the basis of the interpretability of the dimensions, the desire for parsimony, and a scree plot of the eigenvalues which indicated a clear elbow at $t = 2$. Though the third principal axis contributes enough to the total inertia to suggest its interpretation might be worthwhile, we omit plotting it to save

space. The numerical results are reported in Table 8–4 for the soft drinks and Table 8–5 for the individuals. We discuss first the soft drink points.

The display is interpreted with respect to the "positive" (purchase and consumption at least every other week) soft drink points. Because each pair of soft drink points (+ and −) has the same mass (0.125), each pair has its centroid at the origin of the display and consequently each is balanced there with the lighter mass point being proportionately farther from the origin. For example, 7-Up + with mass equal to 0.03 is farther than 7-Up − with mass of 0.09.

The absolute contributions in Table 8–4 indicate that the first principal axis is defined by Tab, Diet 7-Up, and Coke and separates the diet soft drinks (both colas and non-colas) on the right from the nondiet soft drinks on the left. We label this a "diet/nondiet" dimension. The second principal axis, defined primarily by Sprite, 7-Up, and Pepsi, separates the colas on the top from the noncolas on the bottom. We label this a "cola/noncola" dimension. The soft drink locations are based on the profiles of purchase frequency by individuals and provide information on market segments and market structure.

The relative contributions indicate that the first principal axis explains nearly all the variance in Coke (squared correlation = 0.785) and Tab (squared correlation = 0.712), whereas the second principal axis explains the most variance in Sprite (squared correlation = 0.533). Diet Pepsi's quality in two dimensions (quality = 0.405) indicates it has the worst fit in the plane defined by the first two principal axes. However, Coke, Pepsi, and Tab are fit well by two dimensions (quality = 0.803, 0.777, 0.712, respectively).

The display in Figure 8–2 reveals, by their proximities, those soft drinks having similar profiles of purchase and consumption by the 34 individuals. Similarly,

_____Figure 8–2_____

Two-Dimensional Correspondence Analysis of the Doubled Data Matrix Constructed from Table 8–3

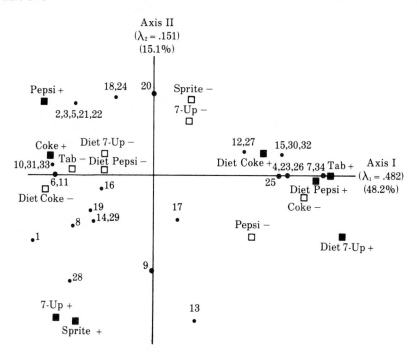

individuals close together in the display share similar patterns of purchase and consumption and thus constitute likely market segments based on purchase behavior. Individuals who share the same point in this display have identical profiles of soft drink usage.

Two segments of consumers are seen on the "diet" side of the first principal axis, those who drink diet colas (individuals 12, 27, 15, 30, and 32) and those who drink diet cola and diet noncola soft drinks (individuals 7, 34, 4, 23, 26, and 25). The absence of any individual points in the lower right region of the space indicates that no one drinks only diet noncolas.

On the left side of the space, we can identify segments of individuals who drink both diet and nondiet colas (18, 24, and 20), who drink only nondiet colas (2, 3, 5, 21, and 22), and who drink both colas and noncolas, skewed either toward colas (e.g., 6, 11, 10, 31, and 33) or toward noncolas (for example, 1, 8, 14, 29, and 19).

The absolute contributions indicate that individuals 13 and 28 are the primary contributors to the second principal axis (contribution = 0.219 and 0.116, respectively). These contributions are "too large" in the sense that these points define, almost solely, the direction of the second principal axis. Such a situation occurs often in correspondence analysis. A remedy is presented in the Discussion section.

Relationship to Other Multivariate Methods

It is relatively easy to show that correspondence analysis is related directly

_____ Table 8–4 _____

Decomposition of Inertia Among the Soft Drinks for the First Two Principal Axes[a]

Soft drink	Quality[b]	Mass	Inertia[c]	Axis 1		Axis 2	
				Squared correlation	Contri-bution[c]	Squared correlation	Contri-bution[c]
Coke+	809	70	55	785	84	18	6
Coke−	809	55	70	785	120	18	9
Diet Coke+	664	62	62	614	80	19	8
Diet Coke−	664	62	62	614	80	19	8
Diet pepsi+	643	25	100	404	80	1	1
Diet Pepsi−	643	100	25	404	25	1	1
Diet 7-Up+	626	25	100	458	94	49	32
Diet 7-Up−	626	100	25	458	24	49	8
Pepsi+	811	62	62	550	76	227	98
Pepsi−	811	62	62	550	67	227	88
Sprite+	826	40	85	149	26	533	298
Sprite−	826	85	40	149	13	533	142
Tab+	751	40	85	712	125	0	0
Tab−	751	85	40	712	60	0	0
7-Up+	727	35	90	181	34	364	221
7-Up+	727	90	35	181	12	364	80

[a] All values are multiplied by 1000 and decimal points are omitted.

[b] Measured over the first three principal axes.

[c] Scaled (before multiplication by 1000) to sum to unity.

to several familiar multivariate methods, including principal components analysis,[4] the biplot [Gabriel, 1971, 1981], canonical correlation analysis, and discriminant analysis, though the generalized singular value decomposition [see Greenacre, 1984, Appendix A.2]. The differences among methods are determined by the type of transformation applied to the original data matrix, the metrics in which the principal axes are defined, and how the basic values are assigned to the left and right basic vectors. In correspondence analysis, the transformation is defined by equation (11), the metrics are the chi square metrics defined by the inverses of equations (2) and (3), and the basic values are assigned according to equations (12) and (13).

A distinct advantage of correspondence analysis over other methods, in terms of obtaining a joint graphical display, is that correspondence analysis produces two dual

---

[4] In fact, the row geometry of the correspondence analysis of a doubled binary data matrix is identical to the row geometry of the principal components analysis of the column-standardized (to unit variance) undoubled data matrix. The row masses and relative distances between row profiles are equivalent in both [Greenacre, 1984; Lebart, Morineau, and Warwick, 1984].

_____ Table 8–5 _____

Decomposition of Inertia Among the Individuals for the First Two Principal Axes[a]

Individual	Quality[b]	Mass	Inertia[c]	Axis 1		Axis 2	
				Squared Correlation	Contribution[c]	Squared Correlation	Contribution[c]
1	911	30	27	701	47	198	42
2,3,5,21,22	909	30	18	520	19	384	44
4,23,26	702	30	40	690	55	0	0
6,11	716	30	18	623	30	1	1
7,34	955	30	49	888	90	1	1
8	453	30	27	322	21	130	27
9	463	30	40	0	0	371	91
10,31,33	808	30	27	593	32	1	1
12,27	776	30	27	490	25	34	6
13	864	30	60	42	5	572	219
14,29	621	30	18	248	12	145	21
15,30,32	704	30	40	688	51	16	3
16	300	30	27	162	9	14	2
17	611	30	27	35	2	129	21
18,24	678	30	18	124	4	541	61
19	428	30	27	245	13	85	14
20	444	30	27	0	0	301	55
25	715	30	40	543	49	1	1
28	908	30	27	347	23	560	116

[a] All values are multiplied by 1000 and decimal points are omitted.

[b] Measured over the first three principal axes.

[c] Scaled (before multiplication by 1000) to sum to unity.

displays whose row and column geometries have similar interpretations. In other multivariate approaches as they are commonly employed, this duality does not exist.

Tenenhaus and Young (1985) have shown that four broad data analytic approaches lead to the equations of correspondence analysis, the "method of reciprocal averages" [Fisher, 1940; Hirschfeld, 1935; Horst, 1935; Richardson and Kuder, 1933], the analysis of variance approach [Bock, 1960; de Leeuw, 1973; Guttman, 1941; Hayashi, 1950, 1952, 1954; Nishisato, 1980; van Rijckevorsel and de Leeuw, 1978], the principal components analysis (PCA) approach [Benzécri, 1969, 1973a, b; Burt, 1950; Greenacre, 1978, 1984], and the generalized canonical analysis approach [McKeon, 1966]. We use the PCA approach to demonstrate correspondence analysis because it illustrates clearly the geometric aspects of the method. However, the equivalences yield additional interpretations of the results of a correspondence analysis (involving the meaning of the eigenvalues), which illuminate other aspects of the method.

The method of reciprocal averages is defined by the transition formulas, where an individual's (row's) scale value (principal coordinate) is the mean of the scale values of the categories (columns) chosen by that individual, and the scale value of a category is the mean of the scale values of the individuals in that category. This renders more intuitive the "barycentric" nature of the transition formulas. The internal consistency of the scale values is maximized and each eigenvalue, is a measure of the internal consistency of each scaling—in other words, dimension—induced on the rows and columns.

In the analysis of variance approach, the ratio of the sum of squares between rows (columns) is maximized and the ratio of the sum of squares within rows (columns) is minimized relative to the total sum of squares. The successive squared correlation ratios (the between sum of squares relative to the total sum of squares) are equivalent to the eigenvalues.

In the generalized canonical analysis approach, the sum of the squared correlations between the scaled individuals and scaled variable categories is maximized. This maximized value equals the sum of the eigenvalues and each eigenvalue is the canonical correlation between each successive joint scaling of the rows and columns.

It is also useful to contrast correspondence analysis with multidimensional unfolding, another approach for the joint display of a data matrix. Correspondence analysis displays the positions of the rows (or columns) of the data matrix relative to the set of rows (or columns) included in the analysis. This is a consequence of using profiles, rather than absolute frequencies. Multidimensional unfolding methods, however, directly approximate the entries in the data matrix, which are assumed to be row-to-column distances (dissimilarities). In this case, there is a direct interpretation of the graphical representation in terms of interpoint distances. If the data can be considered as row-to-column distances,

multidimensional unfolding is an appropriate technique. If the data cannot be considered as such, correspondence analysis may be the more appropriate method for constructing joint representations.

DISCUSSION

Supplementary Points: Fitting External Information Into the Display

The transition formulas in equations (18) and (19) provide the means for fitting external information into the graphical display from a correspondence analysis. These "supplementary points" enrich interpretation of the display, in much the same way that regression procedures assist in the interpretation of multidimensional scaling solutions [Kruskal and Wish, 1978; Schiffman, Reynolds, and Young, 1981].

Suppose we have information about physical characteristics of the eight soft drinks in the preceding example and array these data in a characteristics by soft drinks matrix. It is possible to consider each row of the matrix as defining a point in the space of the row (individual) profiles of the individuals by soft drinks matrix. Through the use of transition formula 18 we can make a transition from columns (the soft drinks) to rows (the physical characteristics) to obtain point locations for each characteristic. Each physical characteristic profile then can be projected onto the plane defined by the first two principal axes to see which characteristics are associated with which soft drinks. If we had information on the individuals, such as demographic data, we could use transition formula 19 and go from rows to columns. In this case, each column of the individuals by demographics matrix defines a column profile in the same space as the profiles of the soft drinks across the individuals. The transition from rows to columns yields a set of points that can be displayed in the original space, thereby providing information on the demographic characteristics of the individuals.

The fitting of supplementary points also can serve as a validity check [Lebart, Morineau, and Warwick, 1984, p. 163]. Because a supplementary variable makes no contribution to the axis, its squared correlation (relative contribution) with each principal axis can be examined. High values indicate good fit into the previously defined display and imply validation of the variables being investigated.

Handling Outliers

Outlier points plague correspondence analysis solutions. Occasionally, a row (or column) profile point is so "rare" (in profile) in its set of points that it has a major role in determining the higher order principal axes. This situation is easily discerned by examining the points' contributions to the axes. When a point has a very large absolute contribution and a large principal coordinate on a major principal axis, it can be considered an outlier.

Two such points are individuals 13 and 28 in the empirical example. These points consume nearly 34 percent of the inertia on the second principal axis, determining its orientation to a large degree. The solution lies in redefining these points as supplementary and performing the analysis again without them, permitting them no influence on the direction of the principal axes. Then the points can be fit a posteriori on the axes calculated for the remaining points with transition formula 18.

Inspection of the data matrix provides information about the nature of the "rarity" of an outlying point. Treating the point as supplementary allows more detailed study of the structure of the remaining points whose multivariate association is not as readily determined by inspection.

A Caveat

Correspondence analysis does have limitations. It is a multivariate descriptive statistical method and is not appropriate for hypothesis testing. Other approaches are better suited to searching for parsimonious models that can account for most of the variance in the data, such as weighted least squares [Grizzle, Starmer, and Koch, 1969] and loglinear modeling [Bishop, Feinberg, and Holland, 1975]. Recently, van der Heijden and de Leeuw (1985) showed that, under certain conditions, correspondence analysis can be interpreted in terms of specific loglinear models. However, statistical tests for correspondence analysis are still being developed; earlier tests were shown either theoretically or through simulations to be unjustified [Lebart, 1976]. Nonetheless, correspondence analysis may be helpful in detecting models that merit further consideration by other methods.

As discussed before, an important caveat for interpreting correspondence analysis results is that the between-set distances cannot be interpreted. The joint display of coordinates shows the relationship between a point from one set and all the points of the other set, not between individual points from each set. [See Carroll, Green, and Schaffer, 1986 for an alternative scaling of the coordinates that provides for comparability of all within-set and between-set distances.] When the correspondence analysis solution has more than two dimensions, proximity with one pair of axes may disappear when other pairs are plotted.

Correspondence analysis also suffers from the "curse of dimensionality." There is no method for conclusively determining the appropriate number of and what combinations of dimensions to plot and inspect. As with other multivariate methods, the researcher must balance parsimony against interpretability in determining the number of dimensions to use.

Finally, it must be recognized that in many ways correspondence analysis is a subjective technique. Many different portrayals of a data set often are possible, leading to different analysis categories and solutions. By its flexibility, correspondence analysis can lead to greater insight into the phenomena being studied because it affords several different views of the same data set. Subjectivity of analysis is part of the price of this flexibility.

Implementation

A variety of computer programs are available for carrying out a correspondence analysis. The SPAD system of FORTRAN programs written by Lebart and Morineau (1982) for mainframe computer systems is particularly applicable to large data sets. A specialized version of this program is described by Lebart, Morineau, and Warwick (1984). Nishisato and Nishisato (1983) have prepared a program that performs correspondence analysis ("dual scaling") on the IBM PC. The program accepts as input up to six different types of data. Greenacre (1984) presents a simple program to do correspondence analysis using the high-level programming language GENSTAT. An extensive collection of computer programs for correspondence analysis and related techniques is provided by Jambu and Lebeaux (1983). If the researcher has access to a matrix subroutine that performs a singular value decomposition, he or she has the tools necessary to implement the method. For example, correspondence analysis is programmed easily with the MATRIX procedure in SAS [SAS Institute, 1982].

Concluding Remarks

As we present it, correspondence analysis is a method of exploratory data analysis that (1) quantifies multivariate categorical data, (2) affords a graphical representation of the structure in the data, and (3) does not pose stringent measure- ment requirements. For many applications, its use is straightforward and unambiguous. When complex multivariate relationships are examined, correspondence analysis is limited only by the researcher's ingenuity in interpreting the derived spatial map. As a graphical method of data analysis, correspondence analysis is applied best as a multivariate descriptive statistical technique supplemental to other forms of analysis.

Correspondence analysis is very flexible. Not only is it flexible in terms of data requirements, but it also allows for the incorporation of marketing knowledge. In studying a product class, say, the researcher can set masses of brands equal to the market share or dollar sales of each, or perhaps to the percentage of consumers who use the product in the population. The technique of fitting supplementary points in the display is an interesting and virtually limitless way to incorporate external information into the analysis. It is also useful as a check on data validity and as a tool for handling troublesome outliers. Though correspondence analysis has limitations, the most important being that between-set distances in the graphical display are not interpretable, its flexibility may render it more suitable than other methods for marketing research applications in many situations.

Categorical data are common products of marketing research. However, the analysis of such data often is hindered by the requirements and limitations of many familiar research tools. Correspondence analysis is a versatile and easily implemented analytical method that can do much to assist researchers in detecting and explaining relationships among complex marketing phenomena.

REFERENCES

Belk, Russell, Painter, John, & Semenik, Richard (1981), "Preferred Solutions to the Energy Crisis as a Function of Causal

Attributions," *Journal of Consumer Research,* 8 (December), 306–12.

Benzécri, J. P. (1969), "Statistical Analysis as a Tool to Make Patterns Emerge from Data," in *Methodologies of Pattern Recognition,* S. Watanabe, ed. New York: Academic Press, Inc., 35–74.

Benzécri, J. P. et al. (1973a), *L'Analyse des Données. Vol. I, La Taxonomie.* Paris: Dunod.

Benzécri, J. P. et al. (1973b), *L'Analyse des Données. Vol. II, L'Analyse des Correspondances.* Paris: Dunod.

Bishop, Yvonne M. M., Feinberg, S. E., & Holland, P. W. (1975), *Discrete Multivariate Analysis: Theory and Practice.* Cambridge, MA: MIT Press.

Bock, R. Darrell (1960), "Methods and Applications of Optimal Scaling," Laboratory Report No. 25, L. L. Thurstone Psychometric Laboratory, University of North Carolina, Chapel Hill.

Burt, C. (1950), "The Factorial Analysis of Qualitative Data," *British Journal of Psychology (Statistical Section),* 3 (November), 166–85.

Carroll, J. Douglas, Green, Paul E., & Schaffer, Catherine M. (1986), "Interpoint Distance Comparisons in Correspondence Analysis," *Journal of Marketing Research,* 23 (August), 271–80.

de Leeuw, Jan (1973), *Canonical Analysis of Categorical Data,* unpublished doctoral dissertation, Psychological Institute, University of Leiden, The Netherlands.

Eckart, C., & Young, Gale (1936), "The Approximation of One Matrix by Another of Lower Rank," *Psychometrika,* 1 (September), 211–18.

Fisher, Ronald A. (1940), "The Precision of Discriminant Functions," *Annals of Eugenics,* 10 (December), 422–9.

Franke, George R. (1983), "Dual Scaling: A Model for Interpreting and Quantifying Categorical Data," in *Research Methods and Causal Modeling in Marketing,* W. R. Darden, K. B. Monroe, and W. D. Dillon, eds. Chicago: American Marketing Association, 111–4.

Franke, George R. (1985), "Evaluating Measures Through Data Quantification: Applying Dual Scaling to an Advertising Copytest," *Journal of Business Research,* 13 (February), 61–9.

Gabriel, K. R. (1971), "The Biplot Graphic Display of Matrices with Application to Principal Component Analysis," *Biometrika,* 58 (December), 453–67.

Gabriel, K. R. (1981), "Biplot Display of Multivariate Matrices for Inspection of Data and Diagnosis," in *Interpreting Multivariate Data,* V. Barnett, ed. Chichester: John Wiley & Sons, Inc., 147–73.

Gower, J. C. (1966), "Some Distance Properties of Latent Root and Vector Methods used in Multivariate Analysis," *Biometrika,* 53 (December), 325–38.

Green, Paul E., with Carroll, J. Douglas (1978), *Mathematical Tools for Applied Multivariate Analysis.* New York: Academic Press, Inc.

Green, Paul E., Rao, Vithala R., & DeSarbo, Wayne S. (1978), "Incorporating Group-Level Similarity Judgments in Conjoint Analysis," *Journal of Consumer Research,* 5 (December), 187–93.

Green, Robert T., Leonardi, Jean-Paul, Chandon, Jean-Louis, Cunningham, Isabella C. M., Verhage, Bronis, & Strazzieri, Alain (1983), "Societal Development and Family Purchasing Roles: A Cross-National Study," *Journal of Consumer Research,* 9 (March), 436–42.

Greenacre, Michael J. (1978), "Some Objective Methods of Graphical Display of a Data Matrix" (English translation of 1978 doctoral thesis), Department of Statistics and Operations Research, University of South Africa.

Greenacre, Michael J. (1984), *Theory and Application of Correspondence Analysis.* London: Academic Press, Inc.

Grizzle, J. E., Starmer, C. F. & Koch, G. G. (1969), "Analysis of Categorical Data by Linear Models," *Biometrics,* 25 (September), 489–504.

Guttman, Louis (1941), "The Quantification of a Class of Attributes: A Theory and Method of Scale Construction," in *Prediction of Personal Adjustment,* The Committee on Social Adjustment, ed. New York: Social Science Research Council, 319–48.

Hayashi, C. (1950), "On the Quantification of Qualitative Data from the Mathematico-Statistical Point of View," *Annals of the Institute of Statistical Mathematics,* 2 (1), 35–47.

Hayashi, C. (1952), "On the Prediction of

Phenomena from Qualitative Data and the Quantification of Qualitative Data from the Mathematico-Statistical Point of View," *Annals of the Institute of Statistical Mathematics,* 3 (2), 69–98.

Hayashi, C. (1954), "Multidimensional Quantification—with the Applications to Analysis of Social Phenomena," *Annals of the Institute of Statistical Mathematics,* 5 (2), 121–43.

Heiser, Willem J. (1981), *Unfolding Analysis of Proximity Data.* Leiden, The Netherlands: Department of Data Theory, University of Leiden.

Hill, M. O. (1974), "Correspondence Analysis: A Neglected Multivariate Method," *Applied Statistics,* 23 (3), 340–54.

Hirschfeld, H. O. (1935), "A Connection Between Correlation and Contingency," *Proceedings of the Cambridge Philosophical Society,* 31 (October), 520–4.

Holbrook, Morris B., Moore, William L., & Winer, Russell S. (1982), "Constructing Joint Spaces from Pick-Any Data: A New Tool for Consumer Analysis," *Journal of Consumer Research,* 9 (June), 99–105.

Horst, Paul (1935), "Measuring Complex Attitudes," *Journal of Social Psychology,* 6 (3), 369–74.

Jambu, M., & Lebeaux, M-O. (1983), *Cluster Analysis and Data Analysis.* Amsterdam: North Holland Publishing Company.

Kruskal, Joseph B., & Wish, Myron (1978), *Multidimensional Scaling,* Sage University Paper Series on Quantitative Applications in the Social Sciences, 07-011. Beverly Hills, CA: Sage Publications, Inc.

Lebart, Ludovic (1976), "The Significance of Eigenvalues Issued from Correspondence Analysis," *Proceedings in Computational Statistics (COMPSTAT).* Vienna: Physica Verlag, 38–45.

Lebart, Ludovic, & Morineau, Alain (1982), "SPAD: A System of FORTRAN Programs for Correspondence Analysis," *Journal of Marketing Research,* 19 (November), 608–9.

Lebart, Ludovic, & Morineau, Alain, and Warwick, Kenneth M. (1984), *Multivariate Descriptive Statistical Analysis: Correspondence Analysis and Related Techniques for Large Matrices.* New York: John Wiley & Sons, Inc.

Levine, Joel H. (1979), "Joint-Space Analysis of 'Pick-Any' Data: Analysis of Choices from an Unconstrained Set of Alternatives," *Psychometrika,* 44 (March), 85–92.

Marc, Marcel (1973), "Some Practical Uses of 'The Factorial Analysis of Correspondence,'" *European Research,* 1 (July), 2–8.

McKeon, J. J. (1966), "Canonical Analysis: Some Relations Between Canonical Correlation, Factor Analysis, Discriminant Function Analysis and Scaling Theory," *Psychometrika,* Monograph No. 13.

Nishisato, Shizuhiko (1980), *Analysis of Categorical Data: Dual Scaling and Its Applications.* Toronto: University of Toronto Press.

Nishisato, Shizuhiko, & Nishisato, Ira (1983), *An Introduction to Dual Scaling,* 1st ed. Islington, Ontario: MicroStats.

Nishisato, Shizuhiko, & Sheu, Wen-Jenn (1984), "A Note on Dual Scaling of Successive Categories Data," *Psychometrika,* 49 (December), 493–500.

Perreault, William D., Jr., & Young, Forrest W. (1980), "Alternating Least Squares Optimal Scaling: Analysis of Nonmetric Data in Marketing Research," *Journal of Marketing Research,* 17 (February), 1–13.

Richardson, M., & Kuder, G. F. (1933), "Making a Rating Scale That Measures," *Personnel Journal,* 12 (June), 36–40.

SAS Institute (1982), *SAS User's Guide: Statistics.* Cary, NC: SAS Institute Inc.

Schiffman, Susan S., Reynolds, M. Lance, and Young, Forrest W. (1981), *Introduction to Multidimensional Scaling.* New York: Academic Press, Inc.

Seber, G. A. F. (1984), *Multivariate Observations.* New York: John Wiley & Sons, Inc.

Tenenhaus, Michel, & Young, Forrest W. (1985), "An Analysis and Synthesis of Multiple Correspondence Analysis, Optimal Scaling, Dual Scaling, Homogeneity Analysis and Other Methods for Quantifying Categorical Multivariate Data," *Psychometrika,* 50 (March), 91–119.

Tukey, John W. (1977), *Exploratory Data Analysis,* Reading, MA: Addison-Wesley Publishing Company, Inc.

van der Heijden, Peter G. M., & de Leeuw, Jan (1985), "Correspondence Analysis Used Complementary to Loglinear Analysis," *Psychometrika,* 50 (December), 429–47.

van Rijckevorsel, Jan, & de Leeuw, Jan (1978), "An Outline to HOMALS-1," Department of Data Theory, Faculty of Social Sciences, University of Leiden, The Netherlands.

COMPARING INTERPOINT DISTANCES IN CORRESPONDENCE ANALYSIS: A CLARIFICATION J. Douglas Carroll, *Bell Laboratories*; Paul E. Green, *University of Pennsylvania*; and Catherine M. Schaffer, *University of Pennsylvania*

Subsequent to the publication of our correspondence analysis article [Carroll, Green, and Schaffer, 1986], we have received a number of letters from industry practitioners, indicating that their computer programs appear to produce plots like those of Figures 2 and 4 in our original paper. The programs referred to are drawn from a number of commercially available packages, as cited by Hoffman and Franke (1986). Clearly, some clarification is needed.

The problem is easily laid to rest when one notes that there is a third type of scaling that appears to be popular in commercial computer packages. Unlike the expositions by Van der Heijden and de Leeuw (1985), Gifi (1981) or Gower (1981), researchers from the "French school" [for example, Greenacre, 1984; Lebart, Morineau, and Warwick, 1984], prefer to apply the matrix of singular values to *both* the P and O orthonormal sections so that our earlier equations (3) and (4), originally expressed as

$$(1) \qquad X = R^{-1/2}P\Delta$$

$$(2) \qquad Y = C^{-1/2}Q$$

now become

$$(3) \qquad X = R^{-1/2}P\Delta$$

$$(4) \qquad \mathring{Y} = C^{-1/2}Q\Delta$$

(*Note*: This is our original equation (11).)

In this case, $\mathring{Y}$ is *not* considered in the sense of Benzécri's barycentric coordinates. Rather, what we now have are two separate distance-based, within-set scalings, plotted in the *same* space.

Greenacre (1984) describes the motivation for this procedure in the following way:

> There are advantages and disadvantages of this simultaneous display. Clearly an advantage is the very concise graphical display expressing a number of different features of the data in a single picture. The display of each cloud of points indicates the nature of similarities and dispersion within the cloud, while the joint display indicates the correspondence between clouds. Notice, however, that we should avoid the danger of interpreting distances between points of different clouds, since no such distances have been explicitly defined. Distances between points within the same cloud are defined in terms of the relevant chi-square distance, while the between-cloud correspondence is governed by the barycentric nature of the transition formulae [p. 65].

Greenacre, however, does mention the existence of the scaling (described in equations (3) and (4) of our original paper) on pp. 93–95 of his text. He points out the following:

> By an *asymmetric display* we mean that the standardizations imposed on the two sets of points is different. Most commonly, one of the sets is represented in principal coordinates while the other is represented in standard coordinates. The transition for-

---

From J. Douglas Carroll, Paul E. Green, and Catherine M. Schaffer, "Comparing Interpoint Distances in Correspondence Analysis: A Clarification," *Journal of Marketing Research*, Vol. XXIV, November 1987. Reprinted by permission of the publisher, American Marketing Association.

mulae between these points are then asymmetric, as is the interpretation of the display [p. 94].

By *principal* coordinates Greenacre means equation (1), above; by *standard* coordinates he means equation (2), above. In any case, the basis for adopting this type of scaling is purely *pragmatic*—better balanced displays appear in the resulting joint space. As Greenacre continues to point out,

> In a principal axes display of the rows, say, in principal coordinates and the columns in standard coordinates, the row points are exactly at barycentres of the column points, where the barycentric weights are the elements of the respective row profiles. This might be advantageous in some practical situations, especially if the principal inertias are fairly high. (When they are low the display in principal coordinates is much smaller than the display in standard coordinates.) [p. 94]

By *principal inertias*, Greenacre refers to the squared singular values.

THE EXAMPLES IN THE CARROLL, GREEN, AND SCHAFFER PAPER

Two examples (one hypothetical and one based on real data) were used in our earlier paper. In both cases the first and second singular values did not differ markedly from each other (for example, in the ratio of 5:1 or higher).

Given the relative closeness between the two sets of first and second singular values, it is not surprising that our industry correspondents found fairly close *visual* agreement with the plots of Figures 2 and 4 in our original paper. This is simply due to the specific data sets that were analyzed. While our scaling and that preferred by Greenacre (p. 65) differ by a diagonal transformation, in general, it will *not* be a scalar transformation.

A COMPARISON OF THE THREE SCALINGS

It would seem to be of interest to show how the three scalings

I. $X = R^{-1/2}P\Delta$; $Y = C^{-1/2}Q$
   (CGS's original equations 3 and 4)

II. $X = R^{-1/2}P(\Delta + I)^{1/2}$;
    $Y = C^{-1/2}Q(\Delta + I)^{1/2}$
    (CGS's original equations (14) and (15), derived from their pseudo-contingency table approach)

III. $\hat{X} = R^{-1/2}P\Delta$; $\hat{Y} = C^{-1/2}Q\Delta$
    (as implied by Greenacre's text, p. 65)

differ in a well-known illustration. While we did not find a dramatic case of disparate singular values, Greenacre's text does provide a useful and easily accessed example (Table 3.1 on p. 55).

For ease of reference his frequency table is reproduced here (see Table 8–6). In this sample problem the first two singular values, 0.2734 and 0.1001, are reasonably (but not dramatically) disparate. Together they account for 99.5 percent of the total inertia; the third singular value (0.0203) is quite small and accounts for only 0.5 percent of the total inertia.

Table 8–7 shows the two-dimensional coordinates for each of the three scaling options. As noted, Option I differs dramatically from the other two options. Option II (based on the pseudocontingency table approach) effectively "stretches" the vertical axis so that the resulting configuration is more spherical than Greenacre's Option III. The configurations of Options III and II are related by the diagonal transformation

$$(5) \quad \frac{(\Delta + I)^{\frac{1}{2}}}{\Delta} = \begin{bmatrix} \dfrac{(1.2734)^{1/2}}{0.2734} & 0 \\ 0 & \dfrac{(1.001)^{1/2}}{0.1001} \end{bmatrix}$$

$$= \begin{bmatrix} 4.1 & 0 \\ 0 & 10.5 \end{bmatrix}$$

_____ *Table 8–6*_____

Greenacre's Sample Frequency Table (Artificial Data)

| | Smoking Category | | | | Row |
	None	Light	Medium	Heavy	Totals
Senior managers	4	2	3	2	11
Junior managers	4	3	7	4	18
Senior employees	25	10	12	4	51
Junior employees	18	24	33	13	88
Secretaries	10	6	7	2	25
Column Totals	61	45	62	25	193

Axis 2 is stretched by 10.5 while axis 1 is stretched by only 4.1, (a ratio of 2.6) in proceeding from Option III to Option II.

Figure 8–3 shows the configuration for Option I. As noted, the four points representing the columns of Table 8–6 are highly stretched relative to the five points representing the rows of Table 8–6. Only the row points can be compared in terms of (squared) interpoint distances.

Figure 8–4 shows the configurations for Options II and III; the plots are placed on the same chart for ease of comparison. (In order to do this, the horizontal (X) axis coordinates of Option II have been adjusted to equal those of Option III.) As noted, the projections of both options on the horizontal axis are the same.

Such is not the case for the vertical (Y) axis, however. We note that Option II stretches the vertical axis considerably greater than Option III. In accord with Greenacre's comments, in the case of Option III (squared) distance comparisons are permissible for both row points and column points separately, but between-set distances are not meaningful. In the CGS formulation (Option II) all (squared)

_____ *Table 8–7*_____

Two-Dimensional Coordinates for Each of the Three Scaling Options

| Plotting Labels | Option I | | Option II | | Option III | |
	X Value	Y Value	X Value	Y Value	X value	Y Value
Sen Mgr	0.066	−0.194	0.066	−0.493	0.066	−0.194
Jun Mgr	−0.259	−0.243	−0.259	−0.620	−0.259	−0.243
Sen Emp	0.381	−0.011	0.381	−0.027	0.381	−0.011
Jun Emp	−0.233	0.058	−0.233	0.147	−0.233	0.058
Secretaries	0.201	0.078	0.201	0.201	0.201	0.078
NONE	1.437	−0.309	0.393	−0.078	0.393	−0.031
LIGHT	−0.366	1.409	−0.100	0.359	−0.100	0.141
MEDIUM	−0.717	0.070	−0.196	0.019	−0.196	0.007
HEAVY	−1.075	−1.078	−0.294	−0.503	−0.294	−0.198

_____ *Figure 8–3* _____

Sample Problem Configuration Based on Option I

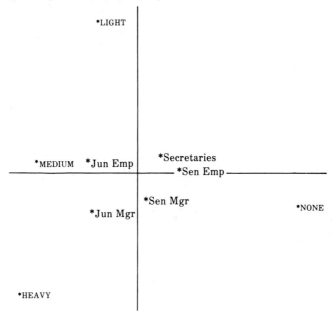

_____ *Figure 8–4* _____

Sample Problem Configuration Based on Options II and III

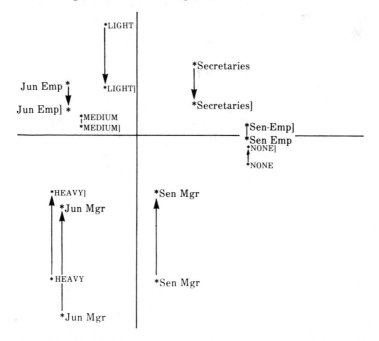

interpoint distances are comparable, both within-set and between-set.

How is the configuration of Option III (Figure 8–4) interpreted? Greenacre first projects all nine points onto the horizontal axis (his Figure 3.4 on p. 69). While the first axis represents only an approximate view of the higher-dimension solution, Greenacre notes that the first axis accounts for 87.8 percent of the total inertia. He also notes that the first axis separates smokers (on the left) from nonsmokers (on the right). Greenacre computes contributions of each point to the total inertia and observes that senior and junior employees contribute over 80 percent of the row-profile inertia while the NONE category contributes 65 percent (itself) to the column-profile inertia (p. 67). He notes that the first axis correctly lines up the five employee groups in terms of their lightness of smoking (left to right) and that the three smoking categories' projections (HEAVY, MEDIUM, and LIGHT) are well separated from the NONE point projection. Greenacre does not provide a separate interpretation for the vertical axis.

In the case of Option II, we note that the same interpretation of the first axis is appropriate, since the points project at the same positions as those of Option III. Moreover, since *all* distances are comparable on this axis, we observe that Senior Employees are very close to NONE followed by Secretaries and Senior Managers. Insofar as HEAVY (smoking) is concerned, Junior Managers represent the closest point, followed by Junior Employees. The point representing LIGHT is not close to any of the five employee groups and is approximately equidistant from Junior Employees and Senior Managers.

Neither Greenacre nor we attempt to interpret the vertical axis; we note that it accounts for only 11.7 percent of the total inertia (while the third axis, not shown, accounts for a minuscule 0.5 percent). However, as illustrated above, our in-

terpretation of axis 1 includes comments on interset distances (employee groups versus categories of smoking), in addition to intraset distances. In contrast, Greenacre's interpretation is restricted to separate intraset comments for each of the two sets of points.

CONCLUSIONS

In summary, depending on what one wishes to do with the matrix of singular values, one could have the representations:

(a) $X = R^{-1/2}P$; $Y = C^{-1/2}Q$
     (both in standard coordinates)

(b) $X = R^{-1/2}P\Delta$; $Y = C^{-1/2}Q$
     (X in principal coordinates; Y in standard coordinates)

(c) $X = R^{-1/2}P$; $Y = C^{-1/2}Q\Delta$
     (X in standard coordinates; Y in principal coordinates)

(d) $X = R^{-1/2}P\Delta$; $Y = C^{-1/2}Q\Delta$
     (both in principal coordinates)

(e) $X = R^{-1/2}P\Delta^{1/2}$; $Y = C^{-1/2}Q\Delta^{1/2}$
     (a splitting of the diagonal matrix of singular values between X and Y)

(f) $X = R^{-1/2}P(\Delta + I)^{1/2}$
     $Y = C^{-1/2}Q(\Delta + I)^{1/2}$
     (the CGS scaling)

From a practical standpoint, it would seem that representations (d), used by the French "school," and (f), suggested by CGS, are the most useful. As discussed above, representation (d), or Option III, constrains the interpretation to separate within-set (squared) distance comparisons, while representation (f), or Option II, does not.

It seems to us that in most practical situations the more casual observer of such configurations will (consciously or not) be prone to interpret *all* distances as comparable, researcher admonitions to the contrary. Only Option II allows this to be done, according to the assumptions described in the CGS proposal.[1]

Whether or not the CGS scaling departs markedly from that used by the French "school" is an empirical matter. If singular values are almost equal, the configurations will look almost the same. But if the first singular value is considerably greater than the second, and so forth, the results can look quite different. In this case, the CGS scaling (Option II) will look more "spherical" than the configuration obtained from Option III.

---

[1]As suggested by a *JMR* reviewer, the reader should be reminded that a two-dimensional representation is considered here for ease of presentation and that the third principal inertia in Greenacre's sample problem is quite small. In other situations, higher-dimensional solutions may be required. As such, lower dimensional representations are only approximations of the (squared) interpoint distances.

REFERENCES

Carroll, J. Douglas, Green, Paul E., & Schaffer, Catherine M. (1986), "Interpoint Distance Comparisons in Correspondence Analysis," *Journal of Marketing Research,* 23 (August), 271–80.

Gifi, A. (1981), *Non-Linear Multivariate Analysis*. Leiden, The Netherlands: Department of Data Theory, University of Leiden.

Gower, J. C., & Digby, P. G. N. (1981), "Expressing Complex Relationships in Two Dimensions," in *Interpreting Multivariate Data,* V. Barnett, ed. Chichester, UK: John Wiley & Sons, Inc., 83–118.

Greenacre, Michael J. (1984), *Theory and Application of Correspondence Analysis*. London: Academic Press, Inc.

Hoffman, Donna L., & Franke, George R. (1986), "Correspondence Analysis: Graphical Representation of Categorical Data in Marketing Research," *Journal of Marketing Research,* 23 (August), 213–27.

Lebart, Ludovic, Morineau, Alain, and Warwick, Kenneth M. (1984), *Multivariate Descriptive Statistical Analysis: Correspondence Analysis and Related Techniques for Large Matrices*. New York: John Wiley & Sons, Inc.

van der Heijden, & de Leeuw, Jan (1985), "Correspondence Analysis Used Complementary to loglinear Analysis," *Psychometrika* (December), 429–48.

PART IV

SOFTWARE APPLICATIONS AND INTERPRETATIONS

A Short Guide to MDPREF: Multidimensional Analysis of Preference Data

Jih Jie Chang and J. Douglas Carroll, Bell Laboratories

NONTECHNICAL INTRODUCTION MDPREF is a program for analysis of preferences. The analysis is usually conducted on a matrix of averaged preference evaluations that have been derived by aggregating preference evaluations for respondents. This data would most often show the average preference for the total sample, or subsample of subjects that we were interested in.

MDPREF analyzes a subject × stimuli matrix containing the preference data. In this situation, the term subject does not necessarily refer to people. Most often we are analyzing a matrix of average preferences for a set of brands that are evaluated on a set of attributes. Again, this attribute by brand matrix contains the average preference evaluations.

Using the nomenclature of MDPREF, the input data matrix is defined as having subjects (rows), which are often defined as attributes that describe the stimuli (columns), which are often brands. In an application that does not involve the attribute-brand matrix, the subjects could take on any number of forms, but are usually attributes descriptive of the stimuli (groups, entities, items) defined by the columns.

MDPREF is what is known as a vector model. This means that the objective of the MDPREF analysis is to identify a perceptual map displaying subject (attribute) vectors. The vector model assumes a linear model such that preference is greatest at the end of the subject vector, and infinitely better as one moves an infinite distance along the vector. To form the subject vectors visually, lines are drawn from the origin of the plot to each subject point. Next, the stimuli (brand) points are plotted by MDPREF. Each stimulus point projects (at a 90 degree angle to the vector) onto each subject vector. This projection shows the average subjects' metric preference of the stimuli with respect to the subject vectors.

The MDPREF program was written by J. D. Carroll and J. J. Chang of Bell Laboratories. This guide is a revision of their paper, made by Scott M. Smith for the PC version of MDPREF. MDPREF copyright 1970 Bell Telephone Laboratories, Incorporated, reprinted by permission.

Operationally, preferences may be measured as a simple ranking (1–8 if 8 items are ranked on attribute 1), or on an evaluative scale.

MDPREF is designed to do multidimensional scaling of preference or evaluation data. MDPREF is a metric model based on a principal components analysis (Eckart-Young decomposition). In this analysis, a data matrix of dimension i subjects by j stimuli is decomposed into two smaller matrices, each of which approximates the original data matrix in a least-squares sense.

The first of these resulting matrices is called a principal component score (or factor score) matrix of size $(i \times r)$, where r is the number of principal components. This matrix depicts the i subjects in the r principal component dimensions and is designated [PCS].

The second matrix is called the principal component loading matrix (or factor-loading matrix), and is of size $(r \times j)$. This matrix depicts the j stimuli in the r principal component dimensions and is designated as [PCL].

THE MDPREF APPROACH   The original MDPREF program recognized two forms of input: paired comparisons data and stimuli evaluation data. The PC-MDS version of MDPREF has deleted the paired comparisons data option because of the infrequent collection and use of such data. Originally it was from the paired-comparison matrices, that MDPREF derived a single matrix called the "first score matrix" of dimension i rows and j columns. In the PC version of MDPREF, the first score matrix is the data matrix input by the user, and is designated S*. Each cell of the S* matrix contains a numerical entry (i,j), which represents the ith subject's rating of the j-th stimuli, as measured by the researcher's survey instrument.

The "first score matrix," which again is a subject by stimuli matrix of evaluation scores, is decomposed into r dimensions or principal components. The first score matrix is additionally used to produce the [PCS] and [PCL] matrices discussed above. Subsequent to this analysis, a second score matrix is produced, having dimensions $(i \times j)$. The second score matrix contains derived projections of stimuli onto subject vectors. The values of the second score matrix agree as near as possible, in a least-squares sense, with the first scores matrix.

MDPREF is valued as an analytical procedure because the resulting values in the [PCS] and [PCL] matrices project the stimuli onto subject vectors within the multidimensional stimuli attribute space. This multidimensional space allows for visual evaluation of the j stimuli, an r dimensional space, where $r < j$.

INPUT PARAMETERS

Input Parameters and Input File Arrangement   The commands must be provided in sequence given below. Each step refers to one line image, or several related images. To read in a data matrix, each row must begin a new image, but may continue on several consecutive lines if necessary.

Parameter Line   Free format.

Parameters and Options

NP = Number of people (Max. NP = 12)

NS = Number of stimuli (Max. NS = 12)

NF = Number of factors (or dimensions)
     NF must be ≤ minimum of NP or NS.

NPF = Number of factors to be plotted
      (NPF must be ≤ NF)

IREAD = 1 Read in the first score matrix (S*),
        which must have NP rows and NS cols. Each row of S^*
        will be normalized by subtracting the row mean.

      = 2 Same as IREAD = 1, except in addition
        each row of S^* will be divided by the
        standard deviation of values in the row

NORP = 0 Normalize subject vectors
     = 1 Do not normalize

Format for Reading the First Score Matrix   The second line in the setup must contain a format statement for reading in the first score matrix. The format statement is read as a string of 80 characters.

Data Images   Next comes the data for the first score matrix. The first score matrix must be entered as an NP by NS matrix, where each subject begins a new line.

SAMPLE MDPREF OUTPUT

```
                    M D P R E F
        MULTIDIMENSIONAL ANALYSIS OF PREFERENCE DATA
     PROGRAM WRITTEN BY DR. J. D. CARROLL AND JIH JIE CHANG
                    PC - MDS VERSION
ANALYSIS TITLE: POP DATA ATTRIBUTE BY BRANDS IN 2 DIMENSIONS
DATA IS READ FROM FILE: ATTXBR.POP
OUTPUT FILE IS: ATTXBR.PRN


NP (NO. OF SUBJECTS)                                      8
NS (NO. OF STIMULI)                                      10
NF (NO. OF DIMENSIONS)                                    2
NFP (NO. OF DIMENSIONS PLOTTED)                           2

IREAD  1=NP X NS SCORE MATRIX WITH ROW MEAN SUBTRACTED    1
       2=SAME AS 1 WITH SCORES DIVIDED BY ROW S. D.

NORP   0=NORMALIZE SUBJ. VECTORS                          0
       1=DO NOT

     *****IDENTIFICATION KEY FOR PLOTS WITH IDENTIFIED POINTS*****

PT #   1   2   3   4   5   6   7   8   9  10  11  12  13  14  15
CHAR   1   2   3   4   5   6   7   8   9   A   B   C   D   E   F

PT #  16  17  18  19  20  21  22  23  24  25  26  27  28  29  30
CHAR   G   H   I   J   K   L   M   N   O   P   Q   R   S   T   U

PT #  31  32  33  34  35  36  37  38  39  40  41  42  43  44  45
CHAR   V   W   X   Y   Z   +   /   =   *   &   $   @   %   ?   <

PT #  46  47  48  49  50
CHAR   (   )   "   ;   @
POINT NUMBERS ABOVE 50 IDENTIFIED AS  >, MULTIPLE POINTS IDENTIFIED AS  #

IN JOINT SPACE PLOTS, THE FIRST  10 POINTS ARE STIMULI
   AND THE NEXT   8 POINTS ARE SUBJECTS

INPUT FORMAT = (10F6.3)


             MEAN OF THE RAW SCORES  (BY SUBJECT)
       4.4543      4.4624      4.3913      4.4703      4.4666    4.4107
       4.4561      4.4860

             FIRST SCORE MATRIX   (SUBJECT  BY  STIMULUS)
  1    1.3347      2.0367      1.3527     -1.5423      -.1563    -.4193
       1.2827     -3.0683      .7737     -1.5943
  .
  .
  .
  .
  8   -1.4160     -1.7670      .2510      1.8470      1.8300    -.2400
      -1.3980      .5840       .6370      -.3280
```

INPUT DATA: 8 ATTRIBUTES X 10 BRANDS
```
 8 10   2   2   1   0
(10F6.3)
5.789 6.491 5.807 2.912 4.298 4.035 5.737 .....
3.421 3.895 4.877 5.667 4.930 4.368 3.140 .....
4.684 5.579 3.368 3.474 3.632 5.404 4.614 .....
3.316 4.246 5.018 6.088 6.228 4.474 2.719 .....
4.561 4.193 5.561 5.088 5.526 4.772 4.158 .....
3.351 2.211 4.053 5.860 6.316 5.105 2.246 .....
3.947 3.702 5.281 5.211 5.614 4.895 3.719 .....
3.070 2.719 4.737 6.333 6.316 4.246 3.088 .....
```

INPUT SPECIFICATIONS:
8 = NUMBER OF SUBJECTS (ATTRIBUTE VECTORS)
10 = NUMBER OF STIMULI (BRANDS)
The parameters call for a 2 dimensional principal components solution. Two dimensions will be plotted.

The data form and normalization option are specified.

Codes for reading the two dimensional plots.

Mean of the subject variables. These are the row variables. In the example the means of each of the 8 attributes are given.

The original data matrix values minus the subject (row) mean. (i.e., 1.3347 = 5.789-4.4543)

The first score matrix is a preference score matrix, where each entry is the preference rating made by the ith subject on the jth stimulus. The first score matrix is decomposed by MDPREF into NF dimensions.

	CROSS PRODUCT MATRIX OF SUBJECTS					
1	24.5385	-6.2786	.7973	-1.8374	7.8784	-14.3155
	.6241	-10.7526				
.						
.						
8	-10.7526	8.6405	-6.5557	11.2627	4.1261	15.7736
	7.3943	14.8171				

The cross products matrix is an intermediate matrix used in the computation of the subject x subject (attribute x attribute) correlation matrix.

	CORRELATION MATRIX OF SUBJECTS					
1	1.0000	-.4985	.0680	-.1042	.5223	-.6536
	.0475	-.5639				
.						
.						
8	-.5639	.8829	-.7200	.8223	.3520	.9268
	.7249	1.0000				

The subject x subject (attribute x attribute) correlation matrix is used as the basis for computing the underlying dimensionality of the data matrix.

	CROSS PRODUCT MATRIX OF STIMULI					
1	7.6801	9.1070	.1489	-9.9256	-8.0465	-.7597
	9.7955	-5.9361	-3.1618	1.0983		
.						
.						
10	1.0983	.5196	-6.0104	-3.2425	-6.6664	-.5405
	3.3761	7.9758	-5.5578	9.0480		

The eigenvalues or characteristic roots of the principal components factor analysis. For principal components analysis, the eigenvalues equal the sum of the squared correlations (squared loadings of the subjects (attributes) on the stimuli (brands). In other words, this is the sum of the r squareds and shows the amount of variance accounted for by each component or dimension underlying the principal components factor analysis.

	ROOTS OF THE FIRST SCORE MATRIX					
	62.5203	30.2225	3.3362	2.0768	.9772	.5864
	.1766	.0212				

PROPORTION OF VARIANCE ACCOUNTED FOR BY EACH FACTOR	
1	2
.6257	.3025

The proportion of variance accounted for by dimensions one and two shows that 62.57% of all variance is accounted for by dimension one and 32.25% of variance is accounted for by dimension two.

CUMULATIVE PROPORTION OF VARIANCE ACCOUNTED FOR	
1	2
.6257	.9282

The cumulative sum of variance accounted for shows that 92.82% of all preference variance is accounted for by the first two dimensions.

	SECOND SCORE MATRIX	(SUBJECT	BY	STIMULUS)		
1	.2667	.3995	.2930	-.2647	-.0529	-.0627
	.2813	-.6385	.1074	-.3291		
.						
.						
8	-.3323	-.4352	.0518	.4608	.4299	.0421
	-.4577	.1791	.1969	-.1354		

The second score matrix is the derived projection of stimuli (brands) onto subject (attribute) vectors. This is as nearly proportional as possible to the first score matrix.

```
POPULATION MATRIX
FACTOR
    1      .6091      .7931
    2     -.9974      .0726
    3      .8406     -.5416
    4     -.8559      .5172
    5     -.3318      .9434
    6     -.9953     -.0972
    7     -.7584      .6518
    8     -.9989      .0460
```

The population matrix is the dimension 1 and 2 plot coordinates of subjects (attributes) vectors.
The coordinates of the subject vectors are on the unit circle (Euclidean distance from origin = 1.0).

```
STIMULUS MATRIX (NORMALIZED)
FACTOR
    1      .3362      .0781
    2      .4431      .1634
    3     -.0336      .3953
    4     -.4604      .0198
    5     -.4186      .2549
    6     -.0442     -.0451
    7      .4583      .0027
    8     -.2090     -.6446
    9     -.1843      .2769
   10      .1125     -.5013
```

The coordinates of ten stimuli (brands) on dimensions 1 and 2. These are the coordinates used in graphs 2 and 3.

```
STIMULUS MATRIX (STRETCHED BY SQ. ROOT OF THE EIGENVALUES)
FACTOR
    1     2.6584      .4291
    2     3.5039      .8983
    3     -.2659     2.1731
    4    -3.6401      .1090
    5    -3.3101     1.4012
    6     -.3496     -.2480
    7     3.6236      .0146
    8    -1.6522    -3.5437
    9    -1.4575     1.5225
   10      .8893    -2.7561
```

By stretching the stimuli (brands) relative to the square root of the eigenvalues, the scales are weighted for the amount of variance explained by each dimension (analogy: to weighting by importance). This matrix is not included in the plots.

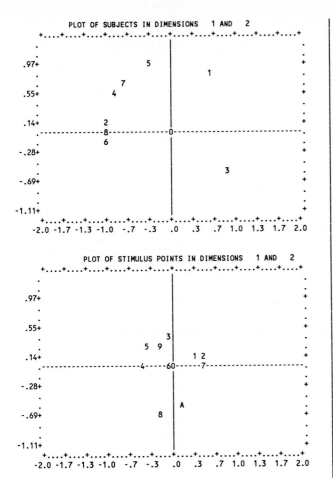

PLOT OF SUBJECTS IN DIMENSIONS   1 AND   2

1-8 = 8 Subjects (attributes)

PLOT OF STIMULUS POINTS IN DIMENSIONS   1 AND   2

1-9 + A = 10 Stimuli (brands)
B - I = 8 subjects (attribute) vectors

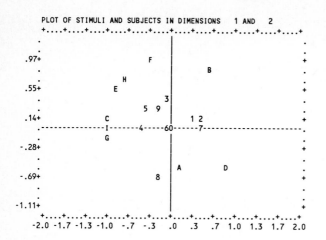

PLOT OF STIMULI AND SUBJECTS IN DIMENSIONS   1 AND   2

1-9 + A = 10 Stimuli (brands)

The projection of stimuli (brands) on
each subject vector is as similar
as possible to the order of preference
expressed by the subject in the
original preference data.

How to Use INDSCAL:
A Computer Program for
Canonical Decomposition of N-Way
Tables and Individual Differences
in Multidimensional Scaling

Jih Jie Chang and J. Douglas Carroll, Bell Laboratories

NONTECHNICAL INTRODUCTION INDSCAL is a program designed for the analysis of individual differences of two or more subjects. INDSCAL does not analyze data for a single subject. INDSCAL requires as input, a separate data matrix for each subject. Broadly defined, a subject may be an actual individual, or a group of individuals aggregated together because of some common characteristic.

INDSCAL performs two types of analysis: an analysis of individual differences and a canonical decomposition analysis. The analysis of individual differences identifies weights that each subject uses to evaluate the stimuli. The stimuli are identified in terms of a set of underlying dimensions that are common to all subjects. In the individual differences analysis, the canonical decomposition analysis is used to identify the perceptual dimensions underlying the stimulus space.

It should be noted that a separate canonical decomposition analysis may be performed. In this case, rectangular data matrices may be analyzed, identifying the underlying dimensions of each of the n-dimensional input matrices.

When performing individual differences analysis, INDSCAL input data is generally of some type of similarity or dissimilarity data. The analysis may be conducted on lower-half or full symmetric matrices. The lower-half matrices may be either similarity, dissimilarity, Euclidean distance, correlation, or covariance measures. The full matrices may be read in as either similarity or dissimilarity measures.

The INDSCAL program was written by J. D. Carroll and J. J. Chang of Bell Laboratories. This guide is a revision of their paper, made by Scott M. Smith for the PC version of INDSCAL.

INDSCAL performs an n-way analysis. The $n =$ three-way analysis is by far the most common. In this situation, n_2 and n_3 define the n_2 by n_3 matrix of similarity judgments, and n_1 defines the number of slices in this three-dimensional matrix. Slices are here defined as respondents or respondent groups.

The INDSCAL solution identifies the underlying dimensions common to the stimuli. The importance of each dimension is reported. Plots of the importance weights used by the individuals in evaluating the stimuli are produced. Also produced are plots of the stimuli in the underlying dimensional space. Plots of the individuals are not produced, but the plot coordinates for the individuals are easy to compute and could be easily graphed in a program such as Lotus 1–2–3.

TECHNICAL INTRODUCTION

INDSCAL is a computer program capable of performing two kinds of analyses, namely, CANDECOMP analysis and INDIFF analysis.

Before going into a more detailed description, it is essential to clarify the relationship of these two analyses. CANDECOMP is used for the more general analysis called canonical decomposition of N-way tables, while INDIFF performs the analysis of individual differences in multidimensional scaling described by Carroll and Chang (1968). Nevertheless, CANDECOMP actually forms the core of INDIFF analysis. By using the appropriate options provided in the program, the user is able to use INDSCAL to do either CANDECOMP or INDIFF analysis. In the ensuing paragraphs, there will be no mention of their specific names when the description applies to both analyses.

CANDECOMP is a method for decomposing arbitrary N-way tables into a kind of product of N matrices of appropriate dimensions. The N-way tables are assumed to have $n_1, n_2, \ldots n_N$ components respectively, where N is less than or equal to 7 (as presently programmed). The N matrices, into which this N-way table is decomposed, will be of the order $r \times n_1, r \times n_2, \ldots, r \times n_N$, respectively, where r is the common dimensionality of the several spaces defined by the matrices CANDECOMP takes as input rectangular data matrices.

INDIFF uses the CANDECOMP method to do individual differences analysis. In this case, the input may be the square matrices of similarities, dissimilarities, Euclidean distances, or scalar product matrices. If any one of the first three serves as input, an early step is to convert the data to scalar products.

INDIFF treats the first of the N matrices into which the N-way table is decomposed as the subjects' weight matrix and matrices 2 and 3 as stimulus matrices. Matrices 2 and 3 should asymptotically be equal. In practice, matrix 2 is set equal to matrix 3 as a last step and the other matrices $(1, 4, \ldots N)$ are recomputed accordingly. The output of INDSCAL consists of the N matrices resulting from the analysis. In addition, plots for each pair of the dimensions in each matrix are generated showing the ni points (where $i = 1, \ldots, N$) in r dimensions.

Input Data Structure CANDECOMP Analysis

Let $n_1, n_2, \ldots n_N$ be respectively the number of components in the N-way tables, where N is less than or equal to 7. The data can be viewed as many rectangular matrices (slices) each of order n_2 (rows) by n_3 (columns). A three-way table would correspond to a stack of n_1 matrices (slices). A four-way table would then be composed of n_4 three-way tables as units. In the same manner, we can construct data for higher-way tables.

The n_2 by n_3 slices described above are read in as follows: The first data line (or lines) has n_3 values corresponding to the first row of the first rectangular matrix (slice) in the first n_1 unit; this is followed by the second row and down to the n_2-th row. Each matrix is followed by the next without interruption.

INDIFF Analysis   The data structure for INDIFF is basically the same as in CANDECOMP. However, in the INDIFF case, n_2 and n_3 are ordinarily assumed to be identical, that is, every two-way matrix derived by holding n_1 and $n_4 \ldots n_N$ constant is symmetric.

The n_2 by n_3 matrix may initially be a similarity, dissimilarity, or Euclidean distance matrix. They can be entered in the form of a full symmetric matrix or a lower-half matrix without diagonal. If so, there are options for converting them to scalar product matrices, by equations given in Torgerson (1958) as referred to in Carroll and Chang (1968).

In the most common situation, say a three-way analysis, the n_1 matrices (each of n_2 rows and n_3 columns) will correspond to individuals, and these matrices will be read in one at a time.

INDSCAL OPTIONS

Initial configuration   The analysis starts with $(N - 1)$ sets of matrices. That is, the program requires that the initial matrices 2 through N be either supplied by the user or generated in the program. If to be read in, the I-th matrix must be entered as an $r \times n_I$ matrix, where r is the common dimensionality specified by the user and $I = 2, 3, \ldots N$.

Option on Method of Analysis   Instead of solving for several dimensions simultaneously, the user may choose the option of doing separate one-dimensional analyses, then combining them to form a single r-dimensional analysis. While this results in a less general solution than does the more usual solution, it assures certain orthogonality properties for successive components.

Solution for Weight Matrices for Fixed Stimulus Matrices (INDIFF analysis)   This option is used when the coordinates of N stimulus points in K dimensions have been obtained, say, from some multidimensional scaling procedure and the user would like to find the subjects' weights for this fixed stimulus space.

The program reads in the initial matrices, proceeds with the iterative procedure, solving for the remaining matrices while keeping matrices 2 and 3 unchanged throughout the analysis. In the case of a three-way analysis, this procedure will converge in one iteration; in higher-way cases, more iterations will be required.

Equating the Stimulus Matrices (INDIFF Analysis)   At the end of the iterative procedure, the program provides the option of equating the two stimulus matrices, matrices 2 and 3. It is essential that in the solution space matrix 2 should be identical to 3 if the input data is in the form of a lower-half or full symmetric matrix.

After equating matrices 2 and 3, the iterative procedure continues, but matrices 2 and 3 are kept fixed while the remaining tables are estimated by the iterative procedure (this is similar to the option in 3 for estimating weight matrices with a fixed stimulus matrix, except that the fixed matrix is an internally computed one rather than one provided as input by the user).

Separate Solutions in Spaces of Different Dimensions   On the parameter line if MAXDIM is set to 4 and MINDIM to 1, the program will compute successively in spaces of dimensions 4, 3, 2, and 1. The initial configuration for each successive dimensions is taken from the solution of the previous computation.

PROGRAM INPUT

1. *Initial configuration.* The analysis starts with $(N-1)$ sets of matrices. That is, the program requires that the initial matrices 2 through N be either supplied by the user or generated in the program. If to be read in, the I-th matrix must be entered as an $r \times n_I$ matrix, where r is the common dimensionality specified by the user and $I = 2, 3, \ldots N$.

2. *Option on method of analysis.* Instead of solving for several dimensions simultaneously, the user may choose the option of doing separate one-dimensional analyses, then combining them to form a single r-dimensional analysis. While this results in a less general solution than does the more usual solution, it assures certain orthogonality properties for successive components.

3. *Option allowing solution for weight matrices for fixed stimulus matrices (INDIFF analysis).* This option is used when the coordinates of N stimulus points in K dimensions have been obtained, say, from some multidimensional scaling procedure and the user would like to find the subjects' weights for this fixed stimulus space. The program reads in the initial matrices, proceeds with the iterative procedure solving for the remaining matrices while keeping matrices 2 and 3 unchanged throughout the analysis. In the case of a three-way analysis, this procedure will converge in one iteration; in higher-way cases, more iterations will be required.

4. *Option for equating the two stimulus matrices* (INDIFF *analysis*). At the end of the iterative procedure, the program provides the option of equating the two stimulus matrices, matrices 2 and 3. It is essential that in the solution space matrix 2 should be identical to 3 if the input data is in the form of a lower-half or full symmetric matrix.

After equating matrices 2 and 3, the iterative procedure continues, but matrices 2 and 3 are kept fixed while the remaining tables are estimated by the iterative procedure (this is similar to the option in 3 for estimating weight matrices with a fixed stimulus matrix, except that the fixed matrix is an internally computed one rather than one provided as input by the user).

5. *Option on obtaining separate solutions in spaces of different dimensions.* On the parameter line, if MAXDIM is set to 3 and MINDIM to 1, the program will compute successively in spaces of dimensions 3, 2, and 1. The initial configuration for each successive dimensions is taken from the solution of the previous computation.

INPUT ARRANGEMENT

Line 1   Parameter Specification: Free format is to be used in reading in the 16 parameter variables.

N, MAXDIM, MINDIM, IRDATA, ITMAX, ISET, IOY, IDR, ISAM, IPUNSP, IRN, IVEC, IP, IA, IS, CRIT

N: Number of ways ($N \leq 3$)

MAXDIM: Maximum number of dimensions (Max. = 3)

MINDIM: Minimum number of dimensions (Min. = 1)
MAXDIM must be ≤ 3 or (MAXDIM $*$ Max. N_1) ≤ 300.

IRDATA: 0 = read in an arbitrary N-way table as described
1 = lower-half similarity matrices without diagonal
2 = lower-half dissimilarity matrices w/o diagonal
3 = lower-half Euclidean distance matrices w/o diagonal
4 = lower-half correlation matrices without diagonal
5 = lower-half covariance matrices with diagonal
6 = full symmetric similarity matrices diagonal ignored
7 = full symmetric dissimilarity matrices diagonal ignored

Scalar products are computed except for options 4 and 5. Additive constants are not estimated for options 3, 4, and 5.

ITMAX: Maximum number of iterations. (Max. = 50) Usually from 15 to 20 iterations is sufficient.

ISET: 1 = At the end of the iterative procedure, set matrix 2 equal to matrix 3, proceed to iterate again but keeping matrices 2 and 3 constant.
0 = Do not set matrix 2 equal to matrix 3.

IOY: 1 = Compute all dimensions simultaneously.
               0 = Do separate one-dimensional solutions.

IDR: 1 = Compute correlations between data and solution
                  for each n_2 by n_3 matrix.

ISAM: 1 = Keep matrices 2 and 3 unchanged and solve for the
                  remaining matrices.
               0 = Solve for all matrices.

IPUNSP: 1 = Output to a file the scalar product matrices.
               0 = Do not output the scalar product matrices.

IRN: 0 = Read in the initial matrices 2 to N.
                  An eight-digit integer for generating the random
                  initial matrices (must be in single quotes).

IVEC: 0 = Read standard data matrix (preferred option).
               1 = The program will read Tricon-type output.

IP: 0 = Do not output normalized A matrices to disk file.
               1 = Yes, output normalized A matrices for a disk file.

IA: 0 = Do not output original data to the output file.
               1 = Yes, output original data to the output file.

IS: 0 = Do not print intermediate matrices (preferred).
               1 = Yes, print intermediate matrices.

CRIT   The criterion for terminating the iterative computation is entered in (F 7.5) format. If $[y - y(I-1)]^2 - [y - y(I)]^2 < \text{CRIT}$ iteration stops, where $y(I)$ stands for estimated y's on I-th iteration.

Line 2 NWT(1), NWT(2)...NWT(N)   The number of objects must be entered in an (18I4) format. NWT is number of components or objects within modes. $\text{NWT}_N(I)$ is the name used in the program for n_i, $i = 1,...N$ $n_i < = 1000$ where n_1 must be $< = 100$, n_2 and n_3 must be $< = 45$.

Line 3   Format for Reading in Data

Line 4   Data Set   in the form specified in option IRDATA.

Line 5   This set of commands is present only if IRN = 0. Required are: (a) the format for reading in the initial matrices, and (b) initial matrices—matrices 2 to N. Each matrix must be entered as a dimension by n_i matrix where $i = 2, 3, ...N$. Read in matrix 2 first then followed by 3 and up to matrix N. Note that if matrix 2 is identical to matrix 3, read in matrix 2 twice followed by matrix 4 ...N.

SAMPLE INDSCAL DATA FILE AND OUTPUT
In this example, three 10×10 lower-half matrices without diagonal are being read in, each with 45 values.

```
3   2   2   2   25   1   0   1   0   0  '12345677'   0   0   1   0 .001
    1    8    8
(7F5.0)
      1     13     17      9     11     22     28
     14     16      8     12     21     27      2
     23     24      7     10     25     26      5
      6      3     18     19     15     20      4
      2     14     16     10     12     21     27
     13     17      7     11     22     28      1
     24     23      8     10     26     25      5
      6      4     19     18     15     20      3
```

INDSCAL SAMPLE DATA

```
3  3  2  2  25  1  0  1  0  0  '12345678'  0  0  1  1  .002
3  10  10
(3X,9F3.0)
COK   1
CCL   3   2
DPE   7   9   8
DSL  27  28  32  22
D7U  41  42  43  29  13
DRP  18  17  19  20  30  40
SLI  24  25  26  31   5  16  23
7UP  35  36  38  44  15   6  37  14
TAB  12  11  10   4  33  34  21  39  45
COK   5
CCL   4   6
DPE   7   9   8
DSL  27  28  32  22
D7U  44  43  42  29  13
DRP  18  17  19  20  30  40
SLI  24  25  26  31   2  16  23
7UP  35  36  38  41  15   1  37  14
TAB  12  11  10   3  33  34  21  39  45
COK   6
CCL   4   5
DPE   7   8   9
DSL  27  28  32  22
D7U  44  43  42  29  13
DRP  18  17  19  20  30  40
SLI  24  25  26  31   2  16  23
7UP  35  36  38  41  15   1  37  14
TAB  12  11  10   3  33  34  21  39  45
```

INDSCAL SAMPLE OUTPUT

```
                    I N D S C A L                              3 3 2 2 25 1 0 1 0 0 '12345678' 0 0 1 1 .002
             INDIVIDUAL  DIFFERENCES  SCALING                  3 10 10
          BY DR. J. D. CARROLL AND JIH JIE CHANG               (3X,9F3.0)
                    PC-MDS VERSION                             COK  1
                                                               CCL  3  2
ANALYSIS TITLE: SAMPLE RUN                                     DPE  7  9  8
DATA IS READ FROM FILE: INDSCAL.DAT                            DSL 27 28 32 22
OUTPUT FILE IS: INDSCAL.OUT                                    D7U 41 42 43 29 13
                                                               DRP 18 17 19 20 30 40
INDIFF- INDIVIDUAL DIFFERENCES ANALYSIS USING CANONICAL DECOMPOSITION   SLI 24 25 26 31  5 16 23
OF  3 WAY TABLE IN  2 DIMENSIONS                               7UP 35 36 38 44 15  6 37 14
PARAMETERS                                                     TAB 12 11 10  4 33 34 21 39 45
N         NO. OF STIMULI                              3        COK  5
NF        DIMENSION OF SOLUTION                        2        CCL  4  6
MAXDIM    MAXIMUM NO. OF DIMENSIONS                    3        DPE  7  9  8
MINDIM    MINIMUM NO. OF DIMENSIONS                    2        DSL 27 28 32 22
IRDATA    TYPE OF DATA INPUT                           2        D7U 44 43 42 29 13
ITMAX     MAXIMUM NO. OF ITERATIONS                   25        DRP 18 17 19 20 30 40
ISET      OPTION TO SET MATRIX 2 EQUAL TO MATRIX 3     1        SLI 24 25 26 31  2 16 23
IOY       SELECT SIMULTANEOUS SOLUTION                 0        7UP 35 36 38 41 15  1 37 14
IDR       CORRELATIONS FOR EACH SUBJECT                1        TAB 12 11 10  3 33 34 21 39 45
ISAM      SOLVE FOR ALL MATRICES                       0        COK  6
IPUNSP    PUNCH SCALAR PRODUCT MATRICES                0        CCL  4  5
IRN       RANDOM NUMBER GENERATOR START SET     12345678        DPE  7  8  9
CRIT      CRITERIA FOR QUITTING ITERATION           .002        DSL 27 28 32 22
IVEC      MATRIX OR VECTOR FORM FOR DATA               0        D7U 44 43 42 29 13
IP        OUTPUT NORMALIZED A-MATRIX                   0        DRP 18 17 19 20 30 40
IA        PRINT ORIGINAL DATA MATRICES                 1        SLI 24 25 26 31  2 16 23
IS        PRINT INTERMEDIATE ITERATIVE MATRICES        1        7UP 35 36 38 41 15  1 37 14
MATRIX SIZES    3  10  10                                       TAB 12 11 10  3 33 34 21 39 45
*************************************************************

   SUBJECT    1
      1.00
      3.00    2.00
      7.00    9.00    8.00
     27.00   28.00   32.00   22.00
     41.00   42.00   43.00   29.00   13.00
     18.00   17.00   19.00   20.00   30.00   40.00
     24.00   25.00   26.00   31.00    5.00   16.00   23.00
     35.00   36.00   38.00   44.00   15.00    6.00   37.00   14.00
     12.00   11.00   10.00    4.00   33.00   34.00   21.00   39.00   45.0

   SUBJECT    3
      6.00
      4.00    5.00
      7.00    8.00    9.00
     27.00   28.00   32.00   22.00
     44.00   43.00   42.00   29.00   13.00
     18.00   17.00   19.00   20.00   30.00   40.00
     24.00   25.00   26.00   31.00    2.00   16.00   23.00
     35.00   36.00   38.00   41.00   15.00    1.00   37.00   14.00
     12.00   11.00   10.00    3.00   33.00   34.00   21.00   39.00   45.0
```

```
MATRIX 1
1      .8545        .8452        .8452
2      .2958        .3008        .3006

MATRIX 2
1     -.2113       -.2182       -.2596       -.2963        .2501
       .2264       -.0366        .4273        .5323       -.4141
2     -.1777       -.1780       -.1299        .2215        .1172
       .6945       -.3686       -.3761       -.0990        .2961

MATRIX 3
1     -.2113       -.2182       -.2596       -.2963        .2501
       .2264       -.0366        .4273        .5323       -.4141
2     -.1777       -.1780       -.1299        .2215        .1172
       .6945       -.3686       -.3761       -.0990        .2961

ITERATION =    1

MATRIX 1
1      .8545        .8452        .8451
2      .2874        .2921        .2919

MATRIX 2
1     -.2537       -.2654       -.2967       -.2749        .3034
       .4712       -.1496        .3229        .5179       -.3753
2     -.4817       -.4713       -.4409        .1215        .3334
       .8950       -.4821        .0015        .4246        .1001
MATRIX 3
1     -.1749       -.1889       -.2319       -.3385        .2546
       .2570       -.0496        .4054        .5198       -.4530

2     -.2470       -.2340       -.1832        .3019        .1090
       .6365       -.3430       -.3342       -.0759        .3699

ERROR =       .15846

ITERATION =    2

MATRIX 1
1      .8515        .8467        .8466
2      .2842        .2936        .2935

MATRIX 2
1     -.2551       -.2666       -.2972       -.2716        .3020
       .4640       -.1538        .3266        .5240       -.3723

2     -.4725       -.4637       -.4375        .1005        .3427
       .9406       -.4541       -.0222        .3859        .0804


MATRIX 3
1     -.1680       -.1835       -.2269       -.3455        .2560
       .2647       -.0525        .3996        .5156       -.4594

2     -.2656       -.2484       -.1966        .3208        .1054
       .6157       -.3351       -.3187       -.0645        .3871


ERROR =       .15586
```

Beginning of Two Dimensional Solution

```
ITERATION =   3

MATRIX 1
1     .8516        .8466        .8466
2     .2843        .2936        .2934


MATRIX 2
1    -.2554       -.2668       -.2973       -.2710        .3018
      .4628       -.1545        .3273        .5250       -.3717

2    -.4691       -.4608       -.4358        .0933        .3448
      .9527       -.4464       -.0285        .3759        .0739


MATRIX 3
1    -.1663       -.1822       -.2256       -.3472        .2564
      .2668       -.0531        .3981        .5143       -.4610

2    -.2703       -.2521       -.2001        .3255        .1043
      .6099       -.3334       -.3144       -.0608        .3914


ERROR =        .15569

REACHED CRITERION    E TEST=   .00017516
CRIT=    .00200000

A MATRICES

MATRIX 1
1     .8516        .8466        .8466
2     .2843        .2936        .2934

MATRIX 2
1    -.2554       -.2668       -.2973       -.2710        .3018
      .4628       -.1545        .3273        .5250       -.3717

2    -.4691       -.4608       -.4358        .0933        .3448
      .9527       -.4464       -.0285        .3759        .0739

MATRIX 3
1    -.1663       -.1822       -.2256       -.3472        .2564
      .2668       -.0531        .3981        .5143       -.4610

2    -.2703       -.2521       -.2001        .3255        .1043
      .6099       -.3334       -.3144       -.0608        .3914

ERROR =        .15569
REACHED CRITERION    E TEST=   .00017516
CRIT=    .00200000
```

```
MATRIX 1
1      .8516         .8466        .8466

2      .2843         .2936        .2934

MATRIX 2
1     -.2554        -.2668       -.2973      -.2710       .3018
       .4628        -.1545        .3273       .5250      -.3717

2     -.4691        -.4608       -.4358       .0933       .3448
       .9527        -.4464       -.0285       .3759       .0739


MATRIX 3
1     -.1663        -.1822       -.2256      -.3472       .2564
       .2668        -.0531        .3981       .5143      -.4610

2     -.2703        -.2521       -.2001       .3255       .1043
       .6099        -.3334       -.3144      -.0608       .3914

ERROR =          .15569
REACHED CRITERION      E TEST=      .00017516
CRIT=   .00200000

A MATRICES

MATRIX 1
1      .8516         .8466        .8466
2      .2843         .2936        .2934

MATRIX 2
1     -.2554        -.2668       -.2973      -.2710       .3018
       .4628        -.1545        .3273       .5250      -.3717

2     -.4691        -.4608       -.4358       .0933       .3448
       .9527        -.4464       -.0285       .3759       .0739

MATRIX 3
1     -.1663        -.1822       -.2256      -.3472       .2564
       .2668        -.0531        .3981       .5143      -.4610

2     -.2703        -.2521       -.2001       .3255       .1043
       .6099        -.3334       -.3144      -.0608       .3914


HISTORY OF COMPUTATION

ITERATION       CORRELATIONS BETWEEN
                Y(DATA) AND YHAT       (R**2)           (1-R**2)
     0             .898880           .807985             .192015
     1             .973231           .947179             .052821
     2             .973676           .948045             .051955
     3             .973707           .948105             .051895
***************************************************************************
```

```
EQUATE MATRIX 2 AND MATRIX 3, ITERATE AGAIN
INITIAL A MATRICES
MATRIX 1
1      .8516        .8466        .8466
2      .2843        .2936        .2934

MATRIX 2
1     -.1663       -.1822       -.2256       -.3472        .2564
       .2668       -.0531        .3981        .5143       -.4610

2     -.2703       -.2521       -.2001        .3255        .1043
       .6099       -.3334       -.3144       -.0608        .3914

MATRIX 3
1     -.1663       -.1822       -.2256       -.3472        .2564
       .2668       -.0531        .3981        .5143       -.4610

2     -.2703       -.2521       -.2001        .3255        .1043
       .6099       -.3334       -.3144       -.0608        .3914

ITERATION =    1
MATRIX 1
1      .8503        .8405        .8405
2      .2911        .2983        .2980

ERROR =         .53521
REACHED MAXIMUM ITERATION      E TEST =   .00017516

A MATRICES

MATRIX 1
1      .8503        .8405        .8405
2      .2911        .2983        .2980

MATRIX 2
1     -.1663       -.1822       -.2256       -.3472        .2564
       .2668       -.0531        .3981        .5143       -.4610

2     -.2703       -.2521       -.2001        .3255        .1043
       .6099       -.3334       -.3144       -.0608        .3914

MATRIX 3
1     -.1663       -.1822       -.2256       -.3472        .2564
       .2668       -.0531        .3981        .5143       -.4610

2     -.2703       -.2521       -.2001        .3255        .1043
       .6099       -.3334       -.3144       -.0608        .3914


HISTORY OF COMPUTATION
ITERATION        CORRELATIONS BETWEEN
                 Y(DATA) AND YHAT       (R**2)          (1-R**2)
        0           .906391            .821544           .178456
        1           .906419            .821595           .178405
```

```
VALUES FOR MATRIX 1: CORRELATION BETWEEN
ORIGINAL (Y DATA) AND COMPUTED
DISTANCES (Y HAT).
VAF = SQUARE OF THE CORRELATION, OR
 1-TRV = 1 - TOTAL RESIDUAL VARIANCE

RESIDUAL VARIANCE =
 1 - CORRELATION BETWEEN Y AND Y-HAT



VALUES FOR MATRIX 2:  (SAME AS MATRIX 1)
```

NORMALIZED A MATRICES

MATRIX   1

1	.85666	.30048
2	.84682	.30794
3	.84677	.30766

MATRIX   2

1	-.16570	-.26600
2	-.18151	-.24813
3	-.22479	-.19692
4	-.34591	.32032
5	.25542	.10266
6	.26579	.60031
7	-.05295	-.32816
8	.39661	-.30941
9	.51234	-.05987
10	-.45928	.38520

MATRIX   3

1	-.16570	-.26600
2	-.18151	-.24813
3	-.22479	-.19692
4	-.34591	.32032
5	.25542	.10266
6	.26579	.60031
7	-.05295	-.32816
8	.39661	-.30941
9	.51234	-.05987
10	-.45928	.38520

MATRIX   1
SUMS OF PRODUCTS

1	2.16798	.77869
2	.77869	.27977
SUM OF SQUARES =		2.44775

MATRIX   2
SUMS OF PRODUCTS

1	1.00000	-.10458
2	-.10458	1.00000
SUM OF SQUARES =		2.00000

MATRIX   3
SUMS OF PRODUCTS

1	1.00000	-.10458
2	-.10458	1.00000
SUM OF SQUARES =		2.00000

SUBJECT WEIGHTS FOR EACH DIMENSION
(SUBJECT 1 AND 2). IF WEIGHTS ARE
NEGATIVE, THEY ARE TREATED AS 0.
IF WEIGHTS ARE LARGE, DIMENSIONALITY
MAY BE TOO LARGE.

THE SUM OF SQUARES OF WGTS FOR
DIM 1 + DIM 2 + ...+DIM K
SHOWS HOW WELL THE WEIGHTED STIMULUS
FITS THE DATA FOR EACH SUBJECT.
SUM OF SQUARES $\approx R^2$
MATRIX 2: GIVES THE NORMALIZED STIMULUS
COORDINATES FOR EACH DIMENSION.
THE SUM OF THE COORDINATES = 0 AND THE
SUM OF THE SQUARED COORDINATES = 1.

MATRIX 3:   SAME AS MATRIX 2

MATRIX 1:
DIAGONAL = SUM OF SQUARES OF SUBJECT WGTS.
FOR EACH DIM. IF EACH ELEMENT IS DIVIDED
BY NWT(1), THE NUMBER OF SUBJECTS, THIS
SHOWS THE RELATIVE IMPORTANCE OF EACH
DIMENSION.
RELATIVE IMPORTANCES DECREASE DOWN THE
DIAGONAL. OFF DIAGONAL ENTRIES ARE IGNORED.
MATRIX 1:
SUMS OF SQUARES: SUM OF MAIN DIAGONAL OF

MATRIX 1: SUM OF SQUARES/NWT(1) =
R-SQUARED (HISTORY OF COMPUTATION).
DIAGONALS SHOW IMPORTANCE OF DIMENSIONS.
MATRIX 2:
OFF DIAGONALS SHOW CORRELATIONS BETWEEN
DIMENSIONS. IF OFF DIAGONALS ARE CLOSE
TO 0, THEN UNCORRELATED.
IF OFF DIAGONALS ARE LARGE, EITHER THE
DIMENSIONS ARE CORRELATED, OR THE
SOLUTION HAS NOT PROPERLY CONVERGED.
IF LARGE OFF DIAGONAL VALUES ARE FOUND,

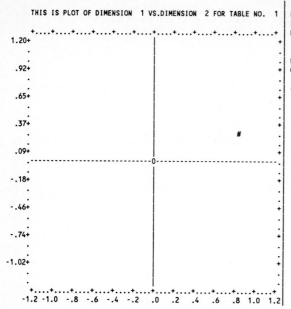

RERUN ANALYSIS IN A LOWER DIMENSIONALITY.
SUM OF SQUARES = # OF DIMENSIONS
MATRIX 3:   SAME AS MATRIX 2

PLOT OF SUBJECT WEIGHTS FOR ALL PAIRS
OF DIMENSIONS OF STIMULUS SPACES

(TABLE 1 IS PLOT OF SUBJECT WGTS)

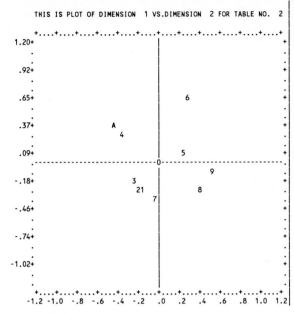

```
     THIS IS PLOT OF DIMENSION  1 VS.DIMENSION  2 FOR TABLE NO.  2
        +....+....+....+....+....+....+....+....+....+....+....+
  1.20+                                                        +
     .                              |                          .
   .92+                             |                          +
     .                              |                          .
   .65+                             |   6                      +
     .                              |                          .
   .37+            A                |                          +
     .                4            |                          .
   .09+                             |     5                    +
     .------------------------------0--------------------------.
     .                              |       9                  .
  -.18+                3            |                          +
     .                21            |    8                     .
     .                      7|                                 .
  -.46+                             |                          +
     .                              |                          .
  -.74+                             |                          +
     .                              |                          .
 -1.02+                             |                          +
     .                              |                          .
        +....+....+....+....+....+....+....+....+....+....+....+
       -1.2 -1.0 -.8  -.6  -.4  -.2  .0   .2   .4   .6   .8  1.0  1.2
```

TABLE 2 GRAPHS SHOW THE GROUP STIMULUS SPACE FOR THE RESPECTIVE DIMENSIONS. THE STIMULI(BRANDS) ARE HERE PLOTTED FOR THE AGGREGATE OF ALL SUBJECTS.

INDIVIDUAL PERCEPTUAL SPACES ARE NOT PLOTTED. THE COORDINATES CAN, HOWEVER BE CALCULATED BY MULTIPLYING THE STIMULUS COORDINATES (MATRIX 2 PLOTTED IN TABLE 2) OF EACH DIMENSION BY THE SQUARE ROOT OF THE SUBJECT'S WEIGHTS FOR THAT DIMENSION. THIS MULTIPLICATION WILL GIVE THE COORDINATE OF THE STIMULUS FOR THE INDIVIDUAL ON THE DIMENSION. THESE PERCEPTUAL SPACES ALLOW FOR THE COMPARISON OF INDIVIDUAL SUBJECTS OR SUBJECT GROUPS IF AGGREGATE SIMILARITIES DATA IS USED.

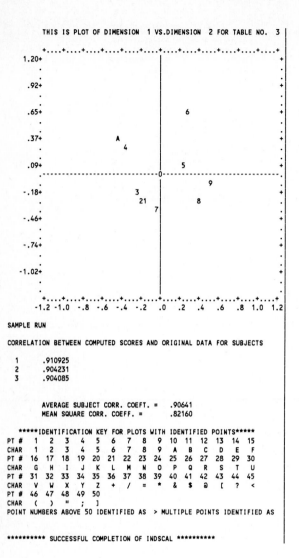

SAMPLE RUN

CORRELATION BETWEEN COMPUTED SCORES AND ORIGINAL DATA FOR SUBJECTS

```
1      .910925
2      .904231
3      .904085


        AVERAGE SUBJECT CORR. COEFT. =    .90641
        MEAN SQUARE CORR. COEFF. =        .82160


     *****IDENTIFICATION KEY FOR PLOTS WITH IDENTIFIED POINTS*****
PT #    1    2    3    4    5    6    7    8    9   10   11   12   13   14   15
CHAR    1    2    3    4    5    6    7    8    9    A    B    C    D    E    F
PT #   16   17   18   19   20   21   22   23   24   25   26   27   28   29   30
CHAR    G    H    I    J    K    L    M    N    O    P    Q    R    S    T    U
PT #   31   32   33   34   35   36   37   38   39   40   41   42   43   44   45
CHAR    V    W    X    Y    Z    +    /    =    *    &    $    @    [    ?    <
PT #   46   47   48   49   50
CHAR    (    )    "    ;    ]
POINT NUMBERS ABOVE 50 IDENTIFIED AS   > MULTIPLE POINTS IDENTIFIED AS


********** SUCCESSFUL COMPLETION OF INDSCAL **********
```

How to Use PREFMAP:
A Program That Relates
Preference Data to
Multidimensional Scaling Solution

Jih Jie Chang and J. Douglas Carroll, Bell Laboratories

NONTECHNICAL INTRODUCTION PREFMAP relates preference data to a stimulus space (the stimulus space must be produced by another PC-MDS program such as KYST or INDSCAL). A hierarchy of vector and ideal point models are calculated. PREFMAP starts with coordinate input describing a stimulus configuration in a specified number of dimensions. Also input is a set of preference rankings, in which each subject ranks the stimuli. In context of this stimulus input, a set of preference scales is evaluated.

PREFMAP finds for each subject, an ideal point for each of three models that is positioned within the stimulus space. For each of these ideal points, the squared Euclidean distances from each stimulus to the ideal point are linearly (for metric model) or monotonically (for non-metric model) related to the preferences expressed by the subject. The ideal point is defined differently in each of the three models. A fourth model, the vector model, assumes the ideal point is at infinity.

Each subject's data is evaluated using any of the four models (called phases). When a model is selected, it is tested for its ability to describe the distance between the subject's ideal points (or preference vector in model 4) and the stimuli.

The PREFMAP output consists of an analysis for each phase requested and a summary table showing correlations within phases, F ratios for each phase and F ratios analyzing differences between phases. It is the analysis of correlations that shows how much of the variance in a subject's preferences are explained by a given phase or model. The F ratios show the improvement attributable to movement to a more sophisticated model.

While the Summary Table is developed for, and is technically correct for

The PREFMAP program was written by J. D. Carroll and J. J. Chang of Bell Laboratories. This guide is a revision of their paper, made by Scott M. Smith for the PC version of PREFMAP. PREFMAP copyright 1972 Bell Telephone Laboratories, Incorporated, reprinted by permission.

evaluating only metric data, the table may be used as a directional indicator of relative improvement attributable to model shifts when non-metric data is analyzed.

TECHNICAL INTRODUCTION PREFMAP relates preference data to a multidimensional solution via a hierarchy of models, ranging from a linear vector model through the Coombs, Bennett, and Hays multidimensional unfolding model, and finally including generalizations of the multi-dimensional unfolding model. The method is described in Carroll's paper (1972).

Given a stimulus configuration of N points in K dimensional space and a set of preference scales in the form of a subject-by-stimulus matrix, the program finds for each individual an ideal point in the given stimulus space such that the squared Euclidean distances (defined differently in each of the four models) from each stimulus to the ideal point are linearly (in the metric case) or monotonically (in the nonmetric case) related to the preferences expressed by the subject.

PREFMAP consists of four phases corresponding to the four models. Phase 1 is the most general model in which each individual is allowed his own orientation and weighting of dimensions. Phase 2 allows each individual differential weighting of dimensions only. In Phase 3 all subjects are assumed to have the same orientation and weighting of dimensions, while Phase 4 corresponds to the vector model. The algorithm for the linear vector model is basically the same as that described in Chang and Carroll (1968) for the case in which linear correlation between the preference scales (data) and the projections of the stimulus points on the fitted vectors is maximized.

INPUT PARAMETERS

Input File Arrangement Each of the numbered lines listed below may refer to a set of images; for example, line 3 is a set of images including the format and the matrix of the scale values.

Line 1: Parameters [Free Format]. There are 15 parameters. The first six parameters are defined as the data parameters which are mandatory. The remaining 9 are option parameters.

N, K, NSUB, ISV, NORS, IRX, IPS, IPE, IRWT, LFITSW, IAV, MAXIT, ISHAT, IPLOT, CRIT

N: Number of stimuli (Max. = 12)

K: Number of dimensions (Max. = 3)

NSUB: Number of subjects (Max. = 10)

ISV: 0 Small-scale value represents greater preference.
     1 Large-scale value represents greater preference.

NORS: 1 Normalize scale values; for each subject make length = 1.
        0 Do not normalize scale values.

IRX: 0 The coordinates of the stimulus points are punched as N by K.
        1 The coordinates are punched as K by N.

IPS, IPE, IRWT: Phase parameters (see Parameters section below).
LFITSW, IAV, MAXIT, ISHAT: Nonmetric parameters (see Parameters section below).
IPLOT: Plotting parameter (see Parameters section below).
CRIT: Present only if doing nonmetric analysis (see Parameters section below).

Lines 2, 3: *Stimulus Space*

Line 2: A format line (use floating-point format).
Line 3: X—a matrix of the coordinates of N stimuli in K
        dimensional space. X must be punched as indicated by IRX.

Lines 4, 5:   These lines are present only when IRWT = 1.

Line 4: A. A format line (using floating-point format).
Line 5: B. Weights—one value for each dimension. There
        should be K values.

Lines 6, 7: *Scale Values*

Line 6: A format line (use floating-point format).
Line 7: S—scale values. S is a matrix of subjects by stimuli.
        Each row represents a subject.

PARAMETERS

Phase Options: *Parameters IPS, IPE, IRWT*   The program computes solutions for Phase 1 to Phase 4 sequentially. However, the starting and the ending phases can be changed simply by setting IPS equal to the phase where computation starts and IPE to the phase where it stops, for example, for IPS = 3, IPE = 4, the program will compute solutions for Phases 3 and 4 only. In case the computation starts on Phase 3, one has the option of applying different weights to the dimensions of the group stimulus space. This can be accomplished by setting IRWT = 1 and the weights are read.

Nonmetric Procedure Options: *Parameters LFITSW, IAV, MAXIT, ISHAT*   The nonmetric analysis employs an iterative procedure. On each iteration the program finds for each subject the best monotone fit of d^2 (the squared Euclidean distances between the stimuli and the ideal point) to data S (the preference scale values).

LFITSW identifies the relationship between d^2 and S.

0 Linearly (or metrically).
1 Monotonically (plan monotone regression, appropriate when there are no ties in the data).

2 Monotonically (block monotone regression using the primary approach of treating ties among values for a group of equal data values, no restriction is placed on ordering within blocks for the fitted values).

3 Monotonically (block monotone regression using the secondary approach of treating the ties among data values for a group of equal data values, the fitted values are required to be equal).

IAV defines the preference scale values of the average subject in each phase. In the metric analysis this option is irrelevant because once the average subject's scale values are computed in the starting phase, they remain the same. However, in the nonmetric case each subject's scale values are replaced in each phase by the best monotone fit values. Therefore, the average subject's scale values are different in each phase.

0 Average subject's scale values are computed in the starting phase and remain the same.

1 Average subject's scale values are computed for each new phase.

MAXIT identifies number of iterations on monotone fit. The default value for MAXIT is 15.

ISHAT decides which set of scale values are used in each phase.

1 At the beginning of a new phase, use the last monotone fit of the scale values from the previous phase.

0 At the beginning of a new phase, use the original scale values.

Plotting Options: IPLOT With respect to the four kinds of plots, option parameter IPLOT designates the kinds of plot to be produced. As default the program generates the average subject's ideal point plot and the composite ideal point plot for Phases 1, 2, and 3; for Phase 4, the vector plot.

The stimulus points are labeled by sequential numbers generated in the program. The ideal points may be labeled by either numbers or letters.

Parameter options on kinds of plot for Phases 1 and 2:

0 Draw ideal point plot for the average subject only.

1 Draw ideal point plot for the average subject only and function plots for each subject.

2 Draw ideal point plot for the average subject and both function plots and ideal point plots for each subject.

Iterative Procedure Stop CRIT is the criterion for stopping iterative procedure on monotone fit. If $(S_I - S_{I-1})^2 \leq$ CRIT, iteration is terminated. (Where I denotes I-th iteration.) CRIT is constrained to .01 or .001 if entered interactively; or, CRIT may be any decimal value if entered in the parameter line of the data file.

SAMPLE PREFMAP DATA

```
                    SAMPLE   PREFMAP   DATA
              CONFIGURATION MATRIX FROM INDSCAL ANALYSIS

  10   2   3   0   1   0   1   4   0   1   1 16   0   2   .001
(6X, 2F12.5)
1            -.16570        -.26600
2            -.18151        -.24813
3            -.22479        -.19692
4            -.34591         .32032
5             .25542         .10266
6             .26579         .60031
7            -.05295        -.32816
8             .39661        -.30941
9             .51234        -.05987
10           -.45928         .38520
(3X, 10F5.2)
001 3.91 3.37 5.00 5.79 5.88 4.39 3.56 4.14 4.67 4.33
002 4.07 3.72 5.28 5.56 5.91 4.86 3.46 3.65 4.79 3.68
003 3.49 2.77 5.05 5.68 6.67 5.25 2.77 5.37 4.83 3.19
```

PREFMAP SAMPLE OUTPUT

```
                    P R E F M A P                          10 2 3 0 1 0 1 4 0 1 1 16 0 2 .001
    MDSCALING VIA A GENERALIZATION OF COOMBS UNFOLDING MODEL  (6X, 2F12.5)
         BY DR. J. D. CARROLL AND JIH JIE CHANG              1     -.16570    -.26600
                  PC - MDS VERSION                           2     -.18151    -.24813
                                                             3     -.22479    -.19692
ANALYSIS TITLE: SAMPLE DATA ANALYSIS                         4     -.34591     .32032
DATA IS READ FROM FILE: PREFMAP.DAT                          5      .25542     .10266
OUTPUT FILE IS: PREFMAP.OUT                                  6      .26579     .60031
*************************************************************7     -.05295    -.32816
N         NO. OF STIMULI                       10            8      .39661    -.30941
K         NO. OF DIMENSIONS                     2            9      .51234    -.05987
NSUB      NO. OF SUBJECTS                       3           10     -.45928     .38520
ISV       0=SMALL SCALE VALUE REPRESENTS GREATER PREF.   0   (3X, 10F5.2)
NORS      1=NORMALIZE SCALE VALUES               1          001 3.91 3.37 5.00 5.79 5.88 4.39 3.56 4.14 4.67 4.33
IRX       0=STIMULUS COORDINATES N BY K, OR 1 = K BY N  0   002 4.07 3.72 5.28 5.56 5.91 4.86 3.46 3.65 4.79 3.68
IPS         STARTING PHASE                       1         003 3.49 2.77 5.05 5.68 6.67 5.25 2.77 5.37 4.83 3.19
IPE         ENDING PHASE                         4
IRWT      1=READ IN WEIGHTS,  0=NO WEIGHTS READ IN  0
LFITSW    HOW D**2 IS RELATED TO SCALE VALUES     1
          0=LINEARLY,
          1=MONOTONE WITH NO TIES,
          2=BLOCK MONOTONE WITH ORDERING IN BLOCKS        INPUT PARAMETERS TO PREFMAP
          3=BLOCK MONOTONE WITH EQUALITY IN BLOCKS
IAV       0=AVERAGE SUBJECTS COMPUTED ONCE FOR ALL PHASES,  1
          1=CALCULATE EACH PHASE
MAXIT     MAXIMUM ITERATIONS, WHEN 0 IT IS SET TO 15    16
ISHAT     0=USE SCALE VALUES FROM PREVIOUS PHASE,        0
          1=USE ORIG VALUES
IPLOT     0=AVERAGE SUBJECTS,                            2
          1=AVERAGE SUBJECTS & SUBJECT FUNCTIONS,
          2=ALL PLOTS
CRIT      CRITERIA FOR STOPPING MONOTONE FIT          .0010
*************************************************************
    *****IDENTIFICATION KEY FOR PLOTS WITH IDENTIFIED POINTS*****
PT #  1   2   3   4   5   6   7   8   9  10  11  12  13  14  15   PLOT IDENTIFICATIONS FOR FIRST 50 STIMULI
CHAR  1   2   3   4   5   6   7   8   9   A   B   C   D   E   F
PT # 16  17  18  19  20  21  22  23  24  25  26  27  28  29  30
CHAR  G   H   I   J   K   L   M   N   O   P   Q   R   S   T   U
PT # 31  32  33  34  35  36  37  38  39  40  41  42  43  44  45
CHAR  V   W   X   Y   Z   +   /   =   *   &   $   @   %   ?   <
PT # 46  47  48  49  50
CHAR  (   )   "   #   @
POINT NUMBERS ABOVE 50 IDENTIFIED AS  >, MULTIPLE POINTS IDENTIFIED AS  THE CONFIGURATION MATRIX INPUT FOR THIS
POINTS 1 TO 10 ARE STIMULI AND POINTS 11 TO  13 ARE IDEAL POINTS      EXAMPLE, WAS PRODUCED BY AN INDSCAL ANALYSIS.
VARIABLE FORMAT (STIMULUS COORDINATES) =  (6X, 2F12.5)
ORIGINAL CONFIGURATION  (X MATRIX)
     1   -.16570    -.26600
     2   -.18151    -.24813
     3   -.22479    -.19692
     4   -.34591     .32032
     5    .25542     .10266
     6    .26579     .60031
     7   -.05295    -.32816
     8    .39661    -.30941
     9    .51234    -.05987
    10   -.45928     .38520

VARIABLE FORMAT  (SCALE VALUES) = (3X, 10F5.2)            PHASE 1 PERMITS EACH SUBJECT TO HAVE A UNIQUE
PHASE  1                                                 ORIENTATION AND PATTERN OF WEIGHTS OF THE ROTATED
SUBJECT   1                                              DIMENSIONS.
SCALE VALUES BEFORE NORMALIZATION FOR SUBJECT    1
      3.91000     3.37000     5.00000     5.79000     5.88000
      3.56000     4.14000     4.67000     4.33000
```

```
S (VECTOR OF SCALE VALUES, E.G. PREFERENCES)
      -.23251      -.44389       .19415       .50339       .53862
      -.36952      -.14248       .06498      -.06811


BEGIN ITERATION ON MONOTONE FIT
END OF ITERATION, REACHED CRITERION

SIGNED DSQ, (SIGNED DISTANCE SQUARED FROM STIMULI TO IDEAL)
    -1.23769     -1.21114     -1.14899      -.64045      -.22497
    -1.23220     -1.26003     -1.08907     -1.09073
*****************************************************************
SUBJECT    1
DIRECTION COSINE OF NEW AXES WITH RESPECT TO OLD
    OLD       1            2
NEW   1         -.57938       .81506
      2          .81506       .57938


COMPOSITE TRANSFORMATION MATRIX
    1      -1.04279       1.46696
    2       1.90728       1.35579

    TRANSFORMED X
  1     -.2174      -.1747      -.0545       .8306      -.1158     .
        -.4262      -.8675      -.6221      1.0440
  2     -.6767      -.6826      -.6957      -.2255       .6263     1.
        -.5459       .3370       .8960      -.3537

COORDINATES OF IDEAL POINT WITH RESPECT TO NEW AXES
          .25502       .33054

COORDINATES OF IDEAL POINT WITH RESPECT TO OLD AXES
          .03304       .19733

IMPORTANCES OF NEW AXES
       -3.23939     -5.47587
*****************************************************************
SUBJECT    2
SCALE VALUES BEFORE NORMALIZATION FOR SUBJECT    2
       4.07000      3.72000      5.28000      5.56000      5.91000
       3.46000      3.65000      4.79000      3.68000

S (VECTOR OF SCALE VALUES, E.G. PREFERENCES)
      -.15947      -.28987       .29136       .39569       .52609
      -.38674      -.31595       .10880      -.30478

BEGIN ITERATION ON MONOTONE FIT
END OF ITERATION, REACHED CRITERION

SIGNED DSQ, (SIGNED DISTANCE SQUARED FROM STIMULI TO IDEAL)
    -1.01460      -.97066      -.86390      -.58799      -.10689
    -1.14878     -1.29548      -.75081      -.98351
*****************************************************************
SUBJECT    2
DIRECTION COSINE OF NEW AXES WITH RESPECT TO OLD
    OLD       1            2
NEW   1          .99962       .02740
      2         -.02740       .99962

COMPOSITE TRANSFORMATION MATRIX
    1       1.64542       .04511
    2       -.05602      2.04348

    TRANSFORMED X
  1     -.2846      -.3099      -.3788      -.5547       .4249     .
        -.1019       .6386       .8403      -.7383
  2     -.5343      -.4969      -.3898       .6739       .1955     1.
        -.6676      -.6545      -.1510       .8129
```

```
S = NORMALIZED SUBJECT PREFERENCE DATA:
EXAMPLE FOR SUBJECT 1:
NORMALIZED      ORIGINAL VALUE
-.44389     =        3.37
-.36952     =        3.56
   .        =         .
   .        =         .
+.53862     =        5.88
```

```
COORDINATES OF IDEAL POINT WITH RESPECT TO NEW AXES
            .15096          .37393

COORDINATES OF IDEAL POINT WITH RESPECT TO OLD AXES
            .08666          .18536

IMPORTANCES OF NEW AXES
          -2.70945       -4.17895
*****************************************************************************
SUBJECT    3
SCALE VALUES BEFORE NORMALIZATION FOR SUBJECT    3
        3.49000      2.77000      5.05000      5.68000      6.67000
        2.77000      5.37000      4.83000      3.19000

S (VECTOR OF SCALE VALUES, E.G. PREFERENCES)
        -.24996       -.42693       .13346       .28830       .53163
        -.42693        .21211       .07939      -.32370

BEGIN ITERATION ON MONOTONE FIT
END OF ITERATION, REACHED CRITERION

SIGNED DSQ, (SIGNED DISTANCE SQUARED FROM STIMULI TO IDEAL)
       -1.29475      -1.28164      -1.25603      -.75343      -.25702
       -1.20632      -1.19937      -1.21746     -1.26753
*****************************************************************************
SUBJECT    3
DIRECTION COSINE OF NEW AXES WITH RESPECT TO OLD
      OLD       1            2
NEW    1       -.45621       .88987
       2        .88987       .45621

COMPOSITE TRANSFORMATION MATRIX
   1       -.79021      1.54138
   2        2.26386     1.16060

    TRANSFORMED X
   1       -.2791       -.2390       -.1259        .7671       -.0436       .
           -.4640       -.7903       -.4971        .9567
   2       -.6838       -.6989       -.7374       -.4113        .6974      1.
           -.5007        .5388       1.0904       -.5927

COORDINATES OF IDEAL POINT WITH RESPECT TO NEW AXES
            .28007          .30718

COORDINATES OF IDEAL POINT WITH RESPECT TO OLD AXES
            .03368          .19897

IMPORTANCES OF NEW AXES
          -3.00027       -6.47204
*****************************************************************************
AVERAGE SUBJECT
S (VECTOR OF SCALE VALUES, E.G. PREFERENCES)
        -.17514       -.17514      -.06107       .33116       .80018
        -.25415       -.22837      -.06107      -.13245

SIGNED DSQ, (SIGNED DISTANCE SQUARED FROM STIMULI TO IDEAL)
       -1.18908      -1.16149      -1.09750      -.66480      -.19988
       -1.19932      -1.25758      -1.03653     -1.12385
*****************************************************************************
SUBJECT    4
DIRECTION COSINE OF NEW AXES WITH RESPECT TO OLD
      OLD       1            2
NEW    1       -.59962       .80028
       2        .80028       .59962
```

```
COMPOSITE TRANSFORMATION MATRIX
   1    -1.09982       1.46788
   2     1.81069       1.35668

   TRANSFORMED X
 1    -.2082     -.1646     -.0418      .8506     -.1302     .
      -.4235     -.8904     -.6514     1.0706
 2    -.6609     -.6653     -.6742     -.1918      .6018    1.
      -.5411      .2984      .8465     -.3090

COORDINATES OF IDEAL POINT WITH RESPECT TO NEW AXES
          .23036         .33746

COORDINATES OF IDEAL POINT WITH RESPECT TO OLD AXES
          .04405         .18994

IMPORTANCES OF NEW AXES
         -3.36426       -5.11917
```
****
```
PHASE  2
X MATRIX, (INPUT CONFIGURATION AFTER NORMALIZATION)
 1    -.2184     -.1726     -.0439      .8921     -.1366     .
      -.4441     -.9338     -.6831     1.1227
 2    -.7698     -.7749     -.7853     -.2234      .7009    1.
      -.6302      .3475      .9859     -.3599


PHASE  2
SUBJECT   1
S (VECTOR OF SCALE VALUES, E.G. PREFERENCES)
      -.21237       -.21237       -.08432       .38481       .80193
      -.21237       -.21237       -.08432      -.08432


BEGIN ITERATION ON MONOTONE FIT
SUBJECT   2
S (VECTOR OF SCALE VALUES, E.G. PREFERENCES)
      -.13996       -.13996        .04820       .26944       .75986
      -.37701       -.37701        .04820      -.13996


BEGIN ITERATION ON MONOTONE FIT
END OF ITERATION, REACHED CRITERION

BETA VALUES  (IN THE MOST GENERAL CASE THERE ARE (2K + K(K-1)/2 + 1) TE
QUADRATIC, LINEAR, THEN A CONSTANT TERM)
      .85959        .44003        .59003       -.96211      -.74883

(CORRELATION)=     .99713


SIGNED DSQ, (SIGNED DISTANCE SQUARED FROM STIMULI TO IDEAL)
     -1.20646      -1.17804      -1.11278      -.70880      -.19890
     -1.22099      -1.30167      -1.06225     -1.19463
```
****
```
SUBJECT    2
COORDINATES OF IDEAL POINT WITH RESPECT TO OLD AXES
          .22868         .39397

IMPORTANCES OF NEW AXES
         -.96211        -.74883
```
****
```
SUBJECT   3
S (VECTOR OF SCALE VALUES, E.G. PREFERENCES)
      -.17308       -.17308       -.14710       .33923       .83874
      -.17308       -.09572       -.14710      -.17308


BEGIN ITERATION ON MONOTONE FIT
END OF ITERATION, REACHED CRITERION
```

PHASE 2 MODEL: ELIPTICAL IDEAL POINT MODEL
EACH SUBJECT REFLECTS DIFFERENTIAL WEIGHTING OF THE
DIMENSIONS ONLY.

X MATRIX=ORIGINAL CONFIGURATION MATRIX AFTER
NORMALIZATION

ITERATION PROCESS BEGINS, SOLVING FOR IDEAL POINT
COORDINATES FOR EACH SUBJECT

ITERATION TO DETERMINE SUBJECT 1'S DISTANCE FROM STIMULI

BETA VALUES ARE IMPORTANCES (OR WEIGHTS) ON EACH NEW
OR ROTATED DIMENSION...NEGATIVE WEIGHTS INDICATE AN
ANTI-IDEAL OR LEAST PREFERRED ITEM IN TERMS OF THAT
PARTICULAR DIMENSION
BETA VALUES ARE THE UNSTANDARDIZED REGRESSION COEFFICIENTS
FOR THE SCALE VALUES ON THE STIMULUS COORDINATES.
THE FIRST BETA VALUE (.85959) IS THE INTERCEPT.
THE SIGN OF THE LAST BETA VALUE (-.74883) SHOWS WHETHER
THE IDEAL POINT IS + OR -. THE INTERMEDIATE
AND LAST BETA VALUES SHOW THE IDEAL POINT COORDINATES.

SIGNED DSQ = SQUARES OF DISTANCE FROM THE IDEAL POINT TO
EACH STIMULUS.

COORDINATES OF THE IDEAL POINT WITH RESPECT TO
THE OLD GROUP STIMULUS SPACE.
COORDINATES OF IDEAL POINT WITH RESPECT TO THE NEW
INDIVIDUAL SPACE ARE THE SAME AS THE LAST BETA.
THE SIGN IS IMPORTANT IN PHASE 2 ANALYSIS ONLY.
IF +, THE IDEAL IS POSITIVE, IF -, THE IDEAL IS NEGATIVE.

```
BETA VALUES  (IN THE MOST GENERAL CASE THERE ARE (2K + K(K-1)/2 + 1) TE  THE SIZE OF THE NUMBER DOES NOT INFLUENCE THE DIMENSIONAL
QUADRATIC, LINEAR, THEN A CONSTANT TERM)                                 WEIGHTS IN THE PHASE 2 ANALYSIS.
     .87330      .40151       .59744      -.91274       -.80294


(CORRELATION)=      .99119


SIGNED DSQ, (SIGNED DISTANCE SQUARED FROM STIMULI TO IDEAL)
    -1.22221     -1.19690      -1.13892      -.69697       -.20286
    -1.20906     -1.21537      -1.04694     -1.17407
**********************************************************************
SUBJECT      3
COORDINATES OF IDEAL POINT WITH RESPECT TO OLD AXES
         .21995        .37203


IMPORTANCES OF NEW AXES
         -.91274       -.80294
**********************************************************************
AVERAGE SUBJECT                                                         S = NORMALIZED PREFERENCES FOR THE AVERAGE SUBJECT.
S (VECTOR OF SCALE VALUES, E.G. PREFERENCES)                            THE AVERAGE SUBJECT'S PREFERENCE ORDER CAN
    -.18348      -.18348       -.08755       .34574        .82563       BE IDENTIFIED.
    -.21048      -.18907       -.08755      -.14221


BETA VALUES  (IN THE MOST GENERAL CASE THERE ARE (2K + K(K-1)/2 + 1) TE
QUADRATIC, LINEAR, THEN A CONSTANT TERM)
     .86310      .43123       .59335      -.92073       -.78141


(CORRELATION)=      .99700


SIGNED DSQ, (SIGNED DISTANCE SQUARED FROM STIMULI TO IDEAL)
    -1.22101     -1.19401      -1.13159      -.68267       -.20720
    -1.22054     -1.25674      -1.06191     -1.15435
**********************************************************************
SUBJECT      4
COORDINATES OF IDEAL POINT WITH RESPECT TO OLD AXES
         .23418        .37967


IMPORTANCES OF NEW AXES
         -.92073       -.78141
**********************************************************************
PHASE 3
X MATRIX, (INPUT CONFIGURATION AFTER NORMALIZATION)
  1      -.2095       -.1656       -.0421       .8560        -.1310        .
         -.4261       -.8960       -.6555      1.0773
  2      -.6805       -.6850       -.6942      -.1974         .6196       1.
         -.5571        .3072        .8715      -.3182


PHASE 3
SUBJECT  1
S (VECTOR OF SCALE VALUES, E.G. PREFERENCES)
    -.21128      -.21128       -.08506       .38064        .80474
    -.21128      -.21128       -.08506      -.08506


BEGIN ITERATION ON MONOTONE FIT
SUBJECT  2
S (VECTOR OF SCALE VALUES, E.G. PREFERENCES)
    -.16702      -.16702       -.05812       .31905        .83171
    -.23647      -.23647       -.05812      -.16941


BEGIN ITERATION ON MONOTONE FIT
END OF ITERATION, REACHED CRITERION


BETA VALUES  (IN THE MOST GENERAL CASE THERE ARE (2K + K(K-1)/2 + 1) TE
QUADRATIC, LINEAR, THEN A CONSTANT TERM)
     .86861      .44733       .67461      1.00639


(CORRELATION)=      .99683
```

```
SIGNED DSQ, (SIGNED DISTANCE SQUARED FROM STIMULI TO IDEAL)
     -1.22575     -1.19879     -1.13658     -.68968     -.20702
     -1.22432     -1.25921     -1.06483    -1.16535
***********************************************************************
SUBJECT    2
COORDINATES OF IDEAL POINT WITH RESPECT TO OLD AXES
          .22225          .33517

IMPORTANCES OF NEW AXES
         -1.00639    -1.00639
***********************************************************************
SUBJECT    3
S (VECTOR OF SCALE VALUES, E.G. PREFERENCES)
     -.17215      -.17215      -.11945      .33752      .84045
     -.18369      -.11945      -.11945      -.17215

BEGIN ITERATION ON MONOTONE FIT
AVERAGE SUBJECT
S (VECTOR OF SCALE VALUES, E.G. PREFERENCES)
     -.18278      -.18278      -.09521      .34773      .82818
     -.20118      -.18090      -.09521      -.14261

BETA VALUES   (IN THE MOST GENERAL CASE THERE ARE (2K + K(K-1)/2 + 1) TE
QUADRATIC, LINEAR, THEN A CONSTANT TERM)
      .86687       .44820       .67063     1.00437


(CORRELATION)=      .99654

SIGNED DSQ, (SIGNED DISTANCE SQUARED FROM STIMULI TO IDEAL)
     -1.22138     -1.19438     -1.13206     -.68578     -.20798
     -1.22065     -1.25858     -1.06566    -1.15979
***********************************************************************
SUBJECT    4
COORDINATES OF IDEAL POINT WITH RESPECT TO OLD AXES
          .22312          .33385

IMPORTANCES OF NEW AXES
         -1.00437    -1.00437
***********************************************************************
STIMULI COORDINATES
DIMENSION       1            2
STIMULI
   1         -.20953      -.68048
   2         -.16563      -.68500
   3         -.04209      -.69415
   4          .85598      -.19745
   5         -.13104       .61959
   6          .59257      1.33407
   7         -.42613      -.55711
   8         -.89598       .30721
   9         -.65546       .87154
  10         1.07729      -.31818

COORDINATES OF IDEAL POINTS
DIMENSION       1            2
SUBJECTS
   1          .24216       .33662
   2          .22225       .33517
   3          .20856       .33046
   4          .22312       .33385
```

IN PHASE 3, BETA VALUES ARE DIMENSION WEIGHTS. THE LAST
BETA WEIGHT IS REPEATED BELOW AS IMPORTANCES OF THE AXES.

```
SUBJECT   4 IS THE AVERAGE SUBJECT
WEIGHTS OF AXES
DIMENSION        1              2
SUBJECTS
   1          -.98799        -.98799
   2         -1.00639       -1.00639
   3         -1.01502       -1.01502
   4         -1.00437       -1.00437

SUBJECT   4 IS THE AVERAGE SUBJECT
```

WEIGHTS OF AXES SHOW THE IMPORTANCE OF NEW AXES AND IF THE IDEAL POINT IS + OR -. THIS IS A REPEAT OF THE FINAL BETA LISTED FOR EACH SUBJECT.
THE SIZE OF THE BETA SHOWS IMPORTANCE OF THE DIMENSION AS A COMPONENT OF PREFERENCE.   A LARGE WEIGHT MEANS THAT A SMALL MOVEMENT ALONG THE DIMENSION WILL HAVE A LARGER EFFECT ON PREFERENCE. A SMALL WEIGHT MEANS THAT LARGER CHANGES IN THE DIMENSION CAN BE MADE WITHOUT INFLUENCING PREFERENCE

THE PREFERENCE CONTOURS AROUND THE POINTS ARE HYPERBOLIC AND NOT ELIPTICAL. THEREFORE, THE MIXED + - IDEAL POSITIONS ARE DIFFICULT TO INTERPRET.

```
      STIMULI AND IDEAL POINTS:  SAMPLE DATA ANALYSIS
      .*....*....*....*....*....*....*....*....*....*....*....*
  1.50**                                                     *
  1.38**                                  6                   *
  1.27**                                                      *
  1.15**                                                      *
  1.04**                                                      *
   .92**               9                                      *
   .81**                                                      *
   .69**                                                      *
   .58**                        5                             *
   .46**                                                      *
   .35**            8              ;B                         *
   .23**                                                      *
   .12**                                                      *
   .00**------------------------------0--------------------- *
  -.12**                                                      *
  -.23**                                  4                   *
  -.35**                                  A                   *
  -.46**                                                      *
  -.58**                   7                                  *
  -.69**                  123                                 *
  -.81**                                                      *
  -.92**                                                      *
 -1.04**                                                      *
 -1.15**                                                      *
 -1.27**                                                      *
 -1.38**                                                      *
 -1.50**                                                      *
      .*....*....*....*....*....*....*....*....*....*....*....*
     .  -1.6667. -1.0000.  -.3333.   .3333.  1.0000.  1.6667.
      -2.0000   -1.3333   -.6667   .0000    .6667   1.3333   2.
```

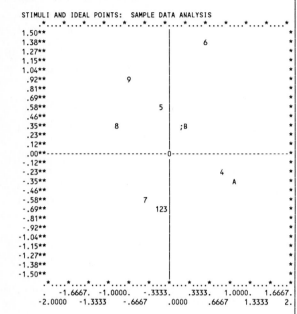

```
PHASE 4
X MATRIX, (INPUT CONFIGURATION AFTER NORMALIZATION)
  1      -.2095      -.1656      -.0421       .8560     -.1310     .
         -.4261      -.8960      -.6555      1.0773
  2      -.6805      -.6850      -.6942      -.1974       .6196    1.
         -.5571       .3072       .8715      -.3182
```

PHASE 4 IS THE VECTOR MODEL PROVIDING DIRECTIONAL COSINES OF THE FITTED SUBJECT VECTOR.

```
PHASE  4
SUBJECT  1
S (VECTOR OF SCALE VALUES, E.G. PREFERENCES)
        .21102      .21102      .08196     -.37049     -.81010
        .21102      .21102      .08196      .09053

BEGIN ITERATION ON MONOTONE FIT
END OF ITERATION, REACHED CRITERION

BETA VALUES  (IN THE MOST GENERAL CASE THERE ARE (2K + K(K-1)/2 + 1) TE
QUADRATIC, LINEAR, THEN A CONSTANT TERM)
     .00000     -.28734     -.23419

(CORRELATION)=     .74852
```

```
PROJECTIONS ON THE FITTED VECTOR
      .59233         .56115         .47117        -.53878        -.28986
      .68228         .50044        -.04253        -.63405

SUBJECT   2
S (VECTOR OF SCALE VALUES, E.G. PREFERENCES)
      .16630         .16630         .08369        -.34385        -.82954
      .21172         .21172         .08369         .16630

BEGIN ITERATION ON MONOTONE FIT
END OF ITERATION, REACHED CRITERION

BETA VALUES  (IN THE MOST GENERAL CASE THERE ARE (2K + K(K-1)/2 + 1) TE
QUADRATIC, LINEAR, THEN A CONSTANT TERM)
      .00000        -.12803        -.25821


(CORRELATION)=       .61531

PROJECTIONS ON THE FITTED VECTOR
      .70273         .68727         .64059        -.20337        -.49688
      .68842         .12280        -.48963        -.19352

SUBJECT   3
S (VECTOR OF SCALE VALUES, E.G. PREFERENCES)
      .17101         .17101         .11998        -.32886        -.84489
      .18082         .11998         .11998         .17101

BEGIN ITERATION ON MONOTONE FIT
END OF ITERATION, REACHED CRITERION

BETA VALUES  (IN THE MOST GENERAL CASE THERE ARE (2K + K(K-1)/2 + 1) TE
QUADRATIC, LINEAR, THEN A CONSTANT TERM)
      .00000        -.05576        -.31335

(CORRELATION)=       .69758
PROJECTIONS ON THE FITTED VECTOR
      .70667         .70342         .69079         .04443        -.58705
      .62315        -.14549        -.74323         .12452

AVERAGE SUBJECT
S (VECTOR OF SCALE VALUES, E.G. PREFERENCES)
      .30483         .36528        -.18462        -.29745        -.34532
      .45625         .08371        -.18462         .09114

BETA VALUES  (IN THE MOST GENERAL CASE THERE ARE (2K + K(K-1)/2 + 1) TE
QUADRATIC, LINEAR, THEN A CONSTANT TERM)
      .00000        -.15510        -.26801

(CORRELATION)=       .72919
PROJECTIONS ON THE FITTED VECTOR
      .69392         .67584         .62188        -.25785        -.47063
      .69563         .18289        -.42602        -.26421

STIMULI COORDINATES
DIMENSION         1                2
STIMULI
   1           -.20953          -.68048
   2           -.16563          -.68500
   3           -.04209          -.69415
   4            .85598          -.19745
   5           -.13104           .61959
   6            .59257          1.33407
   7           -.42613          -.55711
   8           -.89598           .30721
   9           -.65546           .87154
  10           1.07729          -.31818
```

2 DIMENSIONAL COORDINATES OF 10 STIMULI.

```
STIMULI AND IDEAL POINTS:   SAMPLE DATA ANALYSIS
       .*....*....*....*....*....*....*....*....*....*....*....*....* POINTS 1 - 9, A  = STIMULI
 1.50**                                                            * POINTS B - E = IDEAL POINTS
 1.38**                                  6                         *
 1.27**                                                            *
 1.15**                                                            *
 1.04**                                                            *
  .92**                9                                           *
  .81**                                                            *
  .69**                                                            *
  .58**                        5                                   *
  .46**                                                            *
  .35**            8                                               *
  .23**                                                            *
  .12**                                                            *
  .00**------------------------------0---------------------------- *
 -.12**                                                            *
 -.23**                                        4                   *
 -.35**                                        A                   *
 -.46**                                                            *
 -.58**            B    7                                          *
 -.69**                      123                                   *
 -.81**                                                            *
 -.92**              EC                                            *
-1.04**                    D                                       *
-1.15**                                                            *
-1.27**                                                            *
-1.38**                                                            *
-1.50**                                                            *
         .*....*....*....*....*....*....*....*....*....*....*....*....*
         .   -1.6667.  -1.0000.   -.3333.    .3333.  1.0000.  1.6667.
          -2.0000   -1.3333    -.6667     .0000    .6667   1.3333    2.
```

DIRECTION COSINES OF FITTED SUBJECT VECTORS
                          DIMENSION
SUBJECT   1   2
    1   -.7752   -.6318
    2   -.4442   -.8959
    3   -.1752   -.9845
AVG R   -.5009   -.8655

	CORRELATION (PHASE)				F RATIO (PHASE)		
	R1	R2	R3	R4	F1	F2	F3
DF					5 4	4 5	3 6
SUBJ							
1	.998	.998	.997	.749	185.901	308.224	376.663
2	.990	.997	.997	.615	40.239	216.903	314.211
3	.997	.991	.991	.698	119.079	69.996	104.992
AVG	.997	.997	.997	.729	122.103	207.101	287.599

	F RATIO (BETWEEN PHASE)					
	F12	F13	F14	F23	F24	F34
DF	1 4	2 4	3 4	1 5	2 5	1 6
SUBJ						
1	-.229	.465	135.493	1.538	269.662	493.513
2	-2.824	-1.351	41.170	.519	268.621	583.480
3	6.516	3.602	101.240	.327	70.652	158.783
AVG	-.313	.122	94.588	.756	192.631	400.836

ROOT MEAN SQUARE
PHASE
  1   .995
  2   .995
  3   .995
  4   .689
      AN F - VALUE OF 1000.0 IN THE ABOVE TABLE INDICATES
      A POSSIBLE DIVISION BY ZERO. I.E. R IS VERY CLOSE TO 1.00

DIRECTION COSINES:
IF THE VALUE IS > .9, LITTLE ROTATION WILL OCCUR BECAUSE
POINTS ARE ALREADY HIGHLY CORRELATED WITH THE DIMENSIONS.
IF THIS OCCURS, THE PHASE 3 ANALYSIS IS AN APPROPRIATE
PLACE TO START (COMPLETE ANALYSIS FOR PHASES 1-3).

WITHIN PHASE ANALYSIS:

=> MODELS 1,2,3 FIT DATA FOR SUBJECT 1.
=> MODELS 1,2,3 FIT DATA FOR SUBJECT 2.
=> MODELS 1,2,3 FIT DATA FOR SUBJECT 3.
=> MODELS 1,2,3 FIT DATA FOR AVG SUBJECT.

=> MODEL 4 AND 3 FITS DATA FOR SUBJECT 1.
=> MODEL 3 IS BETTER THAN MODEL 4 FOR SUBJECT 2
=> MODEL 4 FITS SUBJECT 3
=> AVERAGE SUBJECT FOR PHASE 4 MODEL IS SIGNIFICANT.

How to Use PROFIT:
A Computer Program for
PROperty FITting by Optimizing
Nonlinear or Linear Correlation

J. J. Chang and J. D. Carroll, Bell Laboratories

NONTECHNICAL INTRODUCTION   The PROFIT program relates a stimulus space to several sets of independently determined physical attributes called properties.

PROFIT starts with coordinate input describing a configuration of stimuli (N) in a specified number of dimensions (K). This input is normally derived from a multidimensional scaling procedure such as KYST or INDSCAL. Also input is the set of independently determined physical measures called properties on which each stimulus is ranked.

PROFIT will find for each property a vector, or direction, in the K-dimensional space such that the projections of the N stimulus points on that vector correspond optimally to the values input for the property vectors.

Two different approaches are employed in finding the vectors, including a procedure based on linear regression (see Miller, Shepard, and Chang, 1964) and a procedure based on optimizing an index of nonlinear correlation, an algorithm devised by J. D. Carroll (1964).

The first procedure is equivalent to a multiple linear regression analysis in which each property plays the role of a dependent variable, while the stimulus coordinates of the multidimensional space are treated as independent variables. The second procedure can be viewed as providing a variety of nonlinear regression analyses in which a very general nonlinear relation is assumed between the dependent variables and a linear combination of the independent variables.

Various plotting facilities are provided by PROFIT, allowing for plotting of best-fitting property vectors against one another and against the coordinates of the multidimensional space.

TECHNICAL INTRODUCTION The particular problem this program deals with can be simply stated as follows:

Suppose we have the coordinates of N stimulus points in K-dimensional space, determined, say, from a multidimensional scaling procedure, and several sets of physical measures, which we call properties. Each property consists of N independently determined measures, one value for each stimulus point in the psychological space. The program will then find for each property a vector in the K-dimensional space such that the projections of the N points on the vector correspond optimally with the given property values. Optimal correspondence is defined in terms of optimizing either linear correlation or a general measure of nonlinear correlation, proposed by Carroll, based on notions of continuity or smoothness.

The approach to this problem devised by Carroll (1964) in the nonlinear regression procedure is quite different from the linear case (Miller, Shepard, and Chang, 1964). However, the input and output of these two analyses are similar. For this reason they are combined into one computer program.

The input to the program consists of the coordinates of stimulus points in a specified number of dimensions and a set of properties.

The program provides output to the screen and to a user-specified disk file.

Description of Methods The mathematics for the linear and nonlinear regression procedures will be briefly stated here. The reader is referred to the references for detailed description.

Property Fitting by Linear Regression We define the following variables:

$X \equiv \|X_{ij}\|$ The matrix of coordinates of N objects in K-dimensional space $(i = 1 \dots N,$ and $j = 1 \dots K)$

The origin of the K-dimensional space is assumed to be at the centroid of the N objects. This means that the columns of the X matrix sum to zero. In practice this is assured by initially subtracting out the column means.

$P \equiv (P_i)$ The row vector of values of one property for the N objects $(i = 1 \dots N)$

$T \equiv (T_j)$ The column vector of direction cosines of the fitted vector $(j = 1 \dots K)$

$H \equiv (H_i)$ The row vector of projections of N points on the fitted vector $(i = 1 \dots N)$

We want to find T and H such that $|P - H|^2$ is minimum where $H = XT$; that is, we seek the least squares solution for T. The solution, by well-known results, is given by

$$T = (X^T X)^{-1} X^T P$$

while

$$H = XT = X(X^TX)^{-1}X^TP$$

Property Fitting by Nonlinear Regression A general index of nonlinear correlation (X) between an independent variable P and a dependent variable X was defined by Carroll (1964) as

$$X = \frac{1}{S^2} \sum_{i \neq j}^{n} \sum W_{ij}(X_i - X_j)^2$$

where

$$W_{ij} = f(|P_i - P_j|)$$

with f a monotone-decreasing function, and

$$S^2 = \frac{1}{N} \sum_{i=1}^{n} (X_i - \bar{X})^2$$

In the current application the independent variable P corresponds to one property and the dependent variable X refers to the projections of the N objects, on a vector in the K-dimensional space, while in most applications $W_{ij} = 1/(P_i - P_j)^2 + \text{CONSTANT}$, X is an inverse measure of nonlinear correlation.

Therefore, the procedure applied in the program aims to *minimize X*. Such a procedure entails finding the direction cosines (with respect to the initial reference axes) of a vector such that the projections of stimuli on that vector are as closely related as possible to the corresponding property values.

As an initial step we must transform the initially given coordinates to a new orthonormal set—i.e., such that $X^TX = I$. We do this by transforming to principal axes and then standardizing each principal axis to unit length.

To find the direction cosines (T) of the fitted vector and the projections (H) of stimuli on the vector, we first construct a symmetric matrix X^TAX, where the elements of A are defined by

$$A_{ij} = -W_{ij} \text{ for } i \neq j$$

and

$$A_{ii} = \sum_{j \neq i}^{n} W_{ij}$$

The smallest characteristic root of X^TAX is the minimum value of X and the corresponding characteristic vector gives the direction cosines (T) of the new vector. As before, $H = XT$. Once we have found the direction cosines with respect to the orthonormal coordinates, we must apply a transformation to find direction cosines with respect to the original coordinate system.

PROCEDURES Since the nonlinear regression procedure embraces a more sophisticated approach, there is some complication in interpreting the nonlinear correlation index, kappa. Hence, a considerable portion of the program has been devoted to nonlinear regression. For this reason we shall describe the procedures adopted respectively by nonlinear and linear regression in succession.

Nonlinear Regression

Step 1 Column means of X are subtracted and X is transformed into a set of orthonormal vectors.

Step 2 For each property the program carries out the following operations:

1. Compute the first four moments of x, as well as skewness and kurtosis. These moments are computed by equations derived by von Neuman (1941), and are appropriate, under the usual normality and independence assumptions, when only a single dependent variable is involved. In our case, where more than one dependent variable is involved, and we have optimized x, the distribution is no longer valid. However, the Z-squared measure discussed below should be at least approximately valid.
2. Compute Z and Z-squared (ZSQ), where Z is a standardized index of nonlinear correlation and ZSQ might be taken as an approximate chi-square measure with K (number of dimensions) degrees of freedom. Z and ZSQ are defined by

$$Z = \frac{x - \mu}{\sigma_x}$$

and

$$\text{ZSQ} = Z^2$$

In these equations, μ_x and σ_x are the mean and standard deviation of x, as computed above. The third and fourth moments (as well as skewness and kurtosis) are computed only to assess how the basic distribution of x departs from normality. If this distribution were normal, skewness and kurtosis would be, respectively, zero and 3.
3. Construct the symmetric matrix $X^T A X$ and find its smallest characteristic root (x). The corresponding characteristic vector (T) defines direction

cosines of the vector on which the projections of N points have the maximum nonlinear correlation (of x) with the given property values.

4. Compute the projections (H) of the N points on the vector defined by T.

Step 3   When all vectors have been found, the program proceeds to compute the cosine of angles between all pairs of vectors.

Step 4   For each pair of vectors, plot the vectors and the projections of N points on the plane formed by the pair.

Step 5   The configuration X is then transformed back to the original coordinates.

Step 6   Compute the direction cosines of all vectors with respect to the original coordinates.

Step 7   Plot the projections of all vectors onto planes defined by pairs of coordinates in the original space, together with the corresponding projections of stimulus points.

Linear Regression

Step 1   Normalize X by columns—that is, subtract the respective column means. Each column represents one dimension. Then compute the matrix *XMAT*, where $XMAT = (X^T X)^{-1} X^T$.

Step 2   For each property the following operations are carried out:

1. Compute the direction cosines (the T_j's) of the fitted vector.
2. Compute the projections of the N points (the H_i's) on the fitted vector.
3. Compute the product moment correlation (RHO) between the projections of N points on the fitted vector and the corresponding property values.

Proceed on to steps 3, 4, and 7 as described in nonlinear regression.

INPUT PARAMETERS   It is essential that the PROFIT input lines be arranged in the order given below. A sample input listing is found at the end of this explanation and in the PROFIT program's help file.

Within the parameter line, each parameter is input under free format. Input sets are also define. These input sets may be a matrix or an array of numbers belonging to a single variable, requiring several lines of input.

Parameters   All parameters except BC0 are integers input under free format

LANA: 1 Do linear regression only.
        2 Do nonlinear regression only.
        3 Do both linear and nonlinear regression treated as two
          independent analyses.

N: Number of stimulus points (Max. = 12)

K: Number of dimensions (Max. = 3)

M: Number of properties (Max. = 12)

IRX: 0   The stimulus matrix is punched N by K. Namely each row consists of the coordinates of one stimulus point. Each row must begin on a new line.

      1   The stimulus matrix is punched K by N. Each row, representing one dimension, begins on a new line and may continue to several lines if necessary.

IWGT: This parameter is relevant only when doing nonlinear regression analysis.

IPLOT: Option on Plots

      0 The program will not generate any plot.

      1 Plot projections of all properties in original space.

      2 Plot projections of all properties in the original space and for each property plot the given property values against the projections of stimuli on its fitted vector.

      3 In addition to the above, plots showing the projections of stimulus points on a plane formed by pairs of fitted vectors.

BC0:   BC0 is a floating point number. It is also relevant only in nonlinear regression analysis.

Input set 2: A format for reading in the stimulus matrix (use floating point format).

Input set 3: Stimulus matrix (X)—This matrix may be entered either K by N or N by K. Option IRX indicates which way it is entered. Each row of the matrix must begin on a new line.

Input set 4: A format for reading in the properties (floating-point format).

Input set 5: Property matrix—Each property must be preceded by a line containing its property name. The property matrix must be arranged in the following order. First property name (restricted to one line). First property values—read in according to format given above. May use several lines if necessary M-th property name, M-th property value.

Input set 6: Relevant only when MIDEN = 1. A format to read in symbols. (Must use A conversion.)

Input set 7: A blank line or repeat of items 1 through 6, one for each additional analysis. A blank line that signals the end of all computation must be the last image.

Further Explanation of Option IWGT concerns the available options on the weight function and BC0 is a constant associated with it. At present there are only three options available:

Option 1 IWGT $= 0$, which is considered the normal case.

$$W_{ij} = 1/[(P_i - P_j)^2 + \text{CONS}]$$

where

$$\text{CONS} = \frac{BC0}{N(N-1)} \sum_{i=j}^{n} (P_i - P_j)^2$$

The reason for the addition of the constant is evident. In the case where $P_i = P_j$, W_{ij} becomes undefined unless this constant is given some nonzero value. It is also felt that the inclusion of this term may improve the measure in many cases. In the case of "noisy" data, there is some reason to believe BC0 should be about equal to the ratio of error variance to true variance.

Option 2 IWGT $= 1$.

$$W_{ij} = \begin{cases} 1 & \text{if } |P_i - P_j| \leq BC0 \\ 0 & \text{otherwise} \end{cases}$$

If the property values correspond to the integer values 1 through N (though not necessarily in that order) and BC0 $= 1.0$, W_{ij} will equal 1 if i and j are adjacent and 0 otherwise. In this case x is equivalent to von Neuman's N, (the ratio of the mean square successive difference to the variance) as defined in von Neuman. Let

$$N_i = \sum_{j=1}^{n} W_{ij}$$

where W_{ij} has been defined in option 2, (with $W_{ii} = 1$). Then we redefine $W_{ij} = W_{ij}/N_i N_j$.

This option has been introduced because it allows, under certain conditions, the equivalence of $1 - x$ and N^2, the so-called correlation ratio. To attain this equivalence, it is necessary only that objects in the same group have property values that differ by no more than BC0, while objects in different groups differ by more than BC0. If this option is used, and the conditions obtain making x equivalent to N^2, the nonlinear regression procedure itself becomes equivalent to finding the best linear discriminant in a discriminant function analysis. There is reason to believe, however, that this option is sensible in more general situations.

OUTPUT   The output provides the following information:

— The normalized configuration of N stimulus points in K dimensional space (printed as K by N matrix)
— For each property, the original values on properties and the projections on fitted vectors
— For the linear case, the maximum correlation between each given property and its fitted vector (For the nonlinear case, the smallest characteristic root associated with each property, as well as Z, ZSQ and the four moments of x.)
— Direction cosines of the fitted vector in normalized space
— Cosines of angles between fitted vectors
— For nonlinear case only—the direction cosines of fitted vectors in the *original* space

SUMMARY OF INSTRUCTIONS

Input Arrangement   Six sets of images may be required.

Image 1   Parameters (requires 8 variables in a free format).

Variable and Description

LANA Linear regression option
N   Number of stimuli (Max. = 12)
K   Number of dimensions (Max. = 3)
M   Number of properties (Max. = 12)

IRX   The matrix configuration
0   If X is entered as N by K matrix
1   If X is entered as K by N matrix

IRWT The weight parameter
0   Ratio of error variance to true variance (DEFLT)
1   Ratio of mean square successive difference to variance

Option on Plots.
   0 The program will not generate any plot.
   1 Plot projections of all properties in original space.
   2 Plot projections of all properties in the original space and for each property plot the given property values against the projections of stimuli on its fitted vector.
   3 In addition to the above, plots showing the projections of stimulus points on a plane formed by pairs of fitted vectors.

BC0 is the maximum allowable difference between property values of objects within a given group. A seven-digit decimal number.

Line 2   Format for reading in the X matrix: A floating-point format must be used.

Line 3 and Successive Lines   The X matrix contains the coordinates of stimuli in K dimensions. X must be entered as indicated by IRX and contain floating-point numbers.

Format for Reading in the Property Matrix   A floating-point format must be used.

Successive Lines   Each property must be preceded by a line containing its property name. The property values are entered on the next card. This sequence continues until the M pairs of cards are entered. When weights are used (when IRWT = 1), use the following; otherwise delete.

IWGT = 0 and BC0 = 1   Equivalent to adding a constant
     BC0, which is the ratio of error to true variance.

IWGT = 1 and BC0 = 1   Equivalent to von Neumans N, the ratio of mean
     square successive differences to the variance.

IWGT = 1 and BC0 = 1   Objects in the same group must differ by no
     more than BC0 and objects in different groups must differ by
     more than BC0. This is equivalent to linear discriminant
     analysis.

SAMPLE DATA SET: POP DATA

```
CONFIGURATION MATRIX FROM INDSCAL ANALYSIS
   1   10   2   8   0   0   3  0.001
   (6X, 2F12.5)
   1          -.16570      -.26600
   2          -.18151      -.24813
   3          -.22479      -.19692
   4          -.34591       .32032
   5           .25542       .10266
   6           .26579       .60031
   7          -.05295      -.32816
   8           .39661      -.30941
   9           .51234      -.05987
  10          -.45928       .38520
   (3X, 10F5.2)
AFTER TASTE
001 4.86 4.61 4.54 1.91 3.49 3.23 4.47 1.54 4.61 2.75
CALORIES
002 4.74 4.81 4.40 3.65 4.33 4.44 4.67 3.51 4.19 4.47
CARBONATION
003 2.28 2.26 5.00 4.77 4.97 2.51 2.97 2.90 5.14 2.84
FRUITINESS
004 4.30 3.98 3.67 3.74 3.07 3.77 4.19 3.42 3.35 3.79
PICK-ME-UP
005 3.16 2.91 3.53 2.68 3.11 3.21 2.90 2.95 3.65 2.40
POPULARITY
006 5.05 5.44 4.61 3.26 4.09 3.95 5.49 3.67 4.09 4.86
SWEETNESS
007 3.91 3.84 3.00 3.40 3.25 3.21 4.07 3.84 2.51 4.51
THIRST QUENCHING
008 5.02 5.19 4.07 3.40 3.21 4.42 5.11 3.58 3.98 3.95
```

PROFIT SAMPLE OUTPUT

```
                    P R O F I T
              PROPERTY FITTING ANALYSIS
   PROGRAM WRITTEN BY DR. J. D. CARROLL AND JIH JIE CHANG
                   PC-MDS VERSION


ANALYSIS TITLE: SAMPLE
DATA IS READ FROM FILE: PROFIT.DAT
OUTPUT FILE IS: PROFIT.OUT


LANA (REGRESSION OPTION):                                1
N    NO. OF STIMULI  ( 12 MAX)                          10
K    NO. OF DIMENSIONS ( 3 MAX)                          2
M    NO. OF PROPERTIES (12 MAX)                          8

IRX  0 = N X K INPUT; 1 = K X N INPUT                    0
IWGT 0 = RATIO OF ERROR VAR. TO TRUE VAR. (USUAL OPTION) 0
     1 = RATIO OF MEAN SQ. SUCCESSIVE DIFFERENCE TO VARIANCE
IPLOT 0 = PROPERTIES ONLY                                3
      1 = PLOT PROPERTIES AND FUNCTIONS
      2 = DO ALL PLOTS
BCO (FLOATING POINT NUMBER FOR NON LINEAR REG.)       0.001


DATA FOR RECORD:     1
-.17E+00-.27E+00

DATA FOR RECORD:    10
-.46E+00 .39E+00

SAMPLE
LINEAR REGRESSION
NORMALIZED CONFIGURATION
   1        -.1657     -.1815     -.2248     -.3459     .2554
             .2658     -.0530      .3966      .5123    -.4593

   2        -.2660     -.2481     -.1969      .3203     .1027
             .6003     -.3282     -.3094     -.0599     .3852

COVARIANCE MATRIX
   1       1.0000    -.1046
   2       -.1046    1.0000

X*(X''X) INVERSE
   1        -.1957     -.2098     -.2481     -.3159     .2691     .3322
             .3683      .5117     -.4236

   2        -.2865     -.2701     -.2229      .2873     .1308     .6350
            -.2709     -.0064      .3409

         PROPERTY  1
INTERMEDIATE SUMS BEFORE SQUARING:     -.2688    -1.6097
SSQ =      2.66350   XL =      1.63202


ORIGINAL VALUES ON PROPERTY  1
        4.8600      4.6100      4.5400      1.9100      3.4900
        3.2300      4.4700      1.5400      4.6100      2.7500


PROJECTIONS ON FITTED VECTORS
         .2897       .2746       .2313      -.2590      -.1433
        -.6359       .3324       .2399      -.0253      -.3043
```

```
PROFIT DATA: CONFIGURATION MATRIX FROM INDSCAL ANALYSIS
   1   10   2   8   0   0   3  0.001
 (6X, 2F12.5)
   1      -.16570      -.26600   PARAMETER LINE IS
   2      -.18151      -.24813   FOLLOWED BY A FORMAT
   3      -.22479      -.19692   STATEMENT FOR
   4      -.34591       .32032   READING THE INPUT
   5       .25542       .10266   CONFIGURATION MATRIX.
   6       .26579       .60031
   7      -.05295      -.32816
   8       .39661      -.30941
   9       .51234      -.05987
  10      -.45928       .38520
 (3X, 10F5.2)    FORMAT STATEMENT FOR READING PROPERTIES
AFTER TASTE
001 4.86 4.61 4.54 1.91 3.49 3.23 4.47 1.54 4.61 2.75
CALORIES
002 4.74 4.81 4.40 3.65 4.33 4.44 4.67 3.51 4.19 4.47
CARBONATION
003 2.28 2.26 5.00 4.77 4.97 2.51 2.97 2.90 5.14 2.84
FRUITINESS
004 4.30 3.98 3.67 3.74 3.07 3.77 4.19 3.42 3.35 3.79
PICK-ME-UP
005 3.16 2.91 3.53 2.68 3.11 3.21 2.90 2.95 3.65 2.40
POPULARITY
006 5.05 5.44 4.61 3.26 4.09 3.95 5.49 3.67 4.09 4.86
SWEETNESS
007 3.91 3.84 3.00 3.40 3.25 3.21 4.07 3.84 2.51 4.51
THIRST QUENCHING
008 5.02 5.19 4.07 3.40 3.21 4.42 5.11 3.58 3.98 3.95
```

```
X*(X'X)$^{-1}$ = COMPUTATION MATRIX USED IN
DETERMINING STIMULUS RATINGS ON THE FITTED
STIMULUS PROPERTY VECTORS.
```

```
PROJECTIONS OF THE 10 STIMULI ON PROPERTY VECTOR 1
```

PLOT OF ORIGINAL (X-AXIS) VERSUS OBTAINED (Y-AXIS) FOR PROPERTY VECTOR | PLOT FOR PROPERTY 1:   PLOT OF ORIGINAL RATINGS
VS FITTED RATINGS (DERIVED BY THE REGRESSION
PROCEDURE TO MINIMIZE THE SUM OF SQUARES
DIFFERENCES BETWEEN THE ORIGINAL AND FITTED RATINGS).
THE CLOSER THE PLOT APPEARS TO AN UPWARD SLOPING
STRAIGHT LINE, THE BETTER THE FIT.

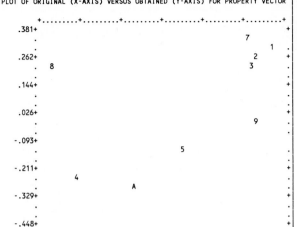

```
PLOT OF ORIGINAL (X-AXIS) VERSUS OBTAINED (Y-AXIS) FOR PROPERTY VECTOR
      +.........+.........+.........+.........+.........+.........+
 .381+                                                           +
 .                                                    7
 .                                                  1   .
 .262+                                            2      +
 .  8                                           3        .
 .
 .144+                                                   +
 .
 .026+                                                   +
 .                                              9
 .
-.093+                                                   +
 .                                   5
-.211+                                                   +
 .         4
 .                      A
-.329+                                                   +
 .
-.448+                                                   +
 .
-.566+                                                   +
 .
 .                               6
-.684+                                                   +
      +.........+.........+.........+.........+.........+.........+
      1.37 1.68 1.98 2.29 2.59 2.90 3.20 3.50 3.81 4.11 4.42 4.72 5.03
```

CORRELATION BETWEEN ORIGINAL AND FITTED VECTORS FOR PROPERTY   1 IS: | CORRELATION BETWEEN THE PROJECTIONS OF THE
N POINTS ON THE FITTED VECTOR AND THE ORIGINAL
RATINGS ON THE PROPERTY VECTOR.

     R =   .441 , RSQ =   .194

          .
          .
          .

          PROPERTY   2 ANALYSIS | OUTPUT IS THE SAME FOR PROPERTIES 2 - 8
          PROPERTY   3 ANALYSIS
          PROPERTY   4 ANALYSIS
          PROPERTY   5 ANALYSIS
          PROPERTY   6 ANALYSIS
          PROPERTY   7 ANALYSIS
          PROPERTY   8 ANALYSIS

          .
          .

TABLE 1. THE MAXIMUM CORRELATION BETWEEN THE PROPERTY
          AND THE PROJECTIONS ON FITTED VECTOR

	RHO	PROPERTY
1	.4408	After taste
2	.3443	Calories
3	.2142	Carbonation
4	.6460	Fruitiness
5	.6305	Pick-me-up
6	.6422	Popularity
7	.5835	Sweetness
8	.4804	Thirst quenching

EACH CORRELATION REPRESENTS THE RELATIONSHIP BETWEEN
THE PROPERTIES OF THE N POINTS ON THE FITTED VECTORS
AND ORIGINAL RATINGS ON THE PROPERTY VECTOR.
TABLE 1 IS TAKEN FROM THE CORRELATION REPORTED AFTER
EACH PROPERTY PLOT.

TABLE 2. DIRECTION COSINES OF FITTED VECTORS
          IN NORMALIZED SPACE

	DIMENSION	
VECTOR	1	2
1	-.1647	-.9863
2	-.8701	-.4928
3	.8866	.4626
4	-.9055	-.4243
5	.9326	-.3609
6	-.6426	-.7662
7	-.9649	-.2625
8	-.5427	-.8399

CORRELATIONS BETWEEN THE PROPERTY VECTOR AND THE
UNDERLYING DIMENSIONAL SPACE. THE SUM OF SQUARED
VALUES ACROSS ROWS EQUALS 1.0.

TABLE 3. COSINE OF ANGLES BETWEEN VECTORS

VECTOR:	1	2	3	4	5	6	7
2	.629						
3	-.602	-.999					
4	.568	.997	-.999				
5	.202	-.634	.660	-.691			
6	.862	.937	-.924	.907	-.323		
7	.418	.969	-.977	.985	-.805	.821	
8	.918	.886	-.870	.848	-.203	.992	.744

B,C,D,E,F,G,H,I CORRELATIONS BETWEEN VECTORS

PLOT FOR FIRST TWO DIMENSIONS OF STIMULUS POINTS AND DIRECTION COSINES
FITTED PROPERTY VECTORS

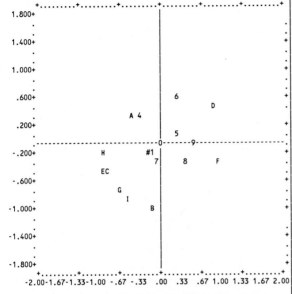

PLOT OF STIMULUS POINTS AND DIRECTIONAL COSINES OF
FITTED VECTORS. THE DIRECTIONAL COSINES DEFINING
THE VECTOR LOCATIONS IN TERMS OF THE X AND Y AXES
ARE FOUND ON THE UNIT CIRCLE.

POINTS = 1 TO A,   VECTORS = B TO I

```
*****IDENTIFICATION KEY FOR PLOTS WITH IDENTIFIED POINTS*****
PT #    1   2   3   4   5   6   7   8   9  10  11  12  13  14  15
CHAR    1   2   3   4   5   6   7   8   9   A   B   C   D   E   F
PT #   16  17  18  19  20  21  22  23  24  25  26  27  28  29  30
CHAR    G   H   I   J   K   L   M   N   O   P   Q   R   S   T   U
PT #   31  32  33  34  35  36  37  38  39  40  41  42  43  44  45
CHAR    V   W   X   Y   Z   +   /   =   *   &   $   @   %   ?   <
PT #   46  47  48  49  50
CHAR    (   )   "   ;   ˜
POINT NUMBERS ABOVE 50 IDENTIFIED AS  >, MULTIPLE POINTS IDENTIFIED
AS  #
```

Howard–Harris Cluster Analysis

N. Howard and B. Harris

The Howard–Harris program forms groups of objects sequentially using data consisting of an objects-by-variables matrix. The program uses the criterion of minimum within-group variance at each level of clustering.

THEORETICAL DISCUSSION   Let the number of objects being clustered be n, each of which is measured on N variables. Let the objects be denoted by x_1, $x_2, \ldots, x_n$, each x_i being a vector $(x_{i1}, \ldots, x_{in})$ in N-dimensional space. Let $P(S, p)$ represent a p-fold partitioning of the set S into disjoint subsets, A, B, and so forth.

With the above notation, the problem of clustering may be stated as follows: Given a set of objects $(x_1, x_2, \ldots, x_n \mid x_i \in S)$ each characterized by a number of variables, to partition S into subsets such that the subsets are as internally homogeneous and at the same time as mutually dissimilar as possible. The dissimilarity between any two objects, x_i and x_j in S can be defined as the squared Euclidean distance

$$d_{ij}^2 \equiv |x_i - x_j|^2 = \sum_{k=1}^{N} (x_{ik} - x_{jk})^2$$

For a group A with n_a members it can be shown that the sum of all squared interpoint distances is directly proportional to the sum of all interpoint deviations from the mean of the group. Mathematically stated,

$$\sum_{(x_i \in A)}^{n_A} |x_i - \bar{x}_A|^2 = \frac{1}{2n_A} \sum_{(x_i, x_j \in A)}^{n_A} \sum^{n_A} |x_i - x_j|^2$$

where $\bar{x}_A$ is the centroid of A, n_A is the number of points in A, and the squared distance between any two points is defined by the previous equation.

The total variance V_T of all n points in S can be written as

$$V_T = \frac{1}{2n_a} \sum_{i=1}^{n} \sum_{j=1}^{n} |x_i - x_j|^2$$

Taken from Appendix B by J. D. Carroll, in *Multiattribute Decisions in Marketing: A Measurement Approach* by P. E. Green and Y. Wind (Eds.) (Hinsdale, Ill.: Dryden, 1973).

For any p-fold partition into p groups, this variance can be divided into two components—a within-group variance, V_W, and a between-group variance, V_B. The total variance within any group A of n_a points has been shown earlier. Thus, the total within-group variance, V_W can be obtained by

$$V_W = \sum_{A \in P(S,p)} V_A$$

The criterion of optimally partitioning S into p groups is simply: Find $P(S,p)$ such that V_W is a minimum.

Unfortunately no algorithm presently exists for finding such a split in N dimensions. However, a locally optimal solution can be found by choosing a good split and then shifting points until a minimum V_W is found by a procedure to be described subsequently. The result will be at least locally optimal, but may be to some degree dependent on the initial split. In the Howard–Harris program an initial split is made on the basis of the maximum variance component of the vectors in the group being split.

COMPUTATIONAL PROCEDURE
The steps involved in finding a $(p + 1)$ fold partitioning of S, such that V_W is minimum given a p-fold partition of S, used in the program are as follows:

1. A group A is chosen for splitting on the basis of maximum within group variance.
2. A component of the vectors x_i in A is chosen to serve as the splitting variable on the basis of maximum variance.
3. New group membership for the vectors x_i (formerly A) is found on the basis of splitting at the mean value of the maximum variance component of x_i in A.
4. Finally, a local optimization is carried out by comparing the distance from each $x_i \in S$ to the centroid of each of the $p + 1$ existing groups. Points are shifted and centroids recomputed. Within group assignments are represented by minimum squared distance to the centroid of each cluster.

It can be shown, using proof by counterexample, that the solution contained in step 4 is locally optimal. The property of the locally optimal solution is: If any single point is moved from its assigned group to any other group, total within-group variance would be increased.

The actual test for final group membership is made by testing for changes in within-group variance that would accompany a hypothetical shift of $x_i \in A$ to any other group B. If the shift would result in decreased variance, it is made.

INPUT PARAMETERS, SAMPLE DATA FILE,

AND SAMPLE OUTPUT This version of the Howard–Harris program will handle 100 objects and 12 variables. Input data can be standardized by column to mean zero and unit standard deviation at the user's option. Furthermore, different scaling factors for each variable can be read in. The user can also specify the maximum number of groups to be formed.

The program does not have a menu or input parameters that must be specified with the data set. Instead, the program interactively requests the following information:

```
ENTER THE MAXIMUM NUMBER OF CLUSTERS TO BE
ALLOWED IN THE SOLUTION   (MAXIMUM = 12)
```

```
ENTER THE NUMBER OF VARIABLES TO BE INCLUDED IN
THE ANALYSIS.  (MAXIMUM=12)
```

```
YOUR DATA WILL BE STANDARDIZED UNLESS INDICATED.
PRESS ENTER TO STANDARDIZE, OR 1 IF NOT DESIRED.
```

```
ARE SCALING FACTORS INCLUDED FOR EACH VARIABLE?
ENTER 1 IF SCALING FACTORS ARE INCLUDED WITH DATA,
   (NOTE: SCALING FACTORS MUST APPEAR IMMEDIATELY
     BEFORE THE DATA AND ARE READ AS  16F5.0 )
PRESS ENTER IF SCALING FACTORS ARE NOT DESIRED.
```

Following this input, execution of the program begins.

```
(F3.0,12X,F3.0,8X,F4.0,F2.0,2F3.0,F4.0,2F3.0,F3.0)
125 6 3 4 08 1 2 300 5 38 46 184 72 53 350   ASTON MARTIN SALOON
110 5 3 2 12 2 2 380 5 39 37 177 78 45 354   FERRARI TESTAROSA
118 5 3 2 12 2 2 420 5 39 33 165 79 42 341   LAMBORGHINI COUNTACH
057 6 3 2 04 2 2 215 4 36 27 169 73 45 194   LOTUS TURBO ESPRIT
059 4 3 2 08 1 2 316 5 38 35 178 72 51 317   PORSCHE 928
026 4 3 2 04 1 2 147 4 34 28 169 68 50 144   PORSCHE 944
014 2 3 2 04 1 2 146 4 33 26 169 67 50 138   MAZDA RX7
018 2 3 2 06 1 2 200 5 32 33 171 68 50 227   NISSAN 300ZX
065 5 3 2 08 2 2 260 5 39 32 169 68 44 213   FERRARI 928 GTS
028 1 2 2 08 1 2 240 5 40 32 176 71 47 345   CORVETTE
                      .
                      .
                      .
012 1 7 4 06 1 2 140 2 32 32 158 68 69 170   BRONCO II
012 1 7 5 04 1 3 085 2 34 29 165 71 63 132   JEEP CHEROKEE
010 1 7 4 04 1 3 085 3 36 29 121 66 72 141   JEEP WRANGLER
011 2 7 5 04 1 3 096 3 35 32 175 65 70 125   ISUZU TROOPER
010 2 7 4 04 1 3 109 3 34 33 157 66 71 142   MITSUBISHI MONTERO
017 2 7 5 04 1 3 125 3 41 42 184 71 70 200   TOYOTA LANDCRUISER
007 2 7 4 04 1 3 063 3 33 21 135 60 66 074   SUZUKI SAMURAI
```

HOWARD–HARRIS SAMPLE OUTPUT

```
                              C L U S T E R
                    HOWARD - HARRIS  CLUSTER  ANALYSIS

          PROGRAM WRITTEN BY PROF. B. HARRIS, ALGORITHM BY PROF. N. HOWARD
                              PC - MDS VERSION
```

ANALYSIS TITLE: CAR DATA SAMPLE RUN	INPUT DATA: 90 CARS BY 10 ATTRIBUTES
DATA IS READ FROM FILE: CLUSTER.DAT	
OUTPUT PRINT FILE IS: CLUSTER.OUT	
DATA FOR RECORD: 1	
.13E+03 .80E+01 .30E+03 .50E+01 .38E+02 .46E+02 .18E+03 .72E+02 .53E+02 .35E+03	PRINT OUT OF RESPONDENT (CAR) #1
DATA FOR RECORD: 90	
.70E+01 .40E+01 .63E+02 .30E+01 .33E+02 .21E+02 .14E+03 .60E+02 .66E+02 .74E+02	PRINT OUT OF RESPONDENT (CAR) #90
TITLE: CAR DATA SAMPLE RUN	

```
NO OF OBSERVATIONS OR CASES      90
NO OF VARIABLES PER CASE         10
MAX NO OF CLUSTERS               6
FORMAT: (F3.0, 12X, F3.0, 8X,   F4.0,F2.0,2F3.0,F4.0,2F3.0,F4.0)

   RAW DATA

      1      2      3      4      5      6      7      8      9     10
 1 125.00   8.00 300.00   5.00  38.00  46.00 184.00  72.00  53.00 350.00      PRINT OUT OF RAW DATA

 2 110.00  12.00 380.00   5.00  39.00  37.00 177.00  78.00  45.00 354.00

 3 118.00  12.00 420.00   5.00  39.00  33.00 165.00  79.00  42.00 341.00
 .     .      .      .      .      .      .      .      .      .      .

 .     .      .      .      .      .      .      .      .      .      .
85  12.00   4.00  85.00   2.00  34.00  29.00 165.00  71.00  63.00 132.00

86  10.00   4.00  85.00   3.00  36.00  29.00 121.00  66.00  72.00 141.00

87  11.00   4.00  96.00   3.00  35.00  32.00 175.00  65.00  70.00 125.00

88  10.00   4.00 109.00   3.00  34.00  33.00 157.00  66.00  71.00 142.00

89  17.00   4.00 125.00   3.00  41.00  42.00 184.00  71.00  70.00 200.00

90   7.00   4.00  63.00   3.00  33.00  21.00 135.00  60.00  66.00  74.00
```

```
        VARIABLE              STANDARD
        NUMBER    MEAN        DEVIATION
        --------------------------------------
           1     22.3889       31.3772
           2      5.1556        1.9259
           3    134.4666       71.9849
           4      2.6333        1.2776
           5     35.8000        3.7274
           6     29.5778        7.2938
           7    175.4889       16.4528
           8     68.4222        4.5092
           9     57.4000        8.5554
          10    162.2000       77.7629
```

MEANS AND STANDARD DEVIATIONS
OF THE 10 VARIABLES

```
**********************************************************************
GROUP    NUMBER OF              SPLIT NUMBER    1
NUMBER   SUBJ. IN GRP.          LIST OF SUBJECTS
--------------------------------------------------------------------
   1        64          6   7  19  21  23  24  25  26  27  28  29  31
                       32  33  34  35  36  37  38  39  40  41  42  43
                       44  45  46  47  48  49  50  51  52  53  54  55
                       56  57  58  59  60  61  66  67  68  69  70  71
                       74  75  76  77  78  79  80  81  82  83  84  85
                       86  87  88  90
   2        26          1   2   3   4   5   8   9  10  11  12  13  14
                       15  16  17  18  20  22  30  62  63  64  65  72
                       73  89
```

FIRST SPLIT INTO 2 GROUPS
THE NUMBER OF RESPONDENTS IN
EACH GROUP AND THE RESPONDENT
IDENTIFICATION NUMBER ARE GIVEN.

```
**********************************************************************
                         .          .
                         .          .
                SPLIT NUMBER    2
                SPLIT NUMBER    3
                SPLIT NUMBER    4
                         .          .
                         .          .
**********************************************************************
GROUP    NUMBER OF              SPLIT NUMBER    5
NUMBER   SUBJ. IN GRP.          LIST OF SUBJECTS
--------------------------------------------------------------------
   1        24         27  28  34  35  36  37  38  39  40  44  46  47
                       48  49  51  53  56  57  58  60  61  74  76  90

   2         4         63  64  65  72
   3        12          5   9  10  11  13  14  16  17  18  20  30  73

   4        25          4   6   7   8  19  21  22  23  24  25  26  29
                       31  32  33  41  42  43  45  50  52  54  55  59
                       62
   5        20         66  67  68  69  70  71  75  77  78  79  80  81
                       82  83  84  85  86  87  88  89
   6         5          1   2   3  12  15
--------------------------------------------------------------------
```

```
        WITHIN GROUP SUM OF SQUARES FOR EACH FINAL GROUP

     900.000   511.828   415.171   334.091   289.858   244.572          | WITHIN GROUP SUM OF SQUARES

TITLE: CAR DATA SAMPLE RUN
****************************************************************************************
                        GROUP SUMMARY TABLE
                     SUBJECT  BY  SPLIT  NUMBER
-------------------------------------------------------------------------------
                                                                        | GROUP IDENTIFICATION CODES
        0   1   2   3   4   5                                           | FOR EACH OF THE 90 RESPONDENTS
   1    1   2   3   3   3   6                                           | AT EACH OF THE REQUESTED NUMBER
   2    1   2   3   3   3   6                                           | OF CLUSTERS.
   3    1   2   3   3   3   6
   4    1   2   1   4   4   4
   5    1   2   3   3   3   3
   .    .   .   .   .   .   .
   .    .   .   .   .   .   .
  85    1   1   1   4   5   5
  86    1   1   1   1   5   5
  87    1   1   1   4   5   5
  88    1   1   1   4   5   5
  89    1   2   2   2   2   5
  90    1   1   1   1   1   1


FINISHED PROCESSING
```

Correspondence Analysis: A Mathematical Algorithm

J. Douglas Carroll, P. E. Green, and C. M. Shaffer

NONTECHNICAL INTRODUCTION   Correspondence analysis is a statistical technique that uses contingency table data, including frequency counts, to derive interpoint distances between the row and column categories.

CORRESP performs correspondence analysis using the Carroll, Green, and Schaffer algorithm for mapping two-way contingency table data. The PC-MDS operationalization of this algorithm has been developed to accept large data sets. The CGS algorithm is described in detail in two articles appearing in the *Journal of Marketing Research*: "Interpoint Distance Comparisons in Correspondence Analysis" (August 1986) and "Comparing Interpoint Distances in Correspondence Analysis: A Clarification" (November 1987).

CORRESP permits squared distance comparisons within row, within column, and between rows and columns. This ability to compare distances between rows and columns differentiates this approach from other commonly available programs.

In nontechnical terms, correspondence analysis could be described as a singular value decomposition (as in factor analysis) of a matrix of chi-square distances. The decomposition produces a set of matrices (eigenvalue and eigenvectors) that are applied to row-and-column distance matrices to produce the interpoint distances for correspondence analysis mapping.

The correspondence analysis map may be interpreted as a point-point model. The distances between points are however, chi-square metric rather than Euclidean metric.

TECHNICAL INTRODUCTION   Correspondence analysis is a metric method of multidimensional scaling for categorical data. The method has been most recently associated with the work of the French school (Benzècri; Lebart, Morineau, and Warwick).

Based on the article "Interpoint Distance Comparisons in Correspondence Analysis" by J. D. Carroll, P. E. Green, and C. M. Shaffer, *Journal of Marketing Research* (August 1986). Used by permission.

Normal methods of analysis for contingency table data entail the computation of a chi-square statistic for the data. Although this approach indicates the independence of row and column variables, the relationships between the rows and columns are not identified. More specifically, they are not identified in terms of a metric space. CORRESP displays these data geometrically.

Mathematical Algorithm

Given a two way contingency table, F, CORRESP normalizes F by pre- and post-multiplication by the reciprocals of the row and column sums. Chi-square distances are then computed on this matrix. It is this matrix of distances that is decomposed, rotated, and again centered to produce the distance matrix. Consider the following:

$$\text{Given} \quad F = \begin{bmatrix} 1 & 5 & 3 \\ 5 & 1 & 3 \\ 2 & 10 & 2 \\ 1 & 1 & 7 \end{bmatrix}$$

F can be normalized using the form

$$H = R^{-1/2}FC^{-1/2}$$

where $R^{-1/2}$ is a 4×4 diagonal matrix and $C^{-1/2}$ is a 3×3 diagonal matrix, whose entries consist of the reciprocals of the square roots of the row and column marginals. The H matrix is next converted to a chi-square distance matrix using the standard $(O - E)^2/E$ formula.

H is next decomposed using the singular value decomposition:

$$H = P\Delta Q'$$

with $P'P = Q'Q = I$, and Δ is a diagonal matrix.

The correspondence analysis next defines the coordinates of the row and column points, X and Y.

$$X = R^{-1/2}P(\Delta + I)^{1/2}$$

and

$$Y = C^{-1/2}Q(\Delta + I)^{1/2}$$

This transformation stretches the vertical axis so that the resulting configuration is more spherical than the more common approach to correspondence analysis.

CORRESP Input

The program CORRESP begins with the standard PC-MDS

input prompts for a title, name of the input data file and output print file. Next the parameter input prompt appears:

```
Parameters may be ENTERED from the keyboard or
READ as the first part of the data file.
 ┌──────────────────┐              ┌──────────────────┐
 │ Type  1  for     │              │ Press ENTER to   │
 │ KEYBOARD ENTRY   │     OR       │ READ as data     │
 └──────────────────┘              └──────────────────┘
```

Line 1: Parameters   If parameters are to be read as part of the data file, two parameters are required:

$$NR = \text{Number of rows}$$

$$NC = \text{Number of columns}$$

These two parameters are read as the first line of the data file. The two values must be separated by a blank space, as they are read under a **FREE** format.

Alternately, if parameters are entered interactively, the following messages appear, to which the user gives appropriate responses.

```
ENTER THE NUMBER OF ROWS IN THE MATRIX   ( 1 to 12)
```

```
ENTER THE NUMBER OF COLUMNS IN THE MATRIX(1 TO 12)
```

Input FORMAT   Like the parameters, the input format may be read as part of the second line of the data file, or specified as **FREE** format from the keyboard.

```
ENTER the INPUT FORMAT for reading the data
 ┌──────────────────┐              ┌──────────────────┐
 │ Press ENTER      │              │ Type FREE        │
 │ if INPUT FORMAT  │              │ if data is in    │
 │ is READ as part  │     OR       │ free format      │
 │ of the data file │              │                  │
 └──────────────────┘              └──────────────────┘
In Free format, data points are separated by spaces
```

Labels Row and column labels may be ignored (not read), entered from the keyboard, or read as part of the data file.

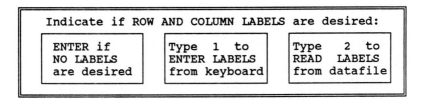

```
Indicate if ROW AND COLUMN LABELS are desired:

ENTER if          Type  1  to        Type    2  to
NO LABELS         ENTER LABELS        READ  LABELS
are desired       from keyboard       from datafile
```

If read as part of the data file, the data file would contain a parameter line, format line, data, and finally labels. There must be as many labels as there are rows *and* columns.

If data labels are to be entered from the keyboard, the program will request labels for each row and then for each column label. Labels must not exceed 8 characters in length.

CORRESP SAMPLE DATA

Example 1

All Parameters, Format, and Labels are part of the data file.

```
 4  3
(3F3.0)
   1   5   1
   5   1   3
   2  10   2
   1   1   7
ROW 1
ROW 2
ROW 3
ROW 4
COLUMN 1
COLUMN 2
COLUMN 3
```

Example 2

Data Only, Parameters entered from keyboard, FREE format, No labels, or Labels entered interactively.

```
1   5   1
5   1   3
2  10   2
1   1   7
```

```
                     TWO  WAY  CORRESPONDENCE  ANALYSIS
       MATHEMATICAL ALGORITHM BY J.D. CARROLL, P.E. GREEN AND C. M. SCHAFFER
                            PC - MDS VERSION

ANALYSIS TITLE:           GREENACRE TEST DATA
DATA IS READ FROM FILE:   GREEN.DAT
OUTPUT FILE IS:           TEST.PRN
INPUT FORMAT: (4F2.0)

INPUT DATA AND EXPECTED CHI-SQUARE FREQUENCIES:
       OBSERVED | NONE  | LIGHT | MEDIUM | HEAVY |
       EXPECTED |   1   |   2   |   3    |   4   |
      ----------+-------+-------+--------+-------+--------
                | 4.00  | 2.00  | 3.00   | 2.00  | 11.00 |
     SENIOR M  1| 3.48  | 2.56  | 3.53   | 1.42  | 11.00 |
      ----------+-------+-------+--------+-------+--------
                | 4.00  | 3.00  | 7.00   | 4.00  | 18.00 |
     JUNIOR M  2| 5.69  | 4.20  | 5.78   | 2.33  | 18.00 |
      ----------+-------+-------+--------+-------+--------
                | 25.00 | 10.00 | 12.00  | 4.00  | 51.00 |
     SENIOR E  3| 16.12 | 11.89 | 16.38  | 6.61  | 51.00 |
      ----------+-------+-------+--------+-------+--------
                | 18.00 | 24.00 | 33.00  | 13.00 | 88.00 |
     JUNIOR E  4| 27.81 | 20.52 | 28.27  | 11.40 | 88.00 |
      ----------+-------+-------+--------+-------+--------
                | 10.00 | 6.00  | 7.00   | 2.00  | 25.00 |
     SECRETAR  5| 7.90  | 5.83  | 8.03   | 3.24  | 25.00 |
      ----------+-------+-------+--------+-------+--------
       TOTALS   | 61.00 | 45.00 | 62.00  | 25.00 | 193.00 |

MATRIX OF CHI-SQUARE DISTANCES
                | NONE  | LIGHT | MEDIUM | HEAVY |
      ----------+-------+-------+--------+-------+-------
     SENIOR M  1|  .28  | -.35  | -.28   |  .48  |
      ----------+-------+-------+--------+-------+-------
     JUNIOR M  2| -.71  | -.58  |  .51   | 1.09  |
      ----------+-------+-------+--------+-------+-------
     SENIOR E  3| 2.21  | -.55  | -1.08  | -1.01 |
      ----------+-------+-------+--------+-------+-------
     JUNIOR E  4| -1.86 |  .77  |  .89   |  .47  |
      ----------+-------+-------+--------+-------+-------
     SECRETAR  5|  .75  |  .07  | -.36   | -.69  |
      ----------+-------+-------+--------+-------+-------

CHI-SQUARE STATISTIC FOR DISTANCE MATRIX =    16.442

EIGENVALUES OF THE CHI-SQUARE DISTANCE MATRIX
                      1         2         3         4
      -----------------------------------------------------------------
     VALUES        .0748     .0100     .0004     .0000 |
     % OF TOTAL   87.7559   11.7587    .4855     .0000 |
     CUMULATIVE % 87.7559   99.5145  100.0000  100.0000 |
      -----------------------------------------------------------------
```

Print out of file information
Input file
Output file
(4F2.0) FORMAT was
 used to read data

Print out of observed input
data file (read as frequencies)
and the expected value of the
cell in the contingency table.

(Note there are 4 columns plus
a column for row Totals).

The Actual data file appears:
(4F2.0)
 4 2 3 2
 4 3 7 4
251012 4
18243313
10 6 7 2

Rows are categories of jobs

1=SENIOR MANAGER
2=JUNIOR MANAGER
3=SENIOR EMPLOYEE
4=JUNIOR EMPLOYEE
5=SECRETARIES

Columns are usage categories
1= NONE
2= LIGHT
3= MEDIUM
4= HEAVY

Matrix of Chi-Square Distances
This matrix is computed from
a transformed (normalized)
frequency matrix, where the
normalization is:

$(R*(-1/2)) * F * (C*(-1/2))$

PLOT COORDINATES OF THE ROW VARIABLES (FIRST 5 DIMENSIONS)

| LABELS | | DIMENSION | | |
		1	2	3
SENIOR M	1	.2714	2.0303	3.5256
JUNIOR M	2	-1.0688	2.5497	-1.6741
SENIOR E	3	1.5708	.1117	-.2561
JUNIOR E	4	-.9614	-.6051	.1642
SECRETAR	5	.8299	-.8270	-.4014

VARIABLE COORDINATES OF THE COLUMN VARIABLES (5 DIMENSIONS)

| LABELS | | DIMENSION | | |
		1	2	3
NONE	1	1.6233	.3195	-.0442
LIGHT	2	-.4105	-1.4783	1.0926
MEDIUM	3	-.8103	-.0771	-1.2745
HEAVY	4	-1.2125	2.0725	1.3019

*****IDENTIFICATION KEY FOR PLOTS WITH IDENTIFIED POINTS*****

PT #	1	2	3	4	5	6	7	8	9	10	11	12	13	14	15
CHAR	1	2	3	4	5	6	7	8	9	A	B	C	D	E	F

PT #	16	17	18	19	20	21	22	23	24	25	26	27	28	29	30
CHAR	G	H	I	J	K	L	M	N	O	P	Q	R	S	T	U

PT #	31	32	33	34	35	36	37	38	39	40	41	42	43	44	45
CHAR	V	W	X	Y	Z	+	/	=	*	&	$	@	%	?	<

PT #	46	47	48	49	50
CHAR	(	)	.	;	^

where the pre and post multiply matrices are diagonal matrices containing transformed row and column totals.

The Chi-Square distance matrix is analyzed and canonical decomposition is performed. Eigenvalues are interpreted as in factor analysis.

The plot coordinates of the varimax rotated solution are given for the first five dimensions of the solution. These coordinates identify the points of both the row and column stimuli.

POINT NUMBERS ABOVE 50 IDENTIFIED AS >, MULTIPLE POINTS IDENTIFIED AS #

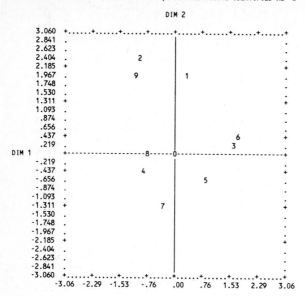

Plot of points in dim. 1 & 2.

The points are identified by codes.

The row points are identified first, starting with 1 and continuing to the end of the rows. The columns then start with the next alpha-numeric character contained in the graph legend.

Plot labels have been entered using a text editor and are not printed by the program.

POINT NUMBERS ABOVE 50 IDENTIFIED AS >, MULTIPLE POINTS IDENTIFIED AS #

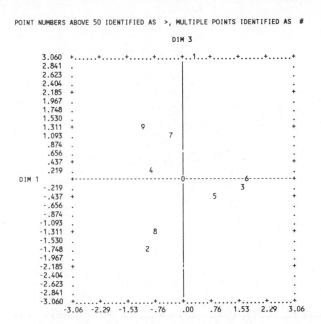

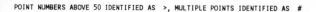

POINT NUMBERS ABOVE 50 IDENTIFIED AS >, MULTIPLE POINTS IDENTIFIED AS #

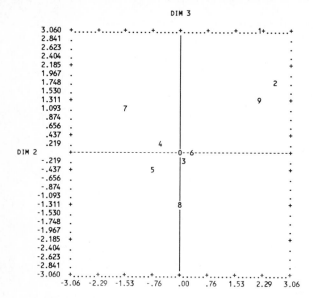

```
                                    DIM 3
       3.060  +......+......+......+......+......+......+......1+......+
       2.841  .                                                      .
       2.623  .                                                      .
       2.404  .                                                      .
       2.185  +                                                      +
       1.967  .                                                      .
       1.748  .                                        2             .
       1.530  .                                                      .
       1.311  +                                     9                +
       1.093  .            7                                         .
        .874  .                                                      .
        .656  .                                                      .
        .437  +                                                      +
        .219  .                         4                            .
DIM 2   +-------------------------0--6------------------------+
       -.219  .                         |3                           .
       -.437  +                    5    |                            +
       -.656  .                                                      .
       -.874  .                                                      .
      -1.093  .                                                      .
      -1.311  +                         |8                           +
      -1.530  .                                                      .
      -1.748  .                                                      .
      -1.967  .                                                      .
      -2.185  +                                                      +
      -2.404  .                                                      .
      -2.623  .                                                      .
      -2.841  .                                                      .
      -3.060  +......+......+......+......+......+......+......+......+
            -3.06  -2.29  -1.53   -.76    .00    .76   1.53   2.29   3.06
```

************** SUCCESSFUL COMPLETION OF CORRESPONDENCE ANALYSIS **************

How to Use KYST:
A Very Flexible Program
to Do Multidimensional
Scaling and Unfolding

Joseph B. Kruskal, Bell Laboratories; Forrest W. Young,
Thurstone Psychometric Laboratory; and Judith B. Seery, Bell Laboratories

NONTECHNICAL INTRODUCTION KYST is an extremely flexible computer program for multidimensional scaling and unfolding. It represents a merger of MDSCAL 5M and TORSCA 9, including the best features of both, as well as some new features of interest. (The name, pronounced "kissed," is an acronym for Kruskal, Young, Shepard, and Torgerson). KYST includes the powerful initial configuration procedure from TORSCA as well as the very helpful practice of rotating solutions to principal components. KYST incorporates the great generality of MDSCAL 5M.

KYST is an extremely general scaling program because of the many options it contains. Many types of metric and nonmetric scaling and unfolding may be conducted. Briefly, KYST is capable of analyzing a set of rank data to produce a metric configuration of points in space. For example, the 45 possible unique pairs of 10 cars $[10 \times (10-1)/2 = 45]$ are ranked according to perceived similarity of the pairs. The pairs are ranked from 1 to 45 and ranks are entered into the lower half of a 10×10 matrix with no diagonal.

KYST uses this rank information about similarities or dissimilarities between the pairs to generate a set of metric distances between objects so that the distances most closely represent the original ranks between pairs.

Unlike the point-vector model of the MDPREF program, which interprets points along a vector, KYST is a point-point model, meaning that distances between any two points plotted may be interpreted as an indicator of similarity or dissimilarity. KYST plots only the stimuli (brands) and does not

---

The KYST program was written by J. B. Kruskal and J. B. Seery of Bell Laboratories and F. W. Young of Thurstone Psychometric Laboratory. This guide is a revision of their paper, made by Scott M. Smith for the PC version of KYST. KYST copyright 1973 Bell Telephone Laboratories, Incorporated, reprinted by permission.

plot both stimuli (brands) and subjects (attributes) (except in unfolding analysis).

KYST analyzes a square symmetric matrix of data containing the evaluation data. Program options, however, allow you to input lower- or upper-half matrices, with or without diagonals, and even rectangular subject by stimuli matrices if unfolding analysis is done. Most often we are analyzing a matrix of average similarity or dissimilarity rankings (nonmetric) or evaluations (metric) for a set of stimuli (brands).

TECHNICAL INTRODUCTION

Unfolding can be thought of as a kind of scaling in which there are two kinds of points (often called subject points and stimulus points), such that the information available compares distances radiating from a single subject point at a time to the various stimulus points. While KYST may be used to do pure unfolding, difficulties are not unusual. (For example, at the most meaningful solution stress may reach a merely local minimum, and it is not unusual for the program to reach a nonmeaningful minimum.) To be recommended for use with KYST are many procedures intermediate between unfolding and ordinary scaling, which use two or more sets of data, only one of which is of the unfolding type. Even where the only direct data available are of the unfolding type, it is generally possible and desirable to derive secondary data of another type for supplementary use.

While this initial configuration works very well in the classical scaling situations, its value in other KYST applications (such as unfolding) is not always clear.

What KYST Does

Only the briefest description of what KYST does can be given here. For a fuller description of the ideas, consult Kruskal (1964a and 1964b) and Young (1972).

KYST places N points in a space of dimension LDIM so as to minimize STRESS, which measures the "badness-of-fit" between the configuration of points and the data. It finds the minimizing configuration by starting with some configuration (perhaps found by the classical scaling procedure of Torgerson), and moving all the points a bit to decrease the stress, then iterating this procedure over and over again until the stopping criterion is reached. Typically, from 15 to 50 iterations may be required. Technically speaking, KYST uses the iterative numerical method of gradients (the method of steepest descent), with a step-size procedure based primarily on the angles between successive gradients.

Let the data values be listed (in any order) and called DATA(1) through DATA(MM). (In the sample discussed above, $MM = 45$.) For a square matrix of size N we have $MM = N^2$ if the diagonal entries are to be included or $MM = N(N - 1)$ if they are not. For a half matrix $MM = N(N + 1)/2$ or $N(N - 1)/2$ depending on whether the diagonal entries are included or not. Each entry in the matrix may be represented by several distinct data values.

If each entry is represented by NREPL1 data values, then *MM* is NREPL1 times as large as it would otherwise be. If some of the data values are missing, *MM* is the same, with minus (zero) entered or the mean value for the data.

For *any* given configuration of N points (it doesn't make any difference where the configuration comes from), let the distances between pairs of points be calculated and listed in DIST(1) to DIST(*MM*) in corresponding positions to those in the data list. If one matrix entry has several data values, then the self-same distance will appear in the distance list several times. If some other matrix entry has no data values (missing data situation, for example), then the corresponding distance never appears on the distance list. Corresponding to diagonal entries of the matrix are distances of zero, of course, and the distances corresponding to (i,j) and (j,i) entries of the matrix are of course the same (automatically).

Now perform a least-squares regression of DIST on DATA. For nonmetric scaling, monotone ascending regression should be used for dissimilarities, and monotone descending regression for similarities. For metric scaling, this regression can be linear or it can be polynomial up to degree 4. Of course, the regression yields the polynomial coefficients.

Ascending or dissimilarities data are characterized by values that increase in dissimilarity as the scale increases. (A higher scale value means less similarity.) Descending or similarities data are characterized by values that increase in similarity as the scale increases. (A higher scale value means greater similarity.)

Let the values of the regression function be listed in DHAT(1) to DHAT(*MM*). Let DBAR be the arithmetic average of the DIST values. Then

$$
\text{STRESS} = \sqrt{\dfrac{\displaystyle\sum_{M=1}^{MM} (\text{DIST}(M) - \text{DHAT}(M))^2}{\displaystyle\sum_{M=1}^{MM} (\text{DIST}(M) - d_0)^2}}
$$

where $d_0 = 0$ for stress formula 1, or $d_0 = \text{DBAR}$ for stress formula 2. It is stress that is minimized by moving the points of the configuration around.

The two formulas will often yield very similar configurations. In using KYST to do multidimensional unfolding, as explained later, the use of formula 2 is in theory vital. However, formula 2 sometimes has problems due to local *maxima* that cannot occur with formula 1.

The interpretation of stress values can be greatly affected by the options used and by various parameters, such as the number of stimuli and the number of dimensions. While actual experience with real data has been the primary source of information so far, fortunately several papers have explored this question by Monte Carlo techniques.

It is possible to transform the data values by a fairly flexible formula, as a preprocessing step prior to the actual scaling computation. This can be a very useful preliminary step, both to help the main scaling procedure when linear or polynomial regression is being used, and to help the TORSCA initial configuration do a better job.

It is possible to weight the squared terms in STRESS. Let $WW(1)$ to $WW(MM)$ be a list of *positive* weights corresponding to the data values. The formula for stress now becomes

$$\text{STRESS} = \sqrt{\frac{\sum WW(M)(\text{DIST}(M) - \text{DHAT}(M))^2}{\sum WW(M)(\text{DIST}(M) - D_0)^2}}$$

KYST permits the weights to be given as a reasonably flexible function of the corresponding data values, or to be read in.

An important element of generality is the ability to "split" the data into separate sublists, and perform separate regressions on each list. (This "splitting" may be used to do unfolding.) When the data are split, a separate regression and a stress is computed for each sublist by the formula above. The overall stress is taken to be the root-mean-square of the several sublist stresses. It is possible to split the data in several different ways. Also, it is possible to use different types of regression for different sublists, a fact that offers some interesting possibilities.

Normally, KYST uses a distance formula that is appropriate for Euclidean space. However, it is capable of using a certain other kind of distance that mathematicians call the l_p-metric, or the Minkowski r-metric. If points x and y have coordinates x_i and y_i, then the Minkowski r-metric distance between them is given by

$$\text{distance } r(x, y) = \left[\sum_i (|x_i - y_i|)^2 \right]^{1/r}$$

For $r = 2.0$, this is ordinary Euclidean distance. For $r = 1.0$, this is the so-called city-block distance, or Manhattan metric. For $r = \infty$, it can be shown that this formula yields the maximum of the absolute coordinate differences, sometimes called the "dominance" metric (which is a simple instance of the important distance mathematicians call the supremum or sup metric.) For any value of r between (and including) 1.0 and ∞, a classical theorem states that the Minkowski r-metric is a true metric because it satisfies the triangle inequality. For values of r between (but excluding) 0 and 1.0, it is known that the Minkowski r-metric does *not* satisfy the triangle inequality (although it does if one omits the outside exponent of $1/r$), but this case has nevertheless received much study. It appears that KYST should be capable of handling values of r in this range also, though we have no actual experience.

OPTIONS AND CONTROL OPTIONS   Table 15–1 shows the complete input to KYST necessary to perform an example of multidimensional scaling.

_____ *Table 15–1* _____

Sample Data: 5×5 Full Matrix

Line Number
Description

1	5	1	1			Parameter
2	(F4.2,4(4X,F4.2))					Format
3	9.3	0.57	6.1	2.0	1.5	Data
4	1.0	8.5	5.5	3.3	4.0	Data
5	2.1	5.3	7.3	3.9	1.1	Data
6	5.0	6.2	1.6	8.9	2.8	Data
7	1.3	4.1	1.0	2.5	8.8	Data

File for Data, Weights, Configuration, and Title   The first line of a data set is a parameter line containing either three or four integer parameters, read in free format.

Before describing the arrangement of parameters, let us describe the general data file as consisting of several groups of rows. Each group has a certain number of rows and columns (the same for every group in a single data file). Unless one of the corner matrix options is in effect, the number of rows is the same as the number of columns.

In addition to the replication possible by using several groups, internal replication is possible. Each matrix entry from a single group may be represented by several adjacent data values; the number of them is constant throughout the data file, and is called the number of replications.

Unless one of the corner matrix options is in effect, the parameter line should contain three parameters as follows:

1. The number of rows and columns in each group (NPART) (Max. = 10)
2. The number of replications (NREPL1)
3. The number of groups (NREPL3)

If one of the corner matrix options is in effect, the parameter line should contain four parameters as follows:

1. The number of rows in each group (NROWS) (Max. = 10)
2. The number of columns in each group (NCOLS)
3. The number of replications (NREPL1)
4. The number of groups (NREPL3)

The internal arrangement of the data set is rigidly specified. The first line of the data set indicates the number of rows (and columns) of the matrix (namely, 5), the number of values provided for each matrix entry (namely, 1), and the number of such matrices included in the data set (namely, 1).

The second line of the data set must give a format (according to the rules for Fortran format statements). This format will be used by the program to read a single row of the matrix. A floating-point format (*F* FORMAT) must be used.

The succeeding lines of the data set (lines 3 through 7 for example) must contain the data matrix itself, entered according to the format you have provided. Note that each row of the matrix must begin on a new line.

There are a great many options that can be chosen when using KYST. Despite the large array of possibilities, however, the user is able to specify the correct options without undue difficulty because of the menu system and defaults that are used. The options and simple control options that invoke them are described in subsequent sections.

MENU OPTIONS One important principle is used throughout. Whenever several alternative possibilities are available, one is always selected to be the "standard" or "default" choice. In the absence of any indication from the user, the program uses these standard choices.

In general, a single data file may contain several "groups" of rows of data (though in the simplest situations, a data file will contain only one such group). Each group may be thought of as a square matrix, or part of a square matrix. Each group has the same size and "shape" as every other in the same data file. Normally, the different groups serve as replicates and contain different data relating to the same objects. However, when the block diagonal option is in effect, the different groups are not replicates but pertain to different objects.

Each group in the data file may have one of five forms, as shown in Figure 15–1. For the two half-matrix forms, the two variations shown in Figure 15–2 are possible.

For the matrix form, the group consists of NPART rows with each row expected to contain NPART matrix entries. The information presented pertains to NPART points or objects.

_____ Figure 15–1 _____
Five Matrix Forms

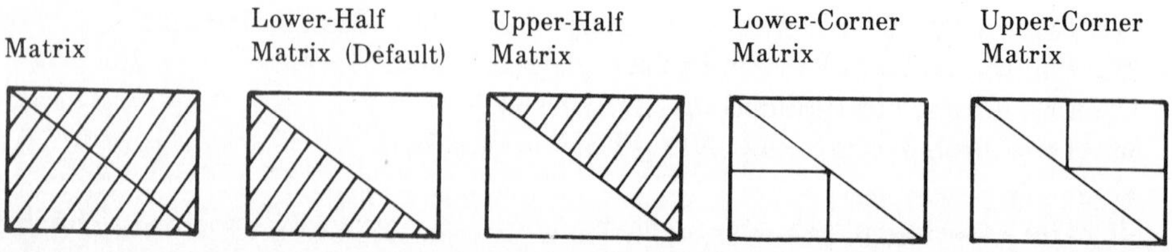

| Matrix | Lower-Half Matrix (Default) | Upper-Half Matrix | Lower-Corner Matrix | Upper-Corner Matrix |

_____ Figure 15–2 _____

Variations of the Lower–Half and Upper–Half Matrix forms

Diagonal   Diagonal Absent
Present   (Default)

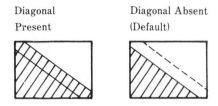

For the lower-half matrix and upper-half matrix forms, the group consists of NPART rows (if the main DIAGONAL is PRESENT) and NPART − 1 rows (if the main DIAGONAL is ABSENT). Each row is expected to contain from 1 up to NPART (or from 1 up to NPART − 1) matrix entries in a regularly varying way. The information pertains to NPART points or objects.

For the lower-corner matrix and upper-corner matrix forms, each group consists of NROWS rows, with each row expected to contain NCOLS matrix entries. The information pertains to NCOLS + NROWS points or objects. As the placement of the corner in the matrix would suggest, the *first* several points in the lower-corner case (and the *last* several points in the upper corner case) correspond to the columns. The sample data sets in Table 15–2 show data values corresponding to the (i,j) matrix entry denoted by ij and should help make these forms clear.

The main use for the half-matrix forms occurs when measured dissimilarity or similarity between objects i and j is experimentally symmetric, so there is no conceptual distinction between the ij entry and the ji entry. One major use for the corner-matrix forms is in unfolding. Because the "splitting" option (see below) is restricted to rows and not available for columns, the columns must correspond to stimuli (or "real" points) and the rows to subjects (or "ideal" points).

When a data set contains more than one group, normally the different groups pertain to the same objects, and contain replicated measurements of the same matrix entries. Thus, if a single group pertains to NPART objects, then normally the whole data set pertains only to $N = $ NPART objects. However, when the block diagonal option is used, each group pertains to a new set of objects, and the several groups should be thought of as blocks down the diagonal of a single larger data matrix. If each group pertains to NPART objects, and there are NREPL3 groups, then the whole data set pertains to $N = $ NREPL3 $\times$ NPART objects. If each group is only part of a square matrix, it is the square matrices that are strung down the diagonal, with each group occupying its appropriate position in its square matrix. The shape of the groups is determined by using the above control options to describe the data.

_____ *Table 15–2* _____

Example Data Sets for KYST Matrix Configurations

Example: Full matrix
with diagonal
```
    4  1  1
  (F2.0,3(3X,F2.0))
   11    12    13    14
   21    22    23    24
   31    32    33    34
   41    42    43    44
```
Example: Lower-half matrix
with diagonal present
```
    4  1  1
  (F2.0,3(3X,F2.0))
   11
   21    22
   31    32    33
   41    42    43    44
```
Example: Lower-half matrix
with diagonal absent
```
    4  1  1
  (F2.0,2(3X,F2.0))
   21
   31    32
   41    42    43
```
Example: Upper-half matrix
with diagonal present
```
    4  1  1
  (F2.0,3(3X,F2.0))
   11    12    13    14
   22    23    24
   33    34
   44
```

Example: Upper-half matrix
with diagonal absent
```
    4  1  1
  (F2.0,2(3X,F2.0))
   12    13    14
   23    24
   34
```
Example: Lower-corner
matrix
```
    3  2  1  1
  (F2.0,3X,F2.0)
   31    32
   41    42
   51    52
```
Example: Full matrix
```
   2  3  2
  (F2.0,5(3X,F2.0))
  11  11  11  12  12  12
  21  21  21  22  22  22
  11  11  11  12  12  12
  21  21  21  22  22  22
```
Example: Block-diagonal
matrix
```
    2  1  3
  (F2.0,3X,F2.0)
   11    12
   21    22
   33    34
   43    44
   55    56
   65    66
```

_____

Note: Entry for (i,j) position in matrix has value ij. Actual data should consist of floating-point numbers.

_____

The block-diagonal option is controlled by the options

BLOCK DIAGONAL: NO   (DEFAULT)
BLOCK DIAGONAL: YES

Two possible configurations using the block-diagonal option are shown in Figure 15–3. As always, the default option applies if no specific indication is given.

_____ Figure 15–3 _____
Block DIAGONAL Configurations

Block Diagonal Matrix

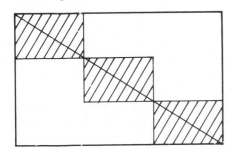

Block Diagonal Lower-Corner Matrix

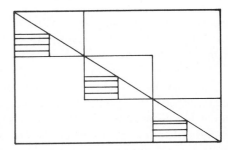

Control Options for Initial Configuration   There are five ways in which the initial configuration may be produced.

1. The TORSCA initial configuration procedure may be used.
2. A random initial configuration may be used.
3. The so-called "arbitrary" initial configuration may be used.
4. A configuration may be read in from a previous run.
5. The solution from a preceding computation may be saved for use as the starting configuration for the next lower dimensionality.

Note that where a single analysis is used to initiate scaling in several different dimensionalities, the choice above applies only to the *first* scaling, which is in the highest dimensionality. For each *subsequent* scaling the solution from the last previous scaling (in a higher dimensionality) is used with the last one or more coordinates dropped off. If rotation to principal coordinates is being used (under the standard option COORDINATES = ROTATE), this procedure usually provides a very good starting configuration.

We list here the five corresponding control options:

— TORSCA   (standard option)
— RANDOM = integer   (standard value for integer is 0)
— ARBITRARY
— CONFIGURATION
— SAVE = CONFIGURATION

Further explanation follows.

Under the control option TORSCA, KYST first uses the classical Torgerson scaling technique to derive a configuration. If the number of points $N \leq 60$, the program then proceeds to use the quasi-nonmetric Young method of improving this configuration. The control option

PRE-ITERATIONS = integer   (standard value is 1)

determines the maximum number of such steps. If more than one data set is used, as described elsewhere, the TORSCA initial configuration calculation will use only the data from the first set. In some cases, the initial configuration obtained from the TORSCA procedure is already quite good.

If RANDOM = integer is used, the program generates its own starting configuration by picking pseudo-random points from an approximately normal multivariate distribution. (Actually, each coordinate is obtained by applying the logistic transformation to a uniform random variable, obtained from a moderate-quality portable generator.) This feature is especially valuable when you wish to generate many solutions starting from different configurations in order to guard against local minimum solutions. Use of RANDOM = integer in each of a successive set of computations *during a single computer run* to produce new and independent starting configurations. However, the pseudo-random number generator naturally produces the same sequence of numbers in each computer run. In order to permit different starting configurations in different runs, the program obtains and discards several random numbers before generating the initial configuration. The integer that follows RANDOM specifies how many random numbers should be discarded. By altering this integer from one run to the next, you can make the program use different starting configurations on different runs.

The control option ARBITRARY is included primarily for historical compatibility. If it is used, the starting configuration (prior to being standardized) is given by

$$r\text{-th coordinate of the } i\text{-th point} = \begin{cases} (0.01)i & \text{if } r \equiv i \text{ mod dimensionality} \\ 0 & \text{otherwise} \end{cases}$$

Some Ways to Use KYST   For nonmetric scaling of the most familiar type, the program may be used as in the preliminary example, with the following simple changes used where appropriate. The options TORSCA and COORDINATES ROTATE are standard options and may be omitted. The PRE-ITERATIONS option will generally be omitted, since the standard option of 1 pre-iteration usually suffices. If the data are dissimilarities, the option REGRESSION ASCENDING should be substituted for the corresponding option in the example. If the data form a lower- or upper-half matrix, the options LOWER-HALF MATRIX and UPPER-HALF MATRIX should be used, with DIAGONAL ABSENT if the diagonal values are missing. For metric scaling, the control option REGRESSION POLYNOMIAL DEGREE should be specified (accompanied by REGRESSION NO

CONSTANT if desired). Also, consider the possibility of transforming the data preliminary to the scaling, by the use of DATA TRANSFORMATION. If the data are transformed in connection with nonmetric scaling (to improve the operation of the TORSCA initial configuration routine), note that the choice of the regression as ASCENDING or DESCENDING should be based on the form of the data *after* transformation.

To do unfolding, the rankings provided by each subject or judge should form one *row* of the data matrix, and the stimuli or objects judged should correspond to the columns. It is necessary to select either LOWER-CORNER MATRIX or UPPER-CORNER MATRIX.

If larger distances from the subject's ideal point should match larger data values, the option REGRESSION ASCENDING should be used, while if a reverse relationship between distances and data values is appropriate, the option REGRESSION DESCENDING should be used. (It is also possible to use KYST for nonmetric unfolding in which the subjects have *negative* ideal points instead of positive ideal points, that is, most disliked central points instead of most liked central points. In fact, the program has no knowledge of which kind of ideal point, regardless of type, should have an ascending or descending relationship to the data values.)

If an unfolding is to be done *nonmetrically*, it is in theory vital to SPLIT BY ROWS and use SFORM2, as otherwise a meaningless zero-stress solution may result. (This solution is one example of what is referred to as "degeneracy.") In practice, however, the situation is not so clear, particularly if a good initial configuration is used. If the unfolding is metric, most often it will be preferable to SPLIT BY ROWS, but where rankings are reasonably comparable among subjects and the data is scanty, it can be sensible to include the rankings of all subjects in a single regression.

Suppose several subjects have provided direct-judged dissimilarities of a single set of objects. Suppose either (a) that the values provided by each subject form a separate data set, or alternatively (b) that there is only one data set and that the values provided by each subject form a group of rows in the set. There are at least four meaningful types of analysis possible, based on two independent choices:

C1: A single configuration is shared by all subjects.
CS: A separate configuration is formed for each subject.
R1: A single regression is shared for all subjects.
RS: A separate regression is done for each subject.

Case C1R1 does not allow for any differences between subjects at all, and treats the different subjects merely as replications. Each of C1RS and CSR1 allows for differences between subjects, though in quite distinct ways. CSRS is conceptually and actually equivalent to performing an entirely separate scaling for each subject.

─────── *Table 15–3* ──────────────────────────────────────

Subject Types and Split Options

	R1	RS
C1	(a) SPLIT = NOMORE (b) SPLIT = BYDECKS 　　　BLOCKDIAGONAL = NO	(a) SPLIT = BYDECKS (b) SPLIT = BYGROUPS 　　　BLOCKDIAGONAL = NO
CS	(a) Not possible (b) SPLIT = BYDECKS 　　　BLOCK DIAGONAL	(a) Not possible (b) SPLIT = BYGROUPS 　　　BLOCK DIAGONAL

Table 15–3 shows how to accomplish the various possibilities. Note that these four cases correspond to McGee's four cells, (McGee, 1968). However he includes a kind of distance between the separate configurations in his badness-of-fit measure, which gives his cases corresponding to our CS cases a somewhat different meaning than ours.

In an unfolding procedure using only linear (or polynomial) regression, KYST places no restriction on coefficients of the regression function. Thus, over the region containing the data values the regression functions can be ascending, descending, constant, or (in the case of polynomials of degree ≥ 2) ascending in part and descending in part. One way to handle situations where this freedom is undesirable is discussed below. One useful possibility that comes with this freedom is that a subject's "ideal" point may be a *negative* ideal, his most disliked possible stimulus, just as easily as a *positive* ideal, and the recovered shape of the regression line indicates which it is. One unfortunate concomitant is that where a subject's ideal point (positive or negative) truly belongs outside or on the edge of the region containing the real stimulus points, it is easy for the program to misplace it on the diametrically opposite position and make it of opposite type.

Sometimes it is desirable to do a scaling or an unfolding using linear (or polynomial) regression, but it is necessary to assure that the regression function is essentially monotone over the region containing the data values. While KYST cannot quite manage this, it can approximate it. The trick is to feed in the selfsame data twice, that is, use duplicate copies of the data set. In the first analysis the option REGRESSION POLYNOMIAL is used. In the second analysis the option REGRESSION ASCENDING or REGRESSION DESCENDING is used. Thus, the overall stress reflects both deviation from the desired polynomial fit and deviation from the appropriate monotonicity.

Some Precautions: Number of Dimensions,
Convergence, and Local Minima　　If there are not very many objects, it
is impossible to recover many dimensions (regardless of whether many dimensions are in fact operative). This is because the number of parameters estimated needs to be considerably less than the number of observations (if

the observations are subject to statistical fluctuation), a general principle of wide application. Blind use of the program can easily extract more dimensions than could possibly be meaningful.

While it is difficult to give hard and fast rules, the bare minimum number of objects for wise use are:

— For a 1-dimensional solution, 5 objects
— For a 2-dimensional solution, 9 objects
— For a 3-dimensional solution, 13 objects

Furthermore, if the number of objects is relatively small, each additional object will increase the accuracy of reconstruction quite a bit.

KYST finds the configuration of minimum stress by using an iterative procedure (of the "steepest descent" type) that starts with an initial configuration and keeps modifying it until, hopefully, it converges to the configuration having minimum stress. Two questions should always be asked about the solution yielded by such a procedure: (1) Is convergence complete? In other words, did the procedure finish converging to a minimum, or did it stop halfway? If convergence is not complete, you may not want to even look at the solution, but rather put it back in for further iteration. (2) Was the right minimum reached? In other words, did the procedure converge to a "local minimum" configuration, from which no *small* modification can decrease the stress, but at which the stress is greater than the true minimum value? If you fear the solution is only a local minimum, you may want to perform further scaling using *other starting configurations* to check this possibility.

Strictly speaking, convergence to an exact minimum is only complete if the partial derivatives of the stress are all *exactly* equal to 0. Because a computer does not represent numbers with perfect precision, this does not happen very often. However, in most practical situations it is possible to come so very close to the minimum toward which the procedure is converging that the difference can have no practical importance. In the vast majority of cases, moreover, other considerations (such as the statistical fluctuations in the data), or the fact that the model is not perfectly appropriate) mean that the achievable precision is far greater than necessary.

Thus the practical question is whether convergence has proceeded far enough to be *practically* complete. The program uses several tests to determine this (such as how fast the stress has been decreasing from iteration to iteration, and the size of the gradient), and declares that a minimum has been reached if it is satisfied. Since rather severe criteria are used, this remark is seldom in error. However, the procedure can terminate itself for other reasons, and it is these that must be remembered. If the maximum number of iterations is reached (normally 50, but easily altered by the user) or if the stress becomes satisfactorily small (normally 0.01, but easily altered by the user), or for several other reasons, the procedure will terminate with a suitable remark.

The reason for termination is always printed. You should always look at this comment. Even where the procedure does not state that a local minimum has been reached, it may often happen that the solution reached is practically indistinguishable from the local minimum that would be reached after a few more iterations. In particular, where the stress is very small, this is generally the case. The "history of the calculation" that may be printed out will often be helpful if convergence is in doubt.

With regard to local minima, there is no feasible way to be mathematically certain that you have found that local minimum that is in fact the true global minimum. (While use of the TORSCA initial configuration reduces the chance of reaching a local minimum in the sort of situations in which it has been tested, KYST offers so many possible modes of use that no universal reassurances can be given. In particular, unfolding is a relatively unexplored area.) However, by using a variety of different random starting configurations to repeatedly scale the same data, it is often possible to obtain practical certainty. For if a variety of different starting configurations yield essentially the same local minimum, with perhaps an occasional exception that yields a substantially worse local minimum, then there is little to worry about. One easy way to provide a variety of different starting configurations is to scale the same data repeatedly, using SAVE = DATA and RANDOM = integer, which will provide a new starting configuration on successive uses (on the same computer run).

In this connection, it is well to remember that rotation and reflection leave a configuration essentially unchanged. Thus to decide whether the solutions obtained as suggested above are essentially the same, you cannot merely compare coordinates. One method you can use is to generate the matrix of distances, since these are unaffected by rotation and reflection. However, a still simpler method that is often adequate is to compare the stress values. If these values agree to three significant figures, the local minima having them are unlikely to be different. In the case of two-dimensional solutions, you can plot the solutions using the control option PLOT-CONFIGURATION-ALL, trace them onto tracing paper, rotate or reflect the solutions by physical motions of the paper, and compare solutions by laying one sheet on top of another.

Note that the likelihood of reaching a local minimum is known by experience to be particularly severe for one-dimensional solutions, or if the Minkowski r-metric is used with r near 1 or ∞, though for ordinary scaling the TORSCA initial configuration greatly alleviates the situation. The one-dimensional case is bad because points cannot easily move past each other during the iterative computation if they lie on a line. The extreme values of r cause trouble because the gradient is a discontinuous function of the configuration if $r = 1$ or if $r = \infty$.

_____ Figure 15-4 _____
KYST Menu Options

```
┌───────────────────────────────────────────────────────────────────┐
│                     K Y S T       M E N U                           │
├───────────────────────────────────────────────────────────────────┤
│                                                                     │
│     1    SELECT PROBLEM DIMENSION/ANALYSIS TYPE:                    │
│             (DIMMAX, DIMMIN, DIMDIF, R, SFORM, TIES, RANDOM)         │
│     2    SELECT DATA FORM OPTIONS                                    │
│             (MATRIX, DIAG, BLKDIAG, SPLIT, CUTOFF, CONFIG, WGTS)     │
│     3    SELECT MODEL OPTIONS                                        │
│             (REGRESSION=MONOTONE, MULTIVARIATE, POLYNOMIAL)          │
│     4    SELECT WEIGHT/DATA TRANSFORMATION OPTIONS, FIX DATA POINTS  │
│                                                                     │
│     5    SELECT TERMINATION/CONVERGENCE SETUP                       │
│             (STRMIN,SFGRMN,SRATST,ITERATIONS,COSAVW,ACOSAV)          │
│     6    SELECT OUTPUT OPTIONS                                       │
│             (CONFIGURATION FILE, PRINT DATA, HISTORY, DISTANCES)     │
│     7    SELECT PLOT OUTPUT OPTIONS                                  │
│                                                                     │
│     8    SELECTIONS COMPLETE, RUN PROGRAM NOW                        │
│                                                                     │
│     9    QUIT PROGRAM                                               │
└───────────────────────────────────────────────────────────────────┘
```

KYST MENU OPTIONS   Figure 15-4 shows the KYST menu.

Option 1 Select Problem Dimension/Analysis Type

1. RETURN   TO VIEW MAIN MENU
2. DIMMAX   MAXIMUM DIMENSIONS (Max. = 3)   (2)
3. DIMMIN   MINIMUM DIMENSIONS   (2)
4. DIMDIF   DIMENSION DECREMENT   (1)
5. R   SELECT DISTANCE MEASURE TYPE   (EUCLIDEAN)
6. SFORM   SELECT STRESS FORMULA TO BE USED   (SFORM1)
7. TIES   SELECT PRIMARY OR SECONDARY   (PRIMARY)
8. RANDOM   SELECT A RANDOM 2 DIGIT STARTING NUMBER   (-99)

DIMMAX, DIMMIN, DIMDIF A single control sequence can initiate several computations all using the same data and same options, in several spaces of different dimension. The first computation is done in the maximum dimension DIMMAX. Then the dimension drops by the dimension difference DIMDIF, and another computation is done This is repeated until finally the computation is done in the minimum dimension DIMMIN, which completes the computation.

R (Distance Function) The kind of Minkowski R-metric distance function used by KYST is controlled by this parameter.

R is equal to a decimal number (standard value is 2.0). For $R = 2.0$, this yields the ordinary Euclidean distance, while for $R = 1.0$, this yields the city-block metric. (For these two special values, the necessary powers and roots are computed in a relatively rapid way, but for other values the general-purpose power operations are used, which behind the scenes requires a logarithm and an exponential to be calculated for each power operation. Thus, for general values of R, the computation will be perceptibly slower.)

S Form (Stress Formula)   Two different stress formulas are available, as indicated earlier. The options are designated 1 and 2. Note that formula 2, which is the newer one, has now become the standard option. As explained in detail above, formula 2 uses a variance-like expression involving DBAR in the denominator, while formula 1 uses 0 in place of DBAR. Formula 2 is used for nonmetric unfolding analysis.

Ties   As explained in detail in Kruskal (1964a and 1964b), there are two ways of treating ties among the data values when performing a monotone regression. Consider the fitted regression values corresponding to a group of equal data values. Either no restriction is placed on the size of these fitted values with respect to one another (the primary approach), or these fitted values may be required to be equal (the secondary approach).

1 = TIES PRIMARY   (standard option)

2 = TIES SECONDARY

Where there are few ties, it hardly makes any difference which is used. Where there are a great many ties, as when the data values represent coarse category judgments, it does make a difference, and the context must be considered in making the choice.

Random   The control option RANDOM is used, to generate a random starting configuration by picking pseudo-random points from an approximately normal multivariate distribution. This feature is especially valuable when you wish to generate many solutions starting from different configurations, in order to guard against local minimum solutions. Use of RANDOM in each of a successive set of computations *during a single computer run* will produce new and independent starting configurations. However, the pseudo-random number generator naturally produces the same sequence of numbers in each computer run. In order to permit different starting configurations in different runs, the program obtains and discards several random numbers before generating the starting configuration. The integer entered when RANDOM is selected specifies how many random numbers should be discarded. Thus by altering this integer from one run to the next, you can make the program use different starting configurations on different runs.

Option 2 Select Data Form Options

1. RETURN	TO VIEW MAIN MENU	
2. MATRIX	SPECIFY MATRIX TYPE	(LOWER-HALF)
3. DIAGON	SPECIFY DIAGONAL OPTION	(PRESENT)
4. CONFIG	INITIAL START CONFIGURATION	(TORSCA)
5. SPLIT	DATA SPLIT OPTIONS	(BY DECK)
6. CUTOFF	MISSING VALUES IF < CUTOFF	$(-1.23E + 20)$
7. WEIGHTS	READ DIRECTLY AFTER DATA	(NO)

Matrix Type   All the options described in this section affect how the data are read, or how they are handled by the program while being read.

In general, a single data file may contain several groups of rows of data (though in the simplest situations, a file will contain only one such group). Each group may be thought of as a square matrix, or part of a square matrix. Each group has the same size and shape as every other in the same data set. Normally, the different groups serve as replicates, and contain different data relating to the same objects. However when the block diagonal option is in effect, the different groups are not replicates but pertain to different objects.

The main use for the half-matrix forms occurs when measured dissimilarity or similarity between objects i and j is experimentally symmetric, so there is no conceptual distinction between the ij entry and the ji entry. One major use for the corner matrix forms is in unfolding. Because the splitting option (see below) is restricted to rows and not available for columns, the columns must correspond to stimuli (or real points) and the rows to subjects (or ideal points).

When a data set contains more than one group, normally the different groups pertain to the same objects, and contain replicated measurements of the same matrix entries. Thus if a single group pertains to NPART objects, then normally the whole data file pertains only to $N =$ NPART objects.

Each group in the data file may have one of five forms:

1 = MATRIX
2 = LOWER-HALF MATRIX   (DEFAULT)
3 = UPPER-HALF MATRIX
4 = LOWER-CORNER MATRIX
5 = UPPER-CORNER MATRIX

SUBMENU: ENTER 1 IF NOT BLOCK DIAGONAL MATRIX   (DEFAULT)
OR 2 IF YES:

Matrix In this case, the group consists of NPART rows with each row expected to contain NPART matrix entries. The information presented pertains to NPART points or objects. (Of course, each matrix entry here and below may be represented by several internal replications, as explained elsewhere.)

Lower-Half–Upper-Half   In these cases, the group consists of NPART rows (if the main DIAGONAL is PRESENT) and NPART − 1 rows (if the main DIAGONAL is ABSENT). Each row is expected to contain from 1 up to NPART (or from 1 up to NPART − 1) matrix entries in a regularly varying way. The information pertains to NPART points or objects.

Lower-Corner–Upper-Corner   In these cases, each group consists of NROWS rows, with each row expected to contain NCOLS matrix entries. The information pertains to NCOLS + NROWS points or objects. As the placement of the corner in the matrix would suggest, the *first* several points in the lower-corner case (and the *last* several points in the upper-corner case) correspond to the columns. The illustrations below, in which a data value corresponding to the (i,j) matrix entry is denoted by ij, should help make these forms clear.

Block Diagonal   When the block diagonal option is used, each group pertains to a new set of objects, and the several groups should be thought of as blocks down the diagonal of a single larger data matrix. If each group pertains to NPART objects, and there are NREPL3 groups, then the whole data set pertains to $N = $ NREPL3*NPART objects. If each group is only part of a square matrix, it is the square matrices that are strung down the diagonal, with each group occupying its appropriate position in its square matrix.

Diagonal   For the two half-matrix forms, two options are given.

1 = DIAGONAL PRESENT
2 = DIAGONAL ABSENT   (DEFAULT)

Configuration

ENTER THE METHOD BY WHICH THE STARTING
CONFIGURATION IS TO BE PRODUCED:
1 = TORSCA   (DEFAULT)
2 = RANDOM CONFIGURATION
3 = ARBITRARILY
4 = CONFIGURATION MATRIX IS TO BE READ IN

introduces a data set containing a configuration of points. This configuration is used to start the computation. If no configuration data set is provided— that is, if the default option is selected—the program generates its own starting configuration by using the classical Torgerson scaling technique. If the number of points $N \leq 60$, the program then proceeds to use the quasi-nonmetric Young method of improving this configuration. The control option

ENTER THE NUMBER OF PRE-ITERATIONS   (DEFAULT = 1)

determines the maximum number of such steps. If more than one data deck is used (split by decks), the TORSCA initial configuration calculation will use only the data from the first deck. In some cases, the initial configuration obtained from the TORSCA procedure is already quite good.

Split   The entire list of data values may be split into sublists, with a separate regression performed on each sublist. There are several ways in which the data can be split. Each *row* of every data file can be a sublist, each *group* of rows can be a sublist, each *data set* can be a sublist. Where there is more than one data set, different sets may be split differently. The options

    1 = SPLIT BY ROWS   (use in unfolding)
    2 = SPLIT BY GROUPS
    3 = SPLIT BY DECK   (DEFAULT)
    4 = SPLIT NO MORE

control splitting. SPLIT BY ROWS, SPLIT BY GROUPS, or SPLIT BY DECK, make each row, each group of rows, or each data file a separate sublist respectively. SPLIT NO MORE is relevant only when several data sets are used. It causes all subsequent data sets to be joined into a single sublist.

Cutoff   If individual data values are missing, this fact may be indicated by using values that are algebraically less than some specific cutoff value specified.

    ENTER CUTOFF
    (MISSING VALUE PARAMETER DEFAULT $= -1.23E + 20$)

Values $\leq$ CUTOFF value will be discarded. This discarding takes place while the data is being read in. The standard value is so large a negative number that it is unlikely to affect anyone's data.

Weights   The control option WEIGHTS introduces a data set containing numerical weights that correspond to the data values. If no weights are provided, the program uses a weight of 1.0 for every data value. When a set of weights is used, it must immediately follow the data set, with no intervening lines. Generally speaking, the arrangement and format of the weights data must be exactly the same as that of the data set, and one weight must appear from every data value, even those which are artificial and indicate missing data. Note that all weights must be > 0. Zero weights may lead to division by 0 in the MFIT subroutine. Where a *data* value is indicated as being missing because it falls below the value of CUTOFF, a corresponding value must nevertheless appear in the weights data set, even though it will not be used. (A blank value can generally be used in this case.)

When more than one data set is used to supply data for a single computation, every data set should be given the same-weights treatment. That is, either no data set should be weighted, or every data file should be accompanied by a weights data set or every data set should use computed weights (all must use the same WTRAN function). The weights data set or WFUNCTION option should be used with the data sets.

Option 3 Select Model Options

1. RETURN TO VIEW MAIN MENU
2. MONOTONE   (DEFAULT)
3. MULTIVARIATE WITH CONSTANT
4. MULTIVARIATE WITHOUT CONSTANT
5. POLYNOMIAL WITH CONSTANT
6. POLYNOMIAL WITHOUT CONSTANT

Monotone   The regression type may be either monotone or polynomial. (The former makes the scaling nonmetric, the latter metric.) The monotone regression may be either ascending (suitable for dissimilarities) or descending (suitable for similarities.). For the monotone option, menu options include

1 = RANK ORDERS INCREASE WITH DISTANCE (DISSIMILARITIES) (DEFAULT)

2 = RANK ORDERS DECREASE AS DISTANCES INCREASE (SIMILARITIES)

Multivariate   The option MULTIVARIATE regression is needed only in special cases. The option MULTIVARIATE may be used to substitute for polynomial regression. (Because a very simple method is used to solve the simultaneous linear equations, it is desirable that the functions f_k not be too terribly far from orthogonal.) Not more than five functions (variates) f_k are permitted when specifying the number of multivariate functions:

ENTER THE NUMBER OF MULTIVARIATE FUNCTIONS (MAX = 5)

Polynomial   The option POLYNOMIAL requires specification of the degree of the polynomial:

ENTER NUMBER OF DEGREE OF THE POLYNOMIAL FUNCTION (MAX = 4)

It is possible to include or exclude the constant term when fitting polynomials by selecting the appropriate regression type. The polynomial regression may be of any degree up to quartic (degree 4), with or without constant term. (The coefficient values are a by-product of the regression.)

When more than one data set is used, a different type of regression may be chosen for each data set, if desired. There are situations where it may be helpful to use monotone and straight-line regression together (thus performing something intermediate between nonmetric and metric scaling).

Option 4 Select Weight/Data Transformation Options, Fix Data Points

1. RETURN TO VIEW MAIN MENU
2. ENTER WEIGHT TRANSFORMATIONS FROM KEYBOARD
3. ENTER DATA TRANSFORMATIONS FROM KEYBOARD
4. FIX DATA POINTS

Weight   Weights associated with the data values are sometimes useful to reflect the varying measurement errors or for other reasons. They are used by KYST to weight the squared terms in the stress formula. Weights may be either computed as a function of the associated data values, or read in immediately following the data. If no weights are provided by either method, the program supplies the default weight of 1.0 for every data value. The weights are effective both during the initial configuration calculation, and during the main scaling computation. It is dangerous to use weights of 0.0, since they may lead to division by zero in the monotone regression algorithm. If a zero weight is desired, use the CUTOFF option to create a missing value in the data.

Five transformation variables are required for the weight transformation: $(T5 + T1*(T2(DATA(i) + T3)**T4)$. The default values are $T1 = 1.0$; $T2 = 1.0$; $T3 = 0.0$; $T4 = 1.0$; $T5 = 0.0$. The maximum transformation input size is F15.7.

In other words, this transformation consists of three stages, a first linear stage using T2 and T3, a second power stage using T4, and a third linear stage using T1 and T5.

Data   When performing metric scaling, a preliminary transformation of the data may be quite important. Also, regardless whether the scaling is metric or not, such a preliminary transformation may be helpful to the classical Torgerson scaling, which is the first step in the TORSCA initial configuration option, by making the data values more like Euclidean distances. Simple transformations can be accomplished from KYST using the data transformation option.

Five transformation variables are required for the weight transformation:

$$T5 + T1*(T2(DATA(i) + T3)**T4$$

The default values are $T1 = 1.0$; $T2 = 1.0$; $T3 = 0.0$; $T4 = 1.0$; $T5 = 0.0$. The maximum transformation input size is F15.7.

In other words, this transformation consists of three stages, a first linear stage using T2 and T3, a second power stage using T4, and a third linear stage using T1 and T5.

Fix   The FIX option "fixes" the first several points of the configuration, so that they do not move during the main scaling computation. In other words, the program treats these points as given, and not subject to adjustment. This option is sensible only if the points of the initial configuration that have been fixed are sensible. Thus, normally this option would be used only if points are read in from a configuration deck, or if the initial configuration has been created by the TORSCA initial configuration routine. Note that the FIX option has no effect on how the TORSCA initial configuration routine operates, but only affects the main scaling procedure. An integer must be entered when requested by the prompt

ENTER 0 = NO FIX (DEFAULT), or K = # OF POINTS TO FIX

Only the initial points of the configuration can be fixed, that is, the points numbered from 1 up to the value of the integer. The means used internally to accomplish this fixing is to set to zero all the coordinates of the gradient vector that correspond to fixed points just before the program starts to make use of the gradient vector. If the user wants these values to appear without change as the coordinate values in the final configuration, the "COORDINATE AS-IS" OPTION should be in effect. Otherwise, the fixed points, along with the rest of the configuration, will be subject to the usual standardization and rotation, and the resultant coordinate values will be different from those fixed.

Option 5 Select Termination/Convergence Setup

1. RETURN	TO VIEW MAIN MENU	
2. STRMIN	MINIMUM STRESS	(0.01)
3. SFGRMN	SCALE FACTOR GRADIENT	(0.0)
4. SRATST	STRESS RATIO STOP	(0.999)
5. ITERAT	MAX. # OF ITERATIONS	(50)
6. COSAVW	COSINE OF ANGLE BETWEEN GRADIENTS	(0.66)
7. ACSAVW	AVERAGE COSINE OF ANGLES	(0.66)

Normally computation stops when the program judges that it has reached the minimum stress value. Of course, the program has no way of distinguishing between a local minimum and a global minimum. That is, any minimum it reaches may be merely the smallest value in some local region (a local minimum) rather than the smallest value everywhere (a global minimum). This difficulty is shared by all procedures for minimizing functions of many variables (except when very special conditions hold, such as convexity). For further information about the likelihood of reaching other than the global minimum in the present context (likelihood varies greatly in different contexts), and what to do if you suspect this difficulty, see Kruskal (1964b). However, note that repeated analyses using the RANDOM option (explained above) makes it very easy to analyze the same data starting from several different starting configurations. The same solution may occur several times (up to such immaterial changes as rotation and reflection).

This solution may have the least stress by a considerable amount, while only a few other solutions occur, all with worse stress and all quite different from one another. In this case, we may have considerable practical confidence in having found the true minimum solution.

At a minimum configuration (whether global or merely local) the gradient vector is 0 (that is, all the partial derivatives of the stress are 0). One test the program uses for determining whether it has reached a local minimum is whether the length of the gradient is small enough.

STRMIN This number-with-decimal-point option provides the criterion value, with the standard value being 0.01. (STRMIN means STRESS MINIMUM.) Usually when stress gets smaller than this (that is, below 1 percent), only negligible further movement of the configuration occurs in achieving a minimum. (For nonmetric scaling, if the stress becomes small enough, in practice it turns out that zero stress is always achievable. However, it may take many iterations of almost infinitesimal movement to achieve it.)

SFGRMN The number-with-decimal-point option provides a criterion value, with the standard value being 0.0. (SFGRMN stands for Scale Factor of the Gradient, MiNimum). When the length (more properly, the scale factor) of the gradient is less than or equal to this criterion, the program decides that a local minimum has been reached. Because computer arithmetic is approximate, it is very unusual for the gradient to become precisely 0. Thus, with the standard value in effect, this test is seldom satisfied.

In practice, primary reliance is placed on how fast the stress is decreasing. If the ratio between present and previous stress is close enough to 1.0, and if simultaneously the weighted average of past values of this ratio is close enough to 1.0, then the program decides that a local minimum has been reached.

STRATST This number-with-decimal-point option has a standard value of 0.999. (SRATST means Stress Ratio Stop). If both the stress ratio and the weighted average stress ratio are between this value and 1.0, then the criterion is met. A more rigorous criterion is achieved by using a value (like 0.999), which is closer to 1.0, while a more generous criterion comes from a value (like 0.99) further from 1.0. If 1.0 itself is used, the criterion becomes virtually unachievable.

Even if a minimum value of stress has not yet been achieved, it is sometimes desirable to stop computing when the stress has become sufficiently small.

ITERAT Whether or not a minimum or a satisfactorily small stress is reached, in practice computation must be terminated after some number of ITERATIONS because computer time is always limited. This control option provides the maximum number of iterations which are permitted in a single computation. After this many iterations, computation is terminated and full normal output provided, regardless of other stopping criteria.

Each computation normally runs through enough iterations to reach a configuration that minimizes stress. To control computation time in case convergence is unduly slow, however, the program will terminate computation after 50 iterations and yield normal output even if a minimum has not yet been reached. (The reason for termination is always indicated.) To change the maximum number of iterations, select the iterations options and input the desired number of iterations:

ITERATIONS = integer   (default value is 50)

More iterations (say 100) may be useful to assure complete convergence, though the further change after 50 iterations is often so small as to be negligible. Fewer iterations (say 25 or even less) may be useful where a great many sets of data are to be analyzed and time is of essence.

Whenever computation is terminated, the reason is always indicated by a remark such as MINIMUM WAS ACHIEVED, MAXIMUM NUMBER OF ITERATIONS WERE USED, SATISFACTORY STRESS WAS REACHED, or ZERO STRESS WAS REACHED.

COSAVW, ACSAVW   During computation, the cosine of the angle between successive gradients plays an important role in several ways. The exponentially weighted average of past cosine values is kept up to date, and so is a similar average of their absolute values.

COSAVW = number-with-decimal-point (default value is 0.66)

ACSAVW = number-with-decimal-point (default value is 0.66)

The control options may be used to alter these parameter values.

Option 6 Select Output Options

1. RETURN TO VIEW MAIN MENU
2. PRODUCE CONFIGURATION FILE AS OUTPUT   (NO)
3. PRINT DATA   (NO)
4. PRINT HISTORY   (YES)
5. PRINT DATA AND DISTANCES   (NO)

The program always provides output to a user-specified disk file. The use of a word processor enables extracting of data for use in related analyses.

The more important input options are printed out, so it is easy to see data and what options were used. The final configuration obtained is also printed, and the corresponding value of the stress. (The stress is the badness-of-fit quantity that is minimized by the program. For further explanation, see the references.) Several other kinds of printed output are available on an optional basis. The options configured in the KYST menu enable the PRINT DATA option, which causes a detailed listing of the input data. The option PRINT DISTANCES will produce a detailed listing that includes the data, the distances, and the fitted regression values. The option PRINT HISTORY will produce a history of the calculation that shows the progress of the iterative numerical calculation.

In KYST, another optional output file is the CONFIGURATION data set. This data set contains the coordinates of the points of the final configuration, together with some preliminary information, which permit it to be used as input to provide a starting configuration in a later scaling computation.

Option 7 Select Plot Output Options

1. RETURN TO VIEW MAIN MENU   (DEFAULT VALUES)

PLOTS OF FINAL CONFIGURATION   (ALL)
    2. ALL PLOTS OF FINAL CONFIGURATION
    3. SOME PLOTS OF FINAL CONFIGURATION
    4. NO PLOTS OF FINAL CONFIGURATION

FINAL CONFIGURATION COORDINATES   (ROTATE)
    5. ROTATE FINAL CONFIGURATION COORDINATES
    6. STANDARDIZE FINAL CONFIGURATION COORD. AS-IS
    7. USE FINAL CONFIG. COORDINATES AS-IS

SCATTER PLOTS OPTIONS   (ALL)
    8. ALL SCATTER PLOTS OF DIST VS DHAT
    9. SOME SCATTER PLOTS OF DIST VS DHAT
    10. NO SCATTER PLOTS OF DIST VS DHAT

Plots of the Final Configuration   Options 2, 3, and 4 control plotting of the final configuration. The use of All produces LDIM*(LDIM − 1)/2 plots of all pairs of dimensions of the configuration, where LDIM is the dimensionality of the configuration. The option SOME is similar, except that each dimension is plotted against only one other dimension. (However, if LDIM is odd, dimension 1 is plotted twice, once with dimension 2 and once with dimension 3). If NO PLOTS are requested, no configuration plotting is done.

Options 4, 5, and 6 control the form of the final configuration. Under the STANDARDIZE option, the configuration has its centroid set to the origin and the mean square distance of the points from the centroid set to 1 after every iteration.

The option ROTATE, besides causing the above standardization on each iteration, also causes the final configuration to be rotated so that its principal components lie along the coordinate axes. (Where the scaling is to be done in several different dimensionalities, this has the desirable effect of causing the least important coordinates to be dropped when going to the next lower dimensionality).

The option AS-IS suppresses both the standardization and the rotation, as may be particularly useful when the initial configuration is read in from a configuration file, particularly if the FIX option is used.

KYST SAMPLE OUTPUT

```
              K Y S T   MULTIDIMENSIONAL  SCALING              | 10  1  1
WRITTEN BY  JOSEPH B. KRUSKAL, FOREST W. YOUNG, WITH JUDITH SEERY | (3X,10F3.0)
                    PC-MDS  VERSION                            | COK  1
                                                              | CCL  3  2
                                                              | DPE  7  9  8
                                                              | DSL 27 28 32 22
                                                              | D7U 41 42 43 29 13
                                                              | DRP 18 17 19 20 30 40
ANALYSIS TITLE: POP DISSIMILARITIES                           | SLI 24 25 26 31  5 16 23
DATA IS READ FROM FILE: KYST.DAT                              | 7UP 35 36 38 44 15  6 37 14
OUTPUT FILE IS: POPSIM.PRN                                    | TAB 12 11 10  4 33 34 21 39 45
                                                              |
                                                              | PRINTOUT OF DEFAULT OR SELECTED OPTIONS
INPUT PARAMETERS:                                             |
                                                              |
MAXIMUM DIMENSIONS                         3                  |
MINIMUM DIMENSIONS                         2                  |
DIMENSION DECREMENT                        1                  |
MINIMUM STRESS                              .01000            |
SCALE FACTOR GRADIENT                       .00000            |
STRESS STEP RATIO                           .99900            |
MAXIMUM ITERATIONS                        50                  |
COSINE OF ANGLE BETWEEN GRADIENTS           .66000            |
AVERAGE COSINE OF ANGLE                     .66000            |
NUMBER OF PRE-ITERATIONS                   1                  |
THE NUMBER OF DATA POINTS TO BE FIXED IS:          0         |
EUCLIDEAN DISTANCE                                            |
STRESS FORMULA 1                                              |
TIES PRIMARY                                                  |
LOWER HALF MATRIX                                             |
NOT BLOCK DIAGONAL                                            |
DIAGONAL ABSENT                                               |
SPLIT BY DECK                                                 |
TORSCA INITIAL CONFIGURATION                                  |
NO WEIGHTS AFTER DATA                                         |
MONOTONE MODEL                                                |
ASCENDING DATA                                                |
ALL PLOTS OF FINAL CONFIGURATION                              |
ALL SCATTER PLOTS OF DIST VS DHAT                             | ASCENDING (DISSIMILARITIES) DATA DEFINED
ROTATE FINAL CONFIG. COORDINATES                              | WHERE RANK ORDER INCREASES AS THE DISTANCE
                                                              | OR SIMILARITY BETWEEN STIMULI INCREASES.
                                                              |
PARAMETERS:  10  1  1                                         |
TITLE: (3X,10F3.0)                                            | PARAMETERS:   10 ROWS/COLS; 1 REPLICATION; 1 GROUP
                                                              | INPUT FORMAT(10 DATA POINTS, EACH 3 COLUMNS WIDE)
DATA FOR RECORD:    10                                        | NO DECIMAL POINTS ARE READ.
 .12E+02 .11E+02 .10E+02 .40E+01 .33E+02 .34E+02 .21E+02 .39E+02 .45E+0
                                                              |
ON THE SHEPARD DIAGRAM THE ORIGINAL DATA (DATA) ARE PLOTTED;  |
ON THE Y AXIS AND DISTANCES (DIST,0) AND ESTIMATED DISTANCES  |
(DHAT,X) ON THE X AXIS. A ; INDICATES TWO VALUES ARE PLOTTED  |
ON TOP OF EACH OTHER AND A > INDICATES POINT NUMBERS GREATER  |
THAN 50.  IDENTIFIERS FOR THE CONFIGURATION PLOT IN 2 DIMENSIONS ARE: |
                                                              | KEY TO PLOT COORDINATES
                                                              |
    *****IDENTIFICATION KEY FOR PLOTS WITH IDENTIFIED POINTS***** |
                                                              |
PT #   1  2  3  4  5  6  7  8  9 10 11 12 13 14 15           |
CHAR   1  2  3  4  5  6  7  8  9  A  B  C  D  E  F           |
                                                              |
PT #  16 17 18 19 20 21 22 23 24 25 26 27 28 29 30           |
CHAR   G  H  I  J  K  L  M  N  O  P  Q  R  S  T  U           |
```

```
PT #  31 32 33 34 35 36 37 38 39 40 41 42 43 44 45
CHAR  V  W  X  Y  Z  +  /  =  *  &  $  @  ]  -  <

PT #  46 47 48 49 50
CHAR  (  )  "  #  '
```

TITLE: POP DISSIMILARITIES	TORSCA PRE-ITERATION TO REDUCE STRESS

```
INITIAL CONFIGURATION COMPUTATION    NO. PTS.= 10    DIM=  3


   PRE-ITERATION       STRESS


        0            .5502
        1            .5781


STRESS STARTING TO INCREASE   BEST VALUE ACHIEVED ON PRE-ITERATION NUMBE


THE BEST INITIAL CONFIGURATION OF 10 POINTS IN  3 DIMENSIONS
HAS A STRESS OF     .550.  STRESS FORMULA 1 WAS USED.

TITLE: POP DISSIMILARITIES

HISTORY OF COMPUTATION:
N= 10 THERE ARE    45 DATA VALUES, SPLIT INTO   1 LIST(S).
DIMENSION(S) =   3

ITERATION STRESS  SRAT SRATAV CAGRGL COSAV ACSAV   SFGR    STEP

     0   .550   .800  .800  .000  .000  .000  .0274  .3771
     1   .383   .696  .764  .552  .364  .364  .0199  .6621
     2   .258   .674  .733 -.288 -.066  .314  .0126  .5251
     3   .191   .739  .735 -.434 -.309  .393  .0109  .3575
     .     .      .     .     .     .     .     .      .
     .     .      .     .     .     .     .     .      .
     .     .      .     .     .     .     .     .      .
    29   .010   .979  .974 -.016  .117  .159  .0001  .0057
    30   .010   .984  .977 -.451 -.258  .352  .0001  .0030
    31   .010   .978  .977  .316  .121  .328  .0001  .0025

SATISFACTORY STRESS WAS REACHED

THE FINAL CONFIGURATION HAS BEEN ROTATED TO PRINCIPAL COMPONENTS.

THE FINAL CONFIGURATION OF  10 POINTS IN  3 DIMENSIONS HAS STRESS OF  .
FORMULA 1 WAS USED.  THE FINAL CONFIGURATION APPEARS:

         1      2      3
 1    -.788  -.609   .176
 2    -.789  -.611   .178
 3    -.797  -.614   .228
 4    -.638  -.069   .263
 5     .987   .747  -.633
 6    1.172  1.046  -.099
 7    -.571  -.991  -.054
 8     .999   .479  -.633
 9    1.224   .827  -.075
10    -.798  -.206   .649
```

Right column notes:

N=# OF STIMULI IN DATA MATRIX
THE NUMBER OF DATA VALUES SHOWS THE NUMBER
OF DATA POINTS READ INTO THE KYST PROGRAM
SHOULD BE THE SAME AS IN THE DATA SET.
SPLIT REFERS TO THE SPLIT OPTION:
BY DECK (DEFAULT) READS ONE INTACT DATA FILE.
BY ROWS (USED FOR UNFOLDING A LOWER CORNER
   DATA MATRIX AND PERFORMS ONE REGRESSION FOR
   EACH SUBJECT'S DATA (i.e., EACH ROW OF THE
   DATA MATRIX)
STRESS = QUALITY OF MODEL FIT (FORMULA 1)

SRAT   = HOW RAPIDLY STRESS IS MINIMIZED

SRATAV = HOW RAPIDLY AVG STRESS IS MINIMIZED

CAGRGL = COSINE OF THE ANGLE BETWEEN CURRENT
         AND PREVIOUS GRADIENT

COSAV = WGTD AVG OF CAGRGL VALUES

ACOSAV = WGTD AVG OF ABSOLUTE VALUE OF CAGRGL

SFGR = SCALE FACTOR (ROUGHLY EQUIVALENT TO
       THE LENGTH OF THE GRADIENT (0 WHEN AT
       THE MINIMUM CONFIGURATION)
STEP = INTERATION STEP SIZE

COORDINATES OF STIMULI (ROWS) IN THE NUMBER
OF DIMENSIONS SPECIFIED FOR THE SOLUTION
 (COLUMNS)
FOR GROUP 1, 25 DATA POINTS WERE READ,
THE FINAL STRESS WAS .010 AND THE
MONOTONE ASCENDING REGRESSION WAS PERORMED
IF THE METRIC (POLYNOMIAL MODEL WAS USED,
THE REGRESSION COEFFICIENTS ALSO APPEAR.

```
DATA GROUP(S)                                                      PLOT OF DISTANCES AND DHAT IN 3 DIMENSIONS
SERIAL  COUNT STRESS REGRESSION COEFFICIENTS (FROM DEGREE 0 TO MAX OF 4  PLOT OF ACTUAL DISTANCES READ IN  (OR RANK
   1     45   .010  ASCENDING                                      DISTANCES IN THIS CASE, VS. DERIVED DISTANCES
                                                                  DISTANCES (DHAT))
************************************************************************
                                                                  O = ORIGINAL VALUES
POP DISSIMILARITIES                                               X = DHAT VALUES
                                                                  + = 2 OR MORE POINTS WERE PLOTTED ON TOP OF
DIST AND DHAT VERSES DATA FOR   3 DIMENSION(S)                          EACH OTHER.
STRESS =    .0099


               .    .1287.    .5889.   1.0492.   1.5094.   1.9696.
                -.1014    .3588    .8190   1.2793   1.7395   2.1997
             * .****.****.****.****.****.****.****.****.****.****.*
       47.20 ..                                                .. 47.2
       45.41 ..                                        X       .. 45.4
       43.61 ..                                       X        .. 43.6
       41.82 ..                                       X        .. 41.8
       40.03 ..                                      X  O      .. 40.0
  S    38.24 ..                                      XO        .. 38.2
  H    36.44 ..                                    OXO         .. 36.4
  E    34.65 ..                                    XXO         .. 34.6
  P    32.86 ..                                 X X            .. 32.8
  A    31.07 ..                                 X              .. 31.0
  R    29.27 ..                                 X              .. 29.2
  D    27.48 ..                                 X              .. 27.4
       25.69 ..                                 X              .. 25.6
       23.90 ..                                 X              .. 23.9
       22.10 ..                             X                  .. 22.1
       20.31 ..                       X                        .. 20.3
  D    18.52 ..             X                                  .. 18.5
  I    16.73 ..             X                                  .. 16.7
  A    14.93 ..             X                                  .. 14.9
  G    13.14 ..            XX                                  .. 13.1
  R    11.35 ..            X+                                  .. 11.3
  A     9.56 ..            X                                   ..  9.5
  M     7.76 ..            X                                   ..  7.7
        5.97 ..       X                                        ..  5.9
        4.18 ..       X                                        ..  4.1
        2.39 ..   X                                            ..  2.3
         .59 .. X                                              ..  .5
       -1.20 ..                                                .. -1.2
             * .****.****.****.****.****.****.****.****.****.****.*
               .    .1287.    .5889.   1.0492.   1.5094.   1.9696.
                -.1014    .3588    .8190   1.2793   1.7395   2.1997
```

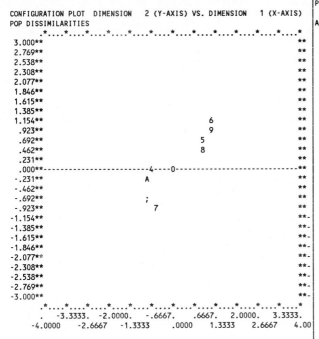

```
                                                        |PLOT OF STIMULUS POINTS
CONFIGURATION PLOT  DIMENSION   2 (Y-AXIS) VS. DIMENSION   1 (X-AXIS)   |; DESIGNATES THAT 2 OR MORE POINTS
POP DISSIMILARITIES                                     |ARE PLOTTED ON TOP OF EACH OTHER.
     .*....*....*....*....*....*....*....*....*....*....*....*....*    |
 3.000**                                                      **      |
 2.769**                                                      **      | CONFIGURATION PLOT:  DIMENSION 2 VS. DIMENSION 1
 2.538**                                                      **      |
 2.308**                                                      **      |
 2.077**                                                      **      |
 1.846**                                                      **      |
 1.615**                                                      **      |
 1.385**                                                      **      |
 1.154**                              6                       **      |
  .923**                              9                       **      |
  .692**                         5                            **      |
  .462**                         8                            **      |
  .231**                                                      **      |
  .000**-------------------------4----0------------------------**      |
 -.231**                    A                                 **      |
 -.462**                                                      **      |
 -.692**                  ;                                   **      |
 -.923**                7                                     **      |
-1.154**                                                      **-     |
-1.385**                                                      **-     |
-1.615**                                                      **-     |
-1.846**                                                      **-     |
-2.077**                                                      **-     |
-2.308**                                                      **-     |
-2.538**                                                      **-     |
-2.769**                                                      **-     |
-3.000**                                                      **-     |
     .*....*...*....*....*....*....*....*....*....*....*....*....*     |
      .   -3.3333.  -2.0000.   -.6667.    .6667.   2.0000.  3.3333.    |
       -4.0000    -2.6667   -1.3333    .0000    1.3333   2.6667    4.00|
```

```
CONFIGURATION PLOT  DIMENSION   3 (Y-AXIS) VS. DIMENSION   1 (X-AXIS)
       .
       .
       .
CONFIGURATION PLOT  DIMENSION   3 (Y-AXIS) VS. DIMENSION   2 (X-AXIS)
       .
       .
       .
HISTORY OF COMPUTATION:
N= 10 THERE ARE    45 DATA VALUES, SPLIT INTO   1 LIST(S).
DIMENSION(S) =   2

ITERATION STRESS  SRAT SRATAV CAGRGL  COSAV  ACSAV    SFGR     STEP

       0   .084  .800  .800   .000   .000   .000   .0058   .0123
       1   .076  .901  .832   .999   .660   .660   .0052   .0333
       2   .054  .716  .792   .986   .875   .875   .0034   .1155
       3   .038  .691  .757  -.709  -.171   .766   .0025   .0610
       .    .     .     .      .      .      .       .       .
       .    .     .     .      .      .      .       .       .
      15   .010  .988  .978  -.147   .018   .215   .0001   .0027
      16   .010  .985  .980  -.102  -.061   .140   .0001   .0019
      17   .010  .989  .983   .476   .293   .362   .0001   .0022

SATISFACTORY STRESS WAS REACHED


THE FINAL CONFIGURATION HAS BEEN ROTATED TO PRINCIPAL COMPONENTS.

THE FINAL CONFIGURATION OF  10 POINTS IN  2 DIMENSIONS HAS STRESS OF  .
FORMULA 1 WAS USED.  THE FINAL CONFIGURATION APPEARS:

        1      2
  1   -.811  -.748
  2   -.811  -.748
  3   -.811  -.748
  4   -.755  -.616
  5   1.133  1.058
  6   1.237  1.219
  7   -.751  -.863
  8   1.148   .986
  9   1.284  1.174
 10   -.864  -.716

DATA GROUP(S)
SERIAL  COUNT STRESS REGRESSION COEFFICIENTS (FROM DEGREE 0 TO MAX OF 4
   1     45   .010  ASCENDING
```

CONFIGURATION PLOT:
DIMENSION 3 VS DIMENSION 1
(PLOT NOT SHOWN IN SAMPLE PRINTOUT)

CONFIGURATION PLOT:
DIMENSION 3 VS DIMENSION 2
(PLOT NOT SHOWN IN SAMPLE PRINTOUT)

AFTER COMPLETION OF THE 3 DIMENSIONAL
SOLUTION, THE TWO DIMENSIONAL SOLUTION
IS SOUGHT.
ALL STAGES IN THE TWO DIMENSIONAL ANALYSIS
ARE THE SAME AS FOR THE THREE DIMENSIONAL
ANALYSIS.

```
DIST AND DHAT VERSES DATA FOR   2 DIMENSION(S)
STRESS =    .0099


              .     .1297.    .6053.   1.0809.   1.5566.   2.0322.
              -.1081     .3675     .8431   1.3187    1.7944    2.2700
              * **** **** **** **** **** **** **** **** **** **** *
       47.20 ..                                            .. 47.2
       45.41 ..                                      X  .. 45.4
       43.61 ..                                  OX     .. 43.6
       41.82 ..                                  X      .. 41.8
       40.03 ..                                  X      .. 40.0
   S   38.24 ..                                  OX     .. 38.2
   H   36.44 ..                                  X      .. 36.4
   E   34.65 ..                                  X      .. 34.6
   P   32.86 ..                               XX        .. 32.8
   A   31.07 ..                               X         .. 31.0
   R   29.27 ..                               X0        .. 29.2
   D   27.48 ..                               X         .. 27.4
       25.69 ..                               X+        .. 25.6
       23.90 ..                               X0        .. 23.9
       22.10 ..                               XX        .. 22.1
       20.31 ..              X                          .. 20.3
   D   18.52 ..            X                            .. 18.5
   I   16.73 ..            XX                           .. 16.7
   A   14.93 ..      OX                                 .. 14.9
   G   13.14 ..      OX                                 .. 13.1
   R   11.35 ..       X                                 .. 11.3
   A    9.56 ..       X                                 ..  9.5
   M    7.76 ..       X                                 ..  7.7
        5.97 ..       X                                 ..  5.9
        4.18 ..      X X                                ..  4.1
        2.39 ..  X                                      ..  2.3
         .59 ..  X                                      ..   .5
       -1.20 ..                                         .. -1.2
              * **** **** **** **** **** **** **** **** **** **** *
              .     .1297.    .6053.   1.0809.   1.5566.   2.0322.
              -.1081     .3675     .8431   1.3187    1.7944    2.2700
```

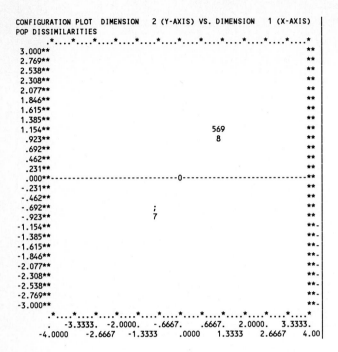

```
CONFIGURATION PLOT  DIMENSION   2 (Y-AXIS) VS. DIMENSION    1 (X-AXIS) |
POP DISSIMILARITIES
        .*....*....*....*....*....*....*....*....*....*....*....*
 3.000**                                                          **
 2.769**                                                          **
 2.538**                                                          **
 2.308**                                                          **
 2.077**                                                          **
 1.846**                                                          **
 1.615**                                                          **
 1.385**                                                          **
 1.154**                            569                           **
  .923**                             8                            **
  .692**                                                          **
  .462**                                                          **
  .231**                                                          **
  .000**-----------------------------0-----------------------------**
 -.231**                                                          **
 -.462**                                                          **
 -.692**                          ;                               **
 -.923**                          7                               **
-1.154**                                                          **-
-1.385**                                                          **-
-1.615**                                                          **-
-1.846**                                                          **-
-2.077**                                                          **-
-2.308**                                                          **-
-2.538**                                                          **-
-2.769**                                                          **-
-3.000**                                                          **-
        .*....*....*....*....*....*....*....*....*....*....*....*
        .    -3.3333.  -2.0000.   -.6667.   .6667.   2.0000.   3.3333.
          -4.0000    -2.6667   -1.3333    .0000   1.3333    2.6667    4.00|
```

APPENDICES

Availability of Computer Programs

Programs for multidimensional scaling are available from the following sources:

BELL LABORATORIES PROGRAMS

Description   MDS Package: 18 programs for MDS and conjoint analysis. Programs are provided with documentation and source code. Source code is set up to run in batch mode and is machine specific, for the IBM 360, Honeywell-6070 or GE-635.

Contact   Joann J. Crawley, Outside Software Distribution, AT&T Bell Laboratories, Room 2F-128B, 600 Mountain Avenue, Murray Hill, New Jersey 07974.

PC-MDS

Description   MDS, Conjoint, Cluster, Regression, Factor, Discriminant, Analysis, etc. (more than twenty programs), including MDPREF, INDSCAL, KYST, PREFMAP, PROFIT MDS. Interactive programs are provided with documentation and EXE files for the IBM compatible PC.

Contact   Scott M. Smith, Ph.D., Institute of Business Management, Brigham Young University, Provo, Utah 84602.

ALSCAL

Description   A general-purpose MDS program that is extremely flexible in analysis. Metric and nonmetric scaling is possible with or without individual differences models.

Contact   Forrest W. Young, L. L. Thurstone Psychometric Laboratory, University of North Carolina, Chapel Hill, North Carolina 27514.

Soft Drink Case Study

Fifty-seven university students completed the questionnaire directed at measuring their preferences for similarities between and evaluations of ten soft drink brands. The data provided by this questionnaire is found on the program diskette accompanying this text.

SOFT DRINK QUESTIONNAIRE

In this project, we are interested in learning more about your perception of soft drinks. We ask that you take the time to complete all questions. As you realize, there are no right or wrong answers—we are interested only in your perceptions.

SECTION I

Listed below are pairs of soft drinks. Please rate each pair on a scale of 1 (not at all similar) to 9 (very similar). Use any value between 1 and 9 to reflect your perception of the degree of similarity of each pair of beverages. Use criteria of your own choice in making these comparisons, but please try to keep these criteria constant for all comparisons.

Brand Pair	Not at all Similar								Very Similar	
PEPSI vs COKE	1	2	3	4	5	6	7	8	9	___
PEPSI vs COKE CLASSIC	1	2	3	4	5	6	7	8	9	_5_
PEPSI vs DIET PEPSI	1	2	3	4	5	6	7	8	9	___
PEPSI vs DIET SLICE	1	2	3	4	5	6	7	8	9	___
PEPSI vs DIET 7-UP	1	2	3	4	5	6	7	8	9	___
PEPSI vs DR. PEPPER	1	2	3	4	5	6	7	8	9	___
PEPSI vs SLICE	1	2	3	4	5	6	7	8	9	___
PEPSI vs 7-UP	1	2	3	4	5	6	7	8	9	___
PEPSI vs TAB	1	2	3	4	5	6	7	8	9	___
COKE vs CLASSIC COKE	1	2	3	4	5	6	7	8	9	___
COKE vs DIET PEPSI	1	2	3	4	5	6	7	8	9	_14_
COKE vs DIET SLICE	1	2	3	4	5	6	7	8	9	___
COKE vs DIET 7-UP	1	2	3	4	5	6	7	8	9	___

Brand Pair	Not at all Similar								Very Similar
COKE vs DR. PEPPER	1	2	3	4	5	6	7	8	9 ____
COKE vs SLICE	1	2	3	4	5	6	7	8	9 ____
COKE vs 7-UP	1	2	3	4	5	6	7	8	9 ____
COKE vs TAB	1	2	3	4	5	6	7	8	9 ____
CLASSIC COKE vs DIET PEPSI	1	2	3	4	5	6	7	8	9 ____
CLASSIC COKE vs DIET SLICE	1	2	3	4	5	6	7	8	9 ____
CLASSIC COKE vs DIET 7-UP	1	2	3	4	5	6	7	8	9 ____
CLASSIC COKE vs DR. PEPPER	1	2	3	4	5	6	7	8	9 ____
CLASSIC COKE vs SLICE	1	2	3	4	5	6	7	8	9 ____
CLASSIC COKE vs 7-UP	1	2	3	4	5	6	7	8	9 ____
CLASSIC COKE vs TAB	1	2	3	4	5	6	7	8	9 ____
DIET PEPSI vs DIET SLICE	1	2	3	4	5	6	7	8	9 ____
DIET PEPSI vs DIET 7-UP	1	2	3	4	5	6	7	8	9 ____
DIET PEPSI vs DR. PEPPER	1	2	3	4	5	6	7	8	9 ____
DIET PEPSI vs SLICE	1	2	3	4	5	6	7	8	9 ____
DIET PEPSI vs 7-UP	1	2	3	4	5	6	7	8	9 ____
DIET PEPSI vs TAB	1	2	3	4	5	6	7	8	9 ____
DIET SLICE vs DIET 7-UP	1	2	3	4	5	6	7	8	9 ____
DIET SLICE vs DR. PEPPER	1	2	3	4	5	6	7	8	9 _35_
DIET SLICE vs SLICE	1	2	3	4	5	6	7	8	9 ____
DIET SLICE vs 7-UP	1	2	3	4	5	6	7	8	9 ____
DIET SLICE vs TAB	1	2	3	4	5	6	7	8	9 ____
DIET 7-UP vs DR. PEPPER	1	2	3	4	5	6	7	8	9 ____
DIET 7-UP vs SLICE	1	2	3	4	5	6	7	8	9 ____
DIET 7-UP vs 7-UP	1	2	3	4	5	6	7	8	9 ____
DIET 7-UP vs TAB	1	2	3	4	5	6	7	8	9 ____
DR. PEPPER vs SLICE	1	2	3	4	5	6	7	8	9 ____
DR. PEPPER vs 7-UP	1	2	3	4	5	6	7	8	9 ____
DR. PEPPER vs TAB	1	2	3	4	5	6	7	8	9 ____
SLICE vs 7-UP	1	2	3	4	5	6	7	8	9 ____
SLICE vs TAB	1	2	3	4	5	6	7	8	9 ____
7-UP vs TAB	1	2	3	4	5	6	7	8	9 _49_

SECTION IIA

In this next section, we would like you to rank order the ten soft drinks on various attributes. Please use the rank of 1 for the most preferred and the rank of 10 for the least preferred on each attribute. Fill in your responses on the grid below. Each row should have one complete set of numbers between 1 and 10.

	Coke	Coke Class.	Diet Pepsi	Diet Slice	Diet 7-Up	Dr. Pepper	Pepsi	Slice	Tab	7-UP	
Fruitiness											50–59
Carbonation											60–69
Calories											70–79
Sweetness											2 / 05–14
Thirst Quenching											15–24
Popularity with Others											25–34
Aftertaste											35–44
Pick-me-up											45–54

SECTION IIB

In this next section, we would like you to rank order the ten soft drinks on various attributes. Please use the rank of 1 for the most preferred and the rank of 10 for the least preferred on each attribute. Fill in your responses on the grid below. Each row should have one complete set of numbers between 1 and 10.

	Coke	Coke Class.	Diet Pepsi	Diet Slice	Diet 7-Up	Dr. Pepper	Pepsi	Slice	Tab	7-UP	
After taste											C2: 35–40
Calories											C1: 70–75
Carbonation											C1: 60–65
Fruitiness											C1: 50–55
Pick-me-up											C2: 45–50
Popularity with Others											C2: 25–30
Sweetness											— — — 2 / C2: 05–10
Thirst Quenching											C2: 15–20

SECTION III.

In this next section, we would like you to rank order the ten soft drinks based on your evaluation under different-use scenarios. Please use the rank of 1 for the most preferred and the rank of 10 for the least preferred for each scenario. Fill in your responses on the grid at the bottom of the page. Each column should have one complete set of numbers between 1 and 10.

Scenario 1: Suppose you are relaxing around your apartment or house when no one else is home. You check the refrigerator as you pass through the kitchen. All 10 brands are present. Rank order your preference for selecting each of the brands of soft drink. (1 is most preferred, 2 is next most preferred, etc.).

    Scenario 2: You have just finished an afternoon of rigorous exercise and find yourself absolutely thirsty. You stand in front of the soft drink cooler at your local convenience store, but before you can have a drink, you must first rank order your preference for selecting each of the brands of soft drink. (1 is most preferred, 2 is next most preferred, etc.).

    Scenario 3:   You are in the grocery store getting munchies and drinks for an evening of entertainment at your place. You expect 8–10 friends to show up. Rank order your preference for selecting each of the brands of soft drink for the party. (1 is most preferred, 2 is next most preferred, etc.).

	Scenario #1 *Home Alone*	*Scenario #2* *Exercise*	*Scenario #3* *Entertaining*
Coke	_____ 55	_____ 65	_____ 05
Coke Classic	_____ 56	_____ 66	_____ 06
Diet Pepsi	_____ 57	_____ 67	_____ 07
Diet Slice	_____ 58	_____ 68	_____ 08
Diet 7-Up	_____ 59	_____ 69	_____ 09
Dr. Pepper	_____ 60	_____ 70	_____ 10
Pepsi	_____ 61	_____ 71	_____ 11
Slice	_____ 62	_____ 72	_____ 12
Tab	_____ 63	_____ 73	_____ 13
7-Up	_____ 64	_____ 74	_____ 14
		_____ 3	

SECTION IV

In this next section we are interested in your perceptions of the ten soft drinks on a number of attributes. Indicate your evaluation of the identified brand on each of the attributes by placing a check on the segment of the line that best indicates your perception.

Coke

A. Fruity Flavor	_____ _____ _____ _____ _____ _____	Nonfruity Flavor	15
B. Low Carbonation	_____ _____ _____ _____ _____ _____	High Carbonation	16
C. High in Calories	_____ _____ _____ _____ _____ _____	Low in Calories	17
D. Very Tart	_____ _____ _____ _____ _____ _____	Very Sweet	18
E. Thirst Quenching	_____ _____ _____ _____ _____ _____	Not Thirst Quenching	19
F. Not Popular	_____ _____ _____ _____ _____ _____	Popular w/Others	20
G. Strong Aftertaste	_____ _____ _____ _____ _____ _____	No Aftertaste	21
H. Not a Pick-me-up	_____ _____ _____ _____ _____ _____	A Pick-me-up	22

Coke Classic

A. Fruity Flavor	_____ _____ _____ _____ _____ _____	Nonfruity Flavor	23
B. Low Carbonation	_____ _____ _____ _____ _____ _____	High Carbonation	24
C. High in Calories	_____ _____ _____ _____ _____ _____	Low in Calories	25
D. Very Tart	_____ _____ _____ _____ _____ _____	Very Sweet	26
E. Thirst Quenching	_____ _____ _____ _____ _____ _____	Not Thirst Quenching	27
F. Not Popular	_____ _____ _____ _____ _____ _____	Popular w/Others	28
G. Strong Aftertaste	_____ _____ _____ _____ _____ _____	No Aftertaste	29
H. Not a Pick-me-up	_____ _____ _____ _____ _____ _____	A Pick-me-up	30

Diet Pepsi

A. Fruity Flavor	___	___	___	___	___	___	Nonfruity Flavor	31
B. Low Carbonation	___	___	___	___	___	___	High Carbonation	32
C. High in Calories	___	___	___	___	___	___	Low in Calories	33
D. Very Tart	___	___	___	___	___	___	Very Sweet	34
E. Thirst Quenching	___	___	___	___	___	___	Not Thirst Quenching	35
F. Not Popular	___	___	___	___	___	___	Popular w/Others	36
G. Strong Aftertaste	___	___	___	___	___	___	No Aftertaste	37
H. Not a Pick-me-up	___	___	___	___	___	___	A Pick-me-up	38

Diet Slice

A. Fruity Flavor	___	___	___	___	___	___	Nonfruity Flavor	39
B. Low Carbonation	___	___	___	___	___	___	High Carbonation	40
C. High in Calories	___	___	___	___	___	___	Low in Calories	41
D. Very Tart	___	___	___	___	___	___	Very Sweet	42
E. Thirst Quenching	___	___	___	___	___	___	Not Thirst Quenching	43
F. Not Popular	___	___	___	___	___	___	Popular w/Others	44
G. Strong Aftertaste	___	___	___	___	___	___	No Aftertaste	45
H. Not a Pick-me-up	___	___	___	___	___	___	A Pick-me-up	46

Diet 7-Up

A. Fruity Flavor	___	___	___	___	___	___	Nonfruity Flavor	47
B. Low Carbonation	___	___	___	___	___	___	High Carbonation	48
C. High in Calories	___	___	___	___	___	___	Low in Calories	49
D. Very Tart	___	___	___	___	___	___	Very Sweet	50
E. Thirst Quenching	___	___	___	___	___	___	Not Thirst Quenching	51
F. Not Popular	___	___	___	___	___	___	Popular w/Others	52
G. Strong Aftertaste	___	___	___	___	___	___	No Aftertaste	53
H. Not a Pick-me-up	___	___	___	___	___	___	A Pick-me-up	54

Dr. Pepper

A. Fruity Flavor	___	___	___	___	___	___	Nonfruity Flavor	55
B. Low Carbonation	___	___	___	___	___	___	High Carbonation	56
C. High in Calories	___	___	___	___	___	___	Low in Calories	57
D. Very Tart	___	___	___	___	___	___	Very Sweet	58
E. Thirst Quenching	___	___	___	___	___	___	Not Thirst Quenching	59
F. Not Popular	___	___	___	___	___	___	Popular w/Others	60
G. Strong Aftertaste	___	___	___	___	___	___	No Aftertaste	61
H. Not a Pick-me-up	___	___	___	___	___	___	A Pick-me-up	62

Pepsi

A. Fruity Flavor	___	___	___	___	___	___	Nonfruity Flavor	63
B. Low Carbonation	___	___	___	___	___	___	High Carbonation	64
C. High in Calories	___	___	___	___	___	___	Low in Calories	65
D. Very Tart	___	___	___	___	___	___	Very Sweet	66
E. Thirst Quenching	___	___	___	___	___	___	Not Thirst Quenching	67
F. Not Popular	___	___	___	___	___	___	Popular w/Others	68
G. Strong Aftertaste	___	___	___	___	___	___	No Aftertaste	69
H. Not a Pick-me-up	___	___	___	___	___	___	A Pick-me-up	70

Slice

A. Fruity Flavor	____ ____ ____ ____ ____ ____ ____	Nonfruity Flavor	71
B. Low Carbonation	____ ____ ____ ____ ____ ____ ____	High Carbonation	72
C. High in Calories	____ ____ ____ ____ ____ ____ ____	Low in Calories	73
D. Very Tart	____ ____ ____ ____ ____ ____ ____	Very Sweet	74
E. Thirst Quenching	____ ____ ____ ____ ____ ____ ____	Not Thirst Quenching	75
F. Not Popular	____ ____ ____ ____ ____ ____ ____	Popular w/Others	76
G. Strong Aftertaste	____ ____ ____ ____ ____ ____ ____	No Aftertaste	77
H. Not a Pick-me-up	____ ____ ____ ____ ____ ____ ____	A Pick-me-up	78
		____ ____ ____ ____	04

Tab

A. Fruity Flavor	____ ____ ____ ____ ____ ____ ____	Nonfruity Flavor	05
B. Low Carbonation	____ ____ ____ ____ ____ ____ ____	High Carbonation	06
C. High in Calories	____ ____ ____ ____ ____ ____ ____	Low in Calories	07
D. Very Tart	____ ____ ____ ____ ____ ____ ____	Very Sweet	08
E. Thirst Quenching	____ ____ ____ ____ ____ ____ ____	Not Thirst Quenching	09
F. Not Popular	____ ____ ____ ____ ____ ____ ____	Popular w/Others	10
G. Strong Aftertaste	____ ____ ____ ____ ____ ____ ____	No Aftertaste	11
H. Not a Pick-me-up	____ ____ ____ ____ ____ ____ ____	A Pick-me-up	12

7-Up

A. Fruity Flavor	____ ____ ____ ____ ____ ____ ____	Nonfruity Flavor	13
B. Low Carbonation	____ ____ ____ ____ ____ ____ ____	High Carbonation	14
C. High in Calories	____ ____ ____ ____ ____ ____ ____	Low in Calories	15
D. Very Tart	____ ____ ____ ____ ____ ____ ____	Very Sweet	16
E. Thirst Quenching	____ ____ ____ ____ ____ ____ ____	Not Thirst Quenching	17
F. Not Popular	____ ____ ____ ____ ____ ____ ____	Popular w/Others	18
G. Strong Aftertaste	____ ____ ____ ____ ____ ____ ____	No Aftertaste	19
H. Not a Pick-me-up	____ ____ ____ ____ ____ ____ ____	A Pick-me-up	20

SECTION V

The last section of the questionnaire contains a series of questions about your demographic characteristics such as age and income. We are asking these questions in order to determine if various groups have different perceptions of soft drinks. Your responses are strictly confidential and no one will ever associate responses with your name.

1. Are you   (a) Female   (b) Male   21
2. What is your age   22
   (a) 16–20   (b) 21–25   (c) 26–30   (d) 31–35   (e) Over 35
3. Are you   (a) Single   (b) Married   (c) Other   23
4. Are you   (a) Undergraduate student   (b) Graduate Student   24
5. What is (was) your undergraduate major?   25

   (a) Business
   (b) Engineering
   (c) Liberal Arts
   (d) Other (please specify) _____

6. What is your graduate school major? (if applicable) 26

    (a) Business
    (b) Engineering
    (c) Liberal Arts
    (d) Other (please specify) ————————————————

(7) Do you 27

    (a) Rent, live alone
    (b) Rent, live with roommates or family
    (c) Live with parents
    (d) Live with other relative
    (e) Own home, live alone
    (f) Own home, live with roommates or family
    (g) Other (please specify) ————————————————

8. How many children (including yourself) are there in your family? ————————28

9. What percentage of your living expenses are you paying yourself by working, scholarship, loans, etc.? 29

    (a) 0%   (d) 26–50%
    (b) 1–10%   (e) 51–75%
    (c) 11–25%   (f) over 75%

10. How often do you participate in physical activities such as aerobics, jogging, court sports, etc.? 30

    (a) almost every day
    (b) about 2–3 times per week
    (c) about once per week
    (d) about twice a month
    (e) about once a month or less often

11. How often do you entertain friends at your home, or attend parties with friends?

31

    (a) about twice per week or more often
    (b) about once per week
    (c) about twice a month
    (d) about once a month
    (e) less than once a month

12. What quantity of soft drinks best describes your consumption for an average week? (assume cans and bottles are 16 oz.) 32

    (a) none   (f) 9–12 cans or bottles
    (b) 1–2 cans or bottles   (g) 13–18 cans or bottles
    (c) 3–5 cans or bottles   (h) 19–24 cans or bottles
    (d) 6–8 cans or bottles   (h) more than 24

13. What is your grade point average up to this term? 33

    (a) less than 2.0
    (b) 2.0–2.5
    (c) 2.51–3.0
    (d) 3.01–3.5
    (e) 3.51–4.0

14. In which income range was your total family income before taxes in 1985?   34
    (a) less than $20,000
    (b) 20,000–25,000
    (c) 26,000–30,000
    (d) 31,000–40,000
    (e) 41,000–50,000
    (f) over $50,000

Thank You For Your Cooperation

Sample Data Sets, Data Matrices, and Program Command Files

INDSCAL INPUT DATA

```
3  3  2  2  25  1  0  1  0  0  '12345678'  0  0  1  1  .002        *
3 10 10                                                            *
(3X,9F3.0)                                                         *
COK  1                                                             *
CCL  3   2                                                         *
DPE  7   9   8                                                     I
DSL 27  28  32  22                                                 N
D7U 41  42  43  29  13                                             D
DRP 18  17  19  20  30  40                                         S
SLI 24  25  26  31   5  16  23                                     C
7UP 35  36  38  44  15   6  37  14                                 A
TAB 12  11  10   4  33  34  21  39  45                             L
COK  5                                                             *
CCL  4   6                                                         *
DPE  7   9   8                                                     I
DSL 27  28  32  22                                                 N
D7U 44  43  42  29  13                                             P
DRP 18  17  19  20  30  40                                         U
SLI 24  25  26  31   2  16  23                                     T
7UP 35  36  38  41  15   1  37  14                                 *
TAB 12  11  10   3  33  34  21  39  45                             *
COK  6                                                             *
CCL  4   5                                                         *
DPE  7   8   9                                                     *
DSL 27  28  32  22                                                 *
D7U 44  43  42  29  13                                             *
DRP 18  17  19  20  30  40                                         *
SLI 24  25  26  31   2  16  23                                     *
7UP 35  36  38  41  15   1  37  14                                 *
TAB 12  11  10   3  33  34  21  39  45                             *
```

KYST INPUT DATA (LOWER HALF SIMILARITIES MATRIX)

```
 10  1  1                                                          *
(3X,9F3.0)                                                         *
COK  1                                                             K
CCL  3   2                                                         Y
DPE  7   9   8                                                     S
DSL 27  28  32  22                                                 T
D7U 41  42  43  29  13                                             *
DRP 18  17  19  20  30  40                                         *
SLI 24  25  26  31   5  16  23                                     *
7UP 35  36  38  44  15   6  37  14                                 *
TAB 12  11  10   4  33  34  21  39  45                             *
```

```
AVERAGE POP BRAND PREFERENCES FOR USAGE SCENARIOS 1-3              M
  3  10   2   2   1   0                                           D
 (10F7.3)                                                         P
  3.912  3.368  5.000  5.789  5.877  4.386  3.561  4.140  4.667  4.333   R
  4.070  3.719  5.281  5.561  5.912  4.860  3.456  3.649  4.789  3.684   E
  3.491  2.772  5.053  5.684  6.667  5.246  2.772  5.368  4.825  3.193   F
                                                                  *
```

```
KYST DATA: ONE RESPONDENT'S CAR DATA AS DISSIMILARITIES (MUSTANG IS 1ST COLUMN)
 11   1   1
(6X,11F3.0)
SEVILL 27
LINCOL 26  1
ESCORT 17 38 39
CORVET 13 28 29 36
CHEVET 25 41 42 10 35
N300ZX 15 32 30 45  9 48
RENAUL 24 40  2 12 43 11 34
POR944 16 33 31 46  8 49 14 44
JAGXJ6 37  7  5 50 18 52 19 51 21
500SEL 47  6  4 53 23 55 22 54 20 03
```

```
PROFIT DATA: CONFIGURATION MATRIX FROM INDSCAL ANALYSIS

    1   10   2    8    0    0   3 0.001                            -
  (6X, 2F12.5)                                                    -
    1        -.16570      -.26600                                 -
    2        -.18151      -.24813                                 -
    3        -.22479      -.19692                                 P
    4        -.34591       .32032                                 R
    5         .25542       .10266                                 O
    6         .26579       .60031                                 F
    7        -.05295      -.32816                                 I
    8         .39661      -.30941                                 T
    9         .51234      -.05987                                 -
   10        -.45928       .38520                                 -
  (3X, 10F5.2)                                                    I
AFTER TASTE                                                       N
001 4.86 4.61 4.54 1.91 3.49 3.23 4.47 1.54 4.61 2.75             P
CALORIES                                                          U
002 4.74 4.81 4.40 3.65 4.33 4.44 4.67 3.51 4.19 4.47             T
CARBONATION                                                       -
003 2.28 2.26 5.00 4.77 4.97 2.51 2.97 2.90 5.14 2.84             -
FRUITINESS                                                        -
004 4.30 3.98 3.67 3.74 3.07 3.77 4.19 3.42 3.35 3.79             -
PICK-ME-UP                                                        -
005 3.16 2.91 3.53 2.68 3.11 3.21 2.90 2.95 3.65 2.40             -
POPULARITY                                                        -
006 5.05 5.44 4.61 3.26 4.09 3.95 5.49 3.67 4.09 4.86             -
SWEETNESS                                                         -
007 3.91 3.84 3.00 3.40 3.25 3.21 4.07 3.84 2.51 4.51             -
THIRST QUENCHING                                                  -
008 5.02 5.19 4.07 3.40 3.21 4.42 5.11 3.58 3.98 3.95             -
```

```
CORRESPONDENCE ANALYSIS: GREENACRE DATA

  5   4
 (4F3.0)
   4   2   3   2
   4   3   7   4
  25  10  12   4
  18  24  33  13
  10   6   7   2
SENIOR M
JUNIOR M
SENIOR E
JUNIOR E
SECRETAR
NONE
LIGHT
MEDIUM
HEAVY
```

```
MDPREF DATA: 8 POP ATTRIBUTES X 10 POP BRANDS

  8  10   2   2   1   0
 (10F5.2)
 5.79 6.49 5.81 2.91 4.30 4.04 5.74 1.39 5.23 2.86
 3.42 3.90 4.88 5.67 4.93 4.37 3.14 5.19 5.25 3.90
 4.68 5.58 3.37 3.47 3.63 5.40 4.61 4.84 3.81 4.51
 3.32 4.25 5.02 6.09 6.23 4.47 2.72 3.74 5.35 3.53
 4.56 4.19 5.56 5.09 5.53 4.77 4.16 2.77 5.25 2.79
 3.35 2.11 4.05 5.86 6.32 5.11 2.25 5.63 5.35 3.98
 3.95 3.70 5.28 5.21 5.61 4.90 3.72 4.04 5.18 2.98
 3.07 2.72 4.74 6.33 6.32 4.25 3.09 5.07 5.12 4.16
```

```
PREFMAP DATA: CONFIGURATION MATRIX FROM INDSCAL ANALYSIS

  2   3   0   1   0   1   4   0   1   1  15   1   2   1
 (6X, 2F12.5)
  1         -.16570      -.26600
  2         -.18151      -.24813
  3         -.22479      -.19692
  4         -.34591       .32032
  5          .25542       .10266
  6          .26579       .60031
  7         -.05295      -.32816
  8          .39661      -.30941
  9          .51234      -.05987
 10         -.45928       .38520
 (3X, 10F5.2)
001 3.91 3.37 5.00 5.79 5.88 4.39 3.56 4.14 4.67 4.33
002 4.07 3.72 5.28 5.56 5.91 4.86 3.46 3.65 4.79 3.68
003 3.49 2.77 5.05 5.68 6.67 5.25 2.77 5.37 4.83 3.19
```

```
(F3.0, 12X, F3.0, 8X,   F4.0,F2.0,2F3.0,F4.0,2F3.0,F4.0)                    *
125 0 1 2 0 0 4 08 1 0 0 1 300 5 38 46 184 72 53 350 ASTON SALOO           C
110 0 1 2 0 0 2 12 1 1 0 1 380 5 39 37 177 78 45 354 FERRARI TES           L
118 0 1 2 0 0 2 12 1 1 0 1 420 5 39 33 165 79 42 341 CONTACH 500           U
057 0 1 2 0 0 2 04 1 1 0 1 215 4 36 27 169 73 45 194 LOTUS TURBO           S
059 0 1 2 0 0 2 08 1 0 0 1 316 5 38 35 178 72 51 317 PORSCHE 928           T
026 0 1 2 0 0 2 04 1 0 0 1 147 4 34 28 169 68 50 144 PORSCHE 944           E
014 1 1 2 0 0 2 04 1 0 0 1 146 4 33 26 169 67 50 138 MAZDA RX7             R
 .  . . . . . . . .  . . . . .   .   .  .  .   .  .  .
 .  . . . . . . . .  . . . . .   .   .  .  .   .  .  .
 .  . . . . . . . .  . . . . .   .   .  .  .   .  .  .
010 1 0 2 0 0 4 04 1 0 1 1 085 3 36 29 121 66 72 141 JEEP WRANGLER         *
011 1 1 5 1 0 5 04 1 0 1 1 096 3 35 32 175 65 70 125 ISUZU TROOPER         *
010 1 1 2 0 0 4 04 1 0 1 1 109 3 34 33 157 66 71 142 MITSUBISHI MONTERR    *
017 1 1 5 1 0 5 04 1 0 1 1 125 3 41 42 184 71 70 200 TOYOTA LANDCRUSER     *
007 1 1 2 0 0 4 04 1 0 1 1 063 3 33 21 135 60 66 074 SUZUKI SAMURI         *
```

POP DATA: QUESTIONNAIRE IS IN APPENDIX B

```
(4X,75F1.0,/,4X,70F1.0,/,4X,74F1.0,/,4X,30F1.0)
00115441151178311311321141157631162343544542378453462785190218674390523867915 04
00124398765102439876520132098754612398765401239876540132978654013498765201
00134358672901244562242543462414611511226242116363651134436531455354331335244 4
00146452651133331666121111135652334
00213171121124211111111111111334223635422672334633907246815321507349864160932587
00223469012785908246715331596820748012469537215968307441596038723467801925
00236135782094652645446614566542663533226223324362255336165433462535551232234 3
00243255353335235234221111133422434
 .  . . . . . . . .  . . . . .   .   .  .  .   .  .  .
 .  . . . . . . . .  . . . . .   .   .  .  .   .  .  .
 .  . . . . . . . .  . . . . .   .   .  .  .   .  .  .
04118573122146532431673253162242267387317833268328971356042524916387089301765 24
04120289751364618795024360798314528541263079204895163731679204858156920374
04132078931645352552354523264545623445126234312364523136242435352316361225523 1
04145552352615436461232211296242 51
04213341111125411111124111113111112513771375114755967152803405387219649810237465
04229052834167748392501608259413767345201698076891532464789350126478935012
042364789350126642365534452234326555222132255455655542244325466343456323433452
042423343225333453542221 1028631161
```

REFERENCES

Ackoff, R. L. 1962. *Scientific Method: Optimizing Applied Research Decisions.* New York: John Wiley & Sons, Inc.

Aldenderfer, M., & Blashfield, R. 1984. *Cluster Analysis.* Beverly Hills: Sage Publications.

American Newspaper Publishers Association, Bureau of Advertising. 1969. "What Can One Newspaper Ad Do? An Experimental Study of Newspaper Advertising Communication and Results." New York.

Arabie, P. 1977. "Clustering Representations of Group Overlap." *Journal of Mathematical Sociology* 5, 113–128.

Arabie, P., & Carroll, J. D. 1980. "MAPCLUS: A Mathematical Programming Approach to fitting the ADCLUS model." *Psychometrika* 45, 211–235.

Arabie, P., Carroll, J. D., & DeSarbo, W. 1987. *Three-Way Scaling and Clustering.* Beverly Hills: Sage Publications.

Arabie, P., Carroll, J. D., DeSarbo, W., & Wind, J. 1981. "Overlapping Clustering: A New Method for Product Positioning." *Journal of Marketing Research* 18 (August), 310–317.

Arnold, S. 1979. "A Test for Clusters." *Journal of Marketing Research* 16 (November), 545–551.

Bennett, J. F., & Hays, W. L. 1960. "Multidimensional Unfolding: Determining the Dimensionality of Ranked Preference Data." *Psychometrika* 25, 27–43.

Benzécri, J. P. 1969. "Statistical Analysis as a Tool to Make Patterns Emerge from Data." *Methodologies of Pattern Recognition,* S. Watanabe (ed.). New York: Academic Press, Inc., pp. 35–74.

Boulding, K. E. 1968. *The Image.* Ann Arbor: The University of Michigan Press.

Bradley, R. A., & Terry, M. E. 1952. "Rank Analysis of Incomplete Block Designs." *Biometrika* 39, 324–345.

Carmone, F. J., Green, P. E., & Robinson, P. J. 1968. "TRICON—An IBM 360/65 FORTRAN IV Program for the Triangularization of Conjoint Data." *Journal of Marketing Research* 5 (May), 219–220.

Carroll, J. D. 1972. "Individual Differences and Multidimensional Scaling." *Multidimensional Scaling: Theory and Application in the Behavioral Sciences. Vol. 1: Theory,* R. N. Shepard, A. K. Romney, and S. Nerlove (eds.). New York: Seminar Press.

Carroll, J. D. 1969. "Polynomial Factor Analysis." *Proceedings of the 77th Annual Convention, American Psychological Association,* 103–104.

Carroll, J. D., & Arabie, P. 1980. "Multidimensional Scaling," in *Annual Review of Psychology,* M. R. Rosenzweig and L. W. Porter (eds.). Palo Alto, Calif.: Annual Reviews, Inc.

Carroll, J. D., & Chang, J. J. 1964. "A General Index of Nonlinear Correlation and Its Application to the Interpretation of Multidimensional Scaling Solutions." *American Psychologist* 19, 540.

Carroll, J. D., & Chang, J. J. 1967. "Relating Preference Data to Multidimensional Scaling Solutions via a Generalization of Coombs' Unfolding Model," unpublished paper. Bell Laboratories, Murray Hill, N.J.

Carroll, J. D., & Chang, J. J. 1969. "A New Method for Dealing with Individual Differences in Multidimensional Scaling," unpublished paper. Bell Laboratories, Murray Hill, N.J.

Carroll, J. D., & Chang, J. J. 1970. "Analysis of Individual Differences in Multidimensional Scaling Via an n-way Generalization of Eckart–Young Decomposition." *Psychometrika* 35, 283–319.

Carroll, J. D., Green, P. E., & Schaffer, C. M. 1986. "Interpoint Distance Comparisons in Correspondence Analysis." *Journal of Marketing Research* 23 (August), 271–280.

Chang, J. J., & Carroll, J. D. 1969a. "How to

Use INDSCAL, A Computer Program for Canonical Decomposition of n-way Tables and Individual Differences in Multidimensional Scaling," unpublished paper. Bell Laboratories, Murray Hill, N.J.

Chang, J. J., & Carroll, J. D. 1969b. "How to Use MDPREF, A Computer Program for Multidimensional Analysis of Preference Data," unpublished paper. Bell Laboratories, Murray Hill, N.J.

Chang, J. J., & Carroll, J. D. 1972. "How to Use PREFMAP and PREFMAP2—Programs which Relate Preference Data to Multidimensional Scaling Solution," unpublished paper. Bell Laboratories, Murray Hill, N.J.

Cliff, Norman. 1966. "Orthogonal Rotation to Congruence." *Psychometrika* **31**, 33–42.

Coombs, C. H. 1950. "Psychological Scaling Without a Unit of Measurement." *Psychological Review* **57,** 148–158.

Coombs, C. H. 1964. *A Theory of Data.* New York: John Wiley & Sons, pp. 80–180.

Coxon, A. P. 1982. *The User's Guide to Multidimensional Scaling.* London: Heinemann Educational Books.

Cronbach, L. J., & Gleser, G. C. 1953. "Assessing Similarity Between Profiles." *Psychological Bulletin* **50,** 456–473.

Davison, M. L. 1983. *Multidimensional Scaling.* New York: John Wiley & Sons, Inc.

De Leeuw, J. 1973. *Canonical Analysis of Categorical Data,* unpublished doctoral dissertation. Psychological Institute, University of Leiden, The Netherlands.

Everett, B. 1980. *Cluster Analysis.* New York: Halsted Press.

Frank, R. E., & Green, P. E. 1968. "Numerical Taxonomy in Marketing Analysis: A Review Article." *Journal of Marketing Research* **5** (February), 83–94.

Friedman, H., & Rubin, J. 1967. "On Some Invariant Criteria for Grouping Data." *Journal of the American Statistical Association* **62,** 1159–1178.

Gleason, T. C. 1967. "A General Model for Nonmetric Multidimensional Scaling." Michigan Mathematical Psychology Program. University of Michigan, Ann Arbor.

Gower, J. C. 1966. "Some Distance Properties of Latent Root and Vector Methods in Multivariate Analysis." *Biometrika* **53,** 315–328.

Gower, J. C. 1967. "Multivariate Analysis and Multidimensional Geometry." *The Statistician* **17,** 13–28.

Green, P. E. 1978. *Mathematical Tools for Applied Multivariate Analysis.* New York: Academic Press.

Green, P. E., Carroll, J. D., & Goldberg, S. M. 1981. "A General Approach to Product Design Optimization Via Conjoint Analysis." *Journal of Marketing* **45** (Summer), 17–37.

Green, P. E., & Carmone, F. J. 1967a. "Perceptual and Preference Mapping of Professional Journals," working paper. University of Pennsylvania, Philadelphia.

Green, P. E., & Carmone, F. J. 1967b. "A Reduced Space and Cluster Analysis of Physicians' Media Reading Habits," working paper. University of Pennsylvania, Philadelphia.

Green, P. E., & Carmone, F. J. 1968. "The Performance Structure of the Computer Market—A Multivariate Approach." *Economics and Business Bulletin* **21** (Fall), 1–11.

Green, P. E., & Carmone, F. J. 1969. "Multidimensional Scaling: An Introduction and Comparison of Nonmetric Unfolding Techniques." *Journal of Marketing Research* **6** (August), 330–341.

Green, P. E., & Carmone, Jr., F. J. 1970. *Multidimensional Scaling.* Boston: Allyn and Bacon.

Green, P. E., Carmone, F. J., & Robinson, P. J. 1968. "A Comparison of Perceptual Mapping Via Confusions Data and Direct Similarity Judgments." *Proceedings of the Denver Conference of the American Marketing Association,* R. L. Kind (ed.). Chicago: American Marketing Association, pp. 323–334.

Green, P. E., & Morris, T. W. 1969. "Individual Differences Models in Multidimensional Scaling: An Empirical Comparison," working paper. University of Pennsylvania, Philadelphia.

Green, P. E., & Rao, V. R. 1972. *Applied Multidimensional Scaling: A Comparison of Approaches and Algorithms.* New York: Holt, Rinehart & Winston, Inc.

Green, P. E., & Srinivasan, V. 1978. "Conjoint Analysis in Consumer Research: Issues and Outlook." *Journal of Consumer Research* **5** (September), 103–123.

Green, P. E., Tull, D. S., & Albaum, G. S. 1988. *Research for Marketing Decisions.* Englewood Cliffs, N.J.: Prentice-Hall.

Green, P. E., & Wind, Y. 1973. *Multiattribute Decisions in Marketing: A Measurement Approach.* Hinsdale, Ill.: The Dryden Press.

Guttman, Louis. 1968. "A General Nonmetric Technique for Finding the Smallest Coordinate Space for a Configuration of Points." *Psychometrika* **33**, 469–506.

Harman, H. H. 1976. *Modern Factor Analysis*. Chicago: University of Chicago Press.

Harris, B. 1981. "Howard–Harris Hierarchical Clustering," unpublished note. University of Pennsylvania, Philadelphia.

Hauser, J., & Koppelman, F. 1979. "Alternative Perceptual Mapping Techniques: Relative Accuracy and Usefulness." *Journal of Marketing Research* **16** (November), 495–506.

Hoffman, D. L., & Franke, G. R. 1986. "Correspondence Analysis: Graphical Representation of Categorical Data in Marketing Research." *Journal of Marketing Research* **23** (August), 213–227.

Jackson, B. 1983. *Multivariate Data Analysis*. Homewood Ill.: Richard D. Irwin, Inc.

Kelly, G. A. 1955. *Psychology of Personal Constructs*. New York: Norton Publishing Co.

Kendall, M. G. 1948. *Rank Correlation Methods*. London: Griffen Publishing Co.

Klahr, David. 1969. "A Monte Carlo Investigation of the Statistical Significance of Kruskal's Nonmetric Scaling Procedure." *Psychometrika* **34**, 319–330.

Klingberg, F. L. 1941. "Studies in Measurement of the Relations Among Sovereign States." *Psychometrika* **6** (December), 335–352.

Kruskal, J. B. 1964a. "Multidimensional Scaling by Optimizing Goodness of Fit to a Nonmetric Hypothesis." *Psychometrika* **29**, 1–27.

Kruskal, J. B. 1964b. "Nonmetric Multidimensional Scaling: A Numerical Method." *Psychometrika* **29**, 115–129.

Kruskal, J. B., & Carmone, Jr., F. J. 1969. "How to Use M-D-SCAL V: A Program to Do Multidimensional Scaling and Multidimensional Unfolding," (Version 5M), unpublished paper. Bell Laboratories, Murray Hill, N.J.

Kruskal, J. B., & Carmone, Jr., F. J. 1971. "How to Use M-D-SCAL (Version 5M) and Other Useful Information." *Multidimensional Scaling Program Package of Bell Laboratories*. Bell Laboratories, Murray Hill, N.J.

Kruskal, J. B., & Wish, M. 1978. *Multidimensional Scaling*. Beverly Hills: Sage Publications.

Kruskal, J. B., Young, F. W., & Seery, J. B. 1973. "How to Use KYST: A Very Flexible Program to Do Multidimensional Scaling and Unfolding." *Multidimensional Scaling Program Package of Bell Laboratories*. Bell Laboratories, Murray Hill, N.J.

Lazarsffeld, P. F. 1950. "The Logical and Mathematical Foundation of Latent Structure Analysis." *Studies on Social Psychology in World War II*. Vol. 4: *Measurement on Prediction,* Stouffer et al., Princeton, N.J.: Princeton University Press.

Lebart, L., Morineau, A., & Warwick, K. M. 1984. *Multivariate Descriptive Statistical Analysis: Correspondence Analysis and Related Techniques for Large Matrices*. New York: John Wiley & Sons, Inc.

Luce, R. D., & Tukey, J. W. 1964. "Simultaneous Conjoint Measurement: A New Type of Fundamental Measurement." *Journal of Mathematical Psychology* **1**, 1–27.

McDonald, R. P. 1962. "A General Approach to Nonlinear Factor Analysis." *Psychometrika* **27**, 397–415.

McGee, V. E. 1968. "Multidimensional Scaling of N Sets of Similarity Measures: A Nonmetric Individual Differences Approach." *Multivariate Behavioral Research* **3** (April), 233–248.

MDS(X) *User's Manual* (SV3). 1980. Edinburgh: Program Library Unit.

Miller, J. E., Shepard, R. N., & Chang, J. J. 1964. "An Analytical Approach to the Interpretation of Multidimensional Scaling Solutions." *American Psychologist* **19**, 579–580.

Neidell, L. A. 1968. "Physicians' Perception and Evaluation of Selected Ethical Drugs: An Application of Nonmetric Multidimensional Scaling to Pharmaceutical Marketing," unpublished doctoral dissertation. University of Pennsylvania, Philadelphia.

Pruzansky, S. 1975. "How to Use SINDSCAL, A Computer Program for Individual Differences in Multidimensional Scaling." *Multidimensional Scaling Program Package of Bell Laboratories*. Bell Laboratories, Murray Hill, N.J.

Punj, G. & Stewart, D. W. 1983. "Cluster Analysis in Marketing Research: Review and Suggestions for Application." *Journal of Marketing Research* **20** (May), 135–148.

Richards, E. A. 1959. "A Commercial Application of Guttman Attitude Scaling Techniques." *Journal of Marketing* **22** (October), 166–173.

Richardson, M. W. 1938. "Multidimensional Psychophysics." *Psychological Bulletin* **35**, 659–660.

Rink, D. R., & Swan, J. E. 1979. "Product Life Cycle Research—A Literature Review."

Journal of Business Research **3**, 219–242.

Roskam, E. E. 1968. Metric Analysis of Ordinal Data in Psychology. Voorscholen, Holland: University of Leiden Press.

Rummel, R. 1970. *Applied Factor Analysis*. Evanston: Northwestern University Press.

Schiffman, S. S., Reynolds, M. L., & Young, F. W. 1981. *Introduction to Multidimensional Scaling: Theory, Methods, and Applications*. New York: Academic Press, Inc.

Shepard, R. N. 1962. "The Analysis of Proximities: Multidimensional Scaling with an Unknown Distance Function," Part One. *Psychometrika* **27**, 125–139.

Shepard, R. N. 1966. "Metric Structures in Ordinal Data." *Journal of Mathematical Psychology* **3**, 287–315.

Shepard, R. N., & Arabie, P. (1979). "Additive Clustering: Representation of Similarities as Combinations of Discrete Overlapping Properties." *Psychological Review* **86**, 87–123.

Shepard, R. N., & Carroll, J. D. 1966. "Parametric Representation of Non-linear Data Structures." *Multivariate Analysis*, P. R. Kirishnaiah (ed.). New York: Academic Press, pp. 561–592.

Shepard, R. N., & Kruskal, J. B. 1964. "Nonmetric Methods for Scaling and for Factor Analysis." *American Psychologist* **19**, 557–558.

Sherman, C. R., & Young, F. W. 1968. "Nonmetric Multidimensional Scaling: A Monte Carlo Study," early version of unpublished paper by Young. *Proceedings of the 76th Annual Convention of the American Psychological Association*, San Francisco. pp. 207–208.

Slater, Patrick. 1961. "Inconsistencies in a Schedule of Paired Comparisons." *Biometrika* **48** (3, 4), 303–312.

Sneath, P., & Sokal, R. 1973. *Numerical Taxonomy*. San Francisco: Freeman.

Spence, I., & Domoney, D. W. 1974. "Single Subject Incomplete Designs for Nonmetric Multidimensional Scaling." *Psychometrika* **39**, 469–490.

Stefflre, Volney. 1960. "Market Structure Studies: New Products for Old Markets and New Markets (Foreign) for Old Products." *Applications of the Sciences in Marketing Management*, Frank Bass, C. M. King, and E. A. Pessemier (eds.). New York: John Wiley & Sons, Inc.

Stenson, H. H., & Knoll, R. L. 1969. "Goodness of Fit for Random Rankings in Kruskal's Nonmetric Scaling Procedure." *Psychological Bulletin* **71**, 122–126.

Takane, Y., Young, F. W., & de Leeuw, J. 1977. "Nonmetric Individual Differences in Multidimensional Scaling: An Alternating Least Squares Method with Optimum Scaling Features." *Psychometrika* **42**, 7–67.

Thurstone, L. L. 1959. *The Measurement of Values*. Chicago: The University of Chicago Press.

Torgerson, W. S. 1958. *Theory and Methods of Scaling*. New York: John Wiley & Sons, Inc.

Torgerson, W. S. 1965. "Multidimensional Scaling of Similarity." *Psychometrika* **30**, 379–393.

Tucker, L. R. 1960. "Dimensions of Preference." E.T.S. Memo RM-60-7. Educational Testing Service, Princeton, N.J.

Tucker, L. R. 1964. "The Extension of Factor Analysis to Three-Dimensional Matrices." *Contributions to Mathematical Psychology*, N. Frederiksen and H. Gullksen (eds.). New York: Holt, Rinehart & Winston, pp. 109–127.

Tucker, L. R., & Messick, Samuel. 1963. "An Individual Differences Model for Multidimensional Scaling." *Psychometrika* **28**, 333–367.

Tversky, Amos. 1965. "Additivity Analysis of Choice Behavior: A Test of Utility Theory," MMPP 52-2, Michigan Mathematical Psychology Program. University of Michigan, Ann Arbor.

Wagenaar, W. A., & Padmos, P. 1971. "Quantitative Interpretation of Stress in Kruskal's Multidimensional Scaling Technique." *British Journal of Mathematical and Statistical Psychology* **24**, 101–110.

Young, F. W. 1968. "TORSCA, An IBM Program for Nonmetric Multidimensional Scaling." *Journal for Marketing Research* **5** (August), 319–321.

Young, F. W. 1988. Multidimensional Scaling of Nominal Data: The Recovery of Metric Information with ALSCAL." *Psychometrika* **43**, 367–379.

Young, F. W., & Lewyckyj, R. 1979. *ALSCAL-4 User's Guide*. University of North Carolina, Chapel Hill.

Young, G., & Householder, A. S. 1938. "Discussion of a Set of Points in Terms of Their Mutual Distances." *Psychometrika* **3** (March), 19–22.

INDEX